The
AMBASSADOR
from
WALL STREET

The AMBASSADOR *from* WALL STREET

The Story of
THOMAS W. LAMONT,
J. P. Morgan's
Chief Executive

EDWARD M. LAMONT

LYONS
PRESS

Essex, Connecticut

An imprint of Globe Pequot, the trade division of
The Rowman & Littlefield Publishing Group, Inc.
4501 Forbes Blvd., Ste. 200
Lanham, MD 20706
www.rowman.com

Distributed by NATIONAL BOOK NETWORK

British Library Cataloguing in Publication Information available

Library of Congress Cataloging-in-Publication Data Available

ISBN 978-1-5683-3018-1 (cloth)
ISBN 978-1-4930-6852-4 (paperback)
ISBN 978-1-4616-9999-6 (ebook)

∞™ The paper used in this publication meets the minimum requirements of American National Standard for Information Sciences—Permanence of Paper for Printed Library Materials, ANSI/NISO Z39.48-1992.

*To Buz
and our children, Ned, Helen and Camille
and all the clan*

Contents

Preface   xi

Acknowledgments   xiii

Introduction   xv

Book I—The Rising Path

Along the Hudson   3

"Huc Verite Pueri, Ut Viri Sitis"   13

Fair Harvard and Its Sons   17

Member of the Press   23

Perils of Business   26

Down a New Road   35

Mr. Morgan's Choice   41

The Money Trust Hearings   48

Changes at 23 Wall   58

Book II—The Trials of Peacemaking

Europe in Flames   67

Arming the Allies   74

Family Affairs   85

America Goes to War   88

Touring the Front   93

"The Whipping Post"   100

The Paris Peace Conference   105

Reparations   108

The Specter of Famine   114

Hard Bargaining   119

A German View, a View of Germany   122

The Allies Dispute and Entertain Each Other   124

Political Flak and Danger Signals   134

The Treaty of Versailles   138

Lobbying for the League   141

Book III—Finance and Diplomacy—Intertwined

The Chinese Consortium   153

Case Closed   165

The Republicans Take Over   170

The Mexican Debt Dilemma   175

Financing European Recovery   186

A New Client   194

A Settlement Unravels   197

The Dawes Loan   201

New Loans and Bad Debts   213

The Good Life   224

Japan's Wall Street Friend   231

Banking on the Corner   238

Egyptian Kings, Past and Present   241

Book IV—Boom and Bust

Domestic Affairs   247

Running With the Bulls   251

The Young Plan 254

Advice for the White House 263

The 1929 Crash 269

The International Inn and Other Diversions 275

Clash Between Friends 280

The Deepening Depression 288

Financial Disarray in Europe 294

The Senate Has Questions 305

Japan's First Target 309

Keeping New York Solvent and Florence Happy 314

Debate Over the Market 318

The Reparations-War Debt Minuet 321

Domestic Banking Crisis 328

Book V—The Defensive Years

Confrontation in Washington 335

Handling the Press 352

Holiday in England; Troubles in New York 360

Dealing with Dr. Schacht 367

The Lord of San Simeon and Other Acquaintances 371

Launching a New Enterprise 378

Senator Nye Attacks 380

The Mexican Muddle 385

A Question of History 391

A Royal Affair 396

South African Safari 398

The Senate Summons Again 403

Mussolini's Olive Branch 406

An After-Dinner Message   410

War in China   414

Partisan Passion   417

Richard Whitney's Shocker   423

Book VI—Again: The Devil's Madness

Calm Before the Storm   435

Conflict Over Neutrality   443

New Look at the Corner   447

The War and American Politics   450

Menace on Both Oceans   457

From Pulpit Harbor to Pearl Harbor   470

On the Home Front   477

TWL II   481

A New Father-Son Team   484

Good Neighbor Policy   487

Pen in Hand   490

Reduce Speed   495

Letters to the Editor   497

"They Are Not Dead, Our Sons Who Fell in Glory"   505

Fitting the Final Pieces   510

Time, Like an Ever-Rolling Stream   517

Sources   525

Bibliography   539

Photo credits   549

Index   551

Preface

My late father, Edward M. Lamont, published this book in 1994 when he was sixty-eight years old, about the same as my age today. He died at eighty-eight in 2016. Dad was an avid history buff and spent many years conducting research for this book on his grandfather, Thomas W. Lamont, and for other books he published in later years. My late mother, affectionately referred to by my father as "Buz" after her maiden name of Buzby, was a huge help to Dad in writing and researching *The Ambassador from Wall Street*.

Dad was a stickler for the truth in writing about his prominent grandfather. He did not want to publish a whitewashed version of Tom Lamont's life. Instead, he sought out family papers, letters, historical materials, old newspapers, and previously published books wherein Tom Lamont appeared—for better or worse. Dad's was the first biography of Thomas Lamont to be published.

I was pleased to be asked to write this brief preface to the new paperback edition of Dad's book. Almost thirty years since its publication, the story remains informative for those of us who did not live through those turbulent years when world wars, a depression, and threats of rising political movements of all kinds roiled the world order. Tom Lamont was a banker, but he also played a role as a negotiator and behind-the-scenes broker on behalf of several U.S. presidents. He sought to remind us that finance cannot live in an ivory tower. It has a broader, public purpose that must include the needs of Main Street as much as Wall Street if it is to be productive and achieve the common good.

In 2014, Rowman & Littlefield published Dad's book *The Forty Years That Created America: The Story of the Explorers, Promoters, Investors, and Settlers Who Founded the First English Colonies*. Writing that book toward the end of his life gave him great pleasure. He was a proud American patriot who relished learning about the earliest Colonial-era men and women who laid the groundwork for our great democracy.

As you read this biography, I hope you'll enjoy learning about a bygone world as much as I did.

—Ned Lamont, Governor of Connecticut

Acknowledgments

I could not have written this book without the daily hands-on assistance of my wife, Camille, known to everyone as Buz. I write with a ballpoint pen and yellow legal pad—with arrows, crossouts, and balloons. From there Buz took over. She mastered and operated the word processor; the hours were long and not without frustrations—mechanical breakdowns, power outages, and the like. Her many suggestions were very helpful. But above all her careful work, patience, and constant encouragement spurred me across the finish line.

I am also indebted to my able agent, Tom Wallace, for his support and expertise. And my editor and old Exeter friend Alan Williams possessed a special insight about my subject, which made his editorial suggestions and questions of tremendous value. He is a real pro. I am also very grateful to the late William Bentinck-Smith, long time Harvard editor and historian, William Sheeline of *Fortune* magazine, and John M. Morris of Citicorp, and formerly with Morgan Guaranty Trust, for reading my manuscript and providing excellent advice.

All the persons I interviewed were gracious and helpful. But one stands out: Franz Schneider, who died in April, 1993 at the age of one hundred and five, appears throughout my story starting with Lamont's purchase of the *New York Evening Post* in 1918. Schneider was on the Wall Street scene throughout TWL's career, and his recollections on many subjects were invaluable.

This book is in a large sense a husband-and-wife team project, and my gratitude to Buz for her help is infinite.

Introduction

It all started when I began to explore the contents of a row of boxes in the attic of my home, a house in which my grandmother had lived at the end of her life. The boxes were filled with bundles of old family letters, mainly from the 1800s, handwritten in ink on rag bond paper and in good condition. My grandfather, Thomas W. Lamont, had had a few key papers typed, most notably the diary of his father, the Methodist parson who guided pastorates throughout the Hudson River Valley in the nineteenth century. The idea of writing a biography of Lamont, the banker who had started life in these country parsonages and led J. P. Morgan & Co. for more than two decades, began to germinate.

I have always been fascinated by that short span of American history wherein our country grew and developed into a modern nation and world power. That the large family reunion my grandfather attended as a six-year-old took place just a few months after the Battle of Little Big Horn was the kind of personal and historic convergence that stirred my imagination and enthusiasm for the project. And Lamont's own books, *My Boyhood in a Parsonage* and *Across World Frontiers*, his account of becoming an international banker, well illustrated America's coming of age.

I was twenty-one when my grandfather died. My contacts with him had been limited to large family gatherings, such as Christmas at my grandparents' country house or picnics in Maine, where they had a summer home. We didn't go fishing or watch baseball games together; in those days I turned to the sports pages while he read Walter Lippmann's column in the *New York Herald Tribune*, or the editorial page of the *New York Times*, which might be running his latest letter to the editor. I knew he was an important and busy man, and we simply had different interests in life. He was kindly and generous, and I admired him for his stature in the community at large and the respect accorded him by his fellow citizens; for his smooth, articulate discussion of weighty matters; and for his obvious enjoyment of a full and gracious life. My lasting impression as I listened with the others to his account of his latest trip to Europe or meeting at the White House was that he seemed to go everywhere worth going and know everyone worth knowing.

My own memories of TWL contribute to the description of Lamont's family life. But the story of his banking career and role in public affairs is based on my research, making use of the sources I will mention here and in detail at the end of the book. I relied on these materials to achieve my objective: a fair and accurate account of Lamont's activities and those of his partners, which provoked public praise and criticism in no small measure for forty-odd years.

All Lamont's business papers and personal correspondence throughout his long career are lodged at the Harvard Business School's Baker Library. My perusal of the index for the collection indicated that it was more than a treasure trove of material about Lamont and the Morgan bank. It also shed new light on some important historic events and figures, such as TWL's conversations with Woodrow Wilson, providing insight into the president's political strategies; the frustrating history of twenty-five years of foreign debt negotiations with the Mexican government; and Walter Lippmann's love-hate relations with the Morgan partners.

Another gold mine of biographic material was available to me—forty years of unpublished letters from Tom and Florence Lamont to their children. They gave a vivid picture of family life and often described business and public events with far more candor than the office papers at Harvard.

No biography of Lamont has been written, although he has figured prominently in many books about his times and the Morgan bank. I thought that his life and career justified a full accounting and that I could add a realistic new dimension in assessing the actions of Lamont and his bank based on special credentials—my first-hand knowledge of the family, the collection of family letters, and my own career experience, including twenty-three years with the World Bank and J. P. Morgan & Co., Inc. Knowing the family and the business would obviously help in researching the life of Thomas W. Lamont, whom J. P. Morgan, Jr.'s, biographer, Professor John Douglas Forbes, described as "the real guiding genius of the Morgan firm for a generation."

John Masefield, England's Poet Laureate, wrote of his friend: "No American of the last half century has shown more fully the wonderful power America has of making a complete man. He was equipped and great in many ways. He lived with enjoyment." And Frances Van Schaik, who edited the family letters, added, "When TWL in the 30's and 40's debarked from his cruiser at Sneden's Landing, returning to his home on the Palisades after a day at 23 Wall Street, he had only to look up river to be reminded how long and interesting a journey . . . down the Hudson could become."

The

AMBASSADOR

from

WALL STREET

Book I

THE RISING PATH

Along the Hudson

IT WAS A CHILLY February night in 1903, and Tom Lamont, a thirty-two-year-old New York marketing executive, was returning to his home in Englewood, New Jersey, after a long day of business in the city. It was about ten o'clock, an hour when most New York commuters were getting ready to retire.

As he walked down the aisle of the swaying New Jersey Northern coach, he passed by Harry Davison and George Case, two of his Englewood neighbors and friends. A banker and lawyer respectively, they were both engaged in organizing the new Bankers Trust Company, whose sponsorship by many of the leading New York bankers boded well for its future. Sitting side by side, they were discussing the filling of executive positions in the new bank. They already had hired enough banking talent and were looking for an experienced and able businessman. Davison spotted Lamont and gave Case a poke. "There's the man," he whispered.

The next morning Davison telephoned Lamont at Lamont, Corliss & Co., his firm on Hudson Street, to ask him to drop by his office at the First National Bank headquarters on Wall Street, which Lamont readily agreed to do. Henry P. Davison was widely viewed in business circles as a rising star; energetic, imaginative, and popular, he was regarded at the age of thirty-five as one of the bright young men in the Wall Street crowd whose successful banking career seemed assured. He was a vice president, and there were only two, of the First National Bank, led by George F. Baker, a venerated Wall Street figure whose bank was a key member of the J. P. Morgan banking group. Furthermore, Davison had conceived the idea of forming the Bankers Trust Company, of which he was chairman of the executive committee. George Case was its general counsel.

Davison outlined for Lamont the promising prospects for the new trust company, which had been established to handle the corporate and personal trust business directed to it by major banks and investment firms. At the time it was located in a two-room office in the Liberty Bank building, but it would probably move to larger offices on Wall Street before long, given the outlook for the rapid growth of its business. The financial community believed in the new venture: the bank's initial stock offering in early February of $1.5 million had been tremendously oversubscribed, and the market quickly doubled the offering price of $150 per share.

After describing the unique role of the new company and its organization, Davison made his proposal to Lamont: "I believe that you are the man for our secretary and treasurer."

TWL was dumbfounded and replied, "But I don't know the first thing about banking. All my life I have been borrowing money, not lending it."

"Fine," retorted Davison, "that's just why we want you. A fearless borrower like you ought to make a prudent lender."

Davison knew Lamont as a friendly neighbor with a charming wife, a respected fellow citizen of Englewood. He also knew that five years earlier, at the age of twenty-eight, Lamont had taken over the management of a failing company that marketed consumer products and with much imagination and hard work transformed it into a profitable and expanding enterprise. He had applied his marketing strategies to several dozen businesses with good results and built an excellent reputation for himself and his firm.

TWL had worked extremely hard over the last decade, taking little time off from a business whose survival had been precarious until recent years. He later described that period of his life: "I had to go through . . . grinding anxiety, with a feeling of living in a house of cards likely to tumble down on my head at any moment."

Lamont had never lacked ambition and firmly believed that the world of finance, centered on Wall Street, offered a golden path to prestige, power, and affluence at this stage of America's burgeoning growth. TWL was delighted to join forces with Davison and become a banker. He spoke later of his "good fortune to alight in the midst of these young Medici, these Fuggers, these Fortunatuses." The job would certainly be more glamorous and remunerative than selling salad oil, Yorkshire Relish, and laundry soap to stock the kitchen shelves of America.

Lamont and his business partner and brother-in-law, Charles Corliss, agreed that TWL should make the move to Bankers Trust, which would enhance the credit and reputation of Lamont, Corliss. Lamont was a major stockholder of the firm, and the brothers-in-law would continue to collaborate in directing the business.

TWL shared the good news with his parents. His father, Thomas, was a Methodist minister, now seventy-one, who had long labored in the Lord's vineyard in a score of parishes in the Hudson River Valley, the setting in which he and his wife Caroline had raised Tom and his older brother and sister. Compared to Lamont's trials over the last decade, growing up in those small towns and villages in the Hudson Valley had been serene.

Thomas William Lamont was born on September 30, 1870, in Claverack, a community of about six hundred inhabitants on the east bank of the Hudson River. The Lamonts lived in the Methodist parsonage, a small white frame house with a porch overlooking the river and Catskill Mountains to the west. Following church practice, the parson was assigned to a new parish every few years, and the family moved on to another valley community when Tom was eighteen months old.

The Methodists of the Hudson Valley were of modest means, and for the parson and his pretty wife, Caroline, it was a life marked by hard work and no frills. "Your mother never ate the bread of idleness," his father once said to Tom. The children were taught early to follow their parents' industrious and economizing habits. "Waste not, want not" was a serious dictum at the parsonage. A regular household chore for Tom as a boy was to sift through the cinders and ashes in the sitting room stove to salvage any unburned coals.

Tom's father enjoyed maintaining close ties with his family, especially his mother and ten brothers and sisters. The family was clannish anyway, perhaps a tendency that came from their Scotch-Irish heritage. Most of them lived in the New York and Hudson River Valley region, and there was a good deal of visiting back and forth, particularly to the old family home in Charlotteville, a little crossroads hamlet nestled in the Catskills west of Albany where the parson's widowed mother lived until her death in 1898.

There Tom's father had worked on the family farm when he wasn't in school. After graduating from Union College in Schenectady he had become a teacher at the New York Conference Seminary in Charlotteville, a Methodist boarding school for about 250 boys and girls that his father had helped establish. He also served as a Methodist preacher for several years before being appointed principal of the seminary and pastor of the Charlotteville church. Ordained a church elder by the bishop in 1861, he often conducted services in neighboring villages.

Eight miles down the narrow valley from Charlotteville lay the hamlet of Fergusonville, home of the Fergusonville Academy founded by two

Ferguson brothers, both Methodist ministers. Pastor Lamont preached often in Fergusonville, and it was there that he met Caroline Deuel Jayne, a niece of the founder, who was visiting the school.

Caroline was from an old New York and Long Island family of Scottish-English background that had long ties with the Methodist church. Indeed Caroline's birth in 1842 had occurred just over nine months after her father's return from Liberia following two and a half years of work there as the printer of a small paper for the Methodist missionaries. At one point near death from recurring bouts of malaria and yellow fever, he survived to spread "the knowledge of Salvation to the heathen tribes of Africa," as he put it. Given her heritage, it was not surprising that the pastor from Charlotteville impressed Caroline as a kindly, upright man of character, strong and solid as a Catskills boulder. The sturdy and solemn parson was charmed by Caroline's sprightliness and good humor. She played the piano; she was also very pretty and ten years younger than the minister. They were married on April 9, 1863.

"The rich Presbyterians" was the way Tom often heard his elders refer to members of that denomination. In one village the president of the Presbyterian board of trustees owned the biggest lumber and coal yard, and the clerk of the board ran the best butcher shop. The Methodist Board president kept only the second-best general store. In another community the Lamonts noted that the Presbyterian Board was installing a new bathroom in the home of their pastor, while trips to the backyard privy remained part of daily living at the Methodist parsonage. Most of the horses and buggies were owned by Presbyterian families, and the Presbyterian church was usually the finest in town, a situation Parson Lamont once found to his advantage.

The Lamonts were very upset by the physical condition of the Methodist church when in 1873 they arrived in Katonah, New York, thirty-five miles north of New York City, for their new parish assignment. It was unpainted, dilapidated beyond repair, and in a poor location. In the words of Tom's mother, writing to her brother, it was "a wreck. . . . I have never seen a church in poorer condition. . . . There is little encouragement for a minister to labor as long as this old church stands, for I cannot believe the Lord in Heaven will ever smile down upon a people who live in palaces themselves and leave Him in worse than a barn." Caroline, unlike her forbearing husband, gave vent to a sharp tongue when aroused.

With much effort over the next six months, Tom's father coaxed the Methodist board of trustees into accepting the idea of building a new church, appealing to their sense of pride and pocketbooks. He pointed out that the Presbyterian board had decided to build a handsome house of worship, which would be a great asset in attracting new members and might even induce some Methodist parishioners to switch over. Furthermore, the old church would need more costly repairs each year.

The Methodist trustees finally agreed to build a new church, but then the project languished for more than a year while they debated over the right location. Meanwhile, the Presbyterians moved ahead vigorously in preparing their building site. "Care-nothing, do-nothing people," Tom's mother fumed in a letter to her brother about the Methodist Church board.

Incited by the Presbyterians' progress, the Methodists finally selected a site, went to work, and completed their new church in January 1875. Tom's mother brought her children to the first service, as her husband preached to an overflowing congregation from the text "Mine house shall be called a house of prayer for all people."

Parson Lamont's fund-raising efforts had also been successful; the new church was debt-free. Feeling real pride in their accomplishment, the Lamonts departed Katonah two months later for their next appointment, the little village of Tremont in the Catskills.

One event in Tom's childhood especially opened his eyes to the world beyond the parsonage—a Lamont family reunion at the home of Uncle George, the parson's younger brother, to honor the matriarch of the family, Tom's widowed sixty-five-year-old grandmother, Elizabeth. Tom's father, his five brothers and five sisters, plus husbands, wives and grandchildren, numbering forty-four in all, had gathered at Uncle George and Aunt Rebecca's large, handsome house in Bound Brook, New Jersey, on a cool November weekend in 1876.

Tom's parents and their three children—Hammond, Lucy, and Tom—were greeted by their host in his usual ebullient fashion. Uncle George was portly and jolly; he had a lively sense of humor and a "smile like a benediction," as Tom later recalled. He had had a successful career in business and now owned and ran a paper manufacturing company. Aunt Bec was from the South, related to the Masons of Virginia. The Bound Brook LaMontes, as they had styled their surname, were charming, cultured, and fond of entertaining. At the reunion banquet Uncle George sat at the head of the long dining-room table, amusing as always.

The Lamont brothers conversed about their plans to visit the Centennial Exposition in Philadelphia, which featured an exhibition of the nation's progress in the new industrial age and a display of the latest

American inventions—the telephone, the typewriter, and a giant steam engine. Tom's father, his older brother, Hammond, and other family members would leave for the fair right after the Bound Brook reunion, and young Tom was exceedingly annoyed at his parents for not letting him join the excursion.

After dinner the gathering adjourned to the parlor. It was time for Tom's father to read the family history he had written for the occasion. The family's forebears, descended from the ancient Lamont clan of Argyllshire in western Scotland, were among the many Scots who emigrated to Northern Ireland in the seventeenth century. About 1745 Archibald Lamont was kidnapped by a ship's captain in the port of Coleraine. Enticed on board to view the vessel, he begged in vain to be put ashore as the ship sailed out of the harbor for New York.

After serving an apprenticeship to a man on Long Island, Archibald obtained his freedom, and at his urging his widowed mother and two brothers joined him in America. The Lamonts settled near North Hillsdale, New York, good farming country in the upper Hudson Valley, an area that was just opening up. The Thomas Lamonts were descended from Archibald's brother Robert.

The thick sheaf of papers in the parson's hand indicated that, like his sermons, this would not be a brief account. Scholarly research and writing was a labor of love for him. It may have been difficult for Tom and his cousins to stay alert as his father's voice droned on: "William, our great-grandfather, was born about 1755, served as a soldier in the Continental Army in the Revolutionary War, was at Saratoga and witnessed the surrender of Burgoyne's army to General Gates in 1777," and there were still a hundred years to go.

The parson's hair was gray, his short gray beard squared off, his demeanor serious. George apparently was paying rapt attention to his brother's recital. The contrast between the two brothers was striking; yet they were very close and respectful of each other. Tom's father once remarked: "Brother George can just about sell anybody anything. I'll bet he could even turn around some of my backsliders!"

While popular books as frivolous as the "rags to riches" stories by Horatio Alger may not have found their way into the parsonage to motivate Tom, surely the Bound Brook LaMontes with their comfortable and affluent lifestyle must have stimulated his thinking about the future. Somehow, as a young man Tom acquired a taste for good books and fashionable clothes, indulgences beyond the reach of plain-living schoolmasters and ministers.

*   *   *

The parson's salary was about $1,200 a year, plus a little extra for performing weddings, less his tithe to the Lord. Combined with free parish housing it was a decent salary for the times, but only occasionally was it fully paid. Many of the church members were farmers who had ample produce but little cash. Accordingly, the practice of having an annual donation party had developed in rural parishes, usually held in December when it had become clear that there was a salary shortfall to be filled.

On the appointed night scores of church members, young and old, would tramp into the parsonage with hearty greetings to the Dominie and his family. Then upon signal gifts of all kinds of foods would be carried in—jelly cakes and doughnuts, bread loaves, barrels of apples and potatoes, slabs of beef, pies, and twenty-gallon cans of milk—and piled about the parlor and kitchen.

After the parson had said grace, the company fell to sampling their own offerings with gusto. The women felt free to wander about the house, upstairs and down, looking in closets and examining and fingering Tom's mother's clothes and keepsakes. The young people often ended up roughhousing in the bedrooms upstairs, leaving things in a mess and sometimes damaging the furnishings and bedclothes.

These not too pleasant occasions became burdensome as Tom's parents grew older. It took days to clean up and repair afterward, and the whole affair seemed demeaning. After one particularly noisy and destructive donation, at which his wife's wedding dress was torn, the pastor declared, "There will never be another donation party in any parsonage of mine. I would rather lose part of my salary than endure it!"

While Tom's father was a reserved man who preferred the quiet company of family and old friends, Tom's mother was sprightly and blessed with a grand sense of humor. Sister Lamont was known as a charming hostess and good provider by visiting clergymen. Tom once recalled a typical Saturday evening: "My mother would bake biscuit and cake and roast the meat for the next day; for on Sunday we had no cooking in the house. And then when we had finished and cleaned up, Mother would sit down and play the piano for an hour or more, with us all singing away for dear life and as happy as larks. She was a young thing in those days, and the liveliest thing you ever knew."

Tom witnessed an incident when he was about fourteen that illustrated well his parents' contrasting personalities. His father, in instructing a new young preacher in future duties, had assigned him the responsibility of calling forward and welcoming into the church thirteen new members. Made visibly nervous by this honor, the young preacher announced in a loud voice: "Will the new members kindly step forward? We shall receive into Holy Communion with us today six adults and seven adulteresses."

The parson's face flushed with embarrassment. He murmured in the young man's ear: "Just call them men and women. That will be better."

Tom looked at his mother, who had had a sudden fit of coughing and held her handkerchief to her face.

At home after church his father said, with a tone of reproach, "Caddie, you should not have smiled." At which his spirited mother threw her head back and burst into peals of laughter.

Methodists for three generations, the Lamonts were as fervent in their fundamentalism and temperance as their sternest parishioners. Dancing and card playing were snares of the Evil One, and demon rum was of course the ultimate snare. Tom's father participated in many a Women's Christian Temperance Union meeting and had a well-honed message, excoriating Satan and his demons and inciting the imbibers in attendance to step up and take the pledge of abstinence. At the tender age of seven, young Tom signed the Blue Ribbon Temperance Pledge, and at age nine, at a revival meeting, he was moved to step forward and confess, of what sins he wasn't quite sure, and was received as a full member of the Methodist Church.

Family prayers were led by Tom's father twice a day—before breakfast and after supper, when the children read aloud a passage from the Scriptures. Tom's mother would often play a hymn on the old rosewood piano in the corner of the parlor. She also played the organ and led the choir at the Sunday morning church service.

Sunday, the Lord's day, started at 9:30 with class meetings for the whole congregation; the main service at 10:30 was led by Parson Lamont in his Prince Albert coat. There were more classes after the service, and finally after lunch came Sunday school for the youngsters. Children of other faiths, such as Presbyterians and Catholics, played in the woods or went skating after church, but not the Methodists. There was an afternoon break after Sunday school, and then back to church for the young people's service at 6:15, followed by the regular evening service and sermon at 7:30. Tom looked forward to Mondays.

Once Tom asked his father how he felt about the Presbyterian young people "taking walks on Sunday afternoon, pairing off, and doing all that other weekday stuff." His father did not seem particularly upset at this conduct, but nevertheless felt he must abide by the strict Methodist practices of his community. Parson Lamont was not one to venture beyond the traditional boundaries.

Another important part of the minister's life was his respect for good books and the pleasure he derived from study and reading. His prize earthly possession was his library, and if a new parsonage lacked adequate shelves for his books, the parson insisted that the Church board have them installed. He also subscribed to the daily *New York Tribune, Harper's Weekly*, and the *Atlantic Monthly*.

The Lamont children inherited their taste for literature from their father. By the time he was fourteen Tom had read the Bible twice, and the list of his favorite authors—Charles Dickens, Sir Walter Scott, Edgar Allan Poe, Jules Verne, James Fenimore Cooper, and others—was long indeed. During the long summer vacations from school other boys clambered down Catskill mountain trails or helped their fathers on the family farm. Young Tom devoured novels by the score.

Tom worshipped his brother Hammond, six years his senior, who possessed a happy, enthusiastic personality and a fine mind. It was Hammond who constantly encouraged his younger brother and sister to read good books, in his opinion the most important part of their education. After attending Albany High School, Hammond had gone on to Harvard, where he excelled in his studies and became an editor of the *Crimson* and the *Harvard Lampoon*.

As time passed, the constant moves to a new parish every few years became more of a trial for Tom's parents. Each year at the closing session of the New York Conference of Methodists, the bishop read aloud the appointments decided on by himself and the presiding elders. For some the announcement brought glad tidings of an assignment to one of the larger churches with a commensurate salary and parsonage. But invariably, Pastor Lamont drew one of the many poorer rural charges, almost all located in the Catskills or on the eastern shore of the Hudson— Monticello, Bullville, Deposit, Claverak, Katonah, Tremont, Catskill, Coxsackie, Saugerties, Goshen, Rodout, and the list went on. He was a modest man who shunned self-seeking advancement. He remained a country parson.

The greatest hardship resulting from such frequent transfers was the physical effort of packing, moving by train and buggy, unpacking, and settling in every few years. Usually, the furniture didn't appear until a week or so after the family's arrival at the new parsonage. It never felt like home to the parson until the piano was in its place and the family could sing a hymn in the evenings.

The physical condition of the newly assigned parsonages varied widely: sometimes new shingling was called for or the vegetable garden had been allowed to deteriorate. Upon arrival at a new parsonage, the parson conducted a thorough inspection of the house, barn, garden, and orchard to determine what work had to be done promptly. Planting the garden was a regular spring task, and fortunately the pastor was an able gardener and carpenter, skills he had learned as a boy on his father's farm in Charlotteville. Tom did his best to help his father even though he loathed household and gardening chores.

While Tom's father was surveying the exterior of the parsonage, his mother was inspecting the interior. Were there enough shelves for her husband's collection of books on theology and philosophy, the source of inspiration for so many of his sermons? Should she replace a badly worn parlor carpet, and would she be able to find a good hired girl to help her out? As Tom's mother grew older she began to dread these physically exhausting moves more and more.

Taking on a new pastorate and new problems so frequently was not an easy undertaking for the parson either. Sometimes he became discouraged about his effectiveness as a preacher and depressed about the high incidence of sickness and death, which in some years seemed almost overwhelming. Adults died from typhoid fever and pneumonia in their prime of life, and children fell victim to epidemics of diphtheria which swept through the valley communities. The parson would christen infants and bury them days later. At times only the cheerfulness and good sense of his wife would bolster him. Once Tom's Aunt Harriet wrote him and asked about his parents. "How is your lovely mother, Tom? Carrie is so quick-witted, so much fun to be with. And your dear father. He's such a saintly man."

In later life Lamont recalled: "To a child the years always stretch out at immense length. The winters, filled with snow and frost, never seemed to end. In my little world, skating began at Thanksgiving and on that small pond in the hollow of the low hills back of the church the ice lingered almost to April. The long vacation days of July and August go by, one by one, peaceful and sleepy, with the humming of the bees. And when the dusk comes dropping down, a small boy, deliciously tired from the swimming and the running and the final household chores is glad to stumble up the stairs and fall drowsily into bed."

He also remembered the mile-long walk to school in zero weather, tapping the fine hard maple trees, and rowing and skating on the river. He recalled his father's prayers from the pulpit Sunday after Sunday for the recovery of President Garfield, who had been shot by a crazy assassin, and remembered him coming up the front path at the Catskill parsonage on a September morning in 1881 bearing the *New York Tribune* with its heavy black mourning borders reporting the death of "our martyred president." In his mind's eye he saw the night boats, the river steamers, moving down the Hudson with their lights all aglow, the great grinding floes of ice floating by in March, the ever-changing river, storm-tossed or peaceful in a summer calm, and "back of us, towering up less than a dozen miles away, the green and blue forested slopes and peaks of the rugged Catskill Mountains."

Lamont's childhood memories, recalled in his book, *My Boyhood in a Parsonage,* written at the end of his life, have a decidedly nostalgic glow. Letters between the adult members of the family circle are filled with accounts of sickness and hard times. Yet it seems clear that the parson's home was filled with mutual affection and that the children grew up sharing their parents' values and their father's respect for scholarship and belief in the importance of obtaining a first-class education.

"Huc Verite Pueri, Ut Viri Sitis"
(Inscription on Academy Building bell at Exeter in 1884)

Brother Hammond had observed that the best-prepared students at Harvard came from Phillips Exeter Academy, the New Hampshire preparatory school founded in 1781 and long noted for its academic thoroughness. Acting on Hammond's strong recommendation, Tom's father decided to send him to Exeter. Just under fourteen, Tom would be one of the youngest boys at the boarding school.

On a September evening in 1884, Tom and his father arrived on the Boston and Maine and went to Tom's small room on the third floor of Gorham Hall, a town inn converted to a school dormitory. Tom's father stayed at Exeter for two days, meeting the principal and teachers. On the last morning he rushed to his son's room to say good-bye, and with a quick hug, hurried off to catch the 7:30 train to Boston.

Extra long hours of study marked Tom's early months at Exeter. There were some wide gaps in the preparation he had received from three different grammar schools. Slackers were not coddled at Exeter but expelled. Latin was emphasized, and fortunately his father's early tutelage helped him through the nine hour-long recitations in that subject each week. Tom's hard work produced good results, and once he had caught up with his peers, he was able to shorten his heavy study schedule. He played tennis and took on some outside jobs—splitting firewood at fifteen cents an hour, snow shoveling, and cleaning furnaces. His earnings reduced his calls on his father for money, and the scholarship grant he was awarded in the spring term eased the financial burden on the family.

Tom wrote his parents weekly letters containing detailed explanations of the expenses that would have to be paid by his father. Tom urged his parents, brother, and sister to write regularly; he confessed that he was homesick, but admonished his parents not to tell anyone.

He found that the boiled beans served in the Abbot Hall dining room gave him stomachaches, and the oleomargarine was so "strong" that he gave up eating it, too. He was outgrowing his clothes, which seemed to be constantly wearing out; his shoes were too small, and his gray everyday pants had a big hole that couldn't be darned.

There was compulsory chapel each morning at 7:45 for the students, and on Sundays they were required to attend one of the town church services. Tom wrote that the Methodist preacher's sermons were boring, definitely not of the caliber to which he was accustomed.

The football game at Andover, Massachusetts, against Phillips Academy, Exeter's traditional rival, was the big event of the fall term, and most of the student body planned to attend the game, about an hour's train ride from Exeter. Tom wrote his father that the train ticket would cost a dollar, and he did not expect to go; incidentally, he reported, three of the best Exeter players attended the Methodist Church. The ploy was successful, and his father sent him a dollar for the ticket.

A few weeks later Tom was mortified by his involvement, albeit tangential, in a student prank in Gorham Hall. He had joined several boys in mixing up and then dousing with water the bedclothes of another student. Professor George A. Wentworth, then in charge of discipline at the academy, had imposed a fine of $5 on each of the miscreants, a stiff penalty to make it clear, Wentworth wrote Tom's father, that hazing would not be tolerated at Exeter.

Tom wrote home: "I did not know what to do, just as I was getting along so well in my studies and everything, to have this come when you are so pressed for money to keep me here. I ask you and Mama to forgive me for acting so. The thought never entered my head but that it would be taken as a joke, but I see that it was a mean trick. . . . I do not know what you and Mama think of me, but I would not have had it happen for the world."

In January Tom suffered the fright and pain of being bitten on the lip by a rat while asleep in his room. The janitor of Gorham Hall stopped up the rat hole with a piece of tin, and Tom went to the doctor with a badly swollen lip. He was upset when the doctor put some court plaster on the wound and charged him fifty cents. He felt Gorham Hall should pay the bill for "allowing such a thing in the house." Tom's lip soon healed, but his health problems were not over.

In February he was struck down by scarlet fever. The same stern Professor Wentworth tenderly wrapped the feverish boy and carried him down three flights of stairs in Gorham Hall to be taken by carriage to a private home in Exeter. After two weeks' recuperation, he was sent home to complete his recovery. He returned to Exeter at the beginning of the spring term, where his spirits were lifted by the warm welcome he received from his classmates and the coming of spring itself after the endless New Hampshire winter.

Tom did not make his class baseball team and turned to tennis. With his father's permission he transferred to the Baptist Church, where he sang second bass in the choir. He spoke on the winning team in a debate at the Golden Branch Literary Society in opposing women's suffrage. His position was that women had been tried and found wanting. "It is a well-known fact," Tom declared at the age of fourteen, "that women cannot think nor feel as deeply or strongly as men," a statement greeted with much applause.

In his upper-class years Tom became even more active in school affairs. He served as an editor of the *Exonian*, the student newspaper, and of the *Pean*, the yearbook report on student activities; he also was managing editor of the *Literary Monthly*. In his senior year he was president of Abbot Hall, his red brick dormitory next to the Academy Building, and became a member of Sigma Pi Alpha, one of Exeter's three secret societies. Not athletic enough to make any of the academy teams, Tom played tennis and, during the winter, skated on the Exeter River.

In Tom's senior year Exeter had an enrollment of 335 boys, more than half coming from New Hampshire, Massachusetts, and New York. Many in his class were older one- or two-year men, some in their early twenties, who were inclined to do pretty much as they pleased. Student pranks and disorderly conduct up to the level of full-scale donnybrooks were not uncommon. During the administration of principal Walter A. Scott, who had also arrived in 1884, there was a serious breakdown in authority over student life, but not in academic discipline. "Complete liberty tempered by expulsion" was an old saying at the academy.

Scott was from Ohio, and his critics said that he never did learn New England's ways and the academy's reverence for its long-standing customs. He was breezy and loquacious; in the class history, the class historian, Tom Lamont, wrote a satirical piece about the principal's long-windedness. Taking over responsibility for parietal discipline from Professor Wentworth, he insensitively sent for the police to break up student fracases, a practice that offended everyone—boys, faculty, and townspeople.

For many years the students had held a huge bonfire on the town square to celebrate the end of the school year, a traditional event that Principal Scott decided to ban; he requested the Exeter police to enforce the order. The result was a noisy brawl in which the students fought with the police. Heads were broken; students were arrested and fined the next day in court. But the townspeople sided with the boys, and the bonfire was reinstituted the following year.

It is unlikely that Tom joined in this melee or the other rumored adventures, such as the goings-on of a worldly-wise group of older fellows, who slipped out of their houses at night to meet girls from the town and canoed up the little Exeter River to a special spot where they drank beer. Given his sheltered upbringing and stern Methodist training, Tom would have considered such conduct disgraceful.

Tom's letters home during this period of his adolescence portrayed a friendly and enthusiastic youth with strong family ties. He was eager to please his parents, especially "Papa," and his older brother and sister and win their praise for his accomplishments. No sign of a maturing sophisticate: Tom was still a small-town boy.

Despite the lack of strong administrative leadership at the school, there were some excellent teachers on the ten-man Exeter faculty, including George Wentworth, the distinguished mathematician, and Bradbury Cilley, the head of the Greek department, who had given Tom a fine new suit and overcoat, which, he said, had been left unexpectedly to him by a friend. Tom thought that George Lyman Kittredge, his instructor in Latin, was the best teacher he had ever had. Exeter's tough academic discipline and its policy of spurring students to be self-reliant had worked for Tom. His grades had been good, and he was ready for the wider world of college.

Fair Harvard and Its Sons

After graduating from Exeter, Tom entered the freshman class at Harvard College in September 1888. What he soon found most exciting about the college was its star-studded faculty, the legendary professors acclaimed as giants in their fields. George Herbert Palmer in ethics and Charles Eliot Norton in art history stirred Tom, and he went to hear the famous and eloquent Phillips Brooks whenever he preached at Appleton Chapel.

Even though Lamont did not consider himself an especially reflective type, he was drawn to Harvard's philosophers, especially William James, the eminent professor of psychology and elder brother of the noted novelist Henry James. William James was erect and dignified, his face kindly and handsomely bearded, his speech quiet and distinguished. His course was immensely popular, and the initial fall lecture had as special an aura as opening night at the opera.

Tom and the other Exeter students had been well prepared academically, but tended to lack the social graces and sophistication of some of their classmates, especially the cosmopolitan young aristocrats who would soon become members of the half dozen exclusive social clubs and Greek-letter fraternities, led by the venerable Porcellian Club. The newest club was the Delta Phi, whose senior-class member J. P. Morgan, Jr., son of the noted banker, had arranged the financing of its new quarters on Mt. Auburn Street.

In their clubhouses members dined sumptuously together, played billiards and backgammon, and smoked their pipes before the fire. Membership, based almost entirely on social background, drew mainly on the sons from old families of Boston, New York, and Philadelphia, who had attended the prestigious New England boarding schools like St. Paul's, St. Mark's, and Mr. Peabody's new school at Groton. Five or six years of rigorous sports activity on the playing fields of boarding school had developed some of these boys into fine athletes, and the leaders were chosen by their teammates to captain the football eleven and other Harvard teams. The prominence and popularity they enjoyed from success in athletics often led to their election to the key class offices.

Tom had gone out for the freshman football team for exercise and to get to know some of the class leaders. However, again his lack of athletic talent led him to abandon football for tennis. Nor did he ever join one of the select clubs. He could not have afforded the luxury anyway; it took a generous allowance from home to pay for the comforts of clubhouse life, and he had no desire to fritter away time with club cronies. He was not overawed by the club crowd.

There was another side of college social life new to Tom—the liberal consumption of spirits, usually beer or punch, by young men at parties or "on the town," graphically symbolized by the arrival scene of the "night car" from Boston. After it clanged to a stop on Massachusetts Avenue opposite Harvard Yard, a band of clubmen singing lustily would descend from it and stagger off toward the elegant dormitory apartments and clubs near Mt. Auburn Street, arms wrapped around each others' shoulders. Tom didn't like the physical effects of liquor, but he was not a prude and enjoyed the camaraderie of his friends in their convivial goings-on.

Determined to earn a good part of his college expenses, Tom had rejected the scholarship route, because he did not want to devote that much time to studying for high grades and thus forgo the rich variety of diversions that beckoned. He found another way.

His work on the editorial staff of Exeter's student newspaper and yearbook had given him the idea of seeking an editorship on the *Crimson*, the daily student newspaper at Harvard. He applied for the position and in February became the first member of his freshman class to be elected an editor of the *Crimson*. He immediately volunteered for a special editorial job that paid $5 a week—coming into the office every night about midnight to correct the final proofs and put the paper to bed. Nobody else was clamoring for this duty, and Tom held it over the next three years. Another financial reward came at the end of the year when the annual profits were divided up among the senior editors, and in his junior year, when he became president of the *Crimson*, his share amounted to $175.

The Boston newspapers always needed a regular correspondent at Harvard. Not only was Tom an able *Crimson* editor, but also, during the summer following his freshman year, he gained valuable experience as a reporter on the *Albany City Evening Journal*, replacing vacationing staff. Starting off as Harvard correspondent for the *Boston Advertiser*, he was hired away by the *Boston Herald*, which agreed to pay him $50 a month. "For me this was a bonanza," he later wrote.

One reporting job led to another. Tom soon was writing "Sunday Specials" on Harvard for the *Herald* that bore his initials and contributing pieces about Harvard events and sports to the *New York Tribune*. Before long he had achieved a modest reputation around Boston as a sports reporter, particularly of Harvard's football program.

In March 1889 the captain of the Harvard team introduced spring football practice for the first time at Harvard, but arch-rival Yale, coached by football mastermind Walter Camp, continued its winning ways in November. Yale had now beaten Harvard in ten of their twelve games. The sports rivalry between Harvard and Yale, and especially the annual football confrontation, had captured the public's enthusiasm, and the series had developed into an embarrassing runaway rout of Harvard teams by Yale. Captain A. J. Cumnock believed that an extraordinary effort was called for to prepare for the 1890 game.

Tom reported in the *Crimson* on Harvard's expanded program of spring and fall football practice in 1890, including the first use of a tackling dummy at Harvard, a device so heavy and hard that a number of players suffered injuries before the captain mercifully decided to spare his teammates from further grief. The football team returned to Cambridge two weeks before college opened in September, and practice was extremely rigorous—two o'clock to dusk, Monday through Friday—all conducted behind a high wooden fence. As a *Crimson* reporter Tom attended team practice sessions, but the managers were on guard against spies from football rivals, who might attempt to steal the secret plays being tested. On Saturdays he covered the games, which were held at Jarvis Field in Cambridge before some 10,000 high-spirited alumni and students.

Harvard rolled over all its ten opponents before the Yale game, and Yale also went undefeated. Spurred on by a rousing article in the *Crimson* and a torchlight rally the night before the game, Tom and a large band of students traveled by special train to Hampden Park Field in Springfield, joining the biggest crowd ever assembled for a Harvard-Yale game, close to 20,000 people. Given the emotional intensity of the teams' supporters, university officials had deemed it wise to choose a neutral site for the confrontation. The *Boston Herald* had assigned Tom to cover "The Game."

The stands were in an uproar as the teams came on the field. The Harvard players were dressed in brown moleskin knee breeches and crimson stockings and jerseys over which they wore tightlaced canvas jackets, uniforms providing little protection against the rough physical combat that followed. Injuries ranging from broken noses to concussions were not uncommon under the current rules and officiating. In the second half two Harvard touchdowns gave the Crimson a lead it never relinquished, and general pandemonium in the Harvard grandstands greeted the first Crimson victory over Yale in fifteen years.

In June 1891 the *Boston Herald* assigned Tom to New London for the week prior to the annual Harvard-Yale regatta on the Thames River to report on the training progress of the crews leading up to race day. In recent years Yale had dominated Harvard in crew as it had in football, and after five successive victories over Harvard, Yale's bigger crew was the clear favorite.

On the day of the race the reporter took in the spectacular scene on the river. A large fleet of vessels lined both sides of the course—graceful sloops with towering masts anchored alongside sleek steam yachts, whose polished mahogany and brass shone in the sunlight. Strings of colorful pennants, flags, and Harvard and Yale banners festooned the rigging of the assorted craft. The stern sections of many boats were filled with girls in white summer frocks and young men in blazers and straw boaters, and other spectators were taking their seats to follow the race on the observation train cars with open sides facing the river.

Tom was in the press boat, which followed just behind the racing shells, from the start—"Ready? Gentlemen, row!"—to the finish twenty-one minutes later in the densest part of the assembled fleet. The Harvard shell, which led from the start, came in ten lengths ahead of Yale. Harvard songs and blasts from horns filled the air, as the crew slumped over their oars, heaving to regain their breaths after four miles of brutal physical effort. Evidently Lamont enjoyed the colorful event, for years later he became a regular spectator at the regatta—from the deck of his own handsome yacht.

To ensure good grades Tom set aside a few days and nights before each examination period to review his courses, and one year he and a friend gave two well-attended seminars to review the History 1 course before the exams. At a price of $3.00 per student, Tom replenished his Christmas-depleted exchequer. He also pursued his bent for literature, becoming business manager and an editor of the literary *Harvard Monthly* and joining two literary societies, the Signet and the O.K., where the members read aloud articles and verse and then engaged in a critique of the selections.

There were other clubs, apart from the socially exclusive ones, whose pursuit of pleasure was far from intellectual. The raison d'être of the Hasty Pudding Institute of 1770 was its annual musical farce written and acted by members whose performance as hairy-legged chorus girls had become a comic tradition at Harvard. Tom sang and danced in the chorus in *The Sphinx or Love at Random*, a musical comedy set in ancient Egypt.

He also was invited to become a member of the D.K.E., known as the Dickey, another club dedicated to having a good time. On initiation night four members of the Dickey came up to his room on the third floor of Thayer Hall and manhandled him downstairs to join the other members in a noisy, chanting procession through the streets. The Dickey also put on shows, and Tom starred as the female lead in a rollicking comedy based on "The Lady or the Tiger." And he eagerly participated in various other student groups and committees at Harvard; he was and would remain a "joiner."

Lamont's friendliness made him a popular companion. His more affluent friends invited him to elaborate four-course dinners accompanied by champagne and witty toasts, served in their luxurious suites on Mt. Auburn Street. Sometimes he took the tramcars to Boston with friends to walk about the Common, explore the winding streets, and browse in the bookstores. He and his chums also got together with the local girls for teas and parties or walks in the country. But Tom had his eye on someone else.

At the June commencement exercises in 1890, Tom had met Miss Florence Corliss of Englewood, New Jersey, who was attending the graduation of a friend. He was quickly captivated by the pretty brown-haired seventeen-year-old charmer. She was gay, quick-witted, and fun to talk to. He had taken her for a stroll in Mt. Auburn Cemetery on Sunday, and on Monday they had taken the tramcars out to Wellesley.

"In spite of what that boy says, I think he is the worst flirt I ever met," Florence confided to her diary. In September she entered the freshman class at Smith College in Northampton, Massachusetts, and invited Tom to the Glee Club concert and dance at Smith on Washington's Birthday weekend.

Florence felt rattled and shy when she first saw Tom at Smith, but he had a way about him that put her quickly at ease. The weekend was blissful, thought Florence, who was persuaded that Tom was not flirting, but quite serious in expressing his affection for her. Tom said he would come back to see her again that spring.

In May *Crimson* reporter Lamont covered the Harvard-Amherst baseball game, which was played at Amherst, not far from Northampton. Florence joined Tom, and after the game they returned to Smith and had dinner at the Inn. On Sunday they went to church and took a walk in the rain, and another walk after supper, "the nicest of all," Florence wrote in her diary. She was almost afraid to admit to herself that she had fallen in love, "after all that has happened to prove how fickle I am."

In September Florence invited Tom to her home in Englewood to meet her parents, Mr. and Mrs. Wilbur Fisk Corliss. Wilbur Corliss headed his own business—Corliss, Coon & Co., Manufacturers of Linen Collars and Cuffs and Ladies' Shirt Waists—and the Corlisses lived comfortably in a pleasant residential neighborhood; in the eyes of small-town Methodists they might even have qualified as "rich Presbyterians." Florence's parents were cordial, Lamont wrote, although "they looked upon me as nothing but one of the crowd of boys who came and went" attracted by Florence's charms.

Tom graduated cum laude from Harvard College with a bachelor of arts degree in 1892. Always a solid student, he was now showing signs of a talent for politics. At Class Day, Neal Rantoul, a popular star athlete and First Marshal of the class, read off the list of class officers: it was headed by Lamont, the newly elected chairman of the Class Committee.

The Class Poet then recited his special poem for the occasion. The Ivy Orator delivered his comic address, and finally, it was the turn of the Class Orator, Hugh McKennan Landon, whose grandiloquent speech met the standard of fulsome rhetoric for this oration. "The heroism we must possess is not the courage to die, but the manfulness to live. Duty says as plainly as ever, 'you must.' It is for us to answer in the true spirit of Harvard men, 'we can and we will.' "

Tom had invited Florence to the commencement festivities. On Saturday evening there was dancing at the gymnasium and Memorial Hall to the strains of the Germania Orchestra and Baldwin's Band. While the Class Day Committee had ruled that caps and gowns must be worn during the day, they could be removed for dancing. A brilliant display of "illuminations" was presented in the Yard; the Glee Club sang, and the Banjo, Mandolin, and Guitar clubs performed on the Law School steps. Clearly the mood was romantic, for that night Tom told Florence how much he loved her. He wanted to marry her as soon as his earnings enabled him to support a family. Florence reported in her diary, "I told him I loved him, too." She would wait until he was ready.

Three days later Lamont performed his first official duty as chairman of the Class Committee, presiding at the Senior Commencement Dinner at the Quincy House, which the *Crimson* reported was a huge success. Tom must have enjoyed being the master of ceremonies, for it was a role that he would enthusiastically seek and perform at scores of banquets for the rest of his life.

On Commencement Day Tom and his classmates in caps and gowns filed into Memorial Hall. President Charles W. Eliot was seated in the traditional Jacobean chair of Harvard presidents, flanked on the commencement stage by several dozen senior faculty, deans, and members of the university's governing boards. Tom and his fellow students had generally viewed Eliot as a rather cold and aloof man as he staidly crossed the yard, but awesome—already a legend in the ranks of Harvard presidents for his introduction of the elective system for courses and his firm organization of the graduate schools.

Tom listened to a great deal of commencement oratory, from President Eliot on down, but he had found the closing words of Professor Josiah Royce in his last philosophy lecture of the year more to the point: "My dear young gentlemen, what I pray is that you may be granted the wisdom and the courage to endure the business of life."

Some of Tom's classmates were planning summer vacations at Newport, Saratoga Springs, and other resorts. Others would attend the World Columbia Exposition in Chicago celebrating the 400th anniversary of the discovery of America. Tom wanted to get on with "the business of life" and, on Monday morning, just two days after graduation, he reported to the city editor of the *New York Tribune*.

He would earn $25 a week, and much as he loved Florence, he knew that he could not afford to marry her. "I was so utterly lacking in worldly goods that I didn't dare to sign her up," he wrote later. Tom was ambitious, and perhaps in the thriving metropolis of New York he would come across some promising business opportunity. Florence, living with her parents in Englewood, would not be far away.

Member of the Press

The heat and humidity in New York in the summer of 1892 were overpowering, whether in the bustling editorial offices of the *Tribune* on Park Row or in the crowded streets. Reporting assignments were handed out by the city editor, Arthur F. Bowers, and Tom covered stories in the grimiest parts of the city—a murder in Hell's Kitchen, an outbreak of cholera on the lower West Side, and gang battles in Chinatown. To earn extra pay he wrote special features for the Sunday edition, such as tales of adventure in the early days of Dutch Manhattan and of Bowery gangster dens and plots.

During the final weeks of the 1892 election campaign, Tom undertook political reporting assignments. The allegations he had heard about corruption at Tammany Hall, the city's powerful Democratic political organization, would provide the basis of a good hard-hitting story on the local races. However, shortly before the election the managing editor circulated a memorandum to the staff suggesting that it did not seem advisable to charge Tammany leaders by name, noting that they allocated among the local papers the valuable election advertising that printed the addresses of hundreds of polling booths throughout the city. Times were hard; advertising revenues were critical, and the reporters did not protest.

Tom's health had never been robust, and he had paid little heed to it that summer and fall, working long hours, sleeping little and eating many meals on the run. Right after the election he woke up in his rooming house on Houston Street feeling miserable—feverish and weak. He took the trolley uptown to his parents' house next to the Amsterdam Avenue Church, his father's first big-city parish. His mother sent for the doctor, who diagnosed Tom's illness as typhoid fever, and he moved into the spare room, where his mother attended him. After a month's recuperation he accepted an invitation from some Harvard friends to visit California. A few months in the benign Southern California climate, where he picked oranges and swam in the Pacific, restored him to full health.

Tom wanted to return to newspaper work, but felt ready to assume more responsible duties than crime reporting in the most wretched parts of the city. Mr. Bowers had been impressed: Tom was accurate and thorough, wrote quickly, and was imaginative in adding descriptive color and giving proper focus to a story. In June 1893, Tom returned to the *Tribune* in a new job: he had been promoted to the position of assistant night city editor, editing the reporters' copy before passing it along to the city editor's desk, with official working hours from 5 p.m. to 1 a.m.

Most Saturdays Tom spent with Florence, taking the train out to Englewood, where they often took long walks on the woodland trails along the craggy rim of the Palisades, the great cliffs looming above the west bank of the Hudson River. They were especially drawn to the spot by the spectacular vistas, both north and south—the vast upper reaches of the river shimmering in the sun and the sprawling city with its downtown hub of massive office buildings.

They usually had supper with Florence's parents. Mrs. Corliss was warm and chatty; Mr. Corliss seemed a bit grim in the beginning, but in time Tom won him over. As for Florence, she and her mother called on the Lamont parents at the Methodist parsonage on Amsterdam Avenue, and the parson, never one given to effusiveness, observed in his diary that they were "pleasant people."

Tom took the train back to New York on Saturday evenings; a new assignment required him to work on Sundays—assisting the financial editor of the *Tribune* to make up the tables of railway earnings for the business section of the Monday paper. It was dull, mechanical work in a dusty basement office on Wall Street, but Tom was glad to take on the job for the extra pay and hoped it would expose him to the workings and people in the world of finance. He did not anticipate a long career in journalism.

Florence and her mother were embarking on the S.S. *Britannia* for a two-month tour of Europe in October, and while looking forward to her first trip to England and the Continent, Florence would desperately miss Tom. Her first letter to him arrived in the mail pouch brought from Sandy Hook by the pilot who had guided the liner out of New York Harbor.

Tom was distressed that he had not been able to leave the city desk for her sailing. The newspaper, forced to lay off staff in the 1893 "Cleveland depression," was too shorthanded to let him out even for a few hours.

Tom took on more and more assignments in business and financial news, but never managed to interview J. P. Morgan or any other leading financier. The moguls only rarely gave interviews, and then when they wished to announce a railway merger or new industrial combination. The bankers especially were extremely close-mouthed, mistrusting the press and its muckraking reporters.

While newspaper life was stimulating, Tom doubted that $35 a week was sufficient to get married and raise a family. One of the veteran *Tribune* editors confided to him that after thirty years of the grind of newspaper work he had not been able to set aside savings to support himself when he retired. He counseled Tom to get into business, where he could earn enough to live well and build up some reserves for old age, advice that made good sense to Tom.

Advancement came too slowly in journalism for Lamont, and he was ready to move on. He had worked closely with the city editor, who wrote a glowing letter of recommendation for him to show to prospective employers.

To whom it may concern:

MR. LAMONT is a newspaper man of wide and varied experience, of remarkable ability, or rare aptness, versatility, discretion, sagacity and judgment. In his talents, capacity and equipment for success in life his endowments are of uncommon worth and merit. For his admirable traits of character I have the highest regard and esteem, and am glad to consider him a personal friend. He is sure to make his mark and to achieve conspicuous success in whatever he may undertake.

(signed) Arthur F. Bowers, City Editor

Perils of Business

In August 1894, Arthur Lockett, an Exeter and Harvard classmate, asked Tom to join him in entering the firm of Cushman Bros., manufacturer's agents for brand-name food and household products in New York. Still a business innocent, Tom did not inquire if the enterprise was profitable. It was not and had been losing money steadily for a year. Furthermore, the capital of the firm was quite inadequate for its size and overhead, and it was impossible to obtain new bank loans. Tom was asked, as a condition of becoming secretary of the firm, to invest $5,000 in the corporation, which he assumed would be added to the firm's working capital. In fact, Tom was purchasing shares from one of the firm's senior officers who wanted to sell out. Tom had to borrow the $5,000 from his Uncle George, secured by a life insurance policy on which the annual premium amounted to 15 percent of his salary, a heavy drain on his slender budget. Lockett invested $10,000 in the firm on the same basis.

It was not an auspicious start in business. But the salary, $2,000, was better, and the prospects for early advancement promising if the company could be kept afloat to survive the worst economic depression the country had experienced in decades. Prices and wages were at rock bottom; there were soup kitchens, and ragged bands of unemployed swarmed the streets of New York; demand was weak for the consumer products handled by Cushman.

The function of Cushman Bros. was to act as the sales representative for out-of-town manufacturers who wanted to sell their products in the New York market but were too small or ill equipped to do it on their own. Cream of Wheat, Trolley Laundry Soap, OPT Self Rising Corn Flour, Sure Catch Sticky Fly Paper, and O.K. Root Beer were valued clients. The firm was located at 78 Hudson Street on the lower west side and had about a dozen salesmen.

Lamont's first job at Cushman Bros. was writing advertising copy for Cream of Wheat. This task grew into developing the overall marketing strategy for Cream of Wheat, as well as for the other products handled by the firm. Before long Tom was negotiating with manufacturers the detailed agreements covering the marketing programs and the terms of Cushman's compensation, which he improved significantly.

Lamont also succeeded in making the firm's procedures more efficient and in cutting costs. An important saving was effected when the senior officers of the firm, the two Cushman brothers, Townshend and William, were persuaded by the major stockholder to accept a reduction in their salaries, which Tom felt was a fully justifiable move in light of their modest contributions.

Tom supplemented his own salary by continuing to take on special reporting assignments for the *Tribune*. Sometimes, after a full day of work at Cushman Bros., Tom edited copy at the *Tribune* office late into the night, when the paper was shorthanded.

Cushman Bros., while not becoming prosperous, added a few customers and survived. At the end of nine months Tom received a $500 raise. In September 1895, after one year on the job, he asked Mr. Cushman, the president, for a $300 increase, which would bring his salary up to $2,800. Tom felt sure that the Cushmans would conclude that they couldn't get along without him if he announced that he was leaving to return to the *Tribune*, where he had a standing offer. Furthermore, the Cushman brothers were obligated to repurchase his stock in the firm for $5,000 if he left. He got the raise.

More certain of his prospects, Tom asked Florence to marry him in October, and having waited over three long years, she happily said yes. The invitation read: "Mr. and Mrs. Wilbur Fisk Corliss request the honour of your presence at the marriage of their daughter, Florence Haskell, to Mr. Thomas William Lamont, on Thursday evening, October the thirty-first, at half after seven o'clock, in The Presbyterian Church, Englewood, New Jersey." The wedding guests were invited back to the home of Mr. and Mrs. Corliss on Hillside Street after the ceremony.

Tom's six ushers included four Harvard classmates, his brother Hammond, and Charles Corliss, his future brother-in-law, who arrived by train from Chicago, where he worked in the branch office of his father's firm. At the bachelor party at the Arena restaurant in Manhattan, Tom handed out his ushers' presents, small initialed silver cuff-links boxes.

Tom's father joined the Presbyterian pastor in conducting the marriage ceremony, and afterward Tom had his best man, Pitts Duffield, give the minister $25 and the sexton $10. The bride and groom spent their honeymoon at a resort in the Great Smoky Mountains, and on their return to Englewood moved into a small rented house on Maple Street, a shady tree-lined thoroughfare running between rows of modest homes with front verandas and well-trimmed lawns. As 1895 came to a close, Tom began a new existence—that of commuter—marked by long weekdays in the city and the precious contentment of weekends at home.

Cushman's business remained poor in 1896, but there was a redeeming feature for Tom. Cushman Bros. was increasingly receiving inquiries from European manufacturers, especially English companies interested in penetrating the huge American market, and Tom persuaded the Messrs. Cushman that he should become the firm's foreign courier, traveling to Europe to develop new business. In June 1896 he and Florence embarked for Glasgow on the *Anchorian*, a small Anchor Line steamer. It was Lamont's first trip abroad.

The twelve-day crossing to Glasgow, bucking northeast winds, was very rough. But for the Lamonts it was a grand adventure, and their traveling companions, mostly college professors and their families, were congenial. They spent hours in the main lounge discussing the travel books they were reading; they compared notes on the costs and quality of different hotels and planned to rendezvous at restaurants in London and Paris. The young couple spent three weeks in London, where Tom succeeded in arranging to represent several English companies exporting products to America. Other business prospects would warrant future trips abroad.

London was the largest city in the world in 1896 and the leading center of business and finance. For Tom it was also the London of Samuel Johnson, Charles Dickens, and Sherlock Holmes, a city filled with an abiding sense of history. The romantic in him was enthralled by the beauty of the city's parks and palaces and its age-old buildings and thoroughfares, crowded with people and carriages.

On this first trip to England, Lamont contracted a severe case of Anglophilia, a romance with the country and its people. He admired their civility, their adherence to principles of human rights, inherited by his own countrymen, and their rich literary heritage. Despite a few lovers' tiffs, his attachment would be lifelong.

After a fortnight's holiday on the Continent, the Lamonts arrived home in late August, and Tom reported to his colleagues at Cushman Bros. on the prospects for obtaining new European accounts. He also learned what had transpired in their business since his departure, and the news was bad. Two of Cushman's biggest accounts had not renewed their agency contracts. Now the firm was draining cash again, and a $5,000 advance from a major customer, whose repayment had already been postponed, was due in two weeks. Tom immediately wrote to one of his wealthy Harvard friends—Edgar Mills of San Francisco. Lamont had visited Mills in California when he was recovering from typhoid fever and had continued to keep in touch with him about class business.

Tom told Mills that he was forced to humiliate himself and write to old friends for help. He was desperate, "so I'm going to put my pride in my pocket and be frank with you."

Tom described the state of Cushman's business. If he couldn't secure a large loan in the next week or so, Cushman Bros. would go under, and he'd be out of a job. What happened to the firm really meant the difference to Florence and him between poverty and comfortable living. Their happiness for many years to come depended on saving the firm. Tom had put his heart and two years of very hard work into the business and could not stand seeing everything lost. "On the other hand, I hate to approach you, Edgar, on something like this, but my own family is poor, as you know, and it's so vitally important to me."

Tom then proceeded to describe the future prospects of Cushman Bros. in decidedly rosy terms. With the ten new clients they expected to sign up, Cushman would have forty agency contracts for first-class consumer products, which would provide the revenue to repay the loans and earn a 25 percent return on capital. Then they would think about expanding— opening up branches in Boston and Chicago for a start.

Securing a $5,000 loan or even more would be the key to turning around this desperate situation. He would be forever grateful for whatever assistance Mills could provide, and Tom would make it his personal responsibility to see that Mills was repaid as promptly as possible. "You know me well enough, Edgar. I won't rest until you're paid back in full. That's a promise!"

Mills replied, "My dear fellow, I am so sorry for what you are going through. For God's sake don't be too downhearted. I just know that with your ability and energy you will win out." Unfortunately, he had had to assist other friends in recent months whose businesses had suffered in the depressed economic environment. Just three weeks earlier he had tied up his last remaining liquid funds, several thousand dollars, in a short-term loan to a friend.

Tom quickly wrote back to Mills asking for his commitment to lend Cushman the money as soon as Mills's friend repaid it. He could make interim financing arrangements. Mills agreed to Tom's proposal, and Cushman Bros., through various economies and rescheduling of debts, weathered the immediate financial storm.

In 1896 the Republicans, led by William McKinley of Ohio, won the White House. The Dingley Tariff of 1897 provided the highest protection for American industry in history. The long depression was over, and American business entered a period of prosperity and growth.

But Cushman Bros. continued to find the going rough. Because the

New York market was so big and growing, larger manufacturers established their own sales forces in the city, and when Cushman Bros. did a
good job in marketing the products of smaller companies, they frequently
dispensed with Cushman's services to carry on by themselves. However,
Tom was optimistic about obtaining more assignments from British
manufacturers exporting to America and planned regular business trips
to England in the future.

Following Townshend Cushman's decision to retire, Lamont decided
to bring his brother-in-law, Charles Corliss, into the firm. Tom's father-
in-law had sold his interest in the linen collar company, and Charles was
ready to make the move. He would invest $2,500 in Cushman Bros.
Lamont thought that he was an able young businessman, and even more
important, Charles was family. Tom wanted someone close to him whom
he could trust completely, someone who would keep an eye on things
when he went abroad. Lamont's views on running the firm now carried
considerable weight, and Corliss was hired.

In the spring of 1898, Tom was very discouraged about Cushman's
business. The firm had lost two more accounts. Tom had not had a raise
in salary for over a year and had to abandon his plan to build a new
house in Englewood.

Howard C. Smith, a wealthy private businessman, was the firm's main
backer, and his patience was wearing thin. In addition to his stock
holdings he had lent $30,000 to Cushman Bros., and payments of interest
and principal were long overdue. An additional $20,000 was owed three
other individuals and a bank. Smith discussed Cushman's dire straits and
Tom's forthcoming trip to Britain with him. It was clear that if business
didn't pick up, the firm couldn't survive for long.

Upon Tom's return to New York from London he was greeted with the
news that his friend Arthur Lockett was leaving to join the Army.
Following America's declaration of war against Spain in April and the
ensuing American victories in Cuba, Lockett had enlisted in the New
York Volunteer Cavalry and would soon sail with his regiment to Puerto
Rico, the other Spanish possession in the Caribbean. The worst news was
that Smith's fears had come to pass: Cushman Bros. was insolvent.
Creditors were demanding payment, and the firm had no funds to pay
them off.

On a humid evening in early August, Tom boarded Howard Smith's
motor yacht at Battery Park for a cruise up the Hudson. Smith, Cushman's major investor, had to decide whether to wind up Cushman Bros.
or try to develop a feasible plan of reorganization. Cushman couldn't

pay its debts, and Smith would not risk additional funds unless a plan could be devised that would put the business back on its feet.

Tom knew that the firm's overhead, especially the three officers' salaries, including his own, were an intolerable drain on Cushman's revenues. He offered his resignation, secure in the knowledge that he had been offered the city editorship of the *New York Evening Post*. Smith asked Tom what he would prefer to do, and he replied that he would like to remain in the business. He had persuaded Charles Corliss, his brother-in-law, to come on board, and he didn't want to abandon him. Second, he hated to admit failure.

Smith said he was pleased with Lamont's answer because he had already decided that he wanted him to stay and run the business. William Cushman would have to leave, and Arthur Lockett could not return to his old job; the firm could no longer afford their salaries. Charles Corliss could stay on, but other expenses would be cut to the bone. The next step was to devise a workable financial plan.

Various bills and customer advances of about $8,000 had to be repaid immediately, and Smith agreed to lend Cushman Bros. this amount. Lamont would personally guarantee repayment of this loan and the existing bank loan to Cushman Bros., additional security the bank now demanded. However, even with the savings from eliminating two salaries, the firm's financial condition was fragile. Ridding Cushman Bros. of its other debts was essential: with the threat of default hanging over the business, customers would be reluctant to advance monies to the company.

Lamont, Lockett, and Cushman were now all significant stockholders of Cushman Bros. Lamont proposed that the individual creditors accept their personal notes in substitution for the notes of the firm, with their holdings of Cushman Bros. stock as collateral. An allocation of Cushman's profits would be set aside monthly to repay these loans, but the three young men bore the ultimate responsibility for repayment. Lamont knew that Lockett and Cushman wanted to protect their investments in Cushman Bros., just as he did. Lockett was a close friend, and he and Cushman had confidence in Lamont's ability to turn the company around. They knew that the large personal risk he was running in backing the loans was not uncalculated. Lamont had done his homework and formed a definite strategy for substantial growth in revenues and income. Everyone bought the plan, and Smith offered Tom a package of first refusal rights and options on Cushman stock. The new chief executive would have a strong incentive to restore Cushman's profitability.

Tom wrote Edgar Mills, his college friend who had lent Cushman Bros.

$3,000, to obtain his approval of the plan. Tom was quite gloomy in describing his overwhelming business worries. "I try to keep cheerful, but it's not easy," he wrote. He also told Mills that Florence was expecting a baby in February.

Mills wrote in reply that Tom could "do anything with my loan." He returned the Cushman check for the latest interest payment and sympathized with Tom's troubles. "Please cheer up, old man! Incidentally, I'm delighted with your domestic news."

Florence had made her family doubly proud and happy. In June 1898 she received her master's degree from Columbia University in philosophy, a subject that would become her life-long passion. Her master's thesis was entitled "A Criticism of Browning's Dramas from the Aristotlelian Point of View: A Study in the Philosophy of Literature."

Lamont was elected president of Cushman Bros. on September 1, 1899. The increase in salary he received was timely: Thomas Stilwell Lamont was born on January 30, 1899, in Englewood Hospital.

A year later Lamont received a note from Howard Smith, who had just reviewed the Cushman Bros. financial statements for 1899. He was pleased with the outcome; his large investment now seemed secure. "I would like to extend my heartiest congratulations to you, Tom. Honesty and hard work make the difference every time."

There was much more to it than that—the wit and imagination to see that extensive and dynamic advertising was the key to selling consumer products as their markets became nationwide. Cushman would now take on new accounts only if the manufacturer was willing to commit funds for a vigorous advertising campaign. Working with J. Walter Thompson and other advertising agencies, Cushman would promote products in national magazines such as *Collier's, Good Housekeeping*, and the *Saturday Evening Post*, as well as the local newspapers.

Furthermore, it was important to have a widespread office network to serve customers well and attract new ones. Within six months Cushman had opened new branches in Washington and Boston, and Lamont planned to establish offices in Pittsburgh, Buffalo, Philadelphia, and Chicago before long.

In August, *Merchant's Review*, the leading business periodical reporting news in the food trade, carried the following news item:

> The remarkable growth of the business of Cushman Bros. Company, the well known manufacturers' representatives of this city, should be set down to the credit of the worthy president, Mr. Thomas W. Lamont, who has worked his way up from an obscure position to the active control of the

company's large and expanding business. . . . We are glad to hear that the Wesson cooking oil and the Wesson salad oil, recently added to the agency list of the Cushman Bros. Co., are giving the utmost satisfaction in this city.

Another new piece of business was the American agency for selling Peter Cailler Kohler Swiss Chocolates. On their visit to Paris in 1900, Tom and Florence discovered the excellent milk chocolate, and Lamont persuaded the management of the Swiss firm to sell its product in the U.S. through Cushman Bros.

New accounts also came to Cushman Bros. from the financial community. Tom's Englewood neighbor, banker Harry Davison, and Howard Smith recognized Lamont's uncommon ability to create successful marketing programs for products with sluggish sales and spread the word to bankers and brokers. Howard Smith frequently told his business friends: "The boy is a business doctor. If you have a sick corporation, send for Lamont. He will make it well."

O'Sullivan Rubber Heels and Pond's Extract were two companies that Tom turned around with vigorous new advertising programs. He negotiated options to obtain stock in Pond's Extract and hoped to gain control of the company in a few years. Lamont was now pursuing a new strategy—to acquire a couple of modest-size manufacturing companies to end Cushman Bros.' dependence on the shifting fortunes of marketing other companies' products. Cushman Bros. must be in control of its own progress.

There was ample reason for the board to change the name of the firm, which became Lamont, Corliss, and Company on January 1, 1902. The president's annual salary was increased to $6,500, and the Lamont family continued to grow, with the arrival of a second son, Corliss, on March 28, 1902.

In June 1902 Tom went to Europe again, spending most of his time in England. Upon his return he met with the editor of the *Merchant's Review*, and a story on Lamont, Corliss soon appeared in that journal.

Mr. Thomas W. Lamont . . . returned on Saturday last per Cunard flyer "Lucania," from a brief trip abroad. One of Mr. Lamont's purposes in visiting England was to open an English branch of his American business. The domestic business . . . controlled and managed by Mr. Lamont and his able colleague, Mr. C. A. Corliss, has grown rapidly of late years, and some of the American manufacturers whose goods they have been successfully handling have been casting longing eyes across the water, where American goods are becoming the vogue. It was at the instance of some of these enterprising American manufacturers that Mr. Lamont went to London to look over the ground, and to establish a branch house there. While in England Mr. Lamont also made arrangements to act as the American selling agents for Yorkshire Relish. This sauce has an enormous sale in Great Britain . . . and Mr. Lamont is sanguine of success in making a market for their product in America.

On a trip through the Midwest to promote his firm's new ability to assist American exporters, Tom visited his Buffalo and Chicago offices and went on to Minneapolis and Pittsburgh to call on old customers and new prospects. Their outlook foresaw a period of strong business growth and expansion to new markets abroad.

Lamont, Corliss needed additional capital to finance the growth of its business, especially the new export department. Howard Smith, one of Smith's friends, and Edgar Mills now felt confident in investing an additional $35,000 in the firm. In 1902 Lamont, Corliss had a net worth of $130,000 and earnings of $30,000. The firm retired much of its debt and paid a dividend to its patient stockholders. After years of heavy going, Tom felt optimistic about his business as he relaxed on the Boston train taking him to his tenth Harvard Class Reunion at Cambridge.

The activities opened with an outing at The Country Club in Brookline, with lunch, golf, and poker for the nonathletes. At the black-tie dinner at the Hasty Pudding Club that evening, after the brandy and cigars had been passed, Lamont, in his role as class chairman, addressed his classmates:

"Ten years have passed since we sat together at our last dinner as undergraduates of Harvard College. We met to say good-bye and then to turn our backs upon Cambridge and upon each other and face the cold, cruel world."

Lamont thanked the Boston members for their hospitality. He then reminded his classmates of their athletic heroes and the victorious football games and crew races against Yale.

> Fine old days! But they are over—never to return. We are all playing in a bigger game now, and most of us have tougher foe to tackle than ever Yale could be. A few of us have died fighting, but these, could they speak to us to-night, would tell us not to let thought of them sadden us, but rather to take up the tasks that they started so well, and to fight on with glad hearts and warm courage. For some of us life has already given us its struggles. We have had to bear the burden and heat of the day; to fight down the hard luck and handicaps that have beset us on every side; to do our best to turn our stumbling-blocks into stepping stones. But whether your lot and my lot in these last ten years has been an easy one or a hard one, I cannot but think that we have grown steadily "wiser to comprehend and stronger to endure the business of life."

The somewhat sanctimonious style was not uncommon at the time; the grandiloquent phrasing would be a Lamont oratorical mannerism for years to come.

Down a New Road

The year 1903 saw remarkable technological achievement in America. A Packard car, driven from San Francisco to New York, completed the first cross-country automobile trip. At Kitty Hawk the Wright brothers successfully made their first flight in a new heavier-than-air craft. The first feature film, *The Great Train Robbery*, was produced. The Pacific cable between San Francisco and Manila was laid, and President Theodore Roosevelt sent the first message over it. And in the grayer world of banking a seemingly modest innovation changed Lamont's life irrevocably.

In January 1903, Henry P. Davison and a group of young bankers agreed at a dinner meeting at the Metropolitan Club to organize a new trust company. Bankers Trust Company was designed to handle the trust business of the customers of commercial banks and investment firms, which were not permitted by law to serve as trustees for individual and corporate funds.

At the time, banks were compelled to refer their customers' trust business to some forty-eight existing trust companies operating in New York. These companies also took in deposits, which they invested in mortgages and other high-yielding loans, and were permitted lower liquidity ratios than the banks. By offering higher interest rates a trust company sometimes attracted the deposits, along with the trust business, of a bank's customers.

The Bankers Trust was conceived by Davison as a bankers' defense against this competition from trust companies. Commercial banks and investment banking firms would refer the trust business of their clients to the new company, which would not bid deposits away from the banks, accepting only secondary inactive accounts. The cream of the banking community was solidly behind the new trust company and represented on its board of directors, which included George W. Perkins of J. P. Morgan & Co.

Bankers Trust company opened for business in a two-room office at 143 Liberty Street on March 30, 1903, the same day that newspaper headlines announced the first news transmission from New York to London by Marconi wireless. The initial staff of nine, including T. W. Lamont, the secretary and treasurer newly recruited by Davison, soon expanded to handle the rapidly growing business. By the end of the year deposits stood at $10 million.

Secretary-Treasurer Lamont noted the promising growth in business at the weekly executive committee meetings held at the Metropolitan Club. The small office on Liberty Street soon proved inadequate, and Bankers Trust moved to large banking offices at 7 Wall Street, near Broadway, where the clanging of the new electric cars and clattering of carriages over the rough pavement created a constant din throughout the day.

In 1904 the newly constructed first section of the New York subway opened to general acclaim, the business of Bankers Trust continued to grow rapidly, and the Lamont family moved into a larger house in Englewood. In 1905, Florence gave birth to a third son, Austin, and TWL was elected to the Bankers Trust board of directors.

Lamont was soon made a member of the executive committee, mainly composed of active young bankers like Davison. The Thursday evening dinner meetings, lasting from 6:30 to 10:30 p.m., brought the outside directors together with the Bankers Trust management to focus on expanding the business of the new trust company. When a sudden financial storm imperiled Wall Street, Davison could call on the cooperation of this group in the bankers' efforts to restore confidence.

In October 1907 a series of crises rocked the financial markets, and the threatening rumors of dire events to come caused more alarm. Public confidence in the soundness of financial institutions was critical. There were no government mechanisms in 1907 to support foundering banks and protect their depositors—no central bank, such as existed in Great Britain and France, to serve as lender of last resort and organize assistance efforts; no system to insure repayment of funds to depositors if a bank failed.

J. Pierpont Morgan, the senior partner of J. P. Morgan & Co., the powerful private banking firm, had long been recognized as the most influential figure in American finance. He was in Richmond, Virginia, attending the annual meeting of the bishops of the Episcopal Church when the storm first broke. Persuaded by phone calls from his partners, Morgan returned promptly to New York to assume command of the effort to quell the mounting panic in the financial community.

The crisis in confidence had been triggered by widespread rumors about the weak financial condition of the Knickerbocker Trust Company, whose president, Charles T. Barney, it was reported, had speculated and lost large sums of company funds in the stock market. Trust company depositors were scared, and the rush to withdraw deposits spread like a virulent epidemic to other institutions, including the healthy.

Back in New York, Morgan at once formed a rescue team led by himself, George F. Baker of the First National Bank, and James Stillman of the National City Bank. This triumvirate selected a team of able younger bankers to examine the condition of the institutions seeking help and to carry out the plans to support those found worthy of assistance. George W. Perkins, from the Morgan firm, Henry P. Davison of the First National Bank, and Benjamin Strong of the Bankers Trust were key members of the group. The command post for the rescue effort quickly became the Morgan Library on 36th Street between Madison and Park avenues. Meetings were held there daily over the next two weeks, mainly in the evening after the close of business.

The financial panic revealed itself in new and disturbing ways during the tumultuous last days of October. The stock market plunged without restraint, with almost no one interested in buying. With confidence collapsing, out-of-town banks began to withdraw the funds they kept on deposit in New York. Credit grew tighter and tighter. Broker loans for purchasing securities, at astronomical interest rates, were virtually unobtainable. Some small brokerage houses failed, and then a new crisis appeared at the major brokerage firm of Moore and Schley. This house, which had financed its customers' large purchases of Tennessee Coal and Iron Co. stock, found itself unable to meet loan calls of $25 million, and it was impossible to sell the stock without massive losses. The mayor of New York and key city officials came to the library to inform Morgan and the bankers that the city needed $30 million to meet its payroll and maturing obligations on November 1. Outside some of the trust companies long lines of frightened depositors waited to withdraw their funds.

Lamont was monitoring the situation closely at Bankers Trust, all day and well into the night; he stayed at a downtown hotel, and Florence packed a suitcase of fresh clothes for him, which was delivered to his office by Harry Davison's chauffeur when he drove into the city. Fortunately, the Bankers Trust was viewed by its depositors—corporations, banks, and people of substantial means—as a strong, well-managed institution, and withdrawals were not serious.

The Knickerbocker Trust Company and several other institutions suffering heavy deposit losses were forced to close their doors and suspend operations. Ben Strong, after examining the books and bundles of collateral for loans presented by the Trust Company of America, had concluded that the firm was still solvent, and Morgan and his colleagues agreed to come to its aid. Funds were advanced to meet the withdrawals, but the run on deposits continued at its headquarters just a few doors down Wall Street from the Morgan offices at the corner of Broad and Wall.

All these emergencies were studied by Morgan and his lieutenants at the library, where plans were formed and implemented to advance funds from the banking pools whenever it appeared that an institution could be saved. The conferences at the library grew longer, often lasting into the early morning hours, and Morgan, not at full strength at age seventy, began to suffer from fatigue and came down with a cold.

On the evening of Saturday, November 2, the Morgan Library was filled with bankers. Judge Elbert Gary, chairman of the United States Steel Corporation, which was considering purchasing the Moore and Schley Tennessee Coal and Iron stock, was also there. Commercial bankers occupied the East Room, and trust company executives the West Room, with Morgan moving from group to group. Davison had asked Lamont to attend the meeting.

"A more incongruous meeting place for anxious bankers could hardly be imagined," TWL wrote later.

> In one room were lofty, magnificent tapestries hanging on the walls, rare Bibles and illuminated manuscripts of the Middle Ages filling the cases. In another, walled with red silk damask patterned with the arms of the Chigi family of Siena, there were Renaissance Florentine masters, a bust by Michaelangelo, two exquisite Donatello statuettes, porcelains, and enamels. An anxious throng of bankers, too uneasy to sit down or converse at ease, paced up and down the lofty chambers and through the lovely marble hall.

"President Edward King of the Union Trust Company had by common consent been selected as the leader of the trust company presidents," Lamont recalled. "After hours of discussion and the display of all the figures by the accountants, Mr. Morgan pointed out to Mr. King and his fellow executives that action must be taken, that a fresh loan of $25,000,000 must be made to save the Trust Company of America or the walls of the other edifices might come crumbling about their ears."

Morgan declared that the experts had just reported that the Trust Company was solvent, and therefore no loss should result from the loan. As the commercial banks were looking after the general situation, it behooved the trust companies to look after their own. Yet, Lamont recalled, the trust company presidents were reluctant to act.

> They felt that in the absence of their directors they had no authority to commit their institutions. They questioned whether their first duty was not to conserve all their assets for the storm which, despite everything, might burst upon them. Mr. Morgan understood well enough their concern . . . but he had a task to accomplish. The situation must not get farther out of hand; it had to be saved. . . . He was satisfied that if each trust company

president present signed for an amount computed fairly on the basis of his company's resources, the several boards of directors would surely ratify the action.

The lawyers had drafted a simple subscription form for the $25 million loan. One of them read it aloud to the assembled bankers and placed it on the table. Mr. Morgan pointed his hand invitingly toward the paper. "There you are, gentlemen," he said.

"The bankers shifted from one foot to another," TWL recalled, "but no one stepped forward. Mr. Morgan waited a few moments. Then he put his hand on the shoulder of his friend, Edward King, and gently urged him forward. 'There's the place, King,' he said kindly but firmly, 'and here's the pen,' placing a handsome gold pen in Mr. King's fingers. Mr. King signed. The ice was broken, and they all signed." The meeting was over at quarter to five on Sunday morning, and the exhausted bankers walked out into the dark and silent streets.

Morgan had taken steps to ensure that no one leave until a satisfactory agreement was reached. After Ben Strong had given his report on the Trust Company of America, he thought that he was free to go home, since he had completed his task and it was three o'clock in the morning. Strong went to the front door of the library and found that it was locked. He was informed that Mr. Morgan had had the door locked and personally pocketed the key. He intended that everyone should stay until the end of the party, and they did.

The outcome of the all-night conference at the library, with the banks and the trust companies coming forward with enough money to meet the banking crisis, restored confidence in New York that spread throughout the country. Morgan alone had possessed the leadership to quell the panic. He had acted privately as a central bank when there was no central bank, and the episode publicly confirmed the unequaled power and influence of the masterful banker.

Edmund C. Converse, president of the Bankers Trust, was an older businessman with many outside interests. He was happy to delegate to Lamont the daily management of the Bankers Trust's operations. Late evenings of work or formal business dinners at elegant establishments like Sherry's restaurant or the Waldorf-Astoria hotel also became a routine part of TWL's life.

Lamont still met regularly with Charles Corliss to go over the affairs of Lamont, Corliss and Co. Business was good; the firm now had a solid roster of manufacturing clients. Corliss had just negotiated an agreement with Peter Cailler Kohler to manufacture its chocolates in Fulton, New York, for sale to the American market. Lamont, Corliss would own the major interest in the American company, Peters Chocolate Co. Other profitable deals came Lamont's way, including the Crowell Publishing Co. stock syndicate, which TWL formed with his friend Arthur Lockett, now a broker. His Englewood cronies Davison and Case, along with several Chase bank executives, were in the investment group. Lamont also managed a small securities portfolio for his parents, now settled in Englewood, and advised a few friends on their investments.

TWL was made a vice president of Bankers Trust in 1908, with a salary of $18,000. That summer he took a business trip to Europe, accompanied by Florence, the three boys, and his parents, who stayed at a cottage Lamont had rented at Seaford on the English Channel.

Bankers Trust had been chosen by the American Bankers Association to organize the issuance of travelers' checks for its member banks, who were eager to get into this lucrative business dominated by the American Express Company. As agent bank, Bankers Trust would deposit funds at selected British and Continental banks, whose branches and correspondents would form a network prepared to accept the travelers' checks. During the summer Lamont successfully negotiated participation agreements with the leading European bankers. The system was put into effect the following year and notably added to the prestige of Bankers Trust in the banking community.

During the panic of 1907, Davison had been the senior general in the field, reporting to Pierpont Morgan, the supreme commander at headquarters. Morgan had been well impressed with Davison's performance and invited him in 1908 to become a partner of the Morgan firm. When Davison resigned from the First National Bank, he recommended to George F. Baker, the president, that Tom Lamont succeed him there, and TWL left Bankers Trust to become a vice president and director of First National Bank at the beginning of 1909. The Morgan-Baker-governed ladder of advancement for promising younger banking executives was operating smoothly.

Later that year Tom and Florence bought Harry Davison's house in Englewood when the Davisons decided to move to Locust Valley, Long Island. It was a comfortable rambling white house crowned with a red stucco roof and well screened by a row of trees from Beech Road. They rejoiced at the birth of their first daughter, Eleanor, in 1910, who joined her three schoolboy brothers, Tommy, Corliss, and Austin. Lamont still caught the 8:22 a.m. train to New York each morning, and now Florence drove him to the Englewood station and picked him up at night in their new automobile.

TWL saw Pierpont Morgan regularly at the monthly board meetings of First National Bank, along with James J. Hill, the pioneering builder of northwestern railroad systems. Lamont joined Hill's Northern Pacific board of directors and soon became expert in the intricacies of railroad finance. First National Bank often collaborated with the Morgan firm on railroad financings, and Morgan was always cordial to Lamont, although if TWL walked by him in the street, Morgan might take no notice of him. Flat-topped derby hat firmly in place, a half-smoked cigar clenched between his teeth, and gold-headed cane in hand, Morgan marched down the sidewalk with piercing eyes fixed straight ahead. People recognized the illustrious banker and kept out of his way, presuming that in his preoccupation he would not heed anything or anyone else.

Mr. Morgan's Choice

Lamont was surprised when he received a telephone message in late October 1910 that Mr. Morgan wanted to see him at his office. He walked down to No. 23 Wall Street, and the guard showed him through the double doors into the partners' enclosure.

As TWL entered the rear room Morgan spoke to him from his desk. "Come over by me," he said, wishing him a good morning. Then he began abruptly, "Lamont, I want you to come down here as a partner on January 1st next."

Lamont was utterly stunned. He had been at the First National Bank for only two years, and he was just forty years old, younger than any Morgan partner. "But what could I do for you?" he stammered.

"Oh, you'll find plenty to keep you busy," Morgan responded. "Just do whatever you see before you that needs to be done." He appeared to think that the interview was over but then added, "You'll come, of course, won't you?"

"Mr. Morgan," TWL replied, "I am pleased beyond words that you should want me. But Mr. Baker has been exceedingly kind and generous to me. I can say nothing to you until I have talked with Mr. Baker."

"Oh, that's all right," said Morgan. "I have already talked with him, of course." He seemed to think imparting that information had settled the matter.

"Nevertheless, I know you'll understand that I must talk first with Mr. Baker, sir," Lamont replied.

"Oh, yes, quite all right," he responded. "Hope to see you here the first of the year."

Then he turned and twisted in his seat a moment. "You know, Lamont," he said, "I want my business done up there," holding his hand high over his head, "not down there," pointing to the floor.

There was never a moment of doubt in TWL's mind about accepting the golden opportunity to become a Morgan partner. He immediately spoke to George F. Baker, the wise old banker with bushy muttonchop whiskers, who had led the First National to the top rank in banking and was Pierpont Morgan's warm friend and staunchest banking ally. At the time Morgan told Lamont: "The First National Bank and J. P. Morgan & Co. occupy adjoining rooms in the same house."

TWL wrote his chief a farewell letter:

Dear Mr. Baker:
    Before I leave my desk at the First National Bank, I want to bear testimony in this brief note, in regard to the happiness that I have had in working with you and your associates. In all my business life, I have never had a personal relationship so pleasant as this. You, Mr. Hine, George, and Backus made me, from the very first day, feel that this was my home, and there has never been among us anything but harmony and good will. It has never fallen my lot to work with men of a higher sense of honor, and in this—as in all other respects—I count myself exceedingly fortunate in having this association.
    I look upon the First National as the greatest bank in this country, by virtue of tradition, character, record and ability; and my best hope for myself is that you will all permit me always to subscribe myself most sincerely and affectionately

Your friend,
Thomas W. Lamont

Baker replied to Lamont that he was convinced that he was making the right decision in joining the Morgan firm. He also warned him that he would have "added cares" and that as "a willing performer" he was "apt to get more than is good for you," a possibility that hardly worried TWL.

A series of steps had led to Lamont's invitation to become a Morgan partner. George W. Perkins, Pierpont Morgan's senior associate, had decided to resign to devote himself to civic affairs. There had been a growing rift between Morgan and Perkins over the handling of firm business, and it was generally assumed on Wall Street that Morgan had pressed Perkins to withdraw.

Morgan had increasingly delegated major tasks to Harry Davison, who became his first officer when Perkins retired. Davison in turn wanted Tom Lamont as his chief lieutenant. Thus following in Davison's footsteps again, Lamont had won the blue ribbon of American banking, a partnership in the House of Morgan.

After the newspaper announcement of the new Morgan partner, TWL received scores of congratulatory letters from friends and business acquaintances. Many referred to the tremendous prestige and influence of J. P. Morgan and his banking house: "the foremost banker of modern times"; "You have achieved the prize of your profession, the summa cum laude of the financial world"; "You have joined the seats of the mighty." Howard C. Smith, who had elevated TWL to the management of Cushman Bros., wrote that at the Morgan firm Lamont would have the opportunity to set a moral standard that would influence the other "lesser lights in the financial community." Arthur Lockett organized a dinner attended by thirty Exeter and Harvard friends at the University Club to celebrate TWL's entrance into the House of Morgan, and there were toasts and songs, including one sung to tune of "Old General Grant."

> *How well I remember the way that Tommy grew,*
> *Till the bank across the street decoyed him in.*
> *He charged six percent, and allowed not more than two,*
> *And started a double chin.*
> *Such a gentle smile, with such a marble heart,*
> *Made them want him badly down at "23."*
> *These nice new days, with a great big black cigar,*
> *A-smoking with old J.P.!*

Lamont had been well aware of the power and influence of the J. P. Morgan banking firm since his days as a reporter at the *Tribune*. Junius Morgan, Pierpont's father, had taken over George Peabody's London merchant banking house in 1864 and, until his death in 1890, had led the firm, of which an integral part was the New York partnership, Drexel, Morgan & Co., headed by Pierpont. When Junius died, Pierpont became the chief executive, or "senior" as his partners referred to him. In 1895 Morgan and the Philadelphia firm of Drexel & Co. merged under the name of J. P. Morgan & Co. in New York. By this time Pierpont Morgan had clearly established himself as the commanding figure in American finance, and his rolltop desk at 23 Wall Street was the center of authority for Morgan's worldwide banking business.

The rise of the Morgan name in American finance came originally through Pierpont's success in raising capital for American companies, especially railroads, by selling their securities in England and on the Continent. Having persuaded people to invest in these ventures from afar, he assumed a large measure of responsibility for their performance. Soon he was intervening in situations where railroads were in financial trouble, and he and his associates undertook reorganizations of a half dozen major rail systems as well as smaller ones.

Around the turn of the century, a series of dramatic events thrust the firm into worldwide prominence. In 1895, Morgan stopped a run on the nation's gold supply by leading a syndicate that raised $65 million in gold for the U.S. Treasury through the sale of an issue of U.S. government bonds, half of them placed in Europe. In 1901, the firm arranged the integration of a complex of individual companies into the giant United States Steel Corporation. An enormous $1.4 billion capitalization was placed on the new company, inflated by a hefty $50 million underwriting fee paid in stock to the Morgan syndicate.

Pierpont Morgan's leadership of the rescue efforts during the money panic of 1907 and his bank's record of success in major undertakings extended the firm's influence well beyond its actual wealth. Morgan commanded the confidence of the financial world in the integrity and judgment of his firm, and no other house surpassed it in the volume and size of issues originated and placed.

But Morgan's power and influence also subjected him to growing public censure. The spreading movement for reform to bring about greater economic and social benefits for labor and the consumer fostered a growing distrust of large concentrations of resources in the hands of giant industrial and banking aggregations. Pierpont Morgan's accomplishments reflected his strongly held belief that combining many smaller units in an industry into one large corporation was beneficial to society. He attached little importance to the theory that keen competition in business provided the best stimulus to promote efficiency in the manufacture and distribution of goods. His economic views were increasingly out of step with the times. Furthermore, his achievements had led many politicians and journalists to conclude that his dominant position in the financial world enabled him to exert hidden influence and control important sectors of American economic life. They felt that so much power in the hands of one man was dangerous.

It was Republican president Theodore Roosevelt who decided to reinvigorate the Sherman Anti-Trust Act, which, though passed in 1890, had been little enforced by earlier administrations. In 1904 Roosevelt shocked Morgan by using Sherman to force the dissolution of the Northern Securities Company, the holding company formed by Morgan to consolidate three large northern railway systems. The president's rhetoric gave Morgan even more cause to wince as he denounced "male-factors of great wealth" and "the tyranny of a plutocracy" and called for a "moral regeneration of the business world." Republican William Howard Taft succeeded Roosevelt as president in 1909, and "Teddy" sailed for Africa to go on safari. "I do hope the first lion he meets does his duty" was a quip popularly attributed to Morgan at the time.

However, under Taft the Justice Department picked up the trust-busting pace, and in the fall of 1911 filed a suit to dissolve the United States Steel Corporation for operating as a monopoly in restraint of trade. It was a heavy blow to Morgan, who had viewed the formation of U.S. Steel as the greatest of his undertakings.

The picture of Pierpont Morgan portrayed by the press to the public was that of a brusque, arrogant man undertaking great projects to enlarge his power and control over vast sectors of the economy for personal gain. Morgan never met with reporters, believing that they would probably misstate the facts and misinterpret his motives anyway. Moreover, he was sure he had every right to keep his business affairs private. He saw no reason to inform the public about these matters; it wasn't their business unless he chose to make it so. He knew he was doing the right thing, so it was best just to get on with the job. Lamont thought that Morgan's policy of ignoring the public was foolish, and the aftermath of an incident which occurred on his first day on the job, January 2, 1911, underlined for TWL why the Morgan firm must foster good relations with the press.

Lamont and William H. Porter, another new partner in the firm, arrived at the office early that morning to be greeted by a delegation of bankers and lawyers from two small institutions on the East Side uptown. The banks had participated in loans set up by the Carnegie Trust Company, a badly managed and failing firm, and many of the loans had gone into default. The word was out, and runs had begun on the two neighborhood banks. If the heavy deposit withdrawals persisted, they would soon have to close their doors.

From a brief examination of their loan portfolio it seemed wise for a prudent banker to stay clear. Lamont and Porter thought there was nothing the Morgan firm could do and explained the situation to Mr. Morgan, whom they telephoned at the library. To some, Lamont's later account of this conversation, contained in his biography of Henry P. Davison, was fanciful. They doubted that the nation's most powerful banker expressed himself in such compassionate terms.

Morgan first inquired about the character of the banks' 30,000 depositors. "Mostly small East Side trade folk, working people, dressmakers, and the like whose entire savings are deposited in those banks" was the answer.

Morgan replied, "Some way must be found to help these poor people. We musn't let them lose all they have in the world. Suppose at the worst we were to guarantee the payment of the $6,000,000 of deposits?" There was also a more hardheaded consideration. Morgan recalled the panic of 1907 in which distrust in the soundness of one or two institutions spread quickly to others.

After considerable effort, a rescue plan was devised. The Morgan bank announced that it would provide financial help to the troubled institutions. The statement and advances from Morgan built up depositor confidence, and the runs on the banks subsided. Morgan also arranged for a stronger bank to absorb the two weaker institutions. When everything was settled, J. P. Morgan & Co. had incurred a loss of about $190,000.

TWL admired J. P. Morgan's attitude in the affair. Here was a man whom everyone thought of as a powerful, tough-minded financier, engaged in major projects for which he would receive handsome compensation. Yet TWL had just watched the same man subject his firm to financial loss because of his concern for the welfare of a local community as well as for safeguarding financial stability. Certainly the public didn't know this side of Pierpont Morgan. One newspaper summed up the episode with the headline: "Morgan Grabs Two More Banks."

During Lamont's first three years at J. P. Morgan, the offices were at 15 Broad Street, next to the "Corner" at Wall and Broad where the old Drexel Morgan brownstone building was being torn down to make way for the new banking house at 23 Wall. During the period of construction Mr. Morgan made his office at his library, and Lamont and the other partners stopped by there to consult with him on important items of business.

Lamont had observed that some of Morgan's associates stood in such awe of him that they were not at their best in his presence. His bearing, stern and dominating, was overwhelming, especially when his blazing dark eyes were piercingly directed at you. TWL soon came to realize that Morgan's abrupt gestures and heavy silences when thinking through a problem were personal mannerisms that did not reflect his feelings toward the bearer of the news. So was his tendency to speak in as few words as necessary to convey his thoughts and decisions. He saw no need for lengthy explanations of the reasons leading to his judgments. At other times he could be charming and affable, especially when discussing such pursuits as yachting and art collecting.

However, there was an occasion early on when even Lamont felt nervous about raising a subject with his senior partner. He had noted that many of the Morgan partners took several months' vacation a year; they also worked extremely long hours when the situation called for it. With some trepidation, he approached Morgan one morning to discuss his annual vacation.

"I've heard said that sometimes Morgan partners have the repute of almost working themselves to death. If I may be so bold, I would like to say that I have no such intent. I'd like to feel free, except in times of emergency, of course, to take three months off each year," said TWL, immediately fearing he had been too brash.

"Why, of course," replied Morgan genially. "Take off as much time as you like. That is entirely in your hands. Lamont, why don't you go to Egypt this coming winter with your family? Just charter a dahabeah at Cairo and spend a few weeks on the Nile. It is a beautiful trip. You will want to go again and again."

Lamont, greatly relieved, demurred, explaining that he had four young children.

"Nonsense," said Morgan, "take along a couple of nurses, and you will be all right. That was what I did with my children when they were young."

From their sessions at the Morgan Library, Lamont came to appreciate his senior's astuteness and sound instincts in business affairs. Morgan had long ago mastered the tools of his trade. He could quickly analyze and spot the danger signals in a corporation's balance sheet and income statements. He knew the markets, foreign exchange, stocks and bonds, and the forces and people that moved and manipulated them. But as he aged Morgan generally did not probe deeply into the terms of a proposal or the creditworthiness of a borrower. At seventy-five, he was surrounded by experienced and expert lieutenants whose ability he fully trusted. The main question that concerned him was whether a proposition was constructive and thus worthy of the firm's undertaking. He wanted solid assurance regarding the integrity and standing of the people involved. Did they have a good name in their city and in their industry? Were they straightforward in their business dealings? Character, Morgan claimed, was the indispensable ingredient, the prerequisite to capital, collateral, or profitability in judging a borrower or a partner in a venture, and the word became engraved in Lamont's mind.

On April 12, 1912, a grand dinner attended by a galaxy of leaders of American business and financial institutions celebrated the opening of the new Bankers Trust building, the pyramid-capped thirty-five-story tower at the corner of Wall and Nassau streets. Director Lamont was asked to contribute a toast to the evening's festivities, and he composed some verses about the bank and its executives. His black-tie audience enjoyed his witty references to old colleagues and friends, but in his final verse he imparted a more dignified and Morgan-influenced theme about the company.

> *It stands for work and honor*
> *Four square to all the world,*
> *It stands for straight-out dealing*
> *With heart that ne'er grows old.*
> *Its aim is more than money,*
> *It works for more than fame,*
> *A monument to character,*
> *A place that truth shall claim.*

The Money Trust Hearings

During the spring of 1912 another force was mounting to confront Pierpont Morgan—the "money trust" investigation conducted by a subcommittee of the Committee on Banking and Currency of the House of Representatives headed by Rep. Arsene P. Pujo of Louisiana. On April 25, the House passed a resolution establishing a subcommittee to investigate "the concentration of money and credit." The investigation had been strongly backed by Minnesota congressman Charles A. Lindbergh, Sr., father of the future aviator hero, who had castigated the "money trust," a code name for J. P. Morgan and his banking clique. The probe had a clear target: the big New York banks which allegedly controlled most of the economy—banks, insurance companies, railroads, industry—through a web of interlocking board directorships and the ability to allocate credit and capital. A small group of men centered in New York City "wield a power over the businesses, commerce, credits, and finances of the country that is despotic and perilous, and is daily becoming more perilous to the public welfare," stated the resolution.

Pierpont Morgan and his partners were the leaders of the banking community, and Morgan would be asked to testify before the committee. The committee chairman and counsel must have looked forward to the publicity that Pierpont Morgan's appearance as star witness would generate.

Davison made a special trip to France to confer with Morgan, who was in Aix-les-Bain taking the waters, and Morgan and Davison cabled back that they thought it would be advisable to retain an outside publicist to present their side to the public. Other schemes were discussed to disseminate the Morgan viewpoint. However, Lamont finally concluded that the bank should handle its own press relations. The firm would furnish publishers, reporters, and columnists with information and ideas for articles that would reflect the Morgan view of the economy and desirable legislation on banking reforms. He and other partners would meet informally with different Wall Street reporters from time to time. Morgan and Davison accepted TWL's plan. A recognized strategy to promote the bank's view and defend it against attacks was born.

Indeed, Lamont hoped that the thrust of the investigation could be diverted away from the money-trust theme to the real sickness affecting American finance—a clumsy and outmoded banking system. The panic of 1907 had been only the latest in a long series of periodic banking collapses. Senator Nelson Aldrich, the chairman of the National Monetary Commission, after investigating the panic, had stated: "Something has got to be done. We may not always have Pierpont Morgan with us to meet a banking crisis." The commission, for which Harry Davison had served as a key adviser, had proposed legislation to establish something similar to the central banking systems in Europe. Lamont hoped that the committee hearings would provide the Morgan partners with the chance to testify on the urgent need for new banking legislation and that this subject would attract the public's attention. But he was running against the grain.

It was a presidential election year, and New Jersey Governor Woodrow Wilson, the Democratic candidate, declared: "The great monopoly in this country is the money monopoly. . . . The growth of the nation, and all our activities, are in the hands of a few men who . . . are necessarily concentrated upon the great undertaking in which their own money is involved, and who necessarily . . . chill and check and destroy genius and economic freedom." The Republican Taft administration had initiated eighty antitrust suits under the Sherman Act compared to forty during the Roosevelt years. To expose malfeasance by Wall Street and big business fitted the national mood.

When Samuel Untermyer, a dapper and successful New York attorney, was selected as counsel to the Pujo Committee, the direction of the inquiry was set. Untermyer believed that a money trust threatened the nation's welfare, and he intended to prove that the financial control of the United States rested largely in the hands of a few Wall Street bankers whose leader was Pierpont Morgan. He had expanded on this thesis in a speech at the YMCA Financial Forum in New York in December 1911, months before the formation of the Pujo Committee. Untermyer had long been readying himself for his role, and the committee had given him broad authority to conduct the investigation.

During the fall of 1912 Lamont and Davison concentrated on organizing the preparation of the information called for by Untermyer. Tables on deposits held by the firm, security issues managed and underwritten, firm stock holdings, directorships, and the like were sent to Washington. By submitting exhaustive data beforehand the Morgan partners and lawyers hoped to free Morgan from hours of questioning by the committee. On the other hand, they were adamant against turning over anything that would breach the confidential relationship that existed between banker and client. To do so would "shock the business world," they told Untermyer.

It was agreed that Morgan would appear before the committee as a witness in December so that he could leave for his regular European trip in January. Meanwhile, on the political front, Teddy Roosevelt and his Bull Moose party had split off a huge segment of Republican voters, resulting in the election victory of Woodrow Wilson in November. The political mood of Washington would not be in Morgan's favor.

Following Thanksgiving, Davison, Lamont, and the lawyers spent many hours at the library briefing Morgan in preparation for his testimony at the Pujo Committee hearings. Morgan sat at his ornate Italian desk in the West Room with its crimson brocade–covered walls and the portrait of his father hanging over the marble fireplace. He had noticeably aged in recent months and was moving more slowly. The briefings seemed to bore him, and he tired easily. Furthermore, he was quite depressed and gloomy about the forthcoming hearing. He expected that the committee would attempt to "make a show" of him, as he told his family. It was not pleasant in the twilight of life to have a government committee attempt publicly to cast doubt on his many substantial achievements in the development of his country's industry and commerce.

Florence Lamont and Kate Davison joined the Morgan group attending the hearings in Washington. The party included their husbands; Morgan and his son, J. P. Morgan, Jr., known as Jack; Morgan's daughter and son-in-law, Louise and Herbert Satterlee; six lawyers; and Morgan's secretary. The hearing was held in the conference room of the House Committee on Banking and Currency at the Capitol on December 18 and 19, and Morgan testified for the best part of two days. On both days the committee room was filled with spectators and the press, and a long queue of people lined the corridor and ran outside the main entrance of the building waiting to get in or just to catch a glimpse of the legendary banker. Pujo and the committee members were silent as Samuel Untermyer, the committee counsel, conducted all the questioning, courteously, but in the style of a prosecutor.

Charts and exhibits prepared by the committee staff purported to demonstrate the strangling concentration of control over American business held by J. P. Morgan and several allied banks through interlocking directorships. The officers or directors of J. P. Morgan & Co., the First National Bank, the National City Bank, the Bankers Trust Company, and the Guaranty Trust Company, the men and institutions representing the Morgan-Baker-Stillman sphere of interest, together held the following directorships:

118 directorships in 34 banks and trust companies
30 directorships in 10 insurance companies
105 directorships in 32 transportation systems
63 directorships in 24 producing and trading corporations
25 directorships in 12 public utility companies

The total added up to 341 directorships in 112 companies having aggregate resources of over $21 billion dollars, with J. P. Morgan & Co. holding 72 of the directorships.

The Morgan-Untermyer exchanges made high drama, suggesting an old grizzly bear fighting off the relentless attacks of a ferocious pack of hounds. Morgan did not budge; he stood his ground unyieldingly. No air of injured innocence for him. He was confident and positive even when his statement seemed to deny a reasonable conclusion drawn from the facts presented. If he could help it, Morgan was not going to provide the government with even a single bullet if it could be used as ammunition against himself or his Wall Street friends. He avoided the carefully planned snares laid by Untermyer to induce him to say something he did not mean or consent to something he really opposed. He answered the questions directly and tersely and did not bother to explain the reasoning leading to his judgments. He granted no easy concessions to Untermyer, who had to probe hard for what little he got. Morgan even denied that he held unusual power.

> Untermyer: That is your idea, is it? Your idea is when a man has vast power, such as you have—you admit you have, do you not?
> Morgan: I do not know it, sir.
> Untermyer: You admit you have, do you not?
> Morgan: I do not think I have.
> Untermyer: You do not feel it at all?
> Morgan: No, I do not feel it at all.

In pursuing his stonewalling style Morgan was uttering nonsense: he would not even acknowledge that he controlled his own firm, that he was the final authority in governing its affairs. However, his account of his purchase of the controlling stock interest in the Equitable Life Assurance Company from the leading shareholder spoke volumes in a few words about the power he denied possessing.

"I told him I thought it was a good thing for me to have. He did not want to sell it, but he sold it."

Morgan's self-confidence was total. In answer to a question he replied that he "dealt with things as they existed. If it is good business for the interests of the country to do it, I do it."

> Untermyer: But, Mr. Morgan, is not a man likely quite subconsciously to imagine that things are for the interest of the country when they are good business?
> Morgan: No, sir.
> Untermyer: You think you are able to judge and impartially differentiate where your own interests are concerned, just as clearly as though you had no interest at stake, do you?
> Morgan: Exactly, sir.

Morgan stated his views on the organization of industry succinctly.

> Untermyer: You are opposed to competition, are you not?
> Morgan: No, I do not mind competition.
> Untermyer: You would rather have combination, would you not?
> Morgan: I would rather have combination.

Untermyer asked whether the House of Morgan, as a private bank, had an unfair advantage in obtaining deposits over other banks which were government regulated.

Morgan replied, "I do not compete for any deposits. I do not care whether they ever come. They come."

His answers illustrated over and over his supreme confidence in his own judgments, his view of how things should be, and his tremendous authority and force. Lamont thought that Morgan had handled himself "frankly and admirably." He was especially impressed by Morgan's testimony that revealed again the heart of his philosophy for business and life. He later wrote in his biography of Henry P. Davison: "Those phrases of Mr. Morgan's, from the witness stand at Washington, uttered by him in entire unconsciousness of their pregnancy and power, have gone ringing down the years ever since."

> Untermyer: Is not commercial credit based primarily on money or property?
> Morgan: No, sir; the first thing is character.
> Untermyer: Before money or property?
> Morgan: Before money or anything else. Money cannot buy it.

Morgan went on to say that no matter how many bonds a man might have it would make no difference to him "because a man I do not trust could not get money from me on all the bonds in Christendom."

The next day Morgan's statement about credit and character made newspaper headlines, such as "Morgan Says Character is the Basis of Credit." Many papers also asserted that the existence of a money trust under Morgan's domination, exerting broad influence over the economy, was proven.

The investigation and hearings had been an ordeal for Morgan, and when he returned to New York from Washington, he was tired and depressed. He had first been astonished at the charges against him, given his record of achievements so beneficial to his country, and then deeply offended. His partners, friends, and family tried to boost his spirits, and he did brighten up when he received congratulatory letters or read complimentary stories and editorials. On January 7, 1913, Morgan and his party, including the Satterlees, sailed for his beloved Egypt, and everyone thought the trip and rest would renew his vigor.

George F. Baker, chairman of the First National Bank and Pierpont Morgan's most trusted business ally, testified in early January, and Lamont again attended the hearings. Baker was a far easier witness than Morgan from Untermyer's viewpoint.

> Untermyer: In your judgment is not Mr. Morgan the dominant power in the financial world today—far above everything else?

Baker: He would be if he were younger. I do not know his superior.

Baker admitted that he thought the concentrated control of credit had "gone about far enough."

> Untermyer: We are speaking of this concentration which has come about, and the power it brings with it, getting into the hands of very ambitious men, perhaps not overscrupulous. You see a peril in that, do you not?
> Baker: Yes.
> Untermyer: So that the safety, if you think there is safety in the situation, really lies in the personnel of the men?
> Baker: Very much.
> Untermyer: Do you think that is a comfortable situation for a great country to be in?
> Baker [replying very slowly]: Not entirely.

The shrewd counsel knew when he had gotten the most benefit out of a witness. "I think that is all," he said, thanking Baker for his participation.

On February 25, J. P. Morgan & Co. released a twenty-seven page letter to the committee, drafted by Lamont, which summarized the firm's views on the Pujo inquiry and banking in the United States. Selfish men had never been able to overcome the main force of economic law, supply and demand, stated the letter. To suggest, as did the resolution establishing the investigation, that a group of such men could engineer a financial panic was false and dangerously alarming to the public. The financial crisis of October 1907 was exacerbated and prolonged by a weak American banking system, and the banking community suffered the most from the severe shrinkage in security values in 1907. Nevertheless, with Morgan's leadership, the stronger banks undertook the responsibility of assisting weaker institutions.

The letter attacked the "interlocking directorship" thesis: "It is preposterous to suggest that every 'interlocking' director has full control in every organization with which he is connected, and that the majority of directors who are not 'interlocking' are mere figure-heads, subject to the will of a small minority of their boards." To sit on a corporation board was a duty, not a privilege, for a private banker. He became a company director when his firm had sponsored the corporation's securities, because it was the bank's moral responsibility to keep an eye on management and protect the interests of the investors.

There was a "demand for larger banking facilities to care for the growth of the country's business. . . . In New York City the largest banks are far inferior in size to banks in the commercial capitals of other and much smaller countries." It was important for banks to cooperate in order to handle the increasingly large security issues needed to finance American business, and there was nothing "sinister and dangerous" about such cooperation. The charge that banking groups tried to eliminate the competitors of enterprises in which they had an interest by denying credit or other means was completely false.

Finally, the letter discussed the critical factor of confidence in banking.

> All power, physical, intellectual, financial or political, is dangerous in evil hands. If Congress were to fall into evil hands the results might be deplorable. But to us it seems as little likely that the citizens of this country will fill Congress with rascals as it is that they will entrust the leadership of their business and financial affairs to a set of clever rogues.

Only Pollyanna herself might have agreed; everyone else knew that rascals and clever rogues were rarely unmasked until after they had done their dirty work.

A copy of a March 1 editorial in the *New York Times* discussing the report of the Pujo Committee was quickly dispatched to Morgan in Cairo. The report stated that the committee had found that a money trust existed—

> an established and well defined identity and community of interest between a few leaders of finance . . . which has resulted in a vast and growing concentration and control of money and credit in the hands of a comparatively few men.

But there was no arrangement among these persons to concentrate control in their hands; there was no conspiracy.

> No evidence of abuse has come to the attention of the committee. . . . the committee slays even its own creation. . . . Its existence is shadowy. Its powers are doubtful, and its ill deeds not proved. . . . The committee deals with fancied troubles, and with imaginary remedies. It is out of its depth, and while wishing to do good would take great risks of doing harm. . . . It is well that we know the worst of the money trust on the very highest authority. We now can sleep more calmly of nights, sharing the repose which may be anticipated for the report.

But the message of the Pujo Committee hearings was far from dormant.

Louise Satterlee, traveling with her father in Egypt, kept her brother, Jack Morgan, in New York informed by cables and radiograms about their father's health. Jack relayed the reports to his partners, and the news was not good. Morgan had been depressed, nervous, and tired much of the time on the excursion by chartered steamer up the Nile. Plans to continue all the way to Khartoum were cancelled, and the party returned to Cairo, where Morgan remained confined to his suite at Shepheard's Hotel. He gained enough strength to move on to Rome, but then his health went downhill rapidly. He died in Rome on March 21, 1913, and in his honor the New York Stock Exchange did not open on the morning of his funeral at St. George's Church two weeks later in New York.

TWL was shocked and bitter about Morgan's sudden death. He had greatly admired the Senior's ability, character, and style of banking that initiated business concepts and projects that were large and bold. In Lamont's opinion the Pujo hearings, more like a trial, had mortally weakened the seventy-five-year-old Morgan, and Samuel Untermyer was the person most responsible. Lamont wrote later:

> I was a witness to Mr. Morgan's growing amazement and indignation to find himself not taking part in a careful, factual inquiry, but being made the subject of innuendoes, charges, and the like by a lawyer acting like a district attorney, whose object never seemed to be to gain the truth but to try to trump up some justification for a thesis all of his own which, flying in the face of clear testimony . . . he embodied in a report, every word of which he wrote himself; the Congressmen who throughout the hearings had hardly ever asked a single question of their own simply attaching their signatures. The effect of all this upon Mr. Morgan's physical powers was devastating. Within three or four months, out of a seemingly clear sky, his health failed and after a two weeks illness, from no particular malady, he died.

Under the provisions of the Morgan partnership, Pierpont's son, J. P. Morgan, Jr., became the senior partner and head of the house.

In May 1913 the *American Magazine* published an article entitled "The Hunt for a Money Trust" by the famous muckraker Ida Tarbell, to whom it was clear that J. P. Morgan and a few other bankers had tremendous influence in the nation's business affairs, but not as a result of obtaining control of companies according to the Pujo interlocking network diagrams.

> Control is not the word. There is something more subtle than brute majorities at work here, something more powerful than numbers concerned. The thing that really interlocks these vast enterprises is a community of interests, the actual advantage they find in cooperation. . . . The actual forces which decide the relative power which one or more of these have—are their judgment, daring, and the confidence they inspire.

Ida Tarbell was persuaded that "a vast power had grown up in the hands of a few men, largely through certain practices which might, in the hands of bad men, be abused." She was impressed by George F. Baker's testimony that the concentration of the control of credit had "gone about far enough" and that of George M. Reynolds, president of the Continental and Commercial Bank of Chicago, who believed that the extent of the concentration constituted "a menace."

Lamont wrote a letter to the editor of the *American Magazine* denying that Wall Street dominated big business. His letter had a somewhat hollow ring, for he was skirting the main point made by Tarbell and even by Baker, Reynolds, and others. But to admit publicly that Morgan possessed enormous power was unthinkable.

In October 1913 the first of a series of articles by Louis Brandeis, entitled "Breaking the Money Trust," appeared in *Harper's Weekly*. The future Supreme Court Justice was then a Boston lawyer long active in business and social reform and one of President Wilson's closest economic advisers. Brandeis was convinced that the power and dominance of Morgan and a few banking allies over the capital issues market should be curbed by new regulations. In December, Norman Hapgood, the editor of *Harper's Weekly*, brought Lamont and Brandeis together for a three-hour meeting at the University Club to discuss their differences. Not surprisingly, neither party persuaded the other to his viewpoint. In 1914, Brandeis's book *Other People's Money and How the Bankers Use It* appeared and made a lasting impression on many public officials, educators, and journalists in their advocacy for public regulation of the securities markets.

While the Pujo Committee report did not lead to the passage of new legislation for securities regulation at the time, the investigation and hearings had a significant public impact in making the nation aware of the widespread influence of Morgan and a few other bankers in American business. The message was not lost on a Congress already considering tough new laws designed to curb business monopolies and anti-competitive practices. Woodrow Wilson, taking office in 1913, believed that he had a strong mandate from the American people to institute social and economic reforms and was vigorous and forceful in presenting his legislative proposals to Congress.

Lamont had a job to do, not just in disputing the money-trust theory, but in improving the Morgan firm's public image. In this he had the assistance of a new colleague, Martin Egan, hired in 1913. Egan was a witty and charming man with a network of friends in journalism and government. A large part of his job was to monitor newspapers and magazines for articles about the Morgan bank, which he and TWL would then discuss to determine what response, if any, should be made by the firm.

Lamont already had a friendly relationship with the editorial staff of the *New York Evening Post*, where his brother, Hammond, had been managing editor for several years until his premature death in 1909. TWL supplied ideas and information to the paper's business editor and was pleased to see his views expressed, sometimes verbatim, in the *Post*'s financial columns and editorials from time to time. Lamont's courtship of the press was well under way.

Changes at 23 Wall

Lamont had become an increasingly active investor over the last few years. The country was growing, and the economy was rapidly becoming industrialized, with many new companies being formed and stock issues floated. As a partner in the Morgan firm TWL received a $500,000 drawing account; other banks, as well, were pleased to grant credit facilities to Mr. Morgan's new colleague. Before long TWL had a portfolio of stocks and a smaller amount of bonds worth well over a million dollars. While, like other Morgan partners, TWL affected to disdain mere money-making, he was an active trader and very good at it.

TWL and other partners were informed about the investment prospects of different companies by the specialists on the Morgan staff or by their friends in business and finance. As a matter of policy, the Morgan bank underwrote only public issues of high-grade government and corporate bonds. However, because of the great prestige of the house, managers of stock issues often invited the Morgan partners as individuals to join in their private syndicates. Because of his growing reputation as an astute businessman and banker, TWL was sometimes asked to advise in the early stages of planning a financing. Often, as an initial investor and adviser he received bonus stock or the right to purchase stock at a discount.

In 1913 Lamont received dividends of $160,000 on his stock holdings.

He earned a fee of $10,000 as chairman of Lamont, Corliss and Co. and some $12,000 in fees for serving as a director of the Astor, Bankers, and Guaranty trust companies of New York, the First National Bank, First Security Company, Westinghouse Electric and Manufacturing Company, International Agricultural Corporation, Northern Pacific Railway, J. G. White and Co., and the Crowell Publishing Company. His share of the Morgan partnership income, which fluctuated from year to year, had been in the $200,000 range, but not in 1913, when the firm's underwriting losses resulted in a year-end deficit of $6.2 million. However, such losses were rare; the last annual deficit had been in 1907, the year of the great financial panic. TWL made a loan of $5,000 to his old friend and Englewood neighbor Arthur Lockett and also gave over $20,000 to various charitable causes in 1913, including $5,000 to the Harvard Dormitories Fund.

That summer Tom and Florence took their children to Europe, along with a tutor to look after the three boys. TWL installed the family in a cottage at Paris Plage on the French channel coast and commuted back and forth between the Morgan Paris office and the beach resort. Later they drove through the hill towns of northern Italy, visited Florence, and went hiking in the Alps at Murren and Chamonix.

Late meetings and dinners now forced TWL to spend many evenings in the city. The time had come to live in town during the week, and Lamont rented a four-story townhouse at 49 East 65th Street. Young Tommy had gone off to Exeter, and his two younger brothers attended St. Bernard's, a private school off Fifth Avenue noted for teaching in the English public school style. The family still spent weekends and some of the summer at their home on Beech Road in Englewood.

The owner of their new house was Franklin D. Roosevelt, who was leaving New York for Washington to become Assistant Secretary of the Navy in the Wilson administration. Roosevelt was a Democratic state senator who had gone to Harvard and, like Lamont, had been chairman of his Class Committee and president of the *Harvard Crimson*.

The Lamont-Roosevelt communications dealt in a friendly fashion with landlord-tenant differences, such as who should bear the expense of repairing the elevator. When Roosevelt at one point advised Lamont that he might decide to leave his post to return to New York, TWL replied, "Privately I was in hopes that Mr. [Josephus] Daniels might desire to retire to private life so that we could have the satisfaction of seeing you Secretary of the Navy!"

J. P. Morgan, Jr., who soon dropped the "Jr." from his name, was a solid, portly banker of forty-six years who appeared to lack his father's tremendous force of personality, drive, and appreciation of power. He enjoyed his privacy and preferred to limit his social contacts to people of his own class and elitist inclinations. Patrician in taste and style, he was little interested in the mundane affairs of common folk and felt the same as his father regarding the public and newspaper reporters. His affairs were not their business. He had not come to realize that the surrender of privacy went hand in hand with the attainment of power.

After graduating from Harvard in 1889, Jack Morgan had lived in England until 1905, working at the firm's London office. He felt quite at home in a country where the separation of the upper class from the rest of society was an accepted condition of life. Morgan loved the life of an English country squire and looked forward to spending a few months each year abroad, mainly at his English country house, Wall Hall, in Hertfordshire.

The new head of the house inherited the same mantle of supreme authority in the partnership that his father had exercised: only Morgan could hire and fire partners and allocate the firm's annual profits among them. While Jack Morgan's powers made him the boss, his style was to seek a consensus of views in directing the firm's activities. He recognized the unique abilities of his partners, especially Davison and Lamont, and would rely heavily on their advice. The role that TWL had played as a subordinate junior partner to the masterful and commanding figure of Pierpont Morgan was a thing of the past.

Like his father, Morgan admired Harry Davison's ability and judgment and looked to him as his chief of staff when he became head of the house in 1913. The old friends Davison and Lamont worked closely and well together at the bank. Davison was frequently away from the bank, often on firm business in London and Paris. Soon after he joined the bank, Lamont started the practice of writing long letters to Davison when he was away, reporting on a wide range of business and personnel matters. He served as Davison's eyes and ears when he was out of the office.

Morgan was soon elected to replace his father as a director on the corporate boards where the Morgan interest was represented by the senior partner. Of these corporations the most troublesome by far was the New York, New Haven, and Hartford Railroad, for which Morgan was the principal banker. J. P. Morgan had been dominant in the line's policy direction over the last decade, a period of rapid and substantial expansion. Huge sums had been spent for the acquisition of other railroads in New England, as well as trolley car lines and steamship companies, funded by a series of bond issues managed by J. P. Morgan & Co. The generation of income had not kept pace, and by 1913 the New Haven line was in serious financial trouble. A couple of bloody train wrecks had outraged the public, and furthermore, users of the line were often angry about poor service, which they assumed Morgan could set right.

"Strange as it may seem, Mr. Morgan has nothing to do with the actual management of the New Haven Road, and little influence with its management except on purely financial questions," TWL wrote a friend who complained about the deterioration of service in Rhode Island. But the press and public perception of his authority was far different: one newspaper cartoon portrayed Morgan as a vulture feeding on the entrails of the New Haven Railroad.

A critical report on the operations of the railroad was released by the Interstate Commerce Commission, and the president of the railroad was replaced. Later, in the face of a U.S. government suit charging that the New Haven had violated the Sherman Anti–Trust Act by monopolizing transport in New England, the railroad agreed to sell off several properties, including steamship and trolley lines. A new Morgan plan in the summer of 1913 to refinance the railroad system with a $67 million issue of convertible debentures only added to the stockholders' anger over the bank's responsibility for the company's sorry financial condition. And then in 1913 the New Haven passed its regular year-end dividend, the first time this had happened in forty years and a heavy blow to thousands of small investors.

J. P. Morgan and his family sailed for England in September 1913 for their annual visit, and that fall Harry Davison, Tom Lamont, Charles Steele, and other partners met frequently to discuss the future course of the firm in the changed political climate in America. The bitter experience with the New Haven Railroad on top of the Pujo investigation and the public reaction to its disclosures called for a thorough reexamination of the bank's strategy, which the partners reviewed with Morgan upon his return in December.

The new look in the partners' approach to banking was soon evident. Given the current public attitudes, it was no longer appropriate for the firm to engage in organizing vast new industrial combinations and railroad systems. Second, the public perception of the concentration of control over banks and credit had to be dealt with: the firm would immediately reduce its stock interest in those few banks where it had a substantial holding to 15 percent, and even lower later on.

Finally, the widely held view persisted that the Morgan firm exerted vast control through a network of directorships and that in serving a company as both banker and director, a Morgan partner had a clear conflict of interest. In January 1914, J. P. Morgan & Co. announced that Mr. Morgan was retiring from the boards of the New Haven and New York Central railroads and their subsidiaries and three banks. Other Morgan partners resigned their directorships from two dozen corporations, including Lamont, who left the boards of the Westinghouse Electric and Manufacturing Co. and the Astor and Bankers trust companies.

The Morgan press release explained that attendance at so many board meetings was taking up too much of the partners' time. They had only reluctantly become corporate directors because they felt an obligation to stay closely informed about the enterprises whose securities they had sold to the public. However, they now felt they could stay "in sufficiently close touch" without becoming directors of these companies, an observation Brandeis had made to TWL in their talk at the University Club.

> Moreover such withdrawals on our part would seem to conform in some measure to a public feeling which regards with apparent disfavor any directorate relationship between merchants in securities on the one hand and, on the other hand, the properties for whose securities such merchants find an investment outlet.

By fall of 1914, President Wilson's key legislative proposals had been passed by Congress. The Federal Reserve Act established a central banking system with twelve district banks under the supervision of the Federal Reserve Board of Governors in Washington. All national banks, plus state banks if they chose, would be members of the system. The reserve banks would discount eligible loans of their members who would look to them for support when needed. The board would be able to influence the nation's money supply by trading government securities to affect the level of bank credit and changing the discount rate. Davison and Lamont, who had strongly argued for the establishment of a modern central banking system, acknowledged that President Wilson had done a superb job in promoting and securing this historic legislation.

The Federal Reserve Act also prohibited private bankers, such as the Morgan partners, from serving on the boards of national banks, and Morgan and his colleagues promptly complied, with Lamont resigning his First National Bank directorship. No one expected this move to disrupt the close cooperation between the two banks. The Morgan-Baker ties were strong and enduring.

In December 1913, Lamont, with Davison's backing, had obtained Morgan's approval to invite his Englewood friend Dwight W. Morrow to join the firm. Morrow, a short, dynamic man of incisive intellect, with a strong inclination for public service, had built up a distinguished record as an attorney at the Wall Street firm of Simpson, Thatcher & Bartlett. After considerable soul-searching Morrow accepted and became a partner on July 1, 1914.

That summer construction went forward on the new Morgan bank building at the corner of Broad and Wall streets, and in November the Morgan staff of 150 moved from the adjacent Mills Building into their handsome new office. The squat corner building reflected the taste and design of the elder J. P. Morgan, who had worked closely with his architects, Trowbridge and Livingston, in planning the new banking house, whose completion he would not live to see. The exterior was of giant blocks of Tennessee marble; the banking floor was spacious with a lofty coffered ceiling and wall sections filled with mosaics of tiny tiles. The partners sat at large, dark, mahogany rolltop desks in a glass-enclosed section on the Broad Street side of the building. A shining brass spittoon was placed alongside each desk.

On the second floor were the partners' private offices, with oak-paneled walls, wood-burning fireplaces, easy chairs, and fine paintings. These retreats, reached by a small private elevator, were most suitable for quiet and discreet meetings with clients. The atmosphere was decidedly subdued, much like a gentleman's club; the junior staff and secretaries spoke in hushed tones. In his office facing the New York Stock Exchange directly across Broad Street, Lamont used a massive Jacobean refectory table for a desk, its oaken surface cracked and worn smooth with age.

On the new building's opening day many callers—clients and friends—dropped by to pay their respects to J. P. Morgan and his partners. They entered at the Corner doorway, where the only identification of the famous banking house was the small inscription of its name in gold on the inner glass front door.

Book II

THE TRIALS OF PEACEMAKING

Europe in Flames

June 1914 brought the assassination of Archduke Franz Ferdinand, and the outbreak of World War I followed inexorably in August. Lamont was firmly inclined to blame the Germans:

> Allied diplomats worked desperately to keep the peace, but not for nothing had the Prussian officers at evening mess been for years pledging to one another "Der Tag." Austria's declaration of war against Serbia on July 28, 1914, was followed by a general scramble for mobilization of troops by most of the leading European countries. Yet even as general war became a certainty, thoughtful men were still asking themselves what in the world there was to fight about. Germany's domestic economy was prospering. Her foreign trade was constantly making new records in volume and profit.

The impact of the war on the United States was quickly felt. In the case of J. P. Morgan & Co., its partners and staff were thrust by the unfolding events into major new roles in international finance, as the early days of battle stretched into long months and years of bloody warfare.

A succession of crises and complex problems stemming from the conflict soon came to rest at the doorstep of 23 Wall, often on the shoulders of Harry Davison, the firm's chief executive officer. Davison provided the initiative and leadership in those hectic and troubled days, increasingly spending more time in London negotiating the firm's new assignments with the British and French governments. J. P. Morgan visited London periodically as well. The New York partners worked out of Morgan's London bank, Morgan Grenfell & Co., whose managing partner, Edward C. Grenfell, was able and well-connected, a Bank of England director providing the house of Morgan an invaluable link to the British government. Back in New York, Lamont spent many hours composing cables to Morgan, Davison, and Grenfell.

On August 18, 1914, President Wilson made a speech urging the

American people to remain neutral regarding the combatants, "impartial in thought as well as action," which TWL described as "rather a tall order." The most influential American ethnic group was of British descent. A common language and the other ties of culture and shared beliefs in principles of law and self-government were age-old bonds with England. The tradition of American friendship with France went back to the Revolution and Lafayette. While no one wanted the United States to join the fighting, most Americans supported the British and French in the conflict, especially after the ruthless German invasion of Belgium and France. However, there were also many other citizens, including millions of German and Irish-Americans, whose feelings ran from strict neutrality to backing the Germans. While interest in the European war was intense in the East, it was only lukewarm to cool in the Midwest and farther west.

The Morgan partners would not embrace President Wilson's advocacy of strict impartiality toward the belligerents. Lamont wrote later: "Those were the days when American citizens were urged to remain neutral in action, in word, and even in thought, but our firm had never for one moment been neutral; we didn't know how to be. From the very start we did everything we could to contribute to the cause of the Allies."

The firm had important long-standing business links to Britain and France—in London, Morgan Grenfell & Co., the prestigious merchant bank successor to the original firm; in Paris, Morgan Harjes & Co., which enjoyed close relations with the French government. J. P. Morgan, who had lived for years in England, where he had many friends, including the royal family, was ardently pro-Ally and pro-British and did not shrink from expressing his strong support for the Allied cause despite the administration's policy of neutrality. Lamont and the other partners fully shared the Senior's views about the war.

As the war settled bloodily into the trenches after the first Battle of the Marne, Britain's military and civilian requirements to purchase vast quantities of commodities and products in the United States rose precipitately, and American industry and agriculture were naturally eager for the business. However, British purchasing methods were proving to be disorganized and uncoordinated. Different branches of government, such as the War Office and the Admiralty, were competing against each other and often with their allies, the French and the Russians. Purchasing agents, who were not carefully selected, were charging exorbitant commissions. Competitive bidding from American suppliers was little used, and as a result Britain and her allies suffered from paying high prices and delays in the shipment of critically needed goods.

Dispatched to London in the fall of 1914, Harry Davison proposed to British government officials that J. P. Morgan & Co. be appointed the purchasing agent for the government in buying supplies in the United States in order to provide the centralized and efficient management that was urgently needed. In a cable to Davison, Jack Morgan wondered if he should also come to London to help present the case, but he did not want to create the impression of "drumming," which was beneath the dignity of the firm. He didn't go.

With the strong support of Lloyd George, the British Chancellor of the Exchequer, the Morgan firm received the appointment in January 1915. As for compensation to Morgan, TWL initially contemplated a 5 percent commission. He was overreaching. It was finally agreed that Morgan would receive 1 percent of the contract price for its services, from which it would pay its expenses, after receiving 2 percent on the initial $47 million of orders. A similar arrangement with the French government was worked out a few months later.

The Morgan firm decided to ask Edward R. Stettinius, president of the Diamond Match Company, to head the new Export Department at the bank, which would handle the massive purchasing operation. Lamont, who knew Stettinius as a fellow board member of the International Agricultural Corporation and admired his business acumen, put the case to him, and he agreed. Stettinius was able and scrupulous about detail; he drove his staff hard in a herculean task. Following Davison and Lamont's recommendation to Morgan, Stettinius became a partner of the firm in January 1916.

Hundreds of companies producing a variety of goods ranging from blankets to artillery shells sought contracts to supply the Allies. Acting on instructions received from the British and French governments through Morgan's London and Paris offices, the Export Department solicited and received bids and, after investigation, selected suppliers and placed contracts. The operation grew quickly in size and complexity.

It had been apparent to the Morgan partners from the start of the war that America could export enormous quantities of commodities to the Allies—grain, cotton, steel, copper—as well as munitions and all kinds of manufactured products, if adequate loans were available to the British and French governments. These countries could not possibly pay for the goods they desperately needed to win the war from their meager wartime exports, foreign investments, and limited gold reserves. The new export trade would be a boon for American business mired in recession.

However, a staggering amount of American loans would be needed to do the job; American exports to Great Britain alone were about $600 million in 1914 and would surely rise to over $1 billion the following year. J. P. Morgan and his partners had no doubt that the Allies would win the war. Therefore there was no reason to question the soundness of loans to Great Britain and France, which had been creditor nations before the war. These would be good loans that J. P. Morgan & Co. could fully support.

But there was another problem in the early days of the war. The American government's official policy, announced by the State Department on August 15, 1914, was that "loans by American bankers to any foreign nation which is at war are inconsistent with the true spirit of neutrality." Secretary of State William Jennings Bryan, who had expressed a keen distrust of bankers and their power throughout his long and populist political career, said at the time: "The powerful financial interests which would be connected with these loans would be tempted to use their influence through the newspapers to support the interest of the government to which they had loaned, because the value of the security would be directly affected by the result of the war. All this influence would make it all the more difficult for us to maintain neutrality."

This position, which the Morgan partners found exasperating, softened before long. Lamont and the other bankers soon found that their plans to extend credit to the Allies received a far more sympathetic hearing from Robert M. Lansing, counselor to the State Department. Lansing, an able international lawyer with friends on Wall Street, was urbane, ambitious, and married to the daughter of former Secretary of State John Watson Foster. He opposed Secretary Bryan's policy of strict neutrality and wanted to assist the Allies, even if he had to undercut his superior to achieve this end. On October 15 he told the bankers that the State Department would not object to the extension of bank credit to belligerent nations, and on October 29, J. P. Morgan & Co. joined National City Bank in a one-year $10 million bank credit to the French government. In March 1915 the Morgan bank informed the State Department of its plan to organize a banking syndicate to make a one-year loan of $30 million to the French government and was told that there was no longer any need to advise the government about bank loans to the warring nations. But public bond issues for the Allies were still banned.

During Davison's meetings in London in December 1914, the subject of a large-scale financing for Great Britain was raised by Lloyd George. Would J. P. Morgan & Co. consider floating a sizable public bond issue for the British government in six months or so to finance the purchase of American products? Davison replied affirmatively with the normal banker's reservations; the bank would not, or course, proceed if the U.S. government objected. He then crossed the Channel to Paris and held similar discussions on the purchase and financing of American goods with French officials.

As the winter months of 1915 slipped by, it became increasingly evident that the British and French would have to borrow huge sums, repayable after the war, to pay for the goods they required. Only public bond issues, not short-term bank credits, could provide the needed funds.

At the same time there was growing sympathy in America for the Allies' cause, mainly aroused by the German submarine attacks on Allied shipping and one American ship that spring. On May 7 the giant British passenger liner *Lusitania* was torpedoed without warning by a German submarine and sank in eighteen minutes off the coast of Ireland. The 1,198 lives lost included 128 Americans. Even though the German embassy had warned American travelers in an advertisement in the New York papers not to sail on the *Lusitania*, Americans were outraged by this act of German callousness.

J. P. Morgan and his partners, so committed to the British cause, were appalled at the news of the *Lusitania* disaster. They were eager to assist the Allies, but the administration still opposed public loans to the warring nations. Moreover, the climate for raising huge loans for the Allies was not encouraging. Many Americans believed they should remain neutral, as their government had recommended. Many bankers saw more attractive investment opportunities than lending to the Allies, whose fortunes, as the war ground on, did not seem all that promising.

In fact, for the first part of 1915, Lamont's main activity was organizing the railroad debt issues sponsored by J. P. Morgan & Co. He remarked that his days seemed filled with one railroad conference after another—a $10 million note issue of the Erie Railroad, to be followed by a convertible bond offering; a $27 million note issue for the New Haven; and a large New York Central offering of convertible debt. In February TWL met with the chairman of the Second District Public Service Commission to explain the terms of the new $100 million loan to fund the large floating debt of the Central. In addition to its share of the underwriting spread, J. P. Morgan & Co. would receive a fee of $1.5

million for managing the financing. The ground was well prepared, and the big issue sold well.

In July a deranged German sympathizer, angry at J. P. Morgan's support for the Allies, attempted to murder Morgan. He broke into the Morgan home at Glen Cove, Long Island, and fired two shots from his pistol at the banker before Morgan was able to throw himself on the man and subdue him. Morgan's servants rushed to his aid and held the intruder for the police. Morgan was struck by two bullets in the groin, but his wounds were not serious, and he was able to return to his office in a few weeks. It was a shattering and sobering experience for Morgan and his partners. They and the public at large were proud of Morgan's physical courage in charging his assailant, and at the end of his first day back at the bank after the attack, a crowd outside 23 Wall Street applauded him as he left the building to return home. From that time on J. P. Morgan was protected by bodyguards. But for most Americans the war still seemed far away; it hardly affected their lives.

Lamont had wanted his children to have the experience of a summer vacation in the rugged Western mountain country. In the summer of 1914 the Lamont party stayed at the Flying D Ranch at Gallatin Gateway, Montana, with their guests, Dr. and Mrs. John Huddleston and their three children. They were a congenial family, and TWL thought that it was wise to have a doctor on hand. Lamont and his party fished for trout, rode horseback, camped out on pack trips, and toured Yellowstone and Glacier National Park.

The outbreak of war in Europe during the first week of August 1914 plunged the commercial and financial markets into uncertainty and confusion. The foreign exchange market was chaotic. The London Stock Exchange was closed, and the governors of the New York Stock Exchange, with the support of J. P. Morgan, followed suit. It was feared that billions of dollars of European-owned American securities might be dumped on the New York market and cause its collapse. The city of New York was afraid that it would be forced to default on its loans from Europe. Difficult new problems, spawned by the conflict, appeared daily for the Morgan partners. Harry Davison telegraphed TWL at the ranch that he and Jack Morgan had discussed asking him to return to the office, but had decided that his presence was not urgently required. They would leave the decision to him.

TWL had been serious about his wish to enjoy long summer vacations with his family and regather his strength for the coming year. He replied that his health was not "up to the mark" and that he would prefer to continue his holiday unless his return was absolutely essential. He did not return to New York until early September.

In the summer of 1915 the Lamonts and Huddlestons headed west again, this time accompanied by five servants—a nurse, a governess, two maids, and a chauffeur. These trips required much advance planning regarding accommodations, horses, pack trips, the availability of pure milk for the children, and the routing of TWL's private Pullman car. After a stay at White Pelican Lodge on Lake Klamath in Oregon, the party visited Crater Lake and then went on to Lake Louise in the Canadian Rockies, where they took a week's camping trip by horseback in the mountains. Lamont rushed back to New York when J. P. Morgan was shot and wounded, rejoining his family later when the Senior's recovery was assured.

In August the family visited the Panama-Pacific Exposition in San Francisco, where TWL attended the annual meeting of the Associated Harvard Clubs. He had been elected president of the association for the coming year and spoke briefly to his Harvard comrades at the final dinner meeting. He concluded with a fulsome description of Harvard's enrollment goal—to attract the best of American youth from all parts of the country to its unparalleled "fountains of learning."

While on vacation, TWL had received a flow of communications from his office keeping him abreast of business developments. On July 23, 1915, the Morgan firm had established a $50 million line of credit for the Bank of England, to be used to stabilize the pound in the foreign exchange market. As the summer progressed there was growing concern on Wall Street that Great Britain's declining gold and dollar reserves would prove inadequate to pay for the large orders from America, and the pound went into a slide on the international exchanges, reaching a low of $4.53 on September 1. France faced the same dilemma. Businessmen, including the Morgan partners, feared that the Allies would sharply curtail their U.S. purchases, a cutback that would be a severe blow to the economy.

Gradually, President Wilson was won over to the views of Lansing, who had become Secretary of State following Bryan's resignation in June, and Secretary of the Treasury William G. McAdoo. The two cabinet members argued persuasively that permitting public loans to the Allies would avoid a serious contraction in American exports, which had brought a new prosperity to the nation. On August 26, 1915, President Wilson agreed that belligerents could now float bond issues in the U.S., and the Allies moved swiftly to arrange the vitally needed financing.

Arming the Allies

On September 2, 1915, the British and French governments announced that they would send a mission to the U.S. to negotiate a large loan to finance their American purchases, a statement that quickly buoyed the sagging pound on foreign exchange markets. The Joint High Loan Commission headed by Lord Reading, Lord Chief Justice of England, sailed for New York and met with Morgan, Davison, and Lamont on September 13 at the Hotel Biltmore, where the commissioners were staying.

The commissioners seemed to have little understanding of the American securities market and apparently believed that American investors would lend enormous sums at an interest rate in the 3 percent range, which was common in Europe. But the American investing public was accustomed to high-grade railroad and corporate issues earning 5 percent interest. Furthermore, the commissioners did not realize how much time and hard work it would take to bring off the huge and extraordinary transaction, by far the largest loan the American public had ever been asked to make, and to foreign borrowers at that. Long days of tough negotiations followed, conferences with the commissioners interspersed with meetings with the officers of leading New York banks and investment houses. These firms would take the biggest underwriting commitments, and they had strong opinions on the terms that would be attractive to American investors.

On September 25 the Morgan partners reached an agreement with the commissioners to form a syndicate to underwrite the purchase of a $500 million bond issue, which would be the joint obligation of the British and French governments. The interest rate would be 5 percent; the bonds would mature in five years and be convertible into long-term bonds at 4½ percent. The managing underwriters, sixty-one banks, trust companies, and investment houses in New York City, for whom J. P. Morgan & Co. was the agent, would forgo their management fee in view of the purpose of the loan.

Now began the intensive effort to educate American investors, unaccustomed to buying foreign bonds, as to why the proposed loan was critical to the prosperity of American agriculture and industry and why it was a perfectly sound undertaking. At the same time the Morgan firm was organizing the huge underwriting syndicate, mainly from east coast cities. The Boston and Philadelphia bankers were solidly behind their

New York confreres, although their smaller size and number limited their commitments to no more than a third of the amount subscribed by the New York institutions. However, it was a different story in the Midwest. In Chicago, Cincinnati, Milwaukee, and St. Louis there were large German-American communities hostile to the Allies.

Other groups throughout the country—pacifist, isolationist, and Irish-American—also opposed the Anglo-French loan and castigated the Morgan bank for sponsoring it. A note to TWL, only one in the stream of hate mail received by the bank, tells the story:

> My dear Mr. Lamont,
>   Your deathdoom is marked by your activity for the British war loan, which will deal death to my brothers on the battlefield in Germany. It shall be a distinct pleasure for me to puncture your black heart with lead some time in the distant future.

Lamont kept in touch with James J. Hill, the St. Paul railroad tycoon with whom TWL and his partners had worked closely in financing the Northern Pacific and other railroad projects. Hill was the most prominent businessman endorsing the loan outside the circle of Eastern financiers. As Hill put it, if the Allies could no longer make purchases because of lack of credit, the American farmers were "likely to secure for their wheat only fifty cents a bushel against the price of a dollar that they might otherwise receive. . . . The country could afford to lose the entire amount of a loan rather than have the Allies forced out of the market here for foodstuffs." The partners counted on Hill's influence through the West and Northwest to build support for the loan.

The Morgan firm drafted a public statement, signed by a number of prominent citizens, which explained why the Anglo-French loan was needed by America's farmers and workers. Great Britain and France were now running an annual trade deficit of almost $1 billion with the United States as the result of their greatly increased wartime purchases and diminished exports. They could not pay for their massive purchases without an American loan, and "if these two great nations are obliged materially to decrease their purchases from us, the logical result will be lowered prices for our farm products, and smaller wages for the workmen in our factories. . . . Not one dollar of the money loaned will leave our shores."

Even though the Eastern banks could underwrite the full loan, if they had to, the Morgan partners wanted to attract the participation of Midwestern banks in the mammoth undertaking. The loan would have a national impact, with an estimated 60 percent of the proceeds to be spent in the Mississippi Valley. However, in the Midwest, and especially in Chicago, its commercial and financial center, the bankers were very cool toward the Anglo-French loan. The banks had thousands of depositors sympathetic to Germany who might withdraw their accounts if their bank joined the syndicate underwriting the loan. Faced with this foot-dragging by the Chicago bankers, the partners decided to send the British and French loan commissioners out to Chicago to try to persuade them to come on board. Lamont was assigned to escort the commissioners.

On September 27, the party, led by Lord Reading, left New York on the Twentieth Century Limited, arriving in Chicago the next morning. According to the Chicago newspapers delivered on board the train, Chicago intended to receive its distinguished foreign visitors with utmost respect and courtesy, but would treat the mission purely as a ceremonial visit.

A white silk handkerchief was waved from the last Pullman car of the train as it rolled into the LaSalle Street station, signaling to the reception committee on the platform the car from which the commission would alight. The car was immediately surrounded by city and Pinkerton detectives. The city did not intend to take any chances with the safety of its eminent foreign guests. The welcoming committee of prominent citizens walked down the length of the platform to greet the commissioners. Lord Reading, dressed in a dark cutaway suit, descended from the train first and was introduced to meatpacker J. Ogden Armour. One of the Armour meat cargoes bound for Europe had been seized by the British under their naval blockade of Germany, and a suit filed by Armour and other Chicago packers was now pending before the British Court of Appeals.

"Happy to meet you, Mr. Armour," Lord Reading exclaimed, immediately paying tribute to the beautiful weather in Chicago, far superior to the rainy conditions in New York. After a round of picture-taking the group was driven to the Blackstone Hotel, where Lord Reading was interviewed by the press. One reporter suggested that because the Chicago bankers were holding aloof from the loan, the mission's visit would turn out to be strictly social.

Lord Reading laughed. "We have come here to offer our terms, and for no other purpose. The details of the negotiations are being arranged. . . . We are awaiting the outcome of our proposals, and in this we do not lack confidence."

Lamont knew the situation was much darker than Lord Reading had presented it. He had expected a big turnout of out-of-town bankers wishing to talk to the commission, but only a half dozen showed up. The

Chicago banks seemed firm in their decision not to participate because of their fear of deposit withdrawals. James B. Forgan, president of the First National Bank, said there already had been a quiet but steady run on his bank by foreign-born depositors who had heard rumors of a plan for a billion dollars to be shipped out of the country.

At 12:30 the reception committee hosted a lunch for the commission at the Chicago Club with about fifteen bankers and businessmen present. Ogden Armour joked to TWL that he would take $15 million in Anglo-French bonds if the bankers would obtain payment from the British in that amount, which corresponded to the value of the meat cargoes they had confiscated. When it was clear that any serious discussion of the loan was being avoided, Lamont raised the subject himself. The leading Chicago bankers, Forgan and George M. Reynolds, president of the Continental Commercial National Bank, both said they'd like to join the loan syndicate but did not dare for fear of a serious run on their deposits. The other Chicago bankers were clearly following the lead of these two large institutions; no cracks appeared in the wall of opposition to the loan.

Lamont then rushed back to his hotel suite for a meeting with thirty-five senior officers from bond houses and bank bond departments. Along with underwriting commitments, it was important to have a good bond distributing network in the Midwest to take down bonds from the syndicate for sale to the public. TWL gave the group a full briefing. No one spoke up to commit his institution, and Lamont decided to adopt a new tactic.

"It looks to me," he said, "that Chicago, which stands to benefit by the operation more than any other one city in the country, is preparing to let Boston and others do her share." He explained how well the deal was shaping up in the Eastern cities. "I predict that regardless of the attitude of the Chicago banks, you will soon be climbing on the band-wagon, because, first, you'll be ashamed not to, and second, the thing will be such a success that you will want to."

The bond men, who had been discouraged by the bankers' refusal to join the underwriting syndicate, seemed to be heartened by TWL's statement. Some said they would participate, and others said they would think seriously about it. Lamont asked Charles G. Dawes, president of the Central Trust Company of Illinois and a former Comptroller of the Currency, to stay behind a moment. TWL believed that Dawes's background had given him a broader perspective and concern for the national interest than most of his fellow bankers.

"Charlie, I've got to say in all frankness that your holding back has been the biggest disappointment to us. You've always had the reputation of having plenty of sand with all of us at 23. Why don't you just jump into the lead and take command of the situation in Chicago? You know, come out with a ringing declaration backing the loan. You would certainly establish a reputation for yourself in the banking world as being strong and independent. You'd be hailed as the new banking leader in Chicago."

Dawes replied that he personally was very tempted to do just that, but first he had to talk to one or two of his directors. Later that afternoon Dawes returned to tell TWL that he would recommend to his board that the Central Trust Company subscribe for an appropriate share of the Anglo-French loan. Lamont brought Dawes down to the commissioners' suite to tell Lord Reading, who was delighted with the news.

Lamont and Reading then discussed the banquet to be given that evening by the Commercial Club in honor of the Lord Chief Justice. In considering the remarks he might make at this dinner gathering, Lord Reading was acutely aware of the generally cool attitude of the Chicago business community toward the Anglo-French loan. His hosts had made it clear that they were honoring him as a distinguished visitor and not as head of the Anglo-French Loan Commission. When he was introduced to speak, he was greeted by measured applause.

Lord Reading proceeded to thaw his audience somewhat by relating how, having failed in a business venture in England as a young man, he had decided to emigrate to America, the land of opportunity, settle in Chicago, and make his fortune. His trunk was packed, and he was ready to sail from Liverpool, when a serious illness in his family forced him to cancel his plans and remain in England to pursue his career. The audience gave him a warm round of applause. After all, but for a stroke of bad luck he might have been their fellow citizen! But even though the bankers agreed that their honored guest was a splendid fellow, he had not changed their minds toward the loan. TWL lobbied hard with the two key Chicago bankers, Forgan and Reynolds, in the course of the evening. If he could turn them around, he was sure that other Chicago banks would follow their lead. He urged that the big Chicago banks get together and come out "as one man" in favor of the loan. It would be hard for their critics, including their depositors, to attack them if they acted together. All to no avail. Forgan said he personally would like to support the loan, but he was "afraid of his board of directors." Reynolds said he was not afraid of his directors but of his depositors.

Lamont and the commission members had a nightcap and postmortem session back at their hotel suite, and TWL got to bed at 1 a.m. It had been a long day, and he had a full morning of conferences ahead before his midday return to New York.

Starting with an eight o'clock breakfast meeting, Lamont was on the run. He had set up another meeting with the officers from the bond houses and bank bond departments at ten o'clock. Twenty-five bond house officers, but only one banker, showed up, and he arrived late. The bankers still worried that their attendance might be construed by the press as indicating that they had decided to join the underwriting syndicate, so they stayed away. The bond house men seemed enthusiastic but again held back from firm commitments.

The meeting adjourned, and TWL went to his sitting room to meet again with Forgan and Reynolds, whom he had asked to join him at eleven o'clock. He was determined to try one last time to overcome their fear of losing deposits and their inborn resentment of Wall Street pressure and dominance.

Once more, Lamont emphasized the prodigious success of the plan in the East. "All that is needed is for you to get together and act as a unit. . . . Not a penny of your deposits will be withdrawn. But if you don't, Chicago will end up sitting on the sidelines making a sorry spectacle of herself." Both bankers professed to be for the loan personally, heart and soul, but they could not act without approval by their boards of directors, which they failed to obtain.

The visit of the Anglo-French Loan Commission to the business center of the American Midwest had not achieved its major objective, but it had won over one important supporter, Charles G. Dawes, who issued a public statement the following day.

> We bankers are coming to realize that this loan is a matter of America first. From the standpoint of the commerce and industry of the American nation it is vital that this loan be made for the preservation of its export trade. . . . of its absolute safety I am in no doubt. I also believe in the real patriotism and neutrality of our German American citizens and do not for a minute think that in any large number they will resent any action taken upon a sound business basis and unquestionably in the interest of our nation to which we all owe our first allegiance and devotion. I shall recommend to our board of directors that we subscribe for our proportional and reasonable share of the loan.

At 4:30 p.m. on October 8, J. P. Morgan marched down the center aisle of the Astor Gallery of the Waldorf-Astoria hotel in New York. Seven hundred bond salesmen were in attendance to hear Morgan explain the terms of the $500 million bond issue of the governments of Great

Britain and France—why the bonds represented a prudent and attractive investment for the customers of the bond houses and banks.

Tom Lamont and Dwight Morrow trailed their senior partner by a couple of steps as he walked toward the speaker's elevated stage. As the trio approached the platform, Lamont and Morrow veered off to take seats in the front row of folding chairs. "I don't want to sit here alone," said Morgan, and he beckoned to Lamont and Morrow to join him on the platform.

"This is a direct loan of $500,000,000 to two of the richest governments in the world," said Morgan, "and I feel that there are only one or two matters we should clear up.

"I think I should speak first as to the neutrality of this loan. I do not consider this a war loan at all. It is commercial. The best customers we have ever had are asking for time on their purchases—the greatest and most resourceful nations of the world, England and France. They have been buying in this country and selling here, but at the present they are buying more than they are selling. We must give them time. We must learn to give credit to our foreign customers . . . if we would keep their trade, if we would become a power in world finance. There can be nothing simpler than that, nothing plainer to every sensible person.

"As to the safety—this loan is an external debt of the two countries. It is a first charge on them; it is to be paid above everything else. It is absolutely imperative for countries to meet external obligations, if nothing else, if they are to escape the worst form of bankruptcy and disgrace." The age of massive defaults by sovereign governments had not yet dawned.

Morgan then described the attractiveness of the investment terms and turned the program over to his partner, Dwight Morrow. Perhaps the primary task, Morrow said, was "educating the American people in a new line of work, of becoming a creditor nation, an investor in the high-grade obligations of foreign nations." In fact the war presented the opportunity of supplanting the English and Germans as the leading international bankers. The American business community had first taken railroad bonds, then electric power bonds; now it had the opportunity to take world bonds. Neither of the countries had ever defaulted even though they had passed through times just as threatening.

After the presentation, the bond salesmen formed a line passing by J. P. Morgan to shake his hand. The feeling among them was that the bonds would sell well.

A week later, the formal agreement between the British and French governments and the American underwriting syndicate was signed at the office of J. P. Morgan & Co. Lord Reading made a gracious speech thanking the Morgan firm and its banking associates for their hard work and cooperation in concluding the transaction.

Lamont, watching the signing, was proud of the job accomplished by his firm. The $500 million Anglo-French loan was the largest bond issue ever floated in America. J. P. Morgan & Co. had not only managed the raising of this huge capital sum, but would also benefit from spending the proceeds of the issue through its role as purchasing agent for the Allies.

The Anglo-French loan was not acclaimed by everyone. The anti-British Hearst newspapers denounced the loan, and men carrying signs reading "Billions for King George" paraded by the Morgan bank on Wall Street. The *New York Sun* reported the statement of a Berlin newspaper: "The *Lokalanzeiger* assures the German-American bankers who in their individual capacities subscribed to the Anglo-French loan that 'their misdeeds will be remembered by the fatherland.' "

The papers also reported a speech by Jeremiah O'Leary, president of the American Peace Society, with many Irish-American backers, who denounced all the participants in the loan. He characterized the bond issue as a "plot to invest the public money in a war loan in the face of the people's protest" and "a war cancer on the financial system of the country. . . . The big financiers who are making large subscriptions aren't actually paying out any money," said O'Leary. "It comes out of the depositors' pockets."

Charles Dawes reported to Lamont that when it was first announced that the Central Trust Company of Illinois would be an underwriter of the Anglo-French loan, several hundred small accounts, amounting to about $230,000, were withdrawn by German-American depositors, but about $5 million in new deposits flowed in, mainly from corporations who supported the loan. He thanked the Morgan bank for its increased correspondent bank balances and for the corporate accounts, including the Pullman Company, which it had referred to Central Trust. When the final tally was made, subscribers in New York State, almost all in New York City, had signed up for $320 million of the $500 million bond issue; the New England states—$50 million; Pennsylvania—$60 million; the rest of the country—$70 million. Only $6 million was subscribed in Chicago and that by the Central Trust Company of Illinois.

Sales to the general public of the Anglo-French bonds went slowly during the fall of 1915. The Morgan firm had to keep $30 million in bonds and pressed several munitions suppliers to the Allies, including the du Ponts and Bethlehem Steel, to take large participations. Nevertheless, the huge loan broke the ice, preparing the way for the enormous financing the British and French would need in their war effort.

During the war, an important service to American companies the bank considered worthy was to introduce them to key British, French, and Russian officials in charge of procurement. In 1915 the bank assisted the Remington Arms Company in presenting its bid to the Ministry of Munitions to supply rifles to the British Army. The agreed-upon $55 million contract called for Remington and the Winchester Repeating Arms Company to supply over three million Enfield .303 Magnum Rifles, bayonets, and scabbards, with Remington producing the bulk of the order.

However, deliveries to the British Army soon fell far below the rate called for in the contract. Flaws in the rifle's design led to numerous design changes, causing the American suppliers to request delays in the contract delivery dates. The British in turn claimed that many of the rifles produced had dangerous defects. The disagreements escalated to a climax when the British threatened to cancel the contract. The Ministry of Munitions had already been forced beyond its wishes to expand the home manufacture of rifles to supply the British soldiers on the Western front. It could not afford to wait longer for deliveries of the American-made rifles of doubtful quality. Remington argued that frequent British design changes had caused the delays and that the unrealistic production and inspection standards set by the British exacerbated the problem.

Lamont and his partners were worried on two counts. The Morgan bank had granted a $9 million credit and then a 25 percent share in a $15 million loan to Remington and also had a $2.3 million loan outstanding to Winchester. Moreover, the British were courting disaster: Remington had kept its American bankers fully informed about the affair, and the general perception that Remington was being treated unfairly by the British severely chilled the climate for British loans in the U.S.

The cables flew back and forth between 23 Wall Street and Edward Grenfell at Morgan's London office. If the Ministry of Munitions cancelled the contract, Lamont warned, American banks would refuse to participate in the forthcoming British loans to be raised in the United States, which would be calamitous for Great Britain. Lamont urged Grenfell to pass the word to the ministry in the strongest terms that it would be wise to renegotiate a mutually satisfactory contract with the American companies. Morgan and Davison, in London during October 1916, pressed home this argument with the British officials. Finally, the ministry gave in. It would purchase 2 million rifles from the American suppliers, guaranteeing them against all financial loss, and the Morgan partners breathed a sigh of relief.

In July 1916, the Morgan bank and Brown Bros. Co. had headed a banking syndicate making a three-year loan of $94.5 million to France through the American Foreign Securities Co. In August, Morgan led a syndicate that floated a $250 million loan to Great Britain, and after the rifle contract dispute was settled another loan for $300 million was made in October. All these bond issues were backed by collateral of American securities or those of neutral countries and non-European belligerents like Canada. After the Anglo-French loan operation it was clear that the American investors would only accept Allied obligations that were fully secured.

The Morgan partners organized other plans to help finance the Allies. Drawdowns under a secured demand loan from several banks, of which the Morgan share was about a half, rose to a high of $400 million; the loan was reduced by the British from the proceeds of the large public bond issues floated from time to time.

In addition, the Morgan firm served as agent for the British and French governments in selling American securities to obtain dollar funds. The British government had acquired about $3 billion in American and neutral countries' securities from its own citizens to use to raise dollars directly or as collateral for loans, and in 1916 Morgan sold $744 million in securities to meet the British Treasury's dollar requirements.

Despite these efforts, by November 1916 the financial position of the Allies was desperate: the British alone needed about $1 billion dollars to pay for their U.S. purchases over the next four months. However, the American investment market was saturated at the time; previous Allies' issues were not yet absorbed. Various small-scale credits made by Morgan and other banks couldn't do the job.

In response, the Morgan partners proposed a new gambit—the large-scale sale of British and French government treasury bills in the U.S. But this project was vetoed by the Federal Reserve Board, which cautioned its member banks in November 1916 that it was not "in the interest of the country at this time that they invest in foreign Treasury bills of this character." The board feared that the purchase of the bills would absorb bank liquidity needed to meet the working capital needs of American industry. The British government quickly agreed to respect the board's wishes, and Morgan terminated the arrangement with the French as well.

Concerned about the sharp price decline of British bonds on the U.S. market following the board's statement, the British announced that all the government's due accounts owed American suppliers would be settled promptly by the sale of American securities or by gold shipments. Over $800 million in gold had already been shipped to the United States since the beginning of the war, and starting in December 1916 the pace accelerated. Over the next four months some $422 million in gold was transported, mainly by swift British cruisers, across the North Atlantic, down the St. Lawrence River to Ottawa, and on to New York. It arrived in a variety of forms and coins—thousands of American eagle coins in canvas bags, English sovereigns, South African gold bars, French Napoleons, Japanese bullion, Russian imperials, and even German twenty-mark pieces.

The Federal Reserve stricture had been disheartening to the Allied governments and their American supporters, as Lamont, Morgan, and Davison made clear to Robert Lansing at the State Department and William G. McAdoo at the Treasury. The availability of ample credit was critical to the Allies: without American supplies they would lose the war. But U.S. investors had not lost confidence in the Allies, and another $250 million British loan was floated by a Morgan-led syndicate in January 1917. On April 1, with the country teetering on the brink of war with Germany, a $100 million loan for the French government was sold successfully. The flow of munitions and supplies to the Allies continued.

The bank's activity as purchasing agent for the Allied governments had developed into a mammoth and complicated task. The Export Department reached a peak staff of 377 people. Some 25,000 cables, all coded, were exchanged each year between Morgan Grenfell and 23 Wall Street. After investigating the capability of hundreds of bidders, four thousand contracts and eight thousand supplemental agreements were executed with American suppliers of a wide range of goods. About $3 billion in orders was placed over a two-year period, roughly two-thirds for the British and one-third for the French. The operation earned the Morgan bank about $30 million in commissions before deducting operating expenses.

To Edward Stettinius and his staff, working late most nights, it seemed that an inordinate amount of time and labor was spent in dealing with unjustified complaints. Rejected business brokers and losing bidders for contracts frequently accused the bank of bias in favor of its client companies.

Morgan later reported to the government that it had a stock interest in only eleven companies that were awarded British government contracts, and in only one case did it amount to more than 3 percent. As for the French contracts, the figures were even more trifling, and the firm always informed the British and French when it had an interest in a company selected to receive a contract. Morgan had refrained from underwriting issues for the large munitions suppliers except in two cases, Remington and Winchester, when their participation had been urged by the Allied governments. The process for awarding contracts was based on the merits of each case, the bank replied to its critics, which did not allay the suspicions of the Morgan-baiters.

Family Affairs

In addition to Lamont's involvement in his firm's work with the Allies, there were other business and pro bono publico activities filling his days and evenings. The bank's domestic business continued to grow, and as an active corporate director, TWL attended monthly board meetings of some nine or ten corporations.

Lamont had become increasingly occupied with Harvard alumni affairs, and in 1912 was elected to the Board of Overseers, the governing council of the university. He was elected president of the Associated Harvard Clubs in 1915 and continued as chairman and treasurer of his class committee, joining his classmates regularly for dinners in New York or Boston and at Harvard-Yale football games and crew races.

Often engaged in securing funds for one Harvard cause or another, TWL led the drive in 1912 to raise endowment funds for the Harvard Graduate School of Business, soliciting his banking friends, including two former bosses—Edmund C. Converse of Bankers Trust and George F. Baker of the First National.

TWL was openhanded in helping his hometown institutions, especially the Englewood Hospital, and charitable causes in New York. In 1913 he was elected a trustee of the Children's Aid Society, the long-established child welfare agency which operated lodging houses to provide temporary shelter, summer camps, and industrial schools where the boys were taught trades. There was also a farm for boys in Westchester and the "Orphan Train" to place homeless youngsters with farm families in the West. Each month TWL would don black tie to attend a dinner meeting at a fellow board member's Park Avenue townhouse to discuss Children's Aid Society affairs, the customary practice for charity board meetings.

The busy father wrote frequently to his son Tommy at Exeter. Perhaps because of his own sicknesses as a youth, he urged his son to follow good health habits—keep his feet dry, don't "get tired and run down." In one letter he encouraged him to play more tennis. "Nobody in school plays tennis," Tommy replied, "for the simple reason that it can't be played under a foot of water! It has rained about every day since September 17."

When Tommy's father rebuked him for flunking two monthly hour exams, his son replied that if his father insisted on top grades, he'd "resign from the musical clubs, debating society, and all other interests, buy some glasses with heavy lenses and keep my door locked all the time."

The correspondence continued in this vein for three years until Tommy graduated—the father urging the son to work harder, not waste time. "As to rough housing, I certainly am the last person in the world not to want you to have fun. However . . ."

Despite the admonishments and exhortations, TWL was a proud father at Tommy's graduation in June 1916. His son had been managing editor of the *Exonian* and delivered the class history at commencement. His classmates enjoyed his humor, laughing and applauding often, which pleased his parents. Young for his class, he planned to return the following year to Exeter for postgraduate study, before going on to Harvard.

After the exercises the Lamonts attended a tea for the families of graduating seniors at the home of Lewis Perry, Exeter's principal since 1914. TWL had been president of the Exeter Alumni Association of New York and followed the affairs of his old school closely. He thought that Perry—wise, witty, and genial—was an outstanding headmaster.

Lamont had now decided to go to sea, and do it in the grand manner, undoubtedly influenced by the example of his senior partner, who owned the magnificent yacht *Corsair*. In the spring of 1916, TWL chartered a ninety-eight-foot motor yacht, complete with captain and seven-man crew. In May, with the warmer weather, the Lamonts moved out from the city to their Englewood house, and each morning the *Nemaha* picked TWL up at the foot of the Palisades and transported him majestically down the Hudson to the tip of Manhattan near Wall Street. He returned home in the same style in the evening and enjoyed his new mode of commuting immensely.

In June Florence took the children to Dark Harbor, Maine, where the

Lamonts had rented a house for the summer. Lamont joined his family in July. On board *Nemaha*, the Lamonts cruised among the spruce-covered rock-rimmed islands in Penobscot Bay, and the boys sailed their gaff-rigged knockabout and swam from rocky beaches in the chilling water. The Lamont family fell in love with the beautiful region and planned to come back.

Florence and the younger children stayed in Dark Harbor through September because of her worry about the large number of cases of infantile paralysis in New York. In the course of the summer Lamont went back and forth between New York and Dark Harbor using the night train service to Rockland, Maine. For their board member, the New York Central provided a comfortable private car in which TWL read and enjoyed a quiet dinner.

Tom and Florence planned to visit their sons at Exeter over the weekend of the Exeter-Andover football game in November, and Lamont's private car would be hitched to the regular Boston and Maine train from Boston. Corliss, now a first-year Exeter student, wrote his mother his opinion of this plan. "I heard yesterday from Tommy that you were coming up to see the Andover game and am very pleased that you are, only I don't like the idea of your coming in a private car and will absolutely refuse to go anywhere near it. If it was known to anybody that my parents and myself had a private car everywhere they went, I would probably be called 'Private Car Lamont' forever afterwards."

When TWL became a banker in 1903, his father had just received a renewal of his appointment from the New York Conference to Lee, Massachusetts, a small town nestled in the Berkshire hills. The parson finally retired, and TWL's parents settled in Englewood, where Tom and Florence attended a Sunday service at which Tom's father was the substitute preacher. TWL had urged his father to don his best black preaching robe trimmed in silk for the occasion, and the minister must have struck an impressive figure in the pulpit. The years of strenuous outdoor work at many parsonages had kept him fit, and his chiseled features, square white beard, and erect bearing gave him an aura of strength and dignity.

TWL's mother, Caroline, died in Englewood on December 28, 1915, and his father answered "heaven's roll call," as he had often expressed it himself, three months later. He was in his eighty-fourth year. Lamont's parents were buried at the Brookside Cemetery in Englewood alongside his brother, Hammond, who had died in 1909. Perhaps TWL's thoughts went back to those years in the parsonage as he stood by his father's grave. As he grew older TWL could gently smile at the traditions and provincialism of the small-town Hudson Valley Methodists. At the same time he knew that beneath the surface there lay a solid bedrock of character and faith. In his own life his father had followed the biblical text from Corinthians XVI on which he had spoken many times: "Watch ye, stand fast in the faith, quit you like men, be strong."

The New York Methodist Conference memorial statement about Thomas Lamont declared, "His Christianity ordered his speech, governed his household, trained his children, and regulated all his relations with his fellow men. . . . He made no claim to oratory, but he was endowed . . . with the genius of common sense. He was a deep thinker and a plain talker. . . . He never posed for admiration and applause." Free from "the least taint of self-seeking or unbecoming ambition," he was "one of the quiet men" to whom American Methodism owed so much.

His father's sincere modesty, shunning the techniques of self-advancement with its gratifying rewards, was not TWL's way, but the example and values of his parents had well shaped his beginnings. That strong start, plus a bold ambition, a keen intellect, and good luck, had brought him to the summit of American finance.

On January 1, 1917, it was announced that Thomas Cochran, former president of the Liberty National Bank, would become a partner of J. P. Morgan & Co. At the same time the firm published an updated list of its partners with descriptive notes in a few cases. Mr. Morgan was "head of the firm"; Charles Steele was "of uncertain health"; Henry P. Davison was described as "closest associate of the late Mr. Morgan and of the present head of the house." Thomas Lamont would join these three senior partners in an area separated by a marble railing from the other partners, and Cochran would take his desk.

America Goes to War

Increasingly strained relations between the United States and Germany reached the breaking point in March 1917 when five U.S. merchant ships were torpedoed by German submarines with loss of American lives. Following passage by Congress of a joint resolution for war, President Wilson formally declared war on Germany on April 6, 1917.

America's entry into the war brought about major changes at the Morgan bank. The purchasing agency for the British and French governments was ended in order to integrate the Allied purchasing into the American government's program; the Allies' buying in the United States would now be financed by U.S. government loans. Edward Stettinius left for Washington to become Surveyor General of Supplies and later Second Assistant Secretary of War. Henry Davison was appointed chairman of the War Council of the American Red Cross, to direct its vastly expanding wartime operations. He, too, moved to Washington.

Morgan, Lamont, and Morrow had hoped to be asked to fill government posts directing important war work. This was not to be. President Wilson was strongly prejudiced against Wall Street bankers, especially the prominent Morgan partners, and believed that it would be politically unwise to appoint them to high government jobs. He had only reluctantly agreed to accept Davison in the Red Cross post because of the strong intervention by a close mutual friend. Stettinius's posts lacked real authority commensurate with his unquestioned experience and ability.

However, Morgan and Lamont were soon devoting their time to war work of a different sort, organizing the multibillion-dollar Liberty Loan issues to finance the American war effort. J. P. Morgan was a member of the Liberty Loan Committee of the Second Federal Reserve District, and there were daily meetings which Lamont often attended as his alternate. There were five Liberty Loan bond issues over a two-year period raising a total of $18.5 billion. The country was prosperous, patriotic feelings were high, and the loans were oversubscribed.

Lamont accepted a number of requests for articles and speeches to encourage the generous support of Americans for their country in its time of need. He enjoyed speaking and writing, and among the Morgan partners soon became known as the one most willing and competent to take on these assignments, with able staff help in research and writing led by Martin Egan.

Lamont's first major speech about the war had been to the American Academy of Political and Social Science in Philadelphia in May 1915— "The Effect of the War on America's Financial Position." His speeches before America entered the war stressed the wisdom of supporting the Allies with loans to purchase the American goods they needed to win the war. TWL ended his Philadelphia talk ringingly: "When the blood red fog of war burns away, we shall see Finance, still standing firm," ready to do the job "in planting new fields, in developing new enterprises, and in rebuilding a broken and wreck-strewn world." This was the public image that Lamont and his partners liked to put forward: they were the statesmen of finance, engaged in great public service in directing huge flows of capital to bolster the world's economies for the common good.

In July 1916, *Harper's Monthly Magazine* carried an article by Lamont entitled "Financial Illusions of the War." England and France had lent billions to America to build up this nation; should the U.S. deny them in their hour of need? In January 1917, *Collier's* published "Shall America's Prosperity Continue?," which was followed by "Foreign Loans, an Essential Instrument of Commerce" in the *Trust Companies Magazine* in February. TWL pointed out America's new role as a creditor nation replacing England and Germany as the leading world traders and bankers, especially in South America and the Far East. Growing exports and imports required strong financial support, and the bankers would be ready. Further articles by TWL ("A Government Bond for Everybody" in *Collier's* and "Pennywise by War" in the *Nation's Business*) and a score of speeches during 1917 promoted investing in sound Liberty Loans.

By March 1917, when it appeared likely that America would be drawn into the conflict, Lamont spoke to the Investment Bankers' Association in Chicago. In closing he looked at his watch and said:

> It is 10 o'clock in Chicago; it is 3 o'clock on the banks of the Somme in France, and it is a starlight night, the cannons are booming, there is a sound of a shell bursting, and another group of young heroes has fought its last fight. It is 3:30 on the frosted peaks of the Alps, where the Italians are sheltering themselves and preparing for the struggle on the morrow; it is 4 o'clock on the frozen fields of Rumania; a little later the gray of dawn will creep up and wake to light the peasant family that has lost its all, its home, its father, brother and son. Still further east it is high noon. It is Sydney, Australia and the sun is blazing there as 20,000 more colonials embark on the transports, to be ferried across the ocean and take their places in that great struggle, which, whatever may be the meaning of it all, has at any rate shown us how men can live and die, simply and nobly for an idea.
>
> If we too are drawn into the struggle, I pray not so much for patriotism and heroism—Americans will always show these qualities—but for wisdom, for the far-sightedness that will show us how best we can help to a speedy ending of the war; for courage to pursue that course unswervingly; and then at the end when peace comes, for the vision that will enable America to take her place at the world's counsel-table, and by her attitude and example contribute her share to the establishment of a world peace that will endure for the ages.

To fellow bankers, such as the New York State Bankers' Association assembled at their annual meeting at Lake Placid, Lamont talked in bankers' terms. He praised the sound investment value of the Liberty bonds, which would carry an attractive interest rate for government obligations—4 percent. He described the great organization of the British and the magnificent response of the English people in floating War Loans. Americans should exercise thrift, "cut down even on necessities," to build a large reservoir of savings to purchase Liberty bonds.

Lamont spoke to a variety of audiences, including the Merchants Association, the Republican County Committee of Newark, and the students of the University of the City of New York, to whom he gave a brief history lesson, tracing the record of Prussian and German militarism from Frederick the Great through Bismarck. He recalled the philosophy teachings of Nietzsche: war had become almost "a holy thing" for Germany, overpowering others and acquiring their territories a way of life. On the other hand, America had fought only for liberty and freedom for oppressed peoples.

To a gathering of local residents at the Brooklyn Academy of Music, Lamont explained why America had finally determined to join the struggle. The cause was imperative, and Lamont did not hesitate to echo the exaggerated wartime propaganda about German atrocities.

> We saw a cruel, rapacious, treacherous government setting out to conquer the world. We saw the Prussians trampling down weaker nations, crushing them as they would a hill of ants, murdering the men, violating the women, maiming the children, committing hideous crimes and exulting in them.
>
> And we saw that if such a government ever succeeded in conquering the heroic French, the sturdy English, the vigorous Italians . . . then next it would be our turn here in America! And we saw that it would be the end of real freedom in America.

The twenty-fifth class reunion has always been a momentous celebration for Harvard men even when curtailed in wartime. It was also a time when alumni reviewed the career report cards of their classmates for the last quarter century, and the consensus was that Lamont had earned all A's. At the '92 reunion in 1917, TWL was appointed to serve as chief marshal of the alumni at the commencement exercises. He was also chairman and treasurer of his Class Committee, an overseer of the college, and chairman of the committee formed to raise capital for the Harvard Graduates Endowment fund. "First and last I have spent a good deal of time on Harvard matters," he stated in the class reunion report.

The class first convened for dinner at the Copley Plaza Hotel in Boston, the reunion headquarters. On Wednesday a stag Field Day was held at Gay Farm in Norwood, the magnificent home of classmate W. Cameron Forbes. Forbes had spared no effort to give his classmates a good time, with three baseball diamonds laid out on the polo field, two lawn tennis courts, a squash court, and polo ponies saddled for riding. TWL and three friends played golf at the Country Club in Brookline and then returned to Gay Farm "to play the nineteenth hole on the south piazza," it was recorded in the post-reunion class report. That evening Lamont presided at the class dinner at the Algonquin Club "with his usual energy, humor, and bonhomie. . . . Lamont himself became the subject of a well deserved toast . . . being rightly acclaimed by his classmates as 'a jolly good fellow.' " The report noted the spirit of friendliness and cordiality that prevailed and added:

> Twenty-five years have made of '92 a splendid body of men. Whatever may have been the complacencies, the intolerance, the cliquishness, that characterized the Class, like all other large undergraduate bodies, twenty-five years ago—these have given way to broader and more human interests and to a greater respect for the rest of the world.

The aristocracy of the club men during college was a thing of the past.

On Commencement Day the officers of the Alumni Association gave a special luncheon spread in a small tent near Appleton Chapel. Chief Marshal Lamont hosted the event, which was attended by the president of Harvard, A. Lawrence Lowell; members of the university governing boards; and the recipients of honorary degrees, including Herbert C. Hoover, U.S. Food Administrator. After lunch the chief marshal led the dignitaries and alumni in the long procession between lines of applauding students to Sever Quadrangle for the alumni meeting.

Later that summer the Lamont family spent six weeks at North Haven, Maine, an island in Penobscot Bay with a growing summer colony composed mainly of old Boston families, such as Cabots, Saltonstalls, and Hallowells. TWL rented a house near the village of North Haven and chartered a motor yacht, the *North Wind*, for the summer. Tom and Florence played golf frequently on the island's new nine-hole course. The Lamonts liked the informal social life, which included lots of boating and picnics. There was some land for sale on the north shore near Pulpit Harbor, and the site had a superb view across the wide bay, dotted with wooded islands, to the Camden Hills on the mainland. Before Lamont returned to New York, he agreed with John Beverage of North Haven to buy his 84-acre farm for $13,500.

Ever since America's entry into the war, the Morgan bank had faced a nagging problem—the prospects for repayment of the British government demand loan of $400 million of which Morgan had a large share, $165 million; the remainder had been parceled out to other banks, and some were becoming restive about its repayment. Furthermore, the banks were being pressed to take big portions of the Liberty Loans, and the outstanding British demand loan seemed to muddy the waters for this top-priority U.S. government financing. However, the British would be hard put to pay back the loan if the bank demanded repayment, as was their right. In the past, drawdowns under this line of credit had been repaid from proceeds of the large British government bond issues organized by Morgan, but when the United States went to war, the U.S. government, it will be recalled, had taken over the task of financing British purchases in America.

Lamont had a number of talks with Secretary of the Treasury William G. McAdoo and Assistant Secretaries Russell C. Leffingwell and Oscar T. Crosby about the problem. Treasury Department policy was that U.S. government advances to the British must be used exclusively for the purchase of military supplies, which ruled out repaying existing bank loans with these funds. The British demand loan was fully secured by American stocks and bonds, and while this collateral could be liquidated to repay the loan, no more than $5 million of securities could be sold weekly without significantly depressing the market. After discussing various schemes, TWL and the Treasury officials finally agreed that if the banks purchased $150 million of a forthcoming offering of U.S. Treasury bills, $81 million would be allocated to the British to reduce the credit, an amount the U.S. government owed the British for the purchase of several British ships. The liquidation of the loan collateral continued steadily, and these proceeds plus a gold payment from the British finally retired the loan, a big plus for Britain's credit standing with Wall Street when the inevitable need for new credits for postwar England arose.

Touring the Front

In the fall of 1917 President Wilson asked his close adviser Colonel Edward M. House to lead a small mission to England and France to consult with Allied officials on a range of economic and financial questions. Lamont, who had developed a good working relationship with the Treasury officials, was requested to be in London and Paris at the same time as the House mission to act as a confidential private adviser to the mission. His acquaintance with many of the leading officials could be especially valuable to the mission. However, Lamont's status must be strictly unofficial; the president preferred that there should be no public mention of his connection with the mission. TWL was angry at Wilson's rude rebuff of the Morgan partners, but he was eager to visit England and France to gain a first-hand impression of wartime conditions and postwar business prospects. Both Morgan and Davison had been over several times. It was agreed at the partners' meeting on November 1 that TWL should go, with his younger colleague George Whitney serving as his aide.

On November 3 he wrote to his son Tommy, now a Harvard freshman:

> Your mother feels dreadfully over the trip I am taking. I shall be back safe and sound for Christmas I trust, and shall feel that I have tried to do a little something more in the war.
>
> If there should ever be any accident your first duty would be to care for your mother. You will not have to support her, but love & cherish and keep her. She is the most wonderful mate, the most devoted mother.

Florence worshipped her husband and was indeed worried about his safety as she waved good-bye from the end of the pier where the S.S. *New York* backed out into the Hudson River to commence the Atlantic crossing. The ship was equipped with two six-inch guns to defend itself against German submarine attacks, and it would pick up an escort of two American destroyers as it approached the British Isles.

Lamont's fellow passengers made the voyage congenial for him. His friend Lord Reading, on board with his wife, was now the British ambassador-designate to Washington. The press baron Lord Northcliffe and his lady were also passengers. He was the owner and publisher of *The Times* in London and had been serving as chairman of the British War Mission based in New York. Lamont usually dined with these couples, and they had long talks together about Anglo-American relations and the postwar world. However, the menace of the German submarines was never far from one's thoughts. TWL was glad when they crossed the bar at Mersey and docked at Liverpool on November 12.

Lamont spent the next ten days working with his colleagues at Morgan Grenfell and meeting with U.S. ambassador Walter Hines Page and members of the House mission. He also negotiated Morgan's compensation with the British Treasury for serving as paying agent for all the British government's U.S. purchases now being handled by the American government. The bank would receive a ⅛ percent commission on all disbursements, a sum, it turned out, almost sufficient to offset all Morgan's expenses incurred earlier as the British government's purchasing agent.

Lamont's mission was not all work. He played a round of golf with Lord Northcliffe at his club and spent a country weekend with Lord Cunliffe, the governor of the Bank of England. Lamont was struck by the manner in which Britain's leading families had adjusted to the austerities mandated by wartime conditions.

At the large country house of Lord Cunliffe, first baron of Headley, the only servants were an ancient butler and maid where seventy people had been employed before the war. Lady Cunliffe and her daughters cultivated the vegetable garden and tended the orchard, picking and preserving large quantities of fruits and vegetables for themselves and dependent families in the village. To conserve gasoline his lordship often walked three miles to the station to catch the London train, and back in the evening.

TWL was impressed with the British spirit—the high morale of the British people despite the tragedy of the appalling casualties on the Western front. Every American should be made aware of Britain's sacrifices at all levels of society to win the war.

On November 23, Lamont and George Whitney took the boat train to Paris. They stayed at the Hotel Ritz on Place Vendome and used the Paris house of the firm, Morgan Harjes & Co., as their base. Lamont joined the House mission members for meetings at the Banque de France and Ministry of Finance. His Chicago banking friend Charles G. Dawes was now a brigadier general and chairman of the General Purchasing Board of the American Expeditionary Force, and the two breakfasted together regularly at the Ritz.

One day General Dawes drove Lamont out to Chaumont, the AEF headquarters, to meet the American commander in chief, General John J. Pershing. At the end of their talk General Dawes made a proposal: "Tom, we want you to stay over here and become the active scouting officer for the procurement division. You know all the people over here. You are a business man. . . . We need you."

Lamont declined politely, saying he felt he could do the cause more good by his work in the United States. But he had in mind a man who was uniquely well qualified for the post, Jeremiah Smith, Jr., a Boston attorney and an old friend from Exeter and Harvard. After listening to Lamont's description of Smith's credentials, the stern, no-nonsense commander immediately cabled a captain's commission for Smith to come to France to fill the position. Smith accepted and would sail from New York at the end of December.

Lord Northcliffe had arranged for Lamont and Whitney to tour the British front and the supply and hospital facilities in Calais to gain a better understanding of the Allied position and strategy. They drove from Paris to Abbeville, where the British army headquarters were housed in an old chateau. Their escort officer presented each of them with a steel helmet and a gas mask. "With the new invisible gas, how do you know when to put them on?" TWL asked. The lieutenant had a macabre sense of humor: "It is often puzzling, you know. The only sure way is if the fellow next to you suddenly falls, you know the gas has got him!"

Early each morning they set out in an open car to visit a different sector, bumping over broken roads crowded with supply trucks, troops, horse-drawn gun carriages, and ambulances returning from the front filled with wounded men on stretchers. They drove through villages and towns devastated by German shelling. In Ypres, where the damaged Cloth Hall and cathedral stood among the ruins around the central plaza, British soldiers were living in the cellars of abandoned houses to enjoy a brief respite from the trenches. Lamont heard the dull booming of the Allied and German artillery and from a hilltop saw the flashes of the guns. In the sky overhead officers in observation balloons spotted and telephoned the location of German gun positions to their command posts.

After visiting Vimy Ridge, Lamont wrote:

> The desolation of the Flanders plain, broken by the water-filled bomb craters, where so many thousands of the Allied troops had laid down their lives, was complete. Had it not been for the boom of artillery, our journey would have seemed to traverse a vast Dantesque Inferno, with frequent flashes from the guns like the fires of the underworld. Nowhere was there a vestige of the glory of war: only the grim and broken land to bring home to us the miseries and sufferings that the Allied troops had endured for months and even years on end. Our daily journeyings across those desolate areas of the Front Line served to show the utter misery, the squalor, the wretchedness that the fighting men had to endure.

Back in Paris after a meeting one afternoon with French officials, Lamont was introduced to Georges Clemenceau, France's new premier, seventy-six years old and known to his countrymen as the "Tiger." Grim and grizzled, wearing gray gloves to cover his eczema, Clemenceau came forward to greet Lamont with outstretched hands. He rejoiced that American soldiers would soon be fighting by the side of his own, and he was grateful for the help that the American Red Cross was already rendering French poilus. Lamont was greatly impressed by France's man of the hour in the critical days of December 1917.

Returning to London on December 6, Lamont spent the weekend with John Masefield, the writer and poet, who lived at Boar's Hill, outside Oxford. In 1916 Masefield had been assigned by the British government to undertake an American speaking tour to arouse support for the Allied cause. After his lecture, "The Tragic Drama," at the Aeolian Hall in New York, he was introduced to Florence Lamont, who was deeply impressed by him. Before his return to England she had guided him about the city and brought him home to meet her husband.

Another new friend was Montagu Norman, deputy governor of the Bank of England, who often joined Lamont and his partner, Edward Grenfell, for dinner. The bearded banker struck TWL as one of the wisest men he had met and clearly destined to become a major figure in postwar international finance. An old friend from Exeter and business, William B. Thompson, head of the American Red Cross mission in Petrograd, was also in London, and he wanted Lamont's help.

By December 1917 the new Bolshevik government headed by Lenin was planning to pull Russia out of the war by signing a separate peace treaty with the Central Powers. Yet the new Russian leaders feared the harshness of the terms that Germany would impose. Thompson was convinced that the new government could be persuaded to keep on fighting the German invaders if the Allies, and especially the United States, provided some tangible evidence of support and friendship, such as food and relief supplies. Lamont agreed to help Thompson present his proposal to senior officials in the British and American governments.

During the next week they made the rounds of high officialdom in London and finally breakfasted at 10 Downing Street with Prime Minister Lloyd George, who listened carefully to Thompson's report. Thompson concluded by stating: "These Bolsheviks are nobodies now. They are fumbling around and need guidance. Let us make them our Bolsheviks!"

Lloyd George responded heartily, "That's it. Let's make them our Bolsheviks!" He waxed enthusiastic over Thompson's ideas, as he walked up and down the breakfast room rubbing his hands. Lamont recorded the prime minister's remarks later:

> A joint Anglo-American Mission . . . should be sent to Petrograd to show the Bolshevik rulers that at least Britain and America still had an interest in Russia, still felt that aid to Russia in keeping her in the war . . . was well worth while if it would add a featherweight to the possible defeat of the German menace that was threatening all the Allies, including Russia.

Mr. Lloyd George said it was no wonder that the soldiers of the Russian Army, with no weapons, food, or warm clothing, badly led almost to the point of treachery—no wonder that they were breaking away and wearily plodding back over the desolate steppes to the homeland. . . . "You will return, both of you, at once," he said to Colonel Thompson and me, "and see your President. He is full of liberal ideas. He will be ready to act with me. . . . We must do the utmost to arouse the war-weary Russians to the German menace, to the impossible terms of peace that Germany is undoubtedly urging. If no help comes from Allied quarters, the Soviet leaders may be forced to accept those terms. Be sure to see the President promptly. This is a situation that Mr. Wilson cannot neglect."

Upon their return to the U.S., Lamont and Thompson immediately attempted to obtain an appointment with President Wilson. The other officials they saw in Washington—McAdoo and Leffingwell of the Treasury; Herbert Hoover, U.S. Food Administrator; George Creel, chairman of the Committee on Public Information; Under Secretary Fred L. Polk of the State Department; Louis Brandeis, now a Supreme Court Justice and still a confidant of President Wilson—seemed impressed by Lloyd George's plan.

But President Wilson refused to see Lamont and Thompson. He had little confidence in the Bolsheviks or their living up to his idealistic standards. Second, he was receiving conflicting reports on Russia and viewed the situation to be so fluid and chaotic that he was reluctant to take any initiative. He wrote Lamont in early February that he found "the changes taking place are so kaleidoscopic" that "information and advice are futile until there is something definite to plan with as well as for."

Thompson, with Lamont's collaboration, submitted a memorandum to the president containing his views: with proper handling Russia could be maintained as a menace to Germany. "Recognition of the Bolsheviks is not essential. Contact is."

The president was not persuaded. The Brest-Litovsk talks between the Central Powers and the Bolshevik government had been proceeding since December 1917, and the peace treaty was signed on March 3, 1918. The harshness of its demands for the surrender of territory and payment of reparations to the Central Powers gave the world an eye-opening picture of Germany's war aims.

Plunging into the promotion of Liberty bonds, Lamont now delivered a vivid message based on his first-hand observations of wartime England, Paris, and the Western Front. To a Boston Chamber of Commerce audience of four hundred businessmen and in a Sunday *New York Times* article, he spoke of the example of Lord and Lady Cunliffe, of the plain and simple way of life this "noble lord" and his family had adopted to help their country's cause.

> On a recent trip to the other side, I found that rich and poor were imbued with the self-same spirit. Women of title, women of position and wealth, women who had been accustomed all their days to having their burdens lifted from their backs, were taking hold of the household tasks and doing them gladly and with a fine and gentle spirit.

The customary adulation of English aristocracy by upper-class Americans obviously took on added potency in wartime, and Lamont and Jack Morgan were leading exemplars. "The practice of economy and thrift" had become the hallmark of the British housewife, declared Lamont, and this "noble self-sacrifice" was most inspiring. So was the cheerfulness and good humor of the British and French people in the midst of hardship and sorrow. "And this despite the fact that there probably isn't a home in either country but has suffered the loss of a dear one; a little grave on the banks of the Marne marks to many an English family a spot of ground that will always be England for them."

Addressing the New York Produce Exchange, Lamont said: "There is one thing I can say to you about the Western Front: The Huns will never break through! . . . Someone asked me whether France was not bled white. Bled white? I tell you France was never more heroic, never more valorous, never more steadfast than today." As for the British soldiers, when they were wounded their concern was whether their wounds would "prevent them from getting back to the trenches soon for another crack at the Boche." He concluded: "We know full well that our men over there have the spirit to hold the line firm, and then, when the time comes, to go over the top."

The parson's son turned banker often stressed the practice of thrift, which he placed on a far higher plane than mere scrimping and penny-pinching. "Its significance is a spiritual significance, just as waste is significant of slackness, of disorder, or a mind and spirit ill-controlled. Thrift means rational living . . . self-control and self-denial and temperance. . . . When each member of the community begins to feel the pinch and realizes that the war is directly affecting him, then, and not till then, shall we all become genuine participants in this mighty struggle."

Such piousness may have sounded hollow coming from Lamont, who hardly led a frugal existence. The Lamonts still rented the comfortable townhouse on East 65th Street from Franklin D. Roosevelt and spent weekends at their home in Englewood, where TWL, who had become an enthusiastic golfer, passed many hours on the green fairways at the Engle-wood Golf Club.

In February, Lamont, a newly elected trustee of Phillips Exeter Academy, attended meetings at the school before going on to join the Harvard Overseers convening in Cambridge. In March the Lamonts took their regular winter holiday at the Grove Park Inn in Asheville, North Carolina.

Two of TWL's good English friends returned to America. John Masefield was a welcome guest, embarking on another lecture tour to inspire Anglo-American solidarity in the crusade to "defeat the Hun." Lord Reading, H.M.G.'s new ambassador to the United States, was guided by Lamont in screening his many invitations for speeches. Lamont undoubtedly had a hand in Harvard's decision to grant honorary degrees to both Masefield and Lord Reading at Commencement on June 20, 1918.

During July TWL and some friends went salmon fishing in Quebec. In August he joined his family for a summer holiday in North Haven, where he oversaw the landscaping and site preparation for his new house. The *North Wind* was again on hand for exploring the coastal waters and Penobscot Bay.

While wartime didn't cramp Lamont's style, an Allied victory and the peace to follow were uppermost in his thoughts. He longed to have a voice that would be heard in the public's consideration of these great issues.

"The Whipping Post"

On August 2, 1918, the press reported that Thomas W. Lamont had purchased the *New York Evening Post*, an afternoon newspaper which traced its origins back to Alexander Hamilton and stood generally in the liberal ranks among the city's dozen papers. Lamont placed his stock in a trust managed by Theodore N. Vail, president of the American Telephone and Telegraph Company; Henry S. Pritchett, president of the Carnegie Foundation for the Advancement of Teaching; and Ellery Sedgwick, editor of the *Atlantic Monthly*. TWL told reporters in an interview:

"I have personally acquired from Mr. Oswald Garrison Villard and his associates all the shares of the stock of the *New York Evening Post*. I have been led to make this purchase partly because of a personal interest in the *Evening Post*, formed when my brother, the late Hammond Lamont, was the managing editor; but chiefly because I have believed that a journal with the sound traditions of the *Evening Post* is an institution of value to the public, if conducted with vigor and independence."

TWL stated that neither he nor the trustees would be responsible for the newspaper's views or its management: "With such management, the editorial staff (as ably led by Mr. Rollo Ogden, the present editor-in-chief) will be completely entrusted; for to command the permanent confidence of the community a newspaper must be free from outside direction, both in its presentation of news and of opinions."

The paper had been in poor financial condition for some years and now was in serious straits, losing $8,000 to $10,000 a month. Villard could no longer afford to keep it going. There were rumors that both Frank A. Munsey, another newspaper publisher, and Bernard M. Baruch, the Wall Street financier and chairman of the War Industries Board, were interested in buying it, and Lamont was concerned for its future if either of them acquired the newspaper. Munsey had not hesitated to close down newspapers he owned when it suited his business strategy. Baruch, TWL wrote a friend, would turn the newspaper into an out-and-out "Democratic organ." However, TWL's most important reason for buying the *Post* was his aspiration to influence public opinion on important issues. Lamont had long appreciated the power of the press, and passive ownership of the *Post* was never his intent, notwithstanding his rhetoric. He paid just under $1 million for the newspaper and by November had advanced another $107,000 to keep it alive.

The trust arrangement was a bit of ornamentation to allay suspicions that Lamont might run the *Post* for his own benefit. It was revocable at any time by TWL and a paper wall that no one took seriously. Lamont was soon regularly communicating his views to Ogden; in the upcoming New York gubernatorial election TWL thought that the major drawback to the Democratic candidate, Alfred E. Smith, was that he was "too close to Tammany Hall."

A number of people—publishing executives, *Post* subscribers, and friends—wrote Lamont that he must make changes in the editorial policy of the paper. TWL agreed with much of the criticism of the *Post* under Villard, who was thought by many to be pacifist and anti-English even after America had gone to war, and who had sharply criticized President Wilson's leadership.

Lamont wrote to several correspondents: "We old friends found ourselves in strong disagreement with his views" and spoke of the "blighting influence of Villard on the *Post*," whose views had driven patriotic advertisers away. Lamont promised that the *Post* would stand for "vigorous prosecution of the war . . . without pussy-footing on side issues." He also made sure that the *Post* supported his views on the peace to follow: Lamont backed President Wilson's goal to conclude a peace treaty that was not so vengeful that it would sow the seeds of future conflict and his plan to form a League of Nations to promote international cooperation and achieve international peace and security.

On September 30, Lamont wrote President Wilson to congratulate him on his recent speech at the Metropolitan Opera House in New York and also to ask for an appointment to discuss his purchase of the *New York Evening Post*. He was "anxious to see no stone left unturned that will help the country and your administration in the conduct of the war" and in dealing with "the problems of peace." On the afternoon of October 4, TWL met with the president in his office at the White House and explained why he had bought the *Post*. He later wrote a memorandum, summarizing the meeting.

Lamont had begun by saying he wanted to accomplish two things with his newspaper.

> Lamont: The first of these is the elimination of a certain fault-finding, or carping, attitude on the part of the Post that has been more or less traditional.
>
> President Wilson: I know just what you mean, Mr. Lamont. In the old days I always used to call the Evening Post the "whipping post."
>
> Lamont: The second point . . . is to help the publication in a constructive attitude, and here is where I come back to the subject of your Opera House speech of September 27. Amidst all the applause that you received . . . two sentiments of yours had little applause: One was when you said that "We must be just to those to whom we do not wish to be just." The other was when you said that "we must conclude a peace satisfactory to all the belligerents." At that there was only one handclap in the whole house, and that was my wife's. I did not applaud that, because I don't see how in the world, Mr. President, you are ever going to conclude a peace satisfactory to Germany.

The president laughed and asked Lamont to continue.

> Lamont: When you come to put into effect throughout the country the practical workings of these two sentiments of yours . . . I think you are going to have difficulty. The country is in a mood just now for war, and that mood is what is making the work of our soldiers in France so effective. We are necessarily intolerant and not ready as a whole to listen to such sentiments as you express.
>
> President Wilson: Yes, not only intolerant, but we are growing revengeful,

which, Mr. Lamont, is a very dangerous attitude and not one calculated to have us conclude the wisest sort of a peace.

Lamont then asked what the *Post* could do to support the president "in attaining a peace that is healing and permanent."

Wilson replied that he believed that the peoples of the Allied nations backed his sentiments, but not necessarily the present administrations of those countries. The British had a narrower viewpoint.

> President Wilson: For instance, you may have noticed that in their plans for an after-the-war trade, the British have appointed a lot of committees, made up of men who are ambitious to maintain Great Britain supreme commercially all over the world. . . . They are reluctant to show even to America their hand on shipping questions, etc. The idea that that group of people has, in the way of peace, is hardly one that would tend toward the permanent satisfaction of the world. For instance, take the case of the German colonies; now we all know that throughout the world there has been a cry that England too completely dominates the sea as it is. Would not that cry be greatly intensified if these additional colonies should be placed in England's hands? Great Britain has certain ideas which she would like us to fall in with, but which we cannot.

Wilson hoped that the *Post* would point out the dangers of a nonhealing peace.

> President Wilson: It is perfectly certain that if we concluded a peace that is not wholly just to every one of the large nations, then each one of those powerful nations will not rest contented until it has righted what it deems to be its wrongs. That, of course, means more wars. In the same way we must lean backwards in being just to the smaller nations, for equally in them lie the seeds of future trouble. If we are not careful we shall leave behind other balkan situations in various parts of the world, smouldering fires that are banked but that will break out if we do not eliminate the cause of the fire beforehand.
>
> Lamont: Let me ask you again, Mr. President: do you think that the allied governments are heart and soul with you in the various points of your speech?
>
> President Wilson: That is very doubtful Mr. Lamont, but the people of those nations are. . . . I believe that at the present time I do enjoy extraordinary prestige abroad, and the maintenance of that prestige I believe to be necessary to the proper handling of the peace problems. . . . Now there is an election coming on, and I want to say to you that I believe it essential to the maintenance of my prestige abroad that we should re-elect a Democratic congress. I am going to be very personal and tell you one or two stories that will throw a little light on what I mean.

Wilson then told Lamont a story about some French schoolgirls whose plea to the headmistress for some privilege had been turned down. After a conference they sent a delegation to the prefect with the message "Unless you allow us to do so we shall take the case up with President Wilson, who is the final Court of Justice."

In another incident some longshoremen in the harbor of Liverpool were on strike. Finally the harbor master called the strikers together, and said, "There are nineteen American vessels in this harbor waiting to discharge their cargoes and to be reloaded and you are holding up that work. Now I want to ask you what President Wilson will think of you when he hears what your attitude is." The longshoremen immediately agreed to return to work.

> President Wilson: You will think me very conceited, Mr. Lamont, to quote these little stories to you, but I have a purpose in doing so. . . . If a Republican congress should be elected, the people of our own country would understand the matter perfectly because we know how our constitution works. We know it is entirely possible, as in times past, for a Democratic president to have a Republican congress on his hands. . . . But the peoples of our Allies would never understand the matter. They would say that I had been repudiated, and such strength and power as I possess among them for the conclusion of the sort of peace that I have set my heart upon, and that I see you are devoted to, would be gone.
>
> There is another suggestion that I wish to make to you as to the domestic situation. When this war is over, Mr. Lamont, there will be great problems to settle, and I want to see them settled by professionals and not by amateurs. I call the radicals the amateurs. I want you and your associates to be assured that I am not a radical, but a moderate. I have the confidence of Labor, however, and I think that, all things considered, I am in a better position to lead in the satisfactory solution of these great problems than is a man like Theodore Roosevelt, for instance. Providentially I have been placed in a position at this time to have great power for good or ill. I see you smile, Mr. Lamont, when I use the word "providentially." I do not mean to indicate that it is necessarily a wise providence that has placed me in this position, but merely that circumstances have done so, and if these considerations . . . appeal to you, perhaps you will wish, upon your return to New York, to bring these views to the attention of certain people over there.

Lamont replied that he was very impressed with the president's observations about his prestige abroad. He added that, frankly, he was not so impressed by Wilson's views on the domestic political situation.

> Lamont: Let me add, Mr. President, that I am Republican, as you perhaps know, and I do not wish to give you the impression that my support will be given to you, thick and thin, for all time to come, but I want to have you know that you have that support to the very limit throughout the war.

Not surprisingly, Lamont resisted the president's partisan pleas for a Democratic Congress in the November 1918 election. On October 25 the president urged Americans to show their confidence in his leadership by voting Democratic. Two weeks later the voters repudiated Wilson: the Republicans retained control of the House of Representatives and captured the Senate as well.

The Second Battle of the Marne in June and July had marked the turning point in the tide of war and led inexorably to Germany's defeat. The German army suffered heavy casualties; its supplies were depleted, and it was exhausted, while fresh American troops were filling the Allied front lines. Germany sued for peace, accepting as a basis for negotiations President Wilson's Fourteen Points, and on November 11 an armistice was signed.

On the night of the armistice celebration in New York, Tom and Florence attended the opera in formal attire and became entangled in a boisterous crowd watching a victory parade up Broadway. A celebrant made off with TWL's top hat. "Oh well," he told his wife, "Mr. Knox the hatter has plenty more!"

On December 4 President Wilson sailed for France. Joining him there were his hand-picked peace commissioners: Secretary of State Lansing; General Tasker H. Bliss, Army Chief of Staff; Colonel House; and Henry White, a career diplomat. Dozens of experts in a variety of subjects ranging from shipping to history were brought along to advise the delegation. Wilson did not include any senators or Republican leaders among his peace commissioners, a strategic misstep in view of the fact that the peace treaty would have to be ratified by the Republican-controlled Senate. Lamont told *Post* editor Ogden that he did not think that Wilson had chosen a strong team but "rubber stamps" for a president who intended to personally direct the peace negotiations.

The Paris Peace Conference

On January 25, 1919, Tom and Florence sailed down New York harbor under fair skies on the S.S. *Lapland* bound for Liverpool, steaming through a large fleet of camouflaged cargo ships and military transports. Lamont had been designated by Secretary of the Treasury Carter Glass to be one of the two representatives of the U.S. Treasury on the American Commission to

Negotiate Peace. Lamont was excited about being a participant in the peace conference and grateful for the endorsement of Assistant Treasury Secretary Russell Leffingwell and Secretary Glass, who had cabled President Wilson recommending Lamont's appointment. Glass wanted a private financier of stature with a solid record of supporting the administration and the Allies in the war effort, and the president had agreed with his choice of Lamont.

Lamont's Morgan colleague George Whitney, who would serve as his deputy, and his wife, Martha, were also on board, and TWL knew a number of his fellow passengers. Many people and organizations were converging on Paris with the hope of advancing their special interests in the negotiations of the comprehensive treaty settlement. There were also dozens of experts assigned to the large American Commission, YMCA workers, and invalided British officers returning to England.

On February 4 the Lamonts arrived in London, where TWL met with Robert Bacon, a former Morgan partner and Whitney's father-in-law, who had just returned from a survey mission to Germany. Bacon reported that the Germans were unrepentant, arrogant, embittered, and as determined as ever to dominate Europe. They did not believe that their armies had been defeated and suffered a military collapse, and they had proposed an armistice only to avoid further losses on both sides, an armistice that Lamont now believed could have been avoided. With its army shattered by the Allies' counterattack, Germany soon would have been forced to surrender anyway. The prospects for a satisfactory peace treaty acceptable without rancor by the Germans seemed considerably less promising in the light of the German attitudes reported by Bacon.

Two days later Tom and Florence crossed over to Paris, where the Hotel Meurice on Rue de Rivoli would be their home for the duration of their stay. The following morning Lamont went over to the Hotel Crillon on Place de la Concorde, the headquarters of the American delegation. During the next few days he met the colleagues with whom he would be working closely over the coming months.

Norman Davis, with Lamont as his alternate, headed the Finance Section. A courtly and able former banker, Davis had served as an adviser on foreign loans to the Secretary of the Treasury for the last two years with the title of Commissioner of Finance to Europe. In addition to Whitney, his deputy, Lamont had arranged for his friend Captain Jeremiah Smith, Jr., to be appointed counsel to this group. Bernard M. Baruch, chairman of the War Industries Board, and Vance McCormick, chairman of the War Trade Board, headed the Economic Section. Baruch, who was very close to the president, had been a highly successful Wall Street investor before the war. McCormick, a former newspaper publisher, had headed President Wilson's 1916 campaign committee. He had appointed John Foster Dulles, a serious young attorney from New York and his assistant at the War Trade Board (who would stamp his imprint on world affairs years later), as counsel to their staff. Another key official was Herbert Hoover, head of the Food Section, which was charged with organizing the relief efforts for war-torn Europe. Hoover had first won acclaim for managing the critical task of supplying food to Belgium, in desperate straits following the German invasion, before becoming wartime Food Administrator in the United States.

On Lamont's very first day of meetings in Paris the deep divisions between the Allies that promised to complicate the treaty negotiations were apparent. With widespread food shortages and hunger reported in Germany, the Americans had drafted a resolution permitting Germany to make payments in gold to purchase food from neutral countries. The French were adamantly opposed to this proposal; they insisted that Germany's gold reserves must remain available for reparations.

Crucial questions at the peace conference were ultimately dealt with at the meetings of the so-called Big Four—Wilson; Prime Minister Lloyd George of Great Britain; Premier Clemenceau of France, and Premier Orlando of Italy. The European leaders were politicians acutely sensitive to public opinion, fearing that if they ignored it, they would promptly be expelled from office. The people of their countries cried for vengeance for the millions of casualties and devastating destruction they had suffered at the hands of the Germans. While Wilson, secure in his four-year term of office, was calling for reasonable and fair reparations, Lloyd George said he agreed with a political cohort who had vowed in the recent British election to "squeeze Germany until the pips squeak."

Clemenceau was even more determined that the Germans should pay fully for their crimes. Northern France had been overrun—its towns in ruins and the countryside laid waste. Furthermore, he would never trust the Germans. French security must be guaranteed. As a young man he vividly recalled Bismarck's defeat of France in 1870, and now it had happened again. Although they had repelled the enemy, a generation of French youth had been slaughtered in the trenches and battlefields of northern France. He was not overly impressed with Wilson's fourteen points either, noting that God Almighty had given mankind only ten commandments.

Reparations

Even as the ideological chasm between the idealistic Woodrow Wilson and the more vengeful Allies widened, Lamont and his colleagues—Baruch, McCormick, Davis, and Dulles—got down to work on the various aspects of the reparations issue. Lamont and Norman Davis were specifically assigned to Sub-Committee No. 2, charged with determining Germany's capacity to pay and how payments should be made. The Americans assumed that they and the British would see eye to eye in handling the issue of German reparations sensibly, despite the British election campaign rhetoric.

The first meeting of Sub-Committee No. 2 was held on the afternoon of February 15 at the French Ministry of Finance, and following nomination by Louis Loucheur, the French representative, Lord Walter Cunliffe, the British delegate, was elected chairman. Lamont, who had been so impressed in 1917 by Cunliffe's personal wartime austerities, considered him an able friend and expected that the committee deliberations would progress smoothly. However, the first several meetings were taken up with lengthy and inconclusive discussions of such items as obtaining accurate data on German supplies of coal, potash, and other commodities. Lamont became increasingly impatient with the proceedings. Several times his suggestion that each delegation submit its estimate of the amount that Germany could pay and how it should be paid was abruptly rejected by the acerbic chairman, who stated that it was premature to take this step.

Finally, in an effort to place the key issue on the agenda while Cunliffe was absent for a short home visit, Lamont privately won over Lord John Sumner, the alternate on the British delegation. On the day of Cunliffe's return to Paris, after further desultory discussions about Germany's potential to export timber and dyestuffs, Lord Cunliffe suddenly turned to Lamont and asked what the charge of the subcommittee was. TWL replied promptly: "To ascertain the amount of reparation which the enemy can pay and to report methods by which such amount can be paid."

"Right!" stated the chairman and asked the delegates to be prepared at the following session to submit their estimates of how much Germany could pay in the twelve-month period following the peace and how much in succeeding years.

Lamont reported to Colonel House on the sudden and welcome change and then met with Norman Davis to formulate the American estimate of Germany's capacity to pay reparations. They agreed on $30 billion. Lamont thought that Germany might manage $40 billion, since its industry had not been damaged, but deferred to his colleague's viewpoint. However, the hopes of the Americans for a rational reparations plan were dashed as soon as the following day's meeting.

Lord Cunliffe was asked by the other countries to lead off with the British estimate of Germany's reparations capacity. With some reluctance he said that he would rely on the figure given out in Prime Minister Lloyd George's election campaign: $120 billion. The Americans thought this estimate was completely unrealistic, but worse was yet to come. Not to be outdone by the British, Loucheur stated that the French estimate was $200 billion. He also whispered to Lamont that after learning the British estimate, the French were forced for domestic political reasons to put forward an even higher figure. Lamont then made the American proposal of $30 billion.

On February 24 Lamont and Loucheur were assigned by the subcommittee to prepare its summary on reparations. Lamont consulted again with Loucheur and Cunliffe and was happy to learn that the British and French had decided to drop their political charade: the French would accept $40 billion, and the British $47.5 billion as the German obligation.

Lamont's relations with Cunliffe had become increasingly strained. Lamont had been frustrated and impatient with Cunliffe's foot-dragging chairmanship, and Cunliffe almost surely resented Lamont's desperate backdoor approach to Lord Sumner. Professor C. K. Leith, one of the experts on the American Commission, wrote in his notes: "Until Mr. Lamont came in, the meetings of the general reparations commission were of the most casual nature."

Lamont was highly provoked at the next meeting, on February 26, when Cunliffe said that if the United States held out and didn't meet his terms, it would be "playing into Boche hands." In Lamont's view Cunliffe was intimating that America was "pro-Boche," and Lamont forcefully expressed his indignation to Cunliffe at this slur. In March he wrote his London partner, Edward Grenfell: "I have been having a difficult time with your friend, Cunliffe, and do not consider it altogether my fault." Bernard Baruch shared TWL's opinion of the British delegate: "Silent Cunliffe" appeared very wise "until he opened his mouth," he observed.

Lamont felt a heavy burden of responsibility during this critical stage of negotiations. If the Americans came up to the figure of $40 billion, this would be the sum demanded. On March 1, Lamont reported to Colonel House, in charge since President Wilson's return to the United

States in mid-February, and recommended that the United States increase its estimate to $40 billion. In his judgment the British and French would not lower their demands further, and the major powers must agree on a single figure. Colonel House concurred. But the reparations caldron was only starting to seethe.

Germany had accepted the provision in the Armistice agreement that "compensation would be made by Germany for all damages done to civilian populations of the Allies and their property by the aggression of Germany by land, by sea, and by air." The American position was that German reparation payments should be limited to compensation for "direct physical damage to property of non-military character and direct physical injury to civilians." The United States would not seek reparations for itself. However, the British delegation promptly argued that damage to the civilian population meant the total actual costs of the war—armies, navies, munitions—everything. The war had placed a tremendous financial burden on the civilian populations of the Allied powers, and the Germans should pay "shilling for shilling, ton for ton," as Prime Minister Lloyd George had said in a political speech. France quickly joined the British in their stand.

Lamont regularly attended the meetings of the Reparations Commission, where the inclusion of war costs in the reparations claims was under intense debate. Bernard Baruch, Vance McCormick, and John Foster Dulles argued the American position that the introduction of war costs would violate the terms of the armistice accepted by Germany and inflate the amount of reparations to a sum that Germany could not possibly pay. Australian Premier William Hughes of the British delegation was especially bitter in denouncing the American viewpoint. At one point the scrawny and feisty Australian leader turned and shook his finger at the American representatives and shouted: "Some people in this war have not been so near the fire as we British have, and, therefore, being unburned, they have a cold detached view of the situation!" Hughes and his countrymen would never forget the appalling Australian casualties at Gallipoli and on the Western Front.

The U.S. delegation stood its ground and telegraphed its recommendation to President Wilson, who was on the high seas returning to America. The president fully supported the position of his advisers and replied in his cable of February 24 that the contention that war costs should be included "is clearly inconsistent with what we led the enemy to expect and cannot now honorably alter simply because we have the power."

Faced with President Wilson's firm stand, the other chiefs of state yielded. However, it was not long before the British introduced a new tactic: to include military pensions and separation allowances in the category of claims to be compensated through reparations, and this was a concept of critical importance to Lloyd George.

If reparations were limited to compensation for injuries suffered by the civilian population and damage to their property, the French and Belgians would be entitled to receive the lion's share, and the British would be virtually left out. The British people, whose armies had suffered such grievous losses in battle, would refuse to support an agreement so unjust and callous to their sacrifice, the prime minister argued.

On March 7 the charming Lloyd George invited Lamont and Norman Davis to lunch. In presenting the British case for including pensions in the claim for compensation, the wily prime minister added, "The only real League of Nations we can depend on for the long future is the action together of America and Great Britain."

Later in March, Lamont and Davis dined again with the prime minister, who urged them to appreciate the political difficulties he faced in England. If public opinion viewed the reparations agreement as unfair to the British, his government would be turned out of office, a new British delegation would be chosen, and the peace negotiations would have to start all over again. The Americans knew that Clemenceau was worried about exactly the same scenario occurring in France.

At the same time another artful spokesman was lobbying persuasively for the British cause on the pension issue—General Jan Christiaan Smuts, the respected South African war hero. The political pressure for including pensions mounted.

Still the American delegation members remained firm in their resistance to including pensions in the reparations obligation. The idea did not conform with the armistice terms accepted by the Germans and would open the door to the whole question of including other war costs.

On April 1 President Wilson, who had returned to Paris in mid-March, summoned his economic and financial advisers to his official residence at Place des Etats Unis to discuss the issue. At two o'clock Lamont, along with Baruch, McCormick, Davis, and Dulles, joined the president in the library.

Lloyd George was unyielding in his determination to include pensions in the reparations agreement, and the president had decided not to buck the British on this question. His advisers protested and urged him to reconsider. Lamont said that no lawyer in the American delegation would give an opinion in favor of including pensions, and Dulles argued that the logic of the situation could force the acceptance of other war costs in the reparations claims.

"Logic? Logic?" Wilson exclaimed. "I don't give a damn for logic, if you will excuse my French! I am going to include pensions." He said that pensions seemed to him to represent a just and equitable basis of claim, and it was especially important to include them so that England would receive a fair share of reparations.

America had not been invaded or suffered the tremendous losses that its Allies had sustained. Wilson felt that they had earned the right to call the tune in this instance and was willing to cast aside technical objections to accommodate their wishes. The experts estimated that the total bill for pensions would amount to about $15 billion. Later that afternoon Lamont chaired a meeting at the president's house with the British, French, and Italians to discuss a reparations formula on the new basis of including pensions in the compensation claims.

Sub-Committee No. 2 had held almost daily meetings throughout February and March, which Lamont had regularly attended. The afternoon sessions, usually held in one of the ornate conference rooms at the Finance Ministry offices on Rue de Rivoli, seemed to grind along at a snail's pace, as delegates from countries large and small felt they must make speeches to impress their associates and to feed the daily printed record of the proceedings. The remarks were all translated into English and French, translations that were often found imperfect, given the importance diplomats attach to delicate shades of verbal meaning. The tedious process gave rise to much misunderstanding and delay. Sometimes after acrimonious debate two delegates found they were defending the same point and apologized with sheepish grins. The 4:30 break for hot chocolate, whipped cream, and macaroons in one of the grand salons of the ministry was welcomed by the delegates as an opportunity to get matters back on the track through informal conversation.

After weeks of discussion Lamont was designated to draft the recommendation from the subcommittee to the overall Reparations Commission. He worked all night in his hotel room writing out the report in longhand. It recommended a minimum of $30 billion to be paid by Germany and a maximum of $40 billion, if justified by economic conditions. However, only half of each installment would be immediately payable in gold or foreign exchange; the other half would be payable in German marks to be converted in the future as the exchange markets became able to absorb these sums.

The experts, in presenting their best economic judgment, had not reckoned with the ongoing force of domestic political considerations. Louis-Lucien Klotz, the French minister of finance, promptly declared that any sum the experts might agree to demand from Germany would still fall far below the expectations of the French people. No government accepting such a low figure for German reparations would long endure. Clemenceau and Lloyd George agreed: no fixed sum for reparations should be specified in the treaty.

Lamont and his colleagues strongly disagreed: it was essential to set an amount in order to remove uncertainty and restore stability to the European financial markets. For their budget planning the Allied governments and Germany itself must know the schedule of forthcoming reparations.

Lloyd George and Clemenceau had been working hard to convert President Wilson to their point of view following his return to Paris. Naming $40 billion or any other amount of reparations on that order would result in the fall of their governments, which would undo all the peace negotiation progress so far, they argued. Wilson found it difficult to question the judgment of these two embattled political leaders.

In the beginning Lloyd George was more open-minded than Clemenceau, and Lamont and Bernard Baruch called on the British prime minister to make a final attempt to convince him of the wisdom of fixing the amount in the treaty.

"Well, Lamont, 'Almost thou persuadest me!' You are right, and I shall probably have to come over to your side," Lloyd George stated at the end of the meeting. However, he then received word of a new eruption in the House of Commons calling for greater demands on Germany, which rekindled his political fears. From then on he was adamant in his opposition to naming a fixed sum.

During the last week of March, Lamont and the other financial and economic advisers met almost daily with the president. Wilson agreed with the logic of his experts in opposing the "blank check" proposal for reparations, but he was beginning to doubt that the Americans would prevail.

On the last day of March, the advisers had an early morning meeting at the Crillon to discuss a formula, originally conceived by John Foster Dulles, that Lloyd George had enthusiastically adopted. The plan called for the establishment of a permanent reparations commission, after the treaty had been signed, to review the claims submitted and set the amounts of compensation to be paid. At eleven o'clock the advisers went over to the president's house to report to their chief, who came out of a Big Four meeting to meet his experts. They told him of the problems they perceived in the Lloyd George formula of postponing the specifics of payment.

Wilson replied that Lloyd George and Clemenceau in their apprehension about their constituents were absolutely determined on the point. There were no vital American interests at stake, as the United States would not share in German reparations except for acquiring some captured German vessels. He instructed his advisers to meet with their counterparts in the other delegations to devise a workable scheme based on the Lloyd George proposal.

On April 1, following the American delegation meeting with President Wilson on the pension question, a Big Four meeting convened with all the economic and financial advisers present. Everyone now endorsed the plan for a permanent reparations commission to set the amounts to be paid by Germany in the future, and the experts were instructed to draft the necessary provisions for the treaty. The struggle to formulate a sound reparations plan was moving onto a new plateau, but Lamont foresaw that there was plenty of hard negotiating still to come.

Others felt the same way. One day Lamont was waiting in an anteroom at one of the government offices when Marshal Foch, France's greatest general in the war, came out of a meeting. They shook hands, and Foch with a melancholy smile observed, "La guerre de la paix, Monsieur Lamont."

The Specter of Famine

Lamont's days, and frequently evenings, were largely consumed by meetings—conferences with his colleagues at the Crillon to formulate the American position on economic and financial questions; meetings with Colonel House and President Wilson to report on the progress of negotiations and obtain their instructions; private sessions with the British delegates in an effort to develop joint Anglo-American positions; the formal conferences of the Reparations Commission and Sub-Committee No. 2; the Supreme Economic Council and its subcommittee dealing with the crucial issue of trade relations between the victors and the vanquished; the Finance Commission, concerned with financing plans to rehabilitate war-ravaged Europe; and the ultimate decision-making meetings of the Council of Four. Lamont also spent long hours at his desk preparing position papers and drafting treaty provisions. He transcribed the highlights of each day in his diary and also wrote letters to his children and the *New York Post* editors.

To his son Tommy, age twenty, he reported in February: "The French want to strip Germany bare, but the question is how far you can pursue that process and still have a machine that can be productive and pay the necessary reparations over a series of years."

TWL told the *Post* editors that France wanted an enormous indemnity for the destruction she had suffered, but by restricting German exports she would prevent Germany from paying her debt. Germany must pay for her crimes, but the treaty should not so cripple the country that the reparations plan became unworkable. The Germans had expected that the treaty would be drawn up on the basis of Wilson's Fourteen Points, but the French clearly had a different agenda.

Despite the grueling work pace, TWL was enjoying himself. It was a heady experience to be working closely with the leaders of the world as they remade its maps and allocated its people and resources in shaping mankind's future. He wrote his daughter Eleanor: "You may tell Uncle Jack that his hero, Woodrow Wilson, has sent for me three times in the last two days, and we are getting quite chummy."

In the evenings Lamont often had working dinners with his American colleagues or their British counterparts. Herbert Hoover and Bernard Baruch gave dinners to introduce their staffs to the American delegation, and TWL and Norman Davis dined with John Maynard Keynes, a British Treasury representative, and Marc Wallenberg, head of the leading Swedish bank, to discuss the possibility of neutral-country financing of German food purchases. After a dinner with the Belgian delegation at the Crillon, the talk over coffee was about special treatment for Belgium in receiving reparations, which the United States favored.

Harry Davison was in Paris to promote his plan for a peacetime international Red Cross organization. As chairman of the new League of Red Cross Societies he gave a large dinner for the press corps at the Hotel Relais d'Orsay, where Herbert Bayard Swope of the *New York World* told TWL that the one hundred or so American journalists could be much more effective in supporting American initiatives like the League of Nations if the reporters were kept better informed about developments at the conference. Following their conversation Lamont saw to it that the journalists were appropriately briefed about financial issues, often by himself.

At a dinner given by the French press corps TWL enjoyed some backstage comments about the American delegation from General Tasker Bliss, one of the American peace commissioners: Wilson had barred the other American commissioners from participating in the negotiations about the League of Nations covenants. The president believed that approval by other national delegations of the plan for the League was the highest priority, and he suspected that Secretary of State Lansing and others were less committed than he to this goal. Part of Wilson's grand design was to regroup much of Eastern Europe into new nations, and General Bliss described the American delegation university professors remaking the map of Europe "like a picture puzzle." He declared that the Paris Peace Conference would make the Congress of Vienna in 1815 after the Napoleonic Wars "look like a prayer meeting."

Florence was excited to be at the scene of the historic conference, although a lingering cold had confined her for some days to her suite. She made friends with a French marquise, a charming old lady born in Boston, who steered her affluent American friend to some dress shops where Florence found the prices unbelievably high—$400 for a simple dress, she wrote her family. On Tom's few free evenings he and Florence dined well at the best restaurants. On Sundays they strolled up the Champs-Élysées for lunch at Fouquets or explored the battle-scarred countryside outside Paris.

Their first excursion was a drive to the shattered little town of Chateau Thierry and Belleau Wood, where the U.S. Army and Marines had repulsed the Germans in 1918. Their U.S. Army captain escort, who had fought in this engagement, described the course of the heavy fighting the previous summer. The next Sunday they drove out to Rheims. Stopping near a hillside that had been bitterly fought over, they clambered through collapsing trenches and dugouts filled with grisly reminders of the recent fighting.

During March a new crisis arose in Germany to absorb Lamont's attention—widespread food shortages and growing hunger among Germans, especially in the cities. While the Allies had continued to maintain an economic blockade of Germany after the armistice, shipments of food and medical supplies were supposed to be let through. In return the Germans were to lease their merchant fleet to the Allies, shipping that was urgently needed for the transport of relief provisions to Europe and the repatriation of American troops. But the delivery of food supplies to

Germany had been blocked, at the initiative of the French, and the specter of famine was becoming real to millions of Germans.

Among the French officials Finance Minister Klotz took the lead in advocating a hard line in the treatment of the defeated enemy. He hoped to crush and suppress the German economy for years to come and apparently ignored the fact that carrying out his policy would prevent Germany from paying its reparations obligations. His attitude reflected the feelings of millions of Frenchmen—a desire for revenge and humiliation of the hated enemy. The French hard-liners also argued that continuing the blockade would make the Germans more disposed to accept the dictated terms of peace without question.

The Allies had first wrangled over how the Germans would pay for the food they purchased. The French proposed that the United States should extend credit to Germany to pay for the bulk of these supplies. Germany's liquid assets—such as its gold reserves, international securities, and commodities available for export—should be held in reserve for the future reparations payments to the Allies. The Americans flatly rejected this French proposal, noting the tremendous new demands for American credit put forward by the Allied nations and newly independent countries in Europe. The Germans were also guilty of some foot-dragging of their own in this affair: no arrangement had yet been made for a single German ship to be turned over to the Allies.

The Americans, supported by the British, now realized that prompt action must be taken to alleviate the growing misery and suffering in Germany; neither country would be party to a deliberate policy of inflicting starvation on Germany. On March 3 a group of Allied representatives, including Lamont, took the night train to Spa, Belgium, to meet the Germans in an effort to break the impasse.

At six o'clock the following evening the Allied and German delegations gathered for their first meeting, the Allied representatives seating themselves on one side of the long conference table, the Germans on the other. The proceedings moved slowly, with the obligatory translations after every few sentences, and ended in an unexpected standoff.

The Germans now declared that they would not turn over any ships unless the Allies agreed to supply Germany's food requirements until the next harvest in the fall. The earlier agreement had committed the Allies only to furnish Germany's immediate needs in return for the ships, and the Allied delegation was not authorized to grant the concession. The talks were deadlocked, and the delegation returned to Paris for consultation and further instructions.

Back in Paris, Lamont and Albert Strauss of the American delegation reported to Colonel House on the Spa meetings. The Americans agreed that the differences must be quickly resolved so that food could be shipped to Germany without further delay, and not only for humanitarian reasons. The Western leaders feared that the Russian-backed German Communists would take advantage of the desperate conditions in Germany.

At lunch that day Lamont reported on the Spa meeting to the British prime minister and his secretary, Philip Kerr. Lloyd George agreed that the German attitude was not unreasonable and that, in any case, the Germans must be fed immediately. He had heard reports from General Plumer, commander of the British occupation forces in Germany, that the Germans were starving. The British people would not stand for this. The French must join in assuring the Germans of sufficient food supplies over the next few months. He had talked with Clemenceau that morning and believed he would go along with this plan in the end, but the proposition must not be presented as a German initiative or the French premier would reject it out of hand.

On the afternoon of March 8, TWL attended a meeting of the Supreme War Council on the subject of feeding the Germans. Lloyd George led the discussion, pointing out that for four months since the armistice not one ton of food had been delivered to Germany and now the German people were starving. These conditions were a dishonor to the Allies. How had this state of affairs come to pass? Who was responsible for this? It was Klotz. "Yes, Monsieur Klotz," said the British prime minister, pointing his finger at the French delegate sitting nearby, "you are the man who has done this thing!" In tones of mounting outrage, more mock than real some thought, Lloyd George read a telegram from General Plumer, who said he feared he might not be able to control the conduct of his men much longer. English soldiers would not stand by watching women and children die of starvation in the streets, especially when there was food in Rotterdam waiting to be shipped to Germany.

Premier Clemenceau felt compelled to give a long speech about the wrongs France had suffered at the hands of Germany, but he had been impressed by the British prime minister's impassioned plea. The War Council appointed a committee, to which Lamont was assigned, to draft a plan for the immediate shipment of foodstuffs to Germany. An Allied delegation would meet the Germans in Brussels to agree on the final arrangements for supplying the food. Herbert Hoover would head the American contingent, and Lamont would be the adviser on financial matters. On the evening of March 12, TWL boarded the night train to Brussels with his aide, George Whitney.

The meetings with the Germans at the Hotel Astoria over the next two days went fairly smoothly. The Allied proposal on shipping food was accepted by the Germans, who would be permitted to use their gold reserves and certain foreign exchange earnings to buy grain and other foodstuffs. Lamont recorded in his diary a tense exchange in which he helped the head of the Allied delegation, British Admiral Sir Rosslyn Wemyss, out of a jam at the closing meeting in Brussels.

> The final plenary session furnished a suspense. After the whole thing had presumably been fixed up Von Braun (head of the German delegation) said that their instructions did not permit them to sign . . . unless we promised to undo the black list [refers to trade blockade]. Admiral W. looked flabbergasted, didn't know the way out. I wrote on the paper table cover in front of me (a Boche twisting his neck off to read it upside down): "In the Finance Commission our people gave the Germans general assurances that we should take up the blockade question actively. Why don't you give a formal declaration to same effect and see if it doesn't go?" I saw the Admiral buck up. As soon as Von B. finished, he cleared his throat, looked with a cold stare at Von B., read out my statement and added in solemn tones: "In presence of this delegation, I declare that I will give my personal attention to this blockade matter." Von B. said, "In view of the Admiral's declaration, we will sign." And sign they did. To me it was illustrative of belief that when it comes to peace they will struggle hard but sign at end.

While the transport logistics and payment arrangements still had to be organized, the main issue had been settled: food would be shipped through to Germany in increasing quantities. Lamont returned to Paris and the other complex and controversial problems demanding attention.

Hard Bargaining

Yielding to the French viewpoint, the Big Four decided against lifting the economic blockade of Germany until the Germans signed and ratified the peace treaty. Nevertheless, the state of Germany's future trade relations with other countries was still a subject of spirited debate. The French, led by Klotz, feared a strong and rapid build-up of German industry and exports enabling the nation to quickly reemerge as a powerful economic force in Europe. French factories and mines had been damaged and destroyed in the war; Germany's had not, giving the recent aggressor a tremendous competitive advantage. Exports of German manufactures and industrial raw material imports in short supply should be under Allied control.

The American delegation, in accord with Wilson's Fourteen Points, was opposed to discriminating against German trade; "the establishment of an equality of trade conditions among all nations" was a basic principle in the president's plan for world peace. Several days after the Brussels meeting, Lamont and Vance McCormick met with the president to confirm his views on the matter. Everyone agreed: no discriminatory embargoes should be placed on German trade, the cornerstone of American policy in negotiating the treaty provisions on Germany's commercial relations.

Lamont often found himself in opposition to Klotz on the issues discussed at the conference meetings and frequently became engaged in debate with him. He was not alone in finding the French official impractical and exasperating. Lloyd George remarked to Lamont one day: "Klotz is the only Jew who knows nothing of finance!" Even his fellow French delegates often disagreed with his extremist hard-line approach toward Germany. One day Clemenceau invited Lamont to sit down with him during the afternoon break of Sub-Committee No. 2. "Be careful, Monsieur Lamont," he whispered. "Klotz will put poison in your chocolate!"

Meeting with President Wilson on the morning of April 3, Lamont and the other economic advisers reported little change in the intransigent French position on reparations. The president appeared tired and discouraged; he was coming down with the flu. He said that he wanted to consult with his advisers about a very serious situation—Clemenceau's unwillingness to abide by the Fourteen Points and the armistice agreement that had been concluded with Germany. Clemenceau insisted that France receive sovereignty over the part of the Saar Basin which Prussia had unjustly annexed in 1815. The Allies had already agreed that France should take control of the Saar coal mines, and the president was determined not to yield further. However, he was at a loss as to how he could break this impasse, and he wondered whether he should leave the conference to return home and report to his countrymen on the reasons for this deadlock in the peace negotiations.

The next day Lamont called Jean Monnet, whom he regarded as one of the most able members of the French delegation, to invite him to lunch. They chose a small, out-of-the-way restaurant where they would not be recognized. TWL recorded in his diary, "I threw the fear of God into him." Lamont told Monnet that the consequences for the peace conference and American-French relations would be disastrous if Clemenceau's unreasonable and stubborn attitude compelled Wilson to return to the United States and inform the American public about his confrontation with the French. Monnet fully shared Lamont's concern: for the Americans to go home now was unthinkable. The following morning Monnet told Lamont that he had consulted with his colleagues, and the Saar Basin issue would not cause a breakdown in the peace talks. The heated dispute was resolved.

In April Lamont was assigned by the Council of Four to draft the text of the reparations section of the treaty with Louis Loucheur of the French delegation. It was agreed that the Inter-Allied Reparations Commission would validate the damage claims and set the amount and payment schedule of German reparations. The equivalent of $5 billion would be paid by May 1921.

The Americans felt strongly that overall reparations should not exceed Germany's capacity to repay within thirty years, about the span of a generation. Preliminary estimates for the total of claims and military pensions were in the $25 to $30 billion range, and Lamont and his American colleagues were doubtful that Germany's foreign earnings could bear this burden. However, the British and French remained adamant: "Public opinion demands that Germany pay all the loss they have caused," said Lloyd George. They must pay "to the extent of their utmost capacity," echoed Klotz.

Even though the Americans had reluctantly agreed to go along with the British and French in accepting the open-ended formula for the total of indemnity payments, they continued to assert their viewpoint on other provisions of the reparations plan. At one Big Four meeting Lamont sat next to Premier Clemenceau. In a draft memorandum TWL argued that Germany be allowed to deduct payments for food from the reparations payment of $5 billion due in May 1921. At this meeting, Klotz was delivering an impassioned harangue against the provision, when Clemenceau leaned over to Lamont and asked, "What do you think?"

Lamont replied, "I do not agree at all. I think France would be cutting off her own nose. It would work to her disadvantage."

Clemenceau then rose and said, "Gentlemen, you know how seldom I overrule my ministers, but in this case I must, and I wish the text of the draft to remain as it is."

Lamont reported in his diary that Premier Orlando, who had observed the incident, whispered to him, "If only you could settle it all, Italy would be so happy!"

On April 10 the advisers went to Wilson to discuss with him whether the United States should be represented on the Reparations Commission. The president thought that America should have a voice in the affairs of this important agency. Baruch and McCormick were against American participation; Davis was on the fence, and Lamont was in favor. TWL said he thought that the Americans would be looked upon as "quitters" if they did not join the commission. After further discussion the president concluded: "I think that sums the matter up, gentlemen. We will go on it."

A German View, a View of Germany

The Allied financial officials were now meeting with the Germans at the Chateau de Villette in Senlis, a suburb north of Paris. On April 16, Lamont presided at a conference to arrange the means by which Germany would pay for her food imports. After the meeting was over, Max M. Warburg, a German delegate whom Lamont had known as a prominent banker before the war, drew TWL aside for a private talk.

Warburg said that "Germany's only hope for a just peace is in America" and that Germans were looking to America and President Wilson as the exponents of fairness who would pursue a policy toward a healing peace. Newspaper stories reported that the treaty's terms would be harsh on Germany—heavy reparations demands and the annexation of the Saar. The people were badly frightened by what they heard, and the danger of Germans turning to Bolshevism was real. No German government would dare sign a treaty whose terms were so harsh.

Lamont replied that Warburg might be wise to wait to receive the peace terms officially, rather than through the newspapers, before forming judgments. He went on: "If you are under the impression that the Allies are divided in their ideas of a just peace, you are greatly mistaken. . . . Furthermore, I might remind you that the feeling in America is exceedingly bitter."

Warburg then left a memorandum of his views with Lamont which contained a long litany of complaints and even threats against the Allies.

After five long months since the armistice, said Warburg, the German people still suffered under the cruel blockade that had been illegally imposed by the Allies as a wartime measure. The economy was in a shambles. Only recently had the Allies permitted foodstuffs to enter Germany, and then on shortsighted and hard terms of payment. In the meantime more than one hundred thousand people had died of starvation.

> Time is wasted with useless discussions about the question of responsibility for the outbreak of the war. May a really neutral court of arbitration decide which and whose deed or deeds actually set the world ablaze. . . . With what right do the Entente powers pronounce the final verdict over the vanquished foe?

Warburg argued that the suffering of the German people may have been equal to that of the French and Belgians because of "the terrible privations they had to endure."

If Wilson's Fourteen Points were applied in the right spirit, he went on, "France would not have to fear for the future that Germany would want to start a war of revenge when her time had come." If the peace was just, the former enemies could "unite in the new spirit and thereby successfully act against the false doctrines of Bolshevism" posing a new threat to France's security. The Allied statesmen must not be satisfied in following public opinion; they must lead it in bringing about a fair and durable peace.

> If these presumptions, under which Germany has signed the armistice are not fulfilled, no Government, which is aware of its responsibility, will be able to sign the preliminary peace or peace itself. The responsibility for the consequences which cannot be foreseen would fall on the victors. But the vanquished would carry the burden, together with the sad consciousness that the big wrong that has been done will have to be righted one day. And then new terror and sufferings would again come over the world.

It was the height or arrogance, TWL thought, for a German delegate to lecture the Allied governments. The Warburg memorandum confirmed his view that there was little, if any, sense of remorse or guilt among the German ruling classes for plunging the world into the most destructive and tragic war in history.

Lamont, eager to get a look inside Germany, had arranged a weekend automobile excursion with some friends to Koblenz via Verdun and Luxembourg. A battle of unparalleled carnage and horror had taken place at Verdun. The devastating German artillery shelling had left broken gray stumps and a vast wasteland of torn-up reddish brown earth, pockmarked with thousands of muddy shell holes and craters. In the shattered town of Verdun the party ate sandwiches at the YMCA canteen and slept on cots in the damaged building, where Lamont could view the starry night through a gaping hole in the roof. The next day they drove through Luxembourg to the old German town of Trier, where they enjoyed a good lunch at the local hotel. The town seemed busy and prosperous. In the afternoon they continued their journey, driving along the banks of the Moselle to its junction with the Rhine and on to Koblenz. The farming country seemed rich and well cultivated. The town itself was untouched by the war. It was Easter weekend. The shops were filled with goods, and the streets were crowded with families in a holiday mood. The children were rosy-cheeked and chubby, and everyone was dressed in their best clothes to attend the Easter church services. The suffering and hunger reported in many parts of Germany was not evident in the Rhenish towns.

TWL wrote in his journal later: "What a tremendous contrast to those desolate wastes of northern France with every town and city razed to the ground, and with nothing but a waste with all the farming machinery stolen and sent to Germany. It made one hate the Boche worse than ever to see such a prosperous contented countryside."

The Allies Dispute and Entertain
Each Other

Lamont was not involved in the tense negotiations to redraw the national boundaries in Europe, but naturally he was fascinated by the process. By April 23 the draft of the reparations section was in its final stage, and the American advisers were scheduled to meet the president at three o'clock that afternoon to brief him in preparation for the Big Four meeting an hour later. When Lamont arrived at the president's house, he found Woodrow Wilson in the library on his hands and knees studying a large-scale map of Italy and the Adriatic Sea spread on the floor.

The president greeted Lamont and then declared that the Fiume situation was just as he thought. Wilson, backed by his experts, believed that the Adriatic port city should belong to the newly created country of Yugoslavia. But the Italian people demanded that Fiume be awarded to Italy, and it was clear to Premier Orlando that he must secure Fiume for Italy at the peace conference or be ousted from office. Despite his earnest pleas, the president would not budge on the Fiume question. The city had been Hungarian for centuries, he explained to TWL, and since that region of the former Austro-Hungarian empire was now part of Yugoslavia, Fiume should belong to Yugoslavia. He intended that day to go over the heads of the Italian leaders in a statement to the people of Italy— namely, that Italy had no rights to Fiume, and Italians should abandon their claim in the interest of justice and peace, albeit in more diplomatic phraseology.

Lamont noted respectfully that Orlando had stated that public opinion in Italy was at a high emotional pitch about Fiume and that an about-face in the people's attitude was out of the question. The president replied, "Ah, Lamont, you do not understand. In every civilized people there is a latent sense of justice that has only to be appealed to in order to assert itself."

The newspapers the next day carried the story of the president's plea to the Italian people, who were as outraged as Lamont had feared. City mobs denounced Wilson's appeal, and Premier Orlando and his chief aides hurriedly returned to Rome. The president's unbending righteousness had provoked a major crisis in the peace conference proceedings.

At the Big Four meeting on April 23, the three remaining chiefs of state present settled virtually all outstanding points in the draft of the reparations section. At the end of the meeting, subcommittees were selected to inform the smaller nations of the reparations plan that had been agreed on, and the following day Lamont attended a meeting to brief several countries, including Belgium.

Even before the armistice the Allied governments had concluded that a priority indemnity payment to Belgium was justified. Germany, in carrying out her ruthless invasion of Belgium in 1914, had wantonly violated the Treaty of 1839, which bound her to respect her neighbor's neutrality. Lamont had informed the Belgian delegation that President Wilson supported a priority payment of $500 million by Germany. However, the

Big Four, occupied with so many urgent matters, had not yet formally concurred. Time passed, and the Belgians grew more anxious. Belgium expected to receive compensation for the full costs of waging war, as well as priority treatment in first claims. Belgian Foreign Minister Paul Hymans finally insisted upon a full-dress hearing at a Big Four meeting on April 29, where he put forward his demands.

Lloyd George was especially adamant in opposing Belgian demands for more than the other Allies would receive, except for the one-time payment of $500 million. Compensation for total war costs had already been rejected by the Big Four after lengthy and acrimonious debate. Achieving a mutually acceptable treaty was difficult enough, and Belgium should not make the situation worse by ill-considered and unwarranted demands. Clemenceau fully agreed, and Wilson backed up his colleagues: A bargain had been struck with Germany on the basis of excluding war costs from the reparations obligation. The Allies could not break their word and with good conscience ask the Germans to sign the treaty.

The meeting appeared to be at an impasse, and the delegates broke up into small groups. At the president's suggestion, Lamont and Norman Davis invited Hymans to join them in a side room, where they tried to convert him by showing the extent to which his demands were already being met. TWL summarized their talk in his diary: "He stuck out, however, very stiffly for war costs. . . . We teased, cajoled, threatened, and implored—all to no avail. Several times it seemed as if he were on the point of yielding, but each time came back to the one question—the necessity of including in some manner the item of the costs of war."

The meeting reconvened, and after further fruitless discussion Hymans declared that he would have to return to Brussels to report on the situation to the Belgian parliament. Lloyd George was furious, muttering loudly, "It amounts to blackmail, pure blackmail, and I won't have it!" Clemenceau, to ease the tense atmosphere, made a long speech in French, which along with the translation allowed time for emotions to cool.

TWL had consulted earlier with French delegate Loucheur about devising a formula that would be acceptable to Lloyd George. It had to be one that he could defend in the House of Commons, a method that would compensate Belgium for the costs of war in a well-camouflaged manner. Now Loucheur beckoned to Lamont and handed him a memorandum containing such a proposal agreed to by Clemenceau. TWL thought the Loucheur formula presented a promising answer to the problem and showed it first to the president and then to Lloyd George. The president would follow the lead of Britain and France.

Germany would be obligated "to reimburse Belgium for all sums borrowed from the Allies as a necessary consequence of the violation of the Treaty of 1839," in which Germany had joined Britain and France in pledging the neutrality of Belgium. In that all the funds borrowed by Belgium had been used for the prosecution of the war, Belgium would receive payment for her war costs as she demanded. All parties agreed that the formula appeared to offer a solution to the deadlock.

After the meeting Lamont was talking with Hymans when Clemenceau approached, took him by the shoulder, and pointing at Hymans, who was standing next to TWL, said, "Mr. Lamont, I charge you to murder this man; nothing less than murder can be done to him. He is a bad man." Clemenceau said it in jest, but he was by no means in an amiable mood.

But the Belgians were not through bargaining. On May 3 Lamont and Norman Davis went to Wilson's house to discuss the latest Belgian demands with the Big Three, Orlando being still absent in Rome. Belgium had obtained loans from the Allies and the U.S. to finance her war effort; she would receive a special issue of German bonds in the same amount representing the reparations owed her by Germany. Foreign Minister Hymans now proposed that the Allies and the U.S. accept these German bonds in substitution for Belgium's debt to them. Thus Belgium's war debt would be immediately extinguished, placing her in a strong position to obtain additional credit to rebuild her shattered economy. The Big Three agreed that this proposition was sensible, although Wilson made it clear that America's acceptance should in no way be considered a precedent for other cases.

The Belgians wanted even more, a fixed 15 percent of the total reparations per annum payment, until the full indemnity owed Belgium was paid off. At this Lloyd George exploded and the other heads of state supported him. Belgium had lost few lives compared to the other Allies and would come out of the war with her debts paid. Lloyd George could not defend this new proposal at home and would not stand for it. Hymans did not press the point.

Along with the financial provisions, there were numerous special covenants, such as the restitution by Germany for the livestock taken from Belgium and the return of the religious art treasures stolen from the churches of St. Bavan at Ghent and St. Peter at Louvain. The Belgium government approved the reparations agreement two days later, and TWL turned his attention to the negotiations that still lay ahead.

It was clear that the war-ravaged European countries would need large sums of new capital to rebuild their impoverished economies, and the

United States was the obvious source. Foreign treasury officials and private bankers descended in force on the offices of the U.S. Financial Section at the Hotel Crillon. Various schemes were put forward to deal with the problem, all engaging United States capital and credit on a massive scale.

At a meeting at the president's house on April 25, Wilson asked TWL for his opinion of the latest plan of John Maynard Keynes of the British Treasury. Earlier, Keynes had circulated a memorandum proposing that all the war debt among the Allied powers be mutually forgiven. The United States was not interested; it held the largest amount of such loans and would be faced with losses amounting to billions of dollars. Now Keynes was advancing a complex scheme involving the guaranty by the U.S. and the Allies of interest on German bonds which could be used to repay the inter-Allied debt. The U.S. was being asked to accept the obligations of Germany, whose postwar prospects were still uncertain, in lieu of the existing firm commitments of Britain and France to repay their American war loans. Once again its creditor position would be undercut. The U.S. Congress would never authorize such a plan, and TWL told the president that the idea was quite impractical. He and Davis drafted a reply to Lloyd George turning aside the Keynes proposal.

However, TWL told the president, the United States must recognize that the Allies as well as the new nations of Eastern Europe would need American loans. In a May 15 memorandum and in follow-up meetings with Wilson, Lamont and the other advisers presented their ideas about financing the rehabilitation of postwar Europe. The president said he agreed with their recommendation that the U.S. government postpone the interest charges on its loans to the Allies for three years.

However, reports from America, including cables from Russell Leffingwell at the U.S. Treasury, warned that the American public and Congress would not support large-scale peacetime government lending to Europe. It would be mainly up to the private sector to undertake the task of supplying new loans to rebuild the shattered European economies.

In TWL's May memorandum to the president he had underlined the interdependence between American prosperity and European stability. He envisaged that the new loans would be organized by committees of bankers and "men of affairs" in the U.S. and Europe cooperating together. A national investment group in the U.S. headed by major banks would operate under the informal approval of the U.S. Treasury Department.

TWL glowingly viewed the new business prospects for the Morgan bank, as did Harry Davison and Edward Stettinius, both in Paris in the spring of 1919. Stettinius, staying on in Europe for a few months, would gather information on economic conditions in the different countries and their requirements for imports and American loans. Davison's Red Cross duties were about completed, and he was ready to focus his energies on this new business. The partners anticipated that the Morgan firm would take the lead once again in organizing American financing for Europe.

The end of the first week in May marked a milestone on the road to peace. On May 6 a plenary session of the Allied delegations approved an abstract of the treaty. The Summary of Conditions of Peace was given to the German delegation the following day at a brief formal ceremony at Versailles. They were given fifteen days to offer their comments on the draft, a period later extended to three weeks. The first German note of comment and protest was received three days later, and for the rest of the month the two sides negotiated by exchanging official memoranda.

The initial draft of the treaty text was finished, and the work pace slackened. Diplomats strolled through the blooming gardens of the Tuileries exchanging political gossip, and TWL found time to play a round of golf at the St. Cloud links with Norman Davis. But even as a beautiful Paris spring unfolded, there were still important tasks to be completed.

Appointed chairman of the Reparations Commission for Austria, Lamont led the meetings to establish the handling of Austrian reparations. When payments could be made was problematical: the Austrian economy was "almost hopeless" and near insolvency, Herbert Hoover wrote TWL on May 24. As for the successor states to the Austro-Hungarian empire, the amounts that could be charged for reparations would be negligible when divided among the creditor nations. To impose reparations would place a heavy burden on the struggling new nations. On May 22 Lamont argued leniency with President Wilson, but the president sided with Lloyd George in demanding reparations from the new states and instructed Lamont to negotiate on this basis.

Lamont and John Foster Dulles met with Foreign Minister Edward Benes of Czechoslovakia in Lamont's rooms at the Hotel Meurice on May 26. Benes, a former history professor, impressed TWL as "a statesman of great acumen and skill" and destined to become the leader of his country, as he later observed to Lloyd George. Lamont and Benes worked out a reparations formula, but the Big Four eventually decided to suspend the modest charges altogether in view of the prostrate economic condition of the new states, as TWL had pointed out in the first place.

With his fiscal counterparts TWL attended meetings with the Germans at the Trianon Palace Hotel in Versailles to discuss financial issues, notably Germany's inability to make timely gold payments for its imports of food. In addition Lamont and Bernard Baruch were assigned responsibility for writing the economic provisions of the treaty and drafting the reply to the German comments on this section and their reparations counteroffer.

The Germans now proposed to fix the amount of their liability at the equivalent of $25 billion. However, under their formula there were substantial offsetting credits and conditions that were unacceptable to the Allies. Nevertheless, the counterproposal offered the opportunity, the Americans felt, to try one more time to persuade the Allies to fix the amount of Germany's obligation. Accordingly, they submitted a memorandum to the Reparations Commission outlining again the advantages of setting the sum of Germany's liability: Germany's commitment to a specific amount of reparations would remove the uncertainty, which was such a deterrent to sound planning by government and business. Moreover, a fixed reparations obligation could become the basis for the extension of credit by the U.S. to the recipient countries.

In the midst of this latest American lobbying effort, Lloyd George dropped a political bombshell. In adopting positions at the conference so far, he had felt bound by the recent election mandate from his countrymen to impose a severe settlement on the Germans. Now in mid-May some English began to fear that Germany would refuse to sign the treaty because of the harshness of its terms. Lloyd George, influenced by growing pressure from British liberals, now submitted concessions to Germany in the terms of the treaty regarding its eastern frontiers and the Allied army of occupation. The British position on German reparations could delay setting the amount for several years.

On June 3 President Wilson summoned all his commissioners and advisers to a meeting in Secretary Lansing's office to discuss the German response to the treaty and the British proposals. Lamont and the other experts were still trying to persuade the French to adopt a fixed-sum formula, and TWL observed that Lloyd George was just trying "to postpone the evil day" of informing the British public about the realistic prospects for receiving reparations.

The president said that at this stage nothing must threaten the unanimity of the Allies in confronting the Germans. He was exasperated with the British who, after insisting on stiffer terms than the United States, now proposed concessions after the treaty had been handed over to the Germans almost a month before. "The Lord be with us," he stated in adjourning the meeting.

Lamont and the other U.S. advisers continued to try to persuade their Allied counterparts during the following week to accept a fixed sum for reparations. All to no avail. The British and French were determined that the reparations provisions should stand as drafted. To fix the sum before examination of the claims was to let the Germans off too easily and was politically unacceptable to their electorates.

On June 7 Tom wrote Florence, who was visiting England, his views on the British performance at the peace conference.

> Whose fault is it that it is not a better Peace? It is the fault of the British, and of the British alone.
>
> The American Delegation came over here determined to do their utmost to have a peace that was just and healing. Mr. Lloyd George and the British Delegation promised us that they would stand by us to that end, and what happened? Every time that a critical juncture arose, every time when a real question of vital principle was involved, the British gave way and flopped over to the side of the French. Of course we all knew the sort of Peace that the French were determined to have, namely, one that would cripple Germany, and after what Germany has done to France, you can have a good deal of sympathy with this view. The difficulty is that crippling Germany means really injuring France, Great Britain and the whole world. We thought that the British were wise enough to see this . . . but when it came to the pinch, they failed us.

The formerly ardent Anglophile was especially angry at the British "commercial interests" represented by the Board of Trade, which was determined to obtain the maximum possible business benefits from the treaty. On the other hand, "America came over here asking not a dollar."

> I came over here pro-British, but I go back anything but that. Talk about liberal minded Englishmen? They all make me sick. If they had one-tenth the courage of their convictions they would have stood by the Americans and helped us get the sort of Peace we wanted. . . .
>
> You say that President Wilson ought to come out and say "The Peace is a poor one, I know; it is the best that I could do." Well, perhaps he ought to say that, and . . . add that "It is the best that I can do in view of the fact that the nobleminded British threw me at every turn, left out my 14 Points, lined up with the French, and wore me out morning, noon and night." This is the real truth, and those liberal-minded British friends of yours might just as well know it.

Lamont and his colleagues had other reasons to be upset with Lloyd George and the British. The prime minister had recently made statements belittling the American role in the war, and on June 13 President Wilson summoned his advisers to discuss a new British proposal—a peacetime

Allied organization to control the international purchase of raw materials and foodstuffs. The Americans firmly opposed the plan: it was quite impractical and would hurt the American farmer by holding down the prices of American food exports to Europe.

The Allies agreed that instead of ceding Upper Silesia outright to Poland, a plebiscite should be held to determine the region's future. They would not make other significant changes in the treaty and so informed Germany on June 16. Now the world would wait for the German answer.

In his diary, Lamont summarized both the formal and informal highlights of each day. One April evening he attended a dinner given by Colonel and Mrs. House, where he had a lively conversation in French with Premier Orlando of Italy and General Joffre of France. Orlando was very pessimistic about the future. Things were in such a mess in Europe and Italy: there was widespread unemployment; the markets were in turmoil; the returning soldiers refused to work. He inquired jokingly if Lamont would give him a job as a typist in his office in New York when he was exiled from his native country.

TWL asked him what the remedy was for this sad situation. Could America help?

"Some," Orlando replied, but it was a problem Europe had to tackle largely for herself, and the solution lay in the simple words "Work, work, work. Everybody must work hard and live small."

Lamont asked him what he thought was the cause of the war. He answered that it lay deep down—the hunger for earth, or territory, that seemed to have possessed so many peoples of the world and caused their undoing.

They speculated as to whether the Germans would sign the treaty. TWL said he believed that the treaty was fair and the Germans would sign it. Even if it was unfair, they should sign it, because in that case it would break down of its own weight as every unjust agreement did. "They will be the gainers, rather than the losers, by signing it, because if they have been unjustly treated, they will gain the sympathy of the world."

The guest of honor was pianist Jan Paderewski, the newly named prime minister of Poland. Paderewski told Lamont that he was touched by the sympathy America had shown for Poland and for the help she had given his country. He had played a concert tour in the United States and longed for a return visit.

As they walked out of the smoking room after dinner, Orlando remarked on the beauty of a large salon they were passing through.

Colonel House replied that they had found the room very convenient and "good for dancing."

"Oh!" exclaimed Orlando, who, TWL had observed, was a bit of a comic and given to making bad puns. "Do you hear that, Paderewski? Good for Danzig!" (He was referring to the disputed Baltic port.)

Paderewski, who did not relish the joke, rolled his eyes upward in despair, and Colonel House patted him on the back. "You realize that it was not our fault, Prime Minister, but, of course, the decision has finally been reached that Danzig is not to be Polish, but a free, independent port."

Lamont's diplomatic social calendar was well-filled. To be on friendly terms with the foreign delegates helped TWL in his job; furthermore, hobnobbing with world leaders at these convivial gatherings was good fun.

In May, TWL gave a small dinner dance at the Precatelain Cafe in the Bois de Boulogne which Vance McCormick pronounced "a good party." Lamont invited General Smuts to dinner, who returned the courtesy. He dined with John Maynard Keynes at the Villa Armenon, Marshal Pétain of France at his home in Chantilly, and the Italian delegation, to whom he forecast a rosy future for Italian-American relations. One evening he and Felix Frankfurter, then a Harvard law professor and legal adviser to the American delegation, had dinner with Alexander Kerensky, the socialist premier of Russia's provisional government in 1917 following the overthrow of the czarist regime. Kerensky had in turn been ousted by the Bolsheviks under Lenin in the October revolution. The charismatic Kerensky claimed to have a plan to replace the Bolshevik government and bring Russia back into the community of Western nations, and President Wilson had asked Lamont and Frankfurter to find out what he had in mind. In the private room of an elegant Paris restaurant, Kerensky talked on into the night, but he had no workable plan, as TWL reported to the Big Four the next day.

At a dinner party given by Herbert Hoover, TWL chatted again with Prime Minister Paderewski, who was worried about the continuing militaristic spirit in Germany and especially East Prussia. Lamont asked him about future relations between Poland and Germany. Would everything be tranquil?

"Oh, Mr. Lamont," he replied, "we shall always be fighting Germany. We have never been at peace with Germany. We never shall be. The two peoples cannot live and work together; they must fight."

Paderewski continued. There was a Latin proverb which stated that man was a wolf gnawing man. "All we can do is file the teeth of the wolf," he added.

Lamont and Hoover disagreed. They saw no reason why war could not disappear from the face of the earth. "Do you think," Lamont asked, "that the League of Nations will succeed in filing the teeth?"

"Well," replied Paderewski, "perhaps it will turn out to be a fair dentist after a long time!"

Political Flak and Danger Signals

On June 9, 1919, Lamont, still in Paris, was subpoenaed by the Senate Foreign Relations Committee, which was investigating the report that a copy of the draft treaty, a classified government document, was in the hands of the Morgan bank. Lamont was worried about this charge, and with reason. After the treaty had been presented to the Germans on May 7, Lamont had given a copy to Harry Davison, who was returning to New York and looked forward to reading the document on the Atlantic crossing. There was no government restriction on the distribution of the treaty at the time, and Lamont felt that Davison had a valid interest in it. Davison had lobbied successfully for the insertion of an article in the treaty important to the future of the international Red Cross movement: the member countries of the League of Red Cross Societies, formed by Davison, undertook to promote the establishment of peacetime Red Cross organizations in their countries. Shortly after Davison's departure it was officially decreed that the treaty's distribution should be restricted to the Allied delegations and governments; Davison, as a private citizen, would not now be eligible to receive a copy.

Lamont and his Morgan partners endorsed the treaty and the historic League of Nations Covenant. They also foresaw that the treaty would be hotly contested in the U.S. Senate once it was presented for ratification. The Republicans held the majority. Some were staunchly isolationist and against participation in the League on any basis, fearing what they perceived as foreign entanglements. Others were seriously concerned about the implications of Article X, which conceivably could commit the country to go to war without congressional approval.

Copies of the treaty were not available in the United States to congressmen or the public at large. Upon his return to New York Davison had given his copy to Elihu Root, a former Secretary of State under President Theodore Roosevelt, an ex-senator, and a highly respected figure in the Republican party, whose support for the treaty would be helpful. Through the Washington grapevine word soon reached Republican senator William E. Borah of Idaho that the Morgan bank had improperly secured a copy of the treaty. Borah was an ardent isolationist. Furthermore he deeply distrusted the powerful Wall Street bankers, and he suspected that the motivation of the Morgan partners in promoting the League was that it would be very beneficial to international finance, with the bankers gaining huge profits. A meeting of the Senate Committee on Foreign Relations was scheduled to hear testimony on the matter, and although Lamont was excused, Morgan and Davison were summoned to appear before the committee on June 13. TWL and Davison exchanged long cables on Davison's forthcoming testimony.

Lamont told the president about his problem and received a brief note in reply: "I am sorry you should be worried by this Senate investigation. You are doing just the right thing and with characteristic frankness."

Vance McCormick observed to Lamont: "That's always the way. The Chief stands by his friends."

Morgan testified briefly that he had never seen the treaty draft, and Davison adroitly used the opportunity to deliver a lecture on the need for peacetime international Red Cross organizations and large-scale financing to rehabilitate postwar Europe. From his standpoint the hearing was a success. He cabled TWL to forget about the charge of leaking the treaty. There was nothing to worry about, he reported, and the incident was closed.

During the course of the peace negotiations Lamont had developed a keen appreciation of Bernard Baruch's ability and value to the delegation. Baruch had an excellent handpicked staff and a house in the country outside Paris, where he could retreat over weekends to work in quiet surroundings or entertain key delegates. Lamont especially envied Baruch's close relationship and easy access to President Wilson, who had great confidence in his judgment. In peacetime the Morgan partners had considered themselves a breed apart from a financier like Baruch, who had amassed a personal fortune as a highly successful Wall Street stock speculator. He was the same age as Lamont, a Jew, a Democrat, and a strong supporter of the president. In the last election he had donated

$10,000 to the Democratic campaign fund, the same amount Lamont had given to the Republicans.

Baruch had had an earlier business run-in with the Morgan partners. In 1916, dealing with Lamont, he had offered the Morgan firm an equity interest in a new company, the predecessor of Texas Gulf Sulphur. The bank purchased a 60 percent interest and soon after sold it to William Boyce Thompson, the successful mining entrepreneur and TWL's friend. Baruch had been angry at Morgan for selling its interest without offering him the chance to buy it back.

Now Norman Davis reported some disquieting news: Baruch had told him that reporters were suggesting that the Morgan influence in the negotiations, represented by Lamont and to a minor extent Davison, could be politically damaging to the president at home. Baruch himself later told TWL that his public support for the treaty might be harmful in the U.S., because some would question the Morgan partners' motivation in backing the treaty. Despite Baruch's partisan jabs at the house of Morgan, at the end of the peace conference TWL, ever the diplomat, wrote him a "Dear Bernie" letter saying he believed that they had become good and loyal friends and expressing his personal esteem for him.

On June 23 the German government officially informed the Allies of its acceptance of the treaty, and the signing ceremony was scheduled for noon on June 28 at the Palais de Versailles. The suspense over acceptance of the treaty by the Germans was over, and now the American delegation turned its attention to the next major hurdle: the problem of persuading the American people and the United States Senate to approve the treaty and the League Covenant.

At the end of President Wilson's brief trip home in March, Lamont had received a cable from J. P. Morgan expressing disappointment that the president had not persuasively presented the League of Nations plan to the American public. After Wilson's return to Paris, American newspaper and political opposition to the League began to crystallize. Over the next several months TWL relayed to the president reports from his partner Dwight Morrow, who told of sharp criticism of the League by leading Republican senators and the concern of many responsible newspapers and public figures about the implications of Article X, whose provisions could involve the country in continuing "participation in European boundary struggles." Morrow also urged that Elihu Root and Supreme Court Justice Louis Brandeis be appointed counselors to the American delegation to help build up bipartisan support for the treaty and Covenant, and Lamont sent Wilson a memorandum containing Root's views on the League. While Root saw many commendable features in the plan, he also believed that Article X, committing the member nations to preserve "territorial integrity and existing political independence," was unwise.

The president turned aside all these suggestions. Appointing Root as counselor would be "a sign of deplorable weakness." He would not countenance any tampering with Article X, which he termed "the heart of the Covenant." He continued to believe that once he returned home with a signed treaty, Americans would rally behind him in support of the League. Despite his rejection of the suggestions forwarded by Lamont, he always responded cordially, as in his letter of June 7:

> I know the disinterested spirit in which you are thinking about these matters which are of such critical and fundamental importance, and hope you will permit me to say that I have more and more admired the liberal and public-spirited stand you have taken in all our counsels.

In a letter to Wilson a few days later, Lamont suggested that when the president returned home he should make a series of speeches explaining the League in simple terms to the American people. "Baruch thinks that once you go back with a Treaty in your pocket, your troubles will be over and the opposition will fade away." Lamont was not so sure that this would happen.

On June 21 Lamont wrote the president that his task was completed and he intended to return to America, if the president agreed, and lobby for the League among Republican senators. "I deplore an attempt on the part of certain Republicans to make a party issue of a matter in which everyone should be first for America and for the world," Lamont declared.

The president, in his letter of June 23, agreed that Lamont should return to America, where he could be influential in informing people about the League and "the necessity for the United States to assume a real leadership in affairs at this turning-point in the history of nations."

> The service you can render in clarifying the situation will, I am sure, be very great, and also in convincing the opponents of the League that it is not within our power now to enter or not to enter the politics of the world. Our only choice is to enter it with advantage and as a leader, or to enter it by compulsion of circumstances and at disadvantages from time to time, as a nation that stands outside the common councils.
>
> I have found that our thoughts run along the same line, and apparently this is the psychological moment to strengthen the tide which now seems to be turning against opposition to the Treaty in any part.

The president had judged Lamont's instincts well. Just a month earlier Wilson had discussed TWL with his friend and doctor, Adm. Cary T. Grayson, who recorded Wilson's comments in his diary: "I chose (Lamont) because I wanted him to see at first hand exactly the plans and purposes and manner of the administration's way of doing business. I wanted him to be a partner for reform."

On June 26, Baruch, McCormick, Davis, and Lamont called on the president to suggest that they sail home with him on June 29. They had arranged for John Foster Dulles to stay on to represent the United States on reparations and financial matters. The president was in a good mood and readily agreed with his advisers; they would all sail on the *George Washington* from Brest the day after the signing of the treaty at Versailles.

The Treaty of Versailles

The morning of Saturday, June 28, 1919, was warm and sunny. Lamont, Norman Davis, and their wives drove out to Versailles in a government car along a highway that had been cleared of normal traffic by French polius guarding the intersections. As they approached the lovely old town thousands of people lined the roadway to watch the dignitaries arrive. Flanking the main avenue to the huge courtyard in front of the chateau were French cavalrymen in steel blue helmets with red and white pennants fluttering from their lances in the breeze. The Lamonts entered the Palais de Versailles and ascended the great staircase leading to the Hall of Mirrors, where the signing ceremony would take place. Chasseurs wearing gleaming brass helmets with long black tassels lined both sides of the stairway with their swords drawn. The Lamonts proceeded through several rooms to the gallery, where Tom took his seat with the other delegation members. Florence's place was on the outside terrace in the section reserved for official guests. In the center of the hall was a horseshoe-shaped table for the heads of state and plenipotentiary peace commissioners. The treaty document, ready for signing, rested on a small table in the center open space. About a thousand people, including delegation staffs and four hundred members of the press, filled the great room.

Soon the heads of state, led by Clemenceau, came in and took their places. The French premier, as Lamont described him later, looked "old and more shriveled than ever, yet full of unquenchable life." At the stroke of noon Clemenceau signaled for silence, and when the room was completely hushed, declared, "Faites entrer les Allemands."

Preceded by four Allied army officers, two German officials, Foreign Secretary Hermann Muller and Johannes Bell, entered the hall and took their seats. They looked utterly woebegone, the paleness of their ashen faces accentuated by the long black frock coats they wore.

"La séance est ouverte," announced Clemenceau, and after a short explanation about the signing procedure, the Germans were led to the small table on which the treaty lay. With visible trembling, they signed it and returned to their seats. President Wilson then led the American peace commissioners to the table to sign the document, and the other heads of state followed. The room again became quiet, and Clemenceau declared, "La séance est levée." The historic ceremony was all over in half an hour, the hall emptied, and the solemnity of the occasion quickly replaced by a mood of joyous celebration. Cannons began to boom, signaling that the peace treaty had been signed by the vanquished Germans.

Lamont introduced his wife to Premier Clemenceau. "Oh, Monsieur Lamont et Madame," he said in a voice filled with emotion, "this is the sound I have been waiting for and that I have wished to hear for forty-eight years!"

Florence was quite taken with the French premier. She described him later as "like an excited little boy at his first party," and she also enjoyed his sly humor. He patted her hand and with a dramatic wink stated, "I am afraid that your husband is not worthy of you! You must have a very bad husband because he is such a good man. He cannot be both a good man *and* a good husband!"

They strolled out on the terrace overlooking the lovely gardens where a throng had gathered to savor the long-awaited moment. The crowds cheered, airplanes flew overhead, and the fountains played and sparkled in the sun for the first time since the war began.

"Yes," said the old premier, "it is a beautiful day!"

That evening, President and Mrs. Wilson, the Lamonts, and other members of the president's entourage left for Brest. Included in the party were Bernard Baruch, Vance McCormick, Norman Davis, and John D. Rockefeller, Jr. There were also hundreds of returning American soldiers on board. The next day as bands played The Star-Spangled Banner and La Marseillaise and artillery fired in salute, the *George Washington* steamed for home.

All in the president's party were delighted to see him so cheerful and relaxed on the ocean crossing, the first respite he had had since the armistice. He paced around the deck and engaged in friendly chatter with anyone who joined him. Around teatime he and Mrs. Wilson settled themselves in deck chairs in a sheltered spot, and his staff and their wives gathered around for an hour or so of congenial conversation led by the president, who often had the group laughing heartily over his stories and limericks.

One afternoon he summoned his advisers to his stateroom to read them his proposed message to the Congress presenting the treaty. Lamont thought it was a good address, a skillfully drafted report of his steward-ship in Paris—how the treaty had been worked out and how its implemen-tation was based on the functioning of the League.

In the ensuing discussion, Lamont noted that the president had referred to the League Covenant as "a definite constitution." TWL said that the phrase gave Wilson's critics the opportunity to attack the covenant as a fixed and final document that was unchangeable, and this was unwise. The president made a note of the point and said he would cover it. The group also discussed whether the president should admit that he did not view the treaty as perfect in all respects. Lamont argued, "Such an apology would give a handle to the more dangerous opponents. . . . The critics who are trying to split the Covenant from the Treaty are the dangerous ones, and we must not say to them that the Treaty is a poor, weak thing," and this view prevailed at the meeting. Before adjourning, the president told his advisers that if it became apparent that he had a fight on his hands in the Senate, he was ready to embark on a nationwide speaking tour to build public support for the League.

On July 8 the *George Washington* was greeted in New York harbor by a huge Navy flotilla, including five battleships and vessels of all kinds. Sirens screamed, horns blew, and flags and pennants fluttered in the fresh breeze. The main decks of the passenger liner were crowded with cheering soldiers. President Wilson stood on the top deck dressed in striped trousers, a dark Prince Albert coat, and a golf cap, smiling and waving at the welcoming craft. An open-car parade to Carnegie Hall followed in which the president received a tumultuous welcome from his fellow citizens. It was a glorious hour, certainly a scene with all the welcoming trappings of a victor's return in triumph, but many Americans, some citing the warning by George Washington in his Farewell Address, remained leary of foreign alliances.

Lobbying for the League

Jack Morgan was glad to have Lamont return to the office, as he wrote his mother: "It's a very great comfort to have Lamont back, too, and we are now pretty well manned again, and I can plan to be away with a fairly easy mind." In late August, Morgan resumed his prewar practice of spending three months in England and Scotland each fall. TWL, again immersed in his firm's business, also had personal causes and problems to attend to.

Both Exeter and Harvard asked their distinguished alumnus to co-chair capital drives—Exeter ($2 million) and Harvard ($11 million). Mingling with his fellow alumni at fund-raising receptions and dinners was a pleasant duty for the gregarious Lamont, whose talks to the Harvard alumni were reported by the Boston and New York papers, including his own newspaper, the *New York Evening Post*. However, owning the *Post* was proving to be a very costly way to promote his views, and the *Post*'s performance was an embarrassment to boot.

The paper had lost $32,000 in the first half of 1919, with no end to the financial drain in sight. The circulation and advertising revenues seemed frozen at a low level, and Lamont had to make up the deficits. And soon after his return the owner received a letter from the editorial staff complaining of their long hours and low salaries.

Furthermore, he was disturbed by the critical comments of readers, which were often justified. The paper lacked personality, and its editorials were querulous rather than positive and constructive. People held TWL responsible for the paper's performance even though he constantly insisted that he was not involved in its management and editorial policy.

His old friend and personal attorney George Case advised Lamont in a letter: "Do make that paper a credit to you or get clean out of it. I hate to see people turn up their noses at the Post and talk about Lamont and his plaything."

Recognizing that to turn the paper around he must hire a top executive to manage it for him, Lamont appointed Edwin Francis Gay to be the *Post*'s new president and chief executive officer. Gay had organized and became the first dean of the Harvard Business School, a job he had held until the war, when he became a member of the War Trade Board. Lamont had known him since the Business School's founding in 1908, when, at Gay's invitation, he had lectured at the school on corporate reorganizations; later he had worked with Gay on the school's fund-raising campaign. Lamont believed that Gay could reinvigorate the paper and anticipated that the *Post* would be politically independent with Republican leanings.

Upon his return, TWL lobbied actively for Senate ratification of the treaty, an effort that was not appreciated by anti-League senators, especially Senator Borah of Idaho, who censured Lamont from the senate floor.

> When this fight was in its beginning, Thomas Lamont, a partner in the firm of J. P. Morgan & Co., bought the New York Evening Post and it immediately was enlisted in the support of the League of Nations. An ably edited newspaper, its propaganda in this cause was backed by an international banker who sat as practically America's official representative at Versailles and was able to send a copy of the peace treaty to his partners.
>
> This newspaper propaganda has been spread all over the country. What does it advocate? The surrender of our traditional foreign policy. . . .
>
> It advocates that a combine controlled by foreigners shall succeed to the control of our international relations; that our foreign affairs shall be placed in the hands of a body whose overwhelming majority are aliens to us. And why? When Mr. Lamont of the firm of Morgan gave a copy of the treaty to his partner, Mr. Davison, he did not say, "Read this over and see if in your opinion it accords with the interests and traditions of America." No, he handed it to his partner and said, "Study this and see if you think it will help this plan we are formulating to finance Europe." That was the object of sending the treaty to Mr. Davison; to determine if the treaty is so drafted that it will assist in carrying out the great schemes of international finance that are being formulated.

TWL showered President Wilson with letters suggesting strategies to build support for the League. Senator Henry Cabot Lodge, the Republican chairman of the Senate Foreign Relations Committee, had announced that he would not approve the treaty unless special reservations were added to protect American interests. In a letter to Lamont, Wilson stated: "I hope now that all the forces will be concentrated upon promoting the policy of keeping all reservations or interpretations out of the formal act of ratification, and embodying those that can reasonably be accepted in a separate document." The battle lines were drawn.

In mid-August, TWL left New York to join Florence and the children in North Haven and work on a new project—drafting a public statement backing the treaty and League Covenant without the Lodge reservations. On August 22 he wrote the president and enclosed a copy.

> Hitherto I have refrained from making any such statement. People, for instance, like Senator Root, with whom of course, I have been in disagree-

ment, as he has been still hanging out for firm reservations, told me that if I made a statement, I might get Borah, et al., so angry it would get their backs up still worse against the Treaty. Then Berney Baruch said that if I were to make a public statement, probably Reed of Missouri would make a public attack against my motives.

To tell the truth, I am getting a little tired of being shut up all the time, just because my motives may be misunderstood, or just because I may get somebody mad. . . . When I arrived in New York I was told it would never do for me to be seen in Washington, etc., etc. . . . I have a little feeling that if I were to say a few things that are the truth about your course over there and about what happened, it might have a favorable rather than an unfavorable effect, even if it made Borah and Reed mad.

The president replied that he thought Lamont should go ahead with the statement and hoped that it would serve to "clear the clouded air that has been thrown about . . . by misapprehensions and misrepresentations of those who have been fighting the Treaty."

On September 3, President Wilson, physically worn and fatigued, embarked by train on a nationwide speaking tour to appeal to his countrymen for their support of the League Covenant. On September 9 Lamont issued his statement, which received widespread newspaper coverage.

Since his return from the Paris Peace Conference, said TWL, he had declined to comment publicly on the debate over the treaty, because he believed that the Republican Senate majority, after careful consideration, would vote for its ratification.

But I . . . have become greatly disturbed at the continued uncertainty and delay, a delay which . . . is already responsible for having rendered social and industrial conditions in both Europe and America distinctly worse.

The whole world is crying for peace, for a chance to renew its normal life and work; and America, by continued inaction, refuses to grant her consent to the settlements necessary. Since it became evident to the world of commerce that the action of the United States Senate might nullify the Treaty, there has been an alarming fall in the rates of foreign exchange. For this no remedy can be had as long as the delay continues at Washington; no plan for the extension of foreign credits, so necessary to maintain America's export trade, can be evolved.

There had been "calamitous fumbling with the most critical situation that the world has ever seen" and "almost incredible misunderstanding . . . of the manner in which the affairs of the world await America's assent to peace."

TWL stoutly defended President Wilson's conduct in Paris:

I hear it repeated that he was unwilling to take counsel with his delegation. That is untrue. He constantly and earnestly sought the advice of his associates. . . . Throughout the complexities and anxieties over there President Wilson acted with moderation, common sense, and great patience. He played no politics and what is more, he showed constantly extraordinary courage in fighting for the idealism that we call American. . . .

As to the Treaty itself, the situation, then, is this: America played an enormously important part in the war. Without her co-operation it could not have been won. In the same way, in making peace her Allies and Associates in the war looked to her for leadership.

The American Commission had finally succeeded in negotiating a just and fair treaty commanding the approval of the delegations of the twenty-two other powers.

The American delegation in the main, then, carried through its ideas, and was enabled to do so because there was openly accorded to it a position of arbiter and dispenser of justice. Repeated instances arose where the other commissions requested the American delegation to prepare a solution which in effect the others would endorse in advance.

So the peace settlement, "upon which all Europe has been hanging for months, for which all industry, all restoration and return to a life of order, have been waiting," was now before the Senate for ratification. The majority of the Senate was disinclined to reject the treaty openly, but contemplated saddling it with alterations which would force the U.S. "to go back to Germany and ask her to have the grace to execute a new Treaty with us." America would also be compelled to "beg" its Allies to reopen negotiations with Germany and to assemble their own parliaments, which in the case of England, Belgium, and a few other nations, had already approved the treaty.

Finally TWL chastised those who argued that the treaty was too severe on Germany. Did they favor treating Germany in a way to encourage her to start another war? Did they forget that

it was Germany who plunged the whole world into darkness and woe, in a struggle that brought death to at least ten million beings; incapacity to twenty million more; the breakdown of law and order; the wasting of over two hundred billion dollars of treasure, and calamities from which the world can hardly recover within a hundred years? The aim of the nations assembled at Paris was to draft a Treaty that was just, but so framed as to prevent Germany or any other nation from repeating such crimes as these.

To this end the Treaty sets up the initial machinery for a League of Free Nations. The United States Senate cannot pull apart that machinery without making the whole Treaty void. Any such action as that will spell renewed

Bolshevist effort throughout Europe, spreading, as there is already evidence, to America.

Unless the Senate approved the treaty, continued chaos among the newly created nations and mass starvation during the coming winter would inevitably follow. By postponing action the U.S. would later face the greatest ignominy: "entering the League of Nations hand in hand with Germany, novitiates together in this wonderful enterprise that is to set the world free from the slavery of war! That may be what the American people want, but I don't believe it."

Some papers praised the Lamont statement; others were skeptical.

The *New York American*: "Find a big financier eager for a chance at world exploitation and you find a friend of the Peace League. That being the case and these men being intelligent, don't you suppose the Peace League contains something particularly attractive for them?"

The *Brooklyn Citizen* described TWL as "the leading member of J. P. Morgan and Company. . . . As Mr. Lamont is certainly well qualified to speak for the business interests of the country at large and is at the same time known to be much more interested in the Republican than the Democratic party, his advice may be expected to carry considerable weight."

The *Holyoke Transcript*: "The inner circles have known how much it meant to the great bankers of New York to come into the new world power as a major part of it. . . . And if Mr. Lamont does not wear the name of Morgan he is the bright particular star of the house of Morgan today. . . .

"There was nothing said about bringing financial leadership to the United States in the fourteen commandments. But that was secured and it is to be presumed that Thomas W. Lamont did the deed. . . . The claim that the United States will benefit hugely in a financial way if the League goes through as planned is certain. We hold the rest of the world financiers in our power and with the League it will be mightly hard for them to get away."

The *Hartford Post*: "The straight-forward warning by Mr. Lamont is further comfort for those who believe that this peaceful future of the world depends upon the ratification of the Treaty substantially as it stands."

The *Easton Express* (Pennsylvania) headlined its story: "Lamont warns of Red Peril," reflecting the incipient national hysteria over an alleged Communist infiltration in America.

TWL received a number of congratulatory letters about his statement. He told his correspondents that he had heard that he had angered Senator Lodge, which didn't bother him, and urged them to tell their senators to vote for the treaty without reservations. He trusted the Allied nations and would sign the treaty even if it were not perfect; it was "a workable instrument and a safe one for America."

Lamont wrote Republican senator Walter E. Edge of New Jersey, assuring him that he was a good Republican. "I want to have you know that Mr. Morgan, Davison, Morrow, myself, and most of our partners are straight out Republicans." But they reserved the right to speak out when they thought certain Republicans were making a mistake: "I was in Paris with our peace mission for five months, and I saw what I saw."

The president wrote Lamont on September 19 from San Diego about his statement: "It ought to do . . . a real service in clarifying matters which I cannot help believing have been deliberately misrepresented and which I find generally misunderstood. The most prominent feeling, so far as I can gather it here in California, is one of resentment on the part of the public that they have been so misinformed and so misled as to the real character and purposes of the Treaty and Covenant.

"Mrs. Wilson joins me in most cordial messages to Mrs. Lamont and yourself. We all have the most delightful recollections of our association on the *George Washington*."

A week later the nation was shocked to learn that the president had suffered a physical collapse after speaking in Pueblo, Colorado. The rest of his tour was cancelled, and Wilson was rushed back to Washington, where he suffered a severe stroke on October 2. The invalid president was confined to the White House living quarters for months, and for much of this period, on the instructions of his physician, Admiral Grayson, he was cut off from all outside contacts except through Mrs. Wilson and his personal secretary, Joseph P. Tumulty.

In November, TWL sent word to Admiral Grayson that he would like five minutes with the president, whenever Grayson felt that the president was up to it, to discuss strategy for winning the battle over the treaty in the Senate. But for months the president's poor condition made this impossible.

Later during the president's confinement it was reported that Bernard Baruch had joined the small group of advisers with access to him, and TWL's jealousy was quickly aroused. In late December, Lamont wrote to Elihu Root that he had expected to be summoned to the White House any day, but had not yet been invited. "Apparently that eminent statesman Bernard M. Baruch, has covered the ground."

The president remained unalterably opposed to Senator Lodge's modifying provisions, and at his instructions on November 19 Democratic senators voted against a treaty including the reservations, dooming it to defeat. But public opinion demanded that the Senate reconsider the treaty and attempt to work out a formula acceptable to the opposing views. TWL believed that the main thing the rest of the world wanted was the assurance of America's cooperation and participation in postwar international councils, even if that commitment were hedged. It was now clear that the Senate would not ratify the treaty without the Lodge reservations. Unless the president was prepared to compromise, as even leading Democrats like Bernard Baruch now advised, the treaty would not be ratified, and America would not join the League of Nations and its sister organizations.

In February 1920, Lamont received the invitation he had been waiting for—to call on the president at the White House. It was a bright sunny day, and the president in his wheelchair had been placed near a large bay window through which the sun was streaming. Lamont was shocked at the change in his physical appearance. He was wasted and frail, his voice weak. But he greeted Lamont cordially and talked whimsically for a moment of his disabilities.

The State Department and the British and French foreign ministries had recently asked Lamont to visit Japan and China on a mission involving international finance, and Lamont discussed his coming trip with the president. One of the complications, Lamont pointed out, was that China itself was basically divided into two great factions—the North with the seat of the national government established at Peking, and the South with Sun Yat-sen's Kuomintang headquarters at Shanghai; independent war lords dominated the hinterland.

"Well," said the president, "I think you must try to devise some formula to bring the North and South together." Alluding to his own southern origins, he added with a chuckle, "You know, Lamont, traditionally I am always for the South."

The president's mind was firmly closed to consideration of reservations to the treaty, as Lamont recalled in *Across World Frontiers*. Wilson was prepared to have the treaty and League Covenant go down to defeat rather than grant concessions that would destroy his ideal concept "of an organization for permanent peace." "He took comfort in the belief that the national idealism of the American people would in due course make itself manifest, and that the high hopes to which he himself had clung so desperately would be attained." As Lamont bade farewell to the president that wintry morning, he realized that Wilson would never compromise.

From his sickroom the president ordered the Democratic senators to vote down Senator Lodge's version of the treaty when it was reintroduced. Four months after the first vote, the Senate once again defeated the treaty containing the reservations, and this time it was irretrievably lost.

By 1920 Lamont, in his fiftieth year, had completed the journey from the parsonage to a station that gave him a respected voice in the highest councils of business and government, a standing that he had eagerly sought and won. Tom's prominence as a former delegate to the Paris Peace Conference and leading international banker also opened a new door for the Lamonts in government and diplomatic social circles. One evening they invited Herbert Hoover to dinner in New York. World-renowned for his leadership of the relief programs for Europe, Hoover, in the view of many Americans, would make a fine president. He and Florence had a lively dinner-table discussion on the issues of the day.

Florence, who considered herself a political liberal, greatly admired Hoover. As he was leaving the party Florence said, "I hope that you do not think I'm a Red, Mr. Hoover. You know I am going to work for you for president."

Hoover, with a twinkle in his eye, replied, "Mrs. Lamont, if ever I am president, my first act will be to jail you as a Bolshevik." At the time, the country was in the midst of a full-blown "Red scare" led by U.S. Attorney General A. Mitchell Palmer, whose agents had rounded up thousands of suspected Communists and radicals.

Florence also reported on a small dinner the Lamonts attended to meet King Albert and Queen Elizabeth of Belgium. Florence had just washed her hair, but it would not dry, she wrote Austin. "It kept getting later and later. Father kept saying 'We must not be *one minute late!*' Oh, it was hectic! But finally got there. I did not know until two minutes before the King and Queen came in, that I had to curtsy to them, and then I fell into a horrible panic because I could not remember whether you put your right leg or your left leg back to make a proper curtsy. But I did it by intuition when the King stood before me. I was perfectly willing to curtsy to the King and Queen . . . but when it came to the little prince, the American Eagle perched on my shoulder and *screamed.* And I thought: Why should a woman of my age bob to this little boy? and I wouldn't, and I was the only one who didn't. And I suppose I was very silly and provincial."

It was time for the Lamonts to own their own home in the city, a larger and more elegant residence that would enable them to entertain and put up houseguests on a far grander scale than the Roosevelt house could accommodate. In the fall of 1919 TWL purchased a lot for $150,000 on the north side of 70th Street just east of Park Avenue. The estimated cost of building the four-story townhouse the Lamonts planned would be about $400,000, and Lamont instructed the architects to proceed.

At the same time, the construction of the Lamonts' large rambling summer home on the north shore of North Haven was nearing completion, and the family expected to enjoy the next summer holiday in their new house. However, TWL had received some bad news about another building project in which he was involved. Ever since his student days at Exeter, when he had contracted scarlet fever, he had recognized the school's need for an infirmary to house sick students. The influenza epidemic that had struck the student body when Corliss was at the school had highlighted the urgency of the need, and Lamont had promised to contribute the $50,000 it was originally estimated the new building would cost. Now Dr. Perry, the principal, informed him that the latest estimate of the construction cost for the infirmary was $100,000, and Lamont would have to donate the additional sum required.

Book III

FINANCE AND DIPLOMACY—
INTERTWINED

The Chinese Consortium

The International Consortium for the Assistance of China had been formed in 1908 by banking groups from Great Britain, France, and Germany. For years these nations, along with Russia and Japan, had been carving out spheres of influence in China where each would be the dominating foreign power in investment and trade. The United States, on the other hand, had favored an "Open Door" policy for China, as enunciated by President McKinley's Secretary of State John Hay, which would protect China's political and territorial integrity and provide equal access to all her trading partners. The Europeans had finally come to recognize that uncoordinated lending under the "sphere of influence" policy was unsound and might even lead to conflict among the foreign groups; accordingly, they had formed the banking consortium as a means of cooperating in making large public loans to China.

In 1909, at the instigation of the State Department, an American group—composed of J. P. Morgan & Co., Kuhn, Loeb, First National Bank, and National City Bank—was formed and joined the consortium. The first loan by the four-power consortium was to the Chinese government in 1911 for $30 million to build the Hukuang Railway. In the following year Japan and Russia were admitted as members.

Immediately after the inauguration of President Wilson in 1913, Harry Davison, representing the American group, met with Secretary of State William Jennings Bryan to inquire if the new administration intended to continue support of the consortium. A negative answer soon came from the White House in a public statement that received front-page coverage.

Wilson suspected that the consortium of Wall Street bankers and their foreign partners was simply a scheme to take advantage of China's weakness, infringe on her sovereignty, and make large profits at her expense. Secretary Bryan stated that the consortium smacked too much of "dollar diplomacy." The American government should not back such activity.

Davison and Lamont were angry at the administration's response. The American bankers had been urged by their government, appealing to their patriotism, to participate in a project that did not appear to be a particularly attractive piece of business. Now the government had abruptly withdrawn its support for the bankers' efforts to assist China. The American bankers would have to drop out of the consortium, and they and the U.S. government would be discredited in the eyes of the other participants. However, the outbreak of war in Europe soon absorbed the world's attention, and investment in China was forgotten by the Western bankers.

But Japan's increasing political and economic penetration of China was causing growing concern at the State Department. Not only was Chinese sovereignty threatened, the future of American trade and investment in China was at stake. In October 1918, the Wilson administration, reluctantly realizing that the bankers were essential to its Far East strategy, did an about-face and sent a note to the British, French, and Japanese governments inviting banking groups from those countries to join with the American bankers in a reconstituted consortium that would operate under a fresh set of principles. At the request of the State Department, J. P. Morgan & Co. and its banking associates from the old consortium had formed a new nationally broad-based American group of about forty banks and investment firms. The American government proposed that the four national banking groups in the new consortium should act together as equal partners in the interests of China; that not only future business, but existing investment commitments and options should be turned over to the consortium for the benefit of all the members, excepting those "upon which substantial progress had been made"; that no country would attempt to establish special spheres of influence in China; that the consortium would make loans to the government of China and its provinces only to finance large public projects and purposes, such as railroad development and currency stabilization.

On May 11, 1919, representatives of the four banking groups convened at the offices of the Banque de l'Indo-Chine in Paris for a meeting chaired by Lamont. They quickly accepted the U.S. statement of principles, and prompt confirmation by their respective governments seemed assured.

In June, however, Lamont received a disturbing letter from Adagiri Masunosuke of the Japanese group. He reported that his government insisted on excluding from the consortium agreement "all the rights and options held by Japan in the regions of Manchuria and Mongolia where

Japan had special interest." The other three groups and their governments which had approved the consortium agreement—the United States, Great Britain, and France—flatly rejected the Japanese reservations. To agree would be to grant a privileged status for Japan in those parts of China, a direct infringement of China's sovereignty and independence, which was simply unacceptable.

Yet the consortium without Japan as a participant subject to its restraints on unilateral operations in China would be an empty shell. A flurried exchange of diplomatic notes all summer and fall between the State Department and the British Foreign Office, on the one hand, and the Japanese foreign ministry produced only further deadlock.

During these months, Lamont kept in close touch with Breckinridge Long, Assistant Secretary of State, and J.V.A. MacMurray, chief of the Bureau of Far Eastern Affairs in the State Department, as they attempted to persuade the Japanese to drop their reservations. The Americans were quite willing to concede that where substantial work or planning was underway, the project would be recognized as being outside the scope of the four-power agreement; South Manchuria Railway being built by the Japanese was one such project. But the American government would not consent to granting any nation exclusive rights over a geographic area. Members of the consortium were equal partners, and none should receive special privileges.

In August, Long and MacMurray proposed to Lamont that the American group make a unilateral loan to the Chinese government to put pressure on the Japanese, but Lamont and his partners declined: a Chinese loan was far too risky a proposition. With President Wilson still incapacitated in the White House and the standoff continuing, Breckinridge Long decided that the only way to settle the issue was for Lamont to go to Japan to explain the Western position directly to the government. In his letter to Lamont of December 12, Long stated that he had long felt that Lamont was the logical person to visit Japan to resolve the problem. As spokesman for the American banking group he could accomplish far more than a government official. "Again, won't you consider favorably the suggestion that you go to Japan and try to straighten this thing out?" pleaded Long. Lamont agreed to go and began planning the mission.

To advise him in the negotiations he would bring his friend Jeremiah Smith, Jr., to serve as mission counsel, and Martin Egan of the Morgan staff to handle press relations. Florence would come, with her personal maid, and two old friends, Mr. and Mrs. Jesse L. Williams, who would keep her company when Tom was busy. Lamont also recruited a doctor to minister to the party's medical needs and an engineering expert.

During January 1920, Lamont visited Washington for talks with State Department officials Robert Lansing, Frank Polk, and Breckinridge Long. It was agreed that TWL would represent the American banking group on a mission, approved by the European banking groups and the U.S., British, and French governments, to secure Japanese acceptance of the consortium agreement and investigate the feasibility of making new loans to China.

On February 12 the Lamont party entrained for the west coast, leaving New York on "The Peacock Point," the Morgan partners' private Pullman car named after the Davison estate on Long Island. A week later they sailed from Vancouver on the *Empress of Russia*, and on March 1 first observed the snow-clad peak of Mt. Fujiyama ringed with clouds. They disembarked the next morning at Yokohama, and several days later proceeded to Tokyo and the Imperial Hotel, their headquarters for the rest of the month.

The leading Japanese banks were the official hosts of the Lamont party and laid out a busy schedule of lunches, receptions, and dinners, which were occasionally enlivened by the graceful dancing of geishas. The Harvard Club of Tokyo gave a large reception, and the Tokyo embassies of the consortium member countries feted them. American ambassador Roland S. Morris gave a grand dinner at the U.S. Embassy for the mission with Prime Minister Takashi Hara, other Japanese government officials, and most of the foreign diplomatic corps in attendance.

Some of the country's most prominent families, including the Mitsuis, Mitsubishis, and Iwasakis, also gave lavish parties to honor the distinguished visitors. Florence described one event that especially impressed her—the splendid luncheon given by Baron and Baroness Iwasaki, reportedly the richest family in Japan, at their villa on the family's twenty-five-acre estate in the middle of Tokyo.

> It is awfully disconcerting at these affairs to sit near a member of your own party, so that you can hear what each other is saying. I could hear Tom saying just exactly the same thing that I was, and a little lower down the table, the doctor started in on the subject of the theatre, and was about five sentences behind me, which rattled me terribly. Jesse was repeating his favorite litany a little lower down on the other side, "Is this your first visit to Japan?" "Yes, but not my last, I hope."
>
> After luncheon we looked at the porcelain collection, and then went for a walk through the beautiful garden, one of the most famous in all Japan. Wild ducks were flying overhead, and some fishermen in a boat were casting a huge circular net—really a wonderful stunt, a little like throwing a lasso. We walked over lovely stone bridges, and sometimes over the water on flat

stepping stones and wandered through the garden which is built around a series of lakes.

The baron had, in fact, staged the fascinating fishing scene for the benefit of his visitors, they later learned. The guests then visited the family's Japanese house (having dined in their European-style house), which was built around a series of secluded small courts connected by graveled walks.

> One of the little Japs was so afraid that I would not appreciate the beauty and value of the various objet d'art that he kept hissing in my ear "He (Baron I.) refused $60,000 for that. That little piece of jade cost $100,000," etc. I could hardly bear it. It showed what he thought of Americans; or did it show his own aesthetic feeling too?
>
> We then walked to a little teahouse on the lake, where tea and cake and candy were waiting for us. Of course, we were starving, as we had only finished a three-hour luncheon half an hour before! Baron I. and I reached there first. He asked me if I would like a cigarette, and I said I should if it was all right for me to smoke there and if it would not be displeasing to the Baroness. He said not at all, as the Baroness herself liked to smoke. So I took a cigarette, and when the Baroness came, the Baron (her nephew; the Baroness was quite old) offered her a cigarette. She refused with considerable astonishment and emphasis. Then the Baron said some of the crossest and sternest Japanese words that I have ever heard, and the Baroness took the cigarette with alacrity. I am sure that she had never touched one before, and the poor old lady's attempts to smoke it aroused all my sympathy. Men are tyrants the world over!

Lamont worked closely with Ambassador Morris, and they both consulted British ambassador Beilby Alston. In addition to his talks with the bankers, TWL met members of the Japanese cabinet, the Diplomatic Advisory Council, and Premier Hara, always emphasizing that the Western banking groups had no intentions regarding Manchuria or Mongolia that would threaten Japan's "economic security or national safety" in any way. Japan's existing undertakings in these regions would not be affected by the consortium agreement. Inosuke Inouye, the governor of the Bank of Japan and spokesman for the banking group, and even Premier Hara told Lamont privately that they wanted Japan to withdraw her demands regarding the two Chinese provinces and join the consortium.

But as Lamont soon learned, there was another important element to contend with, the so-called military clique, whose shadowy and powerful influence was exerted through the General Staff and the Intelligence

Department. This group strongly opposed participation in the consortium without preserving the special claims concerning Mongolia and Manchuria.

Lamont thought he had the answer to calm the military. He proposed that the Western banking groups exchange notes with the Japanese group recognizing Japan's special interests in Mongolia and Manchuria. In theory this banker-to-banker consortium understanding would be free-standing and not compromise the official Western government position barring recognition of spheres of influence. The U.S. banking group would not be giving up anything, TWL thought, because Mongolia and Manchuria would not be of interest to American investors anyway, given the existing Japanese ownership of the South Manchurian Railway and the undeveloped state of the provinces. However, the State Department rejected this suggestion, judging that Lamont's plan would indeed undercut the vital principle banning spheres of influence.

Lamont expressed his irritation at this rebuff in cables to his partners. Manchuria, where the Japanese already dominated trade and investment, would not be attractive to the Western banking groups, in any event, so why not at least grant the Japanese a veto power over railway projects? He asked J. P. Morgan to urge Undersecretary Polk and Breckinridge Long to accept his plan and remind Long that he had undertaken the mission at Long's request "and that I look to him especially for sympathetic approval of solutions worked out here with great difficulty and now offered."

But the State Department remained unmoved. The exchange of notes could contain only a list of specific railroad projects to be excluded from the scope of the agreement, adding three new short lines which the Japanese wanted included.

In the meantime, Lamont made a speech to the American-Japan Society in Tokyo. He had long recognized that Japan, ready to modernize its growing economy, could become a worthy customer for American loans, with the Morgan bank leading the way. Japan was certainly a far more appealing borrower at that time than China. Moreover, during his stay in Tokyo he had learned of Japan's increasing appetite for borrowing in the United States to meet her growing capital needs. In his talk he raised the possibility of American lending to Japan and then quickly observed that naturally the four-power consortium agreement must be concluded before such a loan program could be seriously considered.

Lamont had found Governor Inouye to be congenial; he was serious, astute, and infinitely courteous, and the chemistry between the two bankers was good. On March 26 Inouye announced to the press that

Lamont, representing the American Banking Group of the consortium, had concluded his meetings with the Japanese Banking Group in Tokyo. "As the understanding between them as to the entry of the Japanese Group into the Consortium has been fully arrived at, and the negotiation between the Governments of the United States and Japan is making favorable progress, Mr. Lamont has now left Japan on a trip to China."

The next day Tom joined Florence and the rest of his party in Kyoto for a visit to the ancient temples. That evening they boarded a French steamer at the port of Kobe for the four-day voyage to Shanghai.

The torrent of publicity and attention which greeted the mission's arrival in Shanghai came as a complete surprise. The newspapers devoted columns to the background of the consortium and the mission's purpose. The lobby and corridors of the Astor House Hotel, where the Lamont party was staying, were filled with reporters, Chinese officials, and foreign businessmen all wishing to see Lamont. And it quickly became evident that there were influential groups that distrusted and opposed the consortium.

One of the first people Lamont talked to was a U.S. Army Intelligence Officer based in Peking who had been detailed to assist the mission. He reported that the National Student Movement Association planned to stone the windows of the hotel to demonstrate their defiance of the consortium.

George Sokolsky, an American journalist in Shanghai, who would later ply his trade as a right-wing columnist in the U.S., was also on hand to greet the mission. Sokolsky, who had spent two years in China, had close ties with the student group, which was a significant intellectual and political force. Now he offered to introduce their leaders to TWL, who promptly invited them to tea at the hotel, stating that he was ready to hear their views and answer their questions about the consortium. He trusted that all stone throwing would be postponed.

About thirty students, ten of them women, attended the meeting, moderated by Sokolsky, which went on for two hours. The students were a bright group, and TWL was impressed with their patriotism—the intensity of their desire to see China develop into a great nation. They were highly critical of the national government in Peking, which they regarded as ineffective and corrupt. They distrusted the Japanese, whom they accused of trying to corrupt and undermine the government, and were generally fearful of foreign domination. Consortium loans to the Peking government would serve only to bolster a dishonest and weak regime. The presence of the hated Japanese in the consortium would give them a new base to expand their aggressive campaign to dominate China.

Lamont answered with arguments he would be repeating often over the coming days. The consortium would operate in China only at the express invitation and with the cordial cooperation of the Chinese people. Unless they were convinced of its utility, it would not attempt to function. However, any consortium program must include Japan, because she was China's closest neighbor and already had important interests in parts of China. If the students distrusted Japan's purposes and methods, it seemed wise to have Japan operating as a member of the consortium under the restraints of her agreement with her partners, rather than on her own. Lamont thought that he had convinced most of the students by the end of the meeting as to the honorable objectives of the consortium.

However, it was apparent that an organized propaganda campaign was being conducted in China against the consortium, mainly through newspapers and journals controlled by Japanese interests. Articles, petitions, and letters of protest appeared in the newspapers condemning the consortium, America's role as a member, and the Lamont mission itself. Sokolsky and others told TWL that the Japanese militarists were behind the plot to destroy the mission's credibility.

T'ang Shao-yi, an ex-premier of China, explained the situation to Lamont: "Since the outbreak of the Great War. . . . China has borrowed no less than two hundred and fifty million dollars silver from Japan. What has been done with this vast sum of money?" Nothing constructive. It had gone into the pockets of the very same people who were vociferously opposing the new consortium.

"These men have developed an appetite for Japanese money and are looking for more," said the ex-premier. "When they hear that the new Consortium will lend money only for constructive purposes and will insist that the money be spent for such purposes, they naturally oppose the Consortium from the bottom of their hearts. These men are being backed by a certain element in Japan. Thus they are enabled to buy up newspapers and start propaganda in opposition to the new Consortium, but not for a moment do they really represent our Chinese public opinion."

Lamont defended the consortium at luncheons and conferences organized by businessmen and the local press, in letters to newspapers, and in private conversations with leading citizens and government officials. One day he called on Dr. Sun Yat-sen, the leader of the Nationalist Party, or Kuomintang, at his villa. Sun described the calamitous division between North and South China and observed that the Southern regime was based on democratic processes, which could not be said for the

North. At the time, the Peking government and much of China was dominated by the venal warlords, and Sun Yat-sen's obsession was to unify China—by force if necessary. But as Lamont had already observed, "democratic processes" played little part in the corrupt Kuomintang administration in the South controlled by Sun.

"President Wilson asked me," Lamont said, "to find out whether there was any way to bring peace between the South and North so that, joined together, the two governments could make proper disposition of the Tuchuns, or War Lords, that ravage and bleed the intervening country and leave all China in turmoil."

"Peace between the South and North?" asked Dr. Sun. "Why yes. Just you give me $25,000,000, Mr. Lamont, and I'll equip a couple of army corps. Then we'll have peace in short order."

This answer from a man who professed dedication to peaceful and democratic leadership did not bode well for China's future, TWL concluded.

On April 6 the Lamont party entrained for Peking, Tom and Florence in their own private car. A host of Kuomintang officials saw them off at the station, warning them not to be taken in by their antagonists in the north. Lamont thought he had made progress in Shanghai in gaining acceptance of the consortium, but criticism by the Japanese-controlled press was relentless. TWL's anger at the Japanese effort to undermine the consortium was exacerbated by the dogged presence of two Japanese agents assigned to spy on the mission. Clumsy in disguising their roles, they were easily spotted by mission members on the train, as were their replacements later on. Harmless but annoying, they took up residence at the Grand Hotel in Peking with the Lamonts for three weeks and then followed the party on the final leg of its Chinese excursion back to Tokyo. (Their presence was a mild nuisance: it forced the Lamont party to take special precautions in guarding the Morgan firm's secret code book for sending and deciphering the flow of cables between the bank and the mission. Lamont later asked a Japanese official in Tokyo about his uninvited escorts in China. The functionary apologized profusely, explaining that the surveillance was a routine practice of the secret service. He begged TWL not to mention it to the premier, who would be extremely embarrassed.)

Arriving two days later in Peking, the Lamonts were met by a welcoming throng—mainly Chinese government officials each struggling to hand TWL the card of his particular ministry before another could reach his hand. The President of the Republic had assigned TWL an interpreter for his visit to Peking, whom TWL described in his journal:

He was fearfully excited. I thought he would surely have apoplexy. In order to show his fluent English, he would shriek at the top of his lungs. I would express myself mildly as being glad to reach Peking. This *profound* sentiment the interpreter would at once take up, and, by sheer power of voice would still the din in the station, call for attention, and then in Chinese—with many elaborations and flourishes, state, for the edification of the multitude, that Mr. Lamont was glad to reach Peking.

Peking was the seat of the government of the Republic of China, weak and corrupt as it was, and the mission was showered with attention throughout its three-week stay—official and social gatherings sponsored by government ministries, foreign legations, American and English residents of Peking, and even the Harvard Club of North China. One day the Lamonts were guests of President Hsü Shih-ch'ang at the presidential palace. In the course of luncheon, Lamont said: "Mr. President, I hear considerable talk about the possibility of China turning Bolshevik."

"Oh, no, Mr. Lamont," President Hsü responded seriously. "China tried Bolshevism in the eighth and again in the eleventh century. It did not work. She will not try it again."

Just across the table sat the minister of the interior. At a pause in the conversation the minister leaned over to Lamont and in perfect English said, "Can you tell me who is pitching for the Pittsburgh Pirates this year?" As a young man he had attended a technical institute in Pittsburgh. TWL could not oblige him; he didn't follow professional baseball that closely.

Once again TWL met a student delegation. It was keenly interested in the proposed arrangements for the consortium to supervise the expenditures of loans to China. The opponents of the consortium were spreading the rumor that the consortium would oversee the nation's fiscal and monetary policy, that it was really a device to foster control over China's economy.

Lamont vehemently denied these allegations, although the consortium certainly planned to monitor disbursements closely in view of the well-known local proclivities for graft. Moreover, the consortium intended to stipulate the sources of repayment and security of its loans.

The government officials seemed anxious for the consortium to begin operations and welcomed Lamont's suggestion that each Western group station a representative in Peking who would be in close liaison with the Chinese government. However, while it was important to conclude the consortium agreement promptly for political reasons, TWL and his Morgan partners were cool toward making any loans to China in the near future.

A steady stream of cables from 23 Wall Street had followed Lamont on his travels. The limited supply of investment funds in the United States to meet the growing needs of American industry had already resulted in high interest rates for "sound domestics." Aside from market conditions it was highly doubtful that Chinese securities would appeal to American investors because of the substantial political risk.

Lamont fully agreed: China was in political turmoil. While Sun Yatsen's Kuomintang was plotting to seize control of the national government, the powerful warlords, wooed by both regimes, ruled much of the country. Banditry and extortion were rife in many areas beyond the control of government authority. In Lamont's view the consortium should not consider any new loans until the country was unified and a new national parliament formed that would approve the proposed operations of the consortium.

There was another contentious issue between the American bankers and the Chinese government—the payment of interest coupons on the German share of the 1911 Hukuang Railway bonds, about a quarter of the $30 million issue. When China had declared war on Germany in 1917, she had repudiated the bonds sold to Germans, now subjects of an enemy country, in keeping with international practice. However, many of the bonds purchased originally in Germany had later been sold to American investors, who were angry about not receiving interest payments at both the Chinese and the American bankers who had handled these sales. The Chinese agreed to pay interest to Americans who could prove they had owned the bonds prior to their repudiation, but this validation process would be cumbersome and time-consuming. J. P. Morgan & Co., a paying agent for the loan in the United States, had pressed for full payment of the German bond coupons for months, and Morgan reiterated this position in a cable to TWL: It would be impossible to issue Chinese securities in the American market "unless the government restores complete prewar status to all coupons Hukuang loan." Refusal to pay the interest coupons seriously harmed the credit standing of the Chinese government in the U.S.

Lamont argued this line vigorously in his talks with government officials, but the Chinese cabinet was equally determined not to yield on the matter. In the spring of 1920 the Morgan partners did not want to organize a loan to China because of her shaky creditworthiness. Uncompromising insistence on payment of the Hukuang interest proved a handy means of avoiding consideration of a new Chinese loan.

Political and financial complexities aside, Tom and Florence were enchanted by Peking, as he related in his journal of the trip.

> What is the most beautiful city in the world? Paris, Florence, Rome, Vienna, London, New York? Peking surpasses them all, in a way that I cannot attempt to define. Its loveliness does not rest chiefly in its temples, though the Temple of Heaven in form and coloring is bewildering in its beauty. Does it lie in the Forbidden City, that magnificent cradle of the ancient Manchu dynasties? Or in the old crooked streets that at almost every turn may disclose the walls of a lovely palace that lies hidden and mysterious within? Or does the charm come from the night sounds of the city, the dull tolling of the bells in the Buddhist temples, or in the subdued chatter of the rickshaw boys playing at fan-tan below?

The Lamonts were indefatigable sightseers, and the whole party made the traditional pilgrimage by special train to the Great Wall. Tom and Florence climbed one of the watchtowers to behold a glorious panorama which he described in his journal.

> Winding like a great and impassive serpent for hundreds of miles up and down over the countryside, hill, dale and mountain, the massiveness and permanence of the Great Wall were what struck us most. Through a breach in the Wall where we reached it there was slowly stalking a caravan train of camels laden with furs and rugs, hailing from I know not where beyond the wild Mongolian country, but, as always, following the ancient route of the caravans, and for part of the distance, of Marco Polo himself. This was the China of the ancient of days, ever changing, yet ever the same.

The entry in Florence's diary for April 14 states: "All I can remember of Wednesday is that it was a debauch of shopping, starting in the morning with Mrs. Dan and Mrs. Atherton at a fur shop." Florence had determined to return home ladened with oriental treasures, and the word quickly spread. Each morning local merchants led their heavily burdened donkeys into the hotel courtyard, there to unload and display magnificent bolts of silk, furs, and rugs. The city shopkeepers also made sure that the Lamonts were exposed to their best and most expensive porcelain, jade, and jewelry. In Japan Florence had filled several crates with her purchases—gold-leafed screens, lovely lacquer bowls and trays, brocaded robes, and antique porcelain teacups and vases. In Peking she added to her hoard of riches: jade beads, mandarin embroideries, sable fur wraps, ivory figures, and antique jewelry. The Lamonts bought two red lacquer trunks to carry home their "plunder," in Florence's words. Her final Peking diary entry read: "My last day. Tom and I shopped the length of Jade Street in the afternoon."

Case Closed

Meanwhile the Japanese government had renewed its bargaining for the exclusive right to undertake railway projects in Manchuria. But Lamont was no longer interested in negotiating with the Japanese. In his view a deal had been struck when he left Japan at the end of March, and the discussion should not be reopened. The barrage of anti-consortium propaganda in China launched by the Japanese-controlled press had hardened his disdain for the sinister military group and its scheming to increase its influence over Chinese affairs. TWL urged the State Department to stand fast, even if Japan decided not to join the consortium. The American and British governments rejected the latest Japanese proposal, but neither the State Department nor J. P. Morgan, representing the American group, had any enthusiasm for moving forward without the Japanese; the Americans fervently hoped that they would yield on the matter.

On April 29, Jeremiah Smith, Jr., counsel to the mission, left Peking for Tokyo in order to prepare the banking group letters of agreement for signing. The Lamont party got ready to follow, and TWL issued a statement to the press. His visit had confirmed his belief in the integrity and industry of the Chinese people and marked the first step on behalf of the international banking groups in investigating and planning how they might assist China.

> The situation here is so complex and so important that . . . its study and development must be matters not for a day, but for a patient future that, I trust, may be marked with cordial cooperating between the Chinese people and that great body of investors of the western world which the Banking Groups now represent.

Lamont did not intend to give the Chinese any reasons to expect that consortium loans would be quickly forthcoming.

On May 1, the Lamonts attended their last engagement in Peking, a reception, ironically enough, at the Japanese Legation. They left that evening by train, traversing Manchuria before heading south down the Korean peninsula to Fusan. On May 5, they crossed the Korean Strait by steamer and reached Tokyo by train two days later.

The Japanese had backed off. They now stated that they had received adequate general assurances from the Western consortium members regarding their appreciation of Japan's special economic interests in Manchuria, where several Japanese railway projects were underway. On May 13, the Japanese banking group held a dinner in Lamont's honor at the Tokyo Bankers Club. It was announced that the exchange of notes between the Japanese and the Western banking groups had taken place, and Japan would become a member of the Chinese consortium on the same terms as the other members.

In his remarks Lamont expressed his pleasure at the successful conclusion of the consortium agreement. But he also had a message of warning for his audience of bankers and businessmen. From his visit to China he knew that the Chinese feared Japanese domination, and there was, indeed, growing apprehension among Western nations about the expansionist policy of the Japanese militarists in China, Korea, and Siberia. Their aggressive methods were alienating the West, which had just fought a war to defeat Prussian militarism. Their activities drained Japan's limited fiscal resources and jeopardized her chances to secure capital from the United States. "The essence of every true partnership is equality—equality of opportunity, equality of responsibility, and especially equality of trust and confidence."

Lamont smilingly received the tributes of the Japanese bankers. The president of the Yokahama Species Bank saluted him in completing the formation of the new Chinese consortium, and Governor Inouye, the head of the Japanese banking group, offered a toast: "I propose the health of Mr. Lamont, congratulating him on the success of his most important mission."

The following evening from the deck of the *Korea Maru* bound for Honolulu the Lamonts gazed for the last time at the beautiful snow-clad peak of Mt. Fujiyama in the setting sun.

The warm reception Lamont received in Honolulu, where he gave a talk to a large Chamber of Commerce gathering, was a forerunner of events to follow. The Lamonts arrived in San Francisco on May 30, and TWL addressed a luncheon of several hundred people at the Commonwealth Club the next day. As a senior Morgan partner and recognized figure in public affairs, his views commanded attention. Lamont had successfully concluded a complex and difficult negotiation with the Japanese: the four-power Chinese consortium was now a fact, with preparations underway for the formal conference to ratify the final documents. Washington and the other Western capitals were delighted with the accord that would place restraints on unilateral Japanese expansion in China. The *New York Times* hailed the Lamont mission as "a triumph," a world settlement of major import. A letter from Ambassador Roland Morris especially pleased TWL. "It is the considered judgement of those in Japan in a position to know that you have played 'an errorless game.' I do so admire a piece of work well done," wrote the ambassador.

TWL was now viewed as an "expert" on Far Eastern affairs, and over the coming months he accepted numerous invitations to speak or contribute articles on the subject. He wrote a report on his mission for the *New York Evening Post,* which distributed it to four hundred newspapers throughout the country; it received wide coverage and favorable comment.

By the fall of 1920, it was apparent that China had suffered a third successive year of drought, and the famine that had threatened when Lamont was in Peking became a dreadful reality, with 15 million people reportedly starving. China asked for America's help, and President Wilson appointed Lamont chairman of the Chinese Famine Committee to raise funds for relief. TWL made a number of speeches, helping to raise $8 million for the cause.

Lamont cleared his speeches and articles with the State Department, usually with his friend Norman Davis, now Under Secretary. His public utterances, especially his appeals for famine relief funds, were more glowing about China's prospects than his official reports to the consortium members and the State Department. In these confidential accounts he acknowledged the corruptness and inefficiency of the Chinese government and the bitter political division in the country. In his view the consortium should not undertake new loans to China until the Northern and Southern factions had reconciled their differences and formed a new national parliament and government, which should then approve the proposed operations of the consortium. Second, China must resume interest payments on the Hukuang Railway bonds issued in Germany.

In his speeches about China, Japan, and the consortium, Lamont praised the personal qualities of the Chinese people—their intellect, charm, character, and industry—"four hundred million kindly, honest, highly intelligent people." But the government was weak and incompetent, and the Chinese economy, largely agrarian, was desperately poor. The lack of railway transportation was a major obstacle to growth. China presented a huge market for American capital goods—railway equipment and bridges; agricultural, textile, and mining machinery; and machine tools.

In his talk to the Academy of Political Science at its annual dinner, Lamont said of the Chinese:

They have enormous dynamic force. When we consider how, until nine years ago, they were ruled under an absolute monarchy; when we consider how archaic were their conditions of government, then, indeed, we must be amazed, not because their present government is imperfect, but because the new republic has advanced as far as it has in stability and in administration. We read of disorganized conditions in China, and yet when we are there we feel that it is the safest place in the world. In Peking an American woman can take a rickshaw and jog through the native city, long after midnight, unescorted, alone and yet unafraid. I should feel her much safer there than on the east side of New York City.

Lamont's remarks about Japan lacked his visionary enthusiasm for China. He pointed out that despite "the cleverness of its people" the country was still undeveloped. The nation's leaders were divided into two schools of thought: the liberal-minded men of affairs—bankers, merchants, and manufacturers—and the so-called military party committed to aggressive overseas expansion in East Asia. The militarists, led by the General Staff, were spending huge sums to build up the army and navy, which Japan could ill afford. The Japanese must do away with this tendency toward imperialism. Japan's leaders were eager to modernize the country; however, agricultural development was restricted by the limited land available for cultivation. "Therefore, Japan must become a strong industrial nation and one exporting manufactured goods. To reach this point of attainment she greatly desires American capital, materials, and cooperation," Lamont told the Academy of Political Science audience.

In his speech to the American Manufacturers' Export Association, TWL described the huge market for American goods in the Far East, concluding majestically:

Your operations should be carried out in a spirit of generous tolerance so as to enhance throughout the world the name of America for fair and constructive methods of enterprise. You indeed are among those to whom the gods have granted the opportunity to make "America First"—first not in her own mere safety or freedom from the troubles of a war-torn world, but first, in the eyes of the world, because of her friendliness and helpfulness to the other nations of the earth.

While Lamont had not followed in his father's footsteps as a preacher of the gospel, making use of the "bully pulpit" to sermonize on business morality came easily to him.

On September 16 as Lamont was preparing for an October meeting of the consortium members in New York, a devastating explosion rocked the financial district. A bomb placed in a horse-drawn wagon on Wall Street outside the Morgan bank had been detonated about noon when the street was thronged with office workers on their lunch hour. The blast killed thirty people and wounded many more. The interior of the Morgan banking floor was wrecked, two employees were killed, and more were injured. Morgan's son, Junius, who had recently been made a partner, had been cut by shards of flying glass, but not seriously. Lamont, attending a meeting in his second-floor office overlooking Broad Street, was out of harm's way. Many charged that it was a Bolshevik attack on the headquarters of capitalism, but the perpetrators were never uncovered. The Morgan offices were repaired by the time of the consortium conference, although the scars on the bank's outside wall were grim reminders to the visiting bankers of the bloody and senseless act.

The national banking groups representing the four member countries of the Chinese consortium gathered in New York in mid-October to review and ratify the final consortium agreement. There were nine foreign representatives and dozens of American bankers in attendance. Lamont presided over the meetings and gave a dinner at the Links Club for the visitors. The next day Junius Morgan gave a reception at the Morgan Library, and TWL cabled his father, on his annual fall trip to Europe, that his son had done a first-class job standing in for him. On October 15, the official signing of the agreement of the Consortium for the Assistance of China took place at the New York Chamber of Commerce, followed by a formal banquet at the Metropolitan Club.

Lamont wrote his son Tommy: "We finally signed up and are now ready for business, but whether the conditions will enable us to do business . . . I am doubtful." Lamont and his consortium banking colleagues did not think the time was ripe for making loans to China, and, as recommended by TWL, turned down two American-sponsored proposals favored by the State Department during the next few months.

Some credited Lamont's patience and amiability throughout the protracted negotiations as the key to the successful establishment of the consortium. His counselor on the Far East mission, Jeremiah Smith, Jr., said, "He simply outsmiled the Japanese."

The British banking group gave a dinner at the Reform Club for Lamont when he was visiting London the following spring, and Sir Charles Addis, chairman of the Hong Kong and Shanghai Banking Corporation, paid tribute to the guest of honor. Referring to the negotiations in Japan, he said that it was "before Thomas Lamont's compulsive smile that the militarist party laid down their arms without firing a shot.

He went to China, and the representatives of young China, who had come to throw stones, remained to drink tea in the sunshine of that smile. We met him in New York as the president of the conference, and before the genial rays of his smile doubts and difficulties vanished." Solid preparation and unrelenting charm were TWL's chief negotiating tools.

The Republicans Take Over

In June 1920, Lamont had stopped off in Chicago, on the way back to New York from San Francisco, to attend the Republican national convention for a few days. He personally admired Herbert Hoover and was disappointed that he had not emerged as a strong candidate. TWL went to one session and found the proceedings uninspiring. When he left, the balloting for the presidential nomination was heading toward a deadlock between General Leonard Wood and Governor Frank O. Lowden of Illinois. Two days later the Republican leaders emerged in the early morning hours from their caucus in the famous "smoke-filled room" to announce that they had chosen Senator Warren G. Harding of Ohio to be the Republican nominee.

Harding's Senate record had been conventionally Republican and conservative. TWL was not keen about the selection, and the candidate, campaigning from his front porch in Marion, Ohio, said nothing to ignite Lamont's enthusiasm.

Lamont thought that American membership in the League of Nations was the overriding issue of the campaign. In his speech accepting the nomination, Harding seemed to favor scrapping the whole League plan and starting afresh with a vague new design for an international association of nations. His stand remained obscure throughout the campaign. Edwin Gay, the president of the *New York Evening Post,* interviewed the candidate in Marion and came away no wiser.

On August 23, Lamont wrote Senator Harding to express his views on the League of Nations. He strongly supported approval of the treaty and the League Covenant with the Lodge reservations, and he condemned President Wilson for rejecting this compromise solution. Furthermore,

TWL was sure the other member nations would accept the reservations. While the election support of the *Post* did not rest in his hands, "As a life-long Republican I am bound to tell you that you are making it exceedingly difficult for papers like the Evening Post and for hundreds of thousands of loyal Republicans to come strongly to your support. . . . There is only one way out—the course the Republican Senate voted for all last year: the ratification of the Treaty and League with proper reservations." If Harding came out in support of this course of action, "You will gain thousands of votes that otherwise surely will be lost to you."

The Democrats had chosen Governor James M. Cox of Ohio as their presidential candidate and Franklin D. Roosevelt, the Assistant Secretary of Navy, as his running mate. Cox strongly supported American entry into the League of Nations. Shortly before the election, Lamont, disillusioned with Harding's campaign position on the League, wrote a letter to the *New York Evening Post* supporting its decision to back Cox and Roosevelt.

> My chief reason is, of course, that Cox is for the League of Nations and Harding is against it. The League is admittedly not perfect. But it is the most practicable instrument yet offered for the prevention of future wars. . . .
>
> Shall America, having taken her place in the war as champion of the weaker nations of the earth; shall America, having played her noble part in heroism and sacrifice, now take up the ignoble role of aloofness, of timidity, and of selfishness? Shall America, equipped in intellectual power and material resource to lead a world, now turn her back and, with clouded vision, reject that moral leadership which the lesser nations of the earth entreat her to assume?
>
> There is a call upon America to render high service to the world and to herself. To this call Harding answers No, let us turn back. Cox answers Yes, let us go forward. This is why I vote for Cox.

Lamont's conviction that the United States must assume the mantle of leadership in world affairs had led him to break with his party and Republican business friends and cast his first vote for a Democratic presidential candidate, even though he expected Cox would lose the election. He was right: out of 25,300,000 votes cast, the Republicans won overwhelmingly by 7 million votes, and the completeness of the victory surprised TWL. Nevertheless, he would continue to fight for the League of Nations and so would the *Evening Post*.

However, it was distressingly expensive to own the newspaper, TWL confided to his son Tommy. The losses during 1920 alone, which TWL had to fund, came to over $500,000, and he was beginning to question whether he could reverse the paper's debilitating financial drain.

Florence continued to chronicle the highlights of the Lamonts' social life in her letters to the children. She and Tom attended a gala dinner organized by Harry and Katherine Davison in the ballroom of the Waldorf-Astoria hotel to welcome the Prince of Wales to New York. To the accompaniment of a slow march, a parade of notables, including Elihu Root and General Pershing, walked down the aisle between the tables, followed by the Davisons on either side of the Prince. "Everybody who was anybody in New York was there all dressed up fit to kill," Florence wrote. "The little Prince made an awfully good speech, very boyish, but it won all hearts: New York's skyscrapers were so 'splendid,' his reception had been 'splendid,' he was having a 'splendid' time, etc. But everybody loved his speech, because he seemed like such a nice little boy." The "nice little boy," then age twenty-six, also enjoyed a good party, often into the wee hours of the night.

The next evening Florence attended a ball given by Mrs. Whitelaw Reid at her home to honor the Prince. "It was very, very grand, the most elaborate party I have ever attended. The little Prince danced with all the fluttering 'debs,' made love to all the pretty ones, and was very dignified and prince-like with all the plain ones."

Florence had joined a committee organized by Herbert Hoover to raise funds for the starving children of Central Europe. Lamont still headed the Chinese Famine Committee. "It is going to be hard to raise the money, for everyone seems to be feeling a bit poor," Florence wrote. Meanwhile the Lamonts were dining sumptuously at the homes of New York's prominent and affluent families, such as the Pratts and the Rockefellers. "Huge house, heaps of jewels, too much to eat," Florence reported. "It is horrible to go to dinners like that while ten dollars will save a child from starvation until the next harvest. And yet who am I to throw stones? There is our big house being built on 70th Street."

Florence also reported the Lamonts' lunch in February 1921 with President and Mrs. Wilson at the White House. President Wilson told some amusing stories and, though frail and lame, seemed in good spirits. It was a brave front: everyone knew that Harding's overwhelming victory, which drowned all Wilson's hopes for reviving political support for his cherished League, was a bitter disappointment to the president. Mrs. Wilson took Florence on a tour of the presidential mansion, which the Wilsons would be leaving in just a month to make way for the new tenants.

* * *

Even though Lamont had not supported Harding's candidacy, the senator was soon seeking his advice on the international debt situation. After a visit with the president-elect Lamont wrote his son Austin that he found him "a simple, kindly, likable soul. . . . But his talk about the League of Nations was discouraging." A congenial politician had been propelled by the party bosses into the nation's highest office, which bore responsibilities well beyond the limits of his capacity.

Lamont had told Harding that no secret agreements had been made at the Paris Peace Conference regarding the cancellation of Allied war debt owed the United States. In February 1921 the Wilson administration sought Senate approval of the plan agreed at the peace conference to substitute German government reparations bonds for the Belgian war debt owed to Great Britain, France, and the United States. Senator Harding announced to the press that he was "shocked" at the news of this agreement, which he felt contradicted what Lamont had told him. In his letter of February 24 to Harding, TWL explained that there was nothing secret about the agreement, which had been announced and publicly discussed at the conclusion of the peace conference. Furthermore, no debt was being cancelled. Harding was satisfied with TWL's explanation, and the Senate, running true to form, rejected Wilson's proposal anyway.

But the Allies' problem in repaying the huge war debt to the U.S. was not about to fade away, and soon after his inauguration President Harding invited Lamont to the White House to discuss the question again. TWL described the scene later. "When I went in he was sitting rather gloomily at his flat-topped desk with a disarray of letters on one side of it. The President greeted me cordially, but said almost at once and with weariness in his voice, 'Lamont, this job is just too much for me. Whatever shall I do with all that pile?' He gave a deep sigh as if he did not know just how to tackle the job, and then said, 'Well, I suppose I might as well try to learn something about these debts.' "

Later Lamont observed that Harding was "a pathetic figure, the last man in the world to lead 120 million people from the darkness and confusion of World War I out into the light."

In his talk with the president and later with Secretary of State Charles Evans Hughes, TWL disparaged the idea being advanced by anti-League Republicans that the United States enter into a separate peace treaty with Germany. "Economically, morally, financially, politically, and in every other way, such a step would, I think, be disastrous," said TWL. But as time passed the proposal won growing support in the White House and Senate.

In April the Lamonts sailed for Europe on the S.S. *Adriatic*. Lamont felt that it was important to see his London and Paris partners and inform himself on the spot about the prospects for new loans in the turbulent European political and economic climate. After the war J. P. Morgan & Co. had quickly solidified its position as the premier world bank in organizing huge loans to foreign governments for reconstruction and development. The postwar wave of large American loans led by the Morgan bank had begun with a $250 million convertible gold bond issue of the United Kingdom in October 1919. In September 1920, a twenty-five-year 8 percent gold loan of $100 million was floated for the French government, and in May 1921, Morgan led another French government bond issue of the same amount. While Tom worked on the new loan, Florence shopped for furnishings for the new house, in Paris and in London, where John Masefield took her to see *Othello* performed at the Royal Court Theater.

Upon their return home Tom and Florence attended Tommy's graduation exercises at Harvard. Like his father he had been president of the *Crimson* and had also been elected permanent class secretary and vice president of the Student Council. A year at Cambridge University in England beginning in September would round out his education. Intelligent and popular, Tommy appeared content to travel down the smooth road built by his successful father, a journey that would begin far less stressfully than TWL's early days in business.

Harry Davison had been suffering from increasingly severe and frequent headaches for over a year, a malady that had incapacitated him for an active business life. Retiring to more restful living at Peacock Point and his beloved Magnolia Plantation near Thomasville, Georgia, Davison received a stream of guests, including the Lamonts, whose daily quail shooting he planned with infectious enthusiasm. By the spring of 1921 the patient's condition was worsening. In August the surgeons performed an exploratory operation: Davison had a brain tumor that could not be removed. The operation had brought some relief, which the Davisons and their friends knew was only temporary. The news was a blow to the Lamonts, who had been devoted friends of the Davisons since the early days in Englewood.

In August the United States signed a separate peace treaty with Germany. Lamont shuttled between his office and Sky Farm, the family's new summer home on North Haven, and when the Lamonts finally returned to New York they did not stay put long. On September 30, TWL's fifty-first birthday, they departed by train for San Antonio, Texas, and Mexico City. Lamont, as chairman of the International Committee of Bankers for Adjustment of Mexican Foreign Debt, had been invited to the Mexican capital for discussions with the government. His good friend Jerry Smith accompanied him again as his counselor.

The Mexican Debt Dilemma

The Mexican Revolution had begun in 1911 with the overthrow of Porfirio Díaz, the country's military dictator for the last three decades. The revolutionary forces declared Francisco Madero president, but in 1913 he was deposed by General Victoriano Huerta in the continuing and bloody struggle for power. In the wake of political turbulence and mounting xenophobia, the Mexican government stopped interest and sinking-fund payments on its external debt in 1913, following the coup. This debt, represented by various bond issues held by some 200,000 American and European investors, totaled about $500 million in various currencies, of which almost half represented loans to the National Railways. In addition, the accumulated unpaid interest owed foreign bondholders had mounted to $200 million by 1921. Most of the debt was secured by liens on specific revenues of properties and equipment.

Mexico was wracked by successive revolutions after 1913 as the central thrust of government policy moved more and more to the left against the so-called plutocrats—the big landowners and foreign investors. Article 27 of the 1917 constitution reflected the new nationalistic attitude. It provided for the national ownership not only of all land, but also of all subsoil deposits—minerals and oil. The U.S. government took a dim view of this article and was firmly opposed to its retroactive application, given the extensive American petroleum interests in Mexico. New foreign investment was at a standstill.

In 1919, with the Great War over, the Mexican government realized that the foreign bondholders would have to be accommodated before international investors would consider making badly needed new loans to Mexico. In March an emissary from Mexican president Venustiano Carranza called on J. P. Morgan and his partners to seek their views on how to proceed. The Morgan bank had been a co-manager of Mexican government issues in the prewar period, collaborating with several European investment houses, and was eager for restoration of debt service payments. The first step was to establish an international committee of bankers to represent the foreign holders of Mexican debt. Morgan cabled Lamont in Paris, where he was serving on the American delegation to the peace conference, and TWL promptly convened a meeting of British and French bankers to discuss the problem and organize the new committee. TWL was elected chairman of the committee, which was later enlarged to include Belgian, Dutch, and Swiss members, whose nationals also held substantial amounts of defaulted Mexican bonds.

Over the next two years, the State Department pressed hard for the Mexican government to renounce any retroactive application of Article 27, with special concern for the large investment at stake in Mexico of American oil companies—some $300 million. America would not grant recognition to the new Mexican government until this interpretation of the article was forthcoming. Mexican president Álvaro Obregón, who had deposed Carranza, would not oblige, and the United States, with Great Britain following its lead, withheld recognition.

The Morgan bank followed the practice of informing the State Department of prospective foreign-loan operations and did so again. The International Committee of Bankers was eager to start negotiations with the Mexican government for the resumption of Mexican debt service payments to foreign investors, but Under Secretary Norman Davis advised Lamont against such a move. It might encourage the Mexicans in their resistance to the American wishes regarding Article 27.

In February 1921, Lamont received a letter from the Mexican government inviting him to Mexico City to discuss the external debt problem, which TWL reported to the new Secretary of State, Charles Evans Hughes, and Under Secretary Henry P. Fletcher. However, the Harding administration stuck to the policy of its predecessors: the time was not propitious for such a mission.

On his trip to Paris in May, Lamont met with the bankers' committee, which urged him to accept the Mexican invitation and proceed to Mexico City as soon as possible. The Obregón administration had stated that it would honor the debts contracted by previous Mexican governments, and it was only fair to the foreign bondholders, who had forgone interest payments for nine years, to pursue this initiative without delay. TWL told the State Department that he contemplated making the trip in the fall and would try to persuade the Mexicans to accommodate the American viewpoint regarding Article 27.

On June 30, Lamont wrote President Obregón that he had been authorized by the International Committee to proceed to Mexico City, "subject, however, to any announced action or declaration by the Mexican Congress, or by any other body authorized in the premises, to the effect that Article 27 of the so-called Carranza constitution shall not be construed as being retroactive."

The Mexican reply of July 25 urged Lamont to come to Mexico City as soon as possible; it made no mention of the Article 27 issue. TWL decided to go anyway, and he met with Secretary Hughes, who now agreed that he should undertake the mission. The United States would continue to withhold official recognition of the Mexican government until it acted to protect the rights of foreign investors in Mexico, and Lamont might help achieve this goal. Lamont told Secretary Hughes that he was sure that bankers in America and Great Britain would not make new loans to Mexico until their governments had recognized the Mexican government.

The New York and Mexican newspapers announced the arrival of the Lamont mission in Mexico City on October 5. Florence was exhausted by the trip from San Antonio over the bumpiest roadbed she had ever traveled. However, a few days in the delightful sunny climate lifted her spirits, and she was soon touring the local sights such as the Aztec pyramids and floating gardens of Xochimilco.

Florence and Tom were impressed by Obregón, who had become president in 1920 after joining a successful revolt against President Carranza, who was killed. His means of accession to office was not uncommon over the last decade of Mexican politics: General Carranza had overthrown President Huerta to seize the presidency; General Huerta had taken office after engineering a coup to topple President Madero, who was assassinated. Mexico's current strongman had paid his dues in battle during the revolution, losing his right arm, which had been shattered by an exploding grenade. Obregón was much admired and also feared by many of his countrymen.

One evening Florence was the president's dinner partner at an official affair honoring the Lamont mission. "He is a frank, pleasant-looking, red-faced brigand, and I rather liked him," she wrote her family. "He has lots of dash and verve and life, although I shouldn't think he has much mentality." Perhaps not, according to the standards of the high-brow Smith alumna, but the black-mustachioed caudillo had demonstrated considerable political and military skill in the rough-and-tumble pursuit for power in governing Mexico.

Lamont also liked Obregón's bluff directness and wit. When TWL was first ushered into his private office, the president called out to an attendant: "Bring whiskey, wine, liqueurs! At last, Mr. Lamont you are in a free country," he stated with a beaming smile, referring to the legal prohibition against the sale of spirits in the United States. TWL noted that the president's desk and chair were placed in the middle of the huge room that had a resounding hardwood floor, enabling him, the president genially explained, to hear the stealthiest approach from any quarter. TWL wrote later that "of all the heads that ever wore a crown, his was one of the uneasiest."

Lamont's talk to the American Chamber of Commerce in Mexico City presented a blissful picture of relations between the two nations once Mexico's policy for the just and generous treatment of foreign investors was made manifest:

> All cause for misunderstanding between these two sister Republics will have been removed once and for all. Indeed, as neighbors and as friends, with our boundaries marching together for almost 2,000 miles with every inducement for the increase of trade intercourse, we can count for generations to come upon undisturbed harmony and good will, upon the growing and abundant prosperity in both our lands, and, finally . . . upon that increasing understanding and mutual sympathy that will render as an ideal for the rest of the world the close friendship and solidarity existing between America and Mexico.

However, Lamont's talks with Finance Minister Adolfo de la Huerta, while cordial, were getting nowhere. Under the minister's scheme for retiring Mexico's foreign debt, the government would continue to refrain from paying interest on the debt, using the funds instead to purchase outstanding bonds, which were selling at a fraction of par value. By withholding interest payments the bond prices would remain at a depressed level, enabling the bonds to be bought up cheaply.

De la Huerta hoped to enlist the services of the foreign banks in buying up these bonds. "Why don't you get your customers to turn them in at low prices? For instance, Mr. Lamont, you buy them from your customers at forty cents and sell them to us at fifty cents on the dollar, making the ten cents profit. Also, as time goes on, we will deposit with your firm in New York large sums of money with which to make these purchases."

Lamont rejected the plan out of hand and attempted to explain to de la Huerta the fiduciary relationship the banks had with bondholders, who looked to them to protect their interests. De la Huerta appeared not to understand and persisted in arguing for his scheme. When Lamont realized that further talks were futile, he told de la Huerta he must break off their discussions and return home. Nor would TWL join the minister in a press announcement that the talks had made progress. Lamont issued his own statement.

> A full conference with the Mexican government has failed to result in substantial agreement upon any plan. I am therefore returning to New York to make a full report to the other sections of the International Committee.

Lamont sent a more candid report to his partners, and Morgan cabled a reply: "Congratulate you on getting out before they stole your pocket-book or watch. Congratulations on unmasking the villains."

Lamont's own assessment of the Mexican officials was more charitable. They lacked experience in finance and simply did not understand the importance of honoring financial commitments. De la Huerta, TWL told his friends, had started his career as a cabaret singer.

On the other hand, TWL was shocked by the reports he had heard of pervasive corruption at all levels of government. One Mexican gentleman, in describing the supreme court to TWL, listed the eleven judges and the sums for which each could be "bought"; the three who were honest he referred to as "suckers."

There were other villains afoot in Mexico. The departure of the Lamont group from the capital had been set in advance on a train leaving October 23. Finishing his financial talks earlier than expected, Lamont, without announcing the schedule change, arranged to have his private car attached to another San Antonio-bound train leaving two days earlier. Upon arrival in San Antonio the Lamonts learned that the train on which they were originally scheduled to depart had been held up and wrecked by bandits as it was running through a wilderness area. Later the outlaws were captured and confessed that they had intended to kidnap Mr. Lamont and hold him in a mountain hideaway for ransom—five hundred thousand gold pesos.

The Lamonts, and especially Florence, who had picked up an intestinal bug in Mexico, were glad to be home. The time had come to move into their handsome new residence at 107 East 70th Street. Designed by the firm of Walker and Gillete, the four-story brick and stone dwelling was an architectural tour de force. Built in the Jacobean style, it had lofty twin gables, clustered chimneys of hand-cut bricks, leaded casement and mullioned windows, a walled garden and cloister, and an entrance framed with ornamental carvings.

The final construction cost was $615,000, and Florence and the decorators still had much work ahead in furnishing the spacious residence. For the main hallway, where the stairs ascended behind an antique English oak screen, they selected a fifteenth-century French Gothic tapestry, woven in Touraine, which depicted Old Testament scenes of Moses and the pharoah.

Florence already had a poor impression of her former landlord, Franklin Roosevelt. The Lamonts had recently dined with the Roosevelts at the home of Franklin's mother next door. Florence, who sat next to Franklin, wrote Austin: "He seemed to have rather a poor opinion of women. I mean I am used to having men talk to me about interesting affairs as if I were a man, too, and he didn't." Florence wasn't kidding. It was known that she would much rather join the gentlemen after dinner if given the choice. Now another incident involving the Roosevelts further aggravated Florence.

The Masefields had introduced the Lamonts to H. G. Wells, and it happened that he became their first houseguest on 70th Street. Not knowing the Lamonts had moved, Wells went first to the 65th Street house, now reoccupied by the Franklin Roosevelts. Wells reported that "the colored caretaker" who answered the doorbell was quite brusque with him, slamming the door in his face without telling him the Lamonts' new address. Florence wrote Eleanor Roosevelt, suggesting that her staff treat the Lamonts' friends who might make the same mistake with more respect in the future.

After a string of popular novels, Wells had produced *The Outline of History* in 1920. His fertile intellect bubbled over with ideas on socialism, world peace, and the like; he was a dynamic conversationalist. Florence had mixed feelings about the visit of her distinguished guest. It was "exciting and stimulating having him here," she wrote Austin. But she was not feeling in top form. The Lamonts gave dinners and teas in Wells's honor, and she became quite tired. "It is hard to try to be your best every minute and my mind got desperately dull. . . . This talking to great men when you are having a Mexican germ in your tummy isn't all it's cracked up to be. I was far from brilliant, I assure you."

Tommy's parents wrote him in England about the family's Christmas celebration. His mother observed that "it has grown to be such an orgy of tissue paper, red ribbon, and relatives that the real spirit of it somehow manages to escape." His father added, "H. G. Wells, who seems to have become a sort of permanent guest of ours, was with us, and after the evening dinner he took a very active and successful part in the charades. I think he is even better at charades than he is at novel writing."

* * *

Lamont was now personally soliciting corporate advertising for the *Evening Post* from executive officers he knew. It was a demeaning and inappropriate task for a Morgan partner, but TWL felt impelled to do something to help stem the tide of the paper's losses he was funding. The deficits were getting bigger—about $700,000 in 1921. Late in the year Frank A. Munsey, the publisher of the *New York Evening Sun* and other papers, called to set up a meeting with Lamont. Over lunch, Munsey came quickly to the point: he was willing to buy the *Evening Post* from Lamont for $1,750,000—$250,000 cash and the balance to be paid in six annual installments guaranteed personally by Munsey. While this sum was about $1 million less than TWL had invested to purchase the paper and keep it going, it was still a fair price.

"What do you plan to do with the property, Frank?" Lamont asked.

"Scrap it at once. Save the AP franchise for one of my other papers, and let it go at that," replied Munsey. The *Evening Sun* might absorb some *Post* features, but the *Post*'s long life as an independent newspaper would be over.

TWL was very tempted to take up the offer, but Ellery Sedgwick and others warned him that he would be sharply criticized if he brought about the demise of the fine old paper founded by Alexander Hamilton in 1801.

Lamont turned down Munsey's offer. He couldn't let the staff go and the *Evening Post* die. But he wanted to rid himself of the newspaper, and in January 1922 he did—to Edwin F. Gay, the *Post* president, and his associates, including Marshall Field, Norman Davis, Franklin D. Roosevelt, and Owen D. Young, chairman of the General Electric Corporation. The Gay group was willing to pay the same price that Munsey had offered, but the terms were far less favorable to Lamont. TWL would receive a $125,000 down payment, $125,000 in two years, and mortgage notes repayable in seven and ten years based on the credit and uncertain prospects of the *Post*.

"But," as TWL wrote his eldest son, "I am very glad to get rid of it and have the responsibility on somebody else. It has been the great disappointment of my life that I have never been able to handle this thing as I hoped."

Tommy had good news for his parents when they returned from their midwinter holiday at Grove Park Inn in Asheville. In March, Thomas S. Lamont and Elinor B. Miner of Rochester, New York, announced their engagement to be married, following their summer romance when both were vacationing at North Haven. Ellie's father, Edward G. Miner, good-natured and erudite, was head of the Pfaudler Company, manufacturer of glass-lined tanks in Rochester, and one of the upstate city's leading citizens. TWL thought that his future daughter-in-law was a vivacious charmer, and her father was a grand fellow.

On March 14, Lamont gave a talk at the Dutch Treat Club in New York on the state of America's relations with Mexico. The threat of confiscation of American property in Mexico had led some to suggest that the United States should intervene to defend the interests of its citizens, an idea that TWL said was "unthinkable."

> I do not think we have any right to go into Mexico in an endeavor to straighten out what are not our affairs and to force our point of view upon the Mexicans. Who are we to say that our civilization is perfect, or to say that the highest type of life and of mind is our type? Who are we in America, who live in the midst of rush and turmoil, who are we to say to the Mexicans that their ideas of ease, even of indolence, of keeping time for reflection, or sweet doing nothingness, of playing with their children during long idle hours, of watching the flowers grow, of sitting in the sun and strumming the zither, who are we I say, to force on these people (who had a civilization of their own centuries before Jamestown or Plymouth) the ideas and pace set by our fast-growing Republic? I, for one, am opposed to any force methods.

Perhaps Lamont was subconsciously yearning for a lazy vacation south of the border, but he also had a solid reason to feel upbeat about Mexico. After considerable procrastination Mexican finance minister de la Huerta had agreed to come to New York in June to discuss a debt settlement. In May, Lamont, Jeremiah Smith, Jr., and Arthur M. Anderson, a Morgan staff member, met with the International Committee in Paris to work out a negotiating position.

Before leaving for Europe, TWL had visited Harry Davison at his Georgia plantation, where Davison had talked freely with his partner and old friend about his failing health. While in Paris the Lamonts received the sad news that Davison had died on May 6, 1922, following surgery. Lamont wrote his eldest son: "In affection, loyalty, thought, and generosity he was almost more than any brother could be. To him, more than to myself almost, am I indebted for any advance that I have made, since upon his insistence in 1903 I left Lamont, Corliss & Co. and entered the organization of the Bankers Trust Company. It is a cruel blow." Davison's death was a great loss for J. P. Morgan & Co. His imagination and leadership had formed the cutting edge of the firm for over a decade. Lamont later wrote in his biography of Davison: "He *did* things. He inspired and led in the doing of other things," and spoke of "the love which we bore and still bear for Harry Davison, a leader and inspiration to us all."

The Lamonts moved on to London later in May, staying at the Hyde Park Hotel, where their room overlooked the great verdant park bright with spring flowers. One Sunday they drove out to Boar's Hill near Oxford to have lunch with their good friends the Masefields; John and Florence had been exchanging gossipy letters for several years. In London, a bevy of British writers—novelists, poets, and playwrights—entertained them. Perhaps John Masefield and H. G. Wells had spread the word of the Lamonts' hospitality to visiting literary luminaries in New York. The H. G. Wellses gave a dinner party for them, as did the St. John Ervines, who took them to see *Loyalties,* the latest John Galsworthy play. The following evening, Galsworthy, whose famous trilogy *The Forsyte Saga* was being published in one-volume form that year, took the Lamonts to see *Loyalties* again. Tom and Florence did a bit of playacting themselves, pretending to their host that they were viewing the drama for the first time.

The talks with Mexican finance minister de la Huerta began on June 2, 1922, in New York and lasted two weeks. Thomas Lamont, as chairman of the International Committee of Bankers, led the negotiations in sessions that were sometimes stormy and tense. Said the *New York Commercial*: "On more than one occasion the Mexican Secretary of Finance had his hat on and was about to leave the conference room. It was only through the tactful work of the chairman, Thomas W. Lamont, that disaster was averted time after time."

The question of paying current interest on the outstanding debt was paramount, and Lamont inquired if Mexico was prepared to resume the payments of about $25 million annually. De la Huerta balked stubbornly at this suggestion: the Mexican government recognized its debts, but could only repay them within its capacity. The revolutionary struggle had unsettled the economy, stalled its growth, and caused a substantial increase in the national debt.

After a long and fruitless exchange, TWL finally asked, "Then the minister wants the negotiations to break down at this point?"

De la Huerta replied, "Yes, I regret it extremely, but I guess I will have to take the single peso on my back and go home."

But a compromise was reached the next day, and the talks continued. Mexico's interest payment in 1923 would be $15 million and would increase by increments to reach $25 million in 1928, with the unpaid portion of current interest payable in twenty years. The Mexican government would set aside all oil export taxes, a special surcharge on gross railway receipts, and railway net income to provide the necessary funds for five years. Sinking fund payments would be postponed for five years and repayment of matured notes for ten years.

The next issue to be settled was the treatment of approximately $200 million in interest arrears on Mexico's foreign debt. The Mexican government, stated de la Huerta, felt that this interest obligation should be waived by the foreign bondholders. The International Committee disagreed but was willing to make substantial concessions. Back interest would be waived on the arrears, which would be retired by payments of $5 million annually beginning in 1928. De la Huerta balked, but finally agreed.

A final thorny question was the future management of the Mexican railways, which had been nationalized by the Carranza government. The bankers believed that the disorganized and inefficient operation of the state-run railways represented a serious impediment to economic growth in Mexico. The finance minister reluctantly agreed that the railways should be returned to private management with a private board of directors. The Mexican government would guarantee debt service payments on the railway debt.

The agreement between the Mexican government and the International Committee of Bankers on Mexico was signed on June 16, 1922, at the Mexican Financial Agency by Finance Minister de la Huerta and Thomas W. Lamont on behalf of the International Committee. In an interview, Lamont stated that the best of feelings had prevailed throughout the negotiations and that Señor de la Huerta had handled a difficult situation in a broad and statesmanlike spirit. The press in both countries hailed the accord.

Mexico's main purpose in reaching an agreement with its foreign bondholders was to reestablish its credit so that it could once again borrow abroad. However, when the finance minister broached the subject of a new loan of $25 million, Lamont put him off. It was premature to consider the matter before the United States had recognized the Obregón government, and America's position had not changed: Article 27 of the Mexican constitution must be clarified satisfactorily before recognition would be given. The just protection of American interests in Mexico must be assured.

Lamont spent most of July, along with two of his boys, his sister and brother-in-law, and several friends, at the Island Park ranch on the Snake River in Idaho. In August he joined Florence and the other children at

North Haven, where his office kept him informed daily of Mexican developments.

On August 8, 1922, President Obregón approved the foreign debt agreement; on September 28 the Mexican Senate ratified it. TWL promptly sent his congratulations to Señor de la Huerta: "This is indeed a splendid consummation of your long, arduous work, and I know your countrymen appreciate the fairness that you have shown in this matter and your constant solicitude for the interests of your government."

Lamont kept in close touch with the major American oil companies operating in Mexico. Anxious about the application of Article 27 to their Mexican properties, as well as a new oil export tax, they had suspended the exploration and development of new Mexican fields. There was growing fear that the nationalization of their properties was imminent.

Realizing that the treatment of American oil companies in Mexico, the recognition of the Obregón government by the United States, and the restoration of Mexican credit were all tied together, TWL hoped to influence the Mexican government, through de la Huerta, to take the necessary steps to settle the dispute. He kept Secretary Hughes informed and advised him that it was helpful in dealing with Mexican officials to be not only courteous, but generous with expressions of esteem and cordiality. De la Huerta had once told him, "You can lead us around the world with a lump of sugar, but you can't drive us an inch!" Lamont passed this remark on to Hughes and told him that de la Huerta was "the best bet down there." He was "acting in good faith and was strong politically."

In his letter of November 29 to de la Huerta, Lamont prescribed his own brand of suitably sweetened medicine: "Please don't kill off your friends like the Oil Executives!"

TWL stated that his outlook for Mexico was very poor unless the new oil legislation under consideration was acceptable to the oilmen and led them to continue petroleum development in Mexico. As for Article 27, TWL believed that Mexico had no desire to jeopardize or confiscate the property rights of Americans and other foreigners.

> In times past, as you know, certain Mexicans have been accused of deliberately refraining from meeting a given issue in a clear-cut and decisive manner. I have been predicting to my friends, both abroad and here, that the present administration in Mexico City would certainly not lay itself open to any such accusation, but that it would grasp the situation courageously and by congressional action, or otherwise, make it perfectly clear, to the world at large, that the material interests of the British or Americans in Mexico are to be just as safe as the interests of Mexicans in Great Britain or the United States. . . .

I am exceedingly anxious to see your government take such action as will lead to early recognition. It would have, in a world-wide way, a stabilizing effect much greater than that of the Bankers' Agreement from which, as you know, you have already benefited in the eyes of the world. You are the man that I am counting upon as most effective in meeting this situation and in devising broad-minded oil legislation that will develop Mexico's resources as they ought to be developed. . . . I hardly have to assure you again that my interest in Mexico and in your good self personally always leads me to give you the best counsel of which I am capable. Such counsel may not invariably be just what you want but it is, and always shall be, the best that I have.

Financing European Recovery

In a widely reported speech at the American Bankers Association annual meeting on October 2, 1922, at the Hotel Commodore in New York, Lamont stated his belief that America, now the greatest economic power in the world, should assume a more constructive and responsible role in world affairs.

The shot that was fired at Lexington in 1775 was heard around the world. At that moment America set aglow a new beacon to light the way to freedom and liberty for generations on both sides of the Ocean. But now that we have won so far on the way to a splendid national achievement, to well-ordered freedom, to prosperity and contentment, have we no flaming torch of leadership that we can raise before the eyes of the many millions who, since the Armistice, have been looking in vain for it? . . . But we have been timid and fearful of petty entanglement.

Specifically, Lamont asked his fellow citizens to consider the heavy burden facing the Allies of repaying the war debt owed the American government, about $10 billion, including some postwar loans for relief and reconstruction. The wartime Allies naturally hoped that America would forgive much of the huge obligation, of which about three-quarters was owed by Great Britain and France, which had also made large loans to their wartime associates. If, as many Americans felt, the French should cut back on their demands for reparations from the Germans, wasn't it only fair for the United States to reduce its demands for debt repayment from the Allies?

While Congress in recent legislation had permitted these loans to be stretched out to twenty-five years and reduced the interest charges, TWL still believed that the total amount was well beyond what these nations could repay. Americans should be realistic in determining what debts were in fact uncollectible and should be written off, in order to "quit fooling ourselves." There was also a question of simple equity. Half the debt, about $5 billion, had been contracted between April 4, 1917, when the United States declared war against Germany, and about a year later, when American soldiers in significant numbers first entered the trenches in France. During that period, when America was unable to furnish trained troops to fight its battles, she provided arms and munitions to her Allies, paid for by new U.S. government loans.

> Fate determined that Great Britain and France should give up the lives during that first year, and that we should furnish not our blood but our money. . . . Now that the war is behind us and we can take a long look back, is it wise for us, is it just, is it generous to make some composition of this matter? . . . Shall it not be the generosity as well as the justice that, among all the nations of the earth, will in truth and in name make America First?

Lamont was the first prominent figure to come out in favor of forgiving part of the Allied debt. While his audience, some three thousand bankers, cheered his talk, much of the press comment was critical.

Some thought that Lamont was belittling America's role and sacrifices in the fighting that led to the Allied victory over Germany. Other articles suggested that the Morgan firm was not entirely disinterested in the matter, because it had arranged some $2 billion in loans to the Allies since the beginning of the war. Cancellation of debt owed to the U.S. government would strengthen the ability of European nations to repay the private debt.

Secretary of Commerce Hoover insisted that Europe could repay its debts and should do so. Alluding to Hoover's viewpoint, the *Cincinnati Enquirer* stated:

> Thomas W. Lamont, of J. P. Morgan & Company, holds a different view, and recently he swept the American Bankers' Association off its feet with his plea for the cancellation of these debts. Incidentally, it may be observed, the American people seem still to be holding their footing notwithstanding Mr. Lamont's hectic arguments and appeals.
>
> There is a reason, a reason to which Mr. Hoover pertinently refers: The debt of the Allies is not to this Government, but to the taxpayers of America. The American people by incomparable sacrifices bought $10,000,000,000

worth of Liberty bonds to provide the funds for these loans, and there never was another thought than that the debtor nations would repay their debt of honor in full. . . .

Those publicists and politicians who so strenuously are appealing to Americans to "save" Europe could with greater profit turn their attention to many important problems here at home.

As a result of the speech, Secretary of State Hughes invited TWL to the State Department on October 6. Hughes noted that Lamont saw a direct linkage between the war debt and reparations issues; but TWL seemed to be calling for the U.S. to make the first move in reducing the debt owed the U.S. The administration viewed the matter differently. The European governments should first accept the findings of an expert committee on the amount of reparations Germany was capable of paying, a determination that was essential in considering any reduction in the war debt. The American War Debt Commission, charged with negotiating revised debt agreements with the Allies, would then be armed with the facts it needed to obtain new congressional authority to modify the war debts. The high command had a battle plan, and it was time for the troops to close ranks behind the new strategy.

As 1923 opened, Thomas Stilwell Lamont began his career at J. P. Morgan & Co., where he would join some other offspring and relatives of Morgan partners—Jack Morgan's sons Junius S., Jr., and his younger brother, Henry S.; Henry P. Davison, Jr.; and George Whitney. Junius Morgan and Whitney had already become partners. While enjoying the good life of a Morgan banker, Tommy would have a strong incentive to be diligent in his new job—the Lamont family's significant financial stake in the Morgan partnership.

Most Morgan men were selected on merit alone, and their résumés were impressive. The new partner joining the firm in a few months was just such a person—Russell C. Leffingwell, a New York corporate lawyer and former Assistant Secretary of the Treasury whom TWL knew well from their wartime work together. He was widely regarded as a first-class economist and expert in international finance.

However, the occasional resort to nepotism had advantages for the bank. The sons and relatives chosen to join the Morgan firm had appropriate credentials: they were eminently presentable, Ivy League educated (with a predominance of Harvard graduates), and part of a social network of well-bred young men entering the ranks of big business and finance. In the future the juniors would bring in new accounts from their business friends and provide a lineal continuity in Morgan-client relationships, sometimes replacing their seniors on corporate boards, just as Jack Morgan had done in assuming his father's directorships. Their presence also assured that the trust and investment accounts of the partner's family would remain at the bank from one generation to the next. These contributions would come later; for the present the bank mail room was the first rung on the Morgan career ladder for the young recruits.

TSL's father continued to focus on the bank's foreign loan operations. On a Friday evening in mid-January, Lamont took the night train to Washington. A full schedule of meetings followed on Saturday, starting at the State Department with Secretary Hughes. On the Mexican front the standoff over Article 27 and the treatment of American oil companies continued. In Europe discussions were under way for making a large international loan to Austria for currency stabilization.

The economic condition of Austria was desperate, with widespread unemployment, food shortages, and mounting inflation. When TWL had been in London in May, he and his Morgan Grenfell colleagues met with Austrian treasury officials and ambassador to London Baron Franckenstein to discuss their urgent request for a loan to help the Austrian government meet the huge budget deficits forecast over the next few years. Following these talks a bankers' mission to Vienna concluded that a loan was not feasible under current conditions. The Morgan partners believed that the Austrian government must first institute a comprehensive program of fiscal and monetary reform to show its own people, as well as foreign governments and investors, that it was willing to deal positively with Austria's problems. The partners arranged for the Austrian treasury officials to meet with Sir Arthur Salter, chief of the Economic Section of the League of Nations, in Geneva, with the outcome that an expert League committee was dispatched to study the Austrian situation and prepare a plan for economic recovery.

The Austrian government energetically carried out a tough fiscal program, and within months the value of the Austrian crown was stabilized. At the same time the major European League members began preparations for a large loan to the Austrian government, part of which would be offered by the Morgan firm in the U.S. The European governments would guarantee the major share of the loan.

Lamont suggested to Secretary Hughes that the American government guarantee the portion of the loan to be sold in the United States. But the government did not have legislative authority and the idea was dropped. The guaranty was not critical, TWL decided. The official European backing of the loan and the Morgan sponsorship should ensure a good reception for the American portion.

In the afternoon TWL called on the former president and Mrs. Wilson at their house on S Street in Georgetown. Lamont felt affection and loyalty for his former chief. While Wilson's inflexibility about the terms of American participation in the League had been catastrophic, Lamont still admired his vision for world peace. Moving about on a cane, Wilson was forced by his fragile health to live a quiet and secluded life. Lamont wrote his sons about his visit, describing the former chief of state as a "rather melancholy" figure, sad and frustrated in his inability to engage any more in public affairs. It was the last time Lamont saw the great wartime leader, whose condition steadily declined until his death about a year later.

Lamont, as he confessed, was "addicted" to the game of golf. When playing regularly he shot in the mid 90s. TWL made a point of inserting golf outings on his calendar from time to time, and in February he and his cronies played at the Mid-Pines Country Club in Pinehurst, North Carolina, popular among businessmen-golfers for its scenic courses and informal men's club atmosphere.

Lamont then joined J. P. Morgan and George F. Baker at the very exclusive Jekyll Island Club off the Georgia coast to discuss some Erie Railroad problems. The club, founded by Morgan the elder and a group of friends in 1888, was a favorite of society's old guard of business tycoons, and Baker, the eighty-two-year-old chairman of the First National Bank (and TWL's former boss), was the much respected patriarch in residence. The gentlemen and their ladies were drawn there each winter by the benign climate, long beaches, blooming flowers, and piney woods with mockingbirds singing in the trees, which lined the fairways of the club's golf course.

Lamont and Morgan shared a common enthusiasm for golf and often bantered back and forth about the game. After a minor train accident with no injuries en route to Pinehurst, TWL had wired Jack that he had had trouble keeping his eye on the ball the next day, and Morgan replied that God seemed to take special care of golfers. Lamont was a better golfer than his portly older colleague, and while there is no record of the number of handicap strokes he gave Morgan to make their game an even matchup, presumably TWL was generous. The banking partners enjoyed a few rounds together on the club course before TWL's departure for New York to welcome a new visitor to the city—Lord Robert Cecil.

During the Paris Peace Conference TWL had come to know and admire

Lord Cecil, who was a member of the British delegation and the son of Queen Victoria's late-nineteenth-century prime minister, Lord Salisbury. Many were impressed by Cecil's abilities and character, including Bernard Baruch, who wrote that he "epitomized the best of British aristocracy." Lord Cecil had been one of the chief draftsmen of the League Covenant and was now president of the League of Nations Union, an organization established to promote support for the League. Lamont had heard that Cecil was planning a speaking tour in the United States and wrote inviting him to be the Lamonts' houseguest while in New York. While enthusiastically backing Cecil's mission, he warned him that the American public was far more isolationist than internationalist in its outlook.

Lord Cecil and his secretary stayed with the Lamonts for a week before leaving on a speaking tour. The Lamonts gave a dinner in his honor, and Florence, quite taken with Lord Cecil, had afternoon tea each day with him. The Cecil visit marked the beginning of a warm friendship with the Lamonts.

Following the wedding of Tommy and Ellie Miner on April 14, in Rochester, the Lamonts sailed for Europe on the S.S. *Olympia*. Lord Cecil, Jeremiah Smith, Jr., and Norman Davis were also on board, and the gentlemen had ample opportunity to discuss the affairs of the world before the ladies enticed them away to bridge or dancing. One evening after a concert in the main salon, Lord Cecil gave a short speech urging Americans to overcome their unfounded fear of involvement with the "old world" and join the League to share its responsibilities and the benefits of its accomplishments. The Lamonts heartily applauded their new friend's message. They also knew that the British lord's campaign would have little appeal for most Americans.

After docking in Cherbourg, the Lamonts took the train to Paris where TWL planned the international loan to Austria with his Paris partners, European bankers, and the Austrian Loan Commission. The bulk of the $130 million bond issue would be sold in Europe with an American syndicate headed by J. P. Morgan & Co. underwriting and selling $25 million in the United States.

Before leaving the States, Lamont had touched base with Guido Yung, commercial and financial adviser to the Italian Embassy. TWL planned to go on to Rome in May and hoped to persuade the Italian government to appoint J. P. Morgan & Co. its fiscal agent in organizing Italy's foreign loans. Yung reported he had heard that Dillon, Read, another New York investment firm, was actively attempting to represent the

Italian government in arranging financing abroad. In a letter to Yung, Lamont observed, "It is true that the firm is . . . exceedingly aggressive and has been trying for some time to get in on Italian business. I think that you and I agreed that it would be a pity for your government to start business here in any but the right way."

In mid-May the Lamonts arrived in Rome after a lovely drive along the Mediterranean coast from St. Raphael to Genoa. TWL had written ahead to American ambassador Richard W. Child, who had arranged a meeting for him with the Italian minister of finance and Premier Benito Mussolini. Only six months earlier, with his Fascist party's March on Rome under way, Mussolini had perforce been chosen by King Victor Emmanuel III to head the Italian government.

Lamont told Premier Mussolini that the Italian government should not be in a hurry to borrow abroad. The whole world was watching his accomplishments and Italy's progress under his leadership, said Lamont. He urged Mussolini to support the League of Nations and participate in its councils. It was important to encourage foreign private investment in Italy. If the government wanted financial counsel, Morgan would give its best, and there would be no charge for this service. Great Britain, France, and Belgium were already using the Morgan bank as their financial adviser and fiscal agent. Lamont was sanguine that Mussolini would prove to be the chief of state to lead Italy out of its postwar economic chaos, transforming it into a worthy borrower and prime Morgan client.

Back in New York, TWL completed work on the $25 million Austrian bond issue, which was offered successfully on June 20. He was vacationing in North Haven on August 2 when he received the shocking and sad news of the sudden death of President Harding in San Francisco. At the family farm in Vermont, Vice President Calvin Coolidge took the presidential oath of office, administered by his father, a justice of the peace. Coolidge was an Amherst classmate and old friend of TWL's partner Dwight Morrow, who had actively campaigned for his nomination as the Republican presidential candidate in 1920. Lamont and the Morgan partners had high hopes that Coolidge would adopt a more enlightened approach to foreign affairs than his predecessor.

However, the president and Lamont were clearly on different sides of one issue—whether the United States government should forgive a large portion of the huge debt it was owed by the Allied governments stemming from the World War and its aftermath. President Coolidge expressed his view characteristically: "They hired the money, didn't they?"

*   *   *

The *Evening Post*, which had been sold by Lamont in January 1922 to a group of investors organized by Edwin Gay, continued to struggle. Owen Young, Norman Davis, and Gay, all officers of the *Post* board of directors, asked TWL at various times in 1922 and 1923 to accept a postponement of the interest payments due him on his loans to the newspaper. This Lamont refused to do, pointing out that he had already made "very material sacrifices" in selling the newspaper to the Gay group instead of to Frank Munsey, who had offered far more favorable terms. He had taken this action with the expectation that the Gay group would provide financial support to the *Post* as needed. With considerable strain, the *Post* made the interest payments as they fell due. But the financial fortunes of the newspaper did not improve during the summer and fall of 1923, and the payment of $125,000 due Lamont at the end of the year became more formidable with every passing day. Under the mortgage, Lamont could take over the property in the event of a default, a step that he would not welcome but might find advisable to protect his investment.

Lamont had had a friendly acquaintance for several years with Cyrus H. Curtis, publisher of the *Ladies' Home Journal,* the *Saturday Evening Post*, the *Philadelphia Public Ledger*, and other publications. One day Curtis had lunch with Lamont to seek his advice: "Mr. Lamont, I need a financial editor for the *Public Ledger* badly. Where can I get one?"

"I know the very best," Lamont replied. "But you can't have him. He is Franz Schneider, Jr., and he is the backbone of the *New York Evening Post*." TWL had a high regard for Schneider. On most days when Lamont was at his office, Schneider would come by around noon, and TWL would step out to the anteroom inside the front door at 23 Wall to give Schneider his thoughts on the latest business developments.

As the meeting ended, Lamont said casually, "Why don't you buy the *Post*? There's a whole staff of them," referring to Schneider and his colleagues. Curtis reviewed Schneider's work as the financial editor of the *Post* and was impressed.

After failing to entice Schneider away from the *Post*, Curtis bought the paper in December 1923. He primarily wanted it, he stated, to give his Philadelphia paper the benefit of the *Post*'s excellent financial news staff, and he assured TWL that he would not shut the paper down. The sale of the *Post* to Curtis presented a good solution to the dilemma faced by Lamont and the present owners. TWL wrote Owen Young, chairman of the executive committee of the *Post*, that he admired Curtis as a publisher—"not sensational, no political axes to grind." The sale was a sound step in view of "the embarrassment and difficulties of the last two years." Young and the other owners agreed.

Lamont would receive $500,000 cash from Curtis; his outstanding loan of $1 million to the *Post* would become an obligation of the Curtis organization. TWL wrote: "Money-wise I should have been better off . . . to have accepted Mr. Munsey's offer, yet at least I could sleep with an easy conscience as to my duty to the *Evening Post*."

His newspaper publishing venture had been an embarrassing and costly failure, running up the biggest personal financial loss Lamont had ever suffered—about $1.25 million. However, the foreign policy positions of the *New York Evening Post* under TWL's ownership had impressed President Wilson, which had led to Lamont's participation in foreign affairs at the highest levels of government, an experience that TWL had savored and which considerably enhanced his public stature. There were some benefits from the unfortunate enterprise.

A New Client

Since the formation of the Chinese Consortium in 1920, Lamont, the spokesman of the American Group, had conducted an ongoing dialogue with State Department officials on the subject of making loans to China. The continuing unstable political and economic conditions in China ruled out any lending to that country in the view of the American Group, even for projects backed by the State Department. Nor did the British and French bankers display any enthusiasm for Chinese loan proposals.

Lamont pointed out to Secretary Hughes and other State Department officials that the American Group existed, at considerable expense to itself, only because the State Department believed that its participation in the consortium was necessary to promote American interests in China. The American Group bankers had "little or no active interest in Chinese finance and were following along merely to be good fellows and because they were urged to do so," TWL told department officials at a meeting. Some group members seriously questioned the point of the whole exercise. Lamont, always keen to participate in the inner circle formulating diplomatic strategies, stated that he personally favored carrying on, and Secretary Hughes urged Lamont to persuade his fellow bankers that their continued participation was vital to the American national interest in the Far East.

Despite its unwillingness to make loans to China the consortium remained in existence. The American and British governments thought that it had been valuable in curbing unilateral expansion by Japan in China. Moreover, the improved relations between Japan and America, given impetus by Japan's membership in the consortium, heightened the likelihood of Japanese borrowing in the United States, a prospect that whetted the bankers' appetites.

Lamont had corresponded with Governor Inouye of the Bank of Japan since his visit there in 1920. The Japanese were especially interested in obtaining financing to build the South Manchuria Railroad. The State Department, however, viewed this enterprise as Japan's chief instrument to develop and dominate Manchuria—to the exclusion of American and other foreign interests. The American government emphatically did not want this project assisted with American capital. Nor did Lamont think that it was advisable for Morgan to associate itself with Japanese expansion on the China mainland in its first loan for Japan. Accordingly, he turned aside Inouye's suggestion that the Morgan bank organize a loan for the South Manchuria Railway, to be guaranteed by the Japanese government. The first loan, Lamont wrote Inouye in March 1922, should be "something more purely Japanese, rather than intimately relating to the mainland of Asia." Furthermore, Kuhn, Loeb & Company had served earlier as the American investment banker for the Imperial Japanese Government, and it was not proper for Morgan to intrude on this existing banker-client relationship. "We have in this country and in Wall Street the same unwritten code that I presume exists with you. . . . The leading houses of the community are very scrupulous in refraining from inviting business from one another's clients." Mainly true, but artful and quiet suggestion, perhaps citing changed circumstances such as greatly increased capital needs, could lead a client to switch banks on his own. At the time Lamont contemplated that the Morgan bank might do its first Japanese bond issue with a blue-chip private institution such as the Yokohama Specie Bank rather than the Japanese government.

At the beginning of September 1923, a series of gigantic earthquake shocks caused raging fires and inundating tidal waves that devastated large areas of Japan, including the cities of Tokyo and Yokohama. The human and economic losses to the nation were catastrophic, with hundreds of thousands of casualties and many more made homeless by the disaster.

Lamont wrote to Inouye, who had become finance minister, expressing sympathy on behalf of the Morgan partners over the tragic occurrence. However, he cautioned Inouye against seeking a large foreign loan too soon in a "calamity market." But an outstanding Japanese loan, mainly held in the United States, was maturing in 1925. The need to raise funds to retire this loan and reconstruct the country's earthquake-shattered economy made borrowing abroad imperative and urgent.

A surge of sympathy for the plight of the Japanese people swept over America, as the island nation struggled to rebuild its demolished cities and towns. Dwight Morrow was chosen by President Coolidge to lead a campaign to raise relief funds for Japan, and private donations of over $8 million poured in. The climate for floating a substantial loan to Japan for national reconstruction appeared increasingly favorable, and the Japanese government asked J. P. Morgan & Co., with Kuhn, Loeb's concurrence, to lead the operation in view of its size; it was by far the biggest foreign loan for Japan ever undertaken. Secretary of State Hughes told TWL that the U.S. government fully backed the proposed loan.

"I have never been so busy since war times—at my office until eight or thereabouts every night and then working with the Japs after that until one o'clock in the morning, and I am almost exhausted," TWL wrote his sons. Part of the loan was to be placed in England, and the coded cables flew back and forth between New York, London, and Tokyo, as the negotiations progressed. Lamont was the partner in charge of negotiating the loan because, "I was the only one present who knew the financial layout in all three of the centers and was thus able to try to dovetail the ideas, with my knowledge of the local backgrounds."

The contract for the $150 million Imperial Japanese Government External Loan of 1924, thirty-year sinking fund bonds with a 6½ percent coupon, was signed at the Morgan Library on the evening of February 11. A 25 million pound sterling loan was offered at the same time in London by a Morgan Grenfell syndicate. One of TWL's final duties was preparing draft statements announcing the loan for Treasury officials in Washington and Tokyo. Several days later he was fishing and golfing at the Gasparilla Inn at Boca Grande on the Florida gulf coast.

"I was tired when I left New York," he wrote home, "for I had given everything that was in me to the Japanese loan." Lamont was also very pleased with the results of his hard work. The loan offering had been a great success, and he was confident that the Japanese government would be "a permanent client of the house," joining the illustrious roster of foreign governments already using the bank.

A Settlement Unravels

More than once Lamont observed that the Mexican debt negotiations consumed more of his time than any other bank business. Under the 1922 Lamont-Huerta agreement, the Mexican government was to deposit oil export taxes and a portion of railway revenues in the Banco Nacional de Mexico as they were collected. The bank, on instructions from the finance minister, would then transfer these sums in U.S. dollars to J. P. Morgan & Co. in New York to accumulate the funds needed to pay interest to the foreign bondholders according to the agreed schedule. Mexico would receive the going rate of interest on the deposits until paid out. Morgan held the biggest share, 35 percent, parceling out the balance to several other New York banks that Banco Nacional had selected.

With a few lags the remittance system worked well during 1923, building the funds in New York up toward the first-year requirement of $15 million. President Obregón had finally agreed that Article 27 would not be applied retroactively, and the U.S. had granted official recognition to his government. Mexican-American relations seemed on the mend.

On September 26, de la Huerta resigned as minister of finance and was replaced by Alberto J. Pani, who continued the flow of remittances. With $13.5 million deposited and Pani's assurance that the balance would be transferred prior to year-end, the International Committee felt it could safely declare that the plan for the readjustment of Mexico's foreign debt was officially operative. Then the news broke that de la Huerta, whom TWL had counted on as a moderate and liberal force in Mexican politics, was organizing his supporters for an armed revolt against the government. However, the bankers expected the rebellion to collapse before long, and Lamont, the chairman of the International Committee, went ahead with the press announcement in New York on December 8, 1923.

As reported in the *New York Times*, Lamont described the financial step by Mexico as

> very significant, not only from the standpoint of Mexico and of her creditors, but also from the standpoint of world progress. It marked in effect the restoration of Mexico to the family of nations that are making honest efforts to meet their expenses and pay their bills. It was the largest debt funding agreement ever undertaken for or by any one nation. . . . The whole Mexican Government, he said, has evinced its determination to

support the agreement throughout, and he expressed confidence in its ability to do so.

The balance of $1.5 million was transferred to the Morgan bank by the end of the year, and the first interest payment to the foreign bondholders was made. However, in the early months of 1924, the Mexican treasury was heavily drained by the military expenditures incurred to put down the de la Huerta revolt.

Lamont's private longing to play a large role in diplomatic affairs now led to a surprising suggestion by him. In a talk with Secretary Hughes at the State Department on January 30, 1924, he proposed to attempt to mediate the differences between de la Huerta and President Obregón, in an effort to resolve the insurrection peacefully. He felt he had a good relationship with both men and was prepared to go to Laredo to meet with the interested parties. Secretary Hughes suggested that TWL discuss his idea with the Mexican Embassy officials in Washington, which he did that afternoon. TWL was politely received, but evidently the Obregón administration had no interest; he received no further response to his offer to serve as a peacemaker in the Mexican political clash.

A transfer of $700,000 from Mexico was received by the Morgan bank in January, and then the weeks and months slipped by without further remittances. The sum of $8,750,000 was required for the semi-annual payment to foreign bondholders due July 1. The bankers knew that the oil revenues were being collected and deposited, and Lamont registered with Señor Pani the concern of the International Committee. But the Mexican government continued to block additional transfers to New York.

Throughout the spring of 1924, Lamont and Pani exchanged cables and letters, with TWL's stern protests rising steadily in intensity. However, Pani had now adopted a new approach to the issue: the foreign bankers must make a substantial loan to Mexico to assure continuance of the payments to foreign bondholders.

President Obregón had told Pani that during the 1922 negotiations Finance Minister de la Huerta had assured him that new foreign loans would be forthcoming to establish a Mexican central bank after the agreement was ratified. Without this understanding Obregón would never have approved the 1922 agreement, although he acknowledged that he may have been misled by de la Huerta. Furthermore, not until Pani took over the finance ministry did Obregón learn the true state of the government's finances: the government was running an annual deficit equivalent to $25 million. Salary payments to civil service employees were three months in arrears, and many other government bills remained unpaid. Funds were needed for the severance pay of some 50,000 soldiers recruited to put down the de la Huerta rebellion, troops that had become a troubling menace to the government. There was a strong and growing public feeling that if, having just paid out $15 million to the international bankers, Mexico was unable to obtain a new loan, there was simply no point in continuing the foreign payments, given Mexico's urgent domestic needs. Pani suggested that a foreign loan of at least $20 million, which could be secured by oil production taxes, was called for under the circumstances.

Lamont in turn pointed out to Pani the enormous concessions that the foreign bondholders had made. The outstanding bonds at par value plus accrued interest should be worth $1,358 apiece on the average. Yet they were quoted at $270 on the bond market, representing an 80 percent loss to the bondholder. Would Mexico now deny debt service payments, so substantially reduced by the 1922 agreement, to the long-suffering bondholders who had already sacrificed so much? Such an abrogation of "the solemn agreement" would be disastrous to Mexico's international credit. "All such financial good will toward Mexico will be ruined if the government now defaults."

There was absolutely no enthusiasm among the bankers for any new loan to Mexico. Obviously a public bond issue was out of the question, with Mexico's foreign debt already in default, and a bank loan secured by oil production taxes was a highly risky proposition. The American oil producers, continuing to fear the nationalization of their Mexican properties, forecast declining development and production in that country. Lamont advised Pani that Mexico would do well to satisfy the concerns of the foreign oil companies in order to induce them to increase production of oil, the government's largest source of revenues and foreign exchange. He also informed him that the International Bankers Committee had turned down the proposal for a new loan to Mexico.

Pani wanted a loan, not advice, and flatly told Lamont that if it were not forthcoming, Mexico would suspend foreign debt payments under the 1922 agreement. In his letter of May 5 he stated that a loan would "insure preservation of the New York Agreement . . . a balancing of the budget, and instantaneous disappearance of hostile sentiments in the mind of the Mexican people against the New York Agreement."

An article in *El Universal*, the prominent Mexico City newspaper, confirmed Pani's description of the current public attitude. "The service of the foreign debt must be suspended," read the story's headline. It described "public services unpaid, economic crisis, and widespread misery" facing the country. There was "gold piling up in New York to pay foreign creditors, leaving unpaid national creditors." Government workers were "at the point of starvation," and the government as its first priority must pay the back salaries of thousands of public employees.

Pani was not bluffing: on May 14 President Obregón informed his countrymen that government workers would be paid from the funds reserved for foreign creditors unless Mexico promptly received a new foreign loan. The International Committee through TWL protested vociferously, but it had no loan to offer. On June 29, Obregón issued a decree suspending foreign debt service payments under the 1922 agreement until "a balance in federal public finances" was achieved.

In the absence of Lamont, who had just sailed for England, Thomas Cochran, his partner and alternate chairman of the American Section of the International Committee, issued a statement to the press. The Mexican government had failed to transfer the funds needed to make the $8,750,000 payment to the bondholders due on July 1, and therefore no disbursement would be made. The bankers believed that Mexico's suspension in debt service was temporary, brought on by the expense of putting down the de la Huerta rebellion. The International Committee would not declare Mexico in default. The *New York Times* reported: "The bankers said they realized that Mexico had made a determined effort to live up to its part of the debt agreement, but that unforeseen obstacles had developed in her path, and that they were confident of the good will of Mexico and her desire to live up to the stipulations covering the reorganized debt."

Cochran's private letter to Pani took a considerably harder line. The decree represented "an unwarranted suspension of a solemn agreement." It was illegal because the consent of the other signatory to the agreement, the International Committee, had not been sought or obtained, and it constituted "a breach of the spirit and letter of the agreement." Minister Pani replied calmly that the Mexican government's decision was correct "if not from a legal—certainly from a human standpoint, which is far above the former."

The minister made a good point, but he still needed new foreign loans to improve the lot of his countrymen. The Mexican debt dilemma continued.

The Dawes Loan

The system for German reparations payments to the Allies had broken down by the spring of 1924, five years after the establishment of the Reparations Commission by the Treaty of Versailles. In May 1921, the commission had set the amount for Germany to pay at $33 billion, plus interest, commencing with annual payments of $500 million. Within a year Germany was in default, and in January 1923, France and Belgium occupied the great German industrial area of the Ruhr in an effort to collect the payments due them.

In late 1923, at the suggestion of Secretary of State Hughes, the concerned governments appointed a committee of experts headed by Charles G. Dawes to propose a plan to settle the reparations question. After his service as head of U.S. Army procurement in Europe during the war, Dawes had become in 1921 the country's first director of the Bureau of the Budget. The Dawes Plan proposed internationally supervised controls over German government expenditures. It provided for the Reichsbank, the new central bank, to issue currency backed by appropriate gold reserves. Finally, the handling of reparations payments would be separated into two parts: (1) the collection of government revenues in German marks and (2) the conversion of these marks into foreign currencies, to be supervised by a newly constituted Transfer Committee, which would control the timing and amounts to avoid further depreciation of the mark. Annual payments would start at about $250 million a year, scaling up to $600 million in five years; the total sum was left indefinite.

A key ingredient in implementing the Dawes Plan would be an international loan to Germany of about $200 million, which would enable Germany to commence reparations payments. It was planned that at least half would be placed in the United States, with J. P. Morgan & Co. heading the American syndicate. Great Britain and the major continental countries would take the remainder of the loan. Jack Morgan had banned lending by his firm to the hated wartime foe, but this case was exceptional, because through the reparations route America's former Allies would be aided. Furthermore, Lamont believed that if Germany, the economic hub of Europe, did not prosper, its neighbors would languish as well, causing bad times for everyone.

In July 1924, an inter-Allied government conference was convened in London to work out the agreement for carrying out the Dawes Plan, and

Lamont was on hand to advise on the proposed German loan. At the beginning of July the Lamonts moved into a large townhouse on Audley Square that they had rented for the summer, where George Metcalfe, the wise and urbane Englishman who had served as majordomo of the Lamont household for ten years, handled a stream of official callers with the aplomb and tact of a veteran diplomat.

The Allied governments were anxious to receive assurance from the bankers that the new private loan to Germany, indispensable to the success of the Dawes Plan, would be promptly forthcoming once the revised reparations arrangements had been set by the conference. Accordingly they listened carefully to the advice of J. P. Morgan and his partners, who would be asked to take the lead in managing the complex international loan operation. Throughout the summer TWL exchanged lengthy cables with his key partners in New York—Morgan, Morrow, Leffingwell, and Thomas Cochran—to obtain their views and instructions. After a detailed report on affairs of state or high finance, the cables would end incongruously with such expressions as "Love to all of you" or "Love to you and the family," a long-standing custom of the partners in communicating with each other.

The Morgan partners argued that the reparations plan must not create conditions that American investors would view as threatening to the security or debt service of the German government bonds they would be asked to buy. Lamont and Montagu Norman, the governor of the Bank of England, saw eye to eye on this subject and worked closely together. Next to the United States, Great Britain would assume the largest portion of the German loan.

It was their view that France, in occupying the Ruhr, had already shown its readiness to take unilateral action of the kind that could seriously harm Germany's economic recovery and its ability to repay the proposed new loan. France must agree to evacuate the Ruhr promptly. Furthermore, the power to declare a default should be removed from the Reparations Commission to a new committee, which would be chaired by an American, an arrangement that would give protection to investors against arbitrary French moves threatening the security of the loan. Lamont told the Allied officials that the bankers had no interest in interfering in political matters. But they had been asked for their best advice regarding the feasibility of the German loan, and the conditions they stipulated were necessary to give bondholders adequate financial protection. They could not ask investors to purchase German government bonds unless the security of the loan was safeguarded.

Once again, however, the French threatened to undermine the reparations arrangements as the conference convened in mid-July. The French argued that they had been led to place their faith in the Reparations Commission, under the Versailles Treaty, as the one instrument available to them to force Germany to meet her obligations. Premier Édouard Herriot was under heavy political pressure to resist any change in the authority of the Reparations Commission that would weaken France's freedom of action.

The Morgan firm had granted a six-month $100 million credit to the French government in March to stabilize the weakening franc, and a Morgan-led bond issue was under consideration. Lamont made clear to the French officials that renewal of the credit or proceeding with the bond issue was directly linked to the success of the German loan, which depended on French cooperation on reparations questions.

On July 10, Lamont and Governor Norman met with Prime Minister Ramsay MacDonald at 10 Downing Street. MacDonald, the son of Scottish farming parents and a self-made man, had become the Labor party's first prime minister earlier that year. His otherwise mild appearance was distinguished by a leonine thatch of white hair. Afterward Lamont wrote MacDonald summarizing the views of J. P. Morgan & Co. regarding the German loan.

Regardless of whether the attitude of the American public toward the operations of the Reparations Commission was justified, if the power to declare a default in reparations payments was given to the commission, America would not subscribe to the loan. Therefore, the authority to declare Germany in default should be lodged with a new committee, independent of the Reparations Commission. Furthermore, said Lamont, the German government loan could be successfully issued in the American market only if it carried a first mortgage or charge on Germany's assets and revenues. If this fundamental condition was altered by the Allied governments in a way that would weaken the security or threaten the debt service of the loan, "American investors would reject the loan."

Over the next two weeks as the conference delegates deliberated, TWL followed a heavy schedule of meetings, outlining the bankers' viewpoint to American as well as European officials in London. The U.S. government was keenly interested in seeing the proposed loan go forward. At the same time American officials recognized that it would be disastrous if the French decided to withdraw and break up the conference.

TWL consulted with ambassador to Great Britain Frank B. Kellogg; James A. Logan, the State Department officer assigned as observer to the Reparations Commission; Secretary of the Treasury Andrew W. Mellon; Secretary of State Charles E. Hughes, who was attending the American

Bar Association meeting in London; and Owen D. Young, the leading American expert on the plan on the scene. Young, in private life chairman of General Electric, had been Dawes's chief lieutenant in formulating the Dawes Plan. Kellogg, Young, and Logan did their utmost to smooth the differences between the bankers and the French—conflicting viewpoints that emerged in Lamont's strained sessions with Premier Herriot and Finance Minister Étienne Clémentel.

On July 22, the premier called on Lamont at the Audley Square house, and the ensuing meeting was long and tense. Herriot made an impassioned plea to TWL to be understanding and helpful to France, alluding to the ancient friendship between their two nations. He placed himself at the mercy of the bankers. TWL observed that he did not seem to grasp the fact that the conditions Lamont proposed for the German loan were not set by the bankers arbitrarily, but reflected their best judgment of what private investors in America would demand when asked to purchase German government bonds.

On July 25, the *London Daily Telegraph* reported that Thomas W. Lamont of J. P. Morgan & Co. had presented an ultimatum to the Allied premiers in London: the international bankers would have nothing to do with the proposed $200 million loan to Germany unless their conditions were met. The story was soon published in other British and American newspapers. The *Times* of Madison, Wisconsin, headline, "International Bankers Rule the World," summed up many articles appearing in the American press, which generally supported the bankers' position as sound and fair. The *New York Tribune* headlined its story: "Europe Hails Bankers as True Friends; Sage Advice by Financiers at London Conference Makes History in Adjusting Problems." The article went on to say:

> Five years and more after the armistice European statesmen have been compelled to admit that in the final analysis the dollar really talks. . . .
>
> It was only natural that the Dawes recommendations should be interpreted by bankers and that European statesmen should be compelled to give close heed to what the bankers had to say.

The story identified Governor Norman and Thomas W. Lamont as the two powerful bankers operating behind the scenes at the conference.

> Both Norman and Lamont are second to none of the statesmen in their knowledge of European affairs. All information at the command of the premiers of Britain and France and the State Department at Washington is at their command, even though America occupies no official position.

Not all the press comment was laudatory. Some papers viewed the episode as just another example of Wall Street's sinister influence in world affairs. Others thought that the bankers were being too tough. On July 25, TWL wrote Prime Minister MacDonald that the Morgan partners had been embarrassed by the continued assumptions in the press that the bankers had introduced "new and unforeseen conditions." This was simply not the case: they had been consistent from the beginning in stating their advice, said Lamont.

On the same day Lamont left London to join his family on a motor trip through Devon and Cornwall. A handwritten letter from MacDonald sent from Chequers, the prime minister's official country residence outside London, reached him several days later: "The press is most unfair to blame the bankers for any of our difficulties, and I must find a chance of saying so. We simply must come to an agreement. As you may imagine, I am even busier and carry as heavy and worrying a burden as a Morgan partner."

On Sunday evening, August 3, the prime minister asked Lamont and Governor Norman to confer with him at 10 Downing Street in preparation for his report to Parliament on the progress of the London Conference the following day. At the end of their meeting TWL inquired whether the prime minister would be able to get to sleep easily at that late hour. MacDonald replied: "I shall not have difficulty sleeping if I can once get to bed." Pointing to a side table, he continued, "There is a pile of papers on India; over there is Ireland, and Egypt."

Two days later, J. P. Morgan arrived in London, where he would stay for a week before proceeding to Gannochy in Scotland for grouse shooting. Morgan and Lamont agreed that the bankers had done everything they could to make clear to the Allied officials the conditions they deemed essential for a successful German loan. Now it would be best to rest their case, because it would be unwise for them to appear to be playing too active a role in the Allied governments' meetings.

A new and embarrassing misfire for the Morgan partners had occurred, and the troublemaker this time was their own government. In May, J. P. Morgan had been asked by Governor Norman, on behalf of the Allied governments, to propose an American to fill the new post of Reparations Agent-General, who would have authority over the collection and transfer of reparations payments by Germany. Morgan recommended his partner Dwight Morrow as the best man for the job. In June, Morrow, who was well known and respected in European financial circles, was unanimously chosen by the Reparations Commission for the office, subject to the approval of the American government, which was considered a mere formality. However, the State Department surprisingly vetoed the selection, arguing that the Germans would resent having a partner of J. P.

Morgan & Co., an international banking firm, in a post that would have such important influence over German financial affairs. American ambassador Alanson B. Houghton reported that the German government feared that the appointment might bring about its downfall.

Secretary Hughes informed Morrow, who withdrew his name from consideration. When further checking determined that the State Department opinion was unfounded, Morrow was urged to reconsider his decision by the British, but declined.

In August, Morgan was asked once again to recommend an American for Reparations Agent-General, and he and Lamont consulted by cable with their New York partners. This time the Morgan bank selected S. Parker Gilbert, who had served with distinction in the U.S. Treasury Department, rising to the post of Under Secretary, before recently joining the Cravath law firm in New York. He, too, could be counted on to use his influence to see that the bondholders received fair treatment.

Again, the State Department, represented by James Logan, appeared to drag its feet in approving the Morgan recommendation. However, the Reparations Commission was impressed with Gilbert's credentials and offered him the post. Lamont had gone over to Paris on August 12 to work on a new French government bond issue. At a meeting in Paris with Logan, Young, and Mellon, Lamont successfully made the case for Gilbert's approval by the American government.

Lamont and Logan then had another run-in. TWL had informed Ambassador Kellogg that he planned to consult with the European finance ministers about conditions in the London agreement affecting the proposed German loan, and Logan promptly expressed concern that the Morgan partners might upset the carefully crafted agreement. Lamont did his best to calm his fears, pointing out that it was perfectly normal for the bankers to have such private conversations with the government ministers; the governments of Great Britain, France, and Belgium were, in fact, all clients of J. P. Morgan & Co.

Lamont cabled his partners following the conclusion of the London conference. Ambassador Kellogg and the other American officials were pleased with the agreement, and TWL felt it provided an acceptable basis for considering the German loan. The French had made some significant concessions.

First, France agreed to evacuate the Ruhr within a year, a time frame Kellogg urged Lamont to accept. Second, no member nation of the Reparations Commission could unilaterally declare that Germany was in default. Unless there was unanimous agreement on the question of default, the matter would be referred to a newly formed Arbitration

Committee to be headed by an American. If this committee determined that Germany was in default, sanctions against Germany could be imposed, but they should not affect the creditworthiness of the German loan because the loan would have a first lien on German government revenues, and any claims resulting from sanctions on Germany would be subordinate to that lien.

After five years of struggle and controversy over the handling of reparations, the Allied nations had decided to back the Dawes Plan. The conference had passed a resolution supporting the German loan, and the governments would urge their central banks to help organize the European part of the debt issue. Europeans were enthusiastic about the Dawes Plan and the loan.

In America President Coolidge had publicly expressed support, and the bond market was strong and ready to absorb good new issues. Clarence Dillon of Dillon, Read and Company told TWL he would be interested in leading a syndicate to underwrite the loan, if, by any chance, J. P. Morgan & Co. decided against the undertaking.

The American press generally viewed the Dawes Plan and London Conference agreement as encouraging steps for European prosperity, but there were dissenters who followed the anti-Wall Street line of the *Sacramento Bee*:

> The Dawes Plan is primarily not intended so much to be helpful to Europe as to deliver that continent, body, soul, and spirit, into the hands of the international bankers—the Morgans of America and their allies in London.

At the end of August, the Morgan partners decided that Lamont should remain in Europe to negotiate the German loan. Arthur Anderson would be sent over to assist him. Over the next six weeks TWL shuttled between London and Paris preparing the German loan for offering in mid-October. In Paris he also worked on a proposed new French government loan of $100 million, to be issued later in the fall. J. P. Morgan came down from Scotland to join Lamont and Anderson for the German loan negotiations; Herman Harjes, the senior partner of the Morgan firm in Paris, provided valuable assistance in dealing with the French government. TWL's congenial friend Nelson Dean Jay, the top American partner in the Paris office, was designated as one of the trustees to supervise the future administration of the loan. As Morgan described the German loan: "It's the most important and responsible job we have had to tackle since the end of 1915."

Yet by mid-September the Morgan partners had not firmly decided to proceed with the loan. Governor Norman of the Bank of England believed the Germans would meet their loan obligations "honorably" and that without the loan "Europe will break." But England and the Continent could not go forward without the United States, which would take $110 million, over half of the total loan. If J. P. Morgan & Co. refused to lead the American syndicate, certainly no other house could successfully float the loan in America. Morgan and Lamont were in favor of the loan and cabled their partners in New York for their decision. Unless all the partners agreed that the loan was the best course, Jack Morgan was "not willing to go any further." The key partner then in New York was Dwight Morrow, and he had serious doubts about Germany's future attitude toward the loan. Before J. P. Morgan & Co. committed itself to managing the German bond issue in the United States, he wanted the firm to receive a strong expression of support for the loan from the State Department. In his letter of September 18 to Secretary Hughes, Morrow stated:

> However desirous Germany is of getting the loan at the moment in order to free the hold which France has upon the industries of the Ruhr, it is almost inevitable that this loan will be unpopular in Germany after a few years. The people of Germany, in our opinion, are almost certain, after sufficient time has elapsed, to think not of the release of the Ruhr but of the extent to which what was once a first-class Power has been subjected to foreign control.
>
> The opinion of Governor Norman that unless the loan is made Europe will break, is also of great importance to us. Our main reason for going on with the business would be the heavy responsibility that would rest upon us if our failure to proceed caused a breakdown.

Secretary Hughes replied in his letter the following day that in his view without the Dawes Plan and the German loan there would be "chaotic conditions abroad" and "a feeling of deep despair." He stated that the State Department hoped that the American financiers would "see their way clear to undertake the participation which the world expects and that is essential to the success of the Dawes Plan." The New York partners cabled their colleagues in London that they now agreed that the firm should undertake the German loan, and Morgan replied, "Perfectly delighted that you have decided this way."

There were a number of loose ends to be dealt with. The Morgan bank had decided that it must be officially asked to arrange the German loan by the Allied governments in furtherance of carrying out the Dawes Plan. The house of Morgan did not wish to be viewed as leading a loan on its own initiative to bolster the economy of America's wartime foe. Lamont sent a draft letter to the governments of the sort that J. P. Morgan & Co. wished to receive from them, and the matter was taken care of.

The loan was unusually complex because it would be offered in nine different countries simultaneously. Dollar bonds would be issued in the United States and sterling bonds in Great Britain and all the Continental countries except Italy and Sweden, where lire and kroner bonds would be used. The well-established London exchange would facilitate future trading of the sterling bonds.

The bankers believed that it was essential for the continental countries to have a substantial participation in the loan in order to raise the total amount required, about $190 million. As Morgan told Herman Harjes, his Paris senior partner: "The point of difficulty is that unless the Continent, both neutral and Allied markets, will take a reasonable share of this German loan, they will overstrain the English market, which is already very chilled and is getting more so every day."

Persuading government officials and financiers in each nation to bear their share was the diplomatic task facing Lamont and Governor Norman. In the case of France the assignment was especially difficult. Most French investors abhorred lending anything to the hated Boche.

During the London Conference and on several later occasions, Lamont and Harjes had cajoled Finance Minister Clémentel concerning France's loan allocation, which after much deliberation was set at 3 million pounds sterling, about $13 million. The French claimed that it would be difficult to raise more than half that sum. A widespread public issue was unthinkable, Clémentel said. It would be most unwise to impose a German loan "upon communities still filled with mutilated combatants." It would be up to the French private bankers. But powerful bellwether financier Baron Edouard de Rothschild had told Harjes that he wanted no part of the German loan.

The Morgan bankers persisted, arguing that the German loan would be of direct and immediate benefit to France. The German government would turn over the loan proceeds to the Reichsbank to provide gold reserves to back the German mark. What the government received in exchange would be used to purchase German commodities to make reparations payments in kind, the bulk of which would go to France.

In addition, Lamont pointed out to Clémentel, a successful offering of the upcoming French government bond issue in the United States depended on the success of the German loan, which in turn depended on the behavior of the French. If they did not subscribe to their fair share of the loan, other countries would feel justified in cutting back their allocations, and the loan would be a failure with disastrous consequences for

Europe. The bankers' point struck home, and the French agreed to accept their full share.

As the offering date grew closer, the flood of cables between 23 Wall Street and Morgan Grenfell in London focused on the terms of the German bond issue in the United States—offering price, coupon rate, maturity, sinking fund, and the like. J. P. Morgan & Co. as syndicate manager in America would receive a ¼ percent commission in addition to its compensation as a member of the purchasing and underwriting groups. On all printed documents the Morgan name would appear on a line by itself above the names of the other syndicate members.

There was considerable discussion among the partners over the appropriate position for Kuhn, Loeb & Co. in the purchasing group. Should it rank in the first tier along with First National Bank and National City Bank, as Mortimer L. Schiff, a Kuhn, Loeb senior partner passing through London, told TWL.

Kuhn, Loeb, the distinguished old German-Jewish private bank, whose partners were almost all related, was the second most powerful investment firm on Wall Street. Kuhn, Loeb and Morgan, aggressive rivals in railroad financing at the turn of the century, later found it mutually advantageous to avoid confrontations and collaborate in underwriting syndicates. But not always: during the war Kuhn, Loeb had refused to participate in underwriting the Anglo-French loan led by Morgan. Senior partner Jacob Schiff loathed Russia for her pogroms, and Russia was an ally of the British and French. A few partners did buy bonds as individuals, but Kuhn, Loeb's good name was tarred on Wall Street and in London.

Even though Morgan had individual Jewish friends, he was, in his own words, "not very enthusiastic about Jews," even doubting their patriotism—believing that they did not owe their primary allegiance to their country and its government. The Anglo-Protestant-bred and -educated Morgan partners and their Kuhn, Loeb counterparts did business together, but personal relations were generally not close. Their heritages were completely dissimilar. On the other hand, the ties between the Morgan firm and First National Bank, headed by the venerable and loyal George G. Baker, and National City Bank were long established and strong. The officers, coming from similar backgrounds, went to each other's parties and dined and played golf together at the same clubs. In the end J. P. Morgan, recognizing the merit in Schiff's courteous request, raised Kuhn, Loeb to the higher rank. However, in the case of Speyer & Co., a smaller German-Jewish firm, he took a different tack.

The New York partners, with whom Lamont agreed, felt that for sound business reasons Speyer & Co. should be included in the underwriting syndicate. Jack Morgan had held a poor opinion of the firm over business incidents going back many years: Speyer had won out over Morgan in obtaining the designation to be the American manager of an issue to finance the London subways; later the firm had challenged Morgan's appointment to manage the U.S. portion of Mexican government issues in the prewar period. The senior partner did not want his house to be associated with them. Nevertheless, since all the partners agreed that Speyer should be included in the syndicate, he would allow himself to be overruled.

His partners cabled the next day: "Our loyalty and affection for our chief are so uncompromising" that they had voted to keep Speyer out. Morgan's "peace of mind" was far more important to them than any business consideration. Jack Morgan replied that he was happy with his "kind partners who have patience and understanding with my infirmities and feelings."

October 10 was set for signing the German loan contract in London, with the public offering in New York four days later. The Morgan bankers worked feverishly to have everything ready. The German government was eager to obtain the loan, and the negotiations with the German officials led by Hjalmar Schacht, president of the Reichsbank, went quickly and smoothly. Lazard Freres, a respected private investment firm in Paris, had offered to head the French banking syndicate, solving the earlier problem of leadership of the French group. Lining up the continental portions of the bond issue had been so difficult that the Morgan bank had felt compelled to increase the American share of the issue from $100 million to $110 million.

The signing took place on schedule at the Bank of England. TWL was booked to sail for New York the following day, but there was still an important step to be taken by the Reparations Commission before the offering. Lamont and Owen Young in Paris, who was serving as interim Reparations Agent-General prior to Parker Gilbert's arrival, spent most of the night on the telephone with each other working out the final arrangements. All parties agreed to the loan and its complex security provisions, but the Reparations Commission had not yet formally approved the contract and the subordination of any claims the commission might have on the revenues pledged to secure the bonds. Early on October 11 the commission passed the necessary resolution, and, with two hours' sleep, Lamont boarded the *Mauritania* for the voyage home and a few days of rest—well deserved in the eyes of his partners and others who had worked with him. Owen Young sent a radiogram message to TWL on shipboard: "Please accept my congratulations in bringing this difficult matter through so successfully."

The offering took place in most countries on October 14 on terms that were essentially similar. In the United States the $110 million German External Loan of 1924 7% Gold Bonds were offered at 92. The loan was a huge success. In New York subscriptions of over $500 million poured in—"the largest oversubscription ever received," the Morgan bank stated. The loan was heavily oversubscribed in London as well, and the bonds went to a premium on the markets in both financial centers. Lamont's partners wired him the good news, and he replied, "By Jove, how magnificent!"

French cooperation in the German loan, albeit reluctant, had earned its reward. In November a new $100 million twenty-five-year loan to the French government was floated successfully in the United States by the Morgan-led banking syndicate.

October marked the birth of TWL's first grandchild, Thomas William Lamont II, son of Tommy and Ellie. Upon his return home the proud grandfather lavished gifts, tangible and financial, on his new namesake.

During October, the 1924 presidential election campaign was in its final month, with President Calvin Coolidge the Republican standard-bearer and John W. Davis the Democratic candidate. Davis, who had been solicitor general and ambassador to Great Britain in the Wilson administration, was now a distinguished New York lawyer who numbered the Morgan firm among his clients. Florence supported Davis, which confounded her dinner partners in the conservative social milieu of the Lamonts. According to Florence, election day was grand fun as she brightly approached a couple, of rock-ribbed Republican persuasion, in line to vote. "Good morning! What a beautiful day. I hope you are voting the straight Democratic ticket as I am." She watched with delight "the angry red creeping from his neck to his face" of the man as he sputtered a reply: "I am voting the straight Republican ticket as you should!"

While Lamont liked and admired Davis, he returned to the G.O.P. fold and voted Republican. Hard-working "Silent Cal" won in a landslide victory.

As the year drew to a close the Lamonts celebrated Christmas in Englewood with their family and guests, Lord and Lady Robert Cecil. Cecil had come to America to receive an award from the Woodrow Wilson Foundation for his work toward the establishment of world peace, and TWL had been a member of the award selection jury that chose him. Cecil wrote later about his visit. "We stayed again with our perfect hosts—the Lamonts—and spent Christmas day at their little country house on the Hudson." (The spacious Englewood house with its columned porches, gardens and tennis court could be described as "little" only by the standard of English country houses frequented by Lord Cecil.) "It was very pleasant—a domestic scene. . . . We enjoyed it immensely."

The Cecils' departure for England turned into an unexpected close call. TWL was escorting his guests in a two-car caravan to the 14th Street pier when a sudden blizzard struck the city, stalling the automobiles in heavy traffic. The Cecils and their maid had eighteen minutes to cover the remaining seven blocks to the pier before their steamer's departure. The party abandoned the cars and started off on foot to make their way to the pier in the heavy snow. Cecil described the scene later: "Meanwhile our host was hiring porters to take our luggage down to the ship with a packet of dollar bills in his hand, which he dealt out as if he were playing cards! It was an impressive sight—a typical instance of the marvelous American hospitality." The Cecil party boarded the boat in the nick of time.

New Loans and Bad Debts

No remittances from Mexico for foreign debt service had been received since President Obregón's decree of July 1, 1924, suspending the payments. In January 1925, Finance Minister Pani visited New York. Lunching with Lamont and a colleague in a private dining room at the bank, he announced that Mexico could not resume payments on its foreign debt for another year.

Replying that this was indeed very discouraging news, Lamont indicated that the International Committee, which had been so patient with Mexico over the suspension of payments since July, would now have to declare publicly that the agreement was in default. A memorandum of the meeting described the next exchange.

> When Mr. Lamont explained that foreign bondholders would naturally request the assistance of their various Foreign Offices, Mr. Pani asked if this

meant "intervention." Mr. Lamont replied emphatically that in his view it meant nothing of the kind and that he felt the time when a debt could be collected by force of arms was past. He said that it did mean that Mexico, in the eyes of the world, would be in the same position as Turkey and Russia, and this was something which he did not wish to see.

Pani explained that Mexico's failure to obtain a loan the previous July, after paying out $15 million to the committee, had aroused such public resentment about the international debt agreement that it would be impossible to resume foreign debt service until the government had balanced its budget and provided for repayment of its domestic debts. Meeting with Lamont and several American banker members of the committee a few days later, Pani pursued this argument. Because he had inherited a 50 million peso budget deficit, about $25 million, Mexico could not, without receiving a new loan, pay any foreign debt service for another year.

Lamont said that the committee had discussed the possibility of a $20 million loan to Mexico, but was "still quite in the dark to find a way."

Pani shot back: A $60 million loan was needed, and the bankers could obtain it "right here among the Committee . . . in ten minutes." But the bankers were not interested. There would be no new loan for Mexico.

The finance minister maintained the offensive: the railway loans, whose debt service was guaranteed by the Mexican government, should be separated out of the 1922 agreement. The railways should be returned to private management and made to pay their own way with the government guaranty cancelled.

Impossible, said TWL. While the bankers heartily supported private control of the Mexican railroads, changing the agreement itself at this stage was quite another matter. Purely as a matter of mechanics the committee could not face the separation of the railway and government debt. Rather than trying, which would tear the agreement apart, the committee should "let the whole thing drop. . . . A new agreement would require another committee. . . . We have pledged our good faith to the present job. We can say that we have failed because the government has been unable to carry out the agreement. We cannot come to the bondholders with a new proposition." And there the matter rested, frozen in discord.

At the beginning of February, TWL joined the Dwight Morrows and Martin Egan in Nassau for a winter holiday. He was very tired, more than he had been for many years, he wrote his family, and looked forward to "a complete loaf." The climate and swimming were superb: "I never struck a holiday place quite so perfect."

Florence was also fatigued. In recent years she had often found the rhythm of her life burdened by the stream of houseguests and social events so pleasing to her husband, whom she called a "superman" in a letter to her daughter. "There is no doubt about it . . . that he ought to have two good strong husky wives to spell each other. I'm all for polygamy."

During February, Florence chose her own form of rest cure, entering a small private hospital in New York for three weeks of supervised diet and rest. On February 25 she reported "feeling very much rested in body and spirit."

A month later the Lamonts sailed on the Italian liner *Duilio* for Naples. One evening in preparation for a small dinner with some shipboard friends, Tom and Florence composed jingles for the guests' place cards. TWL wrote of Florence:

> *Woman dark and yet bright,*
> *Always thinks she is right—*
> *Yet angel in everyone's sight.*

In reference to the pasta-dominated shipboard menus, Florence wrote of Tom:

> *His sweet young wife with tearful eyes*
> *Implores him to go slow,*
> *But a different man will walk off the gang plank*
> *Of the good ship Duilio.*

From Naples the Lamonts visited Capri and Pompei and then drove to Rome. Tom paid courtesy calls on King Victor Emmanuel and Premier Mussolini, whom he later described in his Harvard class report as "that impressive figure" in recounting his talk with the premier. Lamont's reaction was not unique among Mussolini's American visitors, from businessmen to journalists, who generally fell under the spell of his unexpected charm and intelligence.

Lamont also talked with the chief officers at the Ministry of Finance, the Bank of Italy, and Credit Italiano, the leading private bank. Italy's strong economic recovery over the last two and a half years under Mussolini merited consideration for an American loan. TWL's job was to nail down the coveted Italian bond issue for Morgan before interested rivals Kuhn, Loeb and Dillon, Read. Lamont proposed that Morgan organize a bank credit to Italy in the near term to be followed by a Morgan-led bond issue in the U.S. later on.

On April 14 the Italian-American Association of Italy gave a dinner in Lamont's honor. TWL complimented Italy on its "manifest progress" since his visit two years earlier. Inflation had been curbed and the national budget was in balance. Americans had much for which they were indebted to Italy:

> for the language of our common speech, for the literature and for the art that lift our lives above the common plain of endeavor and that brings us beauty and delight. . . . Our first insight into the world of the past was gained through your classic writers. With Caesar we fought; with Virgil we travelled; with Cicero we breathed in admiration for noble qualities; with Horace we gained our first sophistications. Thus, with our earliest years we caught that sense of the color and beauty of Italy—as painted by the great artists whom the world reveres today and whose work can never die.

Springtime in Italy—long a magnet for visitors from around the world. Tom and Florence attended services at St. Peter's on Good Friday and were especially moved by the singing of the boy choir. Two days later, the Easter service at St. Peter's was crowded with tourists and lost all spiritual meaning for Florence. The scene reminded her instead of a huge bustling railroad station. Joined by their friends, the Masefields, the Lamonts toured the Italian hill towns by car. In Florence they stayed at I Tatti, the country villa of Bernard Berenson, who naturally excelled as expert guide to the city's art treasures.

In Paris on the way home, TWL's partners at Morgan, Harjes briefed him about the new bank credit for Great Britain in process. Of the total revolving credit of $300 million, the Federal Reserve Bank would lend $200 million to the Bank of England, and Morgan would lead a banking syndicate to provide $100 million to the British Treasury, for which it would be paid a management fee of $250,000.

The dominant Federal Reserve Bank of New York was headed by Benjamin Strong, an Englewood neighbor and good friend of Lamont and Morrow. In earlier years Harry Davison had helped start him out on his banking career, and unsurprisingly, he and the Morgan partners saw eye to eye on the need for U.S. loans to prop up England and the European powers. He had been working closely with Montagu Norman on Great Britain's plans to return to the gold standard in April 1925, and on the 28th of that month the Morgan bank and the Federal Reserve committed to provide the large credit to support the pound, once again tied to gold.

At the end of April, Tom sailed for New York, leaving Florence for a short stay in England, where she visited the Masefields and son Corliss, a student at Oxford. Back at the office Lamont was brought up to date on other foreign government loans in the offing—Argentina, Australia, and Belgium.

During the war years J. P. Morgan & Co. had conscientiously informed the administration of major foreign loans it was considering, to avoid any possible conflict with U.S. foreign policy. At the beginning of the Harding administration in 1921, the president told Lamont and a group of bankers that the government would like this voluntary cooperation by the banks to be continued, and it was. Now, however, Secretary of Commerce Hoover was pressing his cabinet colleagues to formalize foreign loan approval. Loans should be only for productive purposes and not for wasteful programs such as military expenditures; later he argued that loans should lead directly to increased orders for U.S. exports.

In a letter of March 31, 1922, to Secretary of State Hughes, Lamont warned that tying the proceeds of American loans to expenditures in the U.S. was unsound economic policy. American loans would strengthen the economies and bolster the foreign exchange reserves of borrowing countries, thereby increasing their demand for imports. But it would be wrong to force borrowers to purchase goods in the U.S., which in some circumstances might be the most expensive market for them.

Furthermore, a cornerstone of Republican policy, articulated by President Harding on taking office, was "More business in government and less government in business." Lamont warned Secretary Hughes that the Hoover doctrine would place the government "in a bureaucratic position heretofore not assumed by a capital country that we know about," by directly intervening in controlling the expenditures of loaned funds. The United States must be a responsible creditor nation by making sound loans to its foreign customers without earmarking the proceeds for purchases in the United States.

The State Department had been ambivalent about pursuing Hoover's stringent proposals for screening foreign lending, lacking the legal power to force compliance from the banks. Now a new development brought the question of obtaining the government's approval of foreign loans to a head.

In 1923 the U.S. government had begun the process of negotiating agreements with its wartime Allies to fund their American war debt and reduce its interest charges. To enforce this program the State Department decided to veto proposed loans to governments that would not agree to arrange long-term settlements with the United States. Belgium had become a stumbling block in the progress of this major American initiative to set the repayment of the European war debt on a realistic basis.

On May 22, 1925, Lamont phoned Secretary of State Frank B. Kellogg, who had replaced Hughes, to inform him that Morgan intended to head a syndicate to float a $50 million Belgian government bond issue. He was shocked at Kellogg's reply: the administration from President Coolidge on down did not want to see the loan made. Three days later TWL met at the State Department with Secretary Kellogg, Secretary of the Treasury Mellon, and Secretary of Commerce Hoover at a conference requested by Lamont.

The American government was not a party to the Versailles Treaty and did not accept the treaty provision permitting Germany's reparations commitment to Belgium to be substituted for Belgium's debt to her wartime Allies. However, the Belgian government wanted this substitution and was reluctant to negotiate on the premise that Belgium still had to repay the United States directly for its wartime borrowings, about $480 million including accrued interest.

The Belgians had been evasive about a meeting, and Secretary Kellogg was angry at them for stalling. Lamont's memorandum of the meeting recorded that the three cabinet secretaries stated that they had "quite firmly determined to discourage or if possible prevent any private loans direct to governments failing to make attempts to live up to their obligations to the American government, and Belgium was a clear case in point."

Lamont replied that when the Morgan bank had been initially requested to inform the government about prospective foreign loans, it had assumed that the State Department would raise objections only if major political issues were involved. The bankers had never contemplated that the administration would attempt to employ the procedure as a means to collect debts owed it by foreign governments. Accordingly, the bank would submit a formal letter advising the State Department of the proposed loan.

Both sides recognized that the administration, beyond stating its objections, had no authority to block the loan. While the Morgan partners normally wanted to comply with their government's requests, they could not properly and honorably give up the Belgian business. The bankers and the administration were on collision course. Belgium, however, saved the day. After a vigorous diplomatic exchange between Washington and Brussels, the Belgians capitulated and agreed to negotiate a revised debt agreement. The administration dropped its objections to the Belgian loan, and on June 12, 1925, J. P. Morgan & Co. announced the offering of a $50 million Kingdom of Belgium thirty-year bond issue.

At the end of May, Lamont received a cable from the Italian government requesting the $50 million bank credit that he had proposed in Rome. This time the administration cleared the transaction promptly.

During June and July, Lamont manned the office along with Jack Morgan, Morgan's son Junius, and Thomas Cochran. Morrow and Leffingwell were on holiday in France, and Stettinius, in failing health for two years, had not been at his desk in months.

On June 14, J. P. Morgan's wife, Jane Norton, known as Jessie, was stricken with a rare form of sleeping sickness, lethargic encephalitis, and lapsed into a coma from which she never awoke. She died on August 14. Lamont told his London partner, Edward Grenfell, how much he had admired the courage of their senior partner, coming to the office each day and cheerfully attending to his duties despite the terrible strain he was under during the two long summer months of Jessie's illness.

Throughout August, Edward Stettinius's condition steadily worsened, and he died at his home in Locust Valley on September 3. The sympathy and concern of the partners for the Morgan and Stettinius families during the sad summer underlined their affection for their modest senior partner and the strong bonds of personal respect and loyalty among the members of the elite team of bankers.

While Morgan's business with Europe was strong and growing, there had been no progress on the Mexican front: the debt dispute, affecting the savings of some 200,000 foreign bondholders, remained deadlocked. In April 1925, Lamont had met with the European members of the International Committee in Paris, who again rejected the idea of a new Mexican loan, which naturally discouraged the Mexicans from returning to the bargaining table.

While in North Haven in August Lamont kept in close touch with the situation. The Mexican government was establishing a new central bank which required gold-backed reserves to issue new currency. To allocate gold holdings for a wholly new purpose instead of resuming the foreign debt service payments "would indeed excite unfortunate comment upon the government's good faith in fulfilling its external obligations," Lamont wrote Finance Minister Pani in August.

The finance minister replied that the government's plan for the new bank met a national need which would benefit the foreign bondholders in the long run, and the bank began operations on September 1. TWL and his colleagues now realized that without a loan to offer they had little leverage in the financial dispute with Mexico. To negotiate a resumption of the foreign debt service payments, the bankers would have to abandon positions they had stoutly defended earlier, and the sooner the better.

Pani had proposed that the government's guaranty of the railroad loans be cancelled, thus eliminating its responsibility for repayment of this debt, amounting to about 45 percent of the total. TWL and the committee were now ready to concede the point, and Lamont invited Pani to New York to accept their surrender. "I hardly have to state. . . . I am sanguine of an accord with you," he wrote Pani in an effort to secure his prompt acceptance of the invitation. Pani agreed to come and met with the bankers in New York in October.

Leighton H. Coleman, then a young Davis Polk attorney who attended the negotiating sessions with Pani, later recalled Lamont's style in dealing with the finance minister. TWL, in a London-tailored suit with a handkerchief stuffed in his sleeve in the British manner, gestured with his gold-rimmed pince-nez as he suavely addressed the Mexican official in approximately the following terms: "Surely, my dear Mr. Minister, you would not have us believe that the great Republic of Mexico would contemplate further delay in making these modest payments to the thousands of patient bondholders, many of whom are widows and orphans in desperate need of these monies for their very existence. They are investors who still have deep faith in the good name of Mexico and its solemn pledge to honor its commitments. You can't let them down." Tugging at the heartstrings of the finance minister of a country as poor as Mexico seemed unlikely to be effective. Nevertheless, TWL's silky diplomacy and willingness to face up to reality did produce a new accord.

On October 24, 1925, Thomas W. Lamont, chairman of the International Committee of Bankers in Mexico, announced that an agreement had been concluded with Mexican Finance Minister Alberto J. Pani on modifications in the 1922 agreement on Mexico's foreign debt. Under the new accord the national railways would be returned to private control by January 1, 1926, and their bonds would no longer be guaranteed by the Mexican government. The railways would assume full responsibility for paying off their own debt. Mexico would resume the foreign payments called for under the 1922 agreement in January 1926, and the unpaid installments for 1924 and 1925, $37.5 million, would be paid over an eight-year period beginning in 1928. Some bankers were already speculating about how long the pact would survive, given Mexico's record and economic prospects.

*   *   *

On October 28 the Lamonts and a party of friends left New York on the Peacock Point, the Morgan private railway car, for a holiday at Grove Park Inn in Asheville, North Carolina. Pausing in Washington, Lamont went to see Secretary of Commerce Hoover to discuss Italian finance. The Italian Debt Commission was due in to visit Washington in November for talks on recasting their war debt, and Lamont favored a substantial cut in interest charges. Furthermore, the Italian government had requested J. P. Morgan & Co. to organize a large long-term bond issue in America, TWL told Hoover.

In the November 14 revised debt agreement with the U.S., Italy did get a major reduction in annual interest charges to a puny four-tenths of one percent, far lower than the rate set for the other European Allies. This settlement paved the way for the Morgan syndicate to float a $100 million bond issue for the Kingdom of Italy on November 20. The Morgan partners were convinced that the Italian government had become a quality "name," one that American investors would readily accept when asked to buy its bonds. Baron Sardi, a member of the Debt Commission, presented Lamont with a silver-framed signed photograph of Mussolini as an expression of the premier's gratitude.

At the Italy-America Society dinner at the Hotel Biltmore on November 25, Lamont noted with approval the lenient terms granted Italy in the revised U.S. debt agreement. He praised Italy's economic progress over the last three years as extraordinary: "Are we not justified from every point of view in looking forward to a brilliant and glowing future for Italy."

Lamont also noted that some Americans "are unhappy because they feel that the Italian people are not enjoying those ripe and luscious fruits of democracy which we here feed upon. They feel that liberty is on the wane. . . . Perhaps they are right. Yet may it not be that they are wrong? Perhaps the people of Italy do not yet desire our type of democratic government bestowed on them."

Many Americans shared Lamont's admiration for Mussolini's accomplishments. One was Will Rogers, the popular humorist and columnist, who called on the Italian premier. Another was Otto Kahn, the debonair Kuhn, Loeb banker and patron of the arts. Said Kahn in 1925: "I had a long talk with Mussolini and was again profoundly impressed by the greatness and irresistible personality of that wonderful man."

However, there had also been mounting American criticism of Mussolini's actions as premier, culminating in the virtually complete suppression of civil liberties. By the end of 1925 there was only one effective political party, the Fascists, and Mussolini ruled the nation's affairs as a dictator. Political opposition was not tolerated. He had said to the Italian parliament, "Italy wants peace and quiet, work and calm. I will give them these things with love if possible, with force if necessary."

On January 23, 1926, Lamont became engaged in debate about Italy under Mussolini with Professor William Y. Elliott of Harvard at a Foreign Policy Association meeting at the Hotel Astor. Elliott contended that the Mussolini government was based on "force and fear." He pictured Mussolini's rule as "despotic and bloody" relying on "the iron suppression of individual liberty." Fascism was "an organized body of armed thugs."

Lamont did not comment on the totalitarian regime in Italy. Instead he described the chaotic conditions that prevailed in the aftermath of the war and the tremendous improvement in the economy that had occurred since. Unemployment and strikes were now virtually nonexistent, and the government's fiscal management had balanced the budget and curbed inflation, the most oppressive and confiscatory tax on the working people that existed. "In this gathering today we count ourselves liberals, I suppose. Are we sure that we are liberal enough to be willing for the Italian people to have the sort of government which they apparently want?"

A *New York World* editorial the next day quoted the question posed by Lamont and gave this reply:

> But with parliamentary institutions suppressed, free speech muzzled, a free press no longer in existence and a dictator in complete control of every avenue of act and expression, how is Mr. Lamont or any one else to know what sort of government Italy does want? . . .
>
> No land where political liberty is denied by usurpation should be beyond the sympathy of citizens of the Great Republic.

While many newspapers and magazines admired Mussolini's leadership and accomplishments, others had begun to denounce his totalitarian regime and criticized the Morgan-organized loan to Italy. Lamont wrote Herbert Croly, editor of the *New Republic*, that the question was whether American investors "should make an unwarranted attempt to influence the internal affairs of Italy by refusing an economically sound loan to the Fascist government. . . . The admirable principle of non-interference in the internal affairs of one country by the government or business community of another should apply to all countries alike. . . . No banker is wise enough to determine the form of government best suited to such foreign states as he may number among his clients. To presume to dictate the form such government should take in any particular instance is the last attribute which the banker should assume."

Lamont was facing his critics squarely. Should the private sector take the lead in punishing totalitarian regimes by shutting off the flow of goods or capital to countries ruled by dictators? The Morgan bank had worked virtually hand in glove with three U.S. administrations, at their request, on foreign lending operations. In a real sense the firm had become a foreign lending arm of the U.S. government before the days of foreign aid programs and international lending institutions. Lamont believed that his bank should follow, not lead, U.S. foreign policy, and the U.S. government was not advocating curbing loans to Italy.

At an Italy-America Society luncheon in July 1926, TWL, the society's president, reminded his audience that Il Duce had declared to the Italian Senate that "the Fascist government is following and can but follow a policy of peace." Lamont also urged Giovanni Funni, the Morgan representative in Rome, to pass the word to the government that it would be wise to hire an American publicist to interpret its policies and actions to Americans through press releases and media contacts, a function later undertaken by the Italy-America Society.

Why make this extra effort to enhance the American public's opinion of Italy's Fascist government? A mix of motivations came into play for Lamont. Long-standing firm practice, going back to the days of Pierpont Morgan's railroad and industrial combinations, was to maintain responsibility for the performance of the issues that the bank sponsored, and the Italian bond issue of November 1925 had not sold well, leaving the underwriting syndicate stuck with a large block of unsold bonds. Furthermore, the growing distaste in America for Mussolini's repressive rule in Italy would handicap Italy's future ability to borrow in the U.S. In Lamont's view Italy remained a suitable client, and it was the role of international bankers to make sound loans. He looked forward to doing future business with Italy.

The firm's traditional policy was to care for and assist its clients, and they received the full treatment—from good seats to Broadway shows to expediting their luggage through customs; from economic intelligence to advice on public relations. In the case of Italy TWL had been the instrumental partner in winning the account over banking rivals. He was also a master in the art of public relations, and now Italy needed his special expertise.

Second, Lamont was emotionally bound to Italy and its heritage, and he shrank from looking on the dark side. Italy was a magnificent tapestry, and Lamont was loath to acknowledge the spreading stain of Fascism marring its beauty. TWL was a romantic when it came to Italy.

The Good Life

For their separate midwinter holidays in 1926, TWL would sail for Nassau at the end of January, and Florence would go back to the small hospital on 51st Street she had visited a year earlier for her enforced rest cure. She described her hectic pace that called for relief in a letter to Austin at Harvard.

> I am leading a horribly busy life at present, so filled with good works that it is revolting—teas for the League of Nations, a luncheon here at the house to raise money for the Women's Trade Union League, another big luncheon for thirty women who are district leaders of the Non-Partisan Association. That is here at the house, too, and I have got to make them a speech that will "inspire" them. But none of these things is anything compared to this awful debate that I have undertaken for the Colony Club.

According to Florence, her fellow members of the exclusive Park Avenue ladies' club were deadly serious about the upcoming debate on the topic: "Resolved, that the women represented by our club membership have too much leisure." She was glad to be defending the negative side.

> The other day I went to a meeting where it was being discussed, and I said "What I am going to say doesn't worry me nearly as much as what I am going to wear," and they all looked perfectly solemn and said: "You are quite wrong, what you are going to say is much more important." I have made myself the most awful bore at every dinner and every luncheon I have been to, asking everyone for a definition of leisure.
>
> This week I am having the Dinner Club meeting here at the house, and a German professor of psychology, who has been giving some lectures at Harvard, is going to show moving pictures of his work with apes and chimpanzees. I don't know exactly what bearing this has on the subject of our minds and souls, but evidently it has some, and we have some professors of psychology coming to try to refute the German. I think it ought to be a very nice evening.

The following week the Lamonts entertained the *Saturday Review of Literature* editors—Christopher Morley, William Rose Benet, and Henry Seidel Canby—and their wives at dinner. When the *New York Post* had been purchased by Cyrus Curtis, Henry Seidel Canby, the editor of its literary supplement, had resigned and approached Lamont for financial help in starting this new magazine. TWL liked the idea of backing the weekly, which in its own way would become a molder of public opinion. He invested $50,000 in the new enterprise.

Lamont's involvement in good works grew apace. He had been elected to a second term as a Harvard Overseer; he was the chairman of his Harvard class and in 1926 was elected president of the Harvard Alumni Association. He was also a trustee of Smith College, Phillips Exeter Academy, the Carnegie Foundation for the Advancement of Teaching, and the Children's Aid Society. He had endowed a professorship in memory of his father at Union College in Schenectady, which awarded him an honorary Doctor of Laws degree, and was president of the Italy-America Society of New York.

Once again TWL spent a pleasant holiday with the Morrows in Nassau, staying at the palatial New Colonial Hotel. Lamont, Morrow, and their friends cruised grandly through the islands on a motor yacht with a seven-man crew. At the end of February the party visited Havana before returning home via Key West, where Peacock Point, hitched to a Florida East Coast train, was ready to carry them home.

While foreign loans held a special attraction for TWL, domestic business, industrial and railroad financing, had long been the major source of Morgan income. Back at the office following his winter holiday, Lamont went to work readying a Morgan bank loan to the Vaness Corporation, the Van Sweringen brothers' holding company. Orvis P. and Martin J. Van Sweringen from Cleveland, a pair of unprepossessing, reclusive, and hard-working bachelors, had shown themselves to be exceptionally shrewd and successful investors in real estate and railroads. A decade earlier the brothers had started to build a major railway system with their acquisition of the New York, Chicago, and St. Louis line, known as the Nickel Plate. Using a pyramid structure of holding companies and borrowing heavily from banks, the brothers had purchased a controlling interest in several important railroads, including the Erie and the Chesapeake and Ohio. They had been careful to review their acquisition plans with the Morgan partners, who had developed a high regard for them. Their railroad system was well managed and profitable.

In a credit memorandum Lamont wrote of the Van Sweringens: "They are frank and have always commended themselves to us very highly for the way they have handled transactions. They seek advice, listen, are discreet and far-sighted." The Morgan partners believed that the loan, $25 million, secured by railway stock, represented the first step in a growing and profitable relationship with the Van Sweringens, as the brothers turned to the bank for assistance in financing their future expansion plans.

On April 7 the Lamonts left for Europe on the *Mauretania*. TWL wrote his children: "The usual raft of stuff was littering our cabin on departure"—stacks of new books, flowers, fruit, a Virginia ham, and even a container of clams, and the Lamonts went to work writing thank-you notes for their bon-voyage gifts. As usual the planning and preparations for the trip were meticulous. Lamont's secretary, Miss Hoffman, had ordered fresh vegetables and cream delivered on board for the ocean crossing. Weeks earlier she had instructed the Morgan Paris and London offices to make the necessary reservations for the Lamont party. The Lamonts always stayed at the Ritz in Paris and the Hyde Park Hotel in London in their favorite suite overlooking the park. Miss Hoffman requested their regular room arrangement, a suite of two bedrooms and baths with an adjoining sitting room. Single rooms were ordered for Mr. Lamont's "man," George Metcalfe, and Mrs. Lamont's maid. The Paris office attended to the arrangements for the Lamonts' visit to Spain with the Masefields, making reservations on Le Train Rapide from Paris to Madrid.

In Madrid, American ambassador Ogden Hammond arranged a lunch to introduce Lamont to the premier, Primo de Rivera, and an audience with King Alfonso at the Palace of Madrid, later described by TWL in a memorandum. Attired in a cutaway, he was ushered in regulated stages through four anterooms, gilded salons whose crimson brocaded walls were lined with Goya portraits and rich tapestries. Generals and admirals festooned in gold braid, scarlet-robed cardinals and bishops, and frock-coated diplomats stood awaiting their turn. King Alfonso was cordial and disavowed any interest in borrowing abroad, unwilling to accept the exchange risk exposure.

On a motor trip to Seville and Granada the Lamonts and Masefields had admired Spain's beautiful scenery as well as its historic towns, castles, and palaces, noting at the same time a dearth of sightseers. Lamont told the king that he believed that Spain, with proper organization, could attract foreign tourists in great numbers. On his part the king had some advice for TWL to pass along to the French minister of finance, struggling to increase government revenues. He was sure that if the minister were to establish a state lottery, as the king had done in Spain, his troubles would be over.

Returning to Paris, Lamont joined his Paris partners in their talks with French officials on the country's serious financial problems—the large government budget deficit and sharp depreciation of the franc on international exchanges. Lamont wrote son Austin: "The French government was in a panic and wanted me to hold their hand most of the time. There was little I could do to comfort them. They continued to behave as if they had no intelligence, whereas the French are supposed to be highly intelligent."

Russell Leffingwell, the foremost economic expert among the Morgan partners, had prepared a lengthy analysis of the French economy, including his judgment of the appropriate international value for the French franc. In a note to his Paris partner, Herman Harjes, Lamont urged him to share with the French officials "the gospel according to Saint Russell."

The objective of the talks in Paris was to determine the government's financial capacity to take on a major new American loan. When and under what conditions could the Morgan bank proceed with confidence? Not yet, was the partners' conclusion.

Now it was learned that Clarence Dillon, of Dillon, Read, had told the French government that his firm could help it in its financing plans in the United States. Harjes reported this news by radiogram to Lamont on shipboard bound for New York. "France needs only one banker in the United States," Lamont replied, and he urged Harjes to remind the French officials what the Morgan bank had already done for their country.

To Miss Hoffman also fell the task of mopping up after the Lamonts' foreign travels. Florence's shopping sprees in Spain and Paris had produced a princely yield—boxes and crates of antique porcelains and china, silk shawls and gowns, and the like—to be borne home by the travelers or separately shipped to America. The family files in the office were soon filled with bills, paid or in dispute, and letters and cables to art dealers and shops, freight forwarders, and the U.S. Customs office. Who should be responsible for a precious china vase found shattered in its box upon delivery?

The Lamonts regularly moved to their Englewood house in the spring to enjoy the greening countryside and later escape the city's stifling summer heat. Lamont had owned or chartered large motor yachts complete with crew for over a decade and thus was able to avoid the trials facing regular commuters from the area, who coped with train and ferry to reach Manhattan. Gardner Cowles, a distant cousin and college friend of Corliss, visited the Lamonts and later described with awe TWL's daily commuting routine.

> When he arose in the morning, he would put on a dressing gown and, thus attired, would be driven immediately by his chauffeur to his yacht,

which was moored on the west bank of the Hudson River. On board awaiting him would be his barber, his manicurist, and one of his secretaries. As the boat cruised down the river, Lamont would have his shave and shower and enjoy a leisurely breakfast. He then would glance through the morning papers and perhaps dictate a letter or two to his secretary. By this time the boat would be docking at the Battery and Lamont would conclude the routine with a brief walk from the end of Broad Street to the famous Morgan corner at Broad and Wall.

Pierpont Morgan was said to have counseled a young man that if he had to worry about the expense of running a yacht, he shouldn't even think of buying one. TWL, like the Morgans, happily ignored the costs of regal living on land or sea.

However, Lamont's peaceful summer holiday at North Haven was marred by a troublesome maritime incident when his son Austin lent the family sailboat to several friends for a cruise downeast to St. Andrews in Canada. There the college boys had bought a few bottles of Scotch whisky, which were uncovered by the U.S. Customs agent in Jonesport, Maine, upon their return. Under Prohibition the boat was immediately confiscated. Following payment of a fine, the boys regained possession of the boat, and the incident was kept quiet. However, Father Lamont was very upset about the episode and severely reprimanded his son.

Furthermore, TWL was annoyed that Austin felt he had to furnish his college friends with alcoholic drinks from a bar in his room at college. The Lamont parents had heard stories of the drinking parties at Harvard's Porcellian Club, to which Austin belonged, and once the father came across a note from his son to Metcalfe asking him to prepare a thermos of cocktails for Austin to take on a trip.

While Lamont did not object to young people having an occasional cocktail, his own drinking was limited to a ceremonial sip of wine, and, as he wrote his son, he deplored the excessive and gossip-inciting drinking that went on at college. In lieu of cocktails the Lamonts served sherry to their guests before dinner, although it was said that the hospitable and discreet Metcalfe was ready to serve cocktails or whisky to houseguests in their rooms when called upon. The Lamont wine cellar had long been well stocked.

For their winter holiday in 1927 Jack Morgan lent the Lamonts his magnificent black steam yacht, the *Corsair,* for a cruise through the Caribbean. The first port of call for the Lamonts and their guests was Nassau, where Lamont had arranged a full social schedule of parties and luncheons. Then the *Corsair* steamed serenely southward to Puerto Rico and on down the green volcanic chain of islands.

The Lamont party went ashore to tour the local attractions such as San Juan, the El Yunque tropical rain forest, and the village on Saba nestled in a volcanic crater. At Curaçao the *Corsair* turned north, heading for Jamaica, where the party stopped a few days before sailing on to Miami. Florence had found it difficult to sleep through the stifling tropical nights and was glad to get home. Luxury liner trips to Europe each spring with Tom were more her style.

On their annual European trip Lamont attended meetings at the ministry of finance in Paris to discuss the French government's wish to refund its outstanding 8 percent bonds of 1920 at a lower interest rate. This time it was the French who had cause to question the astuteness of their American bankers. Despite their customary meticulousness in drafting cables, a transatlantic misunderstanding had arisen; the talks became confusing, and TWL's final advice to the French on the timing of a new bond issue in the U.S. sharply conflicted with his earlier recommendation. He was embarrassed, and the French decided to postpone the refunding. At least the new transatlantic radio-telephone service between New York and London promised to eliminate the confusion inherent in even the most carefully drafted cables.

The rest of TWL's trip was relaxing—London for a few days and then Scotland for sightseeing, trout fishing, and golf at Gleneagles and St. Andrews. Florence stayed in London, but daughter Eleanor accompanied her father, along with a girl friend. TWL took the occasion to visit the chief of the Lamont clan at his ancestral castle in Argyllshire. At dinner Sir Norman regaled his American kinsfolk with stories of the clan's bloody history. The visitors climbed about the ruins of Toward Castle, the ancient Lamont stronghold. In nearby Dunoon they visited the memorial stone erected to honor the two hundred Lamont captives treacherously slaughtered by the Campbells when they seized the castle in 1646.

Returning to London, Lamont was greeted with news from the Mexican front. The Mexican government had had to borrow $2 million from the International Bankers Committee to complete the June 30 debt service payment due foreign bondholders. The payments owed on the Mexican railway debt had not been made. The defaults did not bode well for the future of the agreement. And there was news of direct importance to the Morgan firm: Dwight Morrow had been requested by President Calvin Coolidge to accept the appointment of U.S. Ambassador to Mexico.

TWL immediately cabled Morrow, urging him to decline the assignment. He foresaw that there would be increasing political turmoil in Mexico as the end of President Calles's term of office approached in

1928. Mexico's serious differences with the United States over the ownership of American oil properties remained unresolved. Morrow would not be able to get anything accomplished; he would be courting failure. Lamont was sailing for New York the next day, and he urged Morrow to postpone his decision until he could talk to him upon his return.

They talked, but Morrow was not persuaded by Lamont's argument. He had long hoped that his old friend from college, Calvin Coolidge, would appoint him to an important government post, and on August 19 he informed the president that he would accept the ambassadorship.

In July, Lamont bought a fifty-four-foot motor yacht from George Baker, Jr., which he named the *Reynard* after the narrative poem about a fox hunt by his friend John Masefield. He had anticipated many happy hours of cruising in the waters around North Haven during August. Unfortunately, this holiday was marred by days of unrelenting fog. In the Pulpit Harbor race for sailing dinghies, some of the little boats completely missed the harbor entrance and had to be rounded up by motorboats.

A poetical poster at the yacht club announced the evening's social event at Sky Farm.

> *As two doth strike, September five,*
> *The Dinghy fleet will fiercely strive*
> *To race around old Pulpit Rock,*
> *Though wind and whale do roughly shock.*
> *After which a sort of supper*
> *(Something more than bread 'n butter)*
> *Will Metcalf serve to Crews and Captains*
> *At the Lamonts—perhaps with napkins!?*
> *Subsequently at eight-thirty*
> *There will be a dancing "pirty"*
> *Given for the young and sprightly*
> *And those who still can trip it lightly.*

At the last moment Florence learned that the small band they had engaged for the dance could not reach the island because of the horrible weather. However, several amateur musicians were drafted, and the young people had a grand time, Florence wrote Corliss, who was traveling in Europe. The flask-sipping and amorous passes in the darkness of the flower garden undoubtedly added to the evening's fun.

Lamont returned to New York on Labor Day. He was scheduled to depart for Japan in two weeks, and there was much to do in preparation.

Japan's Wall Street Friend

When Kengo Mori, the former Japanese finance commissioner in New York with whom Lamont had negotiated the 1924 loan, proposed that Lamont revisit Japan in 1927, TWL was happy to oblige. The time was ripe to make a goodwill trip to strengthen the firm's relations with the government and business community. More foreign bankers were visiting Japan to seek out promising business opportunities, and no Morgan partner had been there since Lamont's earlier trip.

The Morgan bank was held in high esteem in Japan for organizing the urgently needed loan for reconstruction after the 1923 earthquake, and Morgan had subsequently undertaken smaller reconstruction loans for the cities of Tokyo and Yokohama. Furthermore, the Japanese government considered Lamont to be a loyal friend. Just months earlier, TWL had told a Japan Society dinner, "I believe in the Japanese people. Nothing will ever arise in my judgment to break the traditional friendship between America and Japan. That talk of war between these two countries which we sometimes hear is both wicked and silly."

Prior to his departure Lamont met with Secretary of State Frank Kellogg at his vacation office in St. Paul, Minnesota. The secretary was pleased with the current state of U.S.-Japan relations; the Japanese had shown a very cooperative attitude at the recent Geneva Naval Disarmament conference. He assured Lamont that the U.S. government would support new American loans to Japan.

Before sailing, the banker instructed his secretary in New York: "In regard to the ups and downs of my securities in the market, please cable me more rather than less." Even on the high seas Lamont received reports and cabled instructions concerning his personal holding company.

The Lamont party sailed from Vancouver on the *Empress of Russia* on September 22. This time it was an all-male contingent—Lamont; Jeremiah Smith, Jr., his friend and legal adviser; and Martin Egan (both Smith and Egan had accompanied Lamont on his 1920 trip to the Orient); Edward Saunders, a secretary, from the Morgan staff; Dr. E. P. Eglee to minister to the medical needs of the group; and George Metcalfe, Lamont's valet. The *Empress* docked in Yokohama on October 3d, where the Lamont party was met by a large welcoming delegation, headed by the mayor and a horde of reporters.

A reporter for the *Japanese Advertiser* described Lamont as he stood by the stairway on the lower deck of the ship receiving the welcoming committee and responding to the questions of journalists, who were relentless in pressing him to divulge some business purpose for his trip to Japan. Over and over, Lamont patiently explained that he was visiting Japan "at the invitation of friends and for no other reason."

The reporter was impressed by Lamont's calmness and "perfect ease commanding attention and receiving obedience," and he observed that the ladies introduced to TWL were impressed by "his clean-cut appearance and very blue eyes."

> He nodded and spoke a few words to each person. . . . One man persistently tugged at Mr. Lamont's coat to regain his attention and . . . Mr. Lamont revealed that a conversational, soft voice can carry authority: "I am not through with this gentleman yet," he said in a slow monotone, and the persistent gentleman let go of his hold.

> Mr. Lamont does not show his 57 years. He had quietly celebrated his fifty-seventh birthday on September 30, a few days before his arrival in Yokohama.

A press release handed out by Martin Egan stated:

> Mr. Lamont is not visiting Japan to discuss any financial operation, but in response to invitations that he has received from many of his friends here active in banking and finance.

The Japanese press remained skeptical.

The Japanese government had seen to it that Lamont was warmly welcomed. As the visitors drove to the Imperial Hotel in Tokyo from Yokohama harbor, troops of schoolchildren lining the streets shouted "Banzai, Lamontosan" as the party passed by. Large lithographs of Lamont were displayed in shop windows along the route identifying him as "the savior of Japan."

On the second evening of their visit, Governor Inouye of the Bank of Japan and Dr. Takuna Dan, managing director of the Mitsui holding company, hosted a dinner at the Bankers' Club in Lamont's honor attended by ninety government officials, industrialists, and bankers. In his remarks TWL was generous in his praise of Japan and its people. After the great earthquake, the Western world had marveled at the vigor and success of Japan's leaders in overcoming the disaster and at the industry and courage of the Japanese people in rebuilding their country. Furthermore, he believed that the Japanese economy was recovering well following a banking panic and business depression earlier in the year, a view his audience was delighted to hear from the prominent American financier. The *Japan Times* headlined its story on the dinner: "World has

Faith in Japan, States Thomas Lamont. Tokyo Bankers and Business Magnates Welcome Great Financier."

Each day was fully booked. The prime minister, Baron Tanaka, gave a lunch attended by a number of cabinet ministers and former prime ministers. The powerful Mitsui family, American ambassador Charles MacVeagh, and the Harvard Club of Japan entertained the visitors, and the mayor of Tokyo gave them a guided city tour to observe the progress of reconstruction since the earthquake.

TWL and his friends also made sightseeing trips to other parts of the country, and Lamont described a sybaritic experience in Kyoto in a letter to the family. His hosts had organized an outing in a nearby forest to gather the large local mushrooms, a gastronomical delicacy; they were normally well camouflaged and difficult to find.

> But this particular forest had apparently been preserved . . . for weeks before, because we found a great quantity, being actively assisted by about twenty geisha girls imported for the occasion. One of them was a beauty (and she really was beautiful in the American not the Japanese style). She had been brought from Nagoya, a hundred miles away for my special benefit, and at dinner that evening she nestled at my feet and served me all I thought I dared eat or drink.

TWL had indeed elevated his trips combining business and pleasure to an art form.

The Japanese government took the occasion of TWL's visit to confer special honors on him and his New York banking colleagues who had participated in floating the earthquake loans. Imperial decorations were awarded to Lamont, and in absentia to J. P. Morgan; Mortimer Schiff and Otto Kahn of Kuhn, Loeb; Charles E. Mitchell of the National City; and George F. Baker, Jr., of the First National. Lamont received the highest-ranking decoration of the group: the Second Class Order of the Rising Sun with Double Rays.

At 10:15 on October 5, TWL, attired in a long black frock coat with the insignia of his new decoration in his buttonhole, was escorted to the audience chamber of the Imperial Palace to be presented to Emperor Hirohito. The young monarch had ascended to the Chrysanthemum Throne the year before. Lamont described the event in a letter home:

> In accordance with instructions, I made a slight bow just before I crossed the threshold of the audience chamber; a second just over the threshold, a third half way up the chamber, and the fourth about four feet in front of the Emperor, each bow being a little more pronounced than the one before it. The Emperor stood at one end of the room clothed in military khaki, a young man of medium Japanese size with heavy eyebrows and rather

protruding lips. He had a pleasant and cordial expression. At his right stood one of the Japanese noblemen, and at his left fairly close to him Admiral Yamamoto, a very jolly Japanese admiral who was to act as interpreter. After I had made my last bow to the Emperor he gave me a cordial handshake.

The Emperor: I am very glad to welcome to Japan and to the palace so distinguished an American as yourself.

Lamont: Your Majesty, it was very good of you to welcome me so cordially. I have come seven thousand miles in order to show to you and to your people the good will which my house and our friends have for Japan.

The Emperor: I want to take this occasion to express my personal gratitude and that of our people for the great assistance which you rendered to us in the difficult days following the earthquake.

Lamont: Your Majesty, we were glad to be of any assistance and it was the courage the Japanese people showed that in large measure served to encourage us to undertake the heavy loan operation.

After exchanging a few pleasantries the Emperor and Lamont shook hands, and TWL walked backwards from the royal presence, carefully remembering to repeat his ceremonial bows.

Not surprisingly, the Japanese had a more concrete purpose in mind for Lamont's visit than the exchange of mutual expressions of goodwill. On the day before his audience with the Emperor, Lamont received from Governor Inouye a detailed study of the South Manchuria Railway and its financial requirements. The governor proposed that the Morgan bank organize a $30 million loan for the SMR, which the Japanese government would guaranty.

The SMR, controlled and substantially owned by the Japanese government, needed funds to expand its 686-mile system in the Chinese province of Manchuria. There were vast areas of productive agricultural land in the region, and Japan's requirements for imported foodstuffs were mounting steadily. The state of China's administration—divided, corrupt, inefficient, and torn by strife—ruled out any possibility that China could develop the province itself. In fact, the Japanese felt that the presence of the SMR in Manchuria was an important stabilizing influence. Many thousands of Chinese had fled the banditry and lawlessness of other regions to settle in Manchuria.

Lamont cabled Morgan outlining the proposal and stating his support for the loan. Morgan agreed, and the coded cables flew back and forth developing the terms and conditions. Lamont suggested that the SMR bond issue could be offered as early as November 1. After his conversation with Secretary Kellogg in St. Paul, he was confident that the State Department would support the loan, even though it had opposed American loans for the SMR in the past.

American ambassador Charles MacVeagh had preceded Lamont and Jeremiah Smith by several years at Exeter and Harvard; his son, Charlton, was a member of the Morgan bank staff. He would support the SMR loan; to do otherwise would be a setback to improving U.S. relations with Japan, he said. It was still necessary to obtain formal State Department clearance, but the proposition seemed firmly on track as Lamont prepared to sail for San Francisco on October 19.

The American Association held a dinner for the Lamont party on their final evening in Tokyo. In concluding his remarks Lamont said: "As to this country whose beautiful and hospitable shores my associates and I are now leaving, our credo is: We believe in Japan. We believe in her peaceful intentions. We believe in her courage, her patience, her good faith, and her loyal friendship for America."

Ten days later the Lamont party, well rested after a pleasant, sunny voyage, disembarked for a one-day stopover at Honolulu. After a press interview they were royally entertained by local luminaries, attending three receptions and a luau. On November 3 the *President Pierce* steamed into San Francisco Bay. Once more the reporters attempted without success to extract from Lamont some news of future loan operations with Japan. He expressed his standard optimistic assessment of Japan's economic recovery, adding, "Japan is friendly to the United States and this is evidenced on all sides." Later in the day he brought the same message to a large luncheon at the Palace Hotel in his honor, hosted by William H. Crocker, head of the Crocker National Bank, and to a Harvard Club of San Francisco reception.

During the Pacific crossing Lamont had drafted scores of thank-you letters, usually with a personal message, to his Japanese hosts, from Prime Minister Tanaka on down through the ranks. Lamont had found before that sea voyages were an ideal time to write letters to a wide circle of friends and to his children.

Corliss, age twenty-five at the time, was considering doing graduate work in philosophy and contemplating his future career. Of one thing he was certain: his plans did not include banking or business. His father wrote him from shipboard:

> Where did you get this idea that we might think you were "loafing along idly—and being a parasite on society?" Bunk—I'll say. You will never be accused of idleness. . . . But why don't you rejoice that by reason of money independence you can study as long and variously as you please without the

pinch of earning bread and butter; that by reason of your own independent thinking you can achieve great position of your own? But you can't completely cut yourself from your environment and live in the blue Empyrean or like a god on Olympus!

His communications to Tommy on the Morgan staff were more businesslike. From shipboard Lamont cabled TSL: "Please tell mother I want to give men's dinner to French ambassador on November 14 and to college presidents with her present on 16. Ask Leffingwell arrange French dinner list."

For TWL, entertaining was frequently more purposeful than gathering together old chums or playing the customary game of social reciprocity. Wining and dining diplomats and officials was important in cementing good relations between the bank and its clients, and such affairs could also yield useful nuggets of information on government affairs.

On November 10, Lamont called on Under Secretary of State Robert E. Olds to present the case for approval of the South Manchuria Railway loan, and he summarized his views in a letter to Olds the following day. Based on his conversation with Secretary Kellogg in St. Paul, said Lamont, he presumed the State Department would not object to the loan. TWL believed that the SMR presence was a stabilizing influence in Manchuria to the benefit of the large Chinese population growing steadily through immigration from other parts of the country. It was Lamont's firm belief that Japan had abandoned military force as a means of expansion in Asia and had no imperialist design on its neighbor. Friendship and strong ties with the United States were important to Japan, and the SMR project provided an excellent opportunity for the two countries to work together for their mutual benefit and that of China.

On November 17, Lamont, accompanied by Charles E. Mitchell, president of National City Bank, which would be a major participant in the loan, met with Secretary of State Kellogg, Under Secretary Olds, and Assistant Secretary Nelson T. Johnson in Washington to go over the matter again. The State Department had opposed SMR loans in the past because it believed that Japanese expansion in Manchuria would block the development of American interests in the area. But the Japanese had not interfered with American business in the region, and Governor Inouye confirmed the Japanese government's nondiscriminatory policy toward American interests in Manchuria in a cable which Lamont had suggested that he send. The reality was that Manchuria held little investment interest for Americans. The State Department, with the support of Ambassador MacVeagh in Tokyo, was now leaning toward approving the loan. But the SMR loan was no longer a secret in the Far East or the United States, and the American press picked up the story quickly, pinpointing the Lamont-Mitchell meeting with Secretary Kellogg to discuss the proposal.

Over the next few weeks public opposition to the SMR loan mounted. First, the Chinese minister to the United States lodged a protest with the State Department on behalf of the Shanghai Chamber of Commerce and similar groups. Official protests against the proposed loan were made by representatives of both the Kuomintang and Peking regimes. A boycott of American goods in China was threatened, and articles opposing the loan began to appear in liberal American journals. Regarding the SMR loan the *Nation* stated: "It is an insult to China, a provocation to Russia . . . almost an act of war." Various associations—church groups, peace organizations, and Chinese friendship societies—joined the hue and cry. Assisting the South Manchuria Railway was viewed as aiding a Japanese move toward further penetration and dominance over Manchuria. Even the directors of the Standard Oil Company advised Lamont against the loan because of their fear of a Chinese boycott of American imports if it was consummated.

The State Department was cooling toward the loan. On December 1, Lamont cabled Inouye that while the department had not formally objected to the proposition, department officials were uneasy because of the surge of protests about the transaction. The department would like to have the loan postponed until "the storm had blown over. . . . It would be tactful both from your and our point of view to be able to gratify their wishes in this way." Furthermore, the unfavorable press had "soured the market" for the loan. Lamont recommended that the loan negotiations should be quietly suspended until a later time, and Inouye concurred in his cable two days later.

Lamont and Inouye also agreed to say nothing to the press about the status of the loan, but on December 5 both the *New York World* and the *Journal of Commerce* reported that the bankers had tabled the SMR loan because of the storm of protest on behalf of China that it had provoked. Lamont and his partners simply refused to comment on the subject.

Lamont was serious about pursuing the SMR loan at a more opportune time, and he continued to promote his view of Japan's liberal and peaceful intentions in the Far East. In an address at a dinner of the Institute for Pacific Relations on December 13, 1927, TWL said that in their own self-interest the Chinese should "compose their differences to the point of jointly inviting the amicable co-operation of foreign interests, the Americans, British, and Japanese." Lamont added, "We shall see no wars over Japanese interests on the mainland of Asia."

Banking on the Corner

The year 1927 was a good one for TWL in garnering foreign decorations. Earlier in the year the Morgan bank had organized several loans for Italian borrowers, including the City of Rome and the giant industrial company Pirelli. In December, J. P. Morgan & Co. extended a credit of $25 million to the Banco d'Italia as part of an international loan for stabilizing the lire as Italy returned to the gold standard. At year-end royal awards were conferred on Lamont and Morgan, Lamont being appointed a Commander of the Order of the Saints Mauritius and Lazarus.

For the year 1927, Dow Jones & Co., the financial service, reported that the Morgan firm was the leading syndicate manager of bond issues, with just over $500 million to its credit. National City Bank and Kuhn, Loeb were not far behind. Since the war, foreign bond issues had comprised about a third of the Morgan-managed offerings.

First Austria, then Germany, Great Britain, Belgium, and now Italy had returned to the gold standard over the last four years, and the Morgan partners expected that France would shortly follow suit. International loans and credits, in which Morgan's leadership had been instrumental, had buttressed the reserves of these countries as they tied their currencies to gold. The Morgan partners believed that the bankers had played a very constructive role in strengthening the world's economies.

But not all the foreign bonds being sold to American investors were soundly based, especially some of the South American and Balkan government issues. In a talk before the International Chamber of Commerce in Washington on May 2, 1927, Lamont warned investors to be careful: "I have in mind the reports . . . of American bankers and firms competing on almost a violent scale for the purpose of obtaining loans in various foreign money markets overseas. "Naturally it is a tempting thing for certain of the European governments to find a horde of American bankers sitting on their doorsteps offering them money. . . . That sort of competition tends to insecurity and unsound practice."

The profit to bankers in the reckless underwriting of foreign loans was at the public expense. Indeed, weak bank credits, such as advances to Latin American governments, might well be paid off from the proceeds of bond issues sold to trusting investors whose losses came later. The pacesetter among the bankers aggressively underwriting and selling foreign bonds with little investigation and dubious prospects was Charles E. Mitchell, the affable and dynamic head of National City Bank and its investment affiliate. He and others like him paid little heed to TWL's warning.

The Morgan bank, headquartered in the low fortress-like building at the juncture of Wall and Broad streets, was commonly referred to as "the Corner." Directly across Wall Street were the old Sub-Treasury Building and the U.S. Assay Office; the New York Stock Exchange and the Bankers Trust tower stood at the southwest and northwest corners of the intersection. Most of the important New York banks and investment firms were within a few hundred yards. J. P. Morgan & Co. was truly at the financial center of the nation and deserved its premium location. Comparative underwriting statistics understated the powerful influence of the firm, reflecting its standing at the summit of the financial community for over three decades. Its political connections were at the highest levels in Washington and London. In a real sense the Morgan bank was the gatekeeper controlling access to the huge sums of capital needed by the biggest and best corporations and foreign governments. U.S. Steel, General Motors, General Electric, A.T.&T., Great Britain, France, and the list went on—were all Morgan clients. Bankers regularly speculated as to how the Corner would regard a proposal; Morgan's support or rejection could make or break a deal.

All the partners in town tried to be on hand for the daily partners' meeting at ten o'clock, at which strategies and assignments were decided to handle the firm's business. At this session the bankers all gathered around Jack Morgan's rolltop desk in the glass-enclosed partners' row on the Broad Street side of the banking floor. Thomas Lamont presided, and no notes were kept of the decisive discussions.

Wall Street regulars recognized the senior partners as they descended from their chauffeured black limousines each morning, to be greeted by the Morgan doorman as they mounted the short granite steps to the Corner entrance. J. P. Morgan was a shy man who appeared remote and unapproachable to outsiders. While only a few intimates addressed him as "Jack," he was affable with his colleagues and close circle of friends. His word was final in the firm's business, but he almost always accepted the recommendations of his partners, on whose judgment and business acumen he relied. Sometimes Morgan would drive to the office with his son Junius, a congenial yachtsman who did not show signs of inheriting the banking genius of his forebears.

Russell C. Leffingwell was regarded by his colleagues as the firm's leading expert on fiscal and monetary affairs. Lamont often sought his advice on a wide range of political and economic matters. Sometimes Leffingwell had breakfast with George C. Whitney to discuss the firm's business, and the two partners then rode downtown together. Leffingwell, a sharp-nosed man with a shock of white hair and an impressive intellect, and Whitney, slender, handsome, and highly competent, worked closely and well together. Whitney, who had gone to Groton and Harvard and married the daughter of a former Morgan partner, was regarded by his senior colleagues as the most able of the younger partners. In the next rank, Thomas Cochran, Francis D. Bartow, Arthur M. Anderson, and Harold Stanley, while less well known to the public, had important roles in managing the firm's business.

The Morgan partners were a proud lot, proud of their firm's record and standing and of their own abilities as bankers. To some their style seemed arrogant and self-righteous, but the Morgan aura of banking superiority impressed the bank's clients and, combined with good compensation, infused a winning team esprit and strong loyalty down through the ranks.

Lamont was recognized as Morgan's chief executive officer and the guiding light of the Morgan bank, "the ablest and foremost of all of J. P. Morgan's partners," according to *Forbes* magazine. He was also known as the bank's smooth-talking public spokesman and international ambassador. Beneath his congeniality, others could detect an inner steel, ready for use when needed; he had no difficulty in saying no. At the same time he was adept at conveying bad news to a client with the artfulness of a seasoned diplomat.

TWL had an enormous capacity for work. He often quoted a maxim he tried to follow in golf and in life: "Easy does it!" The pitfalls and pressures of business did not seem to upset his calm and unflappable disposition. But there were lapses: an apologetic note to a colleague, found in the files, indicates he had displayed a rare burst of temper in a meeting the previous day.

Lamont's noted charm was not reserved for his peers. In the late twenties, A. Vernon Woodworth, a teenage summer resident, was somewhat awed to be matched against the millionaire Wall Street banker in the North Haven Golf Club championship for two years running. In beating his young opponent, TWL's relaxed and friendly ways put the boy at ease. "Even at my age," said Woodworth, "I could see he had special charm." To those who saw TWL chatting about the weather with the Morgan doorman in the morning, he was genial and democratic, which could not be said for all Morgan partners. Smooth and smiling when communicating with the outside world, TWL could be brutally frank with his colleagues. A Morgan staff member reported a conversation with Lamont about a rival investment banker. "Oh, he's a real son of a bitch," said TWL. "If I ordered a freight train of s.o.b.'s and they shipped that fellow, I would accept him as full delivery of my order."

Lamont's relationship with J. P. Morgan was unfailingly courteous and respectful, as TWL went about his job of directing the firm's affairs. A note from TWL to JPM, after the latter had just departed on a vacation trip, is typical of many: "I stopped down to say good-bye, but you had already gone. . . . Take care of yourself, and give me a game of golf when you return." However, TWL was realistic: to financial editor Franz Schneider he once referred to Morgan as the "grand seigneur."

Morgan in turn recognized TWL's vital importance to the firm. Morgan's business judgment was generally sound, but he was not a clever or imaginative thinker, and ideas surfaced from Lamont and the other partners for his approval. Morgan was away on vacation for lengthy periods, three months or so in England each year, plus *Corsair* cruises and other sojourns for grouse shooting, winter holidays at Jekyll Island, and the like. It was his wish to have Lamont lead the firm, and the working and personal relationship between the two chief partners was friendly, but not the easygoing camaraderie that might exist between old companions. Morgan in his letters to TWL always referred to Florence as "Mrs. Lamont."

Lamont had a fine sense of humor and a light touch. One New York financial editor wrote in his column: "If you were to run into him as he was coming out of the Morgan office at Broad and Wall, he would grab your arm and say: 'Walk up the street with me and help my credit and general public standing!'" Self-confident, bold in self-promotion, and a model of worldly charm, Lamont thoroughly enjoyed his eminence—the full and gracious lifestyle, mingling with glamorous and important figures, and a useful and influential part in world affairs. He especially relished his role as the Morgan bank's roving ambassador.

Egyptian Kings, Past and Present

On January 17, 1928, the Lamonts set out for Egypt with their guests and longtime friends John and Bertha Tildsley. Bertha was a Smith classmate of Florence; her husband was an assistant superintendent of schools in New York City. At Naples, the Masefields and their daughter joined them for the journey up the Nile, the classic tour so warmly recommended to TWL by Pierpont Morgan seventeen years earlier. Florence was delighted to disembark, as she wrote her family: "This is the horridest boat I have ever been on. So noisy that you can't sleep more than a couple of hours at night. I am right under the bar, & so I get my full share of all that is going on. Whenever anyone in the next room uses the wash basin, the pipes in my room give a quick succession of pistol shots and makes me jump nearly right out of my bed. . . . The boat is full of 'Shriners,' all of whom give a certain evidence of belonging to the Porcellian Club. . . . It is the worst trip I have ever had. The boat is managed by lunatics and built by morons. We shall all be glad to leave her. Last night there was a drinking party of men and women in one of the cabins lasting until 4 a.m."

TWL took the shipboard commotion in stride. However, the Lamonts were deeply saddened to receive word during the ocean crossing that Florence's father, Wilbur Fisk Corliss, had died at the age of eighty-six. Lamont wrote his eldest son: "Grandpa was always fine to me. He took a great pride in my modest goings-on, cut out clippings about me in the newspapers and all that. When I told him I wanted to marry your Mother, he said all right—'I hope you love her. Anyway you'll never have a dull moment.' Which was true!"

The American Legation in Cairo had arranged an audience for Lamont with King Fuad, the ruler of Egypt, which had won its independence from Great Britain in 1922. Lamont, in a morning suit and silk hat, was escorted through a series of long halls and reception rooms in the palace to the King's audience chamber. TWL, by now an old hand at meeting royalty, bowed the requisite number of times as the King, wearing a red fez, greeted him cordially. Lamont described the audience in a memorandum afterward. "He was the only man I ever met who could speak as bad French as I could and still make himself intelligible. He was rather amusing . . . starting off by saying, 'Mr. Lamont, I will wager I am the only head of a foreign state who has ever received you without asking for a loan for his government.' "

The King did most of the talking, mainly about "the glories of his country, past, present, and future." TWL thought that the King's glowing vision of Egypt's economic prospects was quite unrealistic. Nevertheless, he was gracious and amiable, had a firm handshake, and "looked you straight in the eye."

The English officials and journalists in Cairo were very skeptical of the newly independent nation's ability to govern itself. A British diplomat conversing with TWL compared the Egyptians to the Mexicans, saying that the two were much alike except that "the Egyptians were worse."

The Lamonts, like the armies of tourists before them, were enthralled by the splendors of ancient Egypt. At Giza, TWL clambered partway up the Pyramid of Cheops, with the aid of two guides pushing and pulling, before Florence's entreaties that he was "too old" for that sort of thing persuaded him to abandon the project. The next day the party boarded the S.S. *Chonsu*, the shallow-draft yacht TWL had chartered to make the trip up the Nile; he had also hired an Arab dragoman who proved to be an excellent guide—knowledgeable about Egyptian history and antiquities and skillful at obtaining fresh vegetables en route. At Luxor, Herbert Winlock, the Metropolitan Museum of Art's noted Egyptologist and a North Haven summer neighbor, guided the group's tour of the great temple of Karnak and the Valley of the Kings, giving them a fascinating insight into the current program of research and excavation. From Luxor the *Chonsu* steamed upriver to Aswan and then on to Abu Simbel, site of the magnificent temple of Ramses II with its four giant statues hewn out of solid rock guarding the entrance. The party returned to Cairo by train from Aswan.

Lamont wrote his children: "It has been a dandy trip. Reading all the books in the world gives you no idea of Egypt as this slow sail on the great river does; with all the life of the river banks (which compose all Egypt) going on before your eyes; and a good part of the life of the ancient Egyptians from 3000 B.C. spread out for your inspection in the temples and tombs and in their vivid and wonderful decorations."

The sun, insects, and dust did not bother TWL. The *Chonsu* chef was excellent, and the twenty-three-man crew took good care of their passengers. "Life on a dahabeah on the Nile is lazy and comfortable," wrote TWL. "The flies are persistent but not vicious; the fleas are vicious but not persistent."

Just before leaving for Egypt Lamont had written Governor Inouye his views on how the South Manchuria Railway loan request should be revised and resubmitted later in the spring, when the anti-SMR clamor had died down. The amount should be reduced to $20 million to be used solely for refunding maturing debt. Thus Morgan and its associates could not be charged with helping to expand the railway itself. All publicity about the SMR should stress its good relations with the Chinese authorities, the "contentment and prosperity" of the Chinese immigrants in Manchuria, and "their desire to have the Japanese continue economic development." Inouye concurred, and on April 18 Lamont submitted the recast loan proposal to the Department of State, which saw no reason to object to the normal refunding operation.

On the same day Prime Minister Tanaka of Japan sent 5,000 troops to

Shantung, allegedly to protect Japanese nationals in the Chinese province, while the army of General Chiang Kai-shek, leader of the Kuomintang regime in the south, drove northward to depose the Peking government. The Chinese and Japanese forces clashed at Tsinan on May 3, and several days later the Japanese seized the city. In the face of this flagrant example of Japanese readiness to employ military force in China, the State Department did a volte-face and withdrew approval of the SMR loan. The incident dealt a blow to Lamont's credibility at the department as the expert who had proclaimed that Japan had forsaken militarism. But although the SMR loan was dead, TWL had no thought of cooling his warm relations with Morgan's client, the Japanese government.

Book IV

BOOM AND BUST

Domestic Affairs

President Coolidge had surprised his fellow citizens by announcing in August 1927 that he did not choose to run for president in 1928, thereby opening up the field to a bevy of Republican hopefuls, among whom Herbert Hoover soon became the frontrunner. He was revered for his brilliant administration of the wartime and postwar relief programs in Europe. Second, the business community admired him as an energetic and progressive Secretary of Commerce. Business was good and the stock market on the rise. TWL, who had had his run-in with Hoover on foreign loans, considered Charles Evans Hughes, the former Secretary of State and 1916 Republican candidate, as more enlightened in international affairs and hoped that he would enter the race.

In a letter to Ambassador Morrow in December 1927, TWL reported a recent dinner conversation with Hughes about his possible candidacy. Hughes had concluded that there was not enough party rank-and-file support for his nomination. Furthermore, he would be too old at age seventy to run for a second term.

Although, most observers thought that the Hoover nomination was a certainty, Lamont still felt Hughes had a chance and went around to his office to make a final attempt to persuade Hughes to announce his candidacy. He told Hughes that there would be an important group at the convention eager to see him nominated and elected and ready to back him to the hilt. "Do you think I could accept a nomination coming in that way?" Hughes asked. Before Lamont left, Hughes had made it very clear that he could not be tempted by Wall Street to throw his hat into the ring.

In June Hoover won in Kansas City on the first ballot, and Governor Alfred E. Smith of New York captured the Democratic nomination. Lamont, without great enthusiasm, planned to vote for his party's candidate and made a substantial donation to the Hoover campaign. Business was thriving, Lamont and his bank were flourishing, and the dour Hoover could be counted on not to rock the boat.

In 1927 the Lamonts had purchased some two hundred acres of woodlands high on the brim of the Palisades overlooking the Hudson and beyond. During the spring of 1928 the family spent weekends exploring their new property, about a dozen miles north of Englewood. Sometimes they made the trip by water, cruising upriver on the *Reynard* to the little village of Snedens Landing nestled at the foot of the cliffs. The family enjoyed hiking in the woods, white with blossoming dogwood, where a rushing brook finally cascaded down a rocky chute to a pool far below. Florence and her architect spent hours together planning the Lamont's stately new country home and grounds.

Following the wedding of second son Corliss and Margaret Irish at Troy in June, TWL went on to the Harvard Commencement exercises, where Dwight Morrow, on leave from his ambassadorial post in Mexico, received an honorary degree and spoke. Morrow had won acclaim for his successful handling of the troublesome problem of the status of American oil properties in Mexico, resulting in the government's recognition of the rights obtained by foreign oil companies before enactment of the 1917 constitution to properties on which they had started work.

The ambassador had developed a warm relationship with President Calles and also demonstrated a real flair for public relations, unlike his striped-pants predecessors. He mingled in friendly and easy fashion with the common folk and had arranged a very popular goodwill flight by Colonel Charles A. Lindbergh to Mexico City, where the famous aviator received a tumultuous welcome and won the heart of Morrow's shy and pretty daughter, Anne.

At the end of June, Lamont went salmon fishing at a camp on the Grand Cassapedia River in Quebec, Canada, with Arthur Lockett, Jerry Smith, and other friends. They had a grand time, he wrote his children, even though the fish weren't biting. In August, TWL joined his family in North Haven and began work on a new project, a biography of Henry P. Davison, his late partner.

Once again the presidential election in November was a Republican landslide. Bucking the trend, Franklin D. Roosevelt, the Lamonts' former landlord, who had eloquently placed Alfred E. Smith's name in nomination at the Democratic convention, was elected governor of New York.

While Lamont voted for Hoover, Florence and even banking son TSL voted for Governor Smith. They objected to the Republicans' isolationist posture, reflected in the party's rhetoric of the day, notwithstanding some noteworthy achievements in international cooperation by recent Republican administrations. Most Americans thought that the Republicans offered the best chance of continuing the nation's prosperous business conditions. Danger signals such as the mounting fever of stock market speculation caused little concern.

While traveling abroad in March 1928, TWL had received a cable from his office: "The market is boiling." After a brief respite early in the year, the stock market was on the march again. Stock prices and trading volume had been advancing for several years, and in the spring of 1928 the bull market took off, buoyed by the news of Hoover's nomination in June, and later by his landslide election victory in November. The volume of trading climbed from 576 million shares in 1927 to 920 million in 1928, reflecting the speculative frenzy seizing the country.

The Morgan partners were not immune to the lure of rapidly rising stock prices, although Russell Leffingwell became increasingly skeptical. Lamont was an optimist. He ran with the bulls, as the family prepared for their own big social event of the year.

On the day before daughter Eleanor's coming-out party in December to introduce her formally to New York society, many of the young men who had been invited had not been heard from, causing the hostess considerable anxiety; however, at the last moment a flood of acceptances came in, followed by a host of stags on the great evening—almost too many, Florence reported to son Austin in England. The 70th Street house was beautiful, trimmed with greens and baskets of roses and chrysanthemums. The music was provided by the Meyer Davis band and dinner by Sherry's restaurant. The whole crowd moved on to another dance around midnight, and Philip Savage, the Lamont chauffeur who drove Miss Eleanor on her party rounds, did not get to bed until seven o'clock the next morning.

TWL wrote Austin: "There had been a long argument between your Mother and me as to whether a stick should be put in the fruit punch or not. I had on hand some prewar Bacardi rum and thought that simply for the psychological effect upon the dinner a little of it should be put in the punch. Your Mother objected, not in practice but in principle. Finally it was compromised by instructions to Metcalfe to put in only enough to give just a tinge of a taste to the punch itself. A little later in the evening one of the boys remarked to Tommy's Ellie that it seemed like a pretty dry evening; whereupon, Ellie, having been conversant with the argument, said 'Oh, no, there is plenty of rum in the punch!' Whereupon, in turn, the boy remarked, 'Well, I guess if anything was put in it must have been with an eyedropper.' "

As the Morgan partner most attentive to cultivating good relations with the press, Lamont had developed a growing respect for Walter Lippmann, the chief of the editorial page of the *New York World*. He was a thoughtful and successful author and speaker, an internationalist, and an avid traveler with entree to the highest councils of government at home and abroad. The *World* and Lippmann, liberal in their viewpoint, had favored the Democratic presidential candidate, Governor Alfred E. Smith. Yet Lippmann knew and highly respected Herbert Hoover and admired the contribution of American business to the nation's welfare. He felt quite comfortable with bankers such as Lamont, Leffingwell, and Morrow, all liberal-minded executives by Wall Street standards. They were unmitigated and powerful capitalists, but certainly not Bourbons. By no means did Lamont and Lippmann agree on everything; for example, their views on Mussolini were far apart. In contrast with TWL's admiration, Lippman and the *World* abhorred Mussolini as a brutal dictator and menace to world peace.

Lippmann was brilliant and entertaining, his wife Faye beautiful and high-spirited. Tom and Florence were charmed by this attractive younger couple, who with growing frequency joined their dinner parties and vacation trips. In December 1928, the Lippmanns visited the Lamonts at their new vacation home at Yeamans Hall, an exclusive private resort on the grounds of a former plantation near Charleston. The old-guard membership preferred a simple, relaxed atmosphere. As one venerable member observed, "It's a sleepy sort of life. If anyone gets here after 9:30 in the evening, he'll find everybody in bed—and in their own beds, too."

Florence had not been consulted by Tom in planning the new "cottage" and was surprised to discover that it contained six bathrooms. The golfing house party was fun, she reported, but the next Lamont social event attended by the Lippmanns was not much fun for Faye.

On New Year's Day, 1929, Tom and Florence gave a dinner party in honor of Dwight and Elizabeth Morrow, home for the holidays from Mexico. After dinner Florence organized a game of charades, and one team decided to act out "Morrow," the name of the guest of honor. Learned Hand, the distinguished federal judge, played the part of Othello, the Moor, in dramatizing an approximation of the first syllable, and lovely Faye Lippmann played Desdemona. The judge, a large man, carried out his role with considerable gusto when he "smothered" Desdemona with a pillow as she lay supine on a couch. Unwittingly, he had performed too well. Poor Faye struggled to her feet, blood gushing from her nose and in great pain. Furthermore, Tom observed that her nose appeared to be slightly off center. A hastily summoned doctor confirmed that Mrs. Lippmann's nose was indeed badly broken. The eminent U.S. Court of Appeals judge was grief-stricken and mortified. "He fears that all the rest of his life his career as a United States judge will be dogged by the fact that he went to a party and broke a lady's nose," Lamont wrote his son Austin.

On January 1, 1929, J. P. Morgan & Co. announced the election to the partnership of three sons of Morgan partners—Henry Sturgis Morgan, the second son of J. P. Morgan to join the firm; Thomas Stilwell Lamont, son of Thomas W. Lamont; and Henry Pomeroy Davison, Jr., son of the late Henry P. Davison. The newspapers commented on the youth of the three new members of the firm, who, said the *New York Times,* had won "the most coveted posts on Wall Street." Davison, barely thirty, was the oldest. "From a financial standpoint a Morgan partnership has always been rated among the chief plums of American banking. . . . It is believed that a partnership in the firm yields at least $1,000,000 a year," added the *Times.* The papers reflected the Wall Street outlook: with no end in sight for the booming financial markets, even Morgan's junior partners became instant millionaires. The three new members brought the total number of partners to fourteen.

Running With the Bulls

Following long-standing policy, J. P. Morgan & Co. had limited its underwriting of securities for public offering to high-grade bonds, government and corporate. It did not underwrite stock issues for public distribution, believing that involvement in the sale of higher-risk securities to unsophisticated smaller investors was not fitting for the Morgan bank. Nor was the firm interested in acting as a broker, retailing securities to the public. "We thought it was slender business," not enough profit, in the words of George Whitney.

But the wave of stock speculation that had swept across the country had affected the Morgan partners as well, who had long traded stocks for their own account. With the Marland Oil issue in 1926 and the Johns-Manville issue the following year, the Morgan bank had begun the practice of privately offering stock it had purchased to a list of selected outside individuals, after allocating a substantial portion to the partners and their families. The firm considered the persons it chose to be knowledgeable investors who well understood the risks involved and could afford to take them. It seemed a good way to effect a broad distribution of a company's stock, thus qualifying it for listing on the stock exchange, without breaking Morgan's traditional rule of not selling stock to the general public.

Now the partners had decided to pursue another corporate and financing strategy, combining several or more companies into a single holding company, with a simultaneous offering of securities to provide the needed financing. While mergers had occurred with growing frequency during the twenties, the Morgan bank had not engaged in putting together these combinations since the days of the elder J. P. Morgan. Partners Whitney, Cochran, and Stanley were the chief architects of the new deals with the firm backing of their seniors, Morgan and Lamont. In January 1929, TWL joined in planning two large financings based on the new strategy. With the stock market strong and bullish, the timing seemed propitious.

The Morgan firm, through its Drexel branch, had held an interest for several years in the United Gas Improvement Co. of Philadelphia, which in turn had holdings in other eastern utilities. In 1928, Morgan acquired from General Electric its interest in the Mohawk Hudson Power Co., a substantial upstate New York utility.

The Morgan partners now decided to set up a large holding company, to be run in effect by the bank, to invest in utility companies. On January 11, Morgan exchanged its utility holdings for a package of preferred and common stock, valued at $50 million of the newly established United Corporation. In addition Morgan and the investment firm of Bonbright and Co., a co-organizer of the project, paid $10 million cash apiece for additional common shares. For their services each received warrants, with perpetual life, permitting the holders to purchase one million shares of common stock at $27.50 a share, an uncommon sweetener of great potential value.

During the second week in January 1929, letters went out from Morgan to a selected group of individuals and several investment firms inviting them to subscribe to a fixed number of United Corporation units consisting of one share of preferred stock and one share of common; the price was $75 a unit, Morgan's cost, without markup. Virtually all the invitees accepted the offer, as the "when issued" price of the units rose to

$99 by January 21, when the bank announced that the sale, amounting to $45 million, had been completed. At the same time the Morgan partners as individuals purchased $5 million of common stock from the firm account for $25 a share.

United shareholders reaped the benefit of the rampaging summer bull market in 1929, as the company's stock rose to 69⅜ by the end of September. In addition to selling some shares, the Morgan bank sold 200,000 stock option warrants for a profit of about $8.5 million. Morgan talent put the deal together; a booming market produced the bonanza.

In recent years the Van Sweringen brothers of Cleveland had been aggressively expanding their ownership of railway systems with the financial cooperation of J. P. Morgan & Co. In May 1927, Morgan had led a $48 million twenty-year bond issue to consolidate the brothers' holdings of the Chesapeake & Ohio in a new company. Now, a year and a half later, a major new scheme to finance the Van Sweringen railroad complex was in the works at the bank.

In January 1929, the Morgan bank organized a large new financing package for the Van Sweringens—a $35 million bond issue combined with $25 million in preferred stock and $25 million in common stock. The funds would be used to consolidate all the major holdings of the Van Sweringen interests in one company, the newly formed Alleghany Corporation, and provide fresh resources for new acquisitions. The brothers now had their eye on the Missouri Pacific, the sprawling railway system in the Southwest. The Morgan firm received 375,000 warrants to purchase Alleghany common stock at $30 a share for arranging the financing. The bond issue managed by Morgan and the preferred stock issue managed by Guaranty Trust were offered successfully in January.

J. P. Morgan & Co. purchased the $25 million in common stock, 1,250,000 shares at $20 a share, which it divided into three parts: 175,000 went into the Morgan vault for the firm's own investment account; 500,000 were sold to the Guaranty for public distribution at $24 a share; 574,900 shares were offered to selected individuals, including Morgan partners and key staff, and to a few investment firms. J. P. Morgan, as senior partner, took 40,000 shares, and T. W. Lamont, with 18,000 shares, received the next largest allocation among the partners.

As in the case of the United Corporation, the Morgan partners made up a list of friends and clients who were invited to subscribe to a fixed number of Alleghany shares. In fact, many of the same people were on both lists. There were a number of family members, including T. S.

Lamont's father-in-law, Edward G. Miner, and George Whitney's brother Richard, a Morgan broker and vice president of the stock exchange; close associates such as John W. Davis, the Morgan counsel, and Giovanni Fummi, the Morgan representative in Rome; leading bankers, including George F. Baker of the First National, Charles E. Mitchell of National City, Albert H. Wiggin of the Chase, and William C. Potter of the Guaranty Trust; prominent industrial leaders, such as Owen D. Young, chairman of General Electric; John J. Raskob, the former General Motors executive and chairman of the Democratic National Committee, and Joseph R. Nutt, treasurer of the Republican National Committee; national heroes General John J. Pershing and Charles A. Lindbergh; and several former high government officials, including William G. McAdoo and Newton D. Baker.

On February 1 letters and telegrams went out to the favored persons offering the Alleghany stock at $20 a share, Morgan's cost. It was a profitable proposition: the Guaranty Trust was offering the stock publicly at $24, and the "when issued" market quotation was $35–$37. Lamont, about to depart for Europe, sent a telegram to Albert H. Wiggin: "The Van Ess boys of Cleveland have just organized Alleghany Corporation. . . . We are making no offering of common stock but have set aside for you and immediate associates 10,000 shares at cost to us, namely $20. The . . . market is quoted at $35. Please wire promptly your wishes. I am sailing for Paris tonight. With best regards, Tom." Wiggin and virtually all the other recipients of the invitation accepted the offer.

Later in 1929 the Alleghany Corporation acquired additional railroad interests, including Missouri Pacific convertible notes, with the Morgan bank assisting in managing a $25 million bond issue for the corporation. The new Alleghany stockholders fared well as the company's stock, buoyed by the strong bull market, soared into the mid-50's. The future of the Alleghany Corporation appeared bright to the Morgan partners.

The Young Plan

In mid-January 1929, the two senior Morgan partners began considering their involvement in a new public task. Under the Dawes Plan of 1924 for handling German reparations, Germany, experiencing a good economic recovery, had made the prescribed payments punctually, her foreign exchange reserves bolstered by substantial borrowing in the

United States. However, after a decade of peace there were still critical reparations questions to be settled. For one thing, Germany was increasingly restive at the external supervision of her fiscal affairs. But the most crucial task remaining was to determine the ultimate term and total amount of Germany's reparations obligation. In September 1928 the Reparations Commission, representing the countries owed reparations, and Germany agreed to establish a new Committee of Experts, two members from each country, to propose a final and definitive solution to the reparations problem. Germany, without representation at the Dawes Plan meetings in 1924, would be a full-fledged participant at the 1929 conference, convening on February 11 in Paris.

The commission first chose Owen D. Young, chairman of General Electric, who had been a key participant in creating the Dawes Plan, as one American member. J. P. Morgan, at the urging of S. Parker Gilbert, the Reparations Agent-General, agreed to serve as the other. Once again the European nations sought the active participation of the United States in their deliberations, even though the Americans would serve unofficially, since the United States had rejected the Versailles Treaty. America's economic might, the large war debt owed the United States by the Allied nations, and the inevitable future commercialization of some part of the German reparations debt all argued for an American presence.

On January 21 the press announced that Morgan had chosen Thomas W. Lamont as his alternate. Young chose Thomas Nelson Perkins, a Boston lawyer and longtime friend and associate, who had been serving as the American unofficial observer on the Reparations Commission. Included on the American staff were Jeremiah Smith, Jr., Lamont's old friend and counselor, and David Sarnoff, an executive of the Radio Corporation of America owned by General Electric.

The Morgan-Lamont party and Owen Young and his associates made the crossing together on the *Aquitania*, arriving in Paris on February 8. Tom and Florence once again settled into a suite at the Ritz, along with Tom's valet, Metcalfe, and Florence's maid, Josephine. On February 11 the committee held its first meeting at the Hotel George V. Owen Young was elected chairman of the Committee of Experts, and Lamont was designated head of a special committee to handle press relations. As the committee and subcommittees went about their work, it soon became clear that agreement on the main question would not come easily.

The conference soon established itself along classic lines, with the creditor nations attempting to hold the debtor close to the Dawes Plan payment level of about $600 million a year and the debtor crying poor. The creditors felt their position was supported by the recently released report of Reparations Agent-General Gilbert, which concluded: "No question can fairly rise, in the light of practical experience thus far, as to the ability of the German budget to provide the full amount of its standard contributions under the Dawes Plan." Paris newspaper headlines trumpeted the news: "Germany Can Pay."

The position of the German government was forcefully stated by its delegation head, Reichsbank president Dr. Hjalmar Schacht, the brilliant and contentious mastermind of Germany's finances. As expected, he underscored the weaknesses of the German economy, especially the unfavorable trade balance and sharp increase in unemployment, as justifying an easier schedule of reparations payments.

There were also continuing differences among the Allied powers themselves over the total amount of reparations and the respective shares each country would receive. The challenge confronting Owen Young and his fellow Americans was to keep the conference on course despite the sharp and bitter exchanges.

In his assignment as press officer Lamont met with a group of reporters almost daily. Owen Young, later interviewed by *Forbes* magazine, described Lamont's role at the conference:

> Perhaps the most important single job in Paris was the Chairmanship of the Joint Press Committee. Day after day it made the issues which were troubling us clear to the whole world and disclosed the material facts so that an intelligent public opinion could be formed. Mr. Thomas W. Lamont was Chairman of that Committee. On him fell primarily the burden of seeing to it that the press of all countries carried a clear and correct story of our problems as they existed each evening. Nothing can be more difficult than to deal with complicated economic and financial questions in such a way as to create correct popular understanding. To do this it is necessary to have not only a clear understanding of the problems, but an appreciation of their news value as well. Mr. Lamont, more than anyone else in Paris, was responsible for the development of a public opinion in all of the countries affected by the settlement, which enabled the Committee to reach a conclusion. . . . Naturally, one who could do this for the public would be persuasive and effective with the Committee itself.

There was little good news to report for over two months. Dr. Schacht was a tough negotiator, in fact, in the view of many Allied delegates, an obstructionist ready to let the conference break up if Germany didn't get what it wanted. In mid-April it appeared to Lamont and others that the conference was deadlocked and in imminent danger of collapse. The delegates were weary and discouraged. J. P. Morgan, suffering from a heavy cold, had left Paris to cruise the Adriatic and the Aegean. Florence

Lamont returned to New York as her husband and his colleagues attempted to deal with a new and disturbing issue raised by the U.S. State Department.

The creditor nations and Germany had agreed from the start that the total German reparations liability would be greater than the amount of war debt the Allies owed the U.S., thus permitting retirement of the Allied debt to be based on future reparation receipts. In drafting the new agreement it seemed reasonable to provide for a reduction in Germany's obligation if the Allies received debt relief from the United States. The Germans were insistent, and the Allies were willing to go along with them on this point.

However, the State Department disagreed, as newly appointed Secretary Henry L. Stimson stated in his cable to Young of April 9. Any linkage in the agreement between the Allies' debt to the U.S. and the German reparations obligation was a violation of long-standing U.S. policy and not in the national interest. The State Department did not want to see Germany aligning itself with the Allies to press the United States for debt relief or perhaps even encouraging the Allies to repudiate their U.S. debts. The message declared that the American delegates had plainly failed in their duty to defend American interests. Young and Lamont, stung and upset at the tone and content of the cable, discussed the problem with Elihu Root, who was passing through Paris. Root, the eminent former Secretary of State and respected Republican elder statesman, was sympathetic to the Young-Lamont dilemma, and a cabled reply was dispatched to Stimson. In it Young pointed out that the American delegates at the conference were not officially representing the U.S. government; they were private citizens who had been invited to serve by the Reparations Commission. As to the substance of the State Department position, it was impossible to ignore the fundamental connection between the Allied war debt and the German reparations obligation, nor could one question the right of the creditor nations to accommodate Germany on this matter. A final settlement of the reparations issue could not be obtained unless a provision enabling Germany to benefit from a reduction in the Allies' war debt was included in agreement. Despite further State Department remonstrances, the American delegates stood fast, and the debt reduction benefit provision remained part of the overall agreement being negotiated.

May had been a productive month for the peace conference in Paris ten years earlier, and it was again in 1929 for the reparations talks. David Sarnoff developed a good rapport with Dr. Schacht, which helped smooth the way in advancing the negotiations, and Owen Young's persistent and determined leadership produced results. In the final days the job of representing the American position often fell on Lamont's shoulders as Young became exhausted from the strain of the long hours of work each day.

All the parties were in accord that there would be constant annuity payments over the first thirty-seven years of the agreement followed by scaled-down payments over the remaining years. The critical figure to be agreed on was the amount of the average annuity to be paid until 1966, and the American delegation's recommendation of about $488 million was finally accepted by Dr. Schacht on May 4 and by the creditor nations on May 22. Although tough negotiations over other German proposals lay ahead, the impasse had been broken.

A feature of the Young Plan dear to the hearts of bankers Morgan and Lamont was the establishment of a new financial institution, the Bank for International Settlements, which would be directed by the central banks or their designees. The main purpose of the bank would be to handle the collection and transfer of German reparations payments, replacing the office of the Reparations Agent-General. The bankers envisaged that the new bank would play a broader role in the future—perhaps as a clearinghouse for central bank transfers, as a stabilizing force in the foreign exchange markets, and as an international agency providing expert advice on world trade and finance.

On June 1 Thomas W. Lamont announced on behalf of the Committee of Experts that a settlement of the reparations question had been reached and the new agreement based on the Young Plan would be ready for signing in a few days. Under the plan Germany's reparations liability was set at about $9 billion, although including interest she would pay about $27 billion over the fifty-nine-year life of the agreement.

Young told his fellow committee members that the last date he could leave Paris to attend his son's wedding in Cleveland was June 8; he wanted to be there. The remaining minor questions were quickly settled, and the signing took place on June 7. Young, Lamont, and Perkins sailed for New York on the *Aquitania* the following day.

It appeared that the major festering wound from the Great War had been healed, and Americans hailed the accomplishments of the Young mission in bringing about the historic accord. Walter Lippmann and his colleagues on the *World* joined in praising the American delegation in an editorial entitled "A Triumph."

> It is a pardonable form of national pride for Americans to feel that their experts at Paris played an indispensable part in what is perhaps the most

successful great negotiation of this age. They may well feel that in Young, Morgan, Perkins and Lamont this country put into the balance not merely its power and prestige but its enlightenment and its good will. The American delegation has brought honor to this country. It deserves honor from this country. No Americans who have returned to it from foreign service in the last ten years have had so great a triumph. The Nation should not fail to celebrate their triumph.

In mid-crossing on the voyage home a message was received from New York Mayor James Walker offering to give the Young delegation an official city welcome, including a ticker-tape parade up Broadway to City Hall. Owen Young modestly declined the invitation in a radiogram.

Young issued a public statement from shipboard praising his colleagues for their dedication and effectiveness. He described Lamont's key role as press officer and added:

> Thomas W. Lamont by his industry, tact and perseverence and his special knowledge of the problems contributed, through unbelievably long hours every day for four months, precision to our work, cleared away misunderstanding and misapprehension, and finally at the end, when the rest of us were largely exhausted, he carried through the plan as the representative of the American group to its ultimate form.

Lamont instructed his office to have the New York Central railroad arrange to transport Owen Young by private car to Cleveland in good time to attend his son's wedding the day after they landed in New York. A New York Central tugboag picked up Young and Lamont at quarantine near the harbor entrance and delivered them to the city in time for Young to make his train departure.

On the morning of June 25, Young, Morgan, Lamont, and Perkins discussed the Young Plan with Secretary Stimson at the State Department before joining President Hoover for lunch at the White House. Young and his associates argued that the new Bank for International Settlements, in stabilizing world foreign exchange markets, would bolster international trade and American exports. But U.S. participation in the B.I.S. was essential to its success.

However, Hoover and Stimson remained adamant in their opposition to having a Federal Reserve representative join the European central bankers on the B.I.S. board of directors, a view held by most members of the Senate as well. Three American administrations had resisted any linkage between Allied war debt owed the United States and German reparations owed the Allies; the U.S. government did not want to be involved in any institution recognizing such a connection.

On July 4 the press covered Lamont's article on the Bank for International Settlements appearing in *World Trade*, the journal of the International Chamber of Commerce. Lamont hailed the new bank's role in handling German reparation monies and as a forum for central bank cooperation as "essential for the continuing stability of the world credit structure," which would promote an expansion in world trade. It was not the first time TWL had challenged Republican orthodoxy to advocate international cooperation.

While in Paris Lamont had received daily cables on the performance and volume of the robust stock market and his own holdings. His son Tommy, or TSL as he was now referred to in the office, kept a close eye on the family investments and reported to his father regularly, as did TWL's executive secretary. Many of the Morgan partners held the same securities, and George Whitney and Thomas Cochran passed on their recommendations to TWL on such matters as participating in new issues or handling stock option warrants. Investors were not barred from using information that had not been made public, and the Morgan partners, who sat on many boards, exchanged corporate data in confidence among themselves.

Lamont's investment view grew more cautious during the spring of 1929 as the market suffered a sharp break and stalled in its forward momentum. By May, after liquidating seven substantial holdings, including Chase National Bank, General Foods, and Humble Oil, he had raised about $4 million cash from the sale of securities. He wrote his son that "prices can go lower, so be sure to keep plenty of cash" and later that "in my spare moments I keep feeling cash is a good asset." He instructed TSL to sell half a dozen other securities, if he agreed. As he prepared to sail for Europe again at the end of June, TWL urged TSL to keep him closely informed about his stock holdings. Most investors were bullish, and the market had resumed its upward march.

The Lamonts first stop was Amsterdam, where TWL attended the Congress of the International Chamber of Commerce in his role as chairman of the American delegation. Following the conference Tom and Florence, joined by their children Eleanor and Austin, vacationed at Saint-Jean-de-Luz near Biarritz. The weather was hot and sunny, the bathing superb. Lamont spent several days in Paris before reaching London on July 29. In both capitals he was quickly immersed in Young Plan discussions as preparations went forward for the governmental conference at the Hague on August 6 to formally approve the plan.

This time the threat of failure—collapse of the conference and abandonment of the Young Plan—came from the British. Chancellor of the Exchequer Philip Snowden repeated to Lamont what he had just told Parliament: he was determined to obtain a significant increase in the share of reparations payments allocated to Great Britain. TWL discussed the divisive issue with his friend and newly appointed U.S. ambassador, Charles G. Dawes, and on July 31 they both called on Prime Minister Ramsay MacDonald to express their concerns. But MacDonald had decided to leave the conduct of the negotiations to Snowden and would not intervene.

On August 2, Tom joined Florence and the children at the Bradbury Hotel in North Berwick, Scotland, for golf and walks in the rain, as it turned out. He was in constant touch by phone and cable with London and the Hague in following the progress of the conference. As he had feared, Snowden's demands were unacceptable to the other Allied delegations. Day after day the French and Belgian delegates tried without success to move the inflexible British. At the request of Governor Moreau of the Bank of France, Lamont arranged to talk again with Prime Minister MacDonald, who was vacationing in Scotland, along with Governor Norman of the Bank of England. At lunch in Edinburgh on August 10 the bankers warned MacDonald of the precarious state of the negotiations.

Concerned by their fears MacDonald drafted a telegram to Snowden advising him to avoid any breakup of the conference and urging him to return to London to confer on the negotiations. As the prime minister later told TWL, the Treasury phoned the message to Snowden instead of sending it by coded cable; the call was tapped, according to Snowden, and its message communicated to other delegations. Snowden's bargaining position was compromised, and he was very upset.

On August 13, Lamont, back in London, called on Ambassador Dawes at the embassy. He had been urged by the French, Belgian, and Italian delegates to come over to the conference to mediate, lend expertise, and by his presence demonstrate America's support for the plan. TWL wanted to go but would not accept the invitation unless the British government agreed. The ambassador received a quick answer to his inquiry: Chancellor Snowden, not surprisingly, did not want Lamont to come to the Hague. The involvement of outside experts, he felt, might undermine his tough negotiating stance. So Tom returned to the Scottish golf links for a few days before sailing for New York.

Time magazine stated that the Hague Conference was in a desperate snarl because of Chancellor of the Exchequer Philip Snowden's demands for a bigger piece of the reparations "sponge cake." It also reported an interview given by Lamont prior to embarking on the *Olympic* on August 21.

> First authoritative word that choleric Chancellor Snowden was losing the support of British financiers came at London from Thomas William Lamont, brisk, decisive, crinkly-eyed partner of J. P. Morgan & Co. chatting with a correspondent of the New York Herald Tribune—a paper on which he once worked as a reporter—Mr. Lamont said that, although "The City" (financial London) at first strongly backed Chancellor Snowden's demand for 2,000,000 pounds per annum more sponge cake, there was now lively apprehension lest that same demand should wreck the Conference and prevent adoption of the Young Plan. "They feel," said Mr. Lamont, allowing himself to be directly quoted. "that failure to reach some agreement would mean international derangement. They feel it would endanger the gold standard (of sterling) and would threaten British financial losses for greater than 2,000,000 pounds a year—or 2,000,000 pounds a day."
>
> Clearly the existence of such a state of mind meant that last week "The City" was putting heavy pressure on the Labor Cabinet of Prime Minister James Ramsay MacDonald, and through him on Chancellor Snowden.

Despite the pressure, Chancellor Snowden stood his ground and, after a climactic late-night session on August 28, got most of what he wanted. The British gains were largely at the expense of France and Italy. The next day Lamont wired his congratulations to Snowden and other key delegates on the official adoption of the Young Plan. There is no reply from Snowden in Lamont's correspondence file, so we can only speculate as to his reaction to the message in the light of TWL's earlier comments to the press.

The successful conclusion of the Young Plan arrangements had still not elevated Germany into the ranks of acceptable clients of the Morgan Bank. While TWL was in London, Dr. Hjalmar Schacht, president of the Reischsbank, had asked him to visit Berlin to discuss a new American loan for the German railroads. Lamont, while interested, had procrastinated. It was a complex subject that must be thoroughly considered by the Morgan partners, once the Young Plan had been ratified. At the end of August, J. P. Morgan cabled his partners from London putting the matter to rest. He had not forgiven the Germans for plunging the world into the havoc of the Great War. "From what I can see of the Germans they are second rate people, and I would rather have their business done for them by somebody else."

Advice for the White House

In June 1929, the level of the Standard Statistics common stock index was about three times higher than it was five years earlier, and the biggest party of the Jazz Age was still going strong. The Morgan firm continued to participate actively in the booming equity market during the summer, establishing dozens of special arbitrage and trading accounts to invest in the swelling flow of transactions. The rising stock prices and a wave of corporate acquisitions and reorganizations spawned a flood of stock splits, new issues, and offers to exchange various classes of securities.

One arbitrage account was set up to trade in the exchange of shares involved in the acquisition of three upstate New York utility companies by Niagara Hudson Power Corp., another new utility holding company formed by Morgan and its associates. The acquisition and related $50 million stock issue on August 29 were immediately followed by Niagara's purchase of the Frontier Corporation, which owned a hydroelectric site on the St. Lawrence River. This move aroused concern at the state capital in Albany, leading Governor Roosevelt to declare that St. Lawrence River power development would remain under state control.

A *New York World* editorial, bearing the mark of Walter Lippmann's friendly feeling toward the Morgan bankers, saw no cause for alarm.

> The State of New York can afford to look upon the power merger confidently and even generously. The fact that this merger will be dominated by J. P. Morgan & Co. . . . is no reason for alarm or hostility. On the contrary, the prospect of a constructive solution is increased if the State can deal with the House of Morgan. For it has been demonstrated within recent years in many significant matters that J. P. Morgan & Co. is able and is willing to pursue an enlightened policy in dealing with the public. In respect to Mexico, to European reconstruction, to reparations, to New York City's transit problem, it has given striking proof of a spirit which is altogether different from the predatory spirit which animated big business a generation ago.

Lamont confirmed in an interview that the question of public versus private development of the St. Lawrence power resources was one for the authorities to decide. The *New York World* was right: a good public image, not public confrontation, was TWL's modus operandi for the Morgan bank.

Throughout the summer of 1929 the leading stocks continued their heady advance despite signs of growing economic malaise in the construction, steel, and automotive industries. Housing starts had declined since 1927, another ominous signal, and farm families had been hurting for years. Nevertheless, despite the fall in the Federal Reserve Index of Industrial Production from 126 to 117 over the summer months, the Dow-Jones index of industrial stocks surged another 14 percent during July and August. Call loans enabling brokers to finance their customers' purchase of stocks on margin soared to a high of $8.5 billion in September, notwithstanding interest rates of 9 percent or more. Direct bank loans to investors climbed to over $7 billion. Economic fundamentals were ignored in the headlong rush to easy street.

On Labor Day, 1929, as TWL relaxed in the cool, if moist, climate of North Haven, thousands of New Yorkers returned from their holidays to the sweltering city. The record heat the following day did not dampen the stock market, with the Dow-Jones index rising to an all-time high of 381.

Two days later the Morgan firm completed the financing for yet another new holding company—Standard Brands, a combination of several food products companies, including Fleischmann's yeast, Chase and Sanborn coffee, and Royal Baking Powder. Morgan bought the Max C. Fleischmann family interest in the Fleischmann Co. for $11 million and raised $23 million in a sale of Standard Brands stock to a list of selected investors, the same practice it followed with the United and Alleghany corporations.

Many of the names in the earlier offerings reappeared on the Standard Brands list along with new names, including Bernard Baruch and Calvin Coolidge. It was indeed a distinguished and nonpartisan company. Lamont was allocated 20,000 shares; his son and junior partner, TSL, took 2,000.

Morgan and the private investors purchased the Standard Brands stock at $32 a share. The Morgan firm account elected to sell most of its shares later in September at prices ranging from 37 to 44⅜, a quick and handsome profit on the deal. Wise market timing paid off on Wall Street.

Thomas W. Lamont had never been shy about offering advice to the nation's leaders. Prime Minister MacDonald of Great Britain planned to visit the U.S. in October 1929 for meetings with President Hoover, and Lamont knew him well from the Dawes and Young negotiations.

On September 20, TWL wrote the president that MacDonald was a man of "excellent good will, high ideals" and great charm. However, he was "pretty sketchy and lacking in thoroughness in his handling of even very important problems. I think he is apt to 'kiss' a thing through if he can."

About the same time he invited MacDonald and his daughter to stay at the Lamont house when they visited New York. The prime minister declined but was pleased to accept TWL's proposal to host a small men's dinner for him. The black-tie affair took place on October 10 at the 70th Street house. In attendance were Elihu Root; Myron C. Taylor, chairman of the U.S. Steel Corp. finance committee; Norman H. Davis, former Under Secretary of State; Owen D. Young; Russell C. Leffingwell; John W. Davis; George E. Harrison, governor of the Federal Reserve Bank of New York; Dr. Nicholas Murray Butler, president of Columbia University; Henry S. Pritchett, president of the Carnegie Foundation for the Advancement of Teaching; Judge Learned Hand; George F. Baker, Jr., vice chairman of the First National Bank; and John D. Rockefeller, Jr.

After dinner Florence eavesdropped as the guests asked the prime minister questions. She and Tom were strong supporters of the Kellogg-Briand Pact, named for Secretary of State Frank B. Kellogg and French foreign minister Aristide Briand and signed on August 28, which Lamont had publicly advocated at the July International Chamber of Commerce conference in Amsterdam. Signed by the United States and fifteen other nations, the pact resolved to outlaw war as a means to settle disputes, substituting world opinion and diplomacy. Just the day before, Hoover and MacDonald had reaffirmed their support for the peace pact. MacDonald was enthusiastic about the prospects of entering a new era of world peace based on the Kellogg-Briand Pact and a new agreement limiting the size of the navies of the major powers.

"It seemed too good to be true," Florence wrote Austin, "too amazing that Ramsay could in all seriousness be saying that a new day had dawned, that war must go, and that sixteen of the leading men in America were listening and agreeing."

Another prominent British politician, Winston S. Churchill, was also in town and accepted Lamont's invitation to lunch with the partners at 23 Wall Street. Churchill, along with some two million other investors, was keeping a wary eye on the stock market. With the advice of the E. F. Hutton brokerage firm, he had invested his recent earnings from writing articles and books in the shares of a few American corporations. But following its post–Labor Day peak, the market had fallen back in fits and starts and continued to sag in October as more conservative investors withdrew and higher margin requirements imposed by bankers and brokers dampened speculation.

Financiers and "experts" were quick to assure the public of their confidence in the stock market. Yale economics professor Irving Fisher told a New York audience that stock prices had reached "what looks like a permanently high plateau," and National City Bank chairman Charles E. Mitchell declared, "Markets are now in a generally healthy condition."

On Saturday, October 19, Lamont sent President Hoover an eighteen-page letter outlining his views on investment trends in the country. TWL said he had heard that the president was wondering what, if anything, should be done about conditions in the securities markets.

> Although certainly there are elements in the situation that have given us all pause and real concern as well, nevertheless, there is nothing in the present situation to suggest that the normal economic forces, working to correct excesses and to restore the proper balance of affairs, are not still operative and adequate.

The protracted bull market in stocks had enabled corporations to finance their needs cheaply by issuing stocks, raising funds to retire debt or improve and expand commerce, industry, and agriculture. TWL noted the large increase in the number of investors in corporate and government bonds during and since the war and wondered if something similar was happening in stocks.

> Is it not just possible that the improved machinery of the Stock Exchanges and the new investment trusts are attracting the savings of small investors all over the country who, induced in the first instance perhaps by merely the hope of a quick speculative profit or by stories of others' winnings, may become in time investors in the best stocks of the best companies? In the not yet forgotten days when such things were possible a jaded appetite was sometimes stimulated by a cocktail to the enjoyment of a hearty meal. If it should turn out that the speculative interest in stocks and the investment trusts are drawing the savings of the American people into partnership in the great and successful American industries, then the problem of waste of capital through the issue of fraudulent securities . . . is being solved by making good stocks available to everyone. The wide distribution of the ownership of our greater industries among tens or hundreds of thousands of stockholders, should go a long way to solve the problems of social unrest and of conflict or imagined conflict between the corporations and the people. . . .
>
> My best belief is . . . that the phenomenon of the "bull market" must find its explanation in the underlying prosperity of the American economy, in the wide distribution of wealth among the American people and in the growing interest and confidence of the American people in common stocks as a long time investment.

Furthermore, there was a great deal of exaggeration about speculation in the press. The theory of the "speculative orgy" was based principally on the rise in brokers' loans and the rise in prices as represented chiefly by the so-called averages.

The "averages" were "misrepresentative" in that they frequently included a picked group of leading stocks, thus obscuring the great diversity of movement among different groups of stocks. The Standard Statistics Company had recently stated that "despite an advance of 28 per cent in our 90-stock index, the majority of issues traded in on the New York Stock Exchange have actually declined since the beginning of the year." In other words, the stock market performance was a mixed bag.

As for brokers' loans, the volume reflected the large increase in the number of shares listed on the stock exchange, over 50 percent in the last four years. Instead of bank funds flowing directly to corporations through commercial loans, they now flowed through the route of brokers' loans and new issues of common stock.

There had been great gains in efficiency, due to improved management and greater use of machinery, and it had been possible to pay high wages and still have low prices. Production costs had been lowered, prices reduced, markets expanded, and purchasing power increased. There had been no inflation and accumulation of inventories. To Lamont the future seemed "brilliant."

The United States had "the greatest and soundest prosperity" and the best prospects of any country in the world, thanks to its natural resources, "selected population," huge domestic market, and American efficiency and capital supplies. The whole world had wanted to buy American stocks or make loans secured by them.

> Our extraordinary prosperity . . . is primarily responsible for the stock market that we have had. When business slackens the stock market will react, and bonds will come back into favor. Experience indicates that the stock market will not fail as long as business rises. . . . There seems to be no reason to attempt to check prosperity now, or break up the relationships that have helped to constitute this prosperity. . . . There is nothing in the present situation to suggest that the normal economic forces working to correct excesses and restore a proper balance are not still operating. Possibly business has been a little too active and is now to become a little less active. If this proves to be the case there will be no need to worry further about possible excesses in the stock market. There will then be something else to worry about.

Finally, Lamont observed, businessmen had been confident that the Coolidge administration could be relied on "not to rock the boat." Now they believed that the Hoover administration intended to pursue conservative and constructive policies, and this feeling would be a "steadying influence" on the economy. While the people whom Lamont had consulted had "varying shades of opinion as to the exact situation now before us, they are all agreed with me that corrective action on the part of public authorities or individuals need not at this time be contemplated."

Lamont and his partners thought that the market had peaked and was on the down slope; they had largely liquidated the firm's stock holdings. Russell Leffingwell's "shade of opinion" about the market led him to be considerably more apprehensive than Lamont about the economic dangers inherent in the protracted bull market. Unsound and unethical stock exchange practices were widespread. While new issues to finance industrial improvement or expansion were offered regularly, the vast bulk of the billions of dollars that had entered the market was engaged in buying and selling existing securities, driving stock prices to unsustainably high levels and creating a massive diversion of credit from American industry. For thousands of players in the market, uniformed speculation whose risks they could ill afford was the financial order of the day.

On the same Saturday that Lamont dispatched his letter to the president, there was a sharp break in the stock market at its half-day session. Sunday newspapers reported a large increase in margin calls from brokers to thousands of investors who had borrowed to purchase stocks.

Funded by the call loan market, supplied by banks and other investors, brokerage houses financed their customers' purchase of stocks, which served as collateral for the broker loans. Typically, large margin speculators paid only 10 percent of the stock purchase price in cash from their own sources, although as the stock market frenzy mounted during the late summer, brokers and bankers, becoming more cautious, raised margin requirements to the 50 percent range. When the value of the stock collateral dropped too low, the brokers demanded that their customers provide additional margin; if they were unable to comply, the brokers sold the stock to recover their loans. The procedure was virtually automatic and could be self-perpetuating. The more stock the brokers sold in the falling market to protect their loans, the more stock prices tumbled, forcing more margin calls and further stock liquidation.

On Monday the market plummeted again in a day of heavy trading, with the stock ticker running an hour and forty minutes late in recording the transactions. A rally at the end of the day carried over into a modest recovery on Tuesday. On Wednesday the market plunged again, hit by an avalanche of sell orders. It was the second-heaviest trading day in history, over six million shares, and the tape was again left far behind as prices closed drastically lower. That evening the mood of Wall Street was all gloom as a torrent of margin calls went out from brokerage offices across the country.

The 1929 Crash

On the morning of Thursday, October 24, throngs of people began to gather in the streets outside the New York Stock Exchange and in the board rooms of Wall Street brokerage offices. The steps of the Sub-Treasury Building across from the exchange were lined with men in business suits, topcoats, and fedoras, waiting tensely in suspense under the statue of George Washington, whose visage inscrutably contemplated the strange goings-on. An atmosphere of impending calamity hung over the area.

Promptly at ten o'clock the stock exchange gong sounded to open the day's trading. Six thousand shares of Montgomery Ward changed hands at 83, down from its earlier high of 156. Soon the losses for other blue-chip stocks—U. S. Steel, General Electric, and many more—were equally staggering. A national stampede to sell was on as an enormous flood of orders drove the market down. Forced sales—brokers liquidating under-margined accounts—set off the first wave of selling, but soon panic—"sell at the market" regardless of price—became an overwhelming force in propelling the market's plunge. In the chaos of the trading floor, it appeared that for many stocks there simply were no bids at all. Around noon Richard Whitney, vice president of the stock exchange, crossed the street to the Morgan offices to report to the bankers, including his brother George, on the disastrous situation. Richard Whitney was acting chief of the exchange in the absence of the president, E. H. H. Simmons, honeymooning in Hawaii.

At the same time a handful of New York's leading bankers, telephoned by Lamont and George Whitney, pushed their way through the frightened crowds at the Corner to enter the Morgan offices. Charles E. Mitchell of National City, Albert H. Wiggin of Chase National, William C. Potter of the Guaranty Trust, and Seward Prosser of the Bankers Trust had come to determine with the Morgan partners what, if anything, they could do to stabilize the stock market debacle. George F. Baker, Jr., of the First National joined the group in a later afternoon conference. J. P. Morgan was still on holiday in England; Lamont presided over the meeting with the bankers, who gathered around his rolltop desk in the partners' enclosure. Bankers had long looked to the Corner to organize rescue parties in times of crisis, such as the panic of 1907. Thomas Lamont was the obvious choice to fill the shoes of Pierpont Morgan in the present emergency.

At the noon conference a list of thirty-seven stocks was drawn up, the prominent and actively traded stocks on the exchange which the group had selected to support. The six banks, including J. P. Morgan & Co., initially committed $120 million, or $20 million apiece, to the rescue effort, an amount later doubled to $250 million. A few additional firms were asked to join in the second go-around, and Bernard Baruch declined Lamont's invitation to participate. "The day was past when the House of Morgan could rally Wall Street in such a crisis," he wrote in *The Public Years*.

When the meeting broke up, Lamont escorted his guests to the door of 23 Wall Street. Their departure was quickly noted by the milling crowd, whose confidence was lifted by word of the conference and its hoped-for consequences—major intervention by the banks to support the market. Then TWL met the press in his office. His demeanor was cool, and his words were soothing as he chose to understate the gravity of the situation in monumental fashion.

> There has been a little distress selling on the stock exchange this morning and we have held a meeting of financial institutions to discuss the financial situation. We have found that there are no houses in difficulty and reports as to the maintenance of margin are very satisfactory.

Lamont also said that it was the bankers' consensus that many of the quotations on the stock exchange did not represent the situation fairly, as a result of so-called air pockets—the complete lack of bids to meet orders to sell. "We consider the situation on the floor of the stock exchange this morning a technical one rather than fundamental and that it will result in a betterment," he declared.

Following the bankers' plan of action, at 1:30 p.m. Richard Whitney strode purposefully through the crowded exchange floor to Post No. 2, where he loudly announced an order to buy 10,000 shares of U.S. Steel at 205, the last sale price, 15 points above the current bid. Other stocks on the list were purchased in the agreed-upon amounts, and the rout was stemmed as the word spread that the bankers' pool was formed and operating.

After the market's close the bankers met again to discuss their strategy, winnowing the list down to about twenty-five pivotal stocks they would support. The Morgan bank would control the operation, reporting daily to the other banks, with partners George Whitney and Francis Bartow in charge under Lamont's supervision.

As darkness fell the lights blazed in offices all over Wall Street where brokers, margin clerks, and bookkeepers coped with the massive paperwork resulting from the heaviest trading day in history, about 13 million shares. Downtown speakeasies were mobbed by investors drowning their losses and fears in bootleg whiskey. Lamont met the press again.

Despite the big losses that day, some $3 billion in stock values, the country's business conditions were basically sound, said TWL. There was no "crisis," he contended, evading direct answers to questions about the operations of the bankers' pool and the outlook for the stock market. The stock ticker recorded the day's final trades at 7:08 p.m., more than four hours after the market's close, as Lamont joined his fellow bankers for yet another conference to plan their defenses for the next day.

Friday morning's papers noted the action of the bankers in restoring confidence and preventing much larger losses in Thursday's tumultuous trading. They reported Lamont's announcement that a bankers' consortium had been formed "to furnish a cushion against the recurrence of any such condition as Thursday." The Morgan partners were cheered by the crowd at the corner of Wall and Broad as they left their limousines to enter the bank. The public did not know that Lamont had told the stock exchange board of governors, when he informed them about the pool, that there was "no man nor group of men that can buy all the stocks that the American public can sell."

President Hoover stated: "The fundamental business of the country, that is the production and distribution of commodities, is on a sound and prosperous basis." Several captains of industry chimed in with their own statements to calm fears and build confidence.

On Friday and Saturday the market pretty much held its own, although prices began slipping again toward the close of Saturday's short session. Lamont and the bankers met again at the Morgan offices to review the operations of the pool and planned to do so each day as long as it seemed necessary.

There was a general feeling that the worst was over. The *New York Times* said that the financial community now felt "secure in the knowledge that the most powerful banks in the country stood ready to prevent a recurrence" of the panic.

Tom wrote his daughter at Smith, "I was a little tired at the end of the week because we had such a hectic time." But on Monday the stock market was again in full retreat, promising more long days of tension and fatigue.

Prices of many higher-priced stocks fell from 20 to 40 points, and by the end of the day the Dow-Jones industrial index had lost 12.7 percent, its largest recorded decline. It was another day of frantic unrestrained selling with over 9 million shares traded. The banks attempted to plug the "air pockets" for issues on their list, buying stocks offered for sale when there were no bids. But nothing could stem the onslaught this time.

The bankers met during the morning and again in the late afternoon, joined by Owen Young of General Electric. Their public statement following this meeting revealed that the plan to intervene in the stock market was now more limited in scope: they would not attempt to support market price levels, but simply try to maintain an orderly market by meeting unanswered offers to sell with reasonable bids.

That evening Lamont attended a men's dinner of financiers and industrialists given by Bernard Baruch at his Fifth Avenue house in honor of Winston Churchill, who from the visitors' gallery had witnessed the debacle on the exchange trading floor the previous Thursday. Charles Mitchell of National City Bank offered a toast to "my fellow former millionaires" before the discussion of the stock market rout grew more serious.

The consensus was that investors who were not forced to sell should hold on to their stocks, a plan of action in the public interest and their own as well. Shares currently at absurdly low prices were sure to recover soon. TWL, who had unloaded a number of his stocks before the market's collapse, held on to his remaining blue chips as their paper value plummeted.

Baruch's guests were premature in their expectation of an early recovery in stock values. On Tuesday, October 29, the market was flooded with sell orders for large blocks of stock from the opening bell and fell off precipitously in an unprecedented volume of trading—16,410,000 shares.

The bankers met at midday on Tuesday and again in the late afternoon. The Dow-Jones industrial index had dropped another 11.5 percent, despite help from a late closing rally, the day's only good news. Then Lamont faced the press, and he was uncharacteristically restrained. He confirmed that the bankers' group would "continue in a cooperative way to support the market and has not been a seller of stocks." But the memory of Pierpont Morgan's successful leadership of the banking fraternity in quelling the money panic of 1907 no longer had any relevance. The present deluge of selling was simply overwhelming. There was no basis for lingering confidence in the power of the banks to stabilize the falling market.

On Wednesday the market rallied and moved forward, reflecting hopeful signals from several quarters. The leading banks, with massive credit backing from the New York Federal Reserve, announced that they were supplying fresh funds for broker loans, at 25 percent margin, a vital support in view of the withdrawal of some $2 billion by out-of-town banks and private lenders from this market over the past week.

U.S. Steel and American Can announced extra dividends, and hearty expressions of confidence in the economy and stock market were voiced by national figures. John D. Rockefeller, for one, announced that "my son and I have for some days been purchasing sound common stocks," a statement that prompted Eddie Cantor, the actor and comedian, to quip, "Sure, who else has any money left?" Lamont immediately wrote John D. Rockefeller, Jr., congratulating him and his father for "an admirable and effective statement" made at an opportune moment, "rendering a real public service."

Wednesday's good performance persuaded the governors to close the exchange until noon on Thursday and altogether on Friday and Saturday. There was a tremendous backlog of paperwork to be processed, and the exhausted employees of the exchange and brokerage firms deserved a rest as well. Lamont told the press that the banking group heartily endorsed the action "in arranging to give the overworked staffs of all the street houses some let-up in a period of extraordinary stress."

During the following week the exchange operated half days only and was closed on Saturday. Mild rallies were quickly overcome by renewed selling as the market descended to new lows. Lamont met with the banking group each day and usually talked to the press afterward. He received a flood of mail congratulating him for his leadership of the bankers' efforts and offering suggestions for new moves the bankers should undertake to steady the market. To these correspondents he regularly replied that "the storm has blown over," "the worst is past," and that extraordinary or novel steps were unnecessary and might be counterproductive in building investor confidence. J. P. Morgan cabled TWL from England, "Very glad indeed you were able to get a strong party to work to act quickly and with judgement in the matter."

On November 11 at a long evening meeting, the bankers decided to end their program of purchasing selected stocks to stabilize the market. Up to that point the bankers' group had purchased 1,407,000 shares for a total cost of $137,752,000. The public would have been surprised: they thought the pool was much larger, even in the billion-dollar range some guessed.

The same day, *Time* magazine in its cover story reported the stock market crash and Lamont's leadership in the bankers' stabilization efforts. Under TWL's photograph on the magazine's cover the caption read, "He felt the helm respond." According to *Time* the selling panic was over, and great credit was due to the banking group for restoring confidence, backed by its tangible and mighty resources.

Nor was there anything intangible about the man who steered the ship of U.S. prosperity through the storm, who at length felt the helm respond. More than most men, Thomas William Lamont can be touched, appraised. In obvious and literal ways, this right hand of John Pierpont Morgan is freely extended among men. A cosmopolite, he knows, understands, and likes the thousands of people of all nations with whom he does business. Because he is patient and urbane, he is the Morgan diplomat. In more subtle ways, Mr. Lamont can be described as a tangible person. Tell him a joke and he will laugh. Offer him an idea and he will develop it. Put him in the middle of a problem and he will begin to solve it. The doors of his mind swing easily ajar. . . .

Liquidate Mr. Lamont tomorrow and many an achievement of his 18 years with Morgan would have a historic value. To him came the financing of the New York Central Railroad and he is today the firm's chief railroad adviser. To him came most of the overseas muddles into which its vast foreign interests plunged the Morgan house. In China (the Consortium), Mexico (International Committee), France (Anglo-French $500,000,000 loan), Austria (1923 joint loan), he has been at one time or another the most important financial factor. When these and many another nation gather together, as at Versailles in 1919 and at Paris in 1929, Mr. Lamont is summoned to speak for U.S. finance. He himself considers his work at Paris last summer the most significant of his life.

Outstanding as a financier (and his chief is the only living banker who might conceivably be said to outrank him), he is scarcely less an intellectual. His friends include John Masefield, with whom he travels—H. G. Wells, who visits him—Ramsay MacDonald, who dined with him last month. A Liberal himself (he supported Cox and Davis because of the League issue, voted for Hoover last fall), he has in his immediate family almost every shade of liberal opinion. His eldest son (Thomas S.) at 31 a Morgan partner, is far more conservative than Corliss, who voted for Smith and now teaches Philosophy at Columbia University. And while Mr. Lamont has received many an honorary degree, it was Mrs. Lamont who after raising four children, earned a Ph.D. at Columbia. [Time was incorrect: Florence has earned a master's degree in philosophy from Columbia in 1898.]

Thus it was an intellectual husband of a Doctor of Philosophy as well as a keen and forceful financier who presided over the most nerve wracking crisis in U.S. business history.

On November 13 the stock market hit its low for the year, with the Dow-Jones index at 199, closing 48 percent lower than its high on September 3. Security values had fallen by over $30 billion during the same period. And then the market picked up moderately.

On November 15 the banking group, now expanded to include a half dozen other bank executives whose institutions had cooperated with the original group, met again at 23 Wall Street. Lamont spoke to the reporters that evening. The bankers considered the stock market as normal during the past few days, he reported, and he understood that several substantial bids had been placed at the closing prices for execution the next day. Everyone welcomed the day's improvement in stock prices. Bernard Baruch cabled Winston Churchill, who had sailed home to England, "Financial storm definitely passed."

The stock market reflects the hopes and fears of investors, or sometimes, as in 1929, their illusions and terrors. However, the "financial storm" didn't sink everyone.

Thanks to the partnership's decision to sell the firm's stock holdings before the market crash, and his own caution, 1929 was a banner year in earnings for TWL. His income before taxes amounted to $6.4 million, reflecting substantial capital gains realized before the market's collapse. He hadn't been taken completely by surprise.

The International Inn and Other Diversions

Having built up a fortune during the roaring twenties, Lamont had every intention of enjoying his elevated level of affluence. At the end of November 1929 the Lamonts began spending weekends and holidays at Palisades, so named because of its site near the edge of the great cliffs. The spacious country manor has plenty of room for children, grandchildren, and houseguests. There were rolling lawns, a tennis court and an adjoining indoor swimming pool, a large vegetable garden, and a cow barn and pasture so that the family could have its own fresh milk supply. There was a lovely walled garden with a center pool filled with goldfish, and a cutting garden and greenhouse to furnish fresh flowers to fill the many vases about the house. The estate superintendent and the family chauffeur both had their own houses flanking a six-car garage. The woods were criss-crossed with hiking trails, some leading to lookouts affording magnificent views of the river and beyond. Now Tom and Florence had a proper place to invite guests for country weekends in the upper-class English style they so admired, replete with elegant dining, good conversation, and long walks in the woods.

However, the outstanding recollection of many visitors during the thirties was not the unsparing care for their comfort or the scenic beauty of the spot. It was the long Sunday lunches around the great dining-room table which became a forum for vigorous discussion of the issues of the day—war and peace in Europe, socialism versus capitalism, FDR versus Wall Street, and the like. Often guests lapsed into silence as an intra-family debate unfolded. With Corliss, in good humor, and his wife, Margaret, usually intense, on hand to argue the viewpoint from the left, a lively exchange was guaranteed.

The Lamonts believed in large dining and living rooms for entertaining on a grand scale. The living room at Palisades was formal, with imported carved pine paneling and an ornately sculpted marble fireplace. It was filled with Chippendale and Hepplewhite, and the windows were framed with heavy golden drapes. Tom and Florence often organized games for their guests after dinner, and charades was the favorite at the Palisades country house.

On the other hand, the Sky Farm living room was Queen Anne and Early American, with deep-cushioned sofas, ship models, bright flowered chintzes, and an enormous fieldstone fireplace. Here the informal setting and holiday mood made Murder the popular choice for evening game-playing. Murder was a lights-out playacting "whodunit" in which the murderer "strangled" his chosen victim. The young men and at least some of the girls enjoyed the clutching and squeezing in the dark, all in the name of the game.

Tom looked forward to sailing on his new yacht, nearing completion, in the Maine waters and at home on the Hudson. With a cruising speed of 18 knots, the 72-foot *Reynard II* would transport TWL in luxury from Snedens Landing to the foot of Manhattan as quickly as its predecessor had made the shorter trip from Englewood. Lamont's *Reynard*, however, was dwarfed by J. P. Morgan's 343-foot *Corsair IV* under construction at Bath, Maine, which was said to be the largest, most expensive, and most elegant private vessel in the world, a veritable seagoing palace.

The Lamonts' New York house had virtually become an international inn, smoothly managed by chief butler George Metcalfe, who saw to the special needs and comforts of the family's houseguests, from martinis to theater tickets. One guest, whose evening shirt was frayed, recalled being led by Metcalfe to a huge closet filled with men's clothing—shirts, socks, business suits, evening clothes in a range of sizes, a miniature Brooks Brothers ready to supply guests with whatever attire the occasion called for.

The Lamonts enjoyed the many visits of the Masefields, good friends and stimulating company, as well as those of ardent socialist H. G. Wells. The latter debated vigorously in his high-pitched voice about economic systems with his capitalist host. On New Year's eve, 1929, the family welcomed Jan Christiaan Smuts, the South African statesman and former prime minister. At the Paris Peace Conference in 1919, Lamont had struck up a friendship with Smuts, who was now visiting America to give a series of lectures to promote American cooperation with the League of Nations. Tom was delighted to see his kindly and neatly goateed friend again.

During the winter months of 1930, the stock market staged an encouraging recovery, and on February 26 J. P. Morgan & Co. announced that the bankers' group had completed the liquidation of the shares it had purchased to help stabilize the market during the worst days of the crash in the fall of 1929. The market's recovery had even enabled the group to make a small profit, about $1 million, on the operation.

However, the decline in the American economy had clearly accelerated since the crash. Recurrent White House conferences attended by industrial leaders were invariably followed by rosy economic forecasts. President Hoover, for one, predicted that the worst effect of the crash on the growing unemployment throughout the nation would soon be over. But the president was becoming increasingly anxious about the future direction of the economy, described as "brilliant" by Lamont in his letter before the crash, and he spoke to TWL about the deteriorating situation from time to time.

At the end of March the Lamonts sailed for Europe on the S.S. *Olympic*. The crossing was rough, but they still found the voyage relaxing and convivial. At the Captain's Dinner a gregarious socialite lady friend, Sybil Walker, told Lamont that he didn't drink enough. People would like him better if he drank more. TWL's affable and outspoken dinner partner enjoyed kidding her image of the perfect, upright, and somewhat stuffy banker (who was virtually a playboy compared to his staid partners and many other senior members of the Wall Street fraternity). TWL replied that unfortunately his "tummy" didn't welcome alcohol.

The Lamonts spent a few days in Paris and then proceeded to Florence, where they had rented a villa in the nearby countryside for two weeks, with Austin and John and Constance Masefield as their guests. On April 14, TWL went down to Rome to keep an appointment with Premier Mussolini. After discussing a possible Morgan-organized loan for highway construction and the plans of International Telephone and Telegraph, a Morgan client, to build a new plant in Italy, Mussolini raised the subject of the London Naval Conference, where delegations from the major naval powers were concluding negotiations on a naval treaty. Italy, which had been granted parity with the French for capital ships at the Washington Naval Conference in 1922, insisted on continuance of this status. "France," the premier added with a charming smile, "is a very rich and proud old lady who looks down rather scornfully upon her poor relations living on the peninsula."

In Lamont's memorandum of the meeting with Mussolini he concluded:

> The P.M. was much more cordial and personal and approachable than ever before. The role that we have from the start endeavored to establish—namely, that of being loyal and disinterested counselors on all external finance problems—seems to be pretty well fixed. He looks upon us not as seeking business, but as honestly desiring to co-operate in the Government's important problems. . . . I hope the next time Mr. J.P.M. is anywhere near here he will go to see the P.M. It would be very helpful.

The holiday at Villa Buoninsegni was a "dream of bliss," Florence wrote to Tommy.

> I do not know when I have had such a lovely time. The villa was delightful with the most divine terraced garden & a pergola covered with wisteria and white clematis. There was a view over the garden wall of distant hills & mountains. The Masefields were at their best, & were so charming & stimulating. They made me feel like a worm, because I felt so like a clod of clay and stupid, but like an aspiring clod, & I know I can do better if I try. Pa had a grant rest, & tho he may have been bored once in a while, yet it did him a world of good.

Then back to Paris, "a nightmare of dining with Americans at restaurants," reported Florence. On April 30, TWL went to Brussels to attend a meeting of the Bank for International Settlements, whose potential for promoting world financial stability he had praised in the April issue of *Foreign Affairs.*

The BIS was a pet project of Lamont's, and he intended to assist its formation despite his government's coolness toward it. When the Federal Reserve was barred from participating in the BIS, J. P. Morgan & Co.

had organized a small American banking group to join the European and Japanese central banks in guaranteeing each country's capital subscription to the new institution, which the bankers discussed in Brussels.

They also reviewed the plans for a new German bond issue of $300 million to be sold in Europe and the United States. The reparations creditor nations would receive $200 million of the proceeds, and future payments under Germany's reparations obligation would be made to the BIS for interest and sinking fund installments on this portion of the thirty-five-year debt. Some $100 million would be used by the German government for the state railways and post office system. The issue would be offered in early June, and J. P. Morgan & Co., despite the senior partner's earlier expression of distaste for a new German loan, had agreed to lead the American syndicate that would sell up to $100 million of the bonds in the United States. The British and French would benefit substantially from the loan.

Tom joined his wife in London after the BIS meeting. On Saturday, May 3, the Lamonts lunched with Prime Minister Ramsay MacDonald at Chequers. After lunch Florence and her host took a walk, climbing a small nearby hill he called "the quarter deck." The view of the meadows and beyond was lovely, Florence wrote her eldest son. "The forget-me-nots under the trees lay in great blue pools." Florence and the prime minister bantered about meeting again at the same enchanting spot.

"Let's make a tryst," MacDonald proposed.

"All right—two years from now," Florence agreed.

"Oh," the prime minister replied. "I hope I shan't be here two years from now. It is too difficult, too much responsibility. It is hard to make decisions and not know what will follow."

"Yes, a man ought to have a single vision and follow it like a steam roller," Florence suggested.

The prime minister agreed. "Yes, a man in my position should have no imagination."

Great Britain's leader was widely regarded as a man of great charm—modest, whimsical, and candid. Florence added her impression of Mac-Donald in her letter: "Altogether he is a sweet person—sensitive, imaginative, rather philosophic in his mind—a strange person to head a Labor cabinet." Men who were sensitive and gentle and not embarrassed to disclose their tenderness and vulnerability to life's trials appealed to Florence, men like MacDonald and John Masefield.

On Sunday the Lamonts visited Lord and Lady Astor at Cliveden, the magnificent Astor family home situated on a hill overlooking the Thames in Buckinghamshire, about twenty-five miles from London. "Liquid history," observed one of the other guests to Lamont as they gazed from an upper terrace at the quietly flowing river in the distance.

Nancy Astor, Waldorf Astor's beautiful and vivacious Virginian-born wife, née Langhorne, has become the first woman Member of Parliament in 1919. Her Cliveden and London dinners and receptions were famous for their largesse and conviviality, the company and conversation sparked by Nancy Astor's noted wit. Tom was captivated by her. Florence reported that TWL and Nancy Astor were "thick as thieves." They were assuredly kindred spirits and became warm friends, exchanging frequent letters filled with political and social gossip. During the Cliveden visit they golfed together, and upon his return to New York TWL ordered and had shipped to Nancy a set of Wilson golf clubs that were custom made to her specifications and identical to a model that she had admired.

Before embarking for New York Lamont worked with his London partners on the upcoming German loan. On June 12, a bond offering of $98,250,000, the American portion of the international issue, was sold successfully by a Morgan-led banking syndicate; the European share of the loan also sold well. The prospects seemed bright for good relations with the nation that had thrust the world into the greatest war in history. Most foreigners did not take seriously the rising popularity of the Nazi party in Germany led by the spellbinding Adolf Hitler.

Clash Between Friends

During Lamont's visit to London in May 1930, bankers and Foreign Office officials had questioned him closely about Mexico's continuing defaults. Payments on the National Railways bonds had been suspended at the end of 1926, and on the Mexican government's direct external debt a year later. Of an outstanding debt of about $500 million, plus accrued interest of some $200 million in 1922, only $40 million, net of administrative expenses, had been remitted. There was a growing feeling among the British and continental bondholders that the International Committee of Bankers, headed by Lamont, should be more forceful in protecting their interests. About 35 percent of Mexico's external debt was held in Great Britain, 45 percent on the Continent, and only 20 percent in the United States.

In November 1927, Finance Minister Louis Montes de Oca had alerted the International Committee that his government would not be able to make the agreed-upon remittances of 1928 of $33,750,000. Nevertheless, he wanted to cooperate with the committee and invited it to send experts to Mexico to study the country's economic and financial situation.

During the following months, the committee dispatched several missions to Mexico to study the country's economy and fiscal position and recommend a new plan for the resumption of foreign debt payments. However, political violence, including armed revolts and the assassination of President-elect Obregón in July 1928, constantly disrupted government planning and budgets, stalling progress on settling the foreign debt problem. As TWL had observed when he first met Obregón in 1921, presidential politics in Mexico was an extremely hazardous occupation.

The bankers also recognized that the huge amount of the government's outstanding domestic obligations, totaling well over a billion dollars, could affect its attitude toward its foreign creditors. The ultimate amounts of two giant loose cannons on the deck of Mexican finance were still undetermined: the agrarian bonds issued in payment for lands confiscated by the government and turned over to local communities, and the claims for injury and damage to foreign persons and properties during the Mexican Revolution, which were being handled officially by the foreign governments involved.

Lamont had written his former partner Ambassador Dwight Morrow regularly about the suspension of payments by Mexico to the foreign bondholders. The Morrow-Lamont friendship went back to the early days in Englewood when the families were neighbors and their children played in each other's backyards. The parents were members of the Shakespeare Club, where they read parts from the plays, and once the Morrows and Lamonts even gave a formal dance together. Lamont had first proposed Morrow for a Morgan partnership, and later they became summer neighbors in North Haven, where they joined forces for boat excursions, picnics, and golf. At the office Morrow was the one other partner who, like Lamont, had yearned to play the statesman. His aspiration was realized, and Lamont was in for a shock.

Morrow's proposal for handling the Mexican debt problem, backed by the State Department, was in direct conflict with the International Committee of Bankers' desire for full resumption of debt service payments as soon as possible. The two old friends were now adversaries, and this time the stakes were higher than in their friendly golf games in the past.

The State Department thought that its primary responsibility was to prevent the private claims of Americans, stemming from losses during the revolution and property expropriations, from being subordinated to the repayment of the Mexican government's other obligations. Ambassador Morrow, a former corporate lawyer, was very familiar with bankruptcy proceedings. He believed that since the Mexican government had been insolvent for several years and unable to repay its overdue obligations, the fairest approach to the problem would be a unified program that took into account the interests of all the creditors, without favoring one particular class, namely the foreign bondholders.

In his letter of February 2, 1929, to Vernon Monroe, secretary of the International Committee and a Morgan officer, Morrow stated, "I regret that the International Committee still feels it desirable to have a contract rather than to use its great influence with the Mexican Government in the formation of a program. . . . The International Committee must realize that its contract can only be kept by the Government's breaking other contracts made by the same authorities to be performed during the same period." The ambassador was now advising Mexican finance minister Montes de Oca to delay making any commitment to the International Committee until a program for settling all the government's debt could be formulated, which would take at least a year and probably longer.

However, the International Committee was not persuaded by the Morrow–State Department reasoning. Starting with the 1922 agreement, the Mexican government had recognized a special responsibility to implement a plan to settle its debt held by foreigners. Much of the foreign debt was secured by a lien on customs revenues now building up to amounts well in excess of debt service requirements. It was the duty of the committee, in defending the interests of the long-suffering foreign bondholders, to negotiate promptly whatever reasonable agreement it could obtain to resume payments on the bonds.

While Lamont was in Paris for the Young Plan negotiations, Vernon Monroe kept him fully informed on developments, and TWL was in touch with the foreign bankers on the committee. Lamont's March 2 cable to his partners stated: "It looks to me as if Ambassador has completely estopped further progress and has now suggested extension of delay. . . . to a whole year. . . . I am sure that the foreign sections and I think the American Section will be by no means content to stand by idly for a year while the Ambassador is perfecting his government's claims. . . . We may have to join issue of this matter pretty promptly."

The tone of TWL's office communications reflected his growing bitterness toward "the Ambassador" as he maneuvered to scuttle Lamont's efforts to reach a new accord. As Morrow well knew, the Morgan partners had invested considerable time and effort to resolve the Mexican foreign debt problem for almost a decade; a prompt and satisfactory settlement was their goal.

In New York on May 31, Ambassador Morrow told his former Morgan colleague Arthur M. Anderson that he wanted a general commission representing all classes of creditors to be established to propose a settlement plan for all the Mexican government debt, foreign and domestic. On the same day Lamont wrote Anderson from Paris that the committee should "proceed as vigorously as possible despite Ambassador's attitude. . . . If we are going to have a head on collision with Ambassador," the time was imminent.

However, the Mexican government was still on the fence. The conflicting advice, another armed revolt, and the upcoming presidential election in Mexico all added to the government's uncertainty about proceeding.

On October 2, 1929, Lamont, Leffingwell, Anderson, and Monroe attended a three-hour meeting at the State Department in Washington presided over by Secretary Henry L. Stimson. Ambassador Morrow presented his proposal to establish a general commission to deal with the Mexican debt problem, and the government officials again stressed the department's responsibility to protect numerous private American claims against the Mexican government. But the bankers had no intention of backing down; their responsibility was to protect Mexico's foreign bondholders, whose patience was wearing exceedingly thin.

The path leading to negotiating a new accord was made easier by the absence of Ambassador Morrow, who had gone to London to serve on the American delegation to the London Conference on Naval Disarmament during the winter of 1930. At the end of April, Morrow returned to New Jersey to campaign as a candidate for the U.S. Senate in the Republican primary election. He won handily and departed for Mexico to wind up his ambassadorial duties.

The attitude of the Mexican government toward negotiating with the International Committee had shifted while Morrow was away. He had advocated delaying any commitment until all the categories of government debt could be settled at the same time. Finance Minister Montes de Oca now believed that this course of action was impractical and not in Mexico's best interest.

Montes de Oca was now under increasing pressure from individual groups of foreign bondholders, who were impatient with the International Committee's lack of progress. They knew that the Mexican government's financial position had improved over the past year and that customs revenues pledged for foreign debt service were well in excess of the sums required. They were ready to negotiate independently with the Mexican government, perhaps with the backing of their respective governments, a prospect de Oca did not welcome. The finance minister knew that it would be far easier to deal with the International Committee before it lost its authority to represent the several national groups of bondholders.

The Mexican government also had come to resent Ambassador Morrow's efforts to intervene in the conduct of its financial affairs. A former embassy attaché in a speech on Morrow's behalf during the New Jersey campaign had stated that the ambassador had advised and directed all departments of the Mexican government. The speaker added, "He took the Secretary of Finance under his wing and taught him finance." The report of the speech, appearing in the Mexican press, predictably produced indignation and wounded pride in government ranks.

Montes de Oca, backed by the new president of Mexico, Ortiz Rubio, was ready to act as he saw fit, regardless of the ambassador's advice. He accepted Lamont's invitation to meet with the International Committee in New York. On June 25 the committee (with representatives from the U.S., Great Britain, and four continental countries) and Montes de Oca, a slender, well-tailored thirty-six-year-old career civil servant, began a new round of negotiations on Mexico's foreign debt.

As in past conferences, the minister argued that the national budget could not possibly accommodate the schedule of foreign remittances proposed by the committee as well as the payments required on the government's large domestic debt of about $1.6 billion. The earlier foreign debt agreements had broken down for this very reason: they imposed too heavy a burden on the government's limited resources. After lengthy debate Lamont observed that it appeared that an irresistible object had met an immovable force and wondered if they should announce to the press that the debt settlement conference had failed. But neither side wanted that to happen. Within ten days they had concurred on the basic principles of an agreement. Most of the European bankers returned home, leaving Lamont and Arthur Anderson to conclude the negotiations.

Tensions at the meetings were well masked from the public and press, with whom Lamont and Montes de Oca met periodically. At a Mexican Chamber of Commerce dinner on July 11, Lamont praised the finance minister as a man of clarity, experience, justness, and patriotism. He rhapsodized over Mexico's many attractions—its beautiful scenery, historic traditions, and art. He admired the special traits of the Mexican people—their mental agility, love of children, flowers, music, and all things beautiful. They truly knew the "art of living."

But in Mexico City, Ambassador Morrow had not quit the fray and continued to lobby strongly against the upcoming foreign debt settlement. According to the New Jersey press, his efforts to defeat the debt settlement plan sponsored by his former colleagues was a blow to the Democratic campaign strategists, who had hoped to pin the House of Morgan–Money Trust badge of opprobrium on him. Morrow was clearly demonstrating his independence from the Morgan bank. When Lamont telephoned him in early July to report on the progress of the negotiations, Morrow questioned the Mexican government's capacity to handle all its domestic debts and foreign claims and sent Lamont a draft statement announcing a postponement of the proposed foreign debt settlement. He hoped that the finance minister and Lamont, on behalf of the International Committee, would concur and release it to the press.

Montes de Oca emphatically declined. It was quite impractical to expect to arrange an omnibus settlement of all the government's debts and foreign claims at the same time. The claims alone consisted of thousands of individual items, which would take years to adjudicate and settle. The minister wanted to make a start by concluding an agreement on the foreign debt, which he regarded as the most pressing obligation to be settled.

On July 23, with the negotiations completed, Lamont and Morrow spoke again on the telephone. The ambassador was highly critical of the debt settlement and predicted that the State Department would lodge a protest with the Mexican government in an effort to block implementation of the pact.

The next day Lamont sent Morrow a seven-page letter summarizing the stand of the International Committee and the minister of finance. First, TWL alluded to the confrontation between the two old friends and colleagues:

> Referring to the talk that you and I had over the telephone yesterday: I am a good deal upset that you and I should have to differ so radically on this Mexican financial and debt problem. You must realize from your side, my dear Dwight, just as I surely do from my side, that the difference is philosophical and in no sense personal. You will continue to be guided by your own judgment and conscience as to how best to represent the interests entrusted to you, and I must follow the same course from my end of the line. I have a feeling that you are a bit disgusted with our mental processes up here and are genuinely upset that we are unable to adopt in toto your point of view. But I may recall to you that the view I have often presented to

you is in no sense personal to me, but is shared and upheld more rigidly perhaps than I uphold it, by all the members of the International Committee; by eminent counsel to the Committee on both sides of the water; and by such sage members of our own firm as Charles Steele and R. C. Leffingwell, both of whom have had competent legal training as well as much practical experience.

At the close Lamont stated the main purpose of his letter:

> Now as to your own attitude in this matter of a proposed direct debt settlement: of course, I realize perfectly well, because you have so often told us all, that you were opposed to the bondholders' making at this time any arrangement to receive some of the money that was owed to them. And I know that you have strongly advised the Mexican Government officials to this end and have given to them what you consider sound reasons for your view. But now it would appear that they have not seen fit to accept counsel on this particular matter, and they have voluntarily come forward, asked for and executed a debt settlement, without urging on the part of the bondholders. That being the case, I hope you can see your way clear to letting the matter rest where it is rather than feeling called upon to attempt to defeat this plan.

On July 25, 1930, Lamont and Montes de Oca executed the foreign debt agreement in the offices of J. P. Morgan & Co. and issued a joint statement to the press. Some $330 million in accrued interest was forgiven on the direct government obligations and national railways debt. The government debt, now set at $267 million with interest at 5 percent, would be consolidated into one bond issue and retired by forty-five annual sinking fund payments. The final arrangements for retiring the railway debt, set at $225 million, would be presented to the bondholders soon along with a plan for a general reorganization of the railways.

Lamont cabled J. P. Morgan, cruising on the *Corsair*, "Signed up new Mexican debt agreement this afternoon, but Dwight very displeased."

Moreover, Morrow had no intention of "letting the matter rest." In his reply of August 20 to Lamont's letter, he said that President Ortiz Rubio had told him that he would submit the foreign debt agreement to the Mexican congress for ratification only as part of an overall program to deal with all the government's debt.

> If, however, the preparation of such a project remains but an aspiration . . . and if it should be proposed to ratify your agreement without any provision for the other creditors of Mexico, foreign and domestic, it will be the State Department, not the Embassy, that will determine what steps it should take for the security of the interests which it represents.

On August 25, Montes de Oca announced that Mexico's national indebtedness and claims would be settled in one integral plan based on Mexico's capacity to pay. The recently concluded external debt agreement would be submitted shortly to congress for ratification as the first component of the plan.

However, Ambassador Morrow continued to lobby against the accord until he left Mexico City in September 1930 to campaign for his Senate race. And there were other forces, such as domestic creditors of the government, hostile to the pact with the foreign bankers. President Ortiz Rubio began to waver and delayed presenting the agreement to the Mexican congress for approval. Lamont's phone calls to the finance minister urging early ratification of the pact by the congress were to no avail. Montes de Oca was powerless as the president continued to procrastinate.

Toward the end of the year a new development militated against ratification of the foreign debt agreement. A sharp drop in the price of silver lowered the international value of the Mexican peso, substantially increasing the cost of making the dollar payments called for by the agreement. On January 30, 1931, Lamont and Montes de Oca amended the July 25 agreement by suspending for two years Mexico's obligation to make the initial debt service payments totaling $25 million. Once again the Mexican government said it planned to submit the new agreement promptly to the national congress for ratification.

Dwight Morrow was elected to the Senate in November. TWL was not one to bear grudges beyond their time, and the Morrow-Lamont friendship blossomed again.

On September 30, Thomas W. Lamont passed a personal milestone, his sixtieth birthday. A newspaper columnist noted that Lamont went to his office on his birthday and that there was "never a day so arduous" that he couldn't spend a few moments answering reporters' questions. Two weeks later TWL, his older sister, Lucy Gavit, and her husband, Jack, drove up the Hudson to Claverack, where, after a bit of hunting, they found the old Methodist parsonage where Tom had been born, the modest box-shaped white house with its pillared veranda overlooking the river and the Catskill mountains.

Lamont enjoyed the lively company of Lucy and her feisty spouse, a writer and former newspaper editor, and regarded with amused tolerance their belief in spiritualism. Lucy purported to be a medium in touch with those "on the other side" and once brought her younger brother good news from J. P. Morgan the elder: "Tom, you are doing a fine job."

While the outcome of TWL's efforts to cut the Gordian knot of the Mexican debt dilemma may not have seemed "a fine job" to 200,000 foreign bondholders, he'd done his best for them.

The Deepening Depression

Notwithstanding the optimistic pronouncements of the White House, it was clear by the summer of 1930 that the nation and the world were in the throes of a serious depression. The music had stopped, and the party was over for hundreds of thousands of American investors who had lost their life savings. Their painful morning-after turned out to be an early symptom of a serious national malady. Personal consumption fell sharply; factories cut back output, slashed wages, and laid off workers. The stock market, which had lost momentum in mid-April, continued to drop. Foreclosures throughout the long-suffering farm belt mounted, and unemployment was at three million and rising.

On November 14, Lamont, as the presiding officer at an Academy of Political Science dinner in New York, spoke of the depression and its causes. There had been a tremendous overproduction of many commodities and manufactured goods. In the United States part of the blame could be attributed to

> our somewhat antiquated Anti-Trust laws. . . . encouraging excessive construction of plant and equipment in the industrial field. The present law constitutes almost a mandate to every wide-awake manufacturer to duplicate the facilities of his rival, and the result is bound to be a great economic waste. . . . this obvious wastage of capital, brought about through almost unbridled competition.

Lamont's distaste for antitrust laws and "unbridled competition" harked back to the business philosophy of Pierpont Morgan, who had paid scant heed to the dangers of eliminating competition in his moves to form huge and dominant industrial combinations. The American people under both Republican and Democratic administrations had supported curbs on monopolistic practices restraining trade for over a generation. Some entrepreneurs and financiers may have erred in their business planning, but antitrust legislation was not the culprit. The devastating depression was taking its toll across the board, flooding industrial giants along with smaller enterprises in red ink, and TWL's observation seemed strangely archaic and ill-conceived.

In general Lamont followed the Hoover line of rejecting large-scale government intervention to ignite the moribund economy.

> We must . . . encourage our recovery to be orderly and step by step. We must not try to over-stimulate ailing business with nitro-glycerine pills; for if we do we may have further explosions!
>
> We must not be impatient for too speedy solutions. We have to contend, as an English writer has pointed out, with revolutionaries who think the world so bad that only violent change can better it, and with reactionaries who consider the safety of our economic life so precarious that we must risk no new experiments upon it.

Clearly, Lamont intended to place himself in the middle of the road, although his Socialist-leaning son Corliss and other liberals may have thought that he and President Hoover fit TWL's own description of a reactionary quite well.

However, TWL and Hoover were far apart on another subject raised by Lamont in this talk—the Smoot-Hawley Tariff, signed into law by the president the previous June, which substantially raised duties on many imported products. TWL had warned Hoover, and a host of leading economists had argued, that the act would trigger retaliation by other countries that would lead to an all-out worldwide trade war. Lamont stated:

> The increased rates have certainly led to a certain feeling of dismay and ill-will abroad and to some retaliatory tariffs. . . . There can be little dispute that we chose a most inopportune time for this particular tariff enactment. With both domestic and foreign trade beginning to show signs of a decline, as they did in the early summer of 1929, it surely was not the time to build up new barriers against world trade. Certainly, too, we did not take a happy method encouraging our foreign customers to buy more of our goods. Nor did we make it any easier for them to pay their Governmental debts to Washington.

Republican Senator Reed Smoot, a co-sponsor of the act, replied to Lamont's charges the next day. Smoot told the press:

I have little patience, with current statements that the new tariff is retarding business recuperation. Thousands and thousands of people are at work today with the boot and shoe and textile and other industries who would be idle except for the new tariff. . . .

Argicultural products in the rest of the world have dropped to such levels that they would be flooding our country if it were not for the tariff. The purchasing power of the farmer is being sustained, thus creating more work for other people. . . .

Since the tariff bill passed wages have been falling in every country in the world except the United States. And, with this widening difference between American and foreign wages, the question is now whether the tariff is high enough, not whether it is too high.

Lamont had told his Academy of Political Science audience that the country was passing through the low point of the business cycle. "Not only shall we win through, but we are winning through!" A month later Lamont reassured the members of the New York Stock Exchange that the banking system was strong despite the recent failure of the largest bank to date, the Bank of the United States, a privately owned institution in New York. "These ill times will pass," said TWL. "I think it must have been after a business depression, 2500 or so years ago, that the Prophet Isaiah gave vent to this utterance. . . . I think it applies to you: 'They helped every one his neighbor and everyone said to his brother, be of good courage.' " The eminent banker still responded to the echoes of his father's sermons.

On the same day the stock market, as measured by the Dow-Jones industrial index, sank to 157.5, its low for the year and 58.7 percent below its 1929 peak. There was growing skepticism in response to messages of hope and confidence by government officials and business leaders. Some also questioned the wisdom of making loans to Europe instead of aiding millions of unemployed Americans, many of whom went to bed hungry. Louis T. McFadden, a Republican congressman from Pennsylvania, who was chairman of the House Banking and Currency Committee, had severely criticized the 1930 German loan and its Morgan sponsors, terming it an "illegal" operation. Lamont tried and failed to persuade the congressman otherwise.

The year 1930 had not been a good one for bankers: some 1,300 banks, mainly of small size, had been forced to shut down since the end of 1929. The Morgan firm suffered substantial securities losses, with a $26 million decline in net worth to $92 million. The partners, who as a group had paid $11 million in income taxes for 1929, paid a trifling $48,000 in 1930.

During January 1931, Lamont followed a brisk social pace often with business-political overtones. He gave a dinner in honor of the new French ambassador at the 70th Street house. The next evening TWL presided at the annual dinner of the Harvard Club, where he gave a generous introduction to New York Governor Franklin D. Roosevelt, the main speaker. The mounting depression was the common topic of conversation among the tuxedo-clad members. Even the Harvard Club was feeling the need to cut costs: its management decided to stop ordering the crimson matchbooks embossed with the Harvard emblem.

Other parties were just for fun, such as one at which guests played Murder after dinner. Edna Ferber, the popular novelist, who at first demurred, saying, "Count me out. I hate games!," later became one of the most enthusiastic participants and was the last to leave the party.

Following a winter holiday in Phoenix, Lamont reported to his children that they had had "a grand time" playing golf and horseback riding in the scenic desert country. But severe hardship and misery faced a growing number of TWL's fellow citizens as the depression deepened. There were now five million people out of work, with more unemployed swelling their ranks each day. President Hoover believed that substantial relief programs to alleviate human suffering were the responsibility of local governments and private charity, not the federal administration, a policy that proved quite inadequate to the task. The official designation of "The Star Spangled Banner" as the national anthem did little to boost the nation's spirits. Nor did Hoover's rigid opposition to repeal of the unpopular Prohibition amendment. The roar of the twenties was becoming a low moan of despair.

Corliss Lamont was now an instructor in philosophy at Columbia University. The dreaded dark side of capitalism—economic depression with its widespread unemployment, misery, and hunger—further strengthened his view that socialism, using central economic planning, presented a superior alternative to free-wheeling private enterprise with its recurring periods of boom and bust. His wife, Margaret, ardently of the same opinion, was a member of the Socialist Party, and both of them looked forward to visiting Russia, where under Communism the socialist experiment was in full swing. Corliss and his father argued over the issue at Sunday lunches at Palisades time and again. Father Lamont thought that socialism had worked poorly where it had been tried. It would not be accepted in the United States, and if by any chance it were, it would not succeed. And Florence observed to Austin: "I wish Corliss would leave Socialism and Russia alone and would tend to his philosophy and get his degree. But he seems fairly daft on the subject of Russia." The left and the right debated, but no one had found the answer to the devastating depression.

On March 25 an Academy of Political Science dinner at the Hotel Astor, organized by Lamont, was given in honor of Walter Lippmann. Lamont, heading a standing ovation for Lippmann, called on the academy to pass a resolution of gratitude to him for his public service: "Big business has always respected Mr. Lippmann's utterances. They have always been constructive. He has those rare qualities of investigation and judgement." The journalist in his speech once again indicated his affinity for "big business," criticizing politically inspired attacks against corporations.

Lippmann had recently decided to leave the *World*, which was being sold to the Scripps-Howard chain, and was considering several newspaper job offers. Ogden Reid, publisher of the conservative *New York Herald Tribune*, wanted Lippmann to write a syndicated column for the paper, and Reid's wife, Helen, enlisted Lamont to help persuade his friend to accept the *Tribune* offer. Lamont was pleased to do this, pointing out the independence Lippmann would enjoy at the *Tribune* and the national exposure his syndicated column would receive, enhancing Lippmann's "already excellent reputation and wide influence." Lippmann agreed to join the *Tribune*.

Two days after the dinner Walter and Faye Lippmann joined the Lamonts on the Italian liner *Saturnia,* bound for Greece, where TWL had organized a well-appointed sightseeing tour for his party. The other Lamont guests were Henry James, son of TWL's former professor, Harvard philosopher William James, and Professor Gilbert Murray, the eminent Oxford classicist. On the ocean crossing the Lamonts and their friends studied books on Greek history and archaeology, sometimes reading out loud to each other in the ship's smoking room. In the late afternoon the Lamonts often played bridge with the Lippmanns before dining with their friends either at their own table or the captain's. Lamont's letter to his children described the party's debarkation in Greece.

The landing at Patras last Wednesday evening was like an Anthony Hope novel, or a light opera. . . . The Governor of the Province, the Captain of the Port in full gold braid, a representative of the Greek cabinet, the American Consul and Vice Consul—all came dashing out to the steamer in a special tender, lined themselves up in formal array in the saloon and tendered us the welcome of Greece. They insisted upon sabotaging all the steamer's landing arrangements—despite our earnest entreaties—and in landing us and our 42 pieces of luggage before anything could happen. It was a struggle between the Governor and Metcalfe as to who should carry your mother's bottle bag and hat box. . . . The whole performance would have made Tommy and Corliss shrink worse even than the rest of us. The Governor marched us up the quay to the hotel, where they gave us a very decent dinner. . . .

After dinner it was discovered that two trunks were missing. Metcalfe was invisible. So I sneaked away from the Government officials and had myself rowed out in the midnight darkness to a lighter out in Patras Harbor. It was loaded with a thousand trunks and loose bed springs, which acted as traps to catch you as you searched with matches through the swaying trunks. But I located the missing ones and got back undiscovered.

The director of the American School of Classical Studies in Athens, of which Lamont was a trustee, accompanied the party on its excursion to Olympia, where, TWL reported, "he made all the ancient glories . . . come to life again" in his description of the historic site of the Olympic games. The next stop for the party was Athens, where the Lamonts visited the Acropolis twice a day—at dawn and at dusk. Returning to the Peloponnesus, Florence reported that the ruins of the palace of Agamemnon, the legandary king of Mycenae, thrilled her "to the bone." But both Lamonts ranked Delphi as the high point of their trip. "The most magnificent spot in the world," Lamont wrote his children, and Florence described the view from the wooded slope of Mount Parnassus: "The blue sea at our feet and range after range of blue mountains glowing in the beautiful light." Professor Murray, the erudite tour guide who had given a short lecture at each archaeological site, was at his best at Delphi. "There at the citadel of the gods, they had lunch on a damask cloth under the cypresses and read aloud poems about Greece from a little book, 'The Englishman in Greece,' Walter had given Florence Lamont," Ronald Steel wrote in his 1980 biography of Lippmann.

From Athens the Lamonts progressed in easy stages via Venice and Paris to London, taking up quarters in their regular suite at the Hyde Park Hotel. Charles G. Dawes, now American ambassador to Great Britain, gave a stag dinner on May 7 in TWL's honor at the embassy. The distinguished guest list of twenty included the Lords Reading and Cecil; Sir Josiah Stamp, a leading economist with whom TWL had worked closely in formulating the Young Plan; Edward C. Grenfell and two fellow partners from Morgan Grenfell; the ambassadors of France and Belgium; the High Commissioner for Canada; and Walter Lippmann. The dinner guests undoubtedly discussed the deepening worldwide depression and growing financial obstacles facing the debtor nations of Central Europe.

Financial Disarray in Europe

As Lamont was leaving England to return home, word was received that the Credit-Anstalt, the largest private bank in Austria, could no longer pay its debts. The tremors from its insolvency were quickly felt throughout Europe and especially in Germany. The Austrian bank failure quickened the fears of foreign investors and lenders to Germany, already concerned about the country's huge foreign liabilities, industrial depression, and growing political unrest. Some refused to renew their German short-term credits, and the Germans for their part were soon protesting that they could not repay these loans and continue their reparations payments to the creditor nations. A major international financial crisis was in the making.

During May 1931 a rescue effort to save the Credit-Anstalt by a group of European financial institutions, including the Bank of England, failed, and the flight from the German mark by foreigners and Germans, anxious to transfer their assets abroad, continued. A massive default by German banks and traders seemed inevitable, with billions of dollars of European and American loans to Germany becoming frozen. According to press reports, the short-term credits to Germany of American banks alone approached a billion dollars, and U.S. corporations and investors held at least equal that amount of German loans and securities.

Over the following days Lamont discussed the developing crisis with his partners, including Russell Leffingwell, who on June 5 gave TWL a memorandum recommending that "the President propose to the Allies that they avail themselves of the provisions in the war debt settlement agreements for delaying payment on the war debts to the U.S., and that to the extent of the relief thus afforded they offer to defer the reparations payments coming to them from Germany." Neither the Allies nor Germany could take the initiative in proposing a moratorium of payments without damaging confidence in their credit and setting off a flight from their respective currencies. Only the United States, the ultimate creditor nation, could take the lead in proposing a moratorium, which would defer some $200 million owed the U.S. in the coming year. Acceptance of the moratorium would provide immediate relief, not a permanent cure, in the threatening financial crisis.

Lamont showed the memorandum to Morgan at lunch, who said that the plan, if carried through successfully, would be "a lifesaver to the world." TWL called the president at 2:30 p.m. to present the idea and recorded the conversation afterward.

> T.W.L.: Mr. President, I am taking the liberty of calling you up to make a suggestion that you will more than likely throw out the window. Nevertheless, my associates and I consider it of such importance that we have no right not to make it to you. It is, in effect, that you should take the initiative in proposing that there should be a holiday of international governmental debt payments.

Lamont then explained that Germany had rejected the idea of declaring a suspension of its reparations payments, fearing that this step would alarm its foreign creditors and cause them to demand repayment of their German loans.

> T.W.L.: With this preliminary, may I point out that under the debt agreements, which the European powers have with you at Washington, they have themselves the right . . . to declare moratoria. Of course, they will not do this, however, unless they are forced to by Germany's declaring a moratorium. Germany cannot declare a moratorium for the very reasons that I have just stated. Yet the crisis today is even more acute than it was a week ago.

The only possible solution, said Lamont, was for America, the chief creditor, to propose a moratorium for intergovernmental debt and reparations payments and urge the debtor nations to accept it. He stressed that he was not talking about any kind of debt cancellation, but a moratorium, which only the U.S. could offer. The debtor nations could not ask for it without precipitating grave difficulties.

> T.W.L.: That is a long speech, Mr. President, what do you think of it?
>
> Hoover: It sounds very interesting, but, offhand, to me not necessary and not feasible. It isn't necessary, because, assuming that it might be dangerous for Germany to declare a moratorium, nevertheless, it would be simple for her to summon the Special Committee of Review into being, and that would do no harm to Germany.

Lamont thought that was a bad idea.

> T.W.L.: When a corporation or government gets to the point where it has to summon its creditors to sit on its corporate body, so to speak, and find out whether it is still alive, that means that the jig is up. No, Mr. President, that is not the proper resort.
>
> Hoover: I will think about the matter, but politically it is quite impossible. Sitting in New York . . . you have no idea what the sentiment of the country at large is on these intergovernmental debts. Added to this, Congress sees

France piling up loads of gold, increasing armaments and encouraging other European armaments among her Allies. I could not make any headway.

Lamont was ready with his own political card. If the U.S. didn't act strongly and quickly, there would be a financial crash in Europe that would prolong "the agony of business depression" in America for years. Hoover should propose the moratorium plan as a major step to assist American farmers and workers. The proposal would not be "a maladroit move politically"; on the contrary it would be a very constructive political step for the administration to take.

> T.W.L.: These days you hear a lot of people whispering about sidetracking the Administration in the 1932 Convention. If you were to come out with such a plan as this, these whisperings would be silenced overnight. It is not a blow at the Administration that I am advocating, Mr. President; it is a gesture that may bring it through.
> Hoover: Well, I am very much obliged. I will think the thing over very carefully, but I am very doubtful about it. . . .
> T.W.L.: One last thing, Mr. President, if anything by any chance ever comes out of this suggestion we should wish to be forgotten in the matter. This is your plan and nobody else's.

President Hoover, as reported in his memoirs, presented the moratorium idea to his cabinet the same day. Presumably he had been encouraged by Lamont's political analysis.

Leaving S. Parker Gilbert, the former Reparations Agent-General, who had just become a Morgan partner, and Russell Leffingwell to monitor the moratorium plan, Lamont attended the celebration of Phillips Exeter Academy's 150th anniversary, where he addressed a throng of alumni in the baseball cage. A week later, after a salmon-fishing outing in Quebec, TWL and a family party of fourteen descended on Cambridge for the Harvard Commencement exercises, at which Harvard's president A. Lawrence Lowell bestowed on Lamont the honorary degree of Doctor of Laws with the following citation: "Thomas William Lamont: By nature a statesman, by occupation a financier; sagacious in council on affairs that affect all nations, he has found time for boundless service to his University."

Back at his office the next day Lamont consulted with Leffingwell and Gilbert on his latest essay in financial statesmanship. They reported that the moratorium plan was moving ahead in Washington. However, it would be unwise for the administration to present a proposal that was too rigid and conclusive in view of the need to win the support of the French, who would be asked to accept a suspension of the largest share of reparations payments from Germany. Once again Lamont phoned the president and later made notes on the conversation.

> Hoover: We are making some progress here. I have been going over the matter with the leading Senators and Representatives. . . . I am having a hard time with some of them, but I am making progress and hope I may be able to reach the point of doing something.
>
> T.W.L.: I have it on my mind to suggest, very respectfully, that if your plan shapes up, it will be by all means best to present it in as general form as possible. Otherwise too specific details are likely to cause trouble. . . .
>
> Hoover: That is all right to say that, but I made an absolute commitment to these Congress people whom I have talked with, and I have got to back up that commitment. We are going to have a clearcut proposition, and the French can take or leave it.
>
> T.W.L.: Well, I hope it will go smoothly.

The next day, Saturday, the president telephoned Lamont at the Palisades house at 8 p.m.

> Hoover: I called you up to explain that so many Congressmen have leaked on this debt suspension plan, that instead of being able to hold it back until Monday or Tuesday, as I had hoped, I have got to make it public tomorrow in the Sunday papers. I feel rather badly about this, because I wanted that extra time to have our people carry on conversations abroad, especially those with the French. But no time affords for that. And, as a matter of fact, after I have read you the gist of my statement I would like you to see what you could do to get the French in line.

The president then read the announcement that he had just released to the press, and Lamont said he would speak to the Bank of France in the morning.

> T.W.L.: I can plainly see that the French are not going to be content to accept your proposition with one gulp. They are not made up that way. Meanwhile let me thank you for the confidence you have shown in calling me up, and congratulate you upon what I hope will turn out to be a most wonderful step.

On June 20, 1931, President Hoover proposed a one-year moratorium on all intergovernmental payments of war debts and reparations. The Allied governments quickly accepted the plan, with the exception of France. Nobody was surprised.

The French, traditionally thin-skinned in matters of diplomatic protocol, were piqued because they had not been consulted before the announcement. Second, as the chief recipient of German reparations, they were worried about Germany's will to resume payments after the mora-

torium. Unstated but very real was the deep-seated French desire to be
an authoritative voice in international affairs, which meant that they
would not docilely follow Anglo-American initiatives, but choose instead
an independent course, and then negotiate. Perversity was power to the
French.

On June 29, Lamont called President Hoover to report on a cable he
had received from his Paris partners who had just returned from a meeting
with French ministry of finance officials. TWL's colleagues believed that
the negotiations between the U.S. and French governments were at a
serious impasse. The French would not accept the Hoover moratorium
unless the plan included special provisions safeguarding their future
reparations payments from Germany.

> T.W.L.: As you see the situation now, is there anything that you think of
> in which we can serve the cause?
>
> Hoover: I don't think that anything can be done. We are all fed up with
> the French. They have placed every obstacle in the way of the agreement. The
> conditions that they have laid down have been multifarious and all of them
> objectionable. It is extraordinary to note the sort of attitude that they could
> take up in a matter of this kind. I think if the public were to be informed of
> the notes that we have received from the French on this matter, there would
> be such a reaction throughout this whole country against the French that
> our people would never want to see them again. Their attitude has been
> intolerable.
>
> T.W.L.: The French are the most difficult people to deal with in the whole
> world. You in your way and I in my smaller way found that out many years
> ago.

Nevertheless, they had to be dealt with, and there were two points to
consider, said Lamont.

> T.W.L.: The first is that just as you have very properly gained the credit
> up to date for doing a wonderful and constructive piece of work, yet, if it
> fails to go through, you are going to get the discredit for the failure.
>
> Hoover: Why should that be? The difficulty lies solely with the French.
>
> T.W.L.: That well may be so, and yet so far as our domestic situation is
> concerned, our people are not going to take any satisfaction in taking it out
> on the French. They are going to pin it down on the Administration. You
> are not responsible for the present depression, and yet the public pins it on
> your Administration. If this thing breaks down, you are going to lose all the
> wonderful credit that you have heretofore gained from it. . . .
>
> The second point that I wanted to make was that you have won such great
> réclame from the whole country that now you can get through Congress any
> final adaption of the Hoover Plan that you declare to be just and fair and
> necessary.

Hoover: I don't agree with you. You are all wrong.

T.W.L.: I usually am wrong, but I doubt whether I am in this particular case. The whole American world has been lifted out of the slough by your action. Members of all political parties are rooting for you. Almost no Congressman is going to have the hardihood to fly in the face of his community by voting to defeat any construction of your Plan that you declare to be the proper one.

Hoover: Well, there can't be any construction of the Plan with the French in their present mood.

T.W.L.: Well, what are the chief difficulties in the way of an agreement?

Hoover: They want to have their cake and eat it too. The whole proposition comes down to this: we have offered to sacrifice $200,000,000 odd for a year, and they are refusing to sacrifice $90,000,000 odd. Now they are trying to twist the postponement payments around, so that they will be turned in to them at the end of the year. That would really mean not a single year's postponement of payments; it would mean only six months.

Lamont and the president then discussed some possible terms that might be offered the French to win their acceptance of the moratorium plan.

Hoover: Well, Mr. Mellon is working [feverishly] over the thing. He can't do any more than he is doing. . . . I don't believe any one man could write out a formula that would satisfy the French. I can't make out what ails these French fellows.

Lamont said that the French were running "true to form." They also recognized that Germany and its states had brought their financial plight on themselves by spending recklessly over the last five years. Germany had made no effort to balance its budget, whereas Great Britain and France "pulled in their belts" and at great sacrifice balanced theirs.

T.W.L.: Naturally the French . . . feel that they should not be called upon to sacrifice too much to pull Germany out of the pit which she has dug for herself. Of course, they are too logical on that, but undoubtedly that fact influences them.

Hoover: Well, we may be driven to drop France out of the whole scheme and just take it up with the other nations and see if we can work something out with them.

T.W.L.: I can see how your mind might be moving that way, but by that arrangement I am fearful that the crisis in Germany might not be tided over.

On July 8 the Morgan partners invited ex-President Coolidge to lunch at the bank. During their conversation in the partners' dining room TWL told Coolidge that early in his administration he had met the president's father while driving through Vermont. Lamont had told the elder Coolidge that everyone expected his son to do a fine job as president. "Time alone will tell," replied the old gentleman.

Coolidge chuckled and said, "Father never was one for endorsing another fellow's note."

TWL enjoyed the former president's dry humor. Coolidge's comment on the Hoover moratorium proposal was "If anybody proposes spending somebody else's money, it is always popular. You will find that this moratorium idea will become quite infectious."

Tough negotiations on the moratorium, led by Secretary of the Treasury Mellon in Paris, in constant contact by phone with the president, finally produced results. On July 9 the French joined the other Allied governments in signing an agreement for a one-year moratorium on intergovernmental debt and reparations payments.

But Germany's financial condition remained precarious despite an advance of $100 million to the Reichsbank from the major central banks in June. An international financial conference on July 20 in London agreed to ask Germany's private bank creditors abroad to maintain their credit lines to Germany until February 1932, in a joint effort to relieve the critical financial crisis. The European and American banks had little choice: Germany was not prepared to repay these loans anyway. However, the "standstill agreement" did not affect the Morgan bank, which had pursued the policy, initiated and strongly backed by the senior partner, of no bank credits for Germany.

Later in July TWL went up alone to his "Maine farm," as he liked to call his summer home in North Haven. Florence was traveling in Europe with family and friends. On July 30 Lamont and his houseguests, Walter and Faye Lippmann, joined the Morrows and the rest of their island neighbors to witness a historic aviation event: in a small red-winged seaplane Charles and Anne Morrow Lindbergh lifted off from the Fox Islands Thoroughfare, lined wth spectators, to start an unprecedented survey flight by the northern great circle route to Japan and China.

Lamont returned to New York after a few weeks to face a new European financial crisis: the banking panic had spread to London, banker to the world. The British economy was severely depressed and suffering from widespread unemployment. The national budget was running a deficit equivalent to $600 million; foreign trade earnings were falling, and millions of pounds of British loans were frozen in Germany, Austria, and Hungary. Nervous foreign investors and businessmen were now transferring their sterling balances out of London into other currencies, especially dollars and French francs, and the efforts of the Bank of England to support the pound at its gold parity had led to an intolerable drain on British gold reserves—$200 million in the last two weeks of July alone. On August 1 the Federal Reserve Bank of New York and the Bank of France granted a $250 million credit to the Bank of England to help stabilize the pound. It was quickly drawn down in the following weeks as the run on sterling continued.

On August 24 the Labor cabinet, unable to come to grips with the budget deficit, resigned. A new coalition cabinet, still headed by Ramsay MacDonald, was quickly formed with the mandate to effect the economies necessary to balance the budget. The new budget proposals were quietly shown to the American bankers via the Bank of England and gave them the assurance they sought for granting a substantial credit to the British government. J. P. Morgan, in England at the time, confirmed that his firm was ready to lead a banking group to provide the American portion of the overall credit.

TWL and his colleagues at 23 Wall Street worked feverishly over the next few days in organizing the large new financing. On August 28, Lamont announced to the press that an American banking group led by J. P. Morgan & Co. would extend a one-year credit of $200 million to the British government. At the same time the French banks would organize $200 million of credits and short-term public loans, making a total of $400 million available to the British to stabilize the pound. Lamont told the press that the new credit facility was an act of "enlightened selfishness." A British financial collapse and a radical devaluation of the pound would have serious consequences for American trade and business.

Lamont denied charges in the British press that the bankers had imposed "political conditions" on the British government, i.e., the new austerity budget. The bankers were relying on press reports that the new national government would propose fiscal reforms that would be enacted by Parliament, said TWL, who had concluded that full candor was not appropriate under the circumstances. They believed that the large new credit, in providing ample resources to defend the pound, would quickly restore confidence in the British currency; the British financial emergency would soon be over. But events over the next three weeks proved otherwise.

Added to Great Britain's already serious economic problems, many foreigners with large amounts of loans and investments blocked in Central Europe were now compelled to withdraw their London balances for domestic liquidity needs. The flight from the pound continued, feeding ever-mounting fears of devaluation, which led to even larger transfers abroad.

Morgan partner Thomas Cochran in London kept in close touch with Bank of England officials on the deteriorating state of Britain's exchange. Lamont talked to him daily by transatlantic phone and also called Ambassador Dawes to discuss the developing crisis. The $400 million credit from the U.S. and France was being drawn down rapidly.

During the third week in September, the pace of foreign transfers from London accelerated. The equivalent of a billion dollars had been withdrawn from the London market since mid-July. Neither the new balanced budget slashing the dole nor the huge foreign credits could stem the outflowing tidal wave of funds. The rapidly depleting Bank of England gold reserves were down to a level of about $650 million. How long would the Bank of England continue to use its dwindling gold stock to support the pound at its official value in a seemingly hopeless cause?

On September 20, 1931, Prime Minister MacDonald announced that the British government would ask Parliament to suspend the Act of 1925 requiring the government to sell gold at a fixed price. Great Britain, the world money center and citadel of sound finance for over a hundred years before the World War, had been forced to abandon the gold standard, delivering a shattering blow to financial confidence on both sides of the ocean. Fears about the future impact of the British move on the world's financial order were real: the international value of the pound, which would now be determined by the myriad transactions on the world's foreign exchange markets, would decline, destabilizing trade and investment relationships around the world. Other countries would surely join the British in deserting the gold standard, and businessmen had no taste for the uncertainties and risks inherent in the muddled new financial environment.

The following day Lamont briefed a group of reporters, not for attribution, at the Morgan office. During the interview a page slipped him a note: the president was on the phone. After talking with Hoover, TWL told the reporters: "I have just been talking over the telephone with President Hoover. He believes England's action will give prices an upward fillip over here." While Lamont privately questioned the president's forecast, he let it pass in the cause of dampening the growing apprehension stemming from the British action. Nor did he disclose his chagrin at having organized, just three weeks earlier, a large syndicate of American banks to extend credit to Britain to preserve the strength of sterling and its tie to gold. Britain's abandonment of the gold standard was plain embarrassing for the Morgan bank, which prided itself on its economic intelligence.

TWL's statement to the press, attributed to an anonymous international banker, said that the British move should not affect repayment of the recent Morgan-led bank credit or earlier loans to the British government, which were all denominated in dollars. The consequences of freeing the pound from gold followed swiftly: within five days the pound sterling fell 20 percent lower than its former gold value, and it fell another 10 percent by year-end.

As the sterling crisis unfolded, Lamont was stunned by the sudden death, from a stroke on October 5, of his old friend Dwight Morrow at the age of fifty-eight. TWL expressed his own personal loss and the nation's great loss on many occasions in the days following his friend's death. The New Jersey senator had served his country with distinction; in recent months he had been a key adviser to President Hoover during the European financial crisis.

Lamont himself continued to offer his advice freely to the president. On October 20, TWL wrote Hoover about the forthcoming visit to Washington of Premier Pierre Laval of France, now the strongest country in Europe—militarily, economically, and financially.

Britain's abandonment of the gold standard was followed by a score or so of nations who devalued their currencies and others who introduced strict foreign exchange controls—moves designed to keep their exports competitive and protect their gold and foreign currency reserves. Among the major Western nations only France and the United States, both holding large gold reserves, remained firmly committed to the gold standard. However, a new development was worrying the American government—growing speculation against the dollar and large and growing gold shipments to Europe, especially to France, which was aggressively adding to its gold holdings. Americans began to hoard gold and withdraw money from banks, and bank closures increased sharply in September and October.

Lamont advised the president that in his talks with Laval he should praise France's unique strength. World recovery depended on the poise, generosity, and self-confidence that France demonstrated in its leadership role. The president should appeal to France's pride, self-respect, and magnanimity. He should assure Laval that the U.S. was determined to maintain the gold standard and that America was "ready to lock arms with them, the two great gold standard countries of the old world and the new." Lamont concluded: "You will as always, I am sure, attribute any excess of zeal which I may show in offering my views upon you to my earnest desire to serve you, even in a trifling degree, in some of the many problems which you are grappling with so much courage and devotion."

TWL called on the black-mustachioed French premier at the Waldorf-Astoria when Laval was passing through New York. Presumably Lamont took the occasion to put forward the same proposals he had suggested to the president.

In the Hoover-Laval talks both countries agreed to maintain their gold standards and work for dollar stability. Speculative attacks on the dollar and the gold drain from the U.S. slackened and finally ceased in the following months.

But the German short-term debt problem was a ticking financial time bomb which Lamont highlighted in a *Saturday Review of Literature* review of Dr. Hjalmar Schacht's new book. While Germany continued to pay debt service on her foreign bonds, the standstill agreement suspended repayment of credits owed foreign banks until February 1932. Said TWL: "Critics will really have sound ground to attack if the German government fails to apply the savings from President Hoover's debt holiday to the liquidation of Germany's short-term obligations both at home and abroad." American banks, as the leading foreign lenders to Germany, had the most cause for worry, but not the Morgan firm, thanks to the long-held bias of its senior partner.

Lamont offered parallel advice to German ambassador F. W. Prittwitz, followed up by his letter of November 9. The standstill agreement completely shut off the granting of new credits to Germany, because foreign investors and banks were confused and worried about Germany's intentions toward their already frozen German loans. The German banks should promptly negotiate with their foreign creditors an orderly plan for the liquidation of this debt, and the government should not intervene. Private claims should not be subject to government agreements involving public debt or political considerations; one class of creditors should not be played off against another.

The United States had been the first to deal a heavy blow to world trade with the erection of the Smoot-Hawley tariff walls in 1930. In 1931 the sterling crisis triggered worldwide protectionism, and world trade shrank precipitously during 1932; business contracted, unemployment spread, and the people's despair over the depression sank to a new low. Government clearly did not have the answers.

The Senate Has Questions

The American railroad industry had been hard hit by the decline in freight and revenues caused by the depression. Among all the debt issues organized by the Morgan bank, railroad bonds were faring the worst. J. P. Morgan & Co. had managed bond issues for a score of railroads, including old clients like the New York Central and more recent ones, notably the Van Sweringen brothers' Alleghany Corporation, which held controlling ownership of the Chesapeake and Ohio, other eastern lines, and the Missouri Pacific. The Morgan bank had made a number of bank loans and floated bond issues for Alleghany and its related companies, of which the latest was a $61.2 million issue for the Missouri Pacific in January 1931. Now the Van Sweringen holding company and railroads were fighting a losing battle to avoid default on their large bonded and floating debt.

Over the past year Lamont had periodically informed President Hoover about developments in the industry. On August 26, 1931, he wrote the president that perhaps 70 percent of outstanding railroad bonds, now selling at deep discounts, might be removed by the New York State authorities from the legal list for investment by New York savings banks and trust funds for failure to meet the interest coverage test. During the second half of 1931, the market for railroad bonds collapsed completely and it was no longer possible to fund railway short-term debt by issuing bonds.

Like Pierpont Morgan in earlier times, Lamont had long thought that a more rational grouping of the major eastern systems was needed to improve their efficiency. In many areas there was wasteful and unprofitable duplication of track and terminals belonging to competing railroads. The need for consolidation was now urgent in view of the tough new competition from pipelines and motor transport facing the railroads. Even air travel would cut into their passenger business some day in the future; two hundred high-paying passengers were now landing daily in New York. Lamont urged Hoover to encourage the railway chiefs to consolidate their lines on a more efficient basis, and the president tried. But the executives failed to take action as their industry's fortunes declined with mounting losses.

American industry's problems were not Lamont's only concern. Along with all New Yorkers, he was moved by the suffering of thousands of individuals in his own city. Believing that relief for the growing army of unemployed should largely be a local community responsibility, he worked as a member of the Emergency Unemployment Relief Committee of New York to raise $12 million in private funds for the city's needy citizens during the coming winter. The number of unemployed seeking relief was much larger than the winter before; many families had long since exhausted their meager savings. There were thousands of homeless people living in "Hooverville" shantytowns, and soup kitchen lines had formed throughout the city.

Speaking at the committee's first meeting on October 2, TWL injected a bit of his own economic philosophy into his plea for donations. Unless private efforts contributed in bringing relief to the unemployed, the whole burden would fall on the state, bringing on "the dole," which was not "the American way." What Lamont and Hoover did not yet grasp was that the swelling numbers needing help were already overwhelming the capacity of local communities and charities to cope.

Many congressmen believed that the country's economic decline, causing widespread unemployment and suffering, had been exacerbated by the reckless selling of foreign bonds, many of which were now in default, to American investors. Lamont was the first witness when the Senate Finance Committee held hearings in December 1931 to investigate "the sale of foreign bonds and securities in the United States."

The weekly newsmagazine *Literary Digest* described TWL as "the suave, urbane, quizzically smiling Lamont, youthfully garbed in double breasted blue suit and polka-dotted bow tie." During three hours of testimony Lamont never failed to address any one of the fourteen senators present by name as he answered their questions. The *Digest* reporter noted: "Quite at ease, as though talking back to a roomful of Senators was no particularly harassing experience, Mr. Lamont occasionally interjected a note of humor, and even ventured to trade witticisms with the deadly serious Johnson"—Senator Hiram Johnson from California, who had introduced the resolution authorizing the investigation.

Lamont related the history of Morgan's activity since the war in floating foreign bond issues in the United States. At times the tone of the hearing resembled a classroom session with Lamont, the learned professor, explaining the mechanics of underwriting securities issues to some graying graduate students eager to explore the mysteries of high finance. The teacher patiently answered questions about the role and compensation of the manager and the allocation of the "gross spread" among the original purchase group, the intermediate banking group, and the distribution syndicate.

In discussing the compensation Morgan received for managing issues, Lamont observed with a smile, "I am sometimes mortified to reveal how small our commission was in some of these cases. I am afraid I may invoke the sympathy of the committee too much."

Since the war Morgan had sponsored offerings of foreign bonds in the United States amounting to about $2.2 billion; the government of France had been the leading borrower with issues totaling $300 million. There were no defaults on any of the Morgan-led bond issues, although Morgan had taken participations in bond issues, now in default, that had been organized by other houses.

Other testimony revealed that of the $7.9 billion of foreign bond issues sold in the United States since 1920, some $815 million of bonds were no longer paying debt service, and Latin American governments were the worst offenders. Wisely, Morgan had largely stayed clear of sponsoring Latin American loans since the war; its outstanding loans to the Republic of Argentina and to Cuba were current.

A Department of Commerce official stated that Morgan and Kuhn, Loeb had conducted their foreign bond business conservatively "in the English tradition," where the borrower seeks the lender. But some other American firms were guilty of overselling—"throwing themselves at foreign governments for the privilege of lending them their money."

"The banks are not loaded up with those bonds to the extent people believe," said Lamont.

"Yes," responded Senator Thomas Gore. "It is Tom, Dick, and Harry who have taken the losses."

"It is true that the brunt of the declines has fallen upon the great investing public and not upon the banks," Lamont replied smoothly. "It is a very deplorable thing that in the present depressed state of world affairs, our private investors have been obliged to witness severe declines in U.S. government bonds, foreign government bonds, railroad bonds, industrial bonds, and every kind of bonds."

The newspaper stories the next day paid special attention to Lamont's reassurances on Germany's finances. The German government had been meticulous in complying with the debt service requirements of the Dawes and Young Plan loans, and Germany's private short-term credits held by American banks constituted no danger to any of these banks, said Lamont. From his checking TWL knew that the largest amount of German credits held by any one bank was $70 million, and that bank's resources were so large that "it was not a matter of danger or even comment." Negotiations were now proceeding in Berlin to arrange a schedule for the gradual liquidation of this short-term debt, Lamont reported. The next day bank shares rallied on Wall Street.

Lamont and his partners had prepared a statement for the committee, and it was clear that the depressed state of railway bonds, not foreign bonds, was uppermost in their minds. Six railway bank issues sponsored by Morgan over the last twenty years had gone into default, and the others were selling at large discounts.

> If we can address ourselves to the domestic situation, the foreign situation will go far in helping to take care of itself. We see railroad bonds, the backbone of the market, under a cloud because the industry's earnings are not sufficient to meet its outgo. We are much pleased by reports of voluntary reduction in wages. That will be one of the great factors lending stability to the bond market. Anything we can do towards facilitating the consummation of that arrangement will help more than any one thing except legislation in Washington.

Some papers praised Lamont's appearance before the committee. The *New York World Telegram* stated: "The banker, speaking quietly and with apparent frankness, obviously made a good impression on committee members, both Democratic and Republican."

Other papers, especially in the nation's hinterland, raised critical questions about what the hearings had disclosed. They noted ruefully that individual investors, not the banks, ended up with the bulk of the defaulted bonds. They suspected that Lamont and the international bankers really wanted lower American tariffs to enable their foreign borrowers to repay their loans, even if American industry suffered from the flood of low-cost goods that would enter the country when the barriers were reduced. In Missouri, the *Jefferson City Post* wondered why the administration had declared a moratorium on the repayment of foreign debt to the U.S. government while "the international bankers have a shrewd way of safeguarding their private loans."

After Christmas the Lamonts retreated to their "cottage" at Yeamens Hall. Florence looked forward to a real rest. Her ankle, broken in an accidental fall in August, had healed painfully and slowly. The dynamic H. G. Wells had been a houseguest for several weeks, which entailed dinner parties in his honor and often, for Florence, breakfast, lunch, and tea as well. Once again the famous novelist had worn out his hostess. "I got awfully tired of talking to him in spite of his wit and brilliance," she wrote her son Austin studying in Oxford. The Lamonts enjoyed the warm Carolina sunshine and the company of their friends and houseguests Walter and Faye Lippmann.

Lippmann's new column, "Today and Tomorrow," appearing in the *New York Herald Tribune*, had quickly won popular acclaim. Newspapers across the country clamored to carry it on a syndicated basis from the *Tribune*. TWL wrote his friend frequently to praise his columns and also to feed him private information on political and economic issues. Over the past two years Lippmann had often been TWL's guest at dinners or on weekends and vacations, and Lamont and Leffingwell had arranged for the columnist to join the fashionable River Club in New York, where he was one of the few Jews to have been admitted to membership. The two successful Harvard graduates of different ages and backgrounds enjoyed each other's company and served each other's interests.

Japan's First Target

J. P. Morgan & Co. had floated bond issues totaling $263 million for Japanese borrowers since 1924, the largest amount for any country outside Europe. The earthquake reconstruction loans had been followed by a loan to the Imperial Government for debt refunding in 1930 and a guaranteed loan in June 1931 to the Taiwan Electric Company. Morgan had also organized a $25 million bank credit to the Yokohama Specie Bank for currency stabilization as Japan prepared to return to the gold standard in 1930. While Lamont and his partners had consistently turned down overtures to grant loans to China, still disorganized and now divided by the struggle for power between the Nationalists and the Communists, the bankers considered Japan to be an important client with excellent prospects for future business. Then on September 19, 1931, the Japanese army struck in Manchuria, seizing the capital city of Mukden.

The Japanese government stated that military action had been initiated only after Chinese soldiers had destroyed part of the South Manchuria Railway track near Mukden; the army's response was necessary to protect the Japanese-owned railway, the economic lifeline of the Chinese province. In fact, the military high command in Tokyo had secretly decided to begin its offensive to take control of the province, and Japanese troops were soon occupying other Manchurian towns and communications centers.

TWL, fed information by Inosuke Inouye, now finance minister, and Japanese banking friends, swallowed it whole and sprang to defend the Japanese action. Inouye was a wise and liberal-minded statesman and friend who needed his help, and TWL advised him on drafting and issuing a press release conveying the official Japanese line that the Chinese were the provocateurs and Japan only wanted peace with China. Lamont and Russell Leffingwell both dispatched letters to Walter Lippmann defending the Japanese presence in Manchuria. Said TWL:

> The reason that the Chinese are piling into Manchuria by the million and settling there is not alone because the land is fertile . . . but because Manchuria is, as matters stand, the only province in Eastern China where it is safe for a farmer to live. . . . Generally the Eastern provinces are overrun and harried by the conflicting armies, and so it is natural that the Chinese should love to go to a land where peace reigns. That peace is due . . . to the care and thoroughness with which the Japanese have developed and kept open means of communication and have policed them well enough to keep them free from banditry. This is a great big white mark for Japan. . . .
>
> Another point is that there are in existence certain treaties under which the Chinese Government agreed not to build fresh railway lines obviously competing with the South Manchurian Railway, without consultation with and consent by the Japanese. These treaties were based on the sound theory that no country—least of all China, could afford to incur deliberate economic wastage in duplicating existing facilities. The Chinese have disregarded these treaties and have been building quite useless railway lines not far from the South Manchurian. The Japanese have protested, but have been terribly decent about the thing, have begged the Chinese to confer with them, and have explained to them that under the treaties they, themselves, would work out with the Chinese trade and transportation routes that would be advantageous to Manchuria and China. . . . But the Chinese have not been interested to adopt this course . . . , withholding payment on any Japanese Government loans and in effect taking the amounts due thereon and applying them to the building of railways in contravention of the existing treaties.
>
> In other words, China, has conducted the most lawless and aggravating course possible. Yet they have an extraordinary knack of making an effective yell to the public when anything happens. They play undoubtedly upon the unwise policies adopted by Japan fifteen or sixteen years ago. They make the world believe that Japan hasn't changed. I think it has.

Japan was changing, but not in the way Lamont expected. Wishful yearning for peace in the Orient and continuing good relations with

Japan, in which he had invested so much effort, had seriously flawed TWL's judgment. In refusing to contemplate that the militarists with their strategy of expansion might be taking over control from the moderates in the Japanese cabinet, he had incautiously leapt to defend Japan's hostile act.

But Lippmann and the U.S. government soon were taking a much harder line toward Japan. When the League of Nations called on Japan to withdraw her troops to the treaty-designated railway zone, Japan not only refused but continued to extend her occupation of Manchuria. On January 7, 1932, Secretary of State Stimson announced that the United States would not recognize any territorial arrangement contrary to the Kellogg-Briand Pact or American treaty rights, placing the United States squarely on record as opposed to the Japanese occupation of Manchuria.

On January 28 a new act of aggression opened TWL's eyes to the nature of the beast and hardened American and world opinion against the Japanese penetration of China. Claiming that the lives of Japanese nationals were threatened, the Japanese navy landed marines at Shanghai, who soon joined combat with the local Chinese troops; Japanese planes bombed Chinese soldiers and civilians, and Japanese ships offshore shelled Chinese positions. The moderate leaders of the Japanese government had been deposed in December by the militarists, and the impact of their ascendency to power was shockingly evident.

On February 9, Lamont, vacationing in Bermuda, received word that Inosuke Inouye had been assasinated at the hands of a nationalist fanatic. Lamont, who had consulted with Inouye for over a decade on Japanese financial affairs, mourned his loss, but the violence was not over: a month later Dr. Takuna Dan, the head of the powerful Mitsui business empire, was murdered under similar circumstances. Inouye and Dan had jointly given the great dinner, attended by the elite from business and government, to welcome Lamont to Japan on his last trip. They had been TWL's best friends in Japan.

After the Shanghai attack Lamont had written Saburu Sonada, the Yokohama Specie Bank agent in New York, that American confidence in Japan had been badly shaken and that it would be virtually impossible for Japan to borrow abroad. Upon hearing of Inouye's death TWL sent another message for Sonada to pass on to his colleagues in Japan, which concluded: "It is time you and all those who think like you must cling together and stand for Japan's highest ideals, attainment of her ends by diplomacy, logic, and peaceful method, not force."

By February 1932 the American public and press were in full cry, condemning Japanese aggression in China. Manchuria had now been completely overrun by the Japanese army, and the Shanghai fighting and wanton bombing of civilians had fanned the flames of public indignation. Sentiment for an embargo on trade with Japan quickly gathered momentum. In early March, A. Lawrence Lowell, president of Harvard, sponsored a petition requesting the U.S. government to inform the League of Nations that it would concur in whatever economic measures the League might take to restore peace in the Orient.

Lowell, only months earlier, had awarded TWL an honorary degree at Harvard, depicting him as "by nature a statesman . . .sagacious in council on affairs that effect all nations." Now he appealed to Lamont to support his petition, but Lamont, after checking with Secretary Stimson, declined. In his letter to Lowell, Lamont agreed that there was no justification for the attack on Shanghai by Japanese forces, who were still occupying the city, and said that he had expressed this view forcefully to his Japanese friends. But Lamont could influence the Japanese more effectively in private as a friend than by taking a public position. He also thought that it was unwise for a private citizens' group to try to force the hand of the administration in an affair of such international consequence; the government should be free to take the lead in the matter. Lamont was against imposing a trade boycott on Japan anyway, which he believed was tantamount to war in causing human suffering. The Japanese people would consider it a warlike move. "We would arouse the very sentiments and passions which as peace lovers it is our purpose to allay," he said.

President Lowell observed in his response that for the first time since the formation of the League of Nations after the war "a great nation has undertaken military action." It was up to the League not just to talk, but to take firm steps. The terms of the boycott would require Japan to withdraw her troops from Shanghai by a certain date, and if she complied, which he expected, there would be no boycott.

Lamont disagreed, although he favored cutting off loans, supporting the administration strategy to restrain Japan's financial capacity for mischief. Also, lending to Japan was no longer attractive for financial as well as political reasons: a sharp decline in foreign trade had led to Japan's abandonment of the gold standard. On March 30, 1932, Lamont wrote Japanese finance minister Korekiyo Takahashi, sending a copy of his letter to Secretary Stimson.

> So far as the general so-called Western public is concerned, nothing will ever convince it that the Japanese military and naval forces at Shanghai have acted with prudence and restraint. It has been a very bad mess, and I should prove myself a poor friend to your country if I did not say so plainly. . . .
>
> It will take all the efforts of our friends on both sides of the water, and a

very considerable space of time, to restore the better feeling that manifestly had begun to exist in this country on all matters Japanese. We must address ourselves to the rebuilding of that good feeling. . . .

It is very necessary that Japan should put herself clearly before the world in the light of a just and humane nation. I am not prepared to discuss your government's policies in South Manchuria, but you will readily see that your government would have had far more chance to work out fair and equitable policies in South Manchuria without undue criticism, if it had not handled the Shanghai adventure with such lack of caution, to say no worse.

TWL then traced the record of the Morgan firm in assisting Japan, starting with the earthquake reconstruction loan of 1924.

You can, therefore, well understand with what anxiety I have viewed recent developments in the Far East. There will come a time in the future when the Japanese Government perhaps, and certainly some of your public utility or industrial corporations, will again desire to arrange credits in the American markets. But naturally for any such future development there will have to be a great change in the picture. It is my earnest hope that you will be able to bring 'about such a change, so that at some time our investment markets and our people generally will be able once more to evince that confidence in the Japanese people which has recently been so sadly shaken.

In March 1932, Japan established Manchuria as a separate puppet state called Manchukuo and routed the Chinese troops in Shanghai in a crushing and bloody defeat. The Japanese finally withdrew their army units from Shanghai in May. In October, when the League-sponsored Lytton Report condemning Japan's occupation of Manchuria was released, Lamont cautioned Secretary Stimson against arousing greater Japanese hostility toward the United States and other Western countries. Inciting world opinion against Japan would not diminish the authority of Japan's military leaders; change could come only from within. At the same time TWL wrote to his Japanese friends praising the Lytton Report as presenting a good basis for negotiations between Japan and China on their outstanding differences.

Lamont had written off the Japanese occupation of Manchuria as a fait accompli, but he still felt it was worthwhile trying to reform Japan's China policy in the hopes of patching together a peaceful settlement which would be beneficial for everyone. However, there were no signs of change in Japan, and she withdrew from the League of Nations in March 1933, as her army pushed into the interior of Manchuria toward the Chinese province of Jehol and the Great Wall.

Keeping New York Solvent and Florence Happy

On January 7, 1932, a *Herald Tribune* front-page headline proclaimed: "Walker's Charges Denied by Banks, City Warned Strict Economy Needed." Underneath was a photograph of Thomas W. Lamont, the bankers' spokesman, smiling amiably.

The City of New York under Mayor James Walker was in trouble. It was confronted by $150 million of maturing short-term debt; an annual budget deficit of over $40 million; 900,000 unemployed and overwhelming demands for relief assistance; a debt service burden of $200 million consuming 30 percent of city revenues; tax arrears of about 20 percent and rising; and a subway system, based on a five-cent fare, generating huge operating losses the city could ill afford. Investors and lenders were very wary about extending additional credit to the city. City Hall, led by its affable and fun-loving mayor, had not demonstrated the seriousness of purpose about economizing that the bankers deemed essential to undertaking a new municipal bond issue.

For his part, Mayor Walker had publicly charged that the bankers had not been cooperative in addressing the city's financial problems and were insensitive to the suffering of the city's poor. "I have visited a great many charitable institutions in this city," the mayor told a dinner audience, "and I never tripped over any bankers as I went in the door or came out."

Lamont's statement was issued on behalf of J. P. Morgan & Co. and seven other large New York banks whose representatives had met to discuss the city's needs. TWL stated that the mayor could not have been referring to the New York bankers in his complaint, who, at the invitation of city officials, had been studying the condition of New York's finances. They would not stipulate specific moves City Hall should take, such as raising the subway fare or cutbacks and postponements in expenditures and construction projects. Only the city officials should initiate such entrenchment proposals. But it was clear that City Hall must introduce "measures of strict economy" and transform enterprises that were not self-supporting into "ones that carry themselves and thus take a heavy burden off the city's budget."

City officials, led by the debonair mayor, and the bankers engaged in tough negotiations over the next two weeks. At a critical evening session held at Lamont's 70th Street house, Mayor Walker was inexplicably over two hours late. The negotiations had come to a halt; the city officials present couldn't proceed without consulting the mayor.

Around ten o'clock, the mayor made a jaunty entrance in evening clothes and top hat; it was clear that he had enjoyed the libations served at the party he had just attended. "Loaded with champagne," observed one banker in attendance. Soon rising to leave, with little accomplished, the mayor announced that he had another engagement: "Mustn't keep a lovely lady waiting, you know," and with a smile and a wink he departed into the night.

The mayor would not budge on raising the subway fare, a promise to voters he intended to keep. But the city would institute other budget cuts and postpone some major construction projects. Accordingly, the bankers agreed to underwrite two bond issues of $100 million each for the city and provide a $151 million line of credit.

On January 22, the *New York Daily News*, in announcing the new program of financial assistance, stated:

> Rather than avail himself of the opportunity to make political capital by shrieking at the bankers, Mayor Walker has chosen to admit frankly that the city must retrench, to put a program of retrenchment in motion, and to talk reasonably with the bankers. That is statesmanship.
>
> Rather than make the politicians sweat in public for past mistakes and super-generosities, the bankers, through Thomas W. Lamont, have agreed to distribute the emergency bonds at par and pay distribution costs. Fine.
>
> This is the way to handle these things in our greatest city. It must keep on being our greatest city; and if we can always settle our difficulties in this broadminded fashion, it will.

But only the city's immediate financial needs were met, and City Hall and the bankers were soon engaged in a long-running and acrimonious debate over the measures of fiscal discipline needed to bolster the city's credit. And the five-cent subway fare, mandated by the city, took its toll. The privately owned Interborough Rapid Transit Company, which ran one of New York's subway lines, couldn't meet a large maturity in 1932 on a Morgan-led bond issue, went into bankruptcy, and was eventually sold by the bankers to the city.

Tom and Florence often had different inclinations about one ongoing aspect of living—how to spend their evenings. Florence was a charming and vivacious hostess. Occasionally her dinner partners might find her conversation a bit laborious when she pursued such topics as the definition of leisure, but she could also be quite mischievous in her repartee. Yet she was most content to retire early with a good book of poetry or philosophy or write letters to John Masefield and her other literary friends, whose volumes filled her bookcases. Once in a letter to his children, Tom described his dear wife's chief shipboard pastime: "Brilliant and Beautiful mère, who however spends almost all her time in bed, getting rested for the literary and philosophical debauch that is awaiting her on European shores."

Florence shunned New York theater evenings unless the offering was serious drama, perhaps the work of one of her British playwright friends. Tom, on the other hand, gregarious by nature, enjoyed attending Broadway musicals and comedies with his friends and the gala parties on opening nights at the theater or opera.

The indefatigable man-about-town, who as a Harvard student could not afford to join one of the select clubs, was now a member of a half dozen or so of the city's most prestigious clubs—the Links, the River, the Metropolitan, the Century, the Union, and, of course, the Harvard Club, where he served a term as president.

Lamont's appetite for attending dinners, meeting notables, and planning far-flung excursions seemed insatiable. TWL admired the attractive and lively ladies he met at these and other affairs, such as shipboard captain's balls and English house parties, and his lady friends included titled blue-bloods and pretty and vivacious divorcées and widows. These charmers in turn aimed to captivate the convivial and wealthy banker. Perhaps an invitation to a country weekend at Palisades, a cruise on the *Reynard* to watch the Harvard-Yale crew races, or some profitable Morgan investment advice for those who needed guidance in their personal finances might be forthcoming. New friends might even be added to Lamont's bounteous gift list for birthdays and Christmas.

The Lamonts' different tastes in nightlife came to a head during their winter vacation in Bermuda with the Gavits and some other friends. The party stayed at the large and luxurious Castle Harbor resort hotel in Tucker's Town.

Florence loved the Bermuda climate and scenery. "No wonder Shakespeare thought the island enchanted," she wrote her children. However, she could be a bit fussy at times, and life at the hotel was quite unappealing to her.

> I do not like this hotel at all. It is very noisy & impossible for sleep. There are too many doors slamming & elevators banging & mosquitoes biting all night, & drunk Americans talking loud till all hours under my window. So now I have turned into a sort of Cinderella & every night about 9:30 I take off my evening dress, don my old golf clothes & drive over to the Mid-Ocean Club where I have the quietest, loveliest room that ever was. After

breakfast, the others will arrive & of course I am with them all day. The other five sleep like tops & never hear a sound & think I am crazy. . . . This hotel is filled with a cheap noisy crowd, there is a dinner dance every single night with the loudest orchestra I have ever heard & we scream at each other from soup till dessert. But Father & the others don't mind the noise and love it here, so of course it's best to stay.

Tom had a different view of resort life, as he wrote TSL:

I find my party a trifle old. A magnificent swimming pool here, sparkling salt water, and temperature perfect. But none of my party wants to go in. They stand around the edges like a lot of chickens and watch me go in all by myself. Then they want to dine at 7:30. I say life does not come into the dining room till 9 P.M. and none of the gay ladies from Hamilton, wearing no stockings, turn up for the dancing till 9:30. Well, I suppose I shall be old some day and like to go to bed at 10 P.M. But you can be young only once!

On March 2, 1932, the shocking story broke of the kidnapping of the baby son of Charles and Anne Lindbergh. The child was taken from his crib at night at the Lindbergh country home near Princeton, New Jersey, and a note demanding ransom was soon received. The Lindberghs had often stayed with the Morrows, Anne's parents, in Englewood and North Haven, and the Lamonts had known Anne since she was a little girl.

The Lamonts were linked unexpectedly to the case in another way. Henry "Red" Johnson, a twenty-two-year-old sailor on TWL's yacht *Reynard*, had phoned his girlfriend Betty Gow, the Lindbergh nurse, on the night of the kidnapping. Johnson was picked up for questioning by the police, and the *Reynard* was searched for clues. It was quickly established that Johnson and Gow had no connection with the kidnapping. The baby's dead body was found in the woods not far from the Lindberghs' home two and a half months later. The Lamonts were stunned by the tragedy and alarmed about the safety of their own growing brood of grandchildren who visited them frequently at Palisades. Steel bars were installed over bedroom windows, and an armed guard, an ex city detective in civilian clothes, was hired to keep an eye on the children.

Debate Over the Market

For some time President Hoover had been provoked by what he viewed as the immoral and damaging manipulation of stock prices by speculators on the stock exchange, especially the practice of "bear raids"—the selling of borrowed stock followed by organized campaigns, including spreading false rumors, to drive stock prices down to a level at which the "shorts" would cover their sales at a handsome profit. Hoover had first spoken to Lamont in 1930 about his concern over bear raids. As neither TWL nor the Morgan firm engaged in short selling, Lamont had arranged for Richard Whitney, president of the New York Stock Exchange, to call on Hoover to discuss the problem. Meetings with Whitney and other exchange officials had been unproductive in the president's opinion; new and strictly enforced regulations were needed to curb stock exchange abuses. In a public statement Hoover reported that the administration had told the exchange officials that "they should take adequate measures to protect investors from artificial depression of the price of securities for speculative profit. Individuals who use the facilities of the exchange for such purposes are not contributing to recovery of the United States." At Hoover's urging the Senate on March 4, 1932, authorized a Banking and Currency Committee investigation of stock exchange practices. On March 16 in a conversation with Lamont at the White House the president reiterated his concern about the harmful economic consequences of short selling.

Lamont demurred. Furthermore, the upcoming Senate investigation into short selling and other stock exchange practices worried him, and he told the president that if the inquiry "was encouraged to run riot" it would create "great uneasiness among investors."

Given the wide extent of abusive stock exchange practices revealed later, Hoover was clearly on the right track in backing the Senate inquiry. Despite his fears of the effect of the investigation on investor confidence, TWL's foot-dragging on the initiative reflected a limited and shortsighted view of a vital public interest—maintaining honest, fair, and efficient securities markets. However, the practice of short selling, conducted ethically, was a valuable trading technique, and Lamont believed that restricting this practice would severely damage the workings of the stock market. Upon his return to the city Lamont asked Richard Whitney to have the exchange staff prepare an analysis of recent stock market performance with statistical data on short and long interests' activity and sent a copy of the study with a covering letter to President Hoover.

TWL noted that the stock market had "followed almost steadily the course of diminishing corporate earnings." The buying and selling of stocks held outright or on credit were by far the dominant force in determining stock prices, not short selling and covering. When depressing news broke, the long interest was almost invariably selling and the short interest covering, operating as a cushion in a declining market with a beneficial stabilizing effect. The lower earnings and dividends of so many companies were the basic cause of heavy selling and falling stock prices, and the market decline would have been much worse had there been no short interest operating.

> If further steps, such as legislative restrictions of short selling, or excessive increase in the Federal tax on stock transfers, are taken to restrict speculation in stocks, we shall have no speculative market at all, and the hope of prompt recovery from the depression . . . will be at an end. Bulls will not buy in a market where bears cannot sell, for today's bull wants to be able to change his foot and sell tomorrow. If the bull knows there are no bears on whose covering he can rely if he changes his mind and wants to sell, the bull won't buy in the first place. Illogical though it may be, a strong stock market encourages general sentiment toward business in general.

There would be no rally until people began buying speculatively again. "That buying has always been the golden key to unlock the door of recovery.'

The president replied to Lamont in his letter of April 2, 1932, thanking him for his memorandum.

> It seems to me, however, that some other factors enter into this consideration.
>
> The first is that prices today do not truly represent the values of American enterprise and property. To base the prices on earnings either at top of a boom or at bottom of a depression is not correct interpretation of values.
>
> The second point . . . is that the pounding down of prices . . . by obvious manipulation of the market and propaganda . . . is an injury to the country and to the investing public. . . .
>
> My third point is that so long as these processes continue, the public, which is willing to invest on the basis of the future of the United States rather than upon immediate bear coloring of earnings, is driven from the market.
>
> My fourth point is that these operations destroy public confidence and induce a slowing down of business and a fall in prices.
>
> My fifth point is that men are not justified in deliberately making a profit from the losses of other people.

I recognize that these points of view are irreconcilable, but I hope you will agree with me that there is here an element of public interest.

Unconvinced by the president's moral conviction, Lamont wrote Hoover back on April 8 agreeing that, of course, "to circulate false or malicious rumors is execrable." But he questioned Hoover's statement that stock prices did not represent "real value" under current conditions. "What can be called 'real value' if a security has no earnings and pays no dividends?" Investors, even the wealthy, needed income.

"The ice is so thin over the whole situation that anything very heavy they throw on it breaks through at once," argued Lamont. The congressional fight over a balanced budget, the threat of the passage of a new large veterans' bonus, and proposals for greater taxes on stock transfers were "projected on it in a body. . . . With all these things thrown on, the ice did break through, and we find ourselves in another alarmingly weak market." A virtually nonexistent bond market and some major corporate failures and near bankruptcies, known throughout the business community, had "led to a wave of real liquidation" on the stock market.

Finally, Lamont said, all that he had in mind about the proposed investigation of stock exchange practices was "to hope that it will be conducted so as to be a constructive rather than a destructive factor." Over the strong opposition of Wall Street, the Senate inquiry went forward with its examination to uncover abuses on the stock exchanges.

On the same day Lamont wrote to the president, the stock market plunged again, perhaps influenced by the rumor of a large new bear raid the next morning. National unemployment was around eleven million and rising, and unemployed businessmen were selling apples from stands on Fifth Avenue and Wall Street. The drain of American gold reserves from foreign withdrawals had begun again, and the dollar's drop in value that day, in response to rumors of an attack against it by French speculators, would accelerate the gold outflow. Furthermore, over a billion dollars, much in gold coin, was being hoarded by frightened Americans increasingly worried about the integrity of their banks.

The Reparations–War Debt Minuet

On the evening of April 8, TWL and Florence sailed for Europe on their annual spring trip. There was a congenial group aboard the *Ile de France*, Lamont wrote TSL. Norman Davis, TWL's colleague at the Paris Peace Conference and a former Under Secretary of State, joined the Lamont table in the ship's dining salon. Indeed the State Department was well represented. "Secretary of State Stimson is agreeable but solemn. . . . Ex-Secretary Frank Kellogg (76) is spry as a cricket and kindly critical of all his predecessors and successors in office." Stimson was on his way to the General Disarmanent Conference being held in Geneva.

The irrepressible Sybil Walker was also at the Lamont table. "Sybil and I fight quite a lot about her bidding at bridge which is as wobbly as her dancing. In the latter she has no sense of time. She therefore dances better when the ship is rolling at an angle of 45 degrees."

The highlight of the Lamonts' spring visit to England was the dedication of the Shakespeare Memorial Theater at Stratford-on-Avon on April 23. TWL was an honored guest in his role as chairman of the Special American Committee which had raised almost $1 million, the bulk of the funds needed to build the new theater. It was a full day, filled with ceremony, luncheon for 670 guests, long speeches, and the performance of *Henry IV*, both parts, in the new theater. The crowd was sprinkled with Lamont friends and acquaintances—George Bernard Shaw; Stanley Baldwin, the former prime minister; American ambassador Andrew Mellon; the Prince of Wales; and the Masefields.

TWL's chance to perform came at the end of the evening performance of the play. Speaking of the thousands of American contributors to the Shakespeare theater project, he said:

They have felt that this great Theatre which we dedicate today stands in memory not alone of a mighty dramatist, of a noble poet, but of that living fount of ideas and aspirations from which our Pilgrim forefathers drank three centuries ago and bore across the Western Ocean, to give out again to the new American commonwealth.

In alluding to the troubles of the world, Lamont stated:

We seem concerned primarily, and perhaps necessarily, with the material affairs of the world. How great a satisfaction then, it must be for us all, princes, ambassadors, British and Americans together, to gather at this shrine and give ourselves over to the contemplation of another life, a more lasting one; to draw breath in a world where ideas of beauty and loveliness reign.

During the Atlantic crossing Lamont had taken the opportunity to present his views to Secretary Stimson on the reparations question, to be reviewed shortly at an international conference in Lausanne. The Hoover moratorium on intergovernmental debt payments was due to expire in two months, and it was again necessary for the creditor nations to reexamine Germany's capacity to pay reparations in view of the severely depressed state of her economy. TWL knew Stimson well from their previous dealings on Japanese and Mexican relations. The studious-looking Stimson was a statesman of wide experience—a former Secretary of War and Governor General of the Phillipines. He had made his mark in diplomatic history in formulating the policy of nonrecognition in the case of Japan's occupation of Manchuria, later known as the Stimson Doctrine.

Lamont thought that Germany's reparations obligation should certainly be reduced but not cancelled. Cancellation would be unfair to those nations who had suffered so much from the war, especially the French. Furthermore, Americans might interpret cancellation as a sign that the Allies intended to repudiate their war debts to the U.S. Stimson concurred with this approach, which he later put forward in his talks with European leaders.

In Paris, Lamont discussed the upcoming Lausanne conference with French premier André Tardieu and his colleagues. They were worried that the British were planning to propose the complete cancellation of Germany's reparations obligation at Lausanne. Crossing over to London, TWL talked with British officials, who confirmed that they did indeed favor cancellation.

Lunching privately at 10 Downing Street on May 3 with Prime Minister MacDonald, TWL said that Germany should not be completely let off the hook, even though her present economy was in a shambles; a grace period of three years or so would be appropriate before reparations payments, in modest amounts, began again. Moreover, it would be politically unwise for the British to intervene on the side of Germany in the negotiations at the expense of France. The settlement should be one that impressed Americans as fair and realistic, and the war debt owed America should not be expected to bear the full brunt of cutbacks in the German obligation. Lamont wrote MacDonald confirming these points and received an appreciative acknowledgment from the prime minister in a letter of May 26: "I often wish you were on this side to discuss in friendly confidence with me some of these problems of which I have no personal experience."

Before going home the Lamonts spent the weekend with Lady Astor at Cliveden and dined with H. G. Wells, who stated, Florence reported, that "the end of the capitalistic system was at hand, and that we should all go through bad times, even be hungry. I came home much depressed and went out and bought two lovely new teagowns this morning. Better enjoy it while you can. If I am going to starve it will be nice to starve in a pretty dress."

Upon his return Lamont briefed President Hoover at the White House and wrote Secretary of State Stimson about his talks in Europe on the reparations–war debts question. Again TWL suggested that the administration signal the Allied governments that it would have a "constructive attitude" about the Allies' war debt, assuming a realistic reparations accord was achieved. In his May 27 letter of acknowledgment Stimson asked Lamont to keep him informed; TWL's diagnosis was "sufficiently close" to his own views to make him feel that they could "exchange views with mutual profit." Lamont understood that President Hoover and Treasury Secretary Ogden Mills also agreed that the administration should recommend to Congress a scaling back of U.S. war debt once a satisfactory reparations agreement was reached at the Lausanne Conference.

On June 18, TWL was awarded an honorary Doctor of Laws degree by Columbia University, presented by his friend and Columbia's president, Dr. Nicholas Murray Butler. Four days later TWL joined his classmates in celebrating the fortieth anniversary of their Harvard class. Speaking to them at the Algonquin Club in Boston, as the American economy plunged to the nadir of depression, he declared that hard work, patience, and courage would set right once again "that great American experiment, the free development and progress of more than one hundred and twenty million people."

TWL was pleased to welcome another Harvard man into the clan, a top athlete and recent captain of the Harvard hockey team who was a refreshing addition to a family of three former *Crimson* editors. On June 25 Eleanor A. Lamont married Charles C. Cunningham in the same Englewood church where her parents had been wed thirty-seven years before. The reception was held in a huge tent on the lawn at Palisades, and this time the champagne flowed freely.

In a lackluster convention the Republicans chose President Hoover to run for reelection. On July 1 New York's ebullient governor, Franklin D. Roosevelt, was nominated by his party to be the Democratic standard-bearer. His enthusiastic reception across the country as the campaign progressed showed that many Americans were ready for a change.

With the economy at a new low there were some thirteen million unemployed, one out of every four workers, and millions more struggling on short pay. Farmers were in rebellion over low crop prices and farm foreclosures; thousands of small-town banks had closed; and an army of unemployed veterans was marching on Washington to demand a special bonus payment from the government. Reflecting the nation's woes on July 8, 1932, the stock market, as measured by the Dow-Jones index, fell to a new depression low of 41, 89 percent below its pre-crash high.

On the same day the Lausanne Conference agreed to a reduction in German reparations to $750 million, plus interest on deferred payments; there would be a three-year moratorium before payments were to begin. The figure was a tiny fraction of the original $33 billion obligation, virtually tantamount to cancellation.

However, it soon came out that the agreement was contingent on a sharp scaling down of the war debt owed the United States. In European eyes German reparations and the repayment of U.S. war debt were inseparable—the former supplying the needed resources for the latter. In the throes of depression, the Europeans were now clamoring for relief from the heavy financial burden, and the debtor nations, led by Great Britain and France, intended to band together in seeking a substantial reduction in the debt owed the United States, whose initials some Europeans claimed stood for "Uncle Shylock."

Lamont, by phone and letter, urged President Hoover to inform Congress that the United States must now be prepared to reduce the European war debt. The Lausanne agreement, a wise settlement, would clearly diminish the capacity of the European countries to repay their debts to the United States.

Hoover, however, was furious at the European nations for combining against the United States, and his viewpoint was passed back to Lamont through a mutual friend, TWL's Morgan colleague Martin Egan.

> Lamont has this matter all wrong. If there is one thing the American people do not like and will not stand for it is a combination of this kind against them. That is precisely what this is. . . . I have had hundreds of messages today from all parts of the country and from important men urging that there be a strong protest against this action. I would be surrendering my power as President if I did nothing about it. It was an unheard of thing for those nations to band themselves into a combination against us. Nothing of the kind ever happened before. They are trying to "gang" us. . . . Maybe they have settled German reparations but they did it

the worst damned way they could. If they settled reparations why didn't they stop there. I hoped we might have done something about the British debt but there is nothing I can do now. It is a Hell of a thing and Lamont cannot appreciate the terrible feeling of resentment that it has stirred up all over the United States.

The president was not exaggerating: the ganging-up strategy of the debtor nations had aroused a storm of protest throughout the country.

Up until the 1931 Hoover moratorium, Germany had paid about $4.5 billion in reparations with the substantial help of over $2 billion in private American loans. No further payments were received. With the German economy in severe depression and Hitler's rise to absolute power, German reparations ended for good while the war debt controversy dragged on.

It was late July, time for TWL to get away cruising on the beautifully appointed *Reynard*. Every piece of the sleek yacht's glass and chinaware was emblazoned with crossed burgees, Lamont's own private signal and that of the New York Yacht Club. In June the vessel had adorned the spectator fleet at the Harvard-Yale crew race in New London, for which TWL assembled a yachting party each year, and now he forsook the overnight train for a voyage from New York to North Haven; next TWL and a group of friends cruised downeast to the Bay of Fundy. Captain Christenson and his four-man all-Scandinavian crew performed as smoothly as ever, as TWL, sporting his gold-braided owner's cap, pointed out the coastal landmarks to his guests.   ·

In August, Florence, who had spent July in England, joined Tom in North Haven. The family gathering was complete except for the Corliss Lamonts traveling in Russia.

The final vacation weeks before the Labor Day exodus were crammed with activity, especially picnics by yacht and sail to neighboring islands in the bay. The Lamont tea at Sky Farm, following the Pulpit Harbor dinghy race, which featured hot cocoa topped with whipped cream, had become a traditional social event; so was the high-spirited softball game between the Pulpit Harbor and Village summer youth the following day. The Lamont household, swollen by guests, including the Lippmanns, sat down nineteen at the table each meal. Florence wrote her traveling son that Lippmann was fascinating in discussing the presidential campaign.

The columnist had earlier viewed Roosevelt as unqualified to be president. "His mind is not very clear, his purposes are not simple, and his methods are not direct," he had told his readers before the Democratic convention. But over the course of the summer, while he still had reservations about Roosevelt, Lippmann became convinced that FDR's optimism, energy, and willingness to take action to cure the nation's ills would provide the kind of leadership the country so desperately needed. The Hoover administration was tired and so discredited that it could no longer function usefully.

Lamont strongly supported President Hoover's reelection and was offering the White House campaign suggestions and assistance in lining up the public backing of newspaper publishers and notables such as Charles Lindbergh. Sensing that Lippmann was about to come out announcing his support for Roosevelt in his column, Lamont wrote him on September 29. "After practically unanimous expressions of approval" of Lippmann's past positions, Lamont somewhat querulously questioned his friend's preference in the upcoming presidential election. Even though Lippmann could list a number of Hoover's failings, what were Roosevelt's qualifications to do a better job? TWL thought that FDR was inadequate for the task.

Roosevelt's personality and cheery outlook were winning over millions of other Americans. On October 1, FDR from his box in Chicago's Wrigley Field exhibited his jaunty enthusiasm to thousands of baseball fans as he threw back his head and laughed like a boy when Babe Ruth signaled his intention with a wave of his bat and then blasted a home run in the third World Series game between the Yankees and the Cubs. A chorus of boos had greeted the sedate Hoover at an earlier game.

Lippmann was not persuaded by TWL's arguments, and a few days later announced in his column that he would "vote cheerfully for Governor Roosevelt." TWL's partner Russell Leffingwell would also vote for Roosevelt for very much the same reasons expressed by Lippmann.

On the day TWL wrote to Lippmann, he spoke to President Hoover on the phone, a conversation he described to his daughter.

> I talked over the telephone with the President last night. A great many people have the feeling that he is surely licked, unless he jumps in and does some real campaigning himself. He explained to me that it has been their strategy, rightly or wrongly, to let Franklin Roosevelt shoot off his mouth until he has said all he could say and had begun to repeat himself, which he seems to be doing now, so that I think the Republicans will now begin to move rather strongly.

Not strongly enough. In the November election Roosevelt won all but six states, 472 out of a total of 531 electoral votes. Lamont immediately wrote to President Hoover:

Please accept my renewed pledges of admiration and friendship. The service you have rendered your country is so great that nothing can deprive you of its satisfaction.

On November 10 Lamont wrote to the president-elect ("Dear Frank") offering "congratulations or perhaps commiserations because of the terrific responsibility" he would bear. "You know . . . that if there is anything in the world I can do, you have only to command me." Rhetoric aside, TWL hoped to initiate the kind of close and useful rapport with FDR that he had enjoyed with Hoover.

In December 1932, with another debt service installment coming due, Britain and France had petitioned the American government for an extension of the Hoover moratorium on war debt payments. President Hoover tried and failed to enlist the support of the president-elect in proposing a general settlement. FDR, wanting to avoid participation in the Hoover administration's decision making anyway, had already stated in an article that he was against a general moratorium, believing that the U.S. should negotiate individually with each country. The moratorium was not extended, and several nations led by France defaulted on the December installments; Great Britain made the payment as called for.

On January 4, 1933, Lamont phoned Governor Roosevelt (and sent a follow-up letter) about dealing with the war debt issue. TWL told FDR that he and his colleagues would be pleased to advise him on the war debt question to lighten the burden of the many complex and serious problems he faced. TWL was not for "letting off debtors" but favored determining what amount of debt repayment was 'within each country's capacity.

In a later call to FDR, Lamont said that he had heard that French officials were saying "We will never pay that installment to Hoover" and were looking for a way to make the overdue payment to the new administration after FDR's inauguration on March 4. It would be easy, TWL suggested, for him to drop by to consult with Roosevelt now or later on at the White House.

In a private letter to TWL of February 17, Prime Minister MacDonald warned that Great Britain would be forced to repudiate its U.S. debt if the Americans did not devise some scheme based on European cooperation toward a general debt settlement. Any British government proposing "a repetition of the December payment" on June 15, the next installment date, would not survive.

The prime minister was not exaggerating. The worldwide depression was driving the debtor nations to the wall. In June 1933, while Britain and Italy made small token payments, there was a general default by the European borrowers, with the exception of little Finland, and the outstanding loans were effectively cancelled by the debtors a year later. The defaults by Mexico and other Latin American nations paled in comparison. Of the original $10.3 billion in war and postwar reconstruction loans to European governments, only $2.6 billion was repaid, and Congress passed the Johnson Act banning American loans to governments that were in default to the U.S.

As the war debt disagreement slid toward its unhappy conclusion, Lamont and his colleagues began to deal with a new and far more serious financial threat facing the nation—the alarming increase in bank failures and state-mandated closures, bank holidays, spreading throughout the country.

Domestic Banking Crisis

On November 18, 1932, Lamont, whom B. C. Forbes in the *New York American* had depicted as "the most influential banker in America," addressed an Academy of Political Science audience on weaknesses in the American banking system, a timely subject in view of the mounting banking crisis, including the first statewide bank closing in Nevada. Lamont proposed two vital steps essential to a badly needed reform of the American banking system.

First, all the nation's banks, large and small, should be brought under the Federal Reserve system, becoming subject to its sound and uniform supervision. Some 60 percent of American banks were now outside the system, subject only to diverse, often inadequate, and loosely administered state regulations. The number of nonmember banks that had failed since 1921 was four and a half times greater than the number of member bank failures.

Second, Lamont suggested establishing "sensible provisions for regional branch banking" of the kind developed successfully in Europe, Great Britain, and Canada. A way must be found to enable the strong institutions in financial centers to extend the benefits of their ample resources and experienced "ordinarily careful management" to the weaker banks in outlying districts.

> The fact is that . . . the country has today *far too many banks*. Our banking units should on the average be far larger than they are today. The small, ill-capitalized institutions should be merged so as to gain the normal stability, diversity, economy and management of the larger concerns.

TWL had also sounded a ringing defense of the gold standard.

> Nothing can or will drive us from that standard. A Democratic administration, just like the steadfast Republican one before it, will continue to uphold the complete integrity of it. Make no mistake: in a dark and troublous world America and the American dollar are, as to material factors, the safest things in all the world to tie to.

TWL was dead right about the inherent danger of having too many small banks, a problem that would plague the banking system for years to come. It was impossible for the regulatory authorities to properly oversee the operations of some 18,000 individual banks. A number of them were burdened by poor management, including officers who periodically experienced a predilection for financing all kinds of building projects whose high leveraged vulnerability in a weak economy resulted in large-scale defaults on real estate loans and bank failures.

Following 1,350 bank failures in 1930, 2,293 banks closed their doors in 1931, and 1,453 in 1932, a year in which the Reconstruction Finance Corporation made loans of almost $1 billion to over 5,000 banks in trouble. Smaller country banks, with frozen real estate loans and farm mortgages, shrinking deposits, and minimal capital, were the main victims. But the banking system as a whole suffered staggering losses. J. P. Morgan & Co., which had taken large securities and loan losses, experienced a decline in net worth from $118.7 million in 1929 to $53.2 million by the end of 1932.

Despite their losses the large New York City banks were better positioned than inland banks to weather the storm. In 1932 their deposits actually increased, reflecting the greater confidence that corporations and other banks had in their stability. The lack of sound lending opportunities and the growing caution of New York bankers in the deteriorating economic environment had led them to build up their liquidity. At the end of 1932, J. P. Morgan & Co. had about 50 percent of its assets in government securities.

January and February 1933, the last days of the lame duck Hoover administration, was a stressful time for the Lamonts. Florence underwent abdominal surgery in early January and did not return home from the hospital until mid-February.

The banking situation rapidly worsened with another 273 banks closing in January. Each closure increased the public's fears about the safety of their deposits in the surviving banks, which struggled to stay liquid as withdrawals mounted. On February 14 the governor of Michigan declared a statewide bank holiday, an action followed by twenty-one other states over the next two weeks. The country was in the throes of a full-scale banking crisis.

Lamont, who had gone down to Yeamans Hall for a brief holiday, was urged by his partners to return to the office. On February 27 he phoned the president-elect five days before his inauguration and followed up with a letter.

> I enclose a memorandum of the points which I made to you over the telephone just after lunch today. I do not wish to be an alarmist. . . . But when I came back this morning from the south, on a hurry call, I found the situation far more critical than I had dreamed. I believe in all seriousness that the emergency could not be greater. . . . The things to be done to save the situation are not complex, but they are vital. And it is your say-so alone that will save the country from a disaster. Every hour in the next few days counts.

Lamont declared that the spread of state-legislated moratoriums must be stopped, likening it to the spread of "an infectious disease."

> It is impossible to contemplate the extent of the human suffering, and the social consequences of a denial of currency and credit to our urban populations. Urban populations cannot do without money. It would be like cutting off a city's water supply. Pestilence and famine would follow, with what further consequences who can tell?

The Federal Reserve must increase its purchase of government securities to supply the banks with adequate currency and credit to meet all demands. The Reconstruction Finance Corporation should make unsecured loans to banks in trouble. (So far the RFC had demanded the best available collateral for its loans, a practice that concerned the depositors left with more doubtful assets backing their deposits.) Finally, the government must act within the week to save the country from "total prostration." But FDR preferred to avoid involvement until he actually took office in a few days, and the Hoover administration was powerless to act in its closing hours.

Even the New York banks were now being hit as frightened depositors, domestic and foreign, rushed to withdraw funds. Foreigners, fearing that

Roosevelt planned to devalue the dollar, converted hundreds of millions to gold for shipment abroad. The financial markets became chaotic, and the Dow-Jones index dropped to 50, off 17 percent since year-end.

On Friday, March 3, the day before Roosevelt's inauguration, TWL attended a meeting at New York Governor Herbert Lehman's Park Avenue apartment to discuss the deteriorating banking situation. That evening Lamont phoned FDR, suggesting that he avoid hasty action in the banking crisis, which might resolve itself on its own by Monday. The banks only had to make it through half a business day on Saturday. But TWL was out of step with the public authorities, who saw far too much risk in letting the banks stay open. On the next day the governors of New York, Illinois, and a half dozen other states shut down their banks. That afternoon, after the inauguration ceremony, President Roosevelt signed a proclamation declaring a national bank holiday closing all commercial banks, the stock and commodity exchanges, and the foreign exchange market.

An Emergency Banking Act was quickly passed broadening the RFC's powers to assist ailing banks. Morgan and virtually all the big city banks reopened in a week, followed by stronger banks throughout the country.

Early in April, Lamont, Leffingwell, and Walter Lippmann lunched together at the bank. In the face of declining prices and wages and growing unemployment TWL was ready to do an about-face on the gold standard. The bankers were especially worried about the growing farm revolt over falling commodity prices; the government had to control the currency, which meant freeing it from gold. Walter Lippmann fully agreed and said so in his influential column.

FDR did not need persuading. Starting with a temporary ban on gold exports, a series of steps led to the U.S. Treasury decree of April 20 severing the fixed-price linkage between the dollar and gold. The international value of the dollar would be allowed to float in response to the demand for dollars around the world, and the expected devaluation should boost American exports and lift domestic prices. The United States had renounced the gold standard, and Lamont sent the president a copy of J. P. Morgan's public statement on the American government's historic action.

> I welcome the reported action of the President and the Secretary of the Treasury in placing an embargo on gold exports. It has become evident that the effort to maintain the exchange value of the dollar at a premium as against depreciated foreign currencies was having a deflationary effect upon already severely deflated American prices and wages and employment. It

seems to me clear that the way out of the depression is to combat and overcome the deflationary forces.

As the administration and the Morgan bankers had expected, the resulting dollar devaluation led to boosting commodity prices. In addition the president's radio "fireside chat," with its reassuring tone and message of hope, and a rapid series of legislative initiatives by the administration to support the economy served to restore confidence. The popularity of the new notion that the government had responsibility for the nation's economic health was soon reflected in the stock market and by other economic signs. TWL and his partners momentarily became enthusiastic fans of the president before they turned their attention to a new trial: the partners had been summoned to testify before the Senate Banking and Currency Committee in its investigation of stock exchange practices.

Thomas Lamont and Caroline Jayne
Lamont, TWL's parents, in the mid-1870s.
The Methodist pastor was assigned
to a series of small town parsonages
in the Hudson River Valley during
Tom's boyhood.

TWL in his senior year at Exeter, 1888. The excellent faculty
and teaching at the old New
Hampshire academy gave
Lamont a solid preparation
for Harvard.

Harvard's Daily Crimson Board of Editors in 1890. Lamont had a bent for journalism and needed earnings from the Crimson and other reporting assignments to pay for his college expenses. TWL last row, far right.

High life at Harvard. The convivial party-goer eagerly attended dinners, receptions, and the like for the rest of his life. TWL third from left.

Invitation to dinner celebrating TWL's entrance to J. P. Morgan & Co., 1911. A partnership in the Morgan firm was considered "the blue ribbon of banking," promising respected stature and the good life for years to come.

Dinner to
Thomas W. Lamont
and his school and college friends
in commemoration of his entrance to
The Banking Firm of
J. P. Morgan & Co.
January 1st 1911
Tendered by Arthur W. Lockett

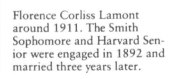

Florence Corliss Lamont around 1911. The Smith Sophomore and Harvard Senior were engaged in 1892 and married three years later.

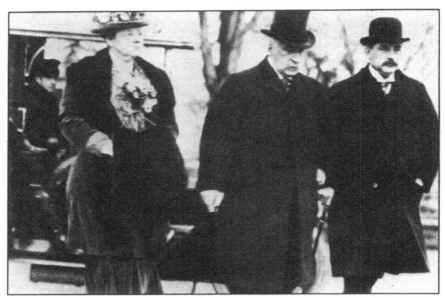

Morgan, his son Jack, and daughter Louise Satterlee arriving at the Pujo hearings in Washington in December 1912.

Henry P. Davison leading Red Cross parade on Fifth Avenue in 1917. The dynamic chief executive for both Morgans and wartime Red Cross leader died prematurely in 1922.

The Reparations Commission at the Paris Peace Conference in 1919. TWL helped negotiate the reparations section of the Treaty of Versailles and lobbied vigorously for American participation in the League of Nations. TWL standing at far left, second row; Herbert Hoover at far left first row; and Bernard Baruch, second from right.

Drawing by J. Mathews, perhaps depicting Lamont's speech in 1922 recommending a reduction in war debt owed the U.S., a highly controversial idea.

TWL and Jeremiah Smith Jr. at Meiji Shinto shrine in Tokyo, 1927. J. P. Morgan & Co. had organized the huge loan to Japan for reconstruction after the 1924 earthquake. Now the Japanese had a new financial proposal to assist their expansionist strategy in Manchuria.

Delegates to the 1929 Young Plan conference in Paris. The world believed that the Young Plan would finally settle the controversial reparations issue and Owen D. Young, Lamont, and Morgan returned to the U.S. in triumph. From left to right: TWL, Jean Parmentier, Emile Moreau of France, and J. P. Morgan.

The Morgan bank on the right hand corner of Wall and Broad streets about the time of the 1929 Crash. The statue of George Washington is on the steps of the Sub-Treasury building across the street.

Dwight and Elizabeth Morrow in the late 1920s. The Morrows and Lamonts were close friends from Englewood and North Haven, and TWL and Dwight were partners. But when Morrow became Ambassador to Mexico, they clashed bitterly over handling the Mexican debt problem.

Jan Christiaan Smuts, South African statesman who led his American friends on a safari in Kruger National Park.

Dr. Lewis Perry, leading procession, and TWL at 150th anniversary of Phillips Exeter Academy, 1931. Lamont became an Academy trustee in 1917 and president of the board in 1935. He was very generous to Exeter and Harvard.

Captain's table on the S.S. Saturnia en route to Greece, 1931. TWL and the powerful columnist were close friends until Lippmann denounced the Morgan firm in his column following disclosures at the 1933 Senate hearings. Florence is fifth from left; Faye Lippmann is fifth from right; TWL fourth from right; Walter Lippmann second from right.

TWL normally met the press on ship-board after his trips abroad. He favored sporty waistcoats and had a large col-lection.

Charles and Anne Lindbergh before their flight to the Orient in 1931. TWL had long admired the aviator hero, but in 1940 he sternly rebuked Lindbergh for preaching isolationism as a leader of the America First movement.

Playing golf at Hot Springs, Va. Lamont, who stated he was "addicted" to golf, scored in the mid-90s. Dwight Morrow is standing to the left of TWL.

1933 Senate Banking and Currency Committee Hearing. Morgan later won praise for his courteous reaction when a lady circus midget was placed in his lap in a press photo session. From left to right: Thomas W. Lamont, George Whitney, Leonard Keyes (standing), J. P. Morgan, John W. Davis (Morgan's counsel), and Russell C. effingwell.

TWL, George Whitney, J. P. Morgan at hearing of Senate Munitions Committee, 1936, which put to rest the charge that financing the Allies had dragged the U.S. into World War I.

Russell C. Leffingwell, Lamont's friend who succeeded him as Chairman of J. P. Morgan & Co., Inc. RCL was recognized as the firm's expert in economic and monetary affairs.

U.S. Steel sometimes honored members of its corporate board of directors in naming vessels in its Great Lakes Fleet of ore carriers. *Thomas W. Lamont*, was 602 feet long and commissioned in 1930.

Reynard at 1941 Harvard-Yale crew races at New London. The luxurious yacht and its efficient crew were used for family excursions and entertaining hosts of friends during the thirties.

TWL and Vice President Henry A. Wallace, 1941, at annual dinner of Academy for Political Science. TWL was a strong backer of FDR's plan to provide Great Britain with the munitions and supplies it needed to fight the Axis powers.

TWL, W. Averill Harriman, later wartime ambassador to Russia, and Allen Wardwell at Russian War Relief dinner, 1941. Lamont was a vocal advocate of aid to Russia in her battle against Hitler's invading armies.

Family photo at North Haven, 1938. Tom and Florence had four children and sixteen grandchildren. TWL center and Florence far right in back row.

TWL and Corliss sailing in North Haven. The vigorous lunch time debates between the capitalist father and socialist son ended when they left the dining room table, and they joined hands in World War II in encouraging support for Russia.

TWL and TWL II on a North Haven picnic in 1941. The grandson liked to discuss world events with his grandfather who felt that his namesake was an unusually promising boy.

Seaman First Class Thomas W. Lamont II. His submarine, the U.S.S. *Snook*, was lost in April 1945 with all hands reported missing in action.

Major Thomas S. Lamont, U.S. Air Force 1943. TSL, who joined the Morgan firm in 1923, shared his father's views and assisted him in numerous ways. After twenty years of banking the excitement of wartime London was an exhilarating new experience.

Palisades, the handsome manor near the great cliffs above the Hudson, was used for country weekends and holidays away from the din of the city. TWL liked to guide his guests on hikes along the leafy trails winding through the surrounding woods.

Sky Farm, overlooking Penobscot Bay in North Haven, Maine. The island home, built in 1920, soon became a summer Mecca for generations of Lamonts. TWL enjoyed cruising on his yacht to picnic on one of the myriad islands in the bay.

The Lamont house, 107 East 70th Street. The city home was an architectural tour de force designed in 1920 for entertaining on the grand scale. For three decades it served as an international inn for hundreds of distinguished guests.

Florence and Tom were devoted to each other for over 50 years, although sometimes she became fatigued from keeping up with his dynamic pace. After TWL's death Florence gave the Palisades estate to Columbia University for the establishment of a geological observatory. She had earned a Master's degree in philosophy from Columbia. Here Florence hands over the deed of Palisades to Dwight D. Eisenhower, then president of Columbia.

Book V

THE DEFENSIVE YEARS

Confrontation in Washington

The 1929 crash and the ensuing catastrophic depression and banking crisis had already badly tarnished the image of the financial community and its leaders. In the early months of 1933 new disclosures of financial improprieties revealed in testimony presented to the Senate Banking and Currency Committee incited further public censure of the bankers' conduct. While the committee had held hearings on and off since the previous April, the appointment in January of its new counsel, Ferdinand Pecora, a bright, Italian-born former assistant district attorney from New York, sparked an energetic and fruitful new phase of its inquiry to uncover stock exchange malpractices and other financial chicanery.

The revelations of the 1933 winter hearings were widely reported: testimony about the formation of stock pools to manipulate the price of stocks to the profit of the pool members; widespread trading by corporate insiders based on information not available to the public; the cases of the reckless issuing of securities, especially by the investment affiliates of banks, of which the National City Company was most prominent in its aggressive underwriting of South American bonds, now in default.

The disclosures about one of Wall Street's pillars, Charles E. Mitchell, the chairman of National City Bank, severely discredited the banking leader. At his direction the National City Company had speculated in the stock of its related bank, engaged in widespread stock speculation, rigged stock pools, and used high-pressure promotion and sales tactics in unloading dubious securities on gullible customers. Mitchell also had collected million-dollar bonuses in personal compensation from his bank for several years before the depression. Facing a federal lawsuit for tax evasion, he was forced to resign the bank's chairmanship in 1933.

Passage of federal legislation prohibiting commercial banks or their affiliates from engaging in securities underwriting became a foregone conclusion following the National City revelations. The Democratic party platform of 1932 had strongly advocated the separation of commercial from investment banking, and even banking leaders like Winthrop W. Aldrich, the new chairman of the Chase Bank, called for separation. Chase, National City, and other banks planned to terminate their investment affiliates.

Aldrich's statement of March 9, 1933, was widely interpreted as a direct challenge to Morgan banking supremacy. The *New York Herald Tribune* headlined its story "Chase Head Hits Morgan Banking Code." In order to absolutely divorce investment banking from commercial banking, Aldrich proposed that all investment banking firms should be prohibited from accepting deposits, a curb that would directly affect J. P. Morgan & Co. Furthermore, no private banker should be permitted to serve as a director of a commercial bank or trust company.

The *Nation's Business* queried: "If Thomas W. Lamont should cease to be a member of the board of the Guaranty Trust Co., who would suffer the most—the Guaranty Trust Co. or J. P. Morgan & Co?"

The Aldrich statement prompted a scathing denunciation of the Morgan firm in the *New York American* in an article entitled "Gabriel over Wall Street." The city daily was a member of the newspaper chain owned by William Randolph Hearst, whose papers had long lambasted Wall Street and "the Morgan interests" with scant attention to factual accuracy.

> Wall Street is in a turmoil. Winthrop W. Aldrich, chairman of the Board of the Chase National Bank, has had the courage and conscience to declare that the banking system of the United States needs radical reform. . . .
>
> America's banking system has been the most reckless, the most unreliable and the most unethical in the world.
>
> There has been an unholy alliance between the banks and their speculative affiliates. . . .
>
> The seemingly reputable banking house has been the decoy in this confidence game. . . .
>
> The public has been the unsuspecting come-on to be relentlessly plucked and plundered. . . .
>
> At the head of the speculative institutions stands the House of Morgan. . . .
>
> Back of wrecked railroads and collapsed power trusts, and various kinds of speculative enterprises inflated to the bursting point, has stood this House of Morgan which for generations has subsisted, and subsisted royally, on pirating from the public and betraying the best interests of the nation.
>
> It has been the propagandist for foreign schemes to exploit the American people.

It has been the fiscal agent of the British Empire, and its influence in American politics has enabled it to be the political agent of England also.

It has dominated both political parties in the United States.

It has nominated candidates and used them for its own advantage and for the advantage of its foreign clients.

But the end has come to these demoralizing and destructive practices.

A President is in office whom the House of Morgan did not nominate.

A party is in power which the House of Morgan does not control. . . .

And, most important of all, the public is aroused.

Reckless and unreliable banking will no longer be permitted.

President Roosevelt himself had led the way in castigating the bankers throughout the election campaign and in his inaugural address: "The rulers of the exchange of mankind's goods have failed, through their own stubbornness and their own incompetences. Practices of the unscrupulous money changers stand indicted in the court of public opinion. . . . They know the rules of a generation of self-seekers."

Such was the prevailing feeling throughout the country about Wall Street as Lamont and John W. Davis, the Morgan attorney, met with Ferdinand Pecora, the Senate committee's counsel, to learn what information the committee wanted to have. Pecora looked forward to interrogating the partners of J. P. Morgan & Co. and was determined that no pertinent facts and figures should be held back for any reason; J. P. Morgan & Co. must open its files for examination by the committee as he deemed necessary to obtain a true picture of the firm's operations. For Morgan and Lamont there was a distinct sense of déjà vu about the upcoming hearing: it was the 1913 Pujo committee investigation, substituting Pecora for Untermyer, all over again.

At a meeting at his New York office Pecora outlined the scope of the data required by the Senate committee. On some subjects the bank was unable to oblige. There was no organization chart defining areas of responsibility for the partners; their work assignments were not formally departmentalized. There was no record of the decisions taken at the daily morning meetings of the partners, as no minutes were kept of these gatherings.

Data on deposits, loans, offerings, and participations in securities issues, the partners' directorships, a listing of bank and corporate executive officers receiving loans from Morgan, and more would be required, plus the firm's balance sheets for the last five years. Davis said that he was "chilly" about the balance sheet request and wanted to think it over.

On March 23 Lamont and Davis called on William H. Woodin, the newly appointed Secretary of the Treasury and a former manufacturing executive well known to the Morgan firm. TWL complained that apparently Pecora wanted the hearings to produce "sensational publicity" at the expense of the Morgan firm. Discrediting the bank would ruin its effectiveness in helping to restore business confidence and strength in the midst of the depression.

Later the same day Lamont met the president at the White House and recorded the conversation in a memorandum. TWL asked the president to tell him "what you want us to do, and we'll come as near as we can to doing it. . . . We want to cooperate along sound and helpful lines."

FDR replied that he hoped the investment affiliates of banks could be "lopped off" within a year.

TWL answered, "Not under two years." Time was needed to make the readjustment, to liquidate their holdings "without breaking the market."

FDR: "Now what about officers' bonuses. That's got to go! My gosh, I feel Charlie took my money," referring to the bonuses Charles Mitchell had received at National City Bank. "Scandalous!"

TWL replied that it was not as bad as it seemed. "But certainly I won't quarrel on that topic."

FDR: "Another thing. If corporate officers and directors speculate in their own shares on inside knowledge, they must tell the public when they're buying and selling."

TWL agreed that insider trading was unfair and should be banned. "But you can't prevent a man from selling his investment if he thinks general conditions are worsening" without regard to the condition of his own company.

FDR then recalled that he had joined a pool to back a certain stock, resulting in a large profit for him. "It was all wrong!" he concluded.

TWL, who had joined stock pools himself, replied: "There must be disclosure," although the administration proposal that corporations should release quarterly financial statements to the public was "kind of rough." Lamont then raised the subject he had come to talk about. He was very worried that "permanent banking changes and doing away with the machinery for furnishing capital to the country" would stall the nation's recovery.

FDR agreed. "We mustn't destroy the machinery."

TWL said that the end of a depression historically was marked by "breaking the ice with a public issue, and J. P. Morgan & Co. were usually the ones to do it." It had been impossible for corporations to raise new capital through public issues for more than a year. "You take away the machinery or cripple it, and you can't start the wheels this time. The trouble with the administration's proposals is that they knock down and don't replace." If the bankers were removed as holders of securities, it "dumped the load" on investment firms, which would then need to seek bank resources to carry it.

FDR: "I didn't realize that."

TWL: "Will you let me send you a memorandum on banking reform, bank investment affiliates, handling securities, private bankers? It will then be yours, if there's any virtue in it, not mine."

FDR: "Fine, but get it to me promptly. Our talks are starting."

TWL then described the meeting with Pecora to discuss the information he wanted for the Senate committee investigation. J. P. Morgan would cooperate in a constructive effort. But it was clear that Pecora was on a fishing expedition. TWL hoped the president could persuade the Senate committee to replace Pecora or at least appoint a responsible assistant counsel. FDR replied that he would speak to the chairman of the committee, Senator Duncan Fletcher of Florida.

TWL: "You see we're called upon in every critical situation, and our usefulness ought not to be impaired by being pilloried for nothing." After all, Morgan had saved other banks from failing. "You know that men like Jack Morgan, Russell Leffingwell, Parker Gilbert, and George Whitney would cut off their right arm before doing anything wrong. But we're not infallible; we've made mistakes." If Morgan were deprecated and denigrated, "The dollar will very likely fly away. . . . Don't put us in City Bank's class. Don't make the mistake of breaking Jack's heart and your own policies at the same time."

FDR: "I get the point, Tom. I do."

TWL: "Pecora wants to make a sensation" over the amount of profits that Morgan had derived from foreign bond issues. The firm had floated over $1.8 billion in foreign issues since 1921, almost all governments, without a default.

FDR: "That's a grand record."

TWL: "Our fingers are crossed."

After briefing the president on the precarious state of New York City's finances, Lamont rose to go.

TWL: "I'll go now. . . . It's the first time I've been here in four years and gone out very heartened and not disheartened. Herbert Hoover was always very difficult."

Politicians from all walks of life tailor their remarks to please the audience they face at the moment. However, FDR's positive optimism did indeed stand out in sharp contrast to Hoover's increasingly careworn and embittered temperament as the economy unraveled disastrously under his stewardship. In his letter of March 27, TWL thanked the president for the chance to visit him at the White House and added, "You have put new heart into the country, and I hardly have to assure you we are all behind you."

Lamont enclosed his promised memorandum on the need for remedial banking legislation. Larger banks with national branch systems should be permitted, in order to obtain the safety of widespread deposit and loan diversification. The powers of states to charter new banks should be discontinued, leaving this field solely to the federal government; too many unnecessary and ill-equipped banks had been authorized in the past, leading to the current banking disaster.

But the main point TWL wanted to make was critical to the future of his own firm. The revival of the moribund capital issues market was essential to economic recovery. If commercial banks dispensed with their securities business, it seemed clear that private investment bankers would be called on to play a large and crucial role in handling capital issues.

The investment bankers must be permitted to accept deposits from their private clients, although not from the general public. Denying them this limited deposit business would severely weaken them just at the time when they were sorely needed, and the loss of this business would make them dependent on the big commercial banks for credit. The Morgan partners did not intend to surrender without a fight.

The partners still hoped to avoid producing the firm's balance sheets for public exposure by the committee. Size and capital strength had long been closely guarded secrets of private bankers. But Pecora disagreed, and in the face of the committee's subpoena powers the bank capitulated.

On May 23, J. P. Morgan led off as the first Morgan partner to testify before the Senate Banking and Currency Committee, with John W. Davis by his side as counsel. In the packed hearing room sat a number of Morgan's partners and staff members. For the next two weeks of hearings the Morgan entourage, including some of the partners' wives, occupied three floors of Washington's Carlton Hotel at a daily cost of about $2,000.

Perhaps the most noteworthy aspect of Morgan's testimony was the famous banker's personality and manner. He was truly "a gentleman of the old school," courteous, patient, open, and eager to cooperate. The guiding principle of the firm "of which I have the honor to be the senior partner" was "doing only first-class business, and that in a first-class way." There was no hint of deception or evasion in Morgan's answers, nor was one reminded of the forceful, self-confident testimony of his father twenty years earlier before the Pujo committee. If Morgan Jr. was unsure of the answer to a question, he called on one of his colleagues to respond; after all, as he pointed out, he was "more or less retired" and had able partners he could rely on.

Over the clicking of photographers' camera shutters, Morgan began his testimony on the role of private bankers and J. P. Morgan & Co., which encompassed the banking houses of Drexel in Philadelphia, Morgan Grenfell in London, and Morgan & Cie in Paris. Morgan's chosen path confined its business to handling the banking needs of its large corporate and government clients, who deposited sizable sums with the firm, and Morgan's depositors made up a roster of leading industrial corporations, railroads, utilities, and financial institutions. But the depression had taken its toll, and the bank's deposits had fallen from half a billion dollars in 1929 to $239 million at the end of March 1933, a level that was modest compared to the deposits of a number of large commercial banks dealing with the public.

The Morgan bank extended credit to its corporate clients and governments and had also made some personal loans, not to the public at large but to prominent businessmen and bank executives. Charles E. Mitchell of National City Bank had received a $10 million Morgan loan in 1929 to buy his bank's stock. This group of loans especially interested Pecora. Didn't these loans make these executives beholden to the Morgan bank, inclined to grant the firm special favors?

Morgan replied that there was nothing unusual about the transactions. "We should loan money if these gentlemen want it. They are friends of ours, and we know they are good, sound, straight fellows."

The firm's main activity at the time was conducting a general commercial banking business, testified Morgan, reflecting the demise of the capital issues market that had occurred as the depression deepened. However, J. P. Morgan & Co.'s power and influence, which so interested Pecora, was based on its role as an investment banker over a half century, and detailed information was placed on the record.

Morgan had been the largest manager of bond issues in 1927, but thereafter the investment affiliates of the big commercial banks had expanded their business to the point of handling close to half of the new bond issues. Of this group National City Company was the pacesetter, and its new issues offerings in 1929 were greater than those of Morgan and Kuhn, Loeb combined.

However, Morgan had long been recognized as the traditional leader of the profession; the firm's prestige and reputation, based on a record that was admirable compared to its peers, was unique. Of course, as

Leffingwell pointed out in a study submitted to the committee, "We have made mistakes. Who has not?"

The Morgan paper and partners' testimony revealed that since 1919 J. P. Morgan & Co. had sponsored and floated securities issues amounting to about $6 billion. Over a third were foreign issues, and none of these were in default. Nor were there defaults in the public utility, industrial, and municipal bond issues floated by Morgan. However, the record of the Morgan-led railroad issues was a different story: of the total of $1.8 billion, some $125 million were in default, including a $61.2 million mortgage bond issue of the Missouri Pacific, controlled by the Van Sweringen brothers.

The recent record of the Morgan partners in paying income taxes especially attracted the committee counsel's attention. The partners had paid a trifling amount in 1930, and none at all in the following two years, a point that Pecora took pains to emphasize in his questioning of Morgan. As Senator Carter Glass, a member of the committee, observed, "Pecora deliberately made the impression on the committee, upon the press and upon the country that this banking firm had been guilty of an irregular if not criminal evasion of the income tax law."

Some newspapers were quick to criticize the Morgan partners, among the country's wealthiest citizens, as shirking responsibility, not doing their share in the midst of hard times—or worse, illegally evading taxes. They were wrong, as Senator Glass had noted.

In their testimony the Morgan partners pointed out that they had paid about $51 million in income taxes since 1917, $11 million in 1929 alone, a substantial part based on capital gains realized during the period. In 1931 and 1932, the partnership's large capital losses had wiped out all income. There was no taxable income; no taxes were paid.

Pecora, like Samuel Untermyer twenty years earlier, hoped to demonstrate that the Morgan bank held a dangerously powerful influence over a substantial part of the nation's business through the directorships of its partners on the boards of American corporations. According to Pecora's calculation, the partners held 167 directorships on the boards of bank and trust companies, railroads, public utilities, insurance companies, and industrial corporations, virtually all of which did business with the Morgan bank. How could the Morgan partner impartially serve two masters, his firm and the corporation, when, as a director, he offered financial advice. Morgan staunchly insisted that there was no conflict of interest, even though the company relied on the Morgan bank to handle its financing requirements. The partners, invited to join these boards to give their expert financial advice, acted in the best interests of the companies and their stockholders.

> Pecora: But the interests of your firm would be best served by doing the financing in the safest possible way and for the greatest amount of profit or commission, would it not?
> Morgan: No; it should not. Certainly not. You seem to think that we do not want to go on doing business. We do want to go on doing business.
> Pecora: You want to go on doing business profitable to yourselves?
> Morgan: Not only profitable to ourselves, but you cannot go on with any good business that only one side makes any money on. . . . When you are dealing with a client for securities both of you have the same object, that is, that the securities shall be put out at the highest possible price . . . that may be creditable so the corporation is satisfied, and second, you must be paid a sufficient amount, not too much, for taking the responsibility of putting it out. Those two things. And your minds always meet with the corporate fellows. Isn't that so, George?

Saying this, Morgan turned to his well-informed younger partner, George Whitney, behind him. Dispassionate and reserved, not a hair on his head out of place, he could, with his superb command of facts and figures, be relied on to handle, or deflect, the counsel's tough questions confidently and coolly. It was Whitney who bore the brunt of the intensive inquiry into Morgan's "preferred lists," a term coined by the press that the Morgan partners themselves disdained.

The term referred to the lists of persons invited by the partners to subscribe to stock in new companies formed by the bank, which comprised about 3 percent of Morgan's total securities offerings since the war. While there were a half dozen such cases over the years, the thrust of the questioning focused on three issues handled by Morgan in 1929—United Corporation, Alleghany Corporation, and Standard Brands. Many of the names of prominent businessmen and bankers, a few investment firms, Morgan partners, and their friends and family appeared on two or all three of the lists.

In the surging pre-crash market the price at which the chosen participants could buy the stock from Morgan was in all three cases considerably lower than its price in trading on a "when issued" basis, or when it was officially listed on the stock exchange, two weeks after the invitations went out in the case of Alleghany. Virtually everyone invited, people of ample means, had accepted the attractive Morgan offer; there was a built-in profit for the taking. The disclosure of the preferred list operation for buying the stock of the Alleghany Corporation, the holding company for the Van Sweringens' vast railroad empire, especially shocked and dismayed the public.

In the Alleghany episode the Morgan partners contacted 227 clients and friends, inviting them to buy stock at $20 a share, Morgan's cost; the "when issued" market price was $35–37 at the time. There were many leaders of business and finance among the invitees, three of whom had later been elected or appointed to high positions in government: William G. McAdoo, a former Secretary of the Treasury and long-time friend of Leffingwell, had been elected to the Senate from California and was a member of the Senate Banking and Currency Committee conducting the investigation; Norman H. Davis was FDR's ambassador-at-large in Europe; William H. Woodin, in 1929 head of the American Car and Foundry Co., was the current Secretary of the Treasury.

The reply of John J. Raskob, chairman of the Democratic National Committee, to such an invitation from George Whitney aroused the curiosity of the examiners, always alert to the potential for political intrigue.

> Dear George:
> Many thanks for your trouble and for so kindly remembering me. My check for $40,000 is enclosed herewith in payment for the Alleghany stock. . . . I appreciate deeply the many courtesies shown me by you and your partners, and I sincerely hope the future holds opportunities for me to reciprocate. The weather is fine.

What did Raskob mean, demanded Pecora, about "opportunities for me to reciprocate"?

"I thought it was just a nice, polite letter," replied Whitney, adding that he and Raskob had been friends ever since they had become fellow directors of General Motors.

In testimony and in a statement submitted to the Senate committee the Morgan partners explained their rationale for the use of "customer lists" in distributing stock.

> As merchants of investment securities of established character, we do not consider that it is sound practice for us to offer common stock over our own name to the general public through banks and dealers. Consequently, in the few equity operations which we undertook, we invited to join us, not primarily institutions and dealers who distribute investment securities to the general public, but individuals capable of sharing and understanding the risk. . . . It would not have been prudent banking to keep all these common stocks in our portfolio.
> Customer Lists. Our lists of private subscribers were naturally composed of men of affairs and position; but they were selected because of established

business and personal relations. . . . We have never had occasion to ask for favors from legislators or persons in public office, nor have we ever done so. We conduct our business through no means or measures of "influence" or favor. We rely upon such confidence as our clients and the business community generally may repose in us.

In fact, investment houses had been offering stock to their own private customers in similar fashion for years, and the bankers naturally hoped that grateful clients would find ways to reciprocate, such as referring new business to their firm. While the Morgan partners considered these offers to be normal business practice, the disclosures raised public concern about the bankers' motivations.

The respected *New York Times* noted almost sadly: "Here was a firm of bankers, perhaps the most famous and powerful in the whole world, which was certainly under no necessity of practicing the small acts of petty traders. Yet it failed under a test of its pride and prestige."

"The scattering of strategic largesse" was the way the *New York Review of Reviews* referred to the practice.

The "favor" was bittersweet for some of Alleghany's new shareholders, depending on how long they held the stock. As the business and earnings of the holding company's railroad interests, principally the Chesapeake and Ohio and Missouri Pacific, fell off sharply during the first three years of the depression, so did the price of Alleghany stock. The Van Sweringens scrambled to meet their obligations by selling off various properties. By 1932 the Alleghany stock had dropped to a low of 38 cents a share, with a sizable amount held by the Morgan bank as collateral for its loans to the Van Sweringens. The market rally in 1933 helped, but not much; Alleghany rose to only 14 percent of its 1929 highest price. Given the public storm of criticism over the practice of using "preferred lists" to sell stock and Alleghany's dismal performance, the Morgan partners surely rued the day they had ever launched the ill-fated holding company.

Lamont testified before the committee on June 9, the final day of hearings assigned to examining the Morgan partners. He believed that Pecora had tried to keep him from testifying, fearing that TWL with his well-known powers of persuasion might damage the case he had adroitly built up against Morgan. However, an unexpected interrogator showed up who wanted to grill Lamont—Senator Huey P. Long, the former governor of Louisiana, who was not a member of the Committee on Banking and Currency. Undeniably popular in his native state for his programs to aid the poor, "the Kingfish" was also considered by many to be an autocratic demagogue, a view which TWL shared and sometimes revealed as the verbal exchange progressed. Senator Long was dressed in a rumpled white linen suit, and his wiry dark hair tumbled down over his perspiring forehead as he warmed to his subject.

Senator Long had just attacked Secretary of the Treasury William H. Woodin on the Senate floor for his links with the Morgan bank: he had been on all three of Morgan's 1929 preferred lists. Referring to his speech, Long addressed TWL:

> You state that it is very possible you have read my statements made on the floor of the United States Senate to the effect that one connected with the House of Morgan should not be in the Treasury Department of the United States Government. . . . Do you remember about how long it would have been, that you remember, if you do remember it, from possibly having read such things before this investigation commenced?
>
> Lamont: Well, Senator Long, I should not have recalled it for very long, because such a statement, if ever made, would not have made the slightest impression upon me.
>
> Senator Long: I see. Then a statement made by a Member of the United States Senate naturally made no impression on you?
>
> Lamont: Any statement made by a Senator of the United States that was founded on anything approaching the facts, would, of course, make a great impression upon me, and I would have great respect for it. But a statement without the slightest foundation in fact would have no effect upon me.

Lamont had long been a director of the Crowell Publishing Co., which owned *Collier's Weekly* and several other magazines. At the beginning of May, *Collier's* had published in serial form parts of TWL's recently completed biography of his former partner, Henry P. Davison, an enthusiastic paean to the Morgan bank. According to Senator Long, *Collier's* had also just mailed a print of a forthcoming article highly critical of Long to all the members of Congress. Long suspected that Lamont, with his connections to *Collier's*, had engineered this latest attack on him and planted pro-Morgan propaganda to appear in the magazine just as the committee's examination of the Morgan partners was to begin.

Lamont emphatically denied the insinuation, but senator continued to hammer away.

> Senator Long: Well, all right. Let us put it in this way: Your writing the series of articles, in which you bring in not only Mr. Davison but other members of the House of Morgan and extol their virtues, occurring just on the eve of this investigation—that is not a matter of publicity or . . . propaganda, but it just happens to be a mere coincidence that it comes just around the time of this investigation? I understand from your answers that that is correct, isn't it?
>
> Lamont: It is correct, as I have stated before, that I know nothing

whatsoever about their editorial policies; that I did my best as a matter of fact to have those articles postponed, but was unable to do so. But as for the article about you, Senator Long, I know nothing whatsoever about it, as I stated before. And I never even read the article, and did not know that it had appeared until you mentioned it.

A half hour later the senator was still hurling the same charges about TWL's article in *Collier's*.

> Senator Long: Now, that happens to break, together with similar articles, along about the time of the investigation . . . and we have hurriedly sent from this same publication through the mails. . . . this stuff to 435 Congressmen and 96 Members of the Senate, a castigation . . . of a Member of the Senate who has denounced the Treasury for being dominated by the preferred employees of the House of Morgan. And yet you cannot understand, you say, this thing, and that it is strictly an accident and something of which you had no notice, and that you undertook in no manner to influence any publication.
>
> Lamont: Absolutely; I have no knowledge of it, Senator.

Senator Long finally wound down, and the committee turned to subjects of greater relevance to its work.

Senator Edward P. Costigan of Colorado next queried Lamont about the extent of Morgan's influence through the many directorships held by its partners on the boards of American companies, plus the business links between Morgan directors and the other members of these boards—the interlocking directorates theory advanced twenty years earlier by Samuel Untermyer at the Pujo committee hearings. Lamont himself sat on ten corporate boards in addition to Crowell, including U.S. Steel, Northern Pacific, and the Guaranty Trust Company. Author Lewis Corey had estimated that Morgan influenced the direction of companies holding as much as a quarter of total corporate assets in America, noted Costigan.

Lamont replied that he had never placed any credence in the interlocking directorates theory.

> Senator Costigan: You feel, then that there is a popular illusion, or perhaps delusion, that the house of Morgan is much more powerful than it is in fact?
>
> Lamont: Yes, exactly, Senator. I feel that there is a very strong popular delusion which has been nourished, I do not say, by people insincerely. I have no doubt that a great many people have followed up this idea and have laid out these graphs and have said "It must be so." But it just isn't so.
>
> I don't want to make a speech here or to attempt it, but if I may point out one or two factors in the situation: We are credited with having what is known as power or influence; and we admit and are glad to admit that we

hope that our counsels are of some avail in certain directions in sound finance. What is that derived from? Is it derived from money? Has the Morgan fortune ever been known as one of the great fortunes of this country? No. With all due respect to Mr. Morgan and his father, it has not been so known.

The stock the firm owned in two New York banks amounted to no more than one half percent in each, and as prudent bankers Morgan held little stock in industrial companies; deposits must be kept liquid. Morgan's alleged pervasive power based on enormous resources was a myth.

Nor was there a growing "concentration of wealth," as the senator suggested. The number of stockholders in American companies had increased steadily, noted Lamont.

But what about a "concentration of the control of wealth"? asked the senator. Lamont didn't see it that way:

> It is true that it is not an easy thing to get as directors of corporations men who, by experience and capacity are equipped to direct the policies of those corporations, and it frequently happens that the same man is drafted over and over again because of his character and capacity as a director, just the same as you will find in the small town, Senator Costigan, such as I was brought up in, or perhaps you, that a few of the leading men of the community are in almost every local industry. You see? And it gives the appearance, therefore, because these men are drafted over and over again, of a concentration, which in fact it does not seem to me exists, and I do not see that the operations of one corporation necessarily impinge at all upon the operations of another corporation.

Lamont stated that directors did not sit on boards "for the purpose of bringing about a concentration or bringing about a control. They sit on those boards because they are invited to in order to serve the community."

There were other incentives to join corporate boards, including the generous fees paid by big companies, whose executives had an important voice in nominating directors who they trusted would be sympathetic to management's goals. But Senator Costigan moved on to fire other rounds at 23 Wall Street before departing the field of battle. Hadn't Morgan directed several subsidiaries of the United Corporation to lobby in Washington against federal development of the Muscle Shoals power project?

Not so, Lamont answered. If the local power companies had lobbied in Washington, they had done so on their own initiative, which was entirely proper. The Morgan firm as a matter of policy did not engage in lobbying with the federal government. Lamont and his partners appeared only when invited to come and express their opinions on financial legislation—"to talk with you, sir, and with your colleagues or members of whatever committee it may be."

"I regret to say that you have not done me the honor of talking to me about any legislation," said Costigan.

"Will you permit me in the future to do so?" replied Lamont.

It was fitting for counsel Pecora, the relentless inquisitor, to conclude the questioning. After fencing over several topics Lamont and Pecora turned to the question of subjecting private banks, like J. P. Morgan & Co., to examination by public authorities.

> Pecora: It is a fact, is it not, that J. P. Morgan & Co. take special care to conduct their banking business, their private banking business, in a manner that will not subject them to the kind of examination at the hands of the State superintendent of banks which that officer is required by law to make of State banks?
>
> Lamont: Oh, I would not put it in that way, Mr. Pecora, would you? All we do is to see to it that we do comply very strictly with the law. The reason that we do that is to comply with the law, and not for the purpose of evading examination by the superintendent of banks. . . . I do not think that there would be the slightest objection on the part of anybody in our firm to periodical examination by duly constituted public authorities.

Lamont's final exchange with Pecora, abetted by Senator Costigan, concerned the quality of TWL's memory. Pecora had earlier questioned Morgan partners on details of stock sales to family members and trusts that had produced tax losses. He now asked Lamont if he recalled a sale of Simms Petroleum Co. stock to his wife in 1930. "I haven't the slightest recollection," TWL replied.

> Pecora: Well, it has been testified to here that the deliberations of the partners of J. P. Morgan & Co. in their daily conferences are not made a matter of written record but rest in the memory of the participants. . . .
>
> [Lamont argreed.]
>
> Pecora: Well, what you want us to believe is that your recollection or memory is a faulty one?
>
> Lamont: Oh, I don't think I have to make any apologies for my memory. I do not think that I have to characterize my memory as a faulty one because I cannot remember some personal transaction three years ago, with all that has happened in between. . . .
>
> Senator Costigan: What I suppose Mr. Pecora was about to inquire was, whether your memory is good as to the action of the board of directors, as to which you keep no minutes, and is bad as to personal transactions. . . .
>
> Lamont: Well, Mr. Costigan, I think I have the average memory on both of those things. But occupied as I am . . . with a great many matters of fairly

large importance I deliberately do not try to carry the details of personal matters in my head. They go out, and if I want to know about them I press a button and they are brought to my attention.

At the close of the Morgan portion of the committee hearing, J. P. Morgan entered a statement for the record which made a strong plea to permit private bankers engaged in securities underwriting to continue to accept deposits from their clients; these deposits should be kept liquid and never used in the firm's securities business. Without the "bread and butter" banking business based on these deposits, the private banks would have to devastate their staffs; they would become "mere dependencies of the commercial banks." But the battle to preserve the status quo of private banks was already over, and Morgan had lost.

The rare appearance of Morgan moved the tabloid *New York Daily News* to report:

> The secret partnership agreement of the House of Morgan, made public by the Senate Investigation Committee late today, revealed the House of Morgan as an American monarchy of finance, whose ruler, John Pierpont Morgan II, exercises power far greater than those of the King in the affairs of the British Empire.
>
> All of the golden strands of the intricate web, which the colossus of American capitalism has woven about the nation's industrial and official life—stock control of giant industries; directorates in scores of industrial firms and banks; "preferred customers," occupying places of the highest political and financial influence—end in Morgan's hands.
>
> He can make or break his partners; in the greatest private banking house in the world—the little three-story marble building at Broad and Wall Streets, where more than a quarter billion dollars reposes in cash and Government bonds—his will is supreme.

J. P. Morgan also received some kudos from the public for his conduct in the hearings. A shy man, he had always shunned publicity and was little known to the public as a person. He had long been glad to have Lamont speak for the firm. Observers at the hearings, counsel, senators, and reporters, were surprised and impressed with Morgan's unassuming manner and earnest efforts to cooperate. And then there was a surprising little drama that won for Morgan the respect and sympathy of millions, who ever after saw him not as another stuffed-shirt, greedy Wall Street banker, but as a kindly, considerate, nice old gentleman.

On June 1, while the committee was absent from the Senate Caucus Room for a brief executive session, a circus press agent suddenly placed a 27-inch woman midget on Morgan's lap as he sat waiting to testify.

The news photographers swiftly went to work. Morgan was understandably surprised but quickly recovered his composure.

"Where do you live, little girl?" asked the banker.

"In a tent, sir," was the squeaky reply.

"I have a grandson bigger than you," Morgan observed, and the two chatted amicably a few moments before the banker carefully lifted the little circus lady to the floor.

The next day the picture of the banker and the midget was in newspapers everywhere. It portrayed a large and heavy man with thick black eyebrows contrasting with his thinning gray hair and white mustache; his expression was gentle and kindly and his petite new friend looked happy. The photograph won the banker many friends and even some new business for his firm.

About a month after the incident, Henry Ford walked into 23 Wall Street and asked to see Mr. Morgan, who was at his desk. Ford admitted that he did not generally admire Wall Street bankers, but he was so impressed by Morgan's testimony and by his calm and courteous reaction to the midget placed on his knee, that he wanted the Ford Motor Company to open a bank account with J. P. Morgan & Co. Soon afterward Morgan Brainard, chairman of the Aetna Life and Casualty Insurance Company, called on Morgan for the same purpose. He, too, had been much impressed by the banker's treatment of the little lady.

Earlier stages of the Senate Committee on Banking and Currency investigation had contributed substantially to the public interest in uncovering harmful financial practices demanding elimination. However, in the view of the Morgan partners, the examination of J. P. Morgan & Co. had turned into a witch-hunt conducted by an ambitious headline-seeking attorney bent on discrediting the bankers to gain maximum publicity. He had pretty well succeeded in his objective.

J. P. Morgan wrote his friend Bishop William Lawrence: "To have to stand before a crowd of people and attempt, by straight answers to crooked questions, to convince the world that one is honest, is a form of insult that I do not think would be possible in any civilized country."

Lamont wrote his daughter: "For the last two weeks Tommy and I and almost all the partners have been down at Washington wading through the mazes of the Pecora Senate Investigation, conducted very unfairly and with a view purely to publicity." TWL had then quoted Senator Carter Glass, a member of the Committee on Banking and Currency. In the course of the hearing Glass had observed with scorn: "We are having a circus, and the only things lacking now are peanuts and colored lemonade."

The Glass-Steagall Act, signed into law on June 16, 1933, prohibited commercial banks and their affiliates from underwriting and dealing in corporate securities. While a one-year grace period was provided, many of the banks had already terminated these operations or were about to; the scandal-ridden affiliates had suffered heavy losses in a business that was moribund during the depression years. Since the new bill prohibited private investment banking firms from serving as commercial bankers and taking deposits, J. P. Morgan & Co. would have to choose between the securities underwriting business, its historic strength, and the commercial banking it practiced for a small number of substantial clients.

The exposure of the multiple abuses by some important commercial banks and their investment affiliates—reckless underwriting, stock prices manipulation, self-dealing, deceptive sales practices, and the pressure on banks to finance the unsold low-grade bonds underwritten by their affiliates—had led directly to the historic financial legislation. Curbs on such harmful practices, whether pursued by the bank affiliates or by independent investment firms and brokers, were urgently needed, and the administration and Congress were already studying measures to regulate the securities markets. The new act also provided for federal insurance of bank deposits, and Congress intended to ensure that they would not be siphoned off to bail out the underwriting losses of bank investment affiliates.

The thousands of banks that had failed and doomed their depositors were generally small, undercapitalized, and located in suburban and rural areas—not big city banks brought down by their investment operations. But the Wall Street banks were an easy first target for restraint; the government was determined to curb their power, and J. P. Morgan & Co. faced the prospect of instituting a fundamental change in its traditional banking activity.

Handling the Press

Among the Morgan partners, Lamont had long assumed primary responsibility for the firm's public relations, and the aftermath of the Pecora hearings kept him busy refuting press criticism of the bank. Office routine was to mark for TWL's attention articles clipped from newspapers and magazines about J. P. Morgan & Co. After consulting with

Russell Leffingwell or Martin Egan, Lamont might call the journalist or invite him to lunch at the bank in order to reform his thinking; other times it seemed best to let the matter drop. There was no rebuttal to newspaper cartoons portraying the portly Morgan with dollar signs covering his ample vest.

Once, Leslie Gould, financial editor of the *New York Journal*, reported that Lamont, a director of Texas Gulf Sulphur, and his son had sold shares of TGS before a cut in the company's dividend. TWL telephoned Gould the next day, and years later Gould recalled their conversation in his column.

> Over the wire came Mr. Lamont's soft voice:
> "Leslie, you had a piece about our selling stock ahead of unfavorable dividend action. I agree that is a reprehensible thing. But the stock I sold was in Texas Gulf Sulphur. The company that cut the dividend was Freeport Sulphur. . . ."
> Our face and ears were red. We apologized and promised an immediate correction. Lamont wanted none of this, but we did correct it the next day in the same space.
> The point of this was that Lamont, instead of going to some of the top brass on the paper . . . phoned us direct and then did not wish a correction. As a one-time newspaper man he knew that was an embarrassing thing to do—even though in this case he had been done a great injustice. It was smart, too, for he made a friend.

Often editors asked for TWL's comments on business articles they planned to publish. Some said that Lamont was adept at taking the sting out of stories that could be damaging to the fortunes of Morgan clients, such as an article exposing the rapidly deteriorating financial health of the Van Sweringen railroad empire. Ralph Hendershot, financial editor of the *New York World Telegram*, wrote that Lamont could "create 'head-line crashers' with the best of them."

Reporters welcomed Lamont's accessibility, easygoing nature, and understanding of their needs. "After all, I'm an old newspaper man myself," he would remind them. Frequently, views attributed to "leading banking opinion" in newspaper stories had been expressed to the reporter by TWL in his office the day before.

Franz Schneider, financial editor of the *New York Sun* following his years in that capacity with the *Evening Post*, described Lamont as "one of the easiest business leaders to interview—pleasant, articulate, unfailingly courteous and suave. Reporters admired his knowledge and integrity" and listened respectfully to his smooth and artful explanations of complex financial problems. The press rarely censured Lamont personally but accorded no such immunity to his easily targeted senior partner.

During the height of the U.S. banking crisis, with its days and nights of long meetings to discuss the emergency, R. E. Knowles, a financial reporter for the *Toronto Star*, called on Lamont at 23 Wall without an appointment.

> Mr. Lamont is even more than the younger Morgan himself, the ruling force of this ancient and world-famed emporium of high finance. To my amazement, access to Mr. Lamont was almost startingly easy. I sent up a card, and in less than five minutes I found myself entering the great man's office.

Lamont quickly put his slightly nervous visitor at ease, and they exchanged pleasantries. "He laughed like a boy. This money king is lots of fun," wrote Knowles. They discussed their backgrounds. Both were minister's sons, and the reporter observed how many successful financiers had come from parsonages.

"I suppose it's because we had to learn the value of a dollar. If we didn't then, by George, we're learning it now," replied Lamont.

After discussing the banking situation, Knowles rose to go, again expressing his appreciation for Lamont's courtesy in seeing him without an appointment. "Why shouldn't I be glad to see the representative of a great Canadian newspaper?" TWL replied. "Besides I was in the newspaper business myself once. I began as a reporter on the New York Tribune."

In his newspaper story the next day, Knowles reflected on the sundry self-important bankers of minor stature who had kept him cooling his heels, waiting in suspense to find out whether he would be granted an interview. "And here was one of the greatest bankers in the world sending me out into the rain with rainbows in my heart."

Lamont had long cultivated his network of friends in journalism—from newspaper owners down through the ranks to Wall Street reporters. Franz Schneider of the *Sun* had been on the 1929 Morgan preferred list. TWL had been a founding member of the Council on Foreign Relations, the prestigious forum for foreign policy discussion, and was on good terms with the editors of *Foreign Affairs*, CFR's quarterly journal, who shared his internationalist outlook. Bertie C. Forbes of *Forbes* magazine had written admiring articles about Lamont, and Walter Lippmann had long since become a close friend. TWL was in close touch with the editors of the *Saturday Review of Literature*, in which he held a large interest and whose deficits he was funding. Harper and Brothers, a longtime Morgan client, had just published Lamont's biography of Henry P. Davison, already serialized in *Collier's*, for whose parent company, Crowell Publishing, TWL served as a director. TWL's cousin Gardner Cowles owned leading newspapers in Des Moines, and for years Lamont had been on friendly terms with New York's foremost newspaper publishers.

On May 27, 1933, Lamont wrote to Adolph Ochs, publisher of the *New York Times*, to challenge the *Times* editorial criticizing Morgan's use of preferred lists to distribute stock. He sent copies of the letter to other newspaper executives, along with reprints of the Morgan statement submitted at the hearing defending the bank's action.

In his personal correspondence TWL vented his wrath in condemning Pecora's handling of the investigation. His contempt for the Senate committee counsel paralleled his scorn for Samuel Untermyer twenty years earlier. To Nancy Astor he wrote that the hearings were more like "the Spanish Inquisition. . . . They misrepresented, distorted, and tortured out of any semblance of truth our firm's transactions." The "young native Sicilian counsel" had tried to embarrass Morgan by badgering him repeatedly with questions about the firm's income tax returns, of which Morgan, in semi-retirement at sixty-six, had little detailed knowledge. Morgan had suggested several times that the firm's tax expert, office manager Leonard Keyes, sitting behind him at the hearing, could readily answer the questions, but only after the intervention of Senator Carter Glass was Keyes called to testify.

To Nicholas Murray Butler, president of Columbia University, Lamont wrote that no effort had been made to obtain the firm's views on "the frightful banking situation. . . . The whole thing was a circus and a publicity stunt. . . . It would astonish even you, the most experienced man I know in the ways of our American democracy."

Newspapers and journals mainly ran true to their political colors and social bias in commenting on the Morgan testimony at the Senate hearing. In the *New York American* Damon Runyon scathingly attacked the Morgan partners' performance: George Whitney had seemed "contemptuous" of the whole proceeding. The *Nation* raked both Morgans, father and son, over the coals, describing J. P. Morgan the elder as "one of the greatest enemies our society ever had. . . . He lived on wrecks. He thrived on depressions."

On the other hand, the *Chicago Daily News*, an important Republican voice in the Midwest, stated:

> The *Daily News* holds no brief for Morgan & Co., but it would be faithless to its readers if it did not point out that thus far the Pecora

investigation had disclosed that neither the Morgan firm nor the Morgan partners pay income taxes when income is lacking; second, that they lend money to reputable people upon what they regard as adequate security, and, third, that in their underwriting of securities they have frequently invited their friends and customers to participate on equal terms with the firm itself. On no one of these three accounts are they susceptible to legitimate criticism. God knows there are enough things in the financial fabric which deserve both criticism and correction about which the senate committee should concern itself.

The staunchly Republican *New York Herald Tribune* noted that the facts regarding the Morgan firm's tax liability and "preferred lists" were unfairly and misleadingly presented in the Senate hearing. The country was "gradually realizing that the innuendos which Mr. Pecora artfully disseminated by his partial presentation of evidence are not standing up."

Ironically, the most telling blow received by Morgan came at the hand of the *Herald Tribune*'s syndicated columnist and Lamont's close friend Walter Lippmann, whom two years earlier TWL had persuaded to accept the *Tribune* post. Lippmann's column, "Today and Tomorrow," was now syndicated in 126 American daily newspapers with a total circulation of about eight million, and he was truly one of America's most powerful molders of public opinion. Lippmann's two columns at the end of May, as the Senate hearing was still unfolding, deeply offended Lamont and his partners, who felt that their erstwhile friend had carelessly and unconscionably betrayed them.

On May 26 the columnist raised a specter that had long haunted the house of Morgan. He first noted that there had been "heavy losses" in the securities issues sponsored by the private bankers during the 1920s. Was the system under which savings were converted into capital investments properly managed and sufficiently regulated? Was the business of long-term capital investment in fact a monopoly—

> whether, in other words, there is a Money Trust directed by J. P. Morgan & Co., or whether the business is in fact highly competitive and dangerously chaotic. . . . If there is a monopoly which directs the flow of American long term capital, then those who direct this monopoly are chargeable with that obvious misinvestment at home and abroad which happened during the '20s. . . .
>
> Suppose there is in fact a Money Trust. Then the rulers of that monopoly are accountable not merely for each particular issue of securities, but for the total volume.

The Morgan partners did not consider their securities underwriting record marred by "heavy losses." Although all bond prices had fallen sharply during the depression, only a few Morgan-sponsored issues, mainly railroad bonds, were in default. But the columnist's reference to a "monopoly" really shocked the Corner: Lippmann had resurrected the bogeyman of the money trust directed by J. P. Morgan & Co. for the public to judge. A Leffingwell memorandum to TWL summed up the Morgan reaction:

> Walter knew that unbridled competition and high-pressure salesmanship—in which we did not participate—were responsible for the bad security issues. Those were not our doing. Using all the influence which we could, we did not have the power to prevent them. We were the victims. It was because we did not have the power, but others did and misused it, that these things happened. . . . For him to imply that we might have possessed Money Trust powers and have therefore been responsible for what happened . . . was cruel. Walter knew and should have said that because we had no such power, we should not be blamed. Walter's reputation was such that it could stand saying favorable as well as unfavorable things about the Morgan firm, if such things were true.

Lippmann struck out again at 23 Wall Street in his May 31 column entitled "The Morgan Inquiry."

> The firm is the center of an immense network of power and influence embracing the largest corporations in almost every line of economic activity. While there is no evidence as yet that the firm has had a monopoly of the investment market, it is abundantly clear that it has controlled a huge pool of capital, and that by its prestige and its connections it has exercised a towering influence upon American corporate financing. . . . The only terms on which such a vast private power could in practice be tolerable would be that it was exercised in the spirit of the most scrupulous trusteeship and with a far-sighted conception of public policy.
> The testimony has shown that at least in the period under investigation, that is to say, in the years of the great boom, the house of Morgan had not only not exercised a wise restraint upon the speculative craze, but participated in it and profited largely by it.

Lippmann acknowledged that Morgan-sponsored bond issues had been "prudent and successful." But the stock offerings, such as the Alleghany and the United Corporation issues involving "the preferred lists and great speculative profits," were a different story.

> It is these transactions which demonstrate the dangers and the social injustice of such great power without full disclosure and complete public accountability. They demonstrate that no set of men, however honorable they may be, and however good their traditions, can be trusted with so much

private power and the opportunities for personal gain which it carries with it.

The most discouraging aspect of the testimony of Mr. Morgan and Mr. Whitney is the assumption that all of these transactions can be explained away and that no important reforms are necessary or desirable.

Lamont prepared an internal memorandum refuting Lippmann's charges, so recklessly and callously hurled, the partners thought, without the slightest attempt to research the facts. It was preposterous to declare now, just as it had been twenty years earlier, that the firm was "the center of an immense network of power" and "controlled a huge pool of capital." For all the boom years, 1926 through 1929, Morgan had ranked only fourth among investment firms in sponsoring securities, after the affiliates of the National City and Chase banks, and Kuhn, Loeb. In those four years Morgan issues amounted to $1,085,000,000, only 7.36 percent of total new securities issues.

Morgan was hardly exercising "a towering influence upon American corporate financing." The firm, from being the leading sponsor of new issues in 1926 and 1927, had sharply cut back this activity in 1928 and 1929, with only $252 million in bond offerings, and became increasingly cautious in its outlook. "As the market became unrestrained, we deliberately hauled in, refused loans, and gave the example of restraint. As our issues lessened in volume others increased. Our example was not followed."

Point by point Lamont challenged Lippmann's charges. Contrary to the Lippmann thesis, Morgan's long record as an investment banking firm was characterized by a regard for "public service"—a long list of loans representing constructive efforts to develop American transportation, industry, and foreign trade, rebuild postwar Europe, and stabilize national currencies. And why should Lippmann criticize Messrs. Morgan and Whitney for not admitting wrongdoing when in their judgment they had done no wrong?

TWL did not intend to drop the matter and might decide to use the memorandum later in refuting the columnist's charges. "What undoubtedly upset me most," he wrote, "was the thought that one of my most intimate friends would readily undertake public criticism before even the so-called evidence was half in, and without making the slightest attempt to clear up points with us that seemed puzzling or open to question."

On June 14 the Lamonts sailed for England, where they planned to spend most of the summer on holiday. By chance, TWL and Lippmann, also visiting Europe, met on July 7 at an affair in London and shared a taxi afterward. Lamont sent a memorandum of their conversation to

Russell Leffingwell in New York. In his letter Lamont said that it would be "hard to forgive" Lippmann; he had "no red blood in his veins."

> Lamont: I have been wondering whether you have ever had any regret . . . about the tone of your pieces on the so-called Inquiry at Washington.
>
> Lippmann: No, I feel just the same now as I did then. I feel I was right in my judgment of the matter.
>
> Lamont: I cannot think of anything that ever cut me really so deeply as those pieces did, and Russell and Parker felt I think about the same.
>
> Lippmann: That is the difficulty in having friends who are in public life. One in my position, who is obliged to make clear-cut comment, can never help offending such friends.
>
> Lamont: I should hardly agree with you on that. We all know perfectly well that at the end of any episode which you deem of importance you must declare yourself without fear or favor. If your most intimate friends have misconducted themselves you must not hesitate to say so. That in itself is no cause for offence. Surely we are enough men of the world to know that. Let me try to give you a picture as it appeared to us. You were amongst our most intimate friends. All of them seemed to be rallying around us most strongly. Some of them, when they saw that we were enduring agony, were expecting some early comment from you recognizing the extraordinary nature of the performance and indicating confidence in us. I did not look for that. I think that Leffingwell and I had simply thought that in accordance with your usual deliberate and cautious way you would at the end of the Inquiry sum it all up and draw from it such lessons as you chose. I did not however expect that you would feel justified only a few days after the start in publicly drawing final lessons from the perverted and distorted testimony.
>
> Lippmann: I said nothing at all in my articles except what was based on the testimony itself and what was admitted by your people in that testimony.
>
> Lamont: Forgive me if I say that several points made by you had no basis in the testimony itself. . . .

Without having attended the hearings Lippmann could not appreciate that the Morgan partners were not permitted by Pecora to tell their story. "Many people were clear that Pecora did not want to let Leffingwell or me go on the stand to discuss the philosophic aspects of our business so to speak. Even at the end apparently Huey Long had to drag me on the stand," said Lamont.

> Lippmann: You observe that I did not so much as touch on the Income Tax phase, but confined my comments to the social implications revealed by the testimony, and to the preferred lists.
>
> Lamont: What puzzled us was this: Here were some of your most intimate friends suffering under a manifestly unjustly conducted inquisition. Some feature of the testimony strikes you as queer or unfavourable, namely, the

lists of our customers. Why then did you not say to yourself—"I know Dwight and Tom and Russell cannot be guilty of improper conduct. . . . I will call up one of them and say that I am puzzled about this or that feature—will they not kindly explain it." Then we would have done so, and I am sure to your satisfaction. . . .

Lippmann: Well, I can only say that I have a duty to perform as a journalist and I must do my duty as I see it.

Lamont: Why, of course, but does that duty sweep away all considerations of trust, loyalty, friendship and affection? . . . Many times during the last two years you had no hesitation in calling Leffingwell for hours at a time and asking him questions that puzzled you as to economics or finance or currency. Why not pursue the same course in a matter which I should have thought would have touched your heart much more nearly? . . . It is not a bit like your usual custom to render judgment on sensationalist and half-baked headlines.

Lippmann: But again, I relied on the testimony which I read carefully.

In charging that the house of Morgan "lacked direction," Lippmann had apparently disregarded all the firm's carefully planned and executed loans for the reconstruction of Europe, said Lamont. "You said that we had given ourselves over to speculation, when even with those few stocks that we sold to our customers the total was only about three per cent of our total security business."

Lippmann: No effort was made by your people to show that they thought things had not been done right. Mr. Morgan said at the start that you had made mistakes, but he failed to confess up to any.

Lamont: Did you expect him to give you a list? Even I should not have been able to do that. . . . However, I must not keep you any longer. I see you are in a hurry and we will just say good-bye.

Holiday in England; Troubles in New York

Tom and Florence were in and out of London during June and the first part of July 1933, visiting the Masefields at their new home at Pinbury Park in Gloucestershire and Lord and Lady Astor at Cliveden. The Astors gave a large party at Cliveden for the delegates to the London Economic Conference and a dinner at their London house on St. James's Square to introduce the Prince of Wales to the American delegation.

The purpose of the conference was twofold: the reduction of trade restrictions and the stabilization of exchange rates. France, still on the gold standard along with Switzerland and the Low Countries, was pushing for an international currency stabilization agreement with some hopes of success when President Roosevelt threw a wrench into the proceedings with a stinging message: currency stabilization was "a specious fallacy"; the United States would have no part of it; it must control its own prices and economic destiny.

Secretary of State Cordell Hull, at the head of the American delegation, was surprised and chagrined by the president's decision. He was also furious at the arrogant way Raymond Moley, FDR's "brain trust" adviser, assumed direction of the delegation.

TWL wrote his son TSL: "At a house party at the Astors where we were over that fateful July weekend (the blast from FDR), Hull was the saddest man I ever met. He sought me out and told me his troubles. . . . The American delegates bicker with one another. . . . The whole bunch strike me as very naive and very talkative."

Senator Key Pittman of Nevada, chairman of the Senate Foreign Relations Committee, was one of the embarrassing performers on the delegation, drunk at both the Astor parties, TWL observed. On the other hand, Lamont thought that former Governor James M. Cox of Ohio, the 1920 Democratic presidential candidate, was "a pretty good fellow." Lamont, Cox, and the Prince of Wales had a happy discussion of the dynamics of a model golf swing at the Astor dinner.

The conference continued to drag on unproductively after the Roosevelt bombshell. Tom and Florence, joined by Austin and Eleanor and their spouses, left London for a month at The Moult, a country house in Salcombe, South Devon.

Packing and moving the Lamonts was no mean task for Metcalfe, the family majordomo. TWL was meticulous in his attire and fond of sporting snappy waistcoats whenever the occasion permitted. In packing TWL's trunk Metcalfe worked from the following list of apparel brought for the trip.

Evening dress coat and best trousers	Two best white waistcoats
Best tuxedo, trousers and waistcoats	Two pair dress shoes
White striped blue suit	Dark striped blue suit
Gray flannel suit and knickers	Blue homespun suit & knickers
Brown gabardine jacket & knickers	Old gabardine trousers
Morning suit, thin trousers	Short black coat & vest
White and brown linen waistcoats	Striped winter waistcoats
White flannel trousers—heavy	Striped blue flannel trousers

Striped brown flannel trousers	Summer black shoes
Two lightweight pair tan shoes	High tan shoes
Shirts—all kinds (3 stiff dress)	Undervests & short drawers
3 pair pajamas—new white silk	Woolen and silk socks
Long stockings	Ties (dress also)
Handkerchiefs, hats and caps	Overcoats, medicines
Golf clubs	Golf & tennis shoes

The Lamonts had great affection for Metcalfe—loyal, efficient, and unflappable even when he regularly banged his bald head in climbing a ladder to his attic bedroom at The Moult. In reference to the rickety old floor of his quarters, Metcalfe tacked a sign on the ladder: "Abandon hope all ye who enter here!"

The family, reported Florence to her children back home, had a most happy time staying in the same house in which Tennyson wrote "Crossing the Bar." The view from the house over the bar and sea to the green headlands beyond was magnificent. The beach and swimming were superb, "much warmer than Maine," the long twilights soft and lovely. "The beauty of this place and the surrounding country takes my breath away," she wrote.

The London Conference had ended inconclusively, leaving Prime Minister MacDonald perplexed and in despair over American policy. As the Lamonts prepared to return home TWL received a letter from MacDonald marked "Very Private and Personal."

> My dear Lamont,
> I am so sorry to note by your letter just received that we are not likely to meet before you return to America, because I wanted very much to have a good talk with you upon the situation. It is very difficult for me here to understand exactly what is going on, but at the moment it looks as though the action of America at the International Conference has about finished me and has certainly been a very serious setback to the work I have been doing for a good many years in building up friendly relations between the two countries. I really cannot understand what the American policy is; whether it really thinks that by closing itself in . . . it is going to improve matters not only internally but in the world; and I was hoping that . . . you might be helpful when you go back to the United States if you would give me your private estimate of what really is going on.

Secretary of State Hull had also found the London Economic Conference frustrating, albeit from a different perspective. TWL wrote his new friend on August 13, expressing his admiration for the way the secretary had handled the difficulties he faced in "the trying days of the Economic

Conference." His conduct had been "creditable both to yourself and your country. . . . Always let me know if I can serve you in any way."

Upon his return to the U.S., TWL's attention was soon drawn to an urgent local problem with dire national ramifications—the latest fiscal crisis facing New York City. Lamont had reported periodically on the city's deteriorating finances to Louis Howe, President Roosevelt's chief political adviser, lately with growing urgency because of the probable widespread and disastrous consequences should New York City default on its outstanding debt. Such an event could trigger a panic in municipal finance nationwide, curtailing or eliminating the ability of a thousand or so cities and towns across the nation to borrow to finance their operations. New York, its credit shattered, would only be able to pay its policemen, firemen, and other operating expenses from the limited funds in hand from current tax receipts. City workers would have to be laid off and capital improvements abandoned.

At the time there was about $2 billion in outstanding city bonds and still no appetite in the market for a new city issue at any price. The New York banks, holding many of these bonds, had been forced to increase their short-term tax anticipation lending to the city from $140 to $236 million, as city tax collections, close to $200 million in arrears, continued to slow down. Current tax receipts, against which revenue notes had been issued, were being used to pay operating expense rather than retire the debt they were pledged to secure.

Such was the state of the city's finances when, after Labor Day, the city comptroller called on the banks for an additional advance of $72 million to meet the city's needs for the rest of 1933. The banks in turn requested a full-scale review of the city's financial condition and prospects with city and state authorities. Governor Herbert Lehman made his uptown apartment available for the meetings, which took place during the last two weeks of September 1933. J. P. Morgan & Co. acted as agent and workhorse for the committee of commercial banks formed to design a financial plan with the city.

With bond financing out of the question, the talks centered on what short-term credit the banks could prudently extend. On October 4, Lamont invited a large group of city editors and reporters to dinner at the Metropolitan Club to announce the new bankers' agreement with New York City: the banks would grant a four-year revolving credit of $400 million to the city, backed by tax revenues. The large amount of new bank credit and the agreement itself, stipulating effective budgetary and borrowing procedures based on realistic revenue forecasts, gradually built up confidence in New York City's credit. Once again the bankers had rescued their city and base of operations from the brink of bankruptcy, but for how long?

In the fall of 1933 the transgressions of Albert Wiggin, another giant of Wall Street, were exposed by the Pecora investigation. He was the recently retired chairman of the Chase National Bank, whose investment affiliate, it appeared, had engaged in the range of securities malpractices revealed in earlier testimony at the hearings. But it was the personal misconduct of the former head of the nation's largest bank that especially shocked the public. The powerful and self-assured banker, who had built up the Chase to its preeminent position, had personally made huge profits through extensive self-dealing with his bank and its subsidiaries. Wiggin had speculated actively in his bank's stock, and during the worst days of the stock market crash in 1929 he was selling Chase stock short, an operation that netted him a $4 million profit. At the time the Chase Bank was publicly recognized as a prominent member of the banking pool, organized by the Morgan firm to stabilize the market and greeted with hope and trust by the public. Four years later the revelations of Wiggin's activities delivered another shattering blow to the already battered public image of bankers, even though Winthrop Aldrich, the Chase's new chairman, publicly disavowed Wiggin's conduct.

As 1933, another dismal year of depression, drew to a close, J. P. Morgan & Co. suffered heavy losses. The partners' drawing accounts were cut in half, and staff salaries were reduced from 10 to 20 percent. As TWL wrote his children, "Business is punk."

Nor had the open wound in Lamont's relationship with Walter Lippmann healed. Lippmann had written TWL a brief note acknowledging that their London taxi conversation had not been fruitful and that they should talk again. Later in the summer Lamont replied:

> I received your note from Paris. I agree that the talk we had was very unsatisfactory. Under such hurried conditions it was bound to be. My mind is always open. But I fear it will be difficult for your old friends at 23 even to understand how you could so readily jump to the conclusion—as your articles indicated—that for years past the operations of friends like Dwight, Russell, Tom Cochran, Parker Gilbert and myself have been non-constructive and their practices "very shocking."

Lamont couldn't let the matter drop and polished up his long memorandum of rebuttal to Lippmann, still unsent, which he circulated to his partners for their comments. In a note to Leffingwell he said, "You see, he was such a terribly good friend I just can't call it a day without a single further word. . . . I do want him to realize how extraordinarily careless and unfounded his articles were."

Son T. S. Lamont commented that "if favors have ever been given away by J. P. Morgan & Co. he leads the list as the recipient who received the most. . . . Does he doubt that the Woodins, Davises, and Schneiders are less independent of us in thought and action than he?"

Moving often in the same social orbit, Lamont and Lippmann met from time to time—at the home of conductor Walter Damrosch; at the annual dinner of the Harvard Club—but not to discuss their differences. On January 26, 1934, TWL sent Lippmann his seventeen-page memorandum bitterly condemning the columnist's charges against the house of Morgan in his May articles.

Lippmann wrote Lamont the next day. He was glad to have the memorandum because it showed how the Morgan partners had misconstrued much of what he had written in the two columns. Still there remained differences in their viewpoints. Lippmann felt that partners Morgan and Whitney should have been more open and forthcoming in discussing the firm's "mistakes." Lamont himself had talked to Lippmann shortly before the hearing about "rotten apples," which the columnist interpreted as mistakes the firm had made "in the crazy days." Lippmann argued, "So far as I know no member of the firm ever admitted that any specific transaction was open to criticism." This was what led him to raise the issue of the "preferred lists" in his column. The correspondence then became a bit ludicrous as TWL fired off a letter explaining what he had meant about "rotten apples" and the difference between "rotten" and "specked" apples.

There the matter rested, with the Lamont-Lippmann friendship severely strained. Nevertheless, TWL decided to renew the outward symbols of their earlier relationship, sending Lippmann a copy of James Hilton's new novel *Lost Horizon* for shipboard reading on his spring trip to Europe.

On June 15, 1934, J. P. Morgan & Co. voluntarily released its financial statement to the public for the first time. It showed that as of June 1 the firm's total assets amounted to $344 million, less than half of the record high figure of $704 million three years earlier.

The disclosure was incidental to the bank's application for a New York State license to continue, as a private commercial bank, to receive deposits. The Glass-Steagall Act compelled banks to choose between commercial banking and investment banking by June 16, 1934. Banks accepting deposits would not be permitted to underwrite securities except for federal, government agency, and municipal general obligation bonds. The Morgan partners had elected to be a commercial bank in the future, a decision that marked a historic turning point for the firm. How could they choose to abandon their supremely powerful role as investment bankers for the mundane activity of a moderate-size commercial bank?

The partners had considered a number of factors. The underwriting business was virtually dead at the time: a total of only $380 million in new corporate issues had been floated in 1933, and the revival of the capital issues market did not seem imminent. Furthermore, Lamont and others thought that a major provision of the Securities Act of 1933, mandating full disclosure of all pertinent facts regarding a securities offering, would deter the sponsorship of new issues. In an internal memorandum Lamont stated that the act "imposed such heavy and formidable penalties upon the seller as to drive him completely out of the market. . . . The Act does not limit the liability of those who issue or sell securities, but makes the liability practically indefinite in amount and extending over many years period in time," a risk the partners had to consider seriously.

The Morgan partners' most important concern was the future welfare of the bank staff of 425, of whom about 400 were occupied in commercial banking. If the firm chose to remain in the securities business, the bulk of its personnel would become surplus, and wholesale layoffs were unthinkable. Morgan's commercial banking business was conducted for a relatively small number of clients—large corporations, financial institutions, and foreign governments. The partners believed that the firm's strong investment banking and research skills would give it a unique advantage in serving its select clientele. But Morgan's size was modest among major commercial banks; it had much lower lending limits than its larger banking rivals. The partners accepted the fact that the Morgan banking supremacy had come to a halt due to a political climate which they confidently expected would turn out to be only temporary. The next Republican administration would surely restore the right of commercial banks to underwrite securities.

There was an important sidebar to the event, another sign of the times. J. P. Morgan & Co. reduced its ownership of Morgan Grenfell to a one-third interest. Morgan Grenfell would no longer be subordinate to Morgan New York.

Dealing with Dr. Schacht

While the firm would no longer underwrite new securities offerings, there were earlier Morgan-sponsored bond issues to be dealt with. On April 7, 1934, Lamont wrote Dr. Schacht, president of the Reichsbank, stating that the firm had heard that Schacht had suggested "a partial default" by the German government on the Dawes and Young Plan loans.

Lamont reminded Schacht of the risks the Morgan firm had taken in sponsoring the two loans; in the Dawes loan Morgan had agreed to increase the American share for which it was responsible by $10 million in the final days before the offering when it became apparent that that portion could not be sold in Europe. The firm, TWL personally, and the other American houses that had participated in the loans would be "shocked" if Germany disregarded its agreements and repudiated the loans.

> It is difficult for us to conceive a final decision such as would force us to inform the most worthwhile portion of the American investment community, which bought these issues, that the international agreements under which they had been issued had been disregarded by the Reich and that its own obligations had, wholly without warrant in our sincere belief, been repudiated.

In his reply to Lamont of April 20, Dr. Schacht said that he did not consider that Germany's proposed action constituted a default, because the reichsmark equivalent of the amounts due would be paid into the Bank for International Settlements at the disposal of the loan trustees. But Germany simply did not have the foreign exchange to make the foreign currency payments called for. The blunt-spoken Schacht then cast aside diplomatic form.

> Whether you call me immoral or stupid . . . it is purely beyond my powers to create dollars and pounds . . . I would be willing to sell my brain and my body if any foreigner would pay for it and would place the proceeds into the hands of the loan trustees.

Throughout May and the first part of June 1934, the cable traffic was intense between 23 Wall Street, Morgan's European offices, and the BIS, as the bankers sought a way to forestall the German government's intention to default on the two loans. On May 29, the Reichsbank announced a suspension of interest transfers for private medium- and long-term debt owed foreigners. Then on June 14 the other shoe dropped: the Germans announced that after July 1, 1934, foreign exchange would not be available for debt service payments on the two international loans of the German government tied to the Dawes and Young plans.

The next day the house of Morgan delivered an aide-memoire to Secretary Hull requesting the diplomatic intervention of the U.S. government to protect the interests of American investors in the two German bond issues. The paper noted that the loans had been issued at the urging of the European powers as part of the German reparations and reconstruction plans and had been fully supported by Secretary Hughes in 1924 and Secretary Stimson in 1930.

During June the State Department fired off notes to the German government protesting the proposed default and resulting losses to American investors. Furthermore, the department had noted that Germany had signified its readiness to negotiate on a bilateral basis the resumption of debt service based on trade concessions from individual countries. The loans were based on "terms of unconditional equality to investors," and the American government wanted assurance that no discrimination against American investors would be permitted.

On June 13 New York University conferred the honorary degree of Doctor of Laws upon the presidents of Harvard, Yale, and Princeton and Thomas W. Lamont. In the introduction Lamont was portrayed as "a banker who could have been a bishop or college president." NYU's chancellor added:

> Thomas W. Lamont, master of one of the most difficult and intricate professions known to man, that of international finance; an expert of first rank who has remained a human being, author, trustee, informed but potent ambassador of international understanding. . . .

TWL would quickly have the chance to exercise these talents in dealing with the German debt problem. A week later the Lamonts sailed for Europe, the same day the Morgan firm dispatched a letter through Morgan Grenfell to Prime Minister MacDonald urging the British government to support the interests of American as well as British bondholders in its negotiations with a German delegation coming to London. Lamont was in London to receive the prime minister's reply of June 28. The British government would press the Germans to honor their obligations on behalf of all the bondholders. Nevertheless, if individual continental countries made their own deals with Germany, HMG must first look out for British bondholders. The Americans would then have to fend for themselves.

On June 29 Lamont met with the dour Chancellor of the Exchequer, Neville Chamberlain, in his office at the House of Commons and later wrote up his notes of their conversation. TWL expressed appreciation for the prime minister's letter expressing willingness to try to help the Americans and then recited the circumstances leading up to the two loans to Germany.

> TWL: I then reminded him of our efforts for Great War loans for Allies especially for British, and then as a corollary great post-War reconstruction loans, beginning with Austria which we went into upon oral urging by Bank of England representing Government opinion here that our cooperation was very necessary; then much more important, Dawes Loan—didn't want to make it—wanted no traffic with the Germans and only on letter from H.B.M. Government and French and Belgium Governments we finally agreed. Then at every critical point in negotiations we came to the rescue and even at very end increased our tranche $10 million to keep loan from failing. All in order, as Bank of England pointed out, to re-establish Reich and put it in position to begin Reparations payments to H.B.M. and other creditor Governments.

Chamberlain agreed with Lamont's summary and asked TWL for his suggestions.

> TWL: Assuming your German negotiations successful, then make representations to Germans that you are concerned about position of U.S.A. tranches, recall to them how the American issue came about and express your desire that same treatment be accorded to the U.S.A. dollar tranches as to pounds.
>
> NC: Yes . . . I will do it. But let us be clear. If we succeed with Germans . . . I should not feel justified in going so far as to cancel my British arrangements if they fail to accede to my request re U.S.A.

TWL agreed and added: "I believe that the representations you make will be so clear and strong as to go far towards getting similar treatment accorded to us.

> NC: Now you have sent letters to French and Belgium governments similar as to us, may I suggest that you report to them attitude that I have pledged myself to take and see if they will be likely to join in.

Lamont agreed, and Chamberlain then asked about the attitude of the American administration toward Germany in the matter. TWL replied that the U.S. government could exercise reprisals against Germany. "But if our advice is asked it will be against the U.S. government going into that field. We don't like embargoes, boycotts, or reprisals. May I add that when knowledge of your attitude comes to the attention of our authorities I am confident it will create a happy impression."

Lamont quickly informed the American Embassy of his conversation with Chamberlain, noting that the European governments were naturally negotiating with the Germans on behalf of their own national interests in the first instance. Accordingly Lamont had urged the British and would urge the French to do "whatever they can to protect American interests, which are otherwise likely to find themselves out on a limb."

Germany and Great Britain concluded an agreement on July 4 under which British bondholders would receive full interest payments in sterling, and similar accords were reached with the continental governments, with Germany receiving export concessions in the bargain. But the British negotiator was unable to protect the American bondholders, who had initially purchased about 42 percent of the two German issues. The State Department would not grant trade concessions as the price of Germany's commitment to continue interest payments in dollars to U.S. investors, and its increasingly sharp notes protesting Germany's discriminatory treatment of American investors went unanswered. The issue was at a diplomatic impasse as TWL headed for home and Sky Farm to join his family.

The rise of the Nazis and Adolf Hitler, who had assumed absolute power in Germany, ruthlessly imprisoning and executing hundreds of former political opponents, was not auspicious for the American bondholders. Hitler had harshly attacked the Treaty of Versailles and the reparations obligation imposed on Germany, for which most of the two German loans, linked to the Dawes and Young plans, had been spent. In a letter to his partner Parker Gilbert, Lamont described Hitler as "an ignorant demagogue . . . and his murderous policies awful."

The next interest payment date was fast approaching, the October 15 coupon of the Dawes loan, and only 50 percent of the required amount had been deposited in dollars to pay the American bondholders. The date came and went with the Americans receiving blocked reichsmarks for the remaining interest, funds that were restricted to approved uses within Germany and worth no more than 50 percent of the currency's par value.

J. P. Morgan & Co., the U.S. coupon-paying agent as well as the sponsor of the two German loans, fired off a stern cable of protest to the German minister of finance—"violation of terms" . . . "default" . . . "grave discrimination against Americans." The State Department also objected vehemently. It was no use. Only one-sixth of the Young loan interest payment of December 1 was made in dollars, and no dollars at all were furnished by Germany for the April 15, 1935, Dawes loan interest payment.

The Lord of San Simeon and Other Acquaintances

By the summer of 1934 Americans were in despair over the economic stagnation casting its pall over the country. Along with widespread urban unemployment and poverty, devastating droughts and dust storms had exacerbated the plight of farmers. As the months of depression lengthened into years people realized that President Roosevelt's New Deal programs provided no easy solution; there were no signs heralding a return to prosperity "just around the corner." The Roosevelt bull market had soon collapsed, and Wall Street felt burdened by the wave of new legislation to regulate and reform its practices. Businessmen generally did not trust the administration's unorthodox fiscal and economic policies—high government spending, heavy taxes, budget deficits, and growing government intervention in the private sector.

TWL had his own doubts, especially his fear of the depressing impact he believed that financial reform legislation would have on capital markets. Nevertheless, he was more positive about FDR's leadership than almost all his conservative Republican business friends, and he wholeheartedly supported the president's plan to lower tariffs between the U.S. and its trading partners.

As the depression ground on, TWL came to recognize the urgent need for a federal safety net to assist the elderly and unemployed reduced to poverty. Harry L. Hopkins, the administrator of federal relief programs, reported that Lamont told him at a New York dinner in September that he expected Roosevelt to remain president until 1940, perhaps even until 1944. Businessmen must look upon FDR as "the only hope and a bulwark for sane policies," said Lamont, and TWL was trying to be helpful in any way possible. Presumably, Lamont was intent on ingratiating himself with the key presidential adviser with these disingenuous remarks, but he carefully stopped short of promising political support to the president following this outburst of praise.

TWL added, "When people complain about government spending, I always answer it by saying: 'Well, if the country was willing to spend $30 billion in a year's time to try to lick the Germans, I don't see why people should complain about its spending $5 or $6 billion to keep people from starving.'"

Tom and Florence got together frequently with their good friend the widowed Betty Morrow, and often saw Charles and Anne Lindbergh. The Lindberghs lived with Anne's mother in Englewood and visited her at Deacon Brown's Point in North Haven, the Morrow summer home. When Lindbergh was in North Haven during August, he invited Florence to join him for a sightseeing flight in his little two-seater plane. Florence was thrilled by the experience, especially the magnificent bird's-eye view of Penobscot Bay. "We went up to 6000 feet all at once and saw the distant White Mountains and the whole world," she wrote Corliss.

The happy days in Maine were a calm before the storm for the Lindberghs. On September 19, 1934, the police arrested Bruno Richard Hauptmann for the kidnapping and murder of their infant son. Once again they were thrust into the dazzling glare of publicity and forced to relive the most tragic episode in their lives.

In October Mrs. Morrow brought her houseguest Harold Nicholson to tea with the Lamonts at Palisades. Nicholson had been commissioned by her to write a biography of Dwight Morrow. The former British diplomat had good political connections and was a highly respected author of history and biography.

In his diary entry reporting the visit to Palisades, Nicholson described Tom as "a nice, intelligent man." But he clearly viewed Florence as a chatterbox. "Now the odd thing about Americans is that they never listen." At the time Ambassador Norman Davis, now a key adviser on foreign policy to the president, was staying with the Lamonts. During tea Davis talked thoughtfully about diplomatic moves in Europe to counter growing German militarism.

"But did they listen? Not for a moment," wrote Nicholson. "'Now let me get you another cup of tea, Mr. Nicholson. I am afraid that our tea here is not as good as the tea you get in England. . . .' Chatter, chatter; interrupt, interrupt."

Nicholson also recorded another exchange about Florence that took place in the Morrow home. Mrs. Morrow quoted Florence as saying that Charles Lindbergh was the only pilot she would fly with. "Now isn't that just like those old dames," Lindbergh replied. "Just because I flew alone to Paris, they think I am a safe pilot. That's just silly."

As his biography of Morrow progressed, Nicholson heard more from TWL and his partners than he wanted. In the book's final stage the Morgan partners, in an exercise organized by Lamont, reviewed the typescript and submitted their comments to the author, who was not grateful for their input, as he wrote his wife:

> I worked practically all yesterday on the Morgan dossier as I want to finish it completely. As you saw, it is immense. Every single partner of J. P.

Morgan and Company has been allowed to have his fling. But it all boils down to the fact that they are furious with the tone I have adopted towards the House of Morgan. Not that I have said a word against it. It is merely that I have not treated it with the awed respect to which they are accustomed. But I dare say that I shall manage to tone it down a trifle. I do not want to create unnecessary ill feeling for Mrs. Morrow.

For the Morgan firm, 1934 was another lean year, and the partners reviewed expenses carefully for future savings. An important staff fringe benefit fell victim to the times: the firm would have to close its summer camp in Maine for Morgan employees and their families.

Lamont and Charles Steele, who had built up their shares of partnership capital through reinvested earnings during the 1920s, now held the largest individual interests in the firm; J. P. Morgan had built the *Corsair IV* instead. His opulent lifestyle was feeling the pinch from the cut in the firm's earnings and higher taxes in the U.S. as well as England, where he stayed at his Herefordshire estate and went grouse shooting in Scotland each year. Early in 1935 Morgan began selling some of his finest paintings and tracts of land in Glen Cove and Locust Valley, Long Island.

Tom was an inveterate tourist. On February 2 he and Florence sailed for Los Angeles via the Panama Canal. The two-week voyage was relaxing and uneventful—"dull enough people not to excite you, not enough feminine beauty to bewilder you, tropical skies and blue-green seas," Lamont wrote his sons. In Guatemala the Lamonts took a day trip to the ancient hill town of Antigua with its "exquisite ruined cathedral at the height of its beauty fifty years before the Pilgrim fathers landed," wrote Florence. The Panana Canal Zone was "something every American should be proud of . . . not only the canal, but the whole zone is marvelous, a miracle of cleanliness and health in the midst of squalor and disease." The local sights were interesting, but on shipboard, one surmises, Tom would have enjoyed seeing a few more pretty girls sunning themselves on deck or chattering over cocktails in the evening. An ambassador or university president might also have made good company.

Lamont had a good time at the ship's fancy dress ball, according to Florence: "Father went as a cardinal in his red dressing gown and a purple cape an old lady had lent him. He looked simply splendid and acted the part so well that I began to wonder if my children were illegitimate. He lost the first prize by only one vote."

After disembarking at Los Angeles, the Lamonts spent a week in La Jolla and then visited some old friends in Santa Barbara, where Florence found the social pace exhausting. "Papa is altogether happy as we go out to luncheon, tea, and dinner every day . . . I manage to keep going but I think I shall have to go away to recuperate and get a rest as soon as I return." Her travel wardrobe of a large trunk, two suitcases, and a shoe bag was inadequate, Florence noted. "No one ever wears the same dress twice out here. Well, I think I am giving them a good example of plain dressing and high thinking, especially the plain dressing."

One day TWL left early for a long drive up the coast to William Randolph Hearst's San Simeon. Though hardly unaccustomed to luxurious living, TWL was dazzled by the baronial estate. He wrote his daughter:

> March 4, 1935 . . . Well, I had a great experience—entre nous. W. R. Hearst, by arrangement, invited me up to his San Simeon ranch for the night. I compromised on luncheon—was motored up the 170 miles and had a vastly entertaining time. San Simeon is a feudal demesne of 100,000 acres, crowned with an enormous two-towered Spanish castle on the very tip top of a 2,000 ft. mountain. The place is like a *glorified* combination of the Arabian Nights, Granada, Versailles, Blenheim and God knows what all. A harbor on the ocean for the yachts to ride in, a landing field and private planes coming and going with guests as thick as most princes have motor cars. A long winding roadway (about 3 miles) up the mountain, past grazing flocks of white deer, buffalo, ostriches et al, with occasional polar bears disporting themselves in grottoes.
>
> Greeted by secretaries and escorted across courtyards and patios, by swimming pools (both outdoor and indoor, the outdoor one large enough to go canoeing on) to a guest house—the sitting room hung in 17th Century crimson brocade, with . . . exquisite bits of Italian sculpture dotted about, the ceiling old carved wood brought from a room in a 14th Century Tuscan villa. . . .
>
> That was merely the guest rooms. When you came to the Castle itself the magnificence was unbounded. The great hall, with huge Gothic tapestries, a ceiling beautiful beyond compare, the dining hall with 16th Century Italian choir-stalls up and down each side, flanking an 80 ft. refectory table and 60 chairs, each a perfect specimen (original) of early Italian.

San Simeon's magnificence was simply mind-boggling for Lamont, as he wandered about:

> One room after another in the same gorgeous magnificence—carved ceilings, all different and brought from ancient castles in Spain, villas in Italy, or chateaux in France. . . . Mille fleurs tapestries beyond compare in the billiard room, beautiful old brocade hangings in the theatre where they have a new moving picture every night.
>
> Italian primitives were as common as ping-pong balls. And pieces of rare

sculpture as frequent as bathroom fixtures. . . . The side tables in the dining room were thirty feet long—each table groaning with the weight of old silver—tankards, trenchers, flagons, everything! . . .

And what about me and Marion Davies? There she was O.K.—very cordial and smiling. She was the hostess and laid herself out to please—still very pretty—had quite evidently striven with considerable success to better her early education.

Marion Davies, a former movie actress and Hearst's longtime mistress, looked after TWL until the host made his appearance for lunch with his forty guests at 2:45, an hour and forty-five minutes after Lamont's arrival. The other guests, including a dozen young screen actors and actresses, were attentive and polite to the distinguished banker. The Hollywood lifestyle was new to TWL, and he was intrigued. The pretty girls in day pajamas and young men kissed each other good morning and lounged about the pool, playing backgammon or ping-pong. Lamont noted that many of the houseguests were still eating breakfast and everyone except TWL had arrived by private plane.

Following lunch Hearst and Lamont had their private talk, and TWL did most of the talking. He had long wanted an opportunity to refute, face to face with the press lord, the reckless and false charges hurled against the Morgan firm in the infamous *New York American* article "Gabriel over Wall Street" two years earlier. He later wrote up brief notes of his talk with Hearst.

J. P. Morgan & Co. was now a "wholesale" bank, handling the commercial banking business of large corporations. But before enactment of the Glass-Steagall Act, Morgan's basic business was managing high-grade bond issues. Its record of sponsoring foreign bond issues was excellent. (Lamont did not mention the current problems with the two German loans.) TWL also reminded Hearst that in 1927 he had cautioned against the rash floating of low-quality foreign bonds by other investment banks, a warning that largely fell on deaf ears.

Moreover, the bank's profits were moderate, around $10 million on a capital of $50 to $60 million in a firm of about twenty partners. J. P. Morgan's own fortune was relatively modest. Nor did the firm control other banks or dominate American political parties. "That's a scream," said Lamont.

TWL described the firm's record of assisting New York City in its recurring financial crises. J. P. Morgan & Co. had compiled a record of seventy years of "fair dealing" in "constructive operations. . . . To sum up, you've got us completely sized up wrong," TWL concluded in defense of his bank.

Lamont then discussed the nation's economic woes. "The trouble is that FDR is prolonging the depression, making it chronic." It was important to "open up the capital markets," which would help create jobs, and to "stop ruining the confidence of the public in all businesses. . . . American business is on the whole honest, and should not be portrayed otherwise. There have been lapses, but look at what businessmen have done in building the nation."

Lamont's notes did not record Hearst's response, but Florence reported to TSL that TWL thought he had had "a satisfactory talk." She also commented on Hearst's belated appearance for lunch. "I think it was a foul way to treat Pa. But he doesn't seem to resent it. I do."

TWL's left-leaning son Corliss was highly critical of his father's chat with the powerful right-wing publisher. TWL replied in a letter to his son:

> I would talk to any dictator in Europe or gangster in America if I thought it would help. I hope I am not so illiberal as to feel that anybody is so beyond the pale that I cannot talk to him if that seems to be my job. Who was it that advised that he who was without fault should cast the first stone?

Germany had continued to refuse interest payments in dollars to the American bondholders of the Dawes and Young loans; the June 1, 1935, Young loan coupon was paid completely in blocked reischmarks, provoking another round of protests from Morgan, the State Department, and the Foreign Bondholders Protective Council.

Dr. Schacht, who had added the portfolio of minister of trade, again stated his government's position. In 1934 Germany had run a large trade deficit with the U.S. Because foreign investment in Germany had dried up, the country could pay interest only in dollars from net export earnings with the U.S.; these were still nonexistent, although the trade balance between the two nations had begun to even out in early 1935 as Germany sharply cut back her imports from America.

Germany's trade surpluses with Great Britain and France enabled those countries to compel her to pay full interest on the German loans; Germany was not willfully discriminating against American investors. If the U.S. agreed to reduce tariffs and ease the anti-dumping restrictions on German imports, the payments to investors would be resumed.

But the State Department had a different agenda: Germany must promptly cure the default in payments to U.S. bondholders, and thus end an unacceptable act of discrimination against American investors, before the U.S. would be prepared to discuss a new trade agreement.

Lamont, planning to be in Europe during July, passed the word through Montagu Norman, governor of the Bank of England, that he would like to meet with Dr. Schacht in an effort to resolve the impasse. TWL had asked his partners for their views, and a long cable to him in London from Parker Gilbert urged caution in initiating any suggestions that American investors would accept interest payments at a lower rate than called for by the loan agreements—7 percent for the Dawes loan and 5½ percent for the Young loan.

Dr. Hjalmar Schacht was stiff-necked, arrogant, and widely regarded at home and abroad as a financial genius. As Hitler's financial czar, no person accomplished more to enable Germany to build its war machine. Yet Schacht was an old-fashioned conservative banker who highly valued his foreign banking ties and friendships, especially in England and America. TWL knew him well from the Young Plan negotiations and Schacht's earlier visits to the U.S.

Lamont and Schacht met at ten o'clock on the morning of July 16 at the Hotel Stephanie in Baden-Baden. After the meeting TWL cabled an account of their discussion to his partners. After reciting Germany's woes, Schacht suggested that American investors accept a moratorium on interest payments pending the implementation of a new trade agreement with Washington, a proposal Lamont quickly rejected.

However, TWL knew that he had to come up with some new formula to break the impasse. The only solution that occurred to him was to propose that the American investors receive U.S. dollar interest payments in an amount that would persuade them and the U.S. government that Germany was acting in good faith to cure the default.

> To such an end I felt that if he were to arrange that hereafter the American holders of Dawes coupons would receive an effective and uncomplicated 5% and of Young coupons 4%, on surrender of current coupons, (meanwhile yielding none of their contractual rights) I for one should feel that the German Government were thereby giving some tangible evidence of their good intent.

Lamont would then inform the State Department that in his view Germany was making an honest effort to solve the problem. Schacht said that he would consider the proposal.

> If he should find a way it would simply mean that our investors would be receiving an . . . amount that might prove not unacceptable. . . . It would mean that we should express the hope to Washington that should the German Government now desire to send a representative to Washington he would . . . be welcomed. I believe that some such course as this is the only possible way to end the present impasse, and I believe that a half loaf is better than no bread at all.

Lamont and Schacht agreed that the new interest formula would be strictly an interim measure until Germany's trade balance with the U.S. enabled it to resume full interest payments. In the meantime the plan offered an immediate benefit to the American bondholders in achieving a modest dollar return for them and doing away with the cumbersome system of converting the blocked reischmarks they currently received. Two weeks later Lamont sailed for New York, where Schacht cabled him on August 14 to confirm Germany's acceptance of the 5%–4% formula.

Lamont sent a full report of his negotiations with Schacht to the State Department, noting that the German government now expected the administration to invite it to send a representative to Washington to negotiate a new trade agreement. Lamont felt that Germany's acceptance of the new formula was evidence of its good intent to resolve the problem. The State Department had no objection, and on August 21 TWL cabled Schacht that the new formula "appeals to us as well as being directed towards the attainment of improved relations."

On October 4 the German government publicly announced the new plan for interest payments to American holders of the Dawes and Young loan bonds, which became operative with the October 15, 1935, coupon of the Dawes loan. Lamont's negotiating initiative with Dr. Schacht, overriding the warning of some of his partners, had paid off—in benefiting the American investors in the two German loans and cooling off a heated dispute between the two countries. But many Americans, including TWL, were growing concerned and angry at Germany and its leader for more overriding reasons—Adolf Hitler's openly avowed militarism and the Nazis' sadistic persecution of Jews.

Launching a New Enterprise

During August 1935, partners Whitney, Leffingwell, Gilbert, and Stanley met with TWL at Sky Farm in North Haven to discuss an important new project, code-named the XYZ Corporation. From this meeting came their decision to establish a new securities firm.

For some time the partners, especially Whitney and Gilbert, had been considering ways in which Morgan's long-acclaimed leadership role in investment banking could be continued. The firm's reputation was peerless, and a new investment banking firm identified with J. P. Morgan & Co. in its origin and bearing the Morgan name would operate with a unique advantage. The timing seemed ripe: total new securities issues were running at more than twice the volume of the same period in 1934 and far ahead of dismal 1933. The Morgan bank and its offspring, which would be independently owned and managed, would find mutually profitable ways to cooperate. Some of J. P. Morgan & Co.'s former investment banking clients were bent on raising capital anew, and their business would get the new firm off to a fast start. Also there were hopes, as Lamont wrote J. P. Morgan, on holiday in England, that "within three years the situation may so far have reversed itself" as to make it possible for J. P. Morgan & Co. to resume its traditional investment banking business. Until that happy time arrived when the Republicans would take over, the new firm would fill the gap. Its president would be the very able Harold Stanley, a Morgan partner since 1927, and its name would be Morgan Stanley & Co.

TWL also cleared the proposal with Charles Steele, the firm's oldest partner, who had long been inactive. Of Morgan Stanley's capital of $7.5 million, $7 million would be in the form of nonvoting 6 percent preferred stock mainly contributed by nine J. P. Morgan partners. Morgan, Lamont, and Steele, holding the largest shares of J. P. Morgan & Co.'s capital, had important personal stakes in the success of the new enterprise. The common stock of $500,000 was held by Morgan Stanley officers.

At four o'clock on September 5, 1935, with Harold Stanley standing beside him near the large fireplace on the banking floor of 23 Wall Street, Lamont met the press to announce the formation of Morgan Stanley & Co. Incorporated. In addition to Stanley, William Ewing and Henry S. Morgan, both Morgan partners, and Perry E. Hall, a Drexel partner, would be senior officers. H. S. Morgan, known as Harry, was J. P. Morgan's second son; his older brother, Junius, remained with the bank. Other Morgan and Drexel personnel transferred to the new firm, which opened its doors for business with a staff of seven officers and thirteen employees.

The Morgan partners' forecast of the new firm's prospects was accurate: for 1936, Morgan Stanley's first full year of operations, it was the leading sponsor of issues for the amazing total of $1 billion, capturing 24 percent of the market, as old Morgan clients, the cream of American industry, flocked to the new investment bank.

But not all of Morgan's clients had withstood the blows of the depression. On September 30, 1935, TWL's sixty-fifth birthday, George Whitney represented a Morgan-led banking syndicate at the sale of its controlling interest in the Alleghany Corporation, which took place at the drab auction rooms of Adrian H. Mullers and Sons on Vesey Street. Five years earlier the Morgan syndicate had made a loan of $39.5 million to the Van Sweringen brothers to enable them to pay off their debts incurred in a futile attempt to support the market price of Alleghany and its related railroad stocks. The loan was secured by the brothers' holdings of Alleghany stock. The Van Sweringens were broke, but the partners still had faith in their ability to manage their railroad empire profitably. They were wrong. Before long the Van Sweringens had stopped paying interest on the loan as the Missouri Pacific, whose revenues were almost halved in the deepening depression, and other Alleghany controlled lines went into receivership. In the late summer of 1935 the bankers thought the time had come to foreclose on their collateral and sell it for whatever they could get—not much, as the market price of Alleghany stock was quoted at a lowly $1.37 per share. A Van Sweringen ally bought the bankers' Alleghany stock for $3.1 million, thus closing a disastrous chapter in the Morgan-Alleghany relationship.

Senator Nye Attacks

For months an increasing barrage of books and articles in the U.S. has castigated the role of American munitions manufacturers during the Great War, alleging that they had propelled the country into the war with the backing of the Wall Street bankers. Perhaps the most widely influential book advocating this thesis was *The Road to War* by Walter Millis, a *Herald Tribune* editorial writer. The huge Allied purchases in the U.S. before America entered the war, financed by the bankers, had given a tremendous boost to the American economy, which was in the doldrums in 1914. Said Millis: "The mighty stream of supplies flowed out, and the corresponding stream of prosperity flowed in, and the U.S. was enmeshed more deeply than ever in the cause of Allied victory."

The most prominent and vocal exponent of this theory was Senator Gerald P. Nye of North Dakota, who was chairman of the Special Committee of the U.S. Senate Investigating the Munitions Industry. The committee, which had begun its hearings in late 1934 with the munitions makers, was now shifting its attention to Wall Street, especially to J. P. Morgan & Co., so dominant in financing Allied purchases. The senator spoke on May 29 to an audience of 5,000, including TWL, at Carnegie Hall, and it was obviously a preview of things to come. He wasted no time in getting around to the Morgan firm: "Our bankers were never opposed to war. Mr. Thomas W. Lamont, who, I understand, has honored us with his presence tonight, has written that J. P. Morgan & Co. were wholeheartedly in back of the Allies from the start."

Nye then described the role of the house of Morgan as purchasing agent and banker for the British and French governments. While U.S. government loans to the Allies were still largely unpaid, "the American bankers got every penny that they had advanced." But by 1917 "the house of Morgan was all done. They couldn't go any further."

After the munitions makers came "Public enemy No. 2: The banker who raises the money to pay for the munitions. . . . What took us into the war? Did the American people know they were fighting to save the skins of the bankers who had loaned $2 billion to the Allies? These $2 billion worth of credits would have been worthless if we had not got into the war. . . . If the Morgans and other bankers must go in for their share of another war, then, for heaven's sake, let them join the Foreign Legion."

Nye continued to censure the house of Morgan and Wall Street in speeches and radio addresses. He also dispatched about a dozen committee staff members to 23 Wall Street to examine the firm's records of the World War period, namely, old files of cablegrams long stored in a Brooklyn warehouse. The senator stated that he soon would summon the Morgan senior partners to appear before his committee. At TWL's direction the Morgan staff prepared research papers covering Morgan's activities during the 1914–1917 period, a chronology of the development of the Wilson administration's policy on loans to the Allies, and the like, to be held ready for public release if necessary at the time of the Senate hearings.

One study tracked and challenged Nye's inaccurate and deceptive statements. The loans to the Allied governments before America joined the war, organized by Morgan and other banks, certainly would not have been "worthless" if America had stayed out of the war. Except for the first $500 million Anglo-French loan, all the loans and the $400 million line of credit to the British government had been amply secured by neutral country collateral, largely American securities. The publicly held loans had commanded a high price and a ready market. It was clear that the bankers did not need to be "saved" by America's entry into the war.

The loans were repaid from the resources of the borrowing governments. "What of it? We all deplore the impasse existing on the intergovernmental debts, but the breakdown there is no justification for Senator Nye's attacks upon our firm for having seen to it that the loans which it issued were carefully and soundly arranged."

As to Nye's suggestion about bankers joining the Foreign Legion, "To what lengths is it permissible for a United States Senator, about to preside at a semi-judicial inquiry . . . to go? How far will public opinion endorse his endeavor to prejudice opinion beforehand, to declare that the case is already closed? Such procedure, we submit, is unfair, un-American, indecent."

As TWL and his partners prepared to defend themselves in Washington once again, Congress passed and FDR reluctantly signed the Neutrality Act of 1935, banning the sale of arms and munitions to belligerents when the president determined that a state of war existed. Along with Germany's escalating militarism under the Nazi regime, another war cloud had been gathering in Europe: Italian premier Mussolini's clear intent to invade Ethiopia. On October 3, 1935, the Duce's army advanced from the Italian colony of Eritrea into the backward and virtually defenseless African nation. This demonstration in Ethiopia of Mussolini's imperial ambitions further heightened American fears of another war in Europe and U.S. involvement.

Harold Nicholson's biography *Dwight Morrow* was published in October 1935, and the *New York Times* carried a book review by R. L. Duffus. In commenting on Morrow's part in J. P. Morgan & Co.'s war work, Duffus referred to "the manner in which our financiers actually made us an ally of the Allies when we were still officially neutral." He added, "Let it be admitted that in helping draw this country into the European war he [Dwight Morrow] had a part in decivilizing the world."

Lamont was not one to let such a denigrating accusation go unchallenged; his lengthy letter to the *Times* appeared on October 18. Lamont acknowledged his firm's role in purchasing supplies, substantially financed by Morgan-led bond issues, for Great Britain and France before America's entry into the war and wrote:

> But does any one, even of the post-war generation, believe that business interest determined the pro-Ally sentiments of Morrow or Morgan or Davison or any of us? Surely not. Like most of our contemporaries and friends and neighbors, we wanted the Allies to win, from the outset of the

war. We were pro-Ally by inheritance, by instinct, by opinion, and so were almost all the people we knew on the Eastern seaboard of the United States, from the moment Germany violated Belgium's neutrality.

The fundamental cause leading to America's declaration of war was Germany's savage submarine attacks against U.S. shipping, despite American warnings; Germany had forced America into the war.

Of late a new version of those causes seems to have struck the popular fancy. Our countrymen are being invited to accept blithely the legend that it was American business men rather than Germany who got us into the war. This notion has been taken up so eagerly and repeated with such engaging embellishments that the most conspicuous facts, readily ascertainable, are being gradually obscured for the American people.

Lamont's statement in the *Times* triggered a series of letters to its editor and articles approving or rebuking TWL's position. R. L. Duffus, the reviewer of *Dwight Morrow*, stoutly maintained that during 1915 and 1916

our bankers, manufacturers and munitions workers were fighting for the Allies . . . as effectively as though they had been standing in the trenches with rifles in their hands. . . . I do maintain, moreover, that the treaty of Versailles, which we made possible, did "decivilize" Europe.

A *New York Times* editorial of October 24 backed Lamont:

The chain of circumstances which led to our declaration of war is a matter of public record. When, notwithstanding our Government's previous warning that such action would mean the severing of diplomatic relations, the Berlin Government announced unrestricted submarine warfare in the stipulated war zone; when, after the subsequent ruthless torpedoing of American ships flying the American flag, the House voted 373 to 50 and the Senate 82 to 6 that a state of war already existed—there was nowhere the least dispute as to what had caused the decision. . . .
To assert, in face of this unmistakable historical record, that the bankers "drove us into war" is to talk absurdity.

Oswald Garrison Villard, from whom Lamont had bought the *New York Evening Post* in 1918, had long been an ardent pacifist. He eagerly joined the attack on the Morgan firm in several articles in the *Nation*. In one he wrote:

Later on when things were going very badly with the Allies and it looked more than doubtful that the British bonds floated in this country would be worth the paper they were printed on, they [the Morgan partners] were perfectly willing that millions of young Americans should be shipped abroad to the shambles which so nearly finished the world and accomplished nothing—not even the destruction of German militarism.

In another article, Villard went so far as to say:

> Secretary Lansing argued that we should go to war in order to preserve prosperity and get back the money loaned abroad. It was the exact viewpoint of the firm of Morgan. These were American traitors of 1915.

The partners decided against suing Villard and the *Nation* for libel. Lamont blistered him in a private letter the next day, but Villard didn't quit. In another article he observed that no Morgan partner had ever entered the trenches during the war. Lamont replied that the youngest partner had been forty-four years old at the time; however, seven sons of partners had joined the armed services; one was killed in action and several had been wounded.

J. P. Morgan, furious at Senator Nye's reckless charges, proposed that the firm take a newspaper advertisement condemning the senator's behavior and explore with counsel the possibility of suing Nye for libel based on his speeches made off the Senate floor. "The fact is I am so tired of letting attacks on our character and our morality of conduct go without a reply," he wrote his partners on October 28 from London. He was enraged that Nye was pronouncing the Morgan partners guilty even before the congressional hearings with the evidence they would produce had taken place.

But cooler heads at 23 Wall Street prevailed. Lamont replied to Morgan that all the partners shared his outrage at Nye's performance. However, the partners decided that it was wisest to take on Nye at the hearings and not give added publicity or currency to his contemptible accusations.

While unwilling to go public in refuting Nye's allegations, TWL expressed his views in letters to friends and journalists such as Lippmann, Arthur Krock of the *New York Times*, and Lewis S. Gannett of the *Herald Tribune*. He also distributed to such opinion makers copies of a book, *American Neutrality 1914–1917*, by Professor Charles Seymour, the distinguished Yale historian who had served on the American delegation to the Paris Peace Conference, that clearly disproved Senator Nye's thesis that munitions makers and bankers had dragged the country into war.

Newton D. Baker, President Wilson's Secretary of War, delivered the most telling denial to Senator Nye's charges in a November 1935 letter to the *New York Times*: "I feel sure that all my surviving associates in President Wilson's cabinet . . . will agree that President Wilson and we, as his associates, did all we knew how to keep our country out of war, and that none of us ever heard the fable, which is now the gospel of the uninformed, that we ever had the slightest concern about the foreign loans of bankers or the industrial ambitions of the few American munition-making companies."

But Americans were concerned about becoming enmeshed in another European war, and Congress was already considering the passage of a tougher Neutrality Act to tighten the ban on the sale of munitions to belligerents. The senior Morgan partners were asked to be ready to testify before the Nye Committee hearings starting January 7, 1936.

The Mexican Muddle

On December 17, 1935, Lamont placed a phone call to Eduardo Suarez, the finance minister of Mexico. Apparently, Suarez was backing off from the latest agreement with the International Committee of Bankers to settle the repayment of the Mexican government's outstanding debt to some 200,000 foreign bondholders. TWL hoped that he could patch up the latest misunderstanding.

Five years had passed since the Lamont–Montes de Oca agreement of 1930 and its supplement of January 1931, the pacts that had cut back Mexico's obligation and stretched it out over forty-five years, with no payments required until 1933. Repeatedly, the government had postponed submitting the agreement to the Mexican Congress, for as early as 1931 it had become clear that that body would not ratify it, citing the worsening economic conditions in Mexico—an adverse trade balance, increasing capital flight, and a substantial deficit in the national budget.

On December 22, 1931, the International Committee and Montes de Oca had signed a new agreement, basically similar in amount and terms to the 1930 agreement, postponing the resumption of debt service to 1934 following the deposit of $5 million with the International Committee by the Mexican government. However, other frictions had soon developed between the bankers and Mexico, and the $5 million deposit had not been forthcoming.

On November 16, 1932, Alberto J. Pani, who had replaced Montes de

Oca as minister of finance, wrote Lamont requesting a $10 million loan to the Banco Agricola, for crop financing. The farm production made possible by the loan would "reflect favorably" on the nation's economy and finances of the government, "placing the latter in a position to expedite the resumption of the service payments on its foreign debt." Mexico was pursuing an earlier strategy: no debt repayment until the foreign lending spigot was turned on again.

Lamont's reply was a smooth paraphrasing of the old truism that throwing good money after bad is unwise. The bankers had given "earnest consideration" to the loan request, recognizing the critical importance of agricultural development in Mexico. TWL applauded the government's efforts in trying to solve "a difficult problem for the betterment of the condition of its people. . . . We should so much wish to help you in your valiant efforts to remedy your country's difficulties. . . . When it comes, however, to the question of a loan, I regret . . ."

The investment market was "almost closed to any new bond issues." Second, investors would not be interested, given the low prices quoted for outstanding Mexican bonds, which reflected the fact that the Mexican government had not lived up to its obligations and established a record of debt service payments.

Finance Minister Pani was not pleased with Lamont's response and was further provoked by another decision of the International Committee of Bankers. Since the Lamont–De la Huerta agreement of 1922, the International Committee had disbursed $33 million to the foreign bond-holders and also paid the legal and other expenses incurred in implementing the agreement out of the funds received from Mexico. However, some $7 million remained on deposit with the International Committee in New York, an amount that was insufficient to distribute complete payments according to the agreement schedule. Legal claims presented by a few bondholders regarding the distribution plan further complicated the situation.

In April 1932, Pani demanded that the $7 million be returned promptly to the Mexican government, and Lamont, speaking for the International Committee, refused. The acrimonious argument ran on with Pani claiming a year later that the International Committee was the agent of the Mexican government, "subject at all times to our authority and orders," and must give up the funds immediately.

On February 7, 1934, Lamont wrote Martes Gomez, the successor finance minister to Pani. Under the agreements with the Mexican government the $7 million in question had been remitted to the committee for the benefit of the foreign bondholders, and the committee served in fact as agent for the bondholders, not the Mexican government. The committee still hoped to negotiate a revised external debt agreement with the Mexican government.

Gomez replied at length on February 27:

> The Department of Finance and I, personally, feel that there is no advantage in adding new agreements to those already rejected [by the Mexican Congress] or in making our agreements more voluminous with a new Gomez–Lamont Agreement which would be added to the De la Huerta–Lamont, Pani–Lamont, and Montes de Oca–Lamont agreements.

On the other hand, the government's repayment of its domestic debt was strengthening its credit and rehabilitating the Mexican economy.

> This last feature is the one which should interest the Committee of Bankers mostly because neither Mexico nor any other country of the world will ever be able to deliver to its creditors amounts which are beyond their capacity to pay, and because each advance made by our domestic economy approximates . . . the date on which Mexico will be able to demonstrate with firm and permanent acts its will to carry out a final agreement with its creditors.

Moreover, Lamont's committee was holding funds which legally belonged to the government of Mexico, because the agreements under which they had been deposited with the committee had been cancelled. The committee must make restitution of these funds to the Mexican government. Mexico would never enter into a new agreement with the committee until the funds were returned, said Gomez.

In September, President Rodriguez, addressing the Mexican Congress, further dashed the prospects for settlement of the dispute:

> The present situation of Mexico does not permit that the External Public Debt be dealt with on the same basis as the Internal Public Debt. In order to amortize the former we would be compelled to export gold and be subject—in the event of concluding arrangements hastily negotiated—to suspend payments after a certain period of time, as we know through the sad experiences of the past.
>
> Furthermore, the Government realizes that public opinion is unanimously opposed to the idea of paying obligations which greatly exceed our capacity to pay . . . particularly at a time when all countries of the earth, struggling to overcome the crisis, must make a true recapitulation of their situation.
>
> The above situation might have been fully discussed with the International Committee of Bankers if the latter had not followed in its dealings with Mexico a totally mistaken line of conduct which has culminated in the retention of our funds in an unjust and illegal manner.
>
> For the time being I merely wish to inform the people's representatives

that inasmuch as the attitude of the International Committee of Bankers was deemed scarcely friendly for our country, and veered from the legal precepts, the Mexican Government officially informed it under date of May 21, 1934 that it would have no further dealings with the Committee.

It was the darkest moment for the International Committee in fifteen years of dealing with Mexico. The Mexican government would not even talk to them and had slammed the door in their face. However, Mexican administrations changed with some frequency, and the committee's mission would continue.

On September 25, Lamont wrote Gomez reiterating that the funds in the hands of the committee belonged to the bondholders, and the committee, as their trustee, merely held them pending their future distribution. Furthermore, a search of the bank's files did not disclose any communication from the president indicating that he would have no further dealings with the committee.

Finally, the comment of President Rodriguez that the attitude of the committee "was deemed scarcely friendly for our country" indicated that he had not been made conversant with the facts.

> If he had had sufficient opportunity to acquaint himself with the past history, he would be the first to appreciate the cooperation of the Committee in its transactions with your Government during all these years, and its efforts to maintain the Government's credit. In fact, the Committee has often been charged by bondholders with adopting too much the Government point of view.

In December 1934, Lamont talked with Eduardo Suarez and Jerome Hess, the senior partners of a Mexico City law firm advising the ministry of finance. The Mexican government's finances were improving, and its customs revenues were more than sufficient to make payments on the foreign debt secured by them. The International Committee would send a representative to Mexico to discuss the external debt question whenever the Mexican government was ready.

On July 1, 1935, Suarez was appointed finance minister. The committee believed he was a man they might do business with—he would at least listen to their viewpoint—and dispatched George Rublee to Mexico City for talks with him. Rublee was a senior partner of the prestigious Washington law firm of Covington, Burling and had been legal adviser to Ambassador Morrow in Mexico and later at the London Naval Conference. He talked with Suarez, who reiterated that the Mexican government first wanted return of the $7 million, or a substantial part of it, before it would enter a new agreement to resume debt service payments.

The committee was now prepared to yield a little to get a new agreement. Many bondholders were pressing for distribution of the $7 million; on the other hand the committee recognized that it ran the risk of provoking a complete breakdown in the debt settlement talks with Mexico if it distributed the funds without the government's approval. The committee felt it could justify giving Mexico about a million dollars representing reimbursement to the government for its debt negotiation expenses and other funds originally designated for a small number of bondholders who had later declined to participate in the committee's distribution arrangements. But the foreign bondholders must first approve any new agreement to release funds to Mexico, or they, too, would have grounds for suing the committee. The committee, caught in the middle, would proceed cautiously.

Based on the Rublee–Suarez talks, the draft of a preliminary agreement was completed in November; however, its interpretation quickly ignited a new argument between Suarez and the committee. Both sides contemplated that a "new permanent agreement" to settle Mexico's external debt would be negotiated and ratified by the Mexican Congress and a majority of foreign bondholders. Moreover, the committee was willing to transfer $1,070,000 of the funds in hand to the Mexican government, again with the bondholders' approval, which the bankers assumed would be forthcoming when they ratified the "new permanent agreement."

However, Suarez in his letter of December 7, enclosing an executed copy of the preliminary agreement, stated that the Mexican government expected to receive the $1,070,000 from the committee immediately. Lamont phoned Suarez on December 17 to explain the committee's perception of the conditions precedent to the release of these funds. The connection was poor, but the gist of Suarez's protest was clear.

Suarez stated that he had been assured by Rublee that the government would receive the funds promptly, which he had told the president in obtaining his approval of the preliminary agreement. "The president expects to get the money and needs it before January 1, 1936."

Lamont replied that the release of the $1,070,000 to the Mexican government must be approved by the bondholders, who would consider it when they reviewed the "new permanent agreement," still to be negotiated and ratified by the Mexican Congress.

Suarez responded that "it is useless to make an agreement of that nature. It puts me in a very difficult position with the president; perhaps I must resign. This agreement would give Mexico nothing at all. It is only an agreement to agree later."

Lamont said that the committee was prepared to send Rublee back to

Mexico City to negotiate a "new permanent agreement" as soon as possible.

Suarez responded: "If Mr. Rublee can bring something useful to Mexico, I will see him; if not, there's no use in seeing him." Rublee made his plans to leave for Mexico in the new year, and there the matter rested, as bankers and bureaucrats alike turned their attention to the Christmas holidays.

It would be a hard Christmas for many American families: there were still at least ten million workers unemployed, and the relief rolls grew daily as the jobless used up their savings. However, TWL had amassed a fortune during the twenties, and his holdings still generated substantial income. The depression had not subdued his living style or philanthropic instincts. On Christmas Day 1935, President James B. Conant of Harvard announced that Lamont had made a gift of half a million dollars to Harvard to endow a new university professorship in economics, which would kick off Harvard's 300th Anniversary Fund handsomely.

Following the death of his friend Jeremiah Smith, Jr., in 1935, Lamont succeeded him as president of the board of trustees of Phillips Exeter Academy. TWL had been a trustee of his old school since 1917, attending two or three meetings a year at the academy, and Exeter's principal, Dr. Lewis Perry, had become a close friend. By 1935 a new Exeter, thanks largely to the generosity of Perry's friend, philanthropist Edward B. Harkness, had replaced the old. The most important change was the major increase in the number of faculty made possible by the Harkness gift, which enabled classes to be conducted through round-table discussions with a dozen or so boys and a teacher. TWL's friend William B. Thompson donated new buildings to the school, and Lamont contributed an annex to the infirmary.

TWL spoke from time to time to the boys at morning chapel. He viewed the academy as a national high school filled with promising boys from all ranks of American society; Exeter's future seemed bright to the new president of the trustees. But the outstanding memory of more than one student was not Lamont's words but his style—the genial and smooth delivery, the double-breasted Saville Row suits, foulard ties, and polished wing-tipped shoes, in stark contrast to the tweedy attire of the academy teachers seated behind him. The boys were impressed.

A Question of History

On the eve of the Senate Munitions Committee hearings, the Morgan partners and their entourage, some thirty-five persons in all, descended on Washington "like an expeditionary force" reported *Time* magazine, taking over an entire wing of the eighth floor of the Shoreham Hotel. The firm estimated that their wartime files containing millions of documents, mostly related to the purchasing agency operation, would amount to forty truckloads. Many of the records were brought to Washington, and messengers went back and forth each day bringing needed documents to the Washington command post.

The Senate hearings, beginning January 7, 1936, and consuming ten days, started off in an atmosphere of high anticipation by much of the press of juicy revelations of wrongdoing in the testimony to follow. The press tables and public seating area in the Senate Caucus Room were filled with reporters and spectators. Senator Nye, the youthful-looking brown-haired committee chairman, and his colleague Senator Bennett Champ Clark, a war veteran and founder of the American Legion, seemed eager to take on the Morgan partners. The committee counsel, Stephen Raushenbush, had sifted through thousands of Morgan documents in preparation for the examination. The chief witnesses, the senior Morgan partners, were notably more elderly than their interrogators as they took their seats at the witness table. Morgan and Lamont, in dark pinstripe suits, and their counsel, John W. Davis, were sparsely white-haired and well into their sixties.

At the chairman's call to order the hubbub of picture-taking died down and the witnesses were sworn in. "Mr. Morgan," began Senator Nye, "will you kindly state for the record what is your connection with J. P. Morgan & Co.?"

To the growing disenchantment of the press corps, the initial tone of scandal-seeking soon changed to one of historical research. The Morgan partners were glad of the chance to set the record straight, to destroy the myth that they had sought to drag America into the war.

The Morgan firm had at all times complied with the administration's evolving policy on loans to the Allies. In August 1915, Secretary of the Treasury McAdoo wrote to President Wilson urging that the Allies be permitted to float public loans in the U.S. to finance their purchases, which had brought prosperity to American farmers and stimulated industry. "The balance of trade is so largely in our favor and will grow even larger if trade continues that we cannot demand payment in gold without eventually exhausting the gold reserves of our best customers which would ruin their credit and stop their trade with us." Secretary of State Lansing was pressing the same argument with the president. On August 26 President Wilson, reversing his previous policy, agreed that belligerents might float public loans in the U.S., thus permitting the large Anglo-French bond issue and other loans that followed it.

Outstanding American bond issues and bank credit for the Allies when the U.S. went to war in April 1917 had financed about a third of U.S. exports to these nations since the outbreak of war. The bulk of Allied purchases was paid for by British and French gold reserves, export earnings, and the sales of their nationals' securities.

Nowhere in the records was there any indication that the Morgan partners had wanted America to enter the war. J. P. Morgan scoffed at the notion: "Do you suppose that because business was good I wanted my son to go to war? He did, though." Junius S. Morgan had served aboard an American destroyer patrolling the English Channel for German submarines.

Another allegation was put to rest: the firm had not owned or financed any newspapers, which might have been used to spread Allied propaganda. Lamont's purchase of the *New York Evening Post* had not occurred until August 1918, long after the U.S. had declared war on Germany.

Nor was any evidence produced that administration officials were unduly influenced by the Morgan partners. In fact, quite the opposite, said Lamont.

"I do not think that we were entirely personae gratae at the White House, Senator, I am sorry to say," TWL told Senator Nye. To the committee counsel Lamont observed, "Mr. Raushenbush, the administration of Mr. Wilson, I would assume, had a very great regard for the general prosperity of the country, and I think they had . . . a pretty tender regard for the feelings of the southern states that wanted to sell their cotton, and the western states that wanted to sell their wheat, but when it came down to tenderness toward bankers and munitions manufacturers, I have never heard of it."

There was no basis for allegations that J. P. Morgan & Co. had made large profits from its stock holdings in companies that had been awarded contracts to supply the British and French. Of 900 companies receiving contracts, the Morgan firm held stock in only fourteen, whose contracts amounted in total to $350 million. The Morgan holdings were small, for the most part less than 1 percent, and were fully disclosed to the British and French governments. The firm had no stock interest in the two largest American suppliers, DuPont and Bethlehem Steel.

Senator Champ Clark, a Missouri Democrat, was the most aggressive examiner of the Morgan partners. The posture of the large, red-faced solon as he questioned Morgan and Lamont was domineering and accusatory. Clark suspected their activities had led President Wilson to abandon the administration's policy of banning American loans to belligerent nations.

During the summer of 1915, when the pound sterling was slipping on the exchange market under the pressure of heavy British purchases in the U.S., the Morgan bank opened a $50 million sterling stabilization credit for the Bank of England. The credit was steadily depleted, and on August 14 the British instructed Morgan to suspend its buying of sterling. The pound continued to decline, causing growing fear in the business community that Great Britain would have to cut back its high volume of U.S. purchases, and when the bank offered to establish a new $50 million credit to renew the support of sterling, the British agreed. At the same time Morgan partner Harry Davison alerted Treasury Secretary McAdoo about the weakening sterling exchange and the damaging consequences for American exports.

Charged Senator Clark: "I think that when Morgan & Co. stepped out from under and permitted the sterling exchange to flop, pressure was brought to bear on McAdoo" for the administration to permit public loans to the Allies.

J. P. Morgan replied, "It's quite clear to me . . . that the idea is in the minds of the Committee that we brought on the exchange panic in order to bring influence to bear on the government. I want to deny in the most clear manner that I can, that such a thing was ever thought of by us or done by us at any time in any way. That is one of the discreditable actions which is foreign to our history . . . and our traditions, and we never did such a thing in our lives."

Organizing the large syndicates to underwrite and sell the $500 million Anglo-French bond issue in 1915 had been a tremendous undertaking, especially "in educating the public," a phrase that appeared often in the Morgan cable files and piqued Senator Clark's interest. Lamont explained that American investors had not been familiar with foreign loans and aware of "the goodness of the obligations of those two foreign governments." They also had to convince investors of the loan's value to the American economy. "It was a big job, a terrific job, and we did everything, very naturally, within the traditions of our house, to make it a success." The bank had even urged American munitions manufacturers to buy the bonds.

Senator Clark: "In the parlance of the Street you 'put the heat on' these people so as to put over the loan."

Lamont: "We don't use that parlance in the Street. . . . We did not, as you have suggested, threaten anybody. That is not our way of doing business. We asked the munitions makers to subscribe, and I think they took something like $88 million of the loan."

J. P. Morgan at age sixty-nine was slowing down. He was not articulate or adroit in many of his responses to questions and made little effort to recall events in detail. Lamont and George Whitney carried the brunt of the testimony in describing the firm's wartime activities, with Whitney usually marshaling the historical data called for. One morning Lamont bore the burden of the examination so completely that Morgan answered only a single question in four hours. Finally committee counsel Raushenbush asked, "I hope you don't feel we are neglecting you, Mr. Morgan?" "Not at all, not at all," replied the aging banker with a chuckle. "Talk to Mr. Lamont."

However, Morgan's sincerity, lack of guile, and amiability served him well in winning the trust and respect of the senators and press. If the integrity of his house seemed to be questioned, he was quick to defend it in tones of forceful and righteous indignation. At other times he showed flashes of humor, as when Lamont misquoted the Bible in referring to money as "the root of all evil." Morgan with a pleased grin corrected his chief partner: "The Bible doesn't say 'money.' It says, 'The love of money is the root of all evil.'" And when the hearings finally ended, there was J. P. Morgan shaking hands all around and saying that he had had "a fine time" and "would not have missed this investigation for the world."

On January 13, 1936, the *Detroit News* ran a story headlined "Show Stolen by Lamont, House of Morgan Partner Silences Big Guns." The article stated that the central figure of the Senate investigation into the wartime activities of J. P. Morgan & Co. was neither North Dakota's publicized prosecutor, Senator Gerald P. Nye, nor the famous banker whose name lent color and headlines to the hearings, J. Pierpont Morgan.

It is, rather, a lithe, urbane, immaculate chap 65 summers young named Thomas W. Lamont, who before the Senate munitions committee is through with him—and before he is through with it—will without much doubt have earned him the name of the nation's leading exponent of that ancient quotation: A gentle answer turneth away wrath.

Lamont is the house of Morgan's shock absorber in this verbal battle of the huge, marble-pillared Senate caucus room. He has been accused of being the "brains" of that organization, but of course could not claim any such monopoly. As the only living partner of the firm who was active during the war, except Morgan himself, however, it has been evident from the start that his facility at repartee is counted on as the ace arrow in the bankers' quiver, whenever the going gets rough and the questions painfully piercing.

Lamont spoke in "a friendly soothing tone." If forced to concede a point—"Why of course, of course, Mr. Raushenbush"—he treated it as "the merest trifle." He was also quick to protest, again in his most urbane manner, when the committee drew some conclusion from the testimony that he felt was unwarranted: "I cannot find it anywhere in the cablegram. It is hardly fair to try to read inferences into what men now dead were saying and thinking about twenty years ago."

As the Senate investigation rambled on without startling disclosures, the press and public grew bored. Finally at a morning session near the end, J. P. Morgan quietly closed his eyes and dozed off, to many a symbolic sign of what the hearings had become.

The Nye Committee hearings ended in an atmosphere of unexpected cordiality between the senatorial examiners and the Morgan partners, in sharp contrast to the chilly beginnings. Senator Nye even observed at the hearings' close, "Nothing in its wartime operations reflected discredit on the Morgan firm."

Dozens of newspapers across the country, from the *Portland Press Herald* of Maine to the *Portland Journal* of Oregon, praised the Morgan partners for their performance before the committee. Said a *New York Herald Tribune* editorial of February 7:

> It is nearly everywhere agreed that the firm of J. P. Morgan & Co. has seldom appeared to a better advantage than in the white light of publicity trained upon it by Senator Nye and his colleagues.

The *New York Daily News,* no friend of bankers and big business, advised its 1 million readers:

> What does Senator Nye think he has proved by digging up all these old facts once more and parading them across the witness stand? . . . It is not a fact that the big bankers got us into the war—any more than it is a fact that all wars are fought for profits . . . We were not tricked out of a sweet dream of peace to go over and fight to make Europe safe for the Morgan loans. The newspapers, for instance, did far more to inflame public sentiment to war heat than the bankers did . . . Let's give the devil his due. Morgan and the rest of the bankers did not get us into that war. And Nye's intimation that they did so is unfair, unhistorical and untrue.

There was still a little mopping up to be done. Rose M. Stein, a Nye Committee staff member, had just completed a book advancing the original Nye thesis of Morgan's war mongering. Advance proofs of *M-Day*, sent to the *Saturday Review*, were forwarded by Canby to Lamont for his advice on an appropriate reviewer. Lamont expressed his low opinion of the book to the publisher, Harcourt Brace & Co., and suggested to Canby that Charles Seymour, as author of a book and articles on American neutrality during the war, would be a good reviewer. As TWL and Canby expected, Seymour denounced *M-Day* as historically unimportant, "discursive and misleading." The book, in any case, sold few copies.

A Royal Affair

The Lamonts were on the move again. For their last Bermuda holiday they had rented a spacious house on the harbor near Tucker Town, a far more peaceful setting than a big hotel for them and their six houseguests. No more late-evening dining and dancing and noisy hotel guests for Florence, and Tom, in his sixties, now agreed. In March 1936 they chose the Mid-Ocean Club in Bermuda, which had a subdued British club atmosphere and a beautiful and challenging seaside golf course. Lots of golf, bridge, and early to bed were the order of the day for hosts and guests.

On May 29 the Lamonts sailed for France—four days in Paris and then on to London at that time of year when the London season was in full swing and the English countryside was at its loveliest. The Astors invited them to Cliveden for the weekend, and TWL wrote his children, "They have settled down to a really quiet life, and there were only forty-six people for lunch yesterday."

"Dearest Nancy," as Tom addressed her in his letters, presided as usual over the splendid house party. In his inimitable style TWL once wrote Lady Astor, "Keep young, keep beautiful, as you always do and are." Flowery sentiment and flattery came naturally to Lamont in addressing attractive ladies, but Nancy Astor did indeed have a special allure for him. He told Giovanni Fummi, his Italian colleague and friend, "Nancy (A.) is an amusing person, the kindest hearted and best friend in the world."

Lady Astor entertained in the grand manner—at tea under a pavilion on the broad south terrace or before the huge stone fireplace in the main hall, and at sumptuous lunches and dinners served by footmen in tailcoats and white ties to several dozen guests in the spectacular eighteenth-century rococo paneled dining room. The French chef was excellent, the wine cellar well stocked, and the conversation stimulating and witty as politicians, bankers, and pundits discussed the great issues of the day.

The next day Lady Sibyl Colefax, one of London society's leading hostesses, invited the Lamonts to lunch. Other guests included Harold Nicholson, now a Labor Member to Parliament; Neville Chamberlain, the Chancellor of the Exchequer; and Winston Churchill, Conservative, MP, now especially reviled and admired for his lonely advocacy of rearming Britain. He led the conversation. When TWL raised the subject of the lingering war debt problem, Churchill argued that the American war loans had supported the British army fighting at the front. If the British had been forced to slacken their vigorous military operations, the American soldiers, when they arrived in France months later, would have suffered far greater casualties. Lamont knew this was so, but suggested that part of the American loans had gone to support the domestic economy of Great Britain. The British should at least pay something to preserve good relations with the U.S., said TWL.

June 1936 was a fraught time, what with Hitler's occupation of the Rhineland, Mussolini's invasion of Ethiopia, and the increasingly apparent failure of the League of Nations, but in London, the royal romance between King Edward VIII and Mrs. Simpson was the main topic of conversation in the upper strata of government and society. Tom wrote his daughter, "London is gossiping about nothing else." The former Prince of Wales, who had become king at the death of his father, George V, in January, had fallen in love with a charming, currently married, and once divorced American, Mrs. Wallis Warfield Simpson, an affair that was bound to provoke public censure as it became more widely known.

On June 10, Sibyl Colefax gave an elegant dinner party—for the Lamonts to meet the King, she told Florence. Argyll House was bathed in candlelight as the guests arrived. The King came with Mrs. Simpson; Mr. Simpson was said to be out of town. TWL, who had met Mrs. Simpson before, told her how beautiful she was looking. "Whereupon she loosened up and told me all about the King. How wonderful he was, etc.," Lamont wrote Eleanor. He also reported on the exquisite jewelry Mrs. Simpson was wearing, given to her by the King, he was told. "Square cut stones, a magnificent ring, a clip at her breast, shaped like a fan—the outer spokes rubies and the inner ones diamonds, and gorgeous earrings of the same." The compliment TWL had paid the King's companion was sincere. Mrs. Simpson, with her jet black hair, pale complexion, lovely evening gown, and dazzling jewels, was a stunning woman. The King was smitten by her, and he showed it.

"When the ladies curtsied their way out after dinner, the King beckoned me to come over and sit by him," TWL wrote. "We talked for twenty minutes, and he was most sensible. Terribly well-bred, always said the right thing."

When the ladies rejoined the men, Arthur Rubinstein played selections from Chopin. Around 12:30, as Rubinstein prepared to start another piece, the King rose and declared, "We enjoyed that very much, Mr. Rubinstein" and started his rounds of "goodnights." But other guests had drifted in, including the Winston Churchills and Noel Coward, who soon took over the piano and began playing, and singing some of his popular songs, such as "Mad Dogs and Englishmen" and "Don't Let Your Daughter Go on the Stage." The King, enjoying himself, stayed on another hour or so, as did the other guests, who couldn't leave before him according to royal protocol. Florence reported she had "a swell time" although she didn't get to bed until 3 a.m.

South African Safari

Lamont now had ample time for the excursions he relished; there was no need for him to involve himself in the routine banking business of his office, ably conducted by younger men. On June 12 the stalwart voyagers embarked on the S.S. *Stirling Castle* from Southampton, bound for Cape Town, South Africa. The Lamonts looked forward to touring a new part of the world and visiting their old friend Jan Christiaan Smuts. The former prime minister had remained a national leader—minister of justice and second in authority to Prime Minister James Hertzog. A longtime advocate of the League of Nations, Smuts was recognized worldwide as a statesman of vision.

Following Smuts's stay with the Lamonts in New York in 1930, he and Florence had struck up a steady correspondence, exchanging a dozen or so letters each year. Smuts sometimes perceived life differently from Florence. When she wrote him of a planned art tour of Italy, the former Afrikaner general in the Boer War and British commander in the 1917 German East Africa campaign replied, "When I think of that country, the thought of Hannibal and his glorious march through it comes before my mind's eye. You see cathedrals and I see battlefields in the haze of the past." However, as their correspondence shows, Smuts and Florence had in common a strong bent for philosophical inquiry. "I want an answer," he once wrote her, "to the insistent question: How has value become a reality?"

The ocean voyage was calm and unexciting. Tom remarked on the dullness of the ship's company: "Mostly colonials returning home . . . They are virtuous and other things like that. . . . That sounds snobbish, but you know what I mean. Not a soul on board you have a yen ever to see again," he wrote his children. However, Tom and Florence enjoyed their invited traveling companions, New York friends Mr. and Mrs. Linzee Blagden. Dorothy Blagden was a great mimic, although not so good as her sister, the Lamonts' friend monologist Ruth Draper, Tom reported. Once again Metcalfe and Josephine were in attendance.

The Lamonts read books on South Africa, including a new biography of Smuts, and entered vigorously into the ship's activities. Florence and her assigned partner won the bridge tournament. He was "a most unattractive gentleman," she wrote, "who wore a soiled white linen suit, missing a button, and no collar." He was also a crack bridge player. Florence went to the fancy dress ball as a nun, a costume assembled from sheets and napkins with the help of Josephine. Tom, who might have turned his collar to become a simple priest, resumed his favorite role of a cardinal at the costume party.

Steaming through the "Cape swell" sixteen days later, the travelers sighted Table Mountain, the magnificent highland overlooking two oceans and the Cape of Good Hope. Disembarking at Cape Town, the party went directly by train to Doornkloof, the Smuts' family home situated on the high veldt at the town of Irene on the main line between Johannesburg and Pretoria. The corrugated-tin-roofed farmhouse was originally built as a British officers' club during the Boer War and remodeled later by General Smuts. Surrounded and shaded by tall trees, it overlooked rolling farmlands and a green valley crossed by a small stream. The sitting rooms were lined with the general's books.

The Smutses enjoyed a peaceful and simple life at Doornkloof. Mrs. Smuts drew two baths for her guests on their arrival, the limit of the hot water tank. Florence described Sybella, or "Isie," Smuts as "a terribly bright and well-educated woman, and a typical Dutch haus-frau. She calls the General 'Papa' or 'Oe Baas' (Old Boss) and trots around the house superintending everything."

The toilet facilities consisted of one outdoor wooden privy. "At times there is quite a run on the bank," the eminent financier wrote home.

"If you go out at night be careful of that old bull Koodoo," warned Mrs. Smuts, referring to one of the wild cattle that sometimes roamed close to the house. "He might put his horns into you."

"Nothing of the kind, Mama," replied the general. "He never butts you badly."

In planning an excursion to Kruger National Park with the Lamonts, General Smuts inquired whether his wife had packed plenty of iodine and carbolic acid. "What are they for?" asked Florence.

"For tick bites," answered the general. "They bore under your skin to lay their eggs, and you have to put on the oil to make them come out."

"Suppose they don't come?" asked Florence.

"Oh well, then you get tick fever, but you always get them out," replied Smuts. "In the old days they dug them out with a knife, but now the oil does it."

Tom did not think that the Smutses were trying to alarm their tender-foot guests. They were just conversing naturally, he told Florence.

During their stay at Doornkloof the party toured Pretoria, Johannesburg, and the Rand gold-mining district. They opted against descending the mile-deep mine shaft, but inspected the refinery and native compound, where the popular general was cheered by 4,000 native mine workers.

After several days at the farm General Smuts led his friends on a motor tour of Kruger National Park, the world-famous game sanctuary in the northeast Transvaal, where lions, elephants, and other wild animals roamed freely over a vast area of forest and grasslands. In his letters Lamont spoke of viewing "the Animal Kingdom," from which, he observed, Noah must have drawn the bulk of passengers for his ark. Four cars and a truck carried the party and their tents and other camping gear. At night around the campfire under a big yellow African moon, the general told tales of his war adventures while his son-in-law contributed stories of his exploits as a big-game hunter, yarns enhanced by a chorus of African night sounds, including the scattered roar of lions which seemed startingly close to the tourists.

They also discussed current political issues, especially South Africa's unique and complex problem in race relations then referred to as the "native question." The Lamonts agreed with Smuts's relatively—compared to most of his white countrymen—enlightened views on race relations in South Africa. In their own country they deplored the segregated facilities and flagrant civil rights violations of the American South, although they, like most white Northerners, even liberal ones, tended to overlook the widespread job discrimination and other forms of racial bias practiced closer to home.

The next weekend the Lamonts stayed at the general's other farm deep in the veldt about seventy miles from Pretoria. The Lamonts were exhilarated by the beauty and serenity of their surroundings—golden brown grasslands and distant mountain ranges—and by the sparkling climate—brilliant sunshine in cloudless blue skies and the dry, pure air of the arid winter months.

Tom wrote his children:

> You walk out at night for a final deep breath under the stars—the Southern Cross now hanging high in the sky and the Milky Way so clear that it seems like a belt of diamond dust, clear across the heaven from one horizon to the other. You see all this infinity of worlds, and then think back on our own little crust of a globe, where men are fighting furiously over a few patches of earth.
>
> Your mother has quite changed her nature on this trip. She drinks strong coffee twice a day, strong tea another time or two, and tosses off a bottle of lager beer before dinner (the only cocktails they have).

Next the Lamonts and the Smutses took a chartered Junkers monoplane to Victoria Falls on the Zambezi River about 650 miles to the north. The party of fifteen included Smuts children and grandchildren, the Blagdens, and Metcalfe and Josephine. Most of the passengers had not flown before, and Tom and Florence had been only on short sightseeing flights. The party first stopped at Fort Victoria in Southern Rhodesia, where they visited the historic Zimbabwe ruins, the stone remains of the old tribal capital and trading post. They next flew to Livingstone, where Sir Hubert Young, the governor of Northern Rhodesia, gave a dinner and tea party for his distinguished visitors. The view from the air of the great falls, with their long cliffs of cascading water, rising clouds of mist, and rainbows arching the turbulence, was spectacular.

At Swartkop Airport back in Pretoria, the Lamonts and Smutses bid each other farewell. Tom wrote in his journal of the trip:

"I have not tried to describe General Smuts and his personality. But he is certainly one of the great ones of the earth—the most many-facetted mind I have come in contact with. On the farm, on our long motor trips, and around the fire in the evening he was full of entertainment—politics, war, love, art, religion, botany, geology, wild game, archaeology, history—all were grist for his hopper. . . . He was more delightful with little children than you can imagine—they all simply adored him, and he would play with them for hours on end.

Alert bankers visiting South Africa arranged to call on Sir Ernest Oppenheimer. South Africa was the world's leading producer of gold and diamonds, and Sir Ernest's Anglo-American and De Beers companies dominated the mining of these minerals. The Lamonts were the house-guests of the Oppenheimers at their magnificent villa on the heights outside Johannesburg, and their hosts honored them with two dinner parties. Not unexpectedly, Lady Oppenheimer's diamonds were out-standing. One morning TWL visited the offices of Anglo-American, in which Morgan Grenfell had a minor interest, to draw up a list of high-grade mining investments in Africa recommended by Sir Ernest and his colleagues. Sir Ernest then took TWL to the Rand Club for drinks at what was said to be the longest bar in the world.

The Lamonts spent four days in Cape Town before sailing for home. Friends of the Smutses and the local bankers gave them a cordial welcome and guided their sightseeing. From the top of Table Mountain they viewed the oceans, Cape, and interior mountain ranges, and TWL wrote in his journal: "The whole combination of ocean, sky, mountain, and sunlight is ravishing, and you can't but feel brooding over it the spirit of Cecil Rhodes," who used to go there "with death stealing upon him, and sit and look out over the oceans—the end of his great career at hand, with work undone and new empires still uncreated—despite all that he had done. Almost his last words were, 'So little done, so much to do!' "

The newspapers in Johannesburg and Cape Town were quite insistent for interviews—no Morgan partner had ever visited South Africa be-fore—and Lamont was happy to oblige. He rhapsodized about the beauty of the country and noted the strength of the nation's economy and public finances based on the richness of its gold deposits and bullion exports, for which foreign demand was assured.

TWL believed in a full schedule. On his final day in Cape Town he played nine holes of golf with the Barclay's Bank manager, did some shopping, visited a museum of native artifacts, lunched at Barclay's with the leading local bankers, and boarded the *Carnarvon Castle* at 3 p.m.

The Lamonts sailed from Cape Town on July 24, and on the seventeen-day voyage to Southampton Tom wrote his journal of the trip and letters to his children. The economic importance of gold mining, whose center was Johannesburg, was an economic fact of life. Cape Town was interesting, charming, and beautiful. But the true heart of the country was something else, Lamont wrote.

> The real South Africa is away up north where the wild animals still roam and the high veldt lures you. . . . I could see why General Smuts and the old Boers who had trekked up from the Cape to get away from the pushing English . . . loved the veldt. The freedom of it, its warmth and vitality, and its variety too, with mountains as rugged as the Dolomites to mark its contours.

Florence had a wonderful time. She described the flight "over glorious mountains with the veldt like a great tawny sea beneath us." She had often written home expressing her gratitude and wonder in viewing God's handiwork in her travels. South Africa was "beautiful beyond words."

The Senate Summons Again

After a short stay in London, the Lamonts were homeward bound. The day after the *Bremen* docked in New York, TWL invited a group of financial reporters to his office. The stock market sell-off the day of his arrival was attributed mainly to the fears of Americans in mid-summer, 1936 over a renewal of hostilities in Europe. One rumor had it that Hitler would soon launch an attack against Danzig. Civil war had broken out in Spain. The rightist Nationalist forces under General Francisco Franco were already occupying growing portions of the country in their drive to overthrow the popular front government, and Franco had appealed to Mussolini and Hitler for aircraft and troops. Other returning travelers had sensed that war was in the air. Lamont disagreed and undertook to calm the war jitters.

He told the reporters that there was more war alarm in America than in Europe: "95% of the people do not want to fight. . . . The men who make the destinies of Europe will go very slowly in dragging their unwilling peoples into major combat. . . . I am not expecting a world war."

"Germany is determined to keep away from serious trouble with Great Britain and France," and Italy and Great Britain were moving to renew their traditional friendly relations. "Tranquillity in Europe is still far off, but I believe that it will beat out the coming of any great war," Lamont told the press.

That evening Tom and Florence left the city for North Haven. The stock market was up the next day, and Lamont's statement discounting the prospects of general war in Europe had reassured investors, reported the *New York Journal*.

The Lamonts had been abroad in July when their North Haven neighbors had welcomed a famous visitor to the island. President Roosevelt, cruising off the Maine coast, had steamed into Pulpit Harbor in the presidential yacht, leaving a flotilla of naval escorts hovering in the bay. The Roosevelt sons borrowed gin and tennis rackets from the Lamonts in residence, and several Lamont parents and children were invited on board the *Potomac* to shake hands with the president. The North Haven high school band serenaded the nation's chief executive from the banks of the harbor, and a local fisherman presented him with a supply of fresh lobsters from the bay.

Most Maine residents, who had given their president a warm and respectful greeting up and down the coast, didn't vote for him in the November 1936 presidential election. It made no difference. FDR overwhelmed Kansas Governor Alfred M. Landon, the Republican candidate supported by TWL, losing only the states of Maine and Vermont.

In early December, Walter and Faye Lippmann joined Tom and Florence at the Yeamans Hall cottage, and the old companions had a cheerful time playing golf and reading aloud the latest Agatha Christie murder mystery. Time had eroded the bitterness and healed the wounded pride of three years earlier.

They also gossiped about the royal love affair coming to a dramatic climax in London after days of mounting speculation and tension. On December 11 King Edward VIII announced that he would renounce the throne for the woman he loved. His stunning message fleetingly divided the world between the defenders of duty and romance, and there was soon to be an unexpected echo nearer home. Married couples can often hide their personal tensions even from good friends, and Tom and Florence had no inkling that Walter and Faye's marriage was shaky. During 1937, Walter fell in love with another woman, Helen Armstrong, the wife of a close friend. A year after the happy get-together at Yeamans Hall, the Lippmanns were divorced.

Tom advised Faye in securing a large financial settlement from Walter and persuaded Lippmann to consent to her requests. Walter's new romance was costly to him in other ways: a number of acquaintances felt he had acted poorly in the affair. He moved to Washington, and while he and Lamont continued to correspond about issues of the day, the former intimacy in their personal relations was over. When the Armstrong divorce was finalized, it was Walter Lippmann's turn to marry the woman he loved, and he did.

TWL's February holiday in 1937 at the Mid-Ocean Club in Bermuda was abruptly interrupted by a summons to appear at still another Senate inquiry in Washington: the Subcommittee on Railroads of the Senate Committee on Interstate Commerce was examining the financial downfall of the Van Sweringen railroad empire. Although half a dozen investigators had been poring over the Morgan files on the subject for close to a year, the committee staff claimed that they had not been given full access to all the relevant documents. Lamont denied the allegation and said that the bank would continue to cooperate fully in the investigation. This rite dealt with, the examination, led by Senator Burton K. Wheeler of Montana, progressed in relatively friendly fashion.

Senator Wheeler and his committee had already scathingly interrogated the Van Sweringen brothers, both of whom had since died. The current investigation focused on the downhill slide of the Van Sweringen railroads after 1930, when a Morgan-led bank syndicate had lent the brothers $39.5 million in an unsuccessful attempt to keep them afloat.

These were not exciting disclosures. The bankers had worked closely with the Van Sweringens in an attempt to rescue a desperate situation. They had failed and, it will be recalled, sold their Alleghany stock collateral at a bargain basement price. Missouri Pacific and Alleghany bond issues were in default, and the Alleghany common stock, initially placed by Morgan at $20 a share, was now quoted at $5.

Lamont summed up the dismal financial impact on J. P. Morgan & Co. of the firm's long relationship with the Van Sweringens. Morgan had led syndicates selling $528 million of Van Sweringen railroad securities, resulting in a profit to the bank of $8,326,000; Morgan's loan losses amounted to $9,621,000, resulting in a net deficit for the firm of $1,295,000. The Van Sweringen–Alleghany relationship had been convincingly calamitous for the bank.

Senator Wheeler did not play the role of the tough and relentless prosecutor this time. In fact, his heart was not really in the effort. He was far more interested in spearheading the opposition to FDR's proposal to "pack" the Supreme Court. He recessed the hearings after several days on March 6.

The Lamont charm was at work again. He said he thought that Senator Wheeler had a "great sense of humor," and the senator returned the compliment. The committee investigators stated that Mr. Lamont was "the pleasantest witness" they had encountered during the hearings.

Sometimes Lamont chose not to be charming. Robert R. Young, a diminutive and daring Texas businessman, and his allies had purchased the controlling interest in the Alleghany Corporation. In testimony before the Wheeler committee, Young had made clear that Alleghany would not be dominated by the Wall Street bankers: "We are absolutely independent." New bond issues for the Alleghany railroads would be awarded to investment bankers through competitive bidding, a policy announcement that did not please Morgan Stanley or J. P. Morgan & Co.

Lamont immediately summoned Young to lunch at 23 Wall Street, and after ducking the engagement with one excuse or another, Young reluctantly appeared. According to Young's version of the meeting, he said he intended to keep the railroads' bankers informed of his plans. TWL replied that Young didn't understand: "I want not only to be informed, but I want to help guide you in your policies." Young was shaken by the confrontation. "He literally put me on the carpet, spanked me, and raked me over the coals," Young reported.

Mussolini's Olive Branch

On April 3, 1937, the Lamonts sailed for Italy to visit their friends Chester Aldrich and his sister Amey; Aldrich, a prominent architect, was director of the American Academy in Rome. He was a marvelous tour guide, taking his guests on delightful picnic outings to ancient churches, monasteries, and Etruscan tombs. He even arranged a close-up view from high scaffolding of the Michelangelo frescoes on the ceiling of the Sistine Chapel in the Vatican. "I shall always feel as if Noah, Isaiah, and the Delphi Sibyl were my intimate friends," wrote Florence, referring to the paintings under which she had lain flat on her back, fifty feet above the ground, gazing upward.

The high point of the visit for TWL was a half hour meeting with Mussolini on April 16, arranged at the Duce's initiative through the Bank of Italy. Lamont, who had been accompanied to the interview by Giovanni Fummi, the Morgan representative in Rome, wrote a memorandum of his talk with the Duce.

After a formal greeting the Duce spoke in effect as follows:

Duce: We have made a great conquest in Africa—that is finished now—I am for Peace, I am for World Peace—I am very strong for Peace. I need Peace. We are satisfied.

TWL: I believe you, Excellency, when you say that; I know it must be so, but the impression in America is very different. There you are pictured as a man who wants war rather than peace; that impression should be corrected. It is very important that in America your real attitude should be understood.

Duce: I tell you that I am very strong for peace. I must have peace. The world must have peace. I am strong for co-operation. I want friendship with Great Britain. We are friends with Germany, America, Great Britain, and with France. (The Duce's expression was not so strong when he mentioned France.)

TWL: I have no doubt of everything you say, Excellency, but I believe it very necessary for you to say such things publicly, and more than once. May I be frank with you? The American world, I repeat, has a distinctly different impression from the one you state to me. I believe that one of the most important things to be done in the world today is for you to make a speech making clear your sentiments of co-operation for world peace. You cannot emphasize them too much or say them too often.

The Duce said he was also for economic cooperation with other countries, and Lamont replied that the U.S. administration firmly believed that freer trade and economic stability were the key to world peace. TWL said that before leaving for Europe he had told Secretary of State Hull that American businessmen felt the same way, and he intended to emphasize this message in his talks with European men of affairs.

Duce: As for myself I repeat again that I am co-operative in economic measures that will assist peace.

TWL: From what you say, Excellency, it is clear to me that now you have made your achievement, what you desire most for your own people is to consolidate your position, to stabilize it. That means economic co-operation with the other leading countries of the world. . . .

Duce: I am doing everything I can to increase the friendship with Great Britain, everything, but Great Britain is always suspicious of what we say or do, and attributes wrong reasons to our speech and actions.

TWL: It pleases me immensely to have you say you are doing all you can to increase the friendship with England. In London last July I heard important expressions along the same line. It happened that when I dined there with the then King Edward VIII, he said to me, "Now that sanctions are to be ended we must get back to the basis of our traditional friendship with Italy." Mr. Neville Chamberlain, the Chancellor of the Exchequer, who is to succeed Mr. Stanley Baldwin as Prime Minister, voiced to me the same sentiments.

Duce: Oh yes, I know that Mr. Neville Chamberlain is well disposed towards us. . . . In my speeches to which you have alluded I must have in mind the domestic situation and the martial spirit of the Italians, but that does not affect my strong attitude towards peace.

Lamont said that he had considered giving Fummi a memorandum, for him to use as he saw fit, regarding Italy's image in the eyes of the world and Mussolini's attitudes toward international peace and economic cooperation.

Duce: Ah yes, I am very grateful for your counsel, and I should be very glad indeed to have you do this; and do not hesitate to advise me direct in regard to these matters. One of my mottoes is "advice from everyone, collaboration by many, decision and responsibility by a few." (T. W. L. and G. F. congratulated him on this formula.)

TWL observed that Italians and Americans had several qualities in common—industry, imagination, and capacity for thrift—and noted the improvements he had observed in Rome since his 1930 visit, including the modern new tuberculosis sanatorium.

I said to the Duce that . . . I felt I could repeat what I had frequently said to my American friends: "We spend much too much time gazing at what the Romans were doing in 100 A.D., and not enough time in looking at what the Romans are doing in 1937 A.D." The Duce smiled pleasantly, and alluded to what the Government is doing in connection with tourist facilities—accommodation in hotels for tourists etc.

I reminded the Duce that while there were many American tourists in Italy just now, the number could be greatly increased . . . with a changed public attitude towards Italy.

The Duce then rose to indicate that the audience was finished, and as we walked out I said to him, "Do not take offense, Excellency, when I tell you that when I was sailing from America some friends asked me whether I was not afraid of going to Italy." When I asked, "Why?" . . . they replied, "Oh, because a war might start . . . or some trouble of that kind." I answered "There is no chance" . . . and continued: "The American people, Excellency, have unbounded admiration for the marvellous achievements you have accomplished for Italy since 1922, unbounded admiration for these great material developments, but as regards yourself, Excellency" (and I smiled) "they are really afraid of you." The Duce smiled in reply, and said that this impression must be corrected, or words to that effect.

In a letter to TSL for circulation to his partners, Lamont summed up his interview with Mussolini:

> He took it all very cordially and said it was hard for him to get an objective opinion, that he was grateful to me because he knew I had been a true friend of Italy.

Mussolini had dispatched hundreds of aircraft, a large supply of arms, and at least 50,000 troops to Spain to join Franco's forces in their drive to overthrow the Loyalist government, a topic TWL had not brought up with the Duce. "You will ask why I did not throw Spain at his head." Spain was "a sore subject," said TWL, and it was unnecessary to raise it. Mussolini knew he had to find a way to get out of Spain.

TWL had informed American ambassador William Phillips about his meeting with the Duce, and he was "simply delighted, made much more of the matter than it deserved."

"I had no desire to see Mussolini, but as he actually sent for me I could not, without discourtesy, decline to see him," explained Lamont.

Mussolini was viewed with repugnance in the West after years of Fascist repression, the bloody conquest of Ethiopia, military support for Franco, and the formation of the Rome-Berlin Axis to collaborate with Hitler. Bond issues for Italy had been out of the question for years, a full decade in the Morgan bank's case. In 1937 TWL clearly was concerned about how others might perceive his willingness to meet the brutal dictator he had once admired for making the trains run on time. But simply berating Mussolini was counterproductive, he felt, and, as Lamont had told his son, "I would talk to any dictator in Europe or gangster in America if I thought it would help."

Back in his hotel in Rome, Lamont drafted a memorandum to Fummi elaborating on his ideas to help Italy present itself to "enlighten American and British opinion." Visitors should study modern Italy—its public works, reclamation projects, and social programs to appreciate how "the Italian people are committed to the pursuits of peace and prosperity." It was not the first time TWL had applied his own spin to shape public opinion.

Lamont believed that the subjugation of Ethiopia was an outrage, but nevertheless in 1937 it was a fait accompli. As he wrote Nancy Astor in June, the dictators hadn't changed their spots, but "raging at them will do no good, and if there is a possibility of methods of appeasement, these are our only chance." It was high time for England and Italy to renew their traditional friendly relations in the interest of keeping the peace in Europe.

TWL still relished the intriguing role of behind-the-scenes peacemaker: He thought that his image-building suggestion to the Duce might enhance Mussolini's trust in his counsel on foreign relations and that a last-ditch effort to wean Mussolini away from the military bond with Hitler and into the Western camp might bear fruit. But touching up the dictator's bloody portrait was a useless and even deceptive exercise if the Duce's actions did not match his declarations of peaceful intent.

An After-Dinner Message

After a week in Paris, Tom and Florence crossed the Channel to their Hyde Park Hotel headquarters to join in the celebration of the coronation of George VI. J. P. Morgan, as head of the firm and a great friend to England, had been invited to the ceremony itself in Westminster Abbey, but a minor heart attack kept him from attending. Tom watched the coronation parade with his friends from two windows in the Canadian National Railway offices on Cockspur Street, which he had rented for the occasion. On his return voyage to New York, Lamont worked hard on a speech he was scheduled to give on the evening of his May 20 arrival. The occasion was a large dinner at the Waldorf-Astoria commemorating the tenth anniversary of Charles Lindbergh's historic transatlantic solo flight. Colonel Lindbergh, unmercifully hounded by the American press since the kidnapping of his son, was living with his family in England, but a host of the popular flyer's admirers were present or listening in across the country to the radio broadcast of TWL's address.

Honoring Lindbergh's flight, which showed how the world had shrunk through expanded communications, led Lamont to expound on one of his favorite themes. He pointed to

> "an alarming increase in that intense nationalism that has spelled economic animosity among the nations, in the raising of those Chinese walls of tariffs and quotas that block international trade to a point where in some countries the standard of living may be reduced so far that men may grow desperate and, regardless of consequences, start to fight before they will starve. . . .
>
> With all our good will and determination to avoid war, even as resourceful and powerful a nation as America is likely to become involved in any great conflict that breaks out unless it plays its full part in building up international good will. If a conflagration breaks out on the street where I live, I shall not keep my house free from fire by slamming my shutters and running down cellar. To avoid trouble I must join in advance in helping construct the fire apparatus that will keep the conflagration from getting under way.

TWL's advocacy of lower trade barriers was right in line with administration policy, spearheaded by Secretary of State Hull. The Reciprocal Trade Agreements Act, first passed in 1934, had already scaled down some of the high Smoot-Hawley tariffs of 1930.

While TWL's Lindbergh speech was well received, he garnered publicity of a different sort shortly afterward. On June 24, Internal Revenue Commissioner Guy T. Helvering presented to the Congressional Joint Committee on Tax Evasion and Avoidance a list of sixty-seven taxpayers who had transferred their personal investment assets to incorporated holding companies, thereby substantially reducing their income taxes. Lamont was listed along with Andrew W. Mellon, the former Secretary of the Treasury, assorted du Ponts, Alfred P. Sloan of General Motors, William S. Paley of the Columbia Broadcasting System, and other leading financiers and businessmen. It was reported that in 1936 Lamont's holding company, the Beech Corporation, received income of $757,174 and paid taxes of $22,107. Florence's considerably smaller holding company served the same purpose. The commissioner admitted that the use of personal holding companies was perfectly legal but illustrated the need to plug "loopholes" with new tax legislation. Newspapers highlighted the story, and New Deal politicians from FDR on down were quick to condemn the practice, which exacerbated the increasingly bitter feelings between businessmen and the administration. Jack Morgan's thoughtless remark to reporters in June had further fanned the flames: "Congress should know how to levy taxes. . . . If stupid mistakes are made, it is up to Congress to rectify them and not for us taxpayers to do so." It was an extraordinary and embarrassing political gaffe.

Nor was TWL pleased with a new book, *America's Sixty Families* by hyperbolic Ferdinand Lundberg. Lundberg first described Lamont as "the brains of J. P. Morgan" and mentor of presidents Wilson and Hoover, who "has exercised more power for twenty years in the western hemisphere, has put into effect more final decisions from which there has been no appeal, than any other person. . . . Lamont, in short, has been the First Consul de facto in the invisible Directory of postwar high finance and politics, a man consulted by presidents, prime ministers, governors of central banks, the directing intelligence behind the Dawes and Young Plans. Lamont is Protean; he is a diplomat, an editor, a writer, a publisher, a politician, a statesman—an international presence as well as a financier."

Lundberg also accused Lamont of wielding vaguely sinister power through the Morgan bank and TWL's own far-reaching network of newspaper and literary connections. *America's Sixty Families* was inarguably more sensational than scholarly, but it was true that for years Lamont as a private citizen had enjoyed extraordinary access to the media and world leaders.

George Whitney now directed Morgan's daily operations, and business was slow at the office, dampened by the dull economy at home and abroad and political tensions overseas. On June 30 the Lamonts ventured forth again, bound for the Scottish Highlands, where TWL had rented Rossdhu, the ancestral home and estate of Sir Ian Colquhoun on the western shore of Loch Lomond. They looked forward to receiving a stream of children, grandchildren, and other houseguests to keep them company over the next two months.

According to Florence, "We all hate it here." It rained steadily, and she didn't get along with the cook, who drank and ran up suspiciously exorbitant grocery bills. She claimed she wanted to go home but couldn't, because the Lamonts had given Sky Farm to the Davison family for the summer. Florence tended to exaggerate.

TWL led his family on a motor tour through the Scottish Highlands. They attended clan games with burly caber throwers and kilt-clad bagpiper marching bands; they observed sheep dog trials and climbed the purple-hued slopes of Ben Lomond; they searched in vain for the Loch Ness monster. Lamont also went down to London and over to St. Moritz for two weeks, staying with his good friend and colleague from Rome, Giovanni Fummi; he returned in high spirits. And like all true Scottish golfers he reveled in his favorite pastime rain or shine. Tom wrote Jack Morgan: "It is jolly here, and I enjoy it."

The experience was memorable for the grandchildren—rowing out to islets in Loch Lomond, climbing about the fallen ramparts and dungeons of ancient castle ruins, or bicycling to the nearby village of Luss to purchase candy and postcards. Grandmother Florence had it all wrong.

During 1937 Europe grew increasingly tense as German rearmament and the Spanish Civil War seemed to propel the continent toward military confrontation. Drawn together in backing Franco with men and arms in Spain, Hitler and Mussolini had joined in formal alliance, the Rome-Berlin Axis, as it came to be known. Lamont, when interviewed on his arrival in New York on September 7, chose to focus on the economic conditions in Europe: they were "gradually improving. . . . As to crises, of course, all of Great Britain goes on a complete holiday in August, so with nobody at home they are strangely disinclined to take any crisis seriously."

But Bernard Baruch, the financier-adviser to Democratic presidents and TWL's fellow passenger on the *Queen Mary*, thought the European situation was indeed serious. Europe was a "tinder-box dominated by fear," said Baruch. There could be neither economic improvement nor prosperity abroad now. He found nothing but "hate, hate, hate." England and France were arming because the armament pace was being set by the dictator countries "who wanted something for nothing."

Lamont wrote his friend Nancy Astor the same day: "Without meaning to be critical of Bernie, I just detest this 'Hate, Hate, Hate' talk. The more hate you talk, the more hate you will have."

Lamont firmly believed that war in Europe would be averted. The *New York Times*, reporting TWL's address to the Commercial Club of Chicago on October 22, 1937, headlined its story: "Lamont Confident War Is Not Coming!" TWL praised the "earnest and strenuous efforts" by European statesmen to preserve the peace. He applauded Britain's avowed policy of following a patient course of appeasement: "There is always the point that measures of appeasement may well possess the seeds of final and peaceful composition. . . . I believe that leaders of State, like the people themselves, have no wish to jump from the frying pan into the fire of war."

Lamont disparaged the latest version of America's Neutrality Acts, signed on May 1, 1937. The sale of munitions and loans to belligerents, except for normal commercial transactions, was already banned. Now certain raw materials essential to running a nation's military machine would have to be paid for in cash and transported only in ships belonging to the belligerent power, the "cash-and-carry" provision. The implementation of the act would build up ill will against the United States and lose valuable markets now supplied by American exporters, said TWL. "We shall be calling down on ourselves a handsome fresh depression of our own," producing large-scale unemployment.

America would adhere to its traditional policy of refusing to mix in the quarrels of foreign nations, said Lamont. "At every step in the development of world affairs, we should calculate, not simply like moralists but like practical men, as to what is the best way to avoid the disaster of war."

War in China

The "disaster of war" had already struck China. Since 1933 the Japanese army had gradually infiltrated the Great Wall and extended its domination over substantial parts of China's northern provinces.

TWL at first harbored hopes that moderate elements in Japan would prevail over the military. In June 1934 Lamont had arranged for Prince Fumimaro Konoye, president of the House of Peers of the Imperial Diet, to have lunch with J. P. Morgan on the *Corsair* at the Harvard-Yale crew races. Later, at a dinner given by Japanese consul general Sawada in New York, TWL told the prince how disturbed Americans were over Japanese aggression in China.

When Admiral Isoroku Yamamoto, the chief strategist of the Japanese navy, visited the U.S., Lamont sent Sawada a memorandum for him to use in briefing the admiral. The English-speaking Yamamoto had done graduate work at Harvard and served as a naval attaché in Washington; maybe he would be more sensitive to American attitudes toward Japan than the rest of his military colleagues. TWL warned him that it would be "erroneous" to think that "the American people would brook any affront which the Japanese military might offer."

In his letter of September 13, 1935, to Governor Eigo Fukai of the Bank of Japan, Lamont stated that Japan must show Americans that "Japan is not embarking on a policy of conquest in China." Japan should slash its military expenditures substantially.

TWL corresponded periodically with the American ambassador to Japan, Joseph C. Grew, and Nelson T. Johnson, minister and later ambassador to China. Johnson had no illusions that Japan would mend its ways. In April 1935 he wrote Lamont that in a year "Japan will have succeeded in establishing control over China's major resources. Japan won't stop there." China was "too poor a market or field to support Japan in the style and manner of life that she has set for herself." The Japanese wanted the Far East rid of all Western influence; it was the duty of Japan alone to maintain peace and order in the region, by military force if necessary.

Following the July 1937 clash between Japanese and Chinese troops at the Marco Polo Bridge near Peking, full-scale fighting led to the fall of that city. In mid-August the Japanese fleet shelled and aircraft bombed Shanghai, which surrendered after two months of savage fighting. Americans were appalled and outraged by the slaughter of civilians and sacking of Shanghai.

On September 17, TWL wrote to K. Wakasugi, the Japanese consul general in New York, with a copy to the Japanese ambassador in Washington, Hiroshi Saito. Americans were "shocked and distressed beyond measure at the manner in which the Japanese military have conducted their operations in and around Shanghai." They would take no stock in Japanese declarations of peaceful intentions or offers to cooperate with the Chinese.

Lamont's patient hopes for enlightened Japanese leadership had ended. He was dismayed by "the cruel and horrifying bombing" which had made "an indelible impression that no explanation by words can eradicate," he wrote a Japanese businessman.

To another Japanese correspondent TWL wrote:

> It is fantastic to suggest that the present conflict is an effort to stamp out Communism. I consider it simply to be part of the long considered policy of Japan in endeavoring to take possession of the East Asian littoral. In the long run I don't believe Japan can succeed in this effort, I sincerely hope not.

Lamont and Ambassador Saito had long enjoyed a friendly relationship. In his letter to TWL of September 27, 1937, Saito stated that Japan had no territorial ambitions in China; the Japanese merely sought Chinese cooperation to the mutual benefit of the two countries, which had not been forthcoming. It had been necessary for the Japanese military to "deliver a telling blow upon the Chinese" to persuade them to reconsider their attitude toward Japan. Said Saito: "It is indeed a very difficult and delicate matter— to beat one hard and tell him to be a good friend immediately. But that is what we are after, and we must do our best to achieve that end. China, being what she is, there will always be ways to do so."

The ambassador's candor was in sharp contrast to the official party line that China had provoked the "incidents" by attacks on Japanese nationals in China. However, it is doubtful that Saito anticipated the unrestrained brutality of the Japanese army as it advanced westward into the heart of China.

On December 12 the U.S. naval gunboat *Panay* was sunk in broad daylight on the Yangtze River by Japanese warplanes; two men were killed and many injured as survivors in the water were repeatedly machine-gunned by the planes. The next day the Nationalist capital of Nanking fell to the attacking Japanese troops, who embarked on an unparalleled orgy of carnage, looting, and rape in which over one hundred thousand Chinese—civilians as well as military—were killed.

In several letters Lamont noted sadly that the liberal elements in Japan had been completely overcome by the militarists, who were carrying out an outrageous aggression against China. Throughout the United States there was overwhelming sympathy for the Chinese in their struggle to resist the Japanese invaders.

However, Lamont saw no reason for the U.S. to provide assistance to China, where U.S. business interests were modest. Furthermore, TWL opposed the imposition of government embargoes on the sale of key commodities, such as oil, to Japan and private boycotts of Japanese goods.

In his Commercial Club of Chicago speech, Lamont had stated that embargoes could succeed only if backed by an armed blockade, which no one recommended. Ineffective embargoes "simply act as irritants" that unite the nation subject to the embargo and inflict "the cruelest kind of war" on the civilian population.

On November 23 Lamont phoned Secretary Hull to ascertain the State Department's attitude toward the private boycott of Japanese imports, such as silk. The secretary replied that economic coercion was definitely contrary to government policy; the administration would pursue "policies of appeasement" in its diplomatic efforts to bring peace to China.

Lamont agreed. He was opposed to economic warfare in all its forms, as he wrote Corliss:

> I have a modest liberal creed of my own. I don't believe in embargoes on individuals or on nations, or in boycotts or ostracism. I don't think coercion works. I don't believe in penalizing nations because their rulers think differently from the way I think, any more than I believe in penalizing my offspring because their ideas are different than mine.

However, TWL was angry and completely disillusioned with Japan and its military rulers. If Lamont had once been ostrich-like in his hopefulness for enlightened leadership in Japan, he had definitely lifted his head from the sands of wishful thinking. In a letter to Ambassador Johnson he said he hoped the Lord would sink the Japanese islands and strike the entire Japanese army with a bolt of lightning.

Partisan Passion

The slowdown in business in August 1937 and the stock market decline, ever steeper after Labor Day, revived fearful memories of the panic and crash just eight years earlier. On October 18 a deluge of sell orders hit the exchange and the Dow-Jones index dropped 7.75 percent. Halloween's frightening demons were once more on the loose on Wall Street, and investors ran for cover as the market continued to fall in the following weeks and months. From 190 on August 27, 1937, it plummeted to 126 on October 18, to 112 on November 23, and reached its bottom at 97 on March 31, 1938. Stock values were halved in eight months. The brokerage business was so bad that the bottom price of a New York Stock Exchange seat ($51,000 in 1938) dropped to the lowest level since the Great War ($45,000 in 1918).

Business contracted rapidly at the same time with the inevitable layoffs: almost two million workers lost their jobs. The Federal Reserve Board Index of Industrial Production, at 117 in August 1937, dropped month after month, reaching a low of 76 in March 1938. Strikes multiplied, dividends were slashed, commodity prices plunged. Corporate securities issues fell off dramatically, amounting to only $628 million in the last half of 1937 compared to over $2 billion during the same period a year earlier.

What was going wrong? In the fall of 1937 credit was easy with the prime rate at 2½ percent and the broker loan rate at 1 percent. The speculative excesses of 1929 were not part of the economic scene. But President Roosevelt had been persuaded by Secretary of the Treasury

Morgenthau to make a real effort to balance the budget. The resultant cutbacks in federal spending were a major cause of the ensuing economic decline. The administration and big business were quick to blame each other angrily for bringing on the new recession.

New Deal orators suggested that business "monopolies" had caused the recession by cutting back their operations instead of lowering prices. They knew that many businessmen were hostile toward FDR and his lieutenants and not unhappy to see the administration floundering in the wake of its failed economic policies.

It was true that corporate executives were angry at FDR, believing that the New Deal had clearly demonstrated its bias against business in major ways, such as the counterproductive tax on undistributed corporate profits. Among the rich, Roosevelt-baiting had reached a peak of viciousness expressed in a spate of insulting and completely fictitious stories about FDR and his wife, Eleanor. Peter Arno humorously depicted the antagonism of the wealthy toward FDR in a *New Yorker* cartoon. It portrayed two blue-blooded Park Avenue couples in evening dress inviting some friends to join them at a movie theater featuring newsreels of current events. "Come along. We're going down to the Trans-Lux to hiss Roosevelt," read the caption.

Arno was funny, but the tales told at businessmen's club bars about the sexual or drinking exploits of the Roosevelts, their Jewish ancestry, or physical and mental infirmities were simply malevolent. The Morgan partners did not indulge in these kinds of scurrilous attacks on FDR. Privately, Morgan and some of his colleagues heaped scorn and contempt on Roosevelt's leadership of the New Deal, but not in public. They were gentlemen, and a few had different agendas. Russell Leffingwell and Parker Gilbert were Democrats, and Leffingwell was also a longtime friend of the president, even though he was becoming disillusioned with the New Deal. Lamont supported the president's foreign policy and greatly valued his periodic access to the White House as the means to advance his proposals to FDR on domestic and foreign affairs.

However, TWL strongly objected to what he perceived as the New Deal's strategy to exert increasing control over the American economy. Extracts from talks he gave in the winter and spring of 1938 expressed his fears.

> There is much validity in the feeling among us today that government, in its effort to correct certain obvious abuses, has seemed to feel itself responsible not merely for regulating the business of the country but for attempting in effect to handle the intimate workings of the industrial machine. . . . It is not difficult to see why this country instinctively shrinks from the tendency

toward over-administration shown by some of our agencies . . . and which instinctively distrusts and repels effort from any central governmental authority, not at suitable regulation of large affairs . . . but at any attempt actually to manage our daily affairs for us; to tell us that there is in government a wisdom so omniscient that it can forsee and handle the varying conditions of commerce and industry throughout the vast areas of our country stretching from the Atlantic to the Pacific.

To another audience TWL stated: "We must not turn our sturdy American workers into robots marching to the goose step of regimentation."

By 1938 the National Recovery Administration's efforts at national industrial planning through hundreds of complex industry codes had failed and been invalidated by the Supreme Court. New Deal legislation had improved workplace conditions, banned child labor, and fostered unionization, and in 1938 the Fair Labor Standards Act established a minimum wage and maximum work week.

Lamont was indulging in gross hyperbole. No one was turning American workers into "robots"; in fact they were gaining greater rights. But if New Deal politicians could lambaste the predatory instincts of big business, two could play the game.

The administration was in a quandary: cutting spending to reduce the federal budget deficit was not succeeding in building business confidence and reversing the economic decline. In December 1937 three former New Deal brain trusters—Charles Taussig, Adolf A. Berle, and Rexford G. Tugwell—conceived an idea to promote cooperation among business, finance, labor, and the government to cure the country's economic ills. They recruited Thomas W. Lamont; Owen D. Young of General Electric; John L. Lewis, head of the CIO, the powerful umbrella organization of labor unions; and Philip Murray, a CIO vice president and chief of the steelworkers union. At two meetings in New York the group agreed on a program to present to the president. FDR, who had already sponsored several unproductive conferences with industrial executives, was willing to try again with this high-level assemblage of business and labor leaders. On January 14, 1938, the group, except for Tugwell, met with the president at the White House to present its recommendations to him.

Ongoing cooperation among business, labor, and government was imperative, said the group. The government must stop cutting back its employment programs like the WPA. In fact, Lewis proposed that there should be an immediate large-scale increase in federal spending.

It was wrong for the administration to press industry to lower the prices for its products. Lower prices would mean lower wages, lower consumption, and further business contraction. Lewis cited the case of U.S. Steel, whose management had recently recognized the CIO as the union organization representing its workers. He had reviewed the corporation's books and was convinced that the company, operating at a loss at only 19 percent of capacity, could not possibly lower its prices without reducing wages. Lamont, a U.S. Steel director since 1927, who had often been called on to defend Big Steel's wage and price policies, couldn't have stated the case better himself, and it was far more effective coming from the politically powerful labor czar. Lewis concluded by forcefully emphasizing the need for industry to operate at a profit and labor's strong interest in seeing such profits assured.

The CIO leader was chosen to be the spokesman for the group in meeting the reporters waiting outside the White House. The press were surprised: "Such acknowledgement of labor leadership by men of interests so mixed cannot be recalled here," stated the *Baltimore Sun*. Some were astonished that the views of Lamont and Lewis were so compatible on important issues.

The *Gloversville Herald* of New York states: "America may take new heart, she may breathe another prayer of thanks for democracy, when a Lewis and Lamont can sit down and talk it over with the President. We're not going to the dogs when such a thing is still possible."

After the White House meeting the group drove back to the Mayflower Hotel to discuss future plans at a private lunch. TWL, sharing a taxi with Philip Murray, started to pay the fare when they arrived at the hotel.

"Just a minute, Mr. Lamont," interceded Murray. "My life's ambition has been to pay a taxi fare for one of the Morgan partners." And so he did.

Despite the president's apparently conciliatory attitude, Lamont had some points to get off his chest, which he delivered in a speech at the University of Pennsylvania three days after the White House meeting. Administration spokesmen had charged that those who directed the investment of capital, businessmen and bankers, were withholding new commitments in order to force the government to alter its policies. However, said Lamont, it would be more proper to say, in the terminology of labor disputes, that capital had been "locked out." Government itself had undertaken a series of measures, such as a changing antitrust policy and punitive taxation on reinvested earnings, which had destroyed business confidence in making new investments.

In the midst of renewed depression it was not surprising "that strident voices should be raised, demanding scapegoats to drive forth into the wilderness . . . and that business and finance have been subjected to violent attack for alleged abuses."

> This leads me to dwell for a moment on the campaign against business men and bankers that has characterized the American scene in recent years. The volume of books and articles and speeches attacking industrialists and bankers has been formidable. . . . Many writers and makers of clever phrases have flooded the market place with articles and books that have little or no basis in fact and that set forth utterly fantastic theses. . . . Such writers seem to have little understanding of men and their work; they distrust everybody and attribute ignoble motives to almost all save themselves.

Lamont believed that an important cause of the current business recession was "the bewilderment and loss of confidence among our citizens, owing to the general attitude of distrust toward business which in the last five years has been cultivated in this country."

> Our country is one whose basic conception has been one of good will among men—never one of a class or group war. Surely this country will come upon evil days if we permit our people . . . to gain an idea that there is some subtle cleavage among us and that some of us must carry on a gladiatorial combat in order to gain our rights.

Business and government must work together with understanding of each other's difficult problems, said Lamont.

Ralph Hendershot in his January 18 column in the *New York World Telegram* noted the contrast between Lamont's apparently harmonious meeting with FDR three days earlier at the White House and his fiery University of Pennsylvania speech. Lamont and the president both claimed a "middle of the road" posture, but "apparently he and Mr. Lamont could both be in the middle of the road and still provide room for a truckload of garlic to pass between them." Despite the hopeful prospects of the plan for cooperation discussed at the White House conference, the idea fizzled out. Opposition within the administration soon doomed it to early abandonment.

But Lamont was already pursuing his own initiative to advise the president, whom he called on at the White House on February 14. It was urgent, TWL told FDR, to reinvigorate the capital markets to arrest the depression. Government securities now represented about 85 percent of new issues; the meager amount of new corporate issues was largely refunding. Lamont recommended three steps. First, the taxes on corporate retained earnings and capital gains should be abolished. There had been arguments for and against every tax instituted since the founding of the republic. The president did not agree with Lamont.

Next, TWL discussed the administration's policy to curb public utility holding companies and the Tennessee Valley Authority program to acquire private power companies, particularly several belonging to Commonwealth and Southern. C. & S., a giant holding company with subsidiaries supplying electric power from Michigan to Florida, had been established in 1929 by the United Corporation and American Superpower Company under the aegis of J. P. Morgan & Co. C. & S. was headed by Wendell L. Willkie, a dynamic and brilliant executive, whom Lamont knew well and admired.

In Lamont's opinion the administration's policy had created a cloud of uncertainty over the nation's public utility industry, dampening the willingness of millions of investors to provide sorely needed new capital for expansion and modernization. It was imperative for TVA to negotiate fair prices for the purchase of private power companies based on realistic appraisals. The scope of TVA's operations should be geographically limited and the results of its program expertly judged within a set period of time. Lamont had considerable doubts about the expected economic efficiency of the "experiment." FDR said he would forward Lamont's memorandum on the subject to David Lilienthal, the head of TVA, who would negotiate the terms of TVA's acquisition of C. & S. properties with Willkie.

Finally, Lamont urged the Federal Reserve Board to alter a "deflationary credit policy" which made no sense in the throes of a depression. The president invited TWL to talk to Marriner Eccles, the chairman of the board of governors of the Federal Reserve, which TWL did. He reported back to FDR on February 25:

> As to credit policies . . . I had quite a visit with Marriner Eccles after my talk with you, but I didn't get even to first base. . . . He talked just as blue to me as he does to you about the immediate outlook.

Credit was already cheap, but there were few creditworthy borrowers in the depression climate of low product demand, operating losses, widespread unemployment, and massive debt and bank loan defaults. Monetary moves would not provide the stimulus to jump-start the faltering economy.

Lamont's expectation that the Tennessee Valley Authority would fail to achieve its goals proved wrong, as the huge project touching seven states went forward. Its multiple programs for flood control, improving the river for navigation, agricultural development, and the production and distribution of low-cost power substantially raised the chronically depressed region's economy. TWL's innate economic conservatism had too quickly closed his mind to an innovative project initiated by the administration.

Richard Whitney's Shocker

Ever since his prominent role in the 1929 crash and its aftermath, Richard Whitney, managing partner of Richard Whitney and Company, had been the most notable leader of the New York Stock Exchange. He had been a governor, vice president, and president of the exchange from 1930 to 1935, after which he continued as a governor, serving on a number of standing committees. He was a power in the exchange's governing councils and had been outspoken in denouncing increasing government investigations and legislation to regulate the securities markets. In addition to his own accomplishments, his position and influence were enhanced by his relationship with his brother George, a high-ranking J. P. Morgan partner right across the street. The Morgan firm, even reduced in size and activity, commanded unique respect on Wall Street for its intellectual and moral leadership. Richard Whitney and Company, primarily an institutional bond house, had long received some 30 percent of the Morgan bank's bond orders for execution and had drawn regularly on a $500,000 unsecured credit from Morgan, which was renewed annually.

Richard Whitney was tall, heavy-set, overbearing, and a snob in the opinion of some exchange members beneath his social rank. He also was a high-living New Jersey country squire, who rode to hounds and raised Ayreshire cattle on his well-staffed 500-acre estate, and kept a Fifth Avenue house in the city.

What Wall Street did not know was that as an investor for his own account, Richard Whitney had failed spectacularly. His personal losses from unsuccessful speculations in long-shot schemes mounted into the millions. Among others, he owed his brother George $2.9 million that he had borrowed over the last sixteen years. Furthermore, his firm, which was effectively a one-man enterprise, had been insolvent for several years, a condition Whitney had coped with by misappropriating securities and cash from his customers' accounts to boost the firm's assets and use as collateral for bank loans.

The Whitney brothers—Boston-bred, Groton- and Harvard-educated, Porcellian Club members—had achieved high positions in the financial community. Yet the brothers were markedly different in intellect and character. George was astute and conservative in business dealings; he was also a man of integrity. Around noon on November 23, 1937,

Richard Whitney called on George at 23 Wall Street to seek his help, and his story appalled and dismayed his older brother.

Richard Whitney had illegally pledged bonds belonging to the Gratuity Fund of the New York Stock Exchange (which provided benefits to the families of deceased members) to the Corn Exchange Bank Trust Company as collateral for a loan from the bank. Whitney had also used Gratuity Fund cash balances for his own purposes. The Whitney firm had had custody, supposedly only temporarily, of the Gratuity Fund assets in its assignment as bond broker for the fund's investments. The fund's trustees had just been alerted that Whitney had retained possession of some of the fund's bonds and cash for a considerable period of time, and they were demanding the immediate return of these assets to the fund. But Richard Whitney did not have the funds to pay off the bank loan to recover the bonds and restore the Gratuity Fund balances. He had pleaded for a day's delay in delivering the bonds, asserting that his office staff was shorthanded.

George Whitney was aghast at the news, "thunderstruck" as Richard later described him. However, he was determined to remain loyal to his brother and help him one more time. George told Richard that he would lend him whatever was required to obtain release of the bonds.

Not having such ready cash at hand, George Whitney went to his senior partner, Thomas Lamont. He told TWL that his brother Richard was in "a very serious jam" as a result of having misappropriated a customer's securities. George needed a temporary loan from TWL to enable him to advance the necessary funds to Richard to correct the situation.

Lamont: "Well, that is a devil of a note, George. Why, Dick Whitney is all right; how could he mishandle securities, even for a moment, no matter what the jam?"

George Whitney: "I don't know, it is an inexplicable thing; it is an isolated instance; but he has got to deliver them tomorrow, and I am going to help him out; I have got to help him out, of course."

Lamont: "I think you are dead right; certainly I will help you to help your brother; certainly."

According to Richard Whitney, it would require $1,082,000 to obtain a release of the Gratuity Fund bonds from the Corn Exchange Bank loan and restore the fund's cash balances taken by Whitney, some $221,000. On November 24 Lamont made a secured loan to George Whitney of $1,082,000, which George relent to his brother. The proceeds were applied as planned, and Richard Whitney obtained and delivered the Gratuity Fund securities and cash to the fund trustees that afternoon.

Only George Whitney and Thomas Lamont knew that Richard Whitney had misappropriated a customer's securities, an incident which, in their belief, was an isolated and now corrected malfeasance.

However, George Whitney told TWL, he did not think that his brother was "capable of handling a business properly and adequately." George would get him "to wind up the business."

Lamont replied that he thought that was "a wise thing."

On Thanksgiving Day 1937, George Whitney persuaded his brother that his firm should be liquidated, preferably sold as a going concern if a buyer could be found. Lamont left for Yeamans Hall the next day for a golfing holiday. On December 28 George Whitney repaid the first installment, $582,000, of TWL's loan to him. His brother reported that progress was slow in his efforts to sell his firm. But Lamont put the Richard Whitney incident from his mind, counting on George Whitney to see to it that his brother's affairs were put in order, that his firm was liquidated or sold.

The Morgan partners' ranks were aging and thinning. In 1936, Thomas Cochran passed away, and on February 23, 1938, S. Parker Gilbert, only forty-five years old, died. Gilbert in his short career had achieved a brilliant record—Under Secretary of the Treasury, Reparations Agent-General, and seven years a Morgan partner. After the Gilbert funeral, Tom and Florence, accompanied by the faithful Metcalfe and Florence's maid, Madeleine, sailed for the French Riviera. TWL had rented an old chateau in the little hillside village of Eze, where their old friends the Arthur Locketts joined them.

Lamont and Lockett often headed for the local golf course, winding through the mountains behind Monte Carlo. The days were sunny, the plum trees in bloom, and the high-fashion stores of Cannes attracted Florence. But the news from home, which TSL phoned his father every night, put a damper on the fun. Florence reported to her oldest son that his father did not sleep well, and "his heart began to 'thump' (he calls it) and make a ringing in his ears." He was quite miserable. "I think it is mostly just strain and worry. . . . He has been dreadfully upset by the Whitney affair. What a terrible thing."

No one had voiced any interest in buying the Richard Whitney firm, burdened by a huge illiquid block of Distilled Liquors stock. Nor had Whitney arranged for an independent financial audit of the firm to enable consideration by a prospective purchaser or lender, and with good reason. The stock exchange comptroller, John Dassau, acting on suspicions aroused by information submitted in an exchange questionnaire by the Whitney firm, had instructed his accountant to investigate further. His findings were damning. The firm not only fell short of exchange capital requirements; it was insolvent, and there was clear evidence that Richard Whitney had misappropriated securities belonging to the New York Yacht Club and two personal accounts under his control to obtain bank loans.

The official Securities and Exchange Commission report of the Richard Whitney investigation summarized the events that followed.

> On the morning of March 8, 1938, Charles R. Gay, President of the New York Stock Exchange, announced from the rostrum of the Exchange that the firm of Richard Whitney & Company had been suspended for insolvency. A statement released by the Exchange immediately thereafter definitely indicated that the firm had been guilty of misconduct. On the same day the firm and its general partners filed voluntary petitions in bankruptcy and were adjudicated bankrupt. On March 17, 1938 Richard Whitney, the senior partner of the firm, was expelled from the New York Stock Exchange. . . . Shortly after March 8, 1938, Richard Whitney was arrested on two separate indictments charging him with grand larceny in the first degree for appropriating to his own use securities entrusted to him in a fiduciary capacity.

Whitney pleaded guilty and on April 11, 1938, was sentenced to a term of five to ten years in Sing Sing prison. About the same time the commission ordered hearings to be held to determine the necessity for further regulations or legislation to improve the operation of the national securities exchanges.

The Lamonts continued their European sojourn, driving from Nice through the French Alps to Grenoble. "A supremely beautiful drive," wrote Florence. "The high snow capped mountains in the background, and near us the bright green meadows, and white and pink apple and peach trees in full bloom—so lovely, so lovely. This beautiful world, and what have we done with God's gift?"

On March 13, Hitler sent his troops into Austria "to preserve order," occupying and annexing Germany's small neighbor. In Paris and London, the next stops on the Lamont itinerary, the consensus was that the days of the Loyalist government in Spain were numbered. Franco's armies, joined by German and Italian ground and air forces, would complete their conquest in a matter of months. In the Far East, Japanese forces, having seized most of the port cities, relentlessly drove into the heart of China.

By the time the Lamonts reached England the countryside was blossoming in April finery. The Lamonts headed directly to Cliveden for the weekend, where Lady Astor gave a huge dinner and reception "for everyone you ever heard of in English political and social life," wrote Florence. At Cliveden and the embassy and social gatherings attended by the Lamonts in London, strong support was voiced for Prime Minister Neville Chamberlain's policy of conciliation. Vigorously opposed were Winston Churchill, Anthony Eden (who had recently resigned in protest from the post of foreign secretary), Harold Nicholson, and others. Great Britain must face up to the reality of Hitler's strategy of aggression, his unswerving intent to seize additional territories, especially in Eastern Europe. Establishing firm alliances with European allies, including Russia, and large-scale rearmament might deter him. Diplomatic missions to accommodate his demands would not.

Opposition to the Nazi menace crystallized in public attacks on the "Cliveden Set," the Astors and their coterie of powerful politicians and journalists, such as Chamberlain and Geoffrey Dawson, editor of the London *Times*, who, it was charged, met at Cliveden to plot their strategy for appeasing Hitler. David Low's cartoons in the *Evening Standard* savaged Lady Astor for alleged pro-Nazi leanings, and Churchill disdained her. But the Astors and their friends, who loathed Hitler, were supporting the policy of the government and most of Parliament and the British people in attempting to avoid the horrors of another war.

Thomas Lamont thought that Chamberlain was pursuing a sound course, and so did the newly appointed ambassador to Great Britain, Joseph P. Kennedy, an outspoken advocate of appeasing Hitler who believed that war with Germany was unthinkable and probably unwinnable. The ambassador was a former highly successful Wall Street speculator and FDR's first chairman of the SEC. The president's selection for the London post puzzled many, including J. P. Morgan, who had recently written a British friend: "I share your wonder that an Irish Papist and a Wall Street punter should have been selected for the London Embassy."

But TWL and the ebullient ambassador hit it off well. After calling on him at the embassy, Lamont wrote TSL that the English were enthusiastic about the Kennedys "because of the wonderful publicity gained in having nine children and his making a golf hole in one at Stoke Poges. Everybody thinks that they are most refreshing and breezy beyond words, especially after the record of their predecessors."

Several reporters met Lamont as he disembarked from the *Bremen* in New York on April 22, and TWL praised his new acquaintance. The new American ambassador had "made a great hit in London. He talks right from the shoulder, and they appreciate it."

A reporter then asked for his views on the disclosures about Richard

Whitney, one of which was that Lamont had made a loan to George Whitney to enable him to help his brother rectify his embezzlement of a client's securities. Lamont replied that he knew no more than had been reported in the press and terminated the interview.

Late in April the Morgan partners were called to testify at the SEC hearings in Washington. The Morgan interrogation was conducted by Gerhard Gesell, a bright twenty-eight-year-old SEC attorney, who years later would become a distinguished federal judge and buy a summer home in North Haven. Gesell focused on the evidence that three and a half months before the public disclosure of Richard Whitney's larceny, George Whitney and Thomas Lamont had known that he had engaged in illegal conduct. George was Richard's brother, which could explain his reluctance to reveal the embezzlement. But why had Lamont remained silent? Gesell questioned Lamont for two hours on April 26.

Q. Did you consider your responsibilities as a citizen toward anyone or your responsibilities as a member of a Stock Exchange firm toward anyone, or did you only consider your responsibilities toward Mr. George Whitney?

A. Well, Mr. Gesell . . . my partner described the need of his brother. He thought it was a perfectly isolated thing. He never dreamed that anything like that could happen again nor did I, and he said he was going to see that the business was liquidated. Well, that was enough for me. . . .

Q. Did you feel you had any obligation to go to anybody—to any public authorities and acquaint them with the facts?

A. No, because I believed . . . that the Exchange people had knowledge that Mr. Whitney had been slow in his deliveries to them and they have adequate machinery for checking up all their houses of that kind, and if the thought had occurred to me, I would have dismissed it and said, "Well, the Exchange will take care of this themselves."

Q. What did the district attorney's office know about this thing—what did any prosecuting agency know about this thing? . . .

A. They did not know anything as far as I am concerned, but would you expect me, Mr. Gesell, to say to Mr. George Whitney, "Yes, George, I will help you out to cure this default, which you believe is a perfectly isolated thing, but I must trot down to the district attorney's office and denounce your brother forthwith"? Did you expect me to say that? . . .

Q. Did you have at that time any reason to believe that anybody connected with the Exchange knew that he unlawfully used his customers' securities?

A. I didn't, Mr. Gesell; you must believe me; I did not give it a minute's thought. I have to reiterate that my friend and partner came to me and he said, "My brother is in this terrific jam; he has misused these securities, and default is going to be made tomorrow, and will you lend the money?" I said, "Yes. . . ." There was the human equation in it, and I handled it in just the way I did.

In previous investigations Lamont had always been confident and indeed eager to spar smoothly with government counsel about financial matters. He knew his business and had command of the facts needed to refute unwarranted charges. But this time he was forced to defend himself against allegations of personal misconduct. At the age of sixty-seven, in the twilight of an illustrious career, his integrity was being challenged; his reputation and that of his firm were at stake. He had no second thoughts about how he had handled the matter, but it was not pleasant to be compelled to persuade the public that he was blameless in the incident.

A. I will go over it again. Here was a question of a man in whom we had the utmost confidence. His brother still had the utmost confidence in him, believing this was an isolated thing. It was a terrible mistake that Dick had made. His brother was going to rectify it—to make good his default—to save him. And that was all there was to it.

It never occurred to me that I should butt in, or that I should denounce Richard Whitney for his terrible mistake or his terrible handling of this thing. Nor did it occur to me that I should run to the Stock Exchange authorities . . . when the chairman of the trustees of the (gratuity) fund knew that Richard Whitney had been delayed in returning the securities and cash. I thought it would be taken care of by the Stock Exchange in their own way. . . .

Q. Did you think a broker guilty of a crime, such as you knew Richard Whitney had then committed, should be allowed to continue as a member of a national security Exchange?

A. In my mind, that was answered by George Whitney's statement to me when he got the money—that liquidation of his brother's firm was to be proceeded with. . . . I had the utmost confidence in the competence of George Whitney, my partner. . . . He said he had told his brother he must liquidate.

Q. Didn't you think you should take a hand in the liquidation since you had loaned Richard Whitney money which enabled him to go on?

A. I did not lend Richard Whitney one cent. I lent my partner $1,082,000, and I considered my partner was competent to handle the matter from there on. I did not lend the money to his brother.

In later testimony Lamont said that he had the utmost confidence in Richard Whitney even after he had learned of his misconduct.

A. The news of what happened in early March came to me when I was abroad as the greatest shock in the world.

Q. Even though you had known on the 23rd of November, 1937, that

Richard Whitney had stolen approximately a million dollars' worth of securities?

A. Mr. Gesell, I don't think I ever put it in . . . the term which you put it now. Do you see what I mean? I did not use—

Q. You thought it was something unwise or improper?

A. No, sir.

Q. You knew it was illegal and unlawful?

A. Sure; but you used the word stealing. It never occurred to me that Richard Whitney was a thief. What occurred to me was that he had gotten into a terrible jam, had made improper and unlawful use of securities; that his brother was proposing to try to make good his default. . . . Even then . . . my confidence in him was such that when the story came out, when I was abroad, it gave me the most tremendous shock in the world. It made me ill almost that all that time he could have been deceiving his brother, deceiving his partners, deceiving his wife and community. Well, it was just— it is inconceivable. . . .

Q. Isn't that the answer to it: you were just unwilling to believe even after what you heard what Mr. George Whitney told you?

A. Well, I don't agree with you, Mr. Gesell. If I had been a lawyer or if I had retained a lawyer, I might possibly have adopted a somewhat different course, but I don't know that I should have, but I am not a lawyer and I did not consult a lawyer and I moved as my heart dictated.

The SEC report of the commission's findings and recommendations condemned the traditions that fostered a perspective held by Lamont and other witnesses: "The attitude of an exchange member . . . who fails to disclose to the proper authorities his knowledge of another member's misdeeds is consistent only with the concept that a national securities exchange is a private club, not a public institution." Lamont's testimony had revealed "a stubborn indifference to the public responsibilities of the Exchange."

TWL received a number of letters supporting his conduct:

"You put it on just the right basis—action of the heart, which every reasoning man would know it was."

"What gentleman would lend money to a man to help his brother and then blab it out to any authority?"

Dave Boone in his *New York Sun* column said "the SEC took an uncalled-for blast at Thomas W. Lamont." Describing the circumstances of Lamont's loan to George Whitney he added, "It's hard to think the manly thing to do would be to yell copper."

Good friends rallied to his side. Lamont had sent some clippings about the Whitney affair to Nancy Astor, who replied: "Dearest Tom, I don't have to read your clippings, or anything else for that matter, to know that you would never do wrong. Such is my affection for you!"

And Wendell Willkie wrote:

> I had followed the Securities and Exchange Commission investigation of the Richard Whitney matter in considerable detail during its progress. I think the statement made concerning you and Mr. George Whitney in the report of the S.E.C. as related in this morning's newspaper is outrageous.
>
> If one were to measure such things solely on the basis of their benefits to society, I still believe that the preservation of the essential loyalties between two brothers and between two partners is essential in any social system worth living in. I certainly would not want to live in a social order where they were absent. In addition, I cannot conceive what further notice the Exchange officials needed as to irregularities on the part of Mr. Richard Whitney over and above the misappropriation of the gratuity fund.

The SEC had its job to do, to see to it that abusive practices on the exchanges were curbed, and its report contained a number of constructive recommendations. The report did not recognize the fundamental moral question facing Lamont: Could he betray his friend and partner who had entrusted him with confidential information about his brother? For him, only one answer was possible.

Book VI

AGAIN: THE DEVIL'S MADNESS

Calm Before the Storm

Business at the Corner was still "flat," in TWL's words, with little corporate activity. Of the bank's total assets on June 30, 1938, of $480 million, $279 million was in U.S. government securities with another $22 million in municipals.

TWL had planned another adventure for July—a pack trip in the Sierra Nevada mountains of California with William Duane, an old friend, a younger couple, all from Santa Barbara, and Susan Hibbard, a widow from Chicago invited by TWL. Mrs. Hibbard was active in good works in Chicago, a trustee of Bryn Mawr, good company and a good sport, Lamont wrote Duane. Nancy and Waldorf Astor had regretfully declined TWL's invitation, and Florence, who had recently had her tonsils removed, did not take to the rustic living conditions of camping out. In planning the trip Lamont wrote detailed letters of instruction to the packer-guide, Earle McKee. Slender of stature, TWL weighed 151 pounds fully clothed and did not want a horse that was too broad-beamed.

TWL was exhilarated by the high mountain scenery of Sequoia National Forest and life on the trail. "Back from a wonderful trip," he wired home when it was over. In a letter to McKee he thanked him and "his boys" for a grand time, with special appreciation to the cook for the fancy cake he had baked to celebrate Duane's sixty-ninth birthday. TWL inquired affectionately about the well-being of his horse, which had developed an abscess in its cheek. Lamont also had his secretary return an air mattress to Abercrombie and Fitch which had sprung a leak the first time it was inflated. In August he headed for North Haven to join Florence and a growing brood of grandchildren.

While Lamont's access to the administration's highest levels was not the same as his open line with President Hoover, TWL put forward ideas from time to time to President Roosevelt and his lieutenants. During the

435

summer Lamont and the president exchanged letters on U.S. Steel's price and wage policy. The steel corporation desperately needed some relief on wages, said TWL. It could not ignore losses running at over $4 million a month that threatened its solvency, and he hoped that John L. Lewis, the head of the CIO, would see the light.

However, resuscitating domestic industry or overseeing the bank in which he had a large interest did not excite Lamont in 1938. International relations—the diplomatic maneuvering that would maintain world peace or lead to war—now absorbed his attention, as it would for years to come. By September 1938 the war-threatening crisis in Europe dominated the daily headlines. Hitler's latest territorial demand was Sudetenland, the western portion of Czechoslovakia containing a large German population, and the Nazi army was poised to invade and occupy it on October 1. Britain and France, who had backed down so far to Hitler's demands, with Chamberlain ignominiously shuttling to Germany for futile meetings with the Fuhrer, were in a quandary. Czechoslovakia, mobilizing its army, had a defense alliance with France, and the British would back the French.

Each morning at eleven o'clock during the days of growing tension Lamont talked to his London and Paris partners on the overseas phone. The mood of frightful suspense, of ominous expectancy that gripped the populations of Britain and France, was palpable. To some war seemed inevitable. However, TWL thought Britain would be foolish to go to war with Germany to help Czechoslovakia hold Sudetenland, whose annexation by Germany would meet Hitler's demands. His partner Russell Leffingwell did not trust Hitler and anticipated that the Nazis would take over all of Czechoslovakia before long.

On September 27 Lamont phoned the president to suggest that he urge Mussolini to propose a four-power conference—the U.K., France, Italy, and Germany—to negotiate a peaceful settlement. FDR replied that Lamont's idea had occurred to him already. TWL said that he hoped the president wouldn't mind if he called him up any time he had "a mild brainstorm" on the situation.

At the infamous four-power conference in Munich during the last two days of September 1938, the leaders of Britain and France, Chamberlain and Edouard Daladier, completely caved in. The Czechs, uninvited, were informed of the Sudetenland area to be ceded to Germany with occupation by the Nazis commencing the next day. Without British and French support resistance was hopeless. Chamberlain went home to announce to cheering London crowds that the Munich pact had brought "peace in our time."

On October 4, after the Nazis had marched into Sudetenland, Lamont wrote to Secretary of State Hull praising Chamberlain's achievement in preserving peace. He also noted that Great Britain and France were not militarily prepared to fight Germany. Negotiating to avoid war bought time the Western democracies desperately needed to rearm.

Nancy Astor wrote TWL in October: "We all feel that Chamberlain has done a great thing. Something new has been born, and I cannot tell you what hope he seems to have brought to all of Europe. . . . Winston Churchill as usual has taken the wrong turning."

At the Astor Hotel in New York, built by Waldorf Astor's Manhattan forebears, the agenda was anything but serious at the December dinner of the Financial Writers' Association, where Lamont received one of the tongue-in-cheek prizes presented to business leaders. The writers had selected a book, *How to Win Friends and Influence People,* by Dale Carnegie, as an appropriate award for TWL. The audience responded gleefully and later roared with laughter at the comic revue put on by the association members, whose opening number was "Doing the Broad and Wall" to the tune of "The Lambeth Walk," the popular new British song and dance step.

> *Any time you're down our way,*
> *Any so-called business day,*
> *You'll find us all*
> *Doing the Broad and Wall!*
>
> *Every little banking guy,*
> *With a profit in his eye,*
> *You'll find them all*
> *Doing the Broad and Wall!*

On January 20, 1939, TWL addressed the annual dinner of the University Club in New York for university presidents, some seventy-two in attendance. The conventional after-dinner speech format TWL followed called for a humorous story before proceeding with the message, his viewpoint on the issues of the day. TWL noted that the audience included his friend Dr. Compton, president of the Massachusetts Institute of Technology, and carried on:

> I should like to tell a story about Hobart College. An old graduate of Hobart, a clergyman, came back to the college and was asked to speak at the Chapel exercises. Whereupon he took upon himself to deliver a long address, using as his text "Hobart." . . . He took about ten minutes in explaining the letter "H" which stood for "honor." He told the students what "honor" meant to their lives, present and future. The next letter "O"

stood for "obedience." He took about ten minutes for that. "B" for "bravery" and so on. The students were a bit fatigued before the hour was over. Shortly after that a senior crossing the campus came upon a freshman, down on his knees and praying.

"Freshy, what are you praying about?" the senior asked. "Oh," said the freshman, "I was just thanking God that my father didn't send me to the Massachusetts Institute of Technology."

The initial reaction of relief after Munich had been supplanted by a backlash of mounting criticism of Chamberlain's abject surrender to the Fuhrer's demands and abhorrence at Germany's new acts of oppression. Czechoslovakians in Sudetenland were persecuted and driven out. On November 10, 1938, the Nazis unleashed the Kristallnacht, a reign of terror against Germany's Jewish population, and Anthony Eden gave an American radio speech warning that all democracies were threatened by Hitler's military aggression.

"Surely iniquity followed Munich," said Lamont at the University Club, "but the iniquity of war would have been infinitely greater." There were important reasons for Chamberlain's "humiliating arrangement," especially the military unpreparedness of Britain and France. TWL was sympathetic to the British and French fear that "in the event of war their world and the world at large would never be the same again."

The American neutrality bill banning the sale of arms to belligerents gave "comfort and aid to the aggressors." The president himself had said that the arms embargo was more likely to lead the U.S. into war than keep the country at peace.

Thomas Lamont, the eternal optimist, concluded by saying,

> Why am I hopeful, you may ask. . . . Dictators can not last forever. To maintain any government you must have more than fear or obedience. . . . The factors of evil—envy, fear, anger, jealousy, hate—all these disparate elements pulling apart and working at cross purposes, with the result that evil as a permanent force has its sure end. That is a credo for us to remember and to count on today.

The parson's sermons about the inevitable triumph of good over evil so many years ago still shaped the thoughts of his worldly son.

George Whitney had been directing the bank's operations since the mid-thirties. The prosaic commercial banking activity of the moderate-size firm during the depression years was a far cry from the heady days of Morgan investment banking supremacy in the twenties, in which he had been a key player. Whitney, often puffing a cigarette, was tall, reserved, and patrician in bearing. He was a staunch Republican whose ill-disguised disdain for the workings of government, its attorneys, and even some elected representatives had not helped the Morgan cause at the Senate hearings during the thirties. Whitney was bottom-line-oriented, all business—an extremely able and hard-working executive who was happy to let his senior partners be the ones to concern themselves with public relations and politics.

On February 17, 1939, the number of Morgan partners was increased to fifteen by admitting three new members, including Henry C. Alexander. For several years the senior partners had had their eye on Alexander, an extremely competent thirty-six-year-old Davis Polk lawyer who had advised them during the Senate investigations. Alexander, a Tennessean and Vanderbilt graduate, had charming manners and a tough, quick legal mind; before long he was serving as deputy to Whitney.

Leaving the office in able hands, TWL headed for the Mid-Ocean Club in Bermuda. He returned well tanned and pleased with his golf game. Back in New York the Lamonts enjoyed the spectacular and futuristic newly opened World's Fair, and on June 15 they left on the *Aquitania* for their annual sojourn in Europe. It would not be all play: a Morgan-sponsored loan was in deep trouble.

The German annexation of Austria in 1938 had aroused new fears among international bankers. Would Austria be permitted by her new masters to honor her foreign loans? The fate of the $25 million American portion of the Austrian loan of 1930, sold by a Morgan-led syndicate, was at stake.

The circumstances were similar to the 1935 negotiations setting new interest payments by Germany to American investors in the Dawes and Young loans. Now Germany was determined to lower interest payments on Austria's foreign loans; future interest charges would be based on each creditor country's trade balance with Germany, which ran a substantial trade deficit with the U.S. On July 1, 1938, the first coupon date following Germany's occupation of Austria, Germany unilaterally reduced the interest payment due American bondholders by one-sixth.

Once again Lamont worked with Secretary of State Hull, the Foreign Bondholders' Protective Council, and Governor Norman of the Bank of England in an attempt to protect the American bondholders and secure for them treatment at least equal to that received by Austria's European creditors. Despite Lamont's entreaty for support, the British quickly struck their own deal with the Germans—new lower interest rates on the Dawes and Young loans and Austrian bonds held by British investors. Governor Norman wrote Lamont that he regretted that Britain had been forced to negotiate on a national basis, but such was the way debtors now treated international loans.

The German position was spelled out in a letter of November 12, 1938, to Lamont from Dr. Rudolf Brinkmann, secretary of state in the Reich ministry of economics. Germany could meet its foreign obligations only from its trade surplus with individual creditor countries, with whom it had negotiated bilateral debt service agreements. Because of Germany's trade deficit with the U.S., it would be impossible to continue debt service on the Austrian loan, "which condition also seems to make the continuance of the special treatment of the Dawes and Young loans hardly bearable." Germany would be ready to negotiate the payment of debt service on the Austrian loan if "conditions should be created on the part of America" leading to the development of a German trade surplus with the U.S.

As Dr. Brinkmann had warned, the January 1, 1939, Austrian loan coupons held by American investors went unpaid, although bondholders in other countries received the payments negotiated by their governments. On February 8, Lamont wrote Brinkmann in language reminiscent of arguments he had advanced to recalcitrant debtors in the past: the nature of Germany's payment arrangement with its European creditors was of no interest to the widows and orphans and other investors holding U.S. dollar bonds. "They know only that they are being discriminated against. That is the outstanding fact. . . .

> The need to borrow arises from an adverse balance of payments, and it seems quite impossible to accept the principle that the same condition which occasioned the borrowing justifies the default. Surely the Reich will have need to borrow to develop her trade and her new acquisitions. Surely then it is to the interest of the Reich to try to rebuild her credit, not to destroy it forever.

America had a large amount of products and commodities that Germans wanted to purchase, much greater in value than American imports from Germany. Therefore, "this theory of paying debts only when you can do so out of a favorable trade balance strikes me as inadmissible. On any such theory the whole world structure of credit on which international trade must be based would fall with a crash."

> As one who was especially active in behalf of the Second Reich in the issuance of the Dawes and Young Plan loans, it is quite impossible for me to contemplate, in the face of an eight-year record of performance on the part of a little nation like Austria, the spectacle of a great nation like the Third Reich declaring its unwillingness or inability to meet such a small

item of foreign exchange as the one involved. Why, my dear Dr. Brinkmann
. . . this particular item is so limited in amount that it is beneath the dignity,
let me say, of a great people like the German nation to discriminate so
openly against American holders of the bonds.

On July 4, Lamont met with Dr. Emil Puhl, a director of the Reichsbank in Brussels, to discuss the Austrian loan. After lengthy debate TWL
finally agreed that the bonds in the American portion of the Austrian
loan, now bearing 7 percent interest, would receive 5 percent from July
1, 1939. The new terms would have to be approved by the U.S. and
German governments and by the Foreign Bondholders' Protective Council
in the U.S. TWL's act of reluctant approval masked his satisfaction at
having concluded a good deal for the U.S. bondholders, if it went
through.

TWL cabled his partners that he thought that Puhl had no better than
a 50-50 chance of gaining approval from the German authorities to the
new proposal in view of the mounting Nazi belligerence in foreign affairs.
"I fear that I have done all I can. The discussion was in good spirit and
. . . we agreed that if the European chiefs of state would be sensible
enough to leave the matters in our hands for settlement, we should soon
reach a basis for permanent peace."

Whereupon TWL crossed over to London. He had a special affection
for England in the spring and early summer and looked forward to
conversing with his friends from the upper echelons of British political
and intellectual life on the perilous state of world affairs.

Despite Hitler's denial of further territorial ambitions at the time, the
Munich pact had signaled the end of Czechoslovakia. In March 1939,
German troops occupied the heart of the country; Hitler paraded trium-
phantly into Prague to officially proclaim a German "protectorate" over
the nation. Chamberlain was shaken by the Nazis' duplicity. In a surprising move Britain, followed by France, announced support for Poland if
she were attacked, but failed to bring Russia into the alliance.

The Fuhrer's next target for acquisition was Danzig, the free seaport
in the Polish corridor to the Baltic; he also wanted German-controlled
transportation access across the corridor to East Prussia. The Polish
government firmly rejected his demands.

At a lunch hosted by Ambassador Joseph Kennedy at the American
Embassy, the guests discussed Hitler's latest moves. After Prime Minister
Neville Chamberlain had departed, Kennedy described him with typical
candor, referring to his "feeble impotence." TWL suggested that Chamberlain might do well to take Winston Churchill into his cabinet.

"Oh, nuts!" replied Kennedy. "Churchill is nothing but a drunken bum!"

The American ambassador, who had favored appeasing Hitler and believed if it came to war Britain would be defeated by Germany, had no use for the outspoken British politician who had repeatedly warned his countrymen about the growing Nazi threat to peace.

The usual gaggle of reporters greeted Lamont when he descended the gangplank of the *Normandie* in New York on July 30. Lamont said that he was optimistic that there would be no war, but then added that he was always optimistic. "Honestly, prime ministers and presidents do not know a thing more about war than you do," he declared. The people of England and France were not "jittery" over the prospects of war. He had had a quiet vacation in France and England, and the only conference he attended was "on the first tee" at the Evian golf club. "There is really nothing significant to report on the European situation," he concluded.

But there were moves afoot during the peaceful holiday month of August that would soon shock prime ministers, presidents, and the world at large. Twenty-one years after the armistice, the armies were ready to march again. On August 23 Germany and Russia signed a nonaggression pact freeing Hitler to invade Poland. German troops attacked Poland on September 1; Great Britain and France declared war on Germany on September 3 but were helpless to defend Poland, which was overrun in a month.

Lamont and his partners were quick to spot good business opportunities. On September 7, Lamont stopped by the White House to inform the president of his firm's intentions. That evening, dining at the British embassy, he proposed his idea, which now had FDR's informal blessing, to Lord Lothian, the British ambassador.

TWL had known Philip Lothian well since the Paris Peace Conference in 1919 when Philip Kerr, who later became the Marquess of Lothian, was Prime Minister Lloyd George's executive assistant. Tall and professorial-looking, the ambassador was kindly and approachable. Lothian had stayed with the Lamonts in New York, and in July Tom and Florence had spent a weekend at Blickling, Lothian's country house. Lady Astor and Lothian were close friends, and Lamont and the British lord often saw each other at her parties.

Great Britain, once more at war with Germany, would again need to purchase huge supplies in the U.S., but this time it planned to establish its own purchasing commission in America. Lamont proposed that the Morgan bank act as depository and disbursing agent for the British government's purchasing program. The bank could be most helpful in providing commercial intelligence to the British, such as evaluations of the physical, managerial, and financial capacity of American companies bidding for contracts. Furthermore, the bank was prepared to handle the sales of U.S. securities by the British government in the American securities markets, as it had done during the World War.

On October 31, Lord Lothian wrote Lamont that his government had decided to use the Federal Reserve Bank as its depository. Nevertheless, TWL felt that his other suggestions were worth pursuing and urged his Morgan Grenfell partners to persuade their government to assign J. P. Morgan & Co. the task of selling its American securities to raise funds to pay for its purchases in the U.S. The solicitation was successful: Morgan won the appointment from the British as well as the French government.

As Lamont had feared, his personal agreement with Dr. Puhl of the Reichsbank regarding the Austrian loan had been rejected at higher levels of the German government. Nor had any payment been made to American bondholders on the July 1, 1939, interest coupon. In his letter to TWL on August 9, Puhl proposed an exchange of bonds that would result in a yield of just under 3 percent to American investors. He hoped that Lamont could agree, "thus proving that even in stirring times there is scope for cooperation in the commercial sphere."

Lamont replied in his letter of August 25 that he could not justifiably urge Puhl's proposal upon the American investors. He was reluctantly prepared to recommend that they accept a 4 percent yield. "To attempt to go below that would be futile." The American bondholders would not agree, and he could not ask them to.

In September Germany went to war. In reply to Lamont's inquiry in October, Puhl said he was working on the matter, but no further interest payments were made on the Austrian loan, and debt service on the Dawes and Young loans was also halted. Hitler's foreign policy firmly ruled out "cooperation in the commercial sphere."

Conflict Over Neutrality

For months President Roosevelt had vigorously advocated the repeal of the 1937 Neutrality Act, which barred the sale of arms to belligerents. After the outbreak of war, Britain and France could not buy a single bullet in the U.S. Lamont strongly supported the president's position; Colonel Charles A. Lindbergh as firmly disagreed.

TWL personally liked the aviator hero, and he had even come to his defense on one occasion in a call to Under Secretary of State Sumner Welles. While living in England Lindbergh had visited Germany several times at the invitation of the German government to inspect the Luftwaffe. He was tremendously impressed by Germany's air strength. In October 1938, at a dinner in Berlin given by the American ambassador, Air Marshal Hermann Goring had presented Lindbergh with a high civilian decoration in honor of his contributions to aviation. Some Americans, including Secretary of the Interior Harold Ickes, had denounced Lindbergh for accepting an award from the Nazis. Lamont pointed out to Welles that the flyer, politically naive in affairs of state, had innocently received the medal without considering the political consequences. In fact, later in November, repelled by the Nazis' vicious new persecution of Jews, Lindbergh had cancelled his plans to return to Germany, said Lamont.

But Lindbergh held strong views about his country's policy toward the warring nations in Europe. Like his father, a Minnesota congressman during the Great War, the celebrated flyer was a strong isolationist. Americans across the country were determined to stay out of the war, but there was a wide gulf between the advocates of a "fortress America" and those who believed that the Allies were America's first line of defense and should be helped in every way possible.

On September 15, 1939, Lindbergh gave a national radio broadcast. He characterized the war as

> an age old struggle between the nations of Europe. . . . We cannot count on victory merely by shipping abroad several thousand airplanes and cannon. We are likely to lose a million men, possibly several million—the best of American youth. We will be staggering under the burden of recovery during the rest of our lives.
>
> Our safety does not lie in fighting European wars. It lies in our own internal strength, in the character of the American people and of American institutions. . . . If Europe is prostrated again by war . . . then the greatest hope for our Western Civilization lies in America. By staying out of war ourselves, we may even bring peace to Europe more quickly. Let us look to our own defenses and to our own character.

Lamont wrote his daughter that he thought that Lindbergh's radio talk was "dreadful." Everyone was anxious to keep America out of the war, but the broadcast would strengthen public support for the isolationists.

> The only argument is what is the best way to keep out of the war. Having studied these matters at close range for a period far longer than Charles Lindbergh's entire lifetime . . . I among many others am convinced that

there is no certainty of our being able to avoid war, but the greatest tangible hope lies in our making it possible immediately for the Allies to get as much here . . . of material supplies as they care to buy. . . . If they were able to do this, they would then indeed be fighting a battle for us and will stand a much better chance of holding off the Germans from themselves and eventually from ourselves as well. . . . Don't let all this isolationist talk fool you.

The best thing the U.S. could do to stay out of war was to arm Britain and France "to fight against the domination of the world by those two notorious gangsters, Hitler and Stalin."

During September and October, Lamont phoned the White House regularly, usually speaking to Colonel Edwin "Pa" Watson, FDR's appointments secretary. Lamont wanted the president to know that he fully backed his foreign policy and was lining up prominent figures such as James B. Conant, president of Harvard; William Allen White, the respected Kansas newspaper editor; and Governor Al Smith of New York to lobby for repeal of the Neutrality Act. Lamont would also work on some of the local congressmen. TWL hoped he might have a brief word with the president at his convenience.

On the day after Lindbergh's broadcast, Lamont, at Palisades for the weekend, spoke on the phone with FDR and immediately dashed off a letter in longhand to him. TWL fully agreed that the Neutrality Act should be repealed; nor should Congress impose any "cash-and-carry" provision—the requirement that belligerents purchase supplies for cash and transport these cargoes in their own ships. The British lacked the shipping to deliver the huge volume of munitions and other products they urgently needed to fight off the Germans.

"The Neutrality Act is not neutral just because its authors call it so." The act helped Germany, which had already built up a large munitions industry, by preventing Britain and France from buying arms in the U.S. The country wanted to stay out of war and would also support ending "these boycotts against the nations of Europe with whose difficulties 95% of our citizens sympathize."

On October 3, Charles Lindbergh visited the bank to discuss some personal business with H. P. Davison and stayed on for lunch with several of the partners. The conversation quickly turned to the war in Europe and America's policy toward the belligerents.

Lindbergh believed that the Allies would be defeated if they attempted to attack Germany across the western front. TWL replied that he expected that Britain and France would wait for Germany to attack, which she would have to do because she couldn't endure a long blockade. Lindbergh disagreed and thought it more likely that Germany would take the offensive in the east. Lamont did not think that it was practicable for Germany to launch an attack in North Africa, the Suez, or Turkey. Furthermore, he was confident that Italy would not join the war on Germany's side. Apparently, Mussolini's seductive talk about his desire for peace had had its desired effect.

The discussion then turned to the national debate over the Neutrality Act. Lindbergh thought that a complete repeal of the arms embargo was unwise. He supported the cash-and-carry restrictions: no American loans for the belligerents; no American ships permitted to sail into the European war zones. Lindbergh described the ensuing exchange between himself and the Morgan partners in his journal:

> That statement started a very warm discussion in which Tom Lamont took the lead. As far as I could tell, I was the only one in the room who was not in favor of unqualified repeal. Obviously, my stand was extremely unpopular. The discussion continued until some of the partners had to leave for meetings. . . . We all parted in a courteous (no personal feelings, you know) but tense atmosphere.

Lindbergh had read the mood of the Morgan partners correctly. A few days later Lamont reported to Colonel Watson at the White House, "I met Lindbergh at lunch the other day and almost had apoplexy over his attitude."

The 1939 Neutrality Act was passed by Congress and signed into law by President Roosevelt on November 4. The arms embargo was lifted, but American ships were forbidden to enter the European war zones and the belligerent nations would have to pay cash for their munitions purchases. A necessary political compromise had been struck, and the president wrote Lamont thanking him for his assistance in promoting repeal of the earlier act. Lamont in turn sent FDR a copy of his speech at the annual dinner of the Academy of Political Science on November 15, 1939, at which he addressed an audience of about a thousand on international affairs.

America should sell military supplies to Britain and France while staying out of the war, and American businessmen wanted peace as badly as all American citizens, contrary to the "false legends" that some promoted, said TWL. The violent rise of Hitlerism had left "all the strange creatures of the underseaworld of society" to rule Germany "with the strange and malevolent practices that have so shocked Western civilization." The Fuhrer could not continue "to overrun one sturdy and independent nation after another, declare it to be German, and expect it to remain a vassal State and part of the Reich. That cannot be done."

England was not decadent, but the same country that had won repeated victories in the past, declared Lamont. Her sea power and "France's wonderful army, magnificently equipped and led, and backed by the calm determination of the whole French people" would bring victory. TWL could almost have lifted the language from his twenty-year-old file of Liberty Bond speeches.

In contemplating the postwar world, international economic cooperation, with the active participation of the U.S., was essential to preserve world peace. European economic planners, like TWL's friend Jean Monnet, the French economist-banker, were increasingly advocating a grand new order—an economic union embracing all of Western Europe. "It is impossible to exaggerate the immensely stabilizing effects upon the world that a great free trade region in Europe would create," said Lamont, endorsing the common market concept that would become a postwar reality.

Not all of TWL's exchanges with the White House were serious. Lamont had sent FDR a letter from a teacher at a women's college in the Bronx whose students had expressed great admiration for the president. FDR replied whimsically:

"Dear Tom:
　You and I are, I believe, at what is known as "the dangerous age," and it is just as well that we do not conduct classes for young ladies in the Bronx.

While TWL's appreciation of feminine pulchritude did not embrace FDR's occasional penchant for hands-on flirting, his rapport with the president was chummy compared to his dealings with FDR's Republican predecessors. They were both sophisticated, Harvard-educated New Yorkers, genial and confident aristocrats of good humor and wit.

New Look at the Corner

In December 1939 the Morgan partners were once again examined by a government committee during the investment banking segment of the hearings of the Temporary National Economic Committee, another lineal descendant of the Pujo hearings. The investigation aimed to demonstrate that, contrary to the objective of the Glass-Steagall Act, J. P. Morgan &

Co., a commercial bank, still exerted control over Morgan Stanley, the investment bank formed in 1935. J. P. Morgan partners had put up 94 percent of the preferred stock representing the bulk of Morgan Stanley's initial capital, and several partners had left the bank to become executives of the new firm. However, there were no overlapping officers and directors, and all of the common stock, carrying voting rights, was held by officers of the new corporation.

Nevertheless, the Morgan firms thought it sound public relations to reduce the "identity of pecuniary interest," as the SEC referred to the investment connection, which culminated in the complete redemption of the preferred stock by Morgan Stanley in November 1941. There was also an important business reason to sever the link: in 1940 Lamont's friend Judge Learned Hand ruled that the bank could not serve as the corporate trustee of Dayton Power and Light's bond issue to be managed by Morgan Stanley, because of its tie to the firm through the preferred stock interest. This obstacle to obtaining trusteeship business had to be removed.

A revealing exhibit emerging from the hearing was the first public listing of the individual J. P. Morgan partner interests in the firm, derived by the SEC from their tax returns. The estate of Charles Steele, who had died in August 1939, held a 36.6 percent share of partnership capital; Thomas W. Lamont held 34.2 percent; J. P. Morgan, the senior partner, only held 9.1 percent.

Morgan had let his capital position decline in order to support his grand manner of living—worldwide cruises on the *Corsair*, houses in Manhattan and Glen Cove and a winter home in Jekyll Island, a lodge in the Adirondacks, a country estate in England, and so forth. He had been lavish in funding the Morgan Library and most generous to numerous good causes. Now his shrinking income, suffering from the bank's decline during the depression and hit by double taxation from the U.S. and Great Britain, compelled him to retrench. He cut back on his giving to charity, resigned from several clubs, and in December 1939 offered the *Corsair* to the British navy.

George Whitney, now acting as the bank's chief executive officer, responded loyally to the obvious question, noting Morgan's suprisingly small interest in the firm. Said Whitney, "Mr. Morgan is still the dominant factor." Whitney also challenged the SEC figures on partnership shares but refused to provide any other breakdown.

On February 15, 1940, J. P. Morgan genially handed out copies of a press release to a group of reporters assembled at the Corner. The firm had decided to end the private banking partnership, whose history went back some eighty years, in order to incorporate the business under New York State law as a bank and trust company, J. P. Morgan & Co. Incorporated. Morgan's Philadelphia branch, Drexel and Co., would close and the Morgan bank would take over its deposits. The Drexel name would be continued in an independent investment banking partnership formed by some of the Philadelphia partners.

The Morgan partners would become officers and directors of the new corporation and receive shares based on their partnership interests. J. P. Morgan would be chairman; T. W. Lamont, chairman of the executive committee; R. C. Leffingwell, vice chairman; and George Whitney, president and chief executive officer. The move marked a watershed in Morgan history and was absolutely essential to the financial health and growth of the firm.

First, the change permitted the Morgan bank to enter the trust business, from which it was barred as a partnership. It would no longer be forced to direct profitable trust accounts to other banks. Most important, incorporation would protect the firm's capital from huge cash withdrawals when partners died. Five million dollars had already been paid out to the Charles Steele heirs, and the next largest interests were held by Lamont, sixty-nine, and Morgan, seventy-two. As Morgan wrote a friend: "We are just in the throes of forming our business into a company, a step made necessary by the fact that so much of the capital is in a few hands, and those few hands are elderly." Under present conditions it was "impossible to make any money to replace lost money quickly. . . . The stock will, I suppose, gradually get into the hands of the public. I only hope they will like it when they get it." In the future, Morgan partners' heirs would wind up with J. P. Morgan corporate stock, not cash, which they could sell.

Changes in the ways of doing business would come about slowly but inevitably. The personalized partnership style of banking with partners' responsibility for gains and losses would be replaced by the more impersonal corporate form with management responsible to a growing body of outside shareholder-owners. However, the Morgan bankers still planned to follow their traditional policy of doing business with blue-chip clients in "a first-class way," and the bank needed a stable and growing capital base to lead the big commercial loans that its major corporate customers would demand when the country recovered from its economic doldrums.

There was a slight glitch in the incorporation process: a plumbing company in Brooklyn was already operating under the J. P. Morgan name, but a friendly state legislator put through a special bill in Albany entitling banking partnerships to keep their names when they converted to corporations. On April 1, 1940, J. P. Morgan & Co., Inc. commenced operations with 33 officers and a staff of 623. The June 29, 1940, balance sheet showed assets of $702 million of which cash, municipals, and government securities accounted for 91 percent of the total. The corporate business was still moribund. Lamont received a number of inquiries from persons who wanted to own some Morgan stock, but for the time being elected to keep his shares in the family.

The War and American Politics

As France fell in the spring of 1940 and the British were evacuated from Dunkirk, Lamont continued to phone the White House, usually talking to "Pa" Watson, to urge repeal of the cash-and-carry provisions of the Neutrality Act which were delaying the shipment of arms to England. On May 15, after the Nazi invasion of the Low Countries, TWL reported to the president by phone on the growing grass-roots support for William Allen White's Committee to Defend America by Aiding the Allies.

At the same time, Charles Lindbergh was becoming increasingly vocal in appealing to the isolationist sentiments of many Americans. He supported the cash-and-carry provisions and opposed the shipment of "offensive weapons," such as bombing planes, to England, even though the Luftwaffe bombers were wreaking heavy damage on British targets.

In his radio broadcast of May 19 Lindbergh stated:

> The only reason that we are in danger of becoming involved in this war is because there are powerful elements in America who desire us to take part. They represent a small minority of the American people, but they control much of the machinery of influence and propaganda. They seize every opportunity to push us closer to the edge.
>
> It is time for the underlying character of this country to rise and assert itself, to strike down these elements of personal profit and foreign interest.

If Lindbergh responded to the memory of the isolationist sentiments of his congressman father, his wife, Anne Morrow, and her mother, Betty,

TWL's old friend, also thought deeply about their own heritage—the policies and beliefs embraced by world banker and statesman Dwight Morrow. Surely he would have supported all-out American aid for the Allies, the course backed by almost all of Morrow's old New York friends and his former Morgan partners. Betty Morrow simply could not support her son-in-law's stand. Anne agonized, faced with reconciling "her divided loyalties in a time of stress," as she wrote later. Her heart went out to England and France, the countries and peoples she loved. But her head told her that America must resist steps that might drag it into a widening conflict, her husband's viewpoint. She wondered if a negotiated peace might not be the answer. Betty Morrow confided to TWL that Anne was "torn in spirit, and it is telling on her health." Lamont decided to write to Lindbergh and, after noting his affection for the Morrow family, came directly to the point.

> I wonder if you would mind naming names or naming groups. Just whom as individuals or as groups have you in mind? Who, for example, are the "powerful elements"? I am in contact with a good many different people, and shades of opinion. I don't know of any such elements.
>
> What is this "machinery of influence and propaganda" that you speak of? I haven't seen it.
>
> Who are the ones who are seizing "every opportunity to push us closer to the edge"?
>
> How are "these elements of personal profit and foreign interest" constituted? Who are the dastardly persons whom you would characterize as wanting to bring this country into the war for the sake of "personal profit"?
>
> Perhaps you will not feel like answering this letter, but so many bewildered people are asking me whom in the world you can be alluding to or what groups you have in mind that I should greatly value a categorical reply if you feel like giving me one.

Lindbergh responded on June 7:

> That there are "powerful elements" in America who desire us to take part in the war seems obvious to me. The Administration in Washington is, I believe far from being the least important of these elements, and it certainly controls much of the machinery of influence and propaganda in this country. It also seems obvious that many organizations and individuals have used the war in an attempt to make personal profit. I believe this can be well substantiated, but I can see no advantage in specific accusations at this time. I believe it is of vital importance for us to avoid the class antagonism and hatred which would arise from such accusations. . . .
>
> I have great respect for your judgment, but I am afraid that our viewpoints differ in regard to the attitude this country should take toward the war in Europe.

The reply could not have pleased Lamont, who presumably surmised that the Morgan bank was a leading "powerful element" in Lindbergh's mind.

However, a fast-rising new star on the political horizon, Wendell L. Willkie, the charismatic dark horse candidate for the Republican presidential nomination, shared Lamont's views on aiding the Allies. Willkie, the prominent utility executive and a business friend of Lamont, had been his industry's most dynamic spokesman in resisting New Deal programs constraining the nation's privately owned utility systems, the 1935 act to curb public utility holding companies, and the Tennessee Valley Authority.

In September 1936, Lamont, Willkie, and a small group of business and government officials had met with the president to discuss the development plans of TVA, and TWL had been tremendously impressed by Willkie's forceful presentation of the private-sector viewpoint. Over the next few years Willkie denounced the administration with growing frequency in articles and speeches, and he no longer limited his remarks to the public power issue. By 1939 he had become the chief spokesman for American businessmen, overwhelmingly Republican, in attacking the Democrats and their programs. Willkie and Lamont, both headquartered in New York, kept in touch.

The front-running candidates for the Republican presidential nomination in 1940 were Thomas E. Dewey, New York's energetic and racket-busting district attorney, and Ohio Senator Robert A. Taft, son of the former president. On January 25, Lamont gave a small stag dinner at his home in honor of Senator Taft. Willkie, who had not yet publicly announced his candidacy, was one of the guests. The discussion centered on U.S. tariff and trade policy. Taft, reflecting orthodox Republican conservativism, favored high tariffs to protect American industry from cheap imports. Willkie, on the other hand, persuasively presented the case for lower trade barriers to increase international commerce, an economic principle fervently espoused by Lamont.

On January 30, 1940, Willkie announced publicly that he would accept the Republican nomination. No Republican candidate had ever so stirred Lamont's enthusiasm. His views on domestic and foreign affairs completely meshed with Lamont's, but TWL believed that it would take a miracle for Willkie to win the nomination. A political outsider, he had not entered a single primary.

Willkie was now speaking to groups across the country, enthusiastic audiences attracted by his unpretentious and dynamic style, wisecracking humor, and magnetic personality. Numerous radio addresses, articles, and good press coverage generated growing momentum for his campaign. Important publishing groups supported him, such as the Luce empire of *Time, Life,* and *Fortune*; the Reids of the *New York Herald Tribune*; and the Cowles brothers of Minneapolis and Des Moines. His quite dazzling performance on the radio quiz show "Information Please" gave his cause a not insignificant fillip as well.

Lamont had long been in close touch with the Cowles family, headed by one of his second cousins. Son John was the publisher of the *Minneapolis Star Journal,* and his brother Gardner published *Look* magazine and the *Des Moines Register and Tribune*. On April 5 Lamont wrote John Cowles his views on the candidates. Taft was "100% wrong on tariffs." He lacked appeal and was "living in another age." Willkie was "a swell fellow," but as a prominent utility executive was probably "ineligible." Cowles replied promptly. He liked Willkie and thought that he could be "built up" to be "a real factor at the Philadelphia convention" and maybe nominated. The Cowles brothers went on to play a major role in the Willkie campaign in lining up delegate support in the Midwest.

On April 14 Lamont met with Oren Root, Jr., a young Davis Polk lawyer who had volunteered to help the Willkie campaign. Root's unique contribution was to organize grass-roots Willkie clubs across the country, a movement that mushroomed with surprising speed. He wrote TWL after their talk, "Somehow we must get rid of the 'Wall Street stigma.' "

TWL had marshaled financial backing for Willkie from his business acquaintances, which was not difficult. Willkie, an internationalist and articulate defender of private enterprise, had many Wall Street friends who preferred him over Taft and Dewey.

Lamont also corresponded with Alfred M. Landon in an effort to influence the former Republican candidate, a member of the Resolutions Committee at the coming convention, toward endorsing adoption in the Republican platform of the flexible foreign policy plank favored by Willkie. Alf and Tom, as they addressed each other, had a cordial exchange, with TWL telling the former Kansas governor that he was "a dirt farmer" at his Maine farm during the summer. Lamont reported that Landon urged him to be available in Philadelphia to offer suggestions on the G.O.P. foreign policy plank.

TWL was alert to the danger posed by what Oren Root had called the "Wall Street stigma." Recognizing Willkie's vulnerability to the charge that he was a captive of Eastern financial interests—"the barefoot lawyer from Wall Street" some Democrats had dubbed him in reference to his Indiana origins—Lamont had not publicly announced his support for him. TWL was concerned about attending the convention in Philadelphia, but finally decided to go, "just to sit around in the background," he wrote a friend. He purchased three tickets in the lower balcony of the visitors' gallery of Convention Hall and reserved a suite at the Barclay Hotel.

On June 24, the first day of the convention, Lamont met Landon in his hotel room and shared a cab to Convention Hall with him. They discussed the Republican foreign policy plank in the light of the latest developments in the European fighting, which had turned rapidly for the worse with the collapse of French resistance after Dunkirk. It was a grim time. On June 10 Italy had declared war on France. Four days later the Germans had marched into Paris, the French sued for peace, and the battle of France was over. TWL was pleased with Minnesota Governor Harold E. Stassen's keynote speech to open the convention which called for full support of the British while staying out of the war.

Lamont was trying to keep a low profile. He never saw or spoke to Willkie, who was wooing delegates around the clock in his sixth-floor suite at the Benjamin Franklin. Nor did TWL attempt to enlist delegates to the Willkie banner. But he was spotted by the press, and some papers, along with the Taft and Dewey camps, made political capital of his presence.

The *Philadelphia Record* of Tuesday, June 25, first raised the hue and cry, in disclosing the presence of Lamont, "a principal Morgan shareholder and Willkie backer."

> The presence of Lamont in the city on the opening day of the convention was vigorously denied as having any connection with the Willkie campaign. It is definitely known, however, that the international banker previously talked frequently by long distance phone with the Willkie headquarters and that he conferred with several influential party leaders. . . .
>
> Lamont's presence here was explained as due to private business affairs with Drexel & Co. Regardless of the explanation, among the delegates the fact that the banker was in the city created a big sensation and was hooked up directly with the Willkie drive.
>
> Also, his opponents saw to it that quietly plenty of capital was made of the fact that Lamont was in town. It was pointed out that there is a close utility tie between Lamont and Willkie through the Morgan-controlled United Corporation, which was a heavy interest in the Commonwealth & Southern, headed by Willkie.

The *New York Daily News* reported,

> Not helpful to Willkie was the sudden appearance in hotel lobbies here of such Wall Street friends and business connections as Tom Lamont, partner

of the House of Morgan, which formerly controlled Commonwealth and Southern and still has an interest in it. . . .

Commented a midwesterner friendly to Willkie: "Those men from Wall Street are just jackasses enough to come here and gum up the works."

The *Brooklyn Eagle,* identifying Lamont and other financiers, said, "Wall Street has invaded Philadelphia in force to sweep Mr. Willkie over the top."

The *Sacramento Bee* talked of "the influence of the House of Morgan, whose top notch partner, Thomas W. Lamont, rushed to Philadelphia to give Willkie a boost when he needed it most."

Charles Michelson, director of publicity of the Democratic National Committee, described the activity of Lamont in Philadelphia as "the most definite evidence of the solidarity of the big industrialists behind Willkie."

Harold Knutson, a Minnesota congressman and leader of the anti-Willkie congressional bloc, merely stated to a reporter, "Tom Lamont is in town."

Lamont left town on Tuesday afternoon to return to New York, much as he would have liked to stay for the balloting, which promised to be an exciting political confrontation. Erwin D. Canham of the *Christian Science Monitor* had the last tongue-in-cheek word:

> We think it was un-American, for instance, for Thomas W. Lamont to be shooed away from Philadelphia during the Republican Convention. Give the poor capitalist, say we, his day in politics along with the professional hacks who have sometimes been his representative, sometimes his foe.

The early ballot strength of Dewey and Taft collapsed before the momentum of the Willkie bandwagon, playing to cheering packed galleries of his supporters. The "miracle" was consummated on the sixth ballot at 1:05 a.m. on Friday: Wendell L. Willkie won the Republican party's nomination to be its candidate for president. Lamont went over the Willkie's office on Pine Street a few days later to offer his congratulations to the candidate and whatever assistance he wished in the campaign. Then he headed for his Maine farm to join Florence and the children, including two young English daughters of a Morgan Grenfell partner who had been evacuated from London.

Sky Farm lived up to its name in 1940. There was an operating dairy, six cows and a bull, supplying milk and cream to the Lamont clan; a couple of dozen sheep in a spacious pasture; chickens, ducks, geese, turkeys; and a vegetable garden dominated by rows of green tasseled corn. After a few days TWL took off for a week's fishing in New Brunswick with his old friend Arthur Lockett and returned with some

fresh salmon for his family. But the Willkie campaign, not farming or
fishing or even his golf game, was uppermost in his mind.

Lamont wrote Willkie on July 5 offering his services, while recognizing
that it probably would not be wise for him to play an active part. "No
cause has ever seemed quite so close to my heart. The thing that would
give me greatest satisfaction would be to have you bother me." He
showered Willkie with memoranda, articles, and suggestions for themes
in his speeches, and spoke to him on the phone a couple of times.

The candidate, while cordial, did not seek any closer connection with
the Wall Street elder statesman. There was no truth to the charge that the
Morgan bank exerted control over Commonwealth and Southern or
United Corporation; commercial banks didn't hold stock. But it made no
difference. The recent press furor at the convention about Lamont
backing Willkie and the constant drumbeat of Democratic attacks on
"economic royalists" and "minions of the House of Morgan" were
enough reason for Willkie to keep his public distance from TWL.

The Italian invasion of France had shocked Lamont: so much for the
Duce's fervent declarations to TWL of peaceful intentions. TWL's outlook on war and peace around the world was largely shaped by his innate
optimism, as he once admitted to a group of welcoming dockside
reporters. Then another country, which Lamont once believed craved
peaceful relations with America, escalated the threat of war.

On September 27 Japan joined Germany and Italy in a Tripartite Pact
to come to each other's assistance if the U.S. entered the war. A few days
later Lamont phoned Willkie. Supplying aid to Britain was the highest
defense priority, and Willkie should be cautious in discussing Japan. It
would be unwise to "embroil ourselves unnecessarily at the drop of a
hat," warned TWL.

TWL joined the huge enthusiastic crowd attending the Willkie rally at
Madison Square Garden on November 2, where chants of "We want
Willkie" resounded through the giant amphitheater. At Willkie's Fifth
Avenue apartment on election night, Lamont and the other guests listened
to the radio reports of the voting results as polls closed across the country:
27,243,000 votes for FDR clinched a third term for the president.
Willkie's total of 22,305,000 was the largest number of votes ever cast
for a Republican presidential candidate, and Lamont wrote Willkie the
next day praising him for having aroused the country "as it has never
been stirred before."

Lamont also wrote his customary letter of congratulations to FDR.
After requesting a meeting the following week, he told the president:

I too did not favor a Third Term. But the situation reminds me a little of
a story Calvin Coolidge told me years ago. He was running for City Solicitor
of Northampton, Mass. and was elected about 5 to 1. Next day one of his
townsmen came up and said: "Cal, I didn't vote for ye.—"No?" says Cal,
"well somebody did."

Menace on Both Oceans

Mussolini's duplicity was quickly brought home to Lamont and his
colleagues: on September 20, 1940, Giovanni Fummi, Morgan's representative in Rome, was arrested by the Fascist police, imprisoned, and
held incommunicado. TWL had a warm affection for "Nino" Fummi, a
sophisticated and wise Italian gentleman and former stockbroker whom
Lamont had hired for the firm in 1920. TWL and Fummi had collaborated closely on the bank's Italian loans, sometimes dining together after
work at the best restaurants of Rome and Paris. Lamont had also visited
the Fummis several times at their vacation home in St. Moritz. They were
charming and considerate hosts, and he enjoyed their company. Lady
Anne Fummi, who was English, had left Rome with her children to live
in England some months before, when the outbreak of war seemed
imminent.

Fummi had been instrumental in securing for Morgan a good portion
of the securities and exchange business of the Vatican. He had good
friends there, who immediately made inquiries about his arrest. After
several days without news, Lamont received word from the papal secretary of state that Fummi had been arrested for expressing sympathy for
England's struggle in a personal letter which had been intercepted by the
police, and Italy was now at war with Great Britain.

There may well have been a more important reason for Fummi's arrest.
As the flames of war spread in Europe during 1939 and 1940, TWL
continued to practice his private diplomacy to keep Mussolini from
irrevocably binding Italy to Germany's campaign of mounting aggression. He dispatched several letters to Fummi for Mussolini's attention,
which were reportedly forwarded to the Duce via the Vatican and Bank

of Italy, messages that warned with growing urgency that all Americans were angered by Hitler's aggression in Europe and persecution of Jews. American sentiment could turn quickly toward joining the war against Germany.

TWL kept President Roosevelt informed, and FDR wrote him on May 23, 1939: "I appreciate the efforts you have made to prevent misunderstanding in Italy of the point of view of the American government and people, and hope that your letter may have borne fruit."

Lamont's letter to Fummi in May 1940 again underlined that all Americans, including Italian-Americans, detested Hitler. However, there was a "deep-seated friendship" for Italy. Americans would be saddened and shocked if Italy allied itself with Hitler in the war. On June 3 Fummi said he would pass the letter to his friend at the Vatican, treasury official Bernadino Nogara, who would have its message transmitted through his own channels to the Duce.

One week later Italy joined Germany in invading France. "The hand that held the dagger has struck it into the back of its neighbor," FDR told the American people in summing up the nation's revulsion over Italy's latest aggression. Italy defaulted on its foreign loans, and the British and Italian armies were soon clashing in North Africa. Mussolini undoubtedly questioned the loyalty of the representative of the prominent American bank with its long-standing British ties, who for months had been passing messages from Lamont denouncing his partner Hitler.

Lamont was shocked by the incident and especially worried about the effect of prison life on his colleague's health, which was not robust. He urged the State Department and the American ambassador in Rome to take steps immediately to secure Fummi's release. He also enlisted the good offices of the Vatican. In these communications and in a letter he drafted to Premier Mussolini, TWL stressed that Fummi had always been completely loyal to the Italian government and had served the interests of Italy with distinction in the negotiations leading to the important loans that had been made to Italy.

On October 1, Fummi was released from prison and wisely fled immediately to his St. Moritz home in neutral Switzerland. He was now considerably more circumspect in his letter writing, thanking TWL profoundly for his help "during my illness."

Ambassador Johnson's letters to TWL had reported at first hand the horror of Japan's ruthless aggression in China: major cities were seized, looted, and burned; the countryside devastated and farmlands ruined, as famine spread across the land. There were millions of casualties, the civilian population terrorized by Japanese troops and air force bombers. Now the signing of the Tripartite Pact publicly confirmed that Japan had joined the aggressor forces intent on dominating the free world, including the U.S.

Lamont, the presiding officer at the Academy of Political Science annual dinner on November 13, chose the occasion to speak out on Japan's latest affront to the U.S. His topic was "The Far Eastern Threat, a Friendly Caution to Japan". TWL had cleared his speech with the State Department and discussed it with Russell Leffingwell, who, while agreeing with his message, noted the irony that Japan's former foremost foreign banker would be the one to chastise her.

TWL observed to the large audience at the Astor Hotel that he had made many friends in Japan, some of whom "because of their liberal views having alas! met death at the hands of assassins." Lamont traced the record of Japanese aggression over the last decade—the seizure of Manchuria in 1931 and then the invasion of the heart of China in 1937 causing widespread destruction and death. The new Triple Axis alliance showed that Japan was still bent on her course of conquest, which was manifestly directed against the U.S. and made Europe and the Far East a single great struggle. "The conflict becomes truly a world war."

America's answer to the threats on both the Atlantic and the Pacific must first be to send more aid to Great Britain, "the pivot of American security," and second to increase its assistance to China in providing planes and military supplies as well as credits. TWL recommended tightening the administration's limited embargo on war materials for Japan, correcting some notable omissions such as materials for the manufacture of bombs.

Lamont had advice for the rulers of Japan: there was nothing to be gained by Japan from the new Axis alliance, because if the time came when Japan needed help, Germany and Italy, 13,000 miles away, neither could nor would provide it. "Japan must abandon once and for all in the Far East the Nazi theory of racial superiority and the idea of 'Asia's new order.' "

Lamont's talk was carried as a front-page story in the *New York Times* and reported in other papers around the country. TWL sent out hundreds of copies of his speech in booklet form to a long list of opinion makers—business executives, government officials and diplomats, publishers and writers, and college presidents.

Frank Knox, Secretary of the Navy, said he liked Lamont's approach to the Far East question. So did Henry Luce, whose *Time* magazine highlighted TWL's talk in its Foreign Relations section. In his replies to the many congratulatory letters he received, TWL continued to emphasize caution in dealing with Japan. Hitler was "the main target." Japan was "part of the same target but not quite so near the bull's eye. I don't believe in precipitating conflict in the Far East that might weaken our effort in aid to Britain." The State Department feared, he wrote, that the clampdown of a complete embargo, including gasoline and oil, might drive Japan to attack the Dutch East Indies and Singapore, which the U.S. and Great Britain were ill prepared to defend.

Ambassador to Japan Joseph C. Grew wrote Lamont that his talk was "the best thing of its kind I have seen, being a restrained and reasonable presentation, expressed in a friendly tone, and carrying irrefutable arguments." Grew asked for twenty more copies to distribute in Japan. "A firm policy will entail inevitable risks of uncalculated strokes by the military extremists which might inflame the American people, but the steadily mounting risks of a policy of laissez-faire on our part would lead to future changes of far greater magnitude."

Lamont also sent a copy to Prince Fumimaro Konoye, Japan's premier, whom TWL had talked to about Japan's growing militarism when the prince visited America in 1934. The prince was a languid intellectual and aristocrat, rapidly becoming a mere figurehead unable to resist the demands of his military chiefs. His reply was philosophical and disheartening.

Yosuke Matsuoka, the foreign minister of Japan, also received a copy of the talk and replied in his letter of December 27, 1940, to TWL. The Triple Alliance was purely defensive in character, he stated, and Japan desired to perpetuate amicable relations with America. "A policy of provocation and pressure, I fear, will only give rise to added tension between Japan and America endangering our traditional friendship, because Japan will not deflect from her settled policy which is based on the creation of the new world order in cooperation with her allies, Germany and Italy."

Taken at face value, it was a chilling prophecy.

In his talk Lamont had said of Britain: "She is fighting for her life, for the freedom of the seas, and for the defense of this hemisphere." For TWL the German conquest of England, the country he loved next to his own, was unthinkable. One way TWL believed that he could be uniquely helpful to the British cause was by offering aid and comfort to Britain's ambassador, his friend Lord Lothian, in his efforts to enlist American sympathy and support for Britain's struggle against the Nazis.

The ambassador frequently visited New York to speak at luncheons or dinners of Manhattan-based organizations. TWL counseled him on which invitations he should accept, or might decline, commenting on the stature and influence of the groups seeking his presence. He urged the ambassador to consider the Lamont residence as his New York hotel, and Lothian and members of his staff stayed at the 70th Street house several times. When the ambassador was scheduled to speak at a lunch or dinner, Lamont took a table at the affair. At the fall dinner of the University Club, Lamont introduced the diplomat before his talk.

In February 1940, Lothian visited the Lamonts at Yeamans Hall, where the two friends played golf on the club course, bordered by giant oaks festooned with Spanish moss. Some had observed that the two things Lothian enjoyed most in life were good conversation and playing golf. The banker and diplomat hit it off well.

TWL's conviction that Britain's successful defense against Hitler was critical to the security of the U.S. clashed with a new initiative launched by ex-President Hoover. Hoover, the acclaimed former administrator of relief programs for Europe during and after the World War, feared that during the coming winter, famine and pestilence would strike the Nazi-occupied parts of Europe, especially the Low Countries and Norway, unless America provided food and medicines to those captive peoples. With food supplies blocked by the British naval blockade, adults and children, especially in the cities, would be starving within months. America must not let this happen. Hoover wanted the British government to permit relief shipments for the occupied countries to pass through the blockade.

During November, Hoover took the first steps to generate public support for his cause, including an in-depth article in *Collier's* on the plight of the captive peoples in Nazi-occupied Europe. Many Americans, guided by religious, humanitarian, or pacifist convictions, were impressed. The blockade, however, was essential to Britain's war plan, and the government, now led by Winston Churchill, naturally felt that large-scale relief for the occupied countries would undermine this strategy. How could the British be sure that the food shipments they permitted to pass through the blockade would not be diverted by the Germans for their own use?

The foremost citizen-advocate of all-out aid to Britain was William Allen White, head of the Committee to Defend America by Aiding the Allies. Known as "The Sage of Emporia," White was the longtime owner and editor of the *Emporia Gazette*. The cracker-barrel wisdom of his editorials in the small-town Kansas newspaper and his many books and magazine articles had given him a large popular following. Affable and straight-talking, White had come to be regarded by his fellow citizens as an American folk hero. White and Lamont, two years his junior, had been friends since the Paris Peace Conference in 1919, which White covered for his paper. In mid-November they joined forces in calling on Hoover to express their concern about his plan. In their opinion Britain alone had the right to decide this question in the light of what she deemed vital to her war strategy.

In his letter of November 22 to President Roosevelt, Lamont asked for a brief meeting to discuss his concern over Hoover's plans for a public campaign to promote his cause, which might disrupt the ranks of aid-to-Britain supporters. The White House response was to invite Lamont to a meeting on November 28 with the president, Secretary Hull, and Norman Davis, now chairman of the American Red Cross, which handled overseas relief programs.

At the White House meeting it was agreed to request permission from the British to ship grain to Spain and condensed milk and medicines for children in unoccupied France through the blockade. Hitler was pressing Spain's Generalissimo Franco to join the Axis powers in the war. The grain supplies, badly needed by Spain to avoid a famine, would help persuade Franco to maintain Spanish neutrality.

After the meeting Lamont went over to the British Embassy to keep a luncheon appointment with Lord Lothian. The British were already in accord with the Spanish strategy and later agreed to the shipments to France. The ambassador appeared very tired to TWL. Just two weeks later, Lothian died in Washington of a kidney disease. A staunch Christian Scientist, he had refused medical treatment to the end.

On December 15, Lamont attended Lord Lothian's funeral service at Washington Cathedral and his burial at Arlington National Cemetery. He wrote a eulogy for his friend, appearing in the *Washington Post*, in which he praised Lothian's service as ambassador in "the last crowning year of his life."

As soon as he heard of Lothian's death, Lamont wrote Lord Halifax, Britain's foreign secretary. Lothian's speeches had been "extraordinarily effective"—"real accomplishments for his country and the cause that he served."

However, Lamont believed that the next ambassador to Washington should be of a different stripe: "What is now urgently needed here is not a politician or a diplomat, but one who is qualified to discuss with some authority, because of his own experience, pressing problems in the financial, economic, and shipping fields."

Prime Minister Winston Churchill had a different set of qualifications for the post in mind—"an outstanding national figure or a statesman versed in every aspect of world politics," he later wrote. The prime minister appointed Lord Halifax, the foreign secretary and former viceroy of India, to the post.

In his letter of December 22, 1940, to Halifax, Lamont adjusted smoothly to the unexpected appointment and delivered his advice to the new envoy.

> I am so glad you are coming. . . . Most Englishmen, unfamiliar with this country through personal visits, have an idea that it is just a New (Anglo-Saxon) World, perhaps not wholly finished and lacking in urbanity here and there, yet essentially the same as England. Any such view has to be accepted with some reserve.

TWL then described the ethnic demographics of American society—the large number of Jews in New York, Irish in Boston and Chicago, Germans in St. Louis and Milwaukee, and other concentrations of hyphenated Americans.

> I say this not to tell you anything new, certainly not to discourage you, but to explain one reason why "America" does not respond at one leap, as many of your countrymen think it should, to a cry from the Anglo-Saxon Motherland to come over and jump into the war as a combatant.

Both political parties were against joining the war, and the isolationists were still a powerful force opposing all-out aid for Britain.

On February 24 Lamont talked to Hoover again about his plan to ship relief supplies to Europe and reported his conversation to Ambassador Halifax in Washington, urging him to explore with Hoover the practicality of his idea. The ex-president fully recognized the importance of a British victory to America and the world and had considerably scaled down his original project: he now proposed to set up soup kitchens in Belgium alone for women and children, who were suffering severely. Hoover's sincere desire to aid the destitute people of Belgium was a sentiment shared by many Americans, which the British should reckon with to avoid creating unnecessary ill will. But the British, with the backing of the administration, continued to block relief projects for Europe. Military strategy ruled the day.

There never had been any question in TWL's mind about William Allen White's determined advocacy of all-out aid to Britain. In September he and Lamont had given enthusiastic support to FDR's trade with Britain of fifty overage destroyers for the right to maintain eight naval bases in Newfoundland, Bermuda, and the British West Indies. Now Lamont and

White agreed that the time had come for the administration to seek authority to provide military aid to Britain—planes, ships, munitions— on a grant basis. After all Britain was already in default on its World War I debt. There was no sense in making new government loans, and private loans to countries in default were prohibited by the Johnson Act. The military aid program for Britain should be perceived as a vital extension of America's own defense build-up to protect itself from the aggressors.

On November 26, 1940, the Committee to Defend America by Aiding the Allies released a declaration of its policy goals. The Atlantic sea route was the lifeline between the U.S. and Britain, and America must be prepared to defend it. Congress should repeal the restrictive statutes which hampered the U.S. in its efforts to aid Britain and other nations under attack. The U.S. and Britain should have a naval plan to enable their fleets to protect the Atlantic for the democracies and stop the spread of war in the Pacific; they must control the seas.

The discussions leading to the policy statement had taken place in New York, where the committee headquarters were located. Many members of the committee's national policy commission were Eastern international- ists, like Lamont, whose support for further steps to aid Britain had advanced beyond the thinking of their fellow citizens in the nation's heartland. After the committee's statement was issued, chairman White returned to his home in Emporia. A native Kansan, White was acutely attuned to the strong isolationist sentiment in the midwestern and prairie states championed by the America First Committee, whose charismatic star was Colonel Charles A. Lindbergh. In a letter to Lamont of Decem- ber 10, White expressed uneasiness about the present course of the Committee to Defend America by Aiding the Allies.

A small group of committee members in New York, dubbed the Century Club because they met at the Century Association clubhouse, were interventionists. They wanted America to declare war against Ger- many which White believed would wreck the committee. "We are getting in Dutch with America," and he was thinking of resigning his chairman- ship of the committee, White added.

On December 23, an article by White appeared in the Scripps-Howard newspapers. The *New York World Telegram* headlined its story: "Sole Purpose of His group Is To Keep America Out of Conflict." White was strongly opposed to sending American escorts to convoy merchant ships carrying supplies to England. He was against efforts to repeal the Johnson Act banning loans to Britain and other countries in default. He opposed repeal of the Neutrality Act forbidding American ships from carrying munitions into the war zones. Such steps would lead America into the war, and "War would defeat the first and last end for which our Committee is organized—to defend America by aiding Great Britain." White's statement seemed to contradict the recently announced policy goals of the committee and immediately caused a bitter rift in its ranks. New York's outspoken mayor, Fiorello H. LaGuardia, a prominent member, led the anti-White charge in his public letter of December 28 to the chairman, dripping with sarcasm.

> It occurred to me that the Committee had better divide. You could continue as chairman of the "Committee to Defend America by Aiding the Allies With Words" and the rest of us would join a "Committee to Defend America by Aiding the Allies with Deeds. . . ."
> With kind personal regards and hoping to have the pleasure of seeing you soon, and with best wishes for as happy a New Year as is possible by simply aiding the Allies with words, I am,
>
> > "Sincerely yours,
> > F. H. LAGUARDIA

Lamont, a member of the committee's national policy commission, and Clark M. Eichelberger, national director of the committee, sprang into peacemaking roles to heal the gaping breach in the committee's public posture. TWL pointed out in an interview that the committee had a great many members throughout the country.

> Naturally, and properly, there are bound to be many shades of opinion. That is one of the advantages of the Committee. It works in a democratic way. But all the members . . . are devoted to the purpose of extending all material help possible to England. . . . Certainly Mr. White was correct when he stated that the Committee was not organized for the purpose of taking this country into war.

In a phone call White told Lamont that in drafting his article he had felt that some compromise was called for to placate the Scripps-Howard chain of newspapers, which had planned to publicly attack the committee for wanting America to go to war. While some Eastern committee members demanded White's immediate resignation as chairman, Lamont disagreed. He felt that White had been an inspiring leader and told the president in a phone call that White was the country's foremost private citizen in promoting aid to Britain.

But the criticism from the major Eastern chapters of the committee had given White second thoughts about his future role. He was not prepared to spend time in New York waging a running battle with some power-hungry Eastern members, who, in his opinion, were "getting out ahead of the President" in promoting aid to the Allies. White submitted his resignation as chairman of the Committee to Defend America by Aiding the Allies effective January 1, 1941. At the same time the president was moving forward at his own pace to transform America into "the arsenal of democracy," as he termed it in a year-end fireside chat.

Britain was rapidly running out of gold and dollars to pay for her war supplies from America, and on January 6, 1941, President Roosevelt called on the Congress to pass a Lend-Lease bill: the U.S. would lend or lease the Allies the arms and other supplies they needed to fight the Axis powers. The proposal was hotly debated in Congress and across the country with the Aid-the-Allies Committee strongly backing it and the America Firsters equally vociferous in denouncing it as a measure that would guarantee war for America.

In vigorously supporting the president's plan, Lamont was again a target of the isolationists' wrath. Hugh Johnson in his *New York World Telegram* column of January 15 accused the House of Morgan, as represented by Thomas W. Lamont, as "active in guiding and propelling our steps toward involvement in this war as they were in 1917." TWL angrily denied the charge in his letter to Johnson the next day.

On January 28 Lamont returned to the familiar podium of the Astor Hotel to speak to six hundred businessmen at a lunch sponsored by the Merchants' Association. TWL warmly endorsed the Lend-Lease bill: the way to avoid war was to arm Britain to help her win the war, a task the bill would expedite.

As to going to war, "The issue rests not with us but with Hitler." TWL gave a new twist to an old subject. There was talk that business favored appeasement, he said, but this was absolutely not so. "Appeasement today means surrender." American industry, management, and labor must step up defense production on a huge scale to meet the crisis confronting the country.

Lamont praised the British people—their heroism in battle and their historic devotion to liberty and freedom. With America's full and speedy aid, they would surely defeat Germany. Equipped with thousands of American-built aircraft they would first gain mastery of the air and then capture the Channel ports, which would spark an uprising against the Nazis by the captive peoples of the Continent. Colonel Lindbergh was dead wrong in arguing that neither side should win the war: German victory would mean semi-slavery for Europe and a terrible new depression in America.

"In such a world as this we cannot forever be the darling of the gods. It is high time that we should shoulder our share of the burden of defeating the despots who threaten our way of life. . . . The salvation of England is for us a matter of self-preservation," declared Lamont.

America's contribution "to help save our world" would be "the final answer." Lamont, while a lifelong Republican, would do everything in his power to support the president in his plans for arming Britain and America. The thrust of TWL's message was a mirror image of his words a generation earlier under similar circumstances. Such talks were bound to arouse the ire of the America Firsters.

The *Chicago Tribune*, published by Colonel Robert R. McCormick, was a powerful voice in the isolationist, antiwar ranks. In March a *Tribune* editorial headlined "Mr. Roosevelt and His Royalists" implied that Lamont and his Morgan associates on the Committee to Defend America by Aiding the Allies favored British interests over those of America because of their vast international holdings. Lamont was furious and arranged a meeting with McCormick. He told the publisher that he was upset and grieved by the editorial, which implied that Lamont and his colleagues were traitors to their country. His memorandum of the conversation stated, "I said my attitude towards aiding England was not one of sentiment for Great Britain, but believing that to be the best method of keeping out of the worst possible trouble ourselves." He knew that McCormick could not have written "such stuff." The Colonel admitted that was so and expressed regret.

In early 1941, TWL believed that the United States could avoid going to war, as he had told James Reston, a young *New York Times* reporter a few weeks earlier at the home of Arthur Hays Sulzberger, the newspaper's publisher. Lamont rejected the notion, put forward by Reston, who had just returned from embattled London, that Great Britain could not survive unless America and the U.S.S.R. joined the conflict.

Beyond speeches, TWL helped his English friends in private ways and through his bank. As the Lamonts prepared to leave for a winter vacation at the Jupiter Island Club in Hobe Sound, Florida, TWL heard from Lady Olive Cubit, the widow of the former governor-general of Bermuda. Could Lamont send a package of food and clothing to her son, Captain Michael Grissell, a POW in Germany? Packages from England to British prisoners did not get through. Her son's only clothes were what he was wearing when he escaped from his burning tank before his capture in May 1940. His mother suggested that Lamont send a blanket, a wool pullover, and several pairs of underwear and socks; chocolate and hard candy; tins of corned beef, sardines, Spam; crackers and water biscuits; tobacco and chewing gum. Address: Olfag VII, Germany. Lamont, who already sent parcels to Nancy Astor and other friends in England, was glad to help and later arranged through the Red Cross to send semi-monthly food packages to Grissell. A year later Lamont received a postcard from the British captain. The Red Cross food parcels, which he shared with his comrades, had come through regularly. "Almost literally you have saved our lives," wrote the young officer.

The securities business which Lamont had solicited from the British government at the outbreak of the war proved to be a delicate and complex operation. Once again the Morgan bank acted as agent for the British and French governments in liquidating American securities purchased from their nationals. In 1939 the two governments held about $1.5 billion in marketable U.S. securities, the bulk of which were owned by the British. During 1940 and 1941 these stocks and bonds were sold to raise funds for the Allied governments' huge purchases in the U.S. John M. Meyer, Jr., directed the operation at the bank, which involved dealing discreetly with scores of brokers and investment firms across the country.

J. P. Morgan & Co. also advised the British in other areas. As Congress debated the Lend-Lease bill in 1941, the administration decided that a large visible gesture by the British was called for to demonstrate the sincerity of their effort to raise funds to pay for their supplies. They asked the British government, which had purchased the interest of U.K. companies in their American operations, to divest itself of the American Viscose Co., the largest American producer of rayon and a subsidiary of Courtaulds Ltd. of London. J. P. Morgan & Co. recommended that the British appoint Morgan Stanley and Dillon Read as joint managers of an underwriting syndicate to offer the shares to the public, and the issue was sold successfully in May 1941, raising $54 million for the British Treasury.

Relations with the British government were cordial but far more routine than the active high-level dealings during the Great War. The Glass-Steagall Act had considerably diminished J. P. Morgan & Co.'s banking stature. The bank could no longer direct the operations of Morgan Grenfell to serve its interests with the British government. There was no purchasing agency assignment with its vast scope of operations and inherent power. But the vigor of TWL's personal advocacy of aid to Britain was not muted.

Lamont, now seventy, had not involved himself in the bank's routine business for some time and now largely devoted his efforts to Exeter, Harvard, and other good works—as well as to embattled Britain and China. On April 28 he spoke at the luncheon meeting of the Economic

Club of Detroit on "China and the Dictators." "We shall defend our Atlantic interests by all aid to Britain, and we shall preserve our Far Eastern defense by all aid to China," declared Lamont. He noted the Japanese threat to British Hong Kong and Singapore, the Dutch East Indies, and all of America's Pacific interests. He called for tougher U.S. trade restrictions—an embargo on shipments of scrap iron and oil—to immobilize Japan's war machine.

> Japan's position reminds me a little of this story: On the cliffs of the Yangtse River, not far above Nanking, there is a bold promontory that juts out over the stream and that for generations has been known as Suicide Rock. So many hundred despairing individuals had leapt to their death that finally the authorities erected on the rock in large Chinese characters this legend: "Stop. Reflect. If you don't do it today, you can still do it tomorrow, but if you do it today, you can't undo it tomorrow."
>
> The Japanese are standing on a suicide rock. Every instinct ought to be telling them to turn back, to take the long view, to join the powers that must eventually gain the world struggle.

The American people were determined "to defend their own freedom by helping other nations defend theirs. . . . The indomitable, unconquerable spirit of the British people, the heroism and dogged resistance of China to Japan, backed by America's determination not to surrender the sea lanes of the Atlantic and the Pacific, will spell the ultimate victory in both East and West," said Lamont.

Japanese foreign minister Matsuoka was one of the hundreds of names on the mailing list to receive a copy of "China and the Dictators." This time there was no reply.

An increasing amount of Lend-Lease aid was ending up at the bottom of the Atlantic as British ships fell victim to German U-boats and surface raiders. In April 1941, FDR took action: the U.S. established a base in Greenland and began air surveillance and naval patrols of the western part of the North Atlantic. Presented by the administration as a move to secure America's Atlantic defense, the patrols helped protect British freighters from German attacks; they were a step removed from escorting British convoys, which could trigger shooting incidents and enrage the isolationists, who still persisted.

FDR, who valued Lamont's public support of aiding Britain, outlined his patrol strategy to Lamont in a phone call on May 1. TWL, in a letter to the president the next day, said he was sure the American people would rally behind the president's move just as they had in backing his Lend-Lease proposal.

Lamont showered the White House with letters and phone calls during the spring of 1941, usually talking to Colonel Watson. The threat of war was mounting, and Lamont yearned to participate in the high councils deciding the nation's fate. In one letter he told the president:

> Naturally this is the last great crisis for our country that I shall probably live to face or take any part in. Today I have no ambition save to be of some service. This, therefore, is only to say again that, as you know, I am completely at your disposal at any time. I have no material or personal interests that command me longer. I only want to be of help.

In another letter TWL told the president that Jack Morgan, who fully supported FDR's foreign policy, had told him that he believed the American people were awaiting a fresh call to action.

> Then, quoting Holy Writ more frequently and accurately than other men I know, he laid on my desk the enclosed text, 1 Cor. XIV-8 which runs: "For if the trumpet give an uncertain sound who shall prepare himself for the battle?"
>
> I was mentioning this to Eve Curie at dinner . . . and I was telling her who it was that handed me the text. "Ah, yes," she said in her quick French way, "is it not amusing? The Morgans getting at Roosevelt through God."

TWL added in a postscript that he hoped the story would give the president a little laugh in the midst of his heavy burdens.

From Pulpit Harbor to Pearl Harbor

Among the various communications from TWL to the president was a brief note sent out to the presidential yacht *Potomac* anchored in Pulpit Harbor, North Haven, Maine, on August 15, 1941. The president and Harry Hopkins, FDR's closest adviser, had just returned from a shipboard meeting with Prime Minister Churchill at Placentia Bay, Newfoundland. With their staffs they had formulated plans for patrolling the North Atlantic and cooperative efforts elsewhere. The two leaders of the free world had also agreed on a statement of principles to preserve world peace after the war, which came to be known as the Atlantic Charter.

Sheltered Pulpit Harbor had long been a favorite of cruisers along the Maine coast. A rocky tower, suggesting a church pulpit and topped by an osprey nest, guarded the harbor entrance. Meadows and spruce woods ran down to its stony beaches, blanketed with brown seaweed at low tide. Here and there a barn, summer houses, and the private docks of their residents dotted the shoreline.

Lamont, whose Sky Farm was perched on a bluff overlooking the bay near the harbor mouth, had inquired if the president was "receiving." He was, and TWL's motor launch whisked him out to the *Potomac*, where he joined FDR and Harry Hopkins on the yacht's fantail. The President, seated in his wheelchair, stretched out his hand and warmly greeted his visitor. A cigarette in its holder was clenched in his teeth; he appeared to be in fine fettle. After their forty-five-minute talk Lamont wrote brief penciled notes of the conversation.

TWL congratulated FDR on his idea of meeting Churchill to discuss strategy to win the war and preserve the postwar peace—"Most wonderful story of the century, a stroke of genius."

The president said the occasion had given him a good chance to get acquainted with Churchill. FDR had not seen him since 1918, although their private cable exchanges had brought them together in recent months.

TWL said he understood that Harry Hopkins was Winston Churchill's "white-haired boy."

"Yes, yes," replied FDR, but even more so Joe Stalin's. He and Churchill had kidded Hopkins about being "Uncle Joe's favorite." After Hitler's invasion of Russia in June, FDR had sent Harry Hopkins to Moscow to confer with Stalin about Russia's needs for Lend-Lease aid. Hopkins then flew to England and accompanied Churchill on the ocean crossing to meet the president in Newfoundland.

Hopkins said he believed that Stalin was a great leader. The Russian people and soldiers were determined to resist the German armies to the end. The Soviet leaders were counting on the Russian winter to turn back the invaders. The Germans would not take either Leningrad or Moscow before "the snow flies," they forecast.

FDR described the four-day meeting: "We were a great assembly"— twenty-seven ships of the U.S. fleet surrounding the heavy cruiser U.S.S. *Augusta*, carrying the president and his staff. Churchill was on board the new British battleship *Prince of Wales*, accompanied by a squadron of corvettes.

FDR and Churchill had lunch together the first day and talked for three hours. Later the Americans hosted a dinner for sixteen on the *Augusta*. Each American and British official and staff officer was matched with his counterpart: Roosevelt and Churchill; Sumner Welles of the State Department and Sir Alexander Cadogan of the Foreign Office; General George C. Marshall, U.S. Army Chief of Staff, and Sir John Dill, Chief of the Imperial General Staff; and so on down the line. FDR instructed each of his aides "to go off with his opposite member and get everything. . . . This they did, not a thing left untold."

The president chuckled. "Well, it is to laugh. You know, in the American Navy supper comes at 6:30. But with these English blokes, not until eight o'clock. And the amount of liquor they'd put away. Four days of it used me up completely."

Lamont's notes then say: "(W. C. Hush)." One can only speculate that the reference was to the prime minister's well-known fondness for whisky and champagne.

The president had been very moved by the Sunday Divine Service conducted on the quarterdeck of the *Prince of Wales*. The crew of the battleship, 1,700 men, 350 sailors from the *Augusta,* and a contingent from every ship in both squadrons attended. The hymn singing of the crews in chorus was magnificent; "Onward Christian Soldiers," "The Navy Hymn," and "O God Our Help in Ages Past" were Churchill's selections. Hopkins added that the commander of the *Prince of Wales* read the service beautifully from the pulpit, which was flanked by the Stars and Stripes and the Union Jack draped closely together. The service had been filmed and would make "great propaganda" when the movie was shown in the U.S., FDR observed.

Lamont inquired if the president felt encouraged by the shipboard conference.

FDR: "More than I have been for many months. We are now furnishing the British X quantities on an ascending scale." The president would probably request Congress for an additional $2.5 billion in Lend-Lease aid. It is a big sum, but halfway measures were no good. "I think I'll get it."

TWL: "Yes, but wasn't that vote in the House dreadful?" He was referring to the marginal 203 to 202 vote cast in favor of extending the period of military service under the Selective Service Act to eighteen months. Lamont then referred to a recent statement of Republican war aims, reflecting the strong isolationist influence and depth of antiwar feeling among the party's leadership. "Terrible! I am a Republican, but the party has gone out the window."

TWL then turned the conversation to the Japanese threat in the Pacific. The talks between Japanese ambassador Kichisaburo Nomura and Secretary Hull were getting nowhere; the aims of the two nations were poles apart. In the course of July the Japanese army completed its occupation of French Indochina. On July 26 the U.S. government, determined that it would no longer tolerate Japanese aggression and conquest, froze all Japanese assets in the United States, effectively ending all trade with Japan, and on August 1 the administration imposed a complete embargo on shipments of oil and gasoline.

"Do you think the Japanese will dare to strike?" asked Lamont.

FDR: "Nobody knows, but on Sunday when I return to Washington, I am going to send for Nomura and talk pretty much up and down to him."

The president had already proposed to Nomura that Indochina and Thailand be neutralized—just like Switzerland, said FDR. Japan would withdraw all her troops from the area. In return she would be guaranteed access to the rice, minerals, and other raw materials in the region that she needed. The Japanese reply, received just before he embarked for New-foundland, had been unsatisfactory.

FDR: "I shall push and may get somewhere."

Harry Hopkins: "I can't be too sanguine about any future deals these days with those fellows."

TWL alluded to the keen press interest in the joint declaration by the president and Churchill of the common policies their countries would pursue to achieve a lasting and just peace in the world.

FDR replied that he had insisted on a provision that Germany must be disarmed and kept disarmed. "We can't trust the old Woodrow Wilson treaty with these fellows."

It was time to go, and Harry Hopkins escorted TWL up to the main deck to see him off. In bidding Lamont good-bye Hopkins observed, "We are going to have some pretty hard bumps ahead."

TWL's campaign of advice and assistance to Lord Halifax was progressing apace. During the first two years of the ambassador's tour, the growing intimacy of their relationship was reflected in the salutations in their letters to each other. Lamont went from "Dear Lord Halifax" to "My Dear Halifax" to "Dear Edward," and the ambassador reciprocated, ending up with "Dear Tom." To help the ambassador present his case to the American public, TWL organized several dinners at the 70th Street house and the Links Club for Halifax to meet some of the nation's media chiefs—Arthur H. Sulzberger and Charles Merz of the *New York Times*, the Ogden Reids and Geoffrey Parsons of the *Herald Tribune*, and Henry Luce of Time-Life, among others. Lamont carefully arranged the table shape and seating plan of these affairs to avoid ruffling the sensibilities of the rival press executives.

Like his predecessor, Halifax spoke in cities across the country to arouse support for the British struggle against the Axis powers. TWL bombarded him with ideas for his speeches: Why not point out the similarity between the Magna Carta and the Bill of Rights—each stating "the same basic utterances marking the beginning of democratic government in each country"?

TWL also advised on the selection of New York groups to be addressed by the ambassador.

> In America, and especially in New York, we have so many public dinners of various kinds that it must be thoroughly bewildering to anyone coming more or less fresh to the scene. Let me explain in a word if I may: The Pilgrims to whom the incoming Ambassador always makes his first address is made up with its guests very largely of New York men of affairs, a strong sprinkling of lawyers, etc. The English-Speaking Union has a somewhat different clientele. Women are largely engaged in its activities as well as men, and you could call it more a central or uptown outfit than the Pilgrims. The Academy of Political Science, while of course over-lapping a little both of the others, is still in a somewhat different category, made up of what I would call the intelligentsia, a great many educators, college professors, etc.

On the other hand, the American Political Science Association, mainly composed of professors, was respectable but "not very exciting." Lord Halifax could decline their invitation.

TWL was on hand when the ambassador was awarded an honorary degree at the Harvard commencement exercises in June. Addressing the large assembly, Harvard's President Conant asked, "How long will the people of the United States think it right to let the British do all the fighting for them?"

Lord Halifax frequently visited New York for speaking engagements, sometimes flying into the city's new La Guardia Airport, and often stayed with the Lamonts or dropped by for breakfast or tea before an appointment. Florence gave her impression of the lean and angular-faced diplomat in a letter to Austin: "Lord Halifax was here for breakfast today. He has a good mind and a wonderful character, but is so lacking in fire. What can we do about it? Vitamins?"

The ambassador did have a good dry wit. More than once he likened the workings of the American government to "a disorderly day's rabbit shooting."

* * *

The talks between Secretary Hull and Ambassador Nomura were deadlocked. The Japanese would not accept the American proposals to bring about a just peace in the Far East; the U.S. would not lift its embargo on trade with Japan. On October 16 General Hideki Tojo became Japan's prime minister, and the die was cast: Tojo was committed to war with the U.S., and, as it turned out, the Washington negotiations were a smoke screen for Japan's war preparations. The president and his chief aides, armed with intelligence from deciphering the Japanese diplomatic code, had reason to suspect that the Japanese were planning new attacks, but where?

Naturally, the rest of the American public was not privy to this secret information. On November 13, TWL sent a memorandum to Walter Lippmann disagreeing with the assertion in his morning column that U.S.-Japanese relations had reached the crisis stage. Japan's ruling principle, said Lamont, was that she must be on the winning side in any world war.

> In September 1940, being convinced of Germany's winning . . . they hop into the Axis. Six months ago, however, the outcome begins to look somewhat doubtful. They have to begin to hedge. . . . They initiate so-called peace talks at Washington that they and we know will not amount to a hill of beans, but they prolong them in order to save their face and put up a front to their own people.
>
> Tojo, knowing that the past so-called peace talks are nil arranges a fresh set-up. He will send out a new emissary. Mark my words; this new emissary will fool around here for another three or four months purely for the sake of stalling. A lot may happen in that time. . . . If at the end of that time the situation is practically unchanged, they will devise another stalling device. I repeat—they will not take such action as will get them into a war where they will be licked, but they will bide their time and jump after the cat has jumped.

But by mid-November it was the imperialistic Japanese cat that was poised to jump upon its unsuspecting prey with feline stealth and ferocity. On November 24, as Admiral Isoroku Yamamoto was assembling his fleet in the Kuriles, Lamont told a United China Relief luncheon in Philadelphia that Japan was bluffing in its war of nerves with the U.S. He did not expect to see her "go on the rampage." On the next day the Japanese carrier force in the Kuriles headed out to sea, bound for Pearl Harbor. The brilliant attack plan was designed by Admiral Yamamoto, the same officer who had served as translator for Lamont's audience with Emperor Hirohito fourteen years before.

On Sunday, December 7, the Japanese struck Pearl Harbor, sinking or damaging a large part of the Pacific Fleet. In New York the incredible news filtered through the crowd watching a professional football game between the N.Y. Giants and Brooklyn Dodgers at the Polo Grounds. Across the Hudson Tom and Florence heard the shocking report on the radio in the library at Palisades.

On the next day, following the president's "day of infamy" speech, Congress declared that a state of war existed with Japan. Three days later Germany and Italy declared war on the United States. The greatest naval disaster in American history had plunged the country into a war that was now truly global.

Norman Davis immediately asked Lamont to become chairman of the Red Cross National Advisory Committee, largely a fund-raising operation, and TWL agreed. But he yearned to play a larger role in his country's war effort, as he wrote the president.

> I do not have to reiterate my anxiety to be of help. . . . I am more or less footloose now for anything that may come up.
>
> In the World War I was able to serve Woodrow Wilson informally and inconspicuously. And even though over twenty years have elapsed since then, I am still just as keen to be of assistance in any direction. . . .
>
> In the midst of all our cares, Mr. President, it must be a source of great inward satisfaction to you to know that at last your patient, courageous handling of foreign affairs over the past few years has now come into its own. Even the most hardboiled isolationist must admit in his heart of hearts that had it not been for your foresight and dogged persistence we should now be lost in any war defense measures.

FDR replied on December 17: "As a matter of fact I did take your offer of service for granted and may have to call on you at any time. Generous words of approval from an old friend like you are heartening."

TWL did not give up easily. On January 26, 1942, he called on the president at the White House. Winston Churchill, who had arrived in Washington just before Christmas, had spent several weeks on and off conferring with the president before flying home to Britain. FDR said that the U.S. and Britain were now following the military strategy that he and the prime minister, along with the combined chiefs of staff, had planned earlier in the month.

But Churchill, said FDR, had not given much thought to preserving international peace in the postwar world. In his memorandum of the conversation, Lamont reported that the president believed that the U.S. would have to join in "the police work. . . . Somebody had to be in a position, if there were signs of Germany breaking loose again, to crack down on them hard."

The president said that Churchill did not have the economic mind that "you and I have," and had mentioned the possibility of establishing a new international commodity dollar. Lamont replied that the U.S. dollar was good enough for him. After the war America would first need to feed the stricken European countries and support their currencies, using part of the ample U.S. gold reserves. However, once the economies of these countries were stabilized, they would become good and steady customers for American goods, triggering "international trade and economic adjustment." The president replied that he fully agreed.

FDR told Lamont that after wracking his brain late into the night, he had thought up the title of "United Nations" for the twenty-six countries at war with the Axis, who had just signed a military alliance to fight the common enemy. In answer to TWL's question, the president replied that both Secretary Hull and Vice President Henry Wallace had formed groups to plan the organization to preserve world peace after the war.

Lamont immediately volunteered to cooperate with either or both groups, "working behind the scenes." The U.S. and Britain would be the decisive players in planning the international organization. His experience at the Paris Peace Conference in 1919 and in dealing with the British for over twenty-five years should be useful.

The president said he would ask Hull and Wallace to call Lamont. "But it will probably rest there," TWL recorded. He was not optimistic that he would be invited to the party. While FDR had appointed prominent Republicans to high posts—Henry L. Stimson as Secretary of War and Frank Knox as Secretary of Navy, Lamont knew he bore a special onus: the strong Wall Street—Morgan bank identification was anathema to New Deal politicians.

On the Home Front

In a letter to his parents Corliss had referred to "the noble mansion" on 70th Street "with its procession of foreign nobles and noble men." In the winter of 1942 the procession was steady. Ambassador Halifax came and went. American poets Edna St. Vincent Millay and Robert Frost were houseguests along with Julian Huxley, the eminent English biologist.

Edna St. Vincent Millay read her poems out loud to Florence one evening. She was "a dear person," but drinking too much for her own good, reported Florence, who was virtually a teetotaler. Robert Frost's conversation was original and refreshing. Huxley was an easy houseguest but tended to dominate conversations with the other visitors; he simply talked too much, observed Florence. Among the guests at the Lamonts' dinner for Huxley were Wendell Willkie and Robert Moses, the New York Parks Commissioner, neither one a shrinking violet. Presumably the dinner conversation was vigorous.

A few days later the Soviet ambassador to America, Maxim Litvinov, came to tea. "He is an intelligent old fox and seems to have nice moral ideals about international relations," wrote Florence. Lamont, who had once called Stalin a "gangster," was determined to help his ambassador boost his country's image with the American public, the same cause ardently advanced by his son Corliss.

Corliss, who had visited Russia twice, had long admired the Soviet-Communist system of government ownership and a centrally planned economy. His views positioned him well to the left of American main-stream thinking, including that of his capitalist father. For some time critics had pinned such labels as "Silk-Shirt Communist" on him. Now he had a fresh and compelling message to deliver about Russia. America's new ally, enduring tremendous suffering, was bravely defending her homeland against the common foe, Hitler's rampaging armies. Russia deserved all-out assistance from America in her desperate struggle. In his role as chairman of the American Friends of the Soviet Union, Corliss was speaking to a variety of groups across the country.

On March 25 Lamont publicly embraced his son's cause, warmly introducing Litvinov before the ambassador's talk to a Council on Foreign Relations dinner in New York. He reminded his audience of Litvinov's advocacy of collective security in Europe to curb Hitler's expansionism before Munich in 1938. Said Lamont: when Hitler is defeated, "Russia will be a great force for permanent peace in the world."

In contrast to the Great War, the Morgan bank's tasks in World War II were relatively tame. One hundred and forty-two men left to join the military services, almost a third of the male staff, and under wartime conditions there was little scope for expansion. The bank continued to absorb large amounts of government bonds, now financing the nation's war effort, and earned a net profit of $4 million in 1941. George Whitney ran the bank, which took several key initiatives during the early war years.

In 1942, J. P. Morgan & Co. became a member of the Federal Reserve system, and a secondary public offering of 8¼ percent of Morgan's outstanding stock, owned by the officers and their families, was made by an underwriting group headed by Smith Barney & Co. For the first time outsiders could buy an interest in the legendary banking house. The time had come to establish a market value for Morgan stock for future estate tax valuations (both Morgan and Lamont were in their seventies) and provide greater liquidity for the stockholders and their heirs. Future stock offerings would take place when the market seemed receptive.

Following incorporation the Morgan bank established a trust department to handle personal trusts, corporate pension funds and the like, and investment advisory accounts. Some renovations were called for to adapt the third floor of the Corner for the new department. J. P. Morgan's barbershop with its marbled and mirrored walls was converted to a waiting room, and a powder room was installed, whose unmarked door led to some confusion and embarrassment.

Soon U.S. Steel, whose board of directors included Morgan and Lamont, and other corporations were assigning their pension funds to the bank for management, as wartime conditions and a favorable IRS tax ruling spawned a mini-boom in trusteed pension plans. The bank also managed a handful of endowment funds, including the Phillips Exeter and Smith College funds (thanks to TWL), and some large personal accounts. For his own investments, mostly common stocks, TWL had retained a full-time expert, John G. Pennypacker, a former Guaranty Trust investment executive, to advise him.

There were plenty of wartime causes to satisfy TWL's penchant for good works and public speaking. Lamont was on the National Board of Directors of United China Relief, working closely with Paul Hoffman, the president of Studebaker and chairman of UCR, about soliciting donations from the country's leading business executives and their corporations. Lamont had always enjoyed a good costume party, and at a gala UCR fund-raiser at New York's River Club TWL came smilingly attired as a court official of the Ching dynasty wearing a long black queue.

Lamont worked hard for his friend Norman Davis, head of the American Red Cross, as chairman of the Red Cross War Fund $50 million appeal. A *Daily Mirror* photograph showed Lamont eating Army chow from a mess kit at the head table of a luncheon for 1,000 at the Commodore Hotel; another one showed two Red Cross nurses demonstrating their skills in gently bandaging his "wounded" arm.

The national appeal, which was strongly supported by Americans, was not without mishap. Pierre S. du Pont, a generous donor, wrote TWL to complain about the Red Cross assignment planned for Eleanor Roosevelt: she would visit Australia for the Red Cross to survey the country's needs for American assistance. Mr. du Pont questioned her qualifications for the job and the use of donations to the Red Cross for this mission, which he clearly viewed as a personal junket for the First Lady. Lamont and Davis did their best to allay his fears: Mrs. Roosevelt's credentials for the assignment were excellent; she had long been active in social work. Furthermore, the Army transport plane that was flying her to Australia was scheduled to make the flight anyway for military purposes.

In June 1942, ninety-five members of the Harvard class of 1892 assembled in Cambridge, breaking all previous records for a fiftieth reunion. TWL played golf Monday and Tuesday at the Country Club with Arthur Lockett and other classmates. On Wednesday the class gathered again at W. Cameron Forbes's Gay Farm for camaraderie and games, including a form of mini-golf laid out on the estate's polo field. Forbes, who had been a governor-general of the Philippines and ambassador to Japan, was suffering from an attack of shingles and received his classmates from a couch in the living room before lunch. A small band played melodies from the Gay Nineties, and the class picture was taken, showing TWL seated front and center, squinting into the bright sunlight.

The class secretary reported later: "The presiding officer? Naturally, inevitably, and, on the whole, beautifully—Tom Lamont," who was chairman and treasurer of the class committee. "It should be added that Tom himself was in fine form, and supplied endless eloquence and poetry."

Other speakers included Hugh Landon, the class orator at the 1892 commencement, who had pledged that the graduating class would not fail Harvard's expectations for it: "We can and we will." Landon, drawing on the biographical data sent in by members of the class, reported on the fulfillment of that promise made a half century before.

For his closing remarks Lamont chose his favorite topic—war and peace and his admiration for the embattled British people. They so loved their land that they would never give it up, said TWL, quoting from Shakespeare's *Richard II*:

> *This happy breed of men, this little world;*
> *This precious stone set in the silver sea,*
> *This blessed plot, this earth, this realm, this England. . . .*

In concluding Lamont said:

In this quiet room, returning from the leafy elms of Cambridge, do we realize how all civilization, all Christendom is hanging in the balance? This is no mere war. It is a gigantic struggle: a war in the souls of men; an immense conflict between light and darkness; evil incarnate trying to overcome the divine principle in the hearts of men.

It is a great turning point in the history of the world; like the fall of Rome; like Runnymede and the Magna Carta; like the discovery of America; or the American Revolution. What threatens us most in this great aggression against men of good will all over the world is the loss not of the material, but of the invisible things of the spirit which are the essence of the community and a civilization.

But, finally, the day will break and the cannon will cease firing. Then America must not fail to fight for the victory of peace. She may have to make great sacrifices, throw away ancient prejudices, but she will have to join the rest of the world in cooperation and collective security or we shall have no world at all.

It was vintage Lamont.

TWL then expressed his affection for his classmates and called for the singing of "Auld Lang Syne" and "Fair Harvard." The venerable gentlemen ended the evening with a rousing cheer for the Class of '92.

The next day TWL joined his classmates in marching in the traditional parade through Harvard Yard to the Alumni Exercises. They happily acknowledged the applause of the large crowd lining their route through the college quadrangle.

TWL II

Thomas W. Lamont was especially proud that another Lamont was bound for Harvard—his oldest grandchild and namesake, TWL II, known as Tommy, who was a seventeen-year-old about to graduate from Exeter. As president of the school trustees TWL signed his grandson's diploma.

Like his grandfather, Tommy had engaged in literary pursuits at Exeter—president of the *Phillips Exeter Review* and feature editor of the *Exonian*. His classmates and teachers remarked on his quick mind and maturity of thought. He was usually "immense fun" and "occasionally irritating," observed a friend. In argument he did not hesitate to let fly his sharp wit to deflate a slower-thinking adversary. He was an effective debater on the academy debating team. He excelled at writing and produced thoughtful analyses of the political and social questions of the day that he had joined his elders in discussing at the Palisades dinner table or on North Haven picnics. His siblings and cousins regarded him with awe.

Tommy was far more worldly than his grandfather had been at the same age—intellectually and socially. Trips to Europe, skiing house parties, debutante coming-out balls, and nightclubs were all part of his life. TWL had grown up in an American Age of Innocence. The times were different, and so were the circumstances, thanks to TWL's own achievements and way of living. Yet TWL's views and style had certainly influenced his grandson, and in a class poll Tommy was voted "the best speaker."

After attending the Exeter commencement exercises in 1942, Lamont showed a copy of Tommy's senior class oration to Russell Leffingwell. The class orator had delivered his address "without a single note before a large and enthusiastic audience of admiring Exeter men and parents. It goes without saying that he never submitted a part of his remarks to either his father, mother, or to me."

Tommy's perspective of the viewpoint of American boys about to go to war was indeed different from his grandfather's oft-expressed spiritual call to arms. The war had changed the thinking of many young Americans. They had been told that Socialism and Communism were evil, but "Russia has vindicated herself in our eyes by unheard-of sacrifice of blood, by heroism which has saved Russia and saved us. In America as well as Britain, the social and economic barriers between fellow-countrymen are crumbling. . . . Some of us already feel that Socialism or a social democracy would be a good thing. . . . The swing is definitely towards the left."

Christian unity and pacifism had failed and "the potency of the church . . . was a nonentity." But youth was not without faith. It had turned to nationalism and the flag had taken the place of the cross. Yet "some of us . . . may gladly ask for the salvation of Christ when death stares us in the face." American boys would fight for the flag—a way of life, a form of government that was "the fairest, most liberal, and most equitable yet devised."

"We are resolved to stamp Fascism from the face of the earth, and, rest assured, we will not leave the peace conference to the wabblings of . . .

old men," declared Tommy. The sacrifice of English and American boys in the Great War was "blasphemed and wasted by inferiors who ruled the peace after the conflict."

In America "our elders" chose national isolation, and weak men still shuddered at the thought of a new and better world organization. "But youth is forever optimistic. . . . We will fight primarily to save the homes and soil of America, but also for the peace and freedom to create something really better. . . .

"It is a rotten thing to die in vain."

There were echoes of TWL, Corliss, and even Lincoln, but the voice was uniquely that of an idealistic and passionate young man ready to join a great crusade.

Florence wrote Austin that Tommy's oration was too radical for her. "It was a young Corliss speaking . . . but it was good. It was nice to see the three Toms there, all Exeter graduates."

Perhaps the three Toms wondered when they would all be together again. In July Thomas S. Lamont received a major's commission in the Army Services of Supply and flew to London, where he was assigned to the Eighth Air Force as a procurement officer. Young Tommy, who would become eighteen on October 1, was planning to join the Navy.

On Labor Day the family picnicked on an island near North Haven. By departure time a strong southwest wind had built up to gale force; the bay was foaming with whitecaps. Tommy elected to skipper the knock-about on the long beat home to Pulpit Harbor with a teenage friend and twelve-year-old brother Lansing. Heading out into the bay, sailing close to the wind, and heeling far over in the gusts, the knockabout soon had water pouring over the leeward rail into the cockpit, much of which found its way through an open companionway into the small forecabin. Tommy headed the boat for shore, and the knockabout disappeared behind a headland from the view of TWL and the family in a motorboat. It never reappeared.

Foundering badly, the knockabout swamped and rapidly sank, bow first. It was impossible to retrieve the life jackets from the water-filled cabin. The three boys swam for shore 150 yards away, an exhausting effort in soaking clothes and chilling Maine water. Austin returned in the motorboat to search for the boys in vain.

It was a frightening half hour for the family until Tommy phoned from a local farmhouse that the boys were safe on shore. TWL summed up the family viewpoint in a letter: "These young boys think they know all about sailing and may get a lesson too much at some time or other."

In the fall of 1942, Tommy, a Harvard freshman, definitely decided to become a Navy flier. His mother, grandfather, grandmother, and Corliss all tried to talk him out of it over an October weekend at Palisades. TWL wrote his daughter, "We are all agreed that for him, because his judgement is not very steady, it would be infinitely better . . . to complete the Naval R.O.T.C. two year course at college and be really qualified to do something, rather than make a poor flier." After the summer sailing incident Tommy's family seriously questioned his readiness for responsibility at sea.

His elders failed in their effort. Volunteering for the Naval Air Force, Tommy was inducted as a Naval Aviation Cadet and, on April 15, 1943, entered the U.S. Navy Flight Preparatory School at Colgate University. Tommy sought the blessing of his father in London: "I wanted to fight and to fight soon. I wanted to fly instead of being on a ship. . . . Harvard's just drudgery now. . . . Can't you see why I want to go?"

TWL's own contribution to the Navy was twofold—a model of a Taiwan hydroelectric dam, financed by a 1931 Morgan-led loan, which was sought by Naval Intelligence, and the *Reynard*, TWL's swift seventy-two-foot motor yacht. After an exchange of letters with Navy Secretary Frank Knox, the Navy bought the *Reynard* for $1, planning to use it for harbor patrols. A marine brokerage firm appraised the yacht at $30,000, the amount TWL would take as a tax deduction for his contribution to the war effort.

A New Father-Son Team

While TWL and TSL viewed the world in harmony, Corliss and his father were poles apart over Russia's totalitarian government and centrally controlled economy. TWL abhorred the socialistic system of economic planning which, as he wrote Corliss, stifled and suppressed individual initiative and endeavors that could bring about a better life for the Russian people. But in 1942 these were of course secondary considerations for TWL: the Russians were now valiant comrades-in-arms.

In a letter of September 20, 1942 to the *New York Times*, TWL denounced Americans who continued to criticize Russia's defects—its economic system, the denial of civil liberties, and suppression of religion. "They fail to realize that on all major counts the Nazis constitute the one urgent menace to the survival of the standards that they hold so dear."

Three times in modern history Russia had joined Great Britain "to preserve Europe from subjugation by a dictator" in the wars against Napoleon, the Kaiser, and now Hitler. . . . "Is it not true today that the ultimate peace of Europe depends on the steadfastness of Russia at the eastern end and of Britain at the western end?"

TWL noted the great contributions Russians had made to civilization in literature—Tolstoy, Dostoevsky, and Chekhov, among others—and in drama, music, ballet, and science. "The racial stock that produced them will not cease to flower," he said.

Too many people felt that it was America's duty "to make the world over in our own image." Others criticized Russia's pact with Germany in 1939 in an attempt to appease Hitler. But at Munich only a year earlier "Britain had tried her hand at appeasement." Russia, like Britain, had had to buy time to prepare herself against "the inevitable invader, Hitler." And in the U.S., Congress enacted "the worse than futile Neutrality Law" declaring that no country drawn into war, even though the victim of atrocious assault, could purchase munitions in the U.S., which gave Hitler "the green light" he was looking for. There were "lots of pots around the world calling kettles black."

It was clear, said TWL, that the four great powers—the U.S., Britain, Russia, and China—had to stand together now and in the future to defeat and prevent new onslaughts from "those traditionally ferocious nations, Germany and Japan."

"Let us be friends with our friends and do our fighting against our enemies. . . . Russia has borne the heat and burden of the bloody battle on land. On her back has been the heaviest load." The U.S. must "do everything in our power to relieve her agony."

Lamont sent out a pamphlet form of the letter to his long mailing list, and the response was generally favorable. But some could not forget Stalin's ruthless purges, and the reaction of a "1917 A.E.F. Vet" to TWL's letter was bitter on another score:

> What do you international bankers know about the problems of the great middle class who make up this country? . . . The boys who fight your wars get damn little after it is over. For before Pearl Harbor men over 30, yes 25, had a hell of a time getting jobs.

> We need a real America presided over by real Americans, not royalty boot
> lickers of your stripe.

Ambassador Litvinov congratulated TWL on his letter, and Lamont
delivered a condensed version of it on a "March of Time" radio broadcast. He declared again that America should support Russia, knowing
that "every German that falls on Russian soil means one less German at
our throats."

While the Russian losses were staggering, the Germans had suffered
over one and a third million casualties and failed to take Moscow and
Leningrad. By early November 1942, German soldiers were fighting their
way into the great industrial city of Stalingrad. German bombing and
shelling and ferocious fighting had left the city in ruins, but Stalingrad
still did not fall.

For some weeks Corliss had been working with former U.S. ambassador to Russia Joseph E. Davies in planning a giant rally to inspire support
for Russia's war effort, the Congress of American-Soviet Friendship. A
distinguished list of patrons was lined up, including Secretary of State
Hull, New York's Governor Herbert Lehman, Mayor La Guardia, Ambassador Halifax, industrialist Owen D. Young, William Green, of the
American Federation of Labor, columnist Dorothy Thompson, singer
Paul Robeson, actor Fredric March, William Allen White, and T. W.
Lamont, sharing a public platform for the first time with his left-wing
son.

On November 8 a huge crowd filled New York's Madison Square
Garden to witness a dramatically staged program of pageantry and
speeches. Corliss Lamont, the chairman of the congress, called the
meeting to order and presented "Book of Friendship" awards to individuals representing different sectors of society—Lamont from business,
Green from labor, and so forth. National groups from each of the nations
allied against the Axis powers paraded to the speaker's platform to
present their flags. Vice President Henry A. Wallace was the main speaker,
and others, including Lamont, spoke briefly.

"I am anything but a Communist," said TWL. However, as a businessman he was glad to stand up and declare his unequivocal support and
friendship for Russia, which was the only nation on the continent of
Europe that could be a great stabilizing influence. Lamont concluded
with a ringing rhetorical flourish:

> How often has it been said that Stalingrad has become a symbol—a
> symbol not of despair but of desperate and unconquerable valor! The city
> on the Volga may be shattered, its streets heaped with rubble. But Russia

will continue indomitable and free. Her heroic stand will have achieved great ends. Despite heavy casualties, Russia's military might still faces Hitler's hordes. Russia's stand will have given precious months to the Allies to prepare for that great offensive which on more than one front is already begun. . . . In saving themselves the Russians have held up Hitler, and in saving themselves may well have saved civilization.

The Volga River may run red with blood. Stalingrad may be in ruins. But whatever happens, that citadel of courage and faith will remain the symbol of Victory. Stalingrad will live to rise again. Down the ages mankind will remember how the Greeks withstood the barbarians at Thermopylae and the Russians at Stalingrad!

Good Neighbor Policy

On November 6, 1942, Lamont invited Mexican finance minister Suarez and his aides to lunch at the bank on the occasion of signing a new foreign debt agreement with Mexico. Suarez was flattered by the Morgan chef's culinary tribute—an artistic confection of red, white, and green ice cream, the colors of the Mexican flag. He was also pleased with the new accord. In toasting the minister Lamont observed that as usual Mexico had gotten "all the candy."

TWL then recalled a boyhood incident on the Hudson River. He had come across an old woman preparing eels for market that her husband had caught. To young Tom's horror he saw that she was skinning the eels alive. When he remonstrated against the practice, she replied, "Oh, they get used to it!" The minister laughed heartily at TWL's characterization of the dealings between the International Committee, led by Lamont, and the Mexican government over the last twenty years.

Following the breakdown of the debt agreement with Mexico in 1936, George Rublee made the first of several trips to Mexico City over the next two years in an attempt to work out a new accord. By 1938 a mutually acceptable deal took shape that was very generous to Mexico. The International Committee proposed to waive 85 percent of the bondholders' claims to principal and accrued interest; the remaining 15 percent would be repaid in twenty-five-year bonds at a 4 percent interest rate.

But a new development severely wounded the Mexican economy. On March 18, 1938, the Mexican government expropriated the American oil properties in Mexico, triggering a bitter row over the amount of compensation to be paid. The two sides were far apart, with the Mexicans willing to consider only a small fraction of the $260 million value the Americans had placed on their assets. Soon the Mexican government's mismanagement of the properties was producing growing operating losses. Instead of providing substantial tax revenues as in the past, the oil industry became a financial drain for the government. After months of delay, Finance Minister Suarez wrote Lamont that he was unable to present a new agreement to the Mexican congress for ratification because of the unresolved compensation issue and the economic setback brought on by expropriation of the foreign oil properties. And there the matter languished over the next three years.

By 1941 the administration's Good Neighbor policy was in full swing, and friendly relations with America's big neighbor south of the border were essential to the united hemispheric defense against the Axis powers. Lamont discussed the Mexican debt problem in January with Secretary Hull at the State Department and wrote him on February 3 characterizing Mexico's conduct as "the uninterrupted attempt to kill the goose that lays the golden egg."

On March 5, TWL met with Under Secretary Sumner Welles at lunch at the Palm Beach home of Myron Taylor, the former head of U.S. Steel, who was FDR's special envoy to the Vatican. The State Department was engaged in talks with Mexico on a range of issues, and Lamont was about to meet Suarez in New York on the foreign debt controversy. Lamont and Welles agreed that if the bankers negotiated a new agreement with Mexico, they would first check with the State Department before signing.

"I have some misgivings lest we shall be making concessions that look much heavier than the ones you make," said TWL.

Welles told Lamont not to make any more concessions than those contained in the draft 1938 agreement. "Make none. They will do whatever you demand in reason!"

TWL's meeting with Suarez was a scene played many times before; the plot was quite familiar. Lamont said that the committee could not accept a reduction to less than 12% to 15% of Mexico's outstanding debt. The minister replied that Mexico needed a greater concession because of the sharp decline in the peso. TWL reported back to Under Secretary Welles and was told to hold firm. Apparently Suarez had similar instructions.

When Suarez returned to Mexico without a new foreign debt agreement, he was asked by reporters when he planned to return to New York to reopen negotiations. He replied with a smile, "Mañana." The International Committee was completely frustrated, TWL informed the State Department, which he fervently hoped would lean on the Mexicans to agree to a new settlement acceptable to the committee.

In November 1941 the oil compensation question was settled, with the American companies ultimately receiving about $42 million. The administration's program of good neighborliness in Latin America was bearing fruit, and following the Pearl Harbor attack, Mexico and other Latin American countries became cooperative allies of the U.S.

On April 15, 1942, Mexican foreign minister Dr. Ezequiel Padilla lunched at the Morgan bank, where he was handed an aide-memoire on the foreign debt problem. The foreign minister, in a letter of thanks for the courtesies extended to him in New York, expressed his hope for a satisfactory settlement of the issue. TWL's reply contained the customary flattery he employed when petitioning officialdom: "I have only to add my own personal expression to the many that we have heard from all sides as to the deep and favorable impress which your personality and liberal views have had upon the American community."

In October Dr. Suarez arrived in New York ready to do business. The new agreement of November 6, 1942, provided that 90 percent of the government's foreign debt would be cancelled; the remaining 10 percent would be paid off in twenty-five-year 4 percent bonds. The bankers and Suarez expected to negotiate a settlement of the defaulted railway debt on approximately the same basis.

In his letter to Lord Bicester, his London partner, Lamont noted that the new agreement had not been received with enthusiasm by the many English investors holding Mexican bonds. The London *Times* had said that the deal could be defended only on the principle that half a loaf was better than no bread. "Nobody pretends that this is a first-rate settlement. . . . But I was in constant consultation with the Department of State and on the whole thought this was the best thing to be done."

The Mexican congress ratified the new foreign debt agreement on December 28, 1942, and another well-skinned eel joined its ancestors. The fisherman's wife was right: it didn't hurt so much anymore.

Pen in Hand

The Lamonts' causes kept them on the go during the fall of 1942. Florence's committees were in full swing: "I am busy with Russian War Relief and next week open my house for Greek War Relief," she wrote. TWL presided at the Pilgrims' dinner in honor of Mackenzie King, the prime minister of Canada, and crossed Wall Street to speak on the steps of the Sub-Treasury building at a Red Cross rally on the anniversary of Pearl Harbor.

Families throughout the country celebrating Christmas in 1942 missed their menfolk in the armed services, many of whom were already fighting overseas. In the Lamont family TSL was stationed in London with the Air Force and Eleanor's husband, Charles Cunningham, was a Navy lieutenant headed for duty in the Pacific.

A dozen grandchildren, accompanied by assorted parents and relatives, joined their grandparents for Christmas at Palisades. The family sang carols by the candle-lit Christmas tree in the long front hall, while waiting for the arrival of Santa Claus, played by grandson Ted. Before receiving a gift from Santa each child recited a poem or sang a song, in a production smoothly directed by Grandmother Florence. The older family members performed at the festive Christmas dinner table, with Tom and Florence singing in duet "My Bonnie Lies Over the Ocean."

Florence was always ready to play games or read out loud to her grandchildren, who adored her—even the older ones, who found her to be an understanding and discreet confidante. The children did encounter a mild cultural barrier with Grandmother from time to time. Florence was baffled by the message of a granddaughter who wrote that Palisades would not be a "neat" place to visit without her, and a grandson was surprised to learn that she had no idea who Babe Ruth was.

Grandfather was kindly and most generous, and his grandchildren accepted the fact that he had little time to spare from the affairs of the world to play games. One morning he stunned a grandson standing nearby who became the lucky beneficiary when TWL decided to dispose of several wrinkled and dirty dollar bills from his silver money clip. All the other bills were crisp and new, the boy noted.

The Lamonts relished their country weekends at Palisades, and the restriction on pleasure driving because of gas rationing gnawed at Florence's conscience. However, there was also a wartime shortage of dairy products, and each Sunday the chauffeur-driven limousine was loaded with full milk cans for the return trip to nourish the Lamont household in New York—clearly an essential mission, reasoned Florence.

Lamont, arguably the nation's most prominent Anglophile, felt that the cause of American-British solidarity needed a boost. The *New York Times* obliged once again in publishing his letter of February 9, 1943.

Some American "reformers" wished to "wrench apart" the British empire with its far-flung colonies spanning the globe. But, said TWL, Britain's strategic foreign outposts, such as Gilbralter, Malta, and the Suez, and its colonies were vital to the defense of the free world. "It would be the act of madmen to demand that all backward peoples are promptly cut loose from their present moorings" and left to fend for themselves.

It was said that the sun never set on the British empire. Nor should it, thought Lamont, notwithstanding growing nationalist aspirations in some parts, at least until the war was won.

"Whether we like or dislike individual Englishmen, whether we think they are inclined to high hat us or not, whether we look upon ourselves as innocents abroad and easy marks for the English trader—or on the other hand monarchs of all we survey," America and Britain had to work together to preserve world peace in the future.

> The mutual respect, the forbearance and the understanding that we have for each other spring from common roots deep in the past; roots so intimately interwoven and united in history that no man can sunder them. We can work together because of our common acceptance of certain fundamentals—our instinct for justice and fair play, our preference for an orderly world where each branch of the human family may work out its own salvation in its own way, our convictions that individual enterprise and democracy are inextricably dependent each upon the other.

The Anglo-American principles for national governance, revered by TWL and Americans in general, were still well ahead of their time in much of the world. Close to half a century would pass before most branches of "the human family" would begin to accept the proposition that the union of "individual enterprise and democracy," free markets and free ideas, presented the most promising path for mankind's welfare.

Following his customary practice TWL sent a pamphlet form of the letter to his long mailing list drawn from the ranks of journalism, academe, business, and government. The American ambassador to Ireland asked for 20,000 additional copies. Mindful of the traditional Irish disdain for the English, TWL wrote Ambassador Halifax that he doubted that the pamphlet would please even one of the 20,000 Irishmen to whom it was addressed.

In mid-February the Lamonts left the winter weather of New York to spend a month at Yeamans Hall, where TWL hoped the more benign climate would clear up a lingering cold. This time Tom and Florence did not invite any guests; they looked forward to a complete rest.

Lamont had already had good reason to contemplate his mortality. His older sister, Lucy, had died in 1941, and his longtime London partner Edward C. Grenfell (Lord St. Just after his elevation to peerage) and other old friends had since passed away. Nevertheless, the news of J. P. Morgan's death on March 13, 1943, at Gasparilla Inn in Boca Grande, Florida, came as a shock. Morgan's condition had deteriorated rapidly since he suffered a heart attack about two weeks earlier. He died at the age of seventy-five, the same age at which his father had died thirty years earlier.

Lamont had always felt affection for his senior partner, admiring his genuine modesty and kindliness and the steadfast integrity that had been the hallmark of the Morgans, father and son. In his letter of March 25 to Peter Vermilye, a young Morgan staff member, TWL praised Morgan's "intimate personal qualities" that for so many years "made us feel that we were friends working together in a common cause." Morgan's naivete in public utterances was occasionally embarrassing, and some of his private prejudices were wrongheaded and distasteful. But he was fundamentally a decent and very generous person. Jack Morgan had given Lamont virtually a free rein to run the bank, and TWL was grateful to him for a fulfilling and bountiful career.

The Lamonts attended Morgan's funeral at St. George's Church in New York on March 16. TWL was elected chairman of the board of J. P. Morgan & Co. Incorporated, while George Whitney continued as president and chief executive officer.

In the spring of 1943 Florence felt that TWL was working too hard at the office. There were administrative matters to be dealt with following Morgan's death and endless conferences to plan the bank's participation in the government's war bond issues. "He has amazing vitality but looks thin," Florence wrote TSL. "He never rests. I can't see how he does it all. He's always in a hurry."

Lamont also was mad, and the object of his wrath was John L. Lewis, president of the United Mine Workers. The banker and the labor czar no longer saw eye to eye—far from it.

Six weeks of meetings between Lewis and the Appalachian coal mine operators to negotiate a new wage contract for some 400,000 miners had been fruitless: the talks were completely deadlocked. Two weeks before the old contract was due to expire on April 30, Lewis went public, lashing out at "a conspiracy" to "lock out" the miners from their jobs on May 1. The negotiations were being sabotaged by the representatives of the "captive mines" owned by the U.S. Steel Corporation, said Lewis.

> The mine workers assert that a settlement of this problem can be made in this conference providing the United States Steel Corporation will take its foot off the neck of the mine workers. We have advised Dr. Steelman as the President's representative that the government in our judgment should call on Thomas W. Lamont of J. P. Morgan & Co., which controls the financial and industrial policies of United States Steel, to desist from this mad effort and to exercise constructively instead of destructively the great influence of that powerful financial group.

In another statement Lewis asked, "Why not give the farmers and miners a part of this profit that the Graces, the Lamonts, the Girdlers, the du Ponts and others of their ilk are taking from the public purse?"

Lamont, a longtime U.S. steel director, angrily drafted a letter to Lewis which excoriated Lewis's inflammatory rhetoric and concluded, "Normally I would wind up a letter to you with the phrase, 'Personal regards,' but for the life of me, after a blast like this of yours, I don't see it."

Upon reflection TWL decided not to dispatch his letter, recognizing that the demagogic mine workers' chief was no longer swaying public opinion or the administration. In an earlier round with Lewis, when he ordered the workers to strike in the steel company mines, President Roosevelt had written Lamont:

> When you see Jack [Morgan] tell him for me not to concern himself any more about Lewis' attack, for after many years of observation, I have come reluctantly to the conclusion that Lewis is a psychopathic condition.

The *Charleston* (West Virginia) *Mail*, in the heart of the mining country, published an editorial under the title of "Tiresome."

> Mr. John L. Lewis' frenetical posturings upon the national scene every two years when the Appalachian wage contract expires often hit new highs in originality, daring and sheer showmanship. His latest act, however, leaves a taste of disappointment in that he has had to revert to a rather thread-bare device. He has resurrected the old cry that "big business" is engaged in a "conspiracy" to "lock out" the miners on May 1 when the current negotiations are to end.
>
> The "conspiracy," Mr. Lewis says embraces that old, established minion of entrenched wealth, J. P. Morgan and Company, and he suggests that Mr. Thomas Lamont, a Morgan partner, be called on the carpet to explain why the firm should wish to keep the miners in grinding poverty.
>
> Frankly, this begins to look as though Mr. Lewis is losing his grip. Like

fashions in clothes, styles in name-calling change. Forty years ago, Mr. Lewis could have obtained a large and enthusiastic audience by pillorying Mr. Lamont and the Morgan company. Today, the shoe is on the other foot.

It is not the Morgan interests who are engaged in a "conspiracy" to defraud the working man out of his just rewards. It is not Mr. Lamont who is in a position to strangle the United Mine Workers of America.

On May 1 Lewis called a strike of the United Mine Workers, and President Roosevelt ordered Secretary of the Interior Ickes to take over the bituminous coal mines. The next day Lewis called off the strike.

Lamont was still advancing his favorite themes from different podiums. To Red Cross audiences he voiced the need to rehabilitate the war-torn world when peace came and the importance of international cooperation to prevent future wars. To a Committee for Economic Development luncheon meeting he discussed the prospects of the postwar American economy.

"The only chance our government will have to keep its own head above water is to encourage business morning, noon, and night, and then begin by encouraging it all over again the next day," stated Lamont. "More than once it has been well pointed out that none of the world's great ages has been based on striving for security; that something more positive and dynamic is needed to bring out the best in man; that the nation that wants to become and remain great must place enterprise ahead of security."

To a symposium in a series called "For This We Fight" on NBC radio, Lamont stated, "Never shall we Americans dare to be isolationists again. . . . Powerful as America may be, she can never by her own force alone insure herself against war." The U.S. and other nations had made "colossal blunders" in establishing tariffs and embargoes that clogged the channels of world trade and led to reprisals and antagonisms. "Now we are waking up, realizing that our great industrial nations are sick or well together. . . . Trade is a two-way street. Open up our own markets, and we shall build up the markets of others." In his letter of June 10, 1943, the president thanked Lamont for his support for renewing the Trade Agreement Act.

Earlier in June, TWL had come down with a bad case of bronchitis which sapped his energy for weeks. By mid-July he was more than ready to escape a New York heat wave and seek relief in the calmer and cooler atmosphere of North Haven.

Reduce Speed

In the last week of July 1943, Lamont was stricken: about 5 a.m. he awoke in distress with severe difficulty breathing; he felt weak and exhausted. Florence sent for the North Haven island doctor, who believed that TWL had suffered a heart attack. Florence phoned Austin, now a doctor at Johns Hopkins in Baltimore, and TWL's New York physician, Dr. James A. Miller, who then talked with the local doctor about the patient's condition.

During the day TWL rested fairly comfortably, but that evening suffered two more attacks. The doctor attended to his patient and then went into the next room, dropped to his knees, and started to pray. Florence asked if her husband was desperately ill, and the good doctor replied, "All we can do now is trust in Him."

Once again Florence called the mainland doctors, including a Boston heart specialist, who agreed to come to the island the next day. Florence and the local doctor kept a bedside vigil throughout the night. A thunderstorm arose and the lights went out. Flashlights and candles, flickering in drafts from the high winds outside, glimmered in the bedroom's gloom.

The Boston specialist arrived the next afternoon, and his confident presence relieved Florence's foreboding. An electrocardiogram and a blood count indicated that TWL had not suffered a coronary attack; he was suffering from severe anemia.

Lamont's blood count and overall condition improved steadily with rest and medication. By mid-August he was permitted to sit outdoors in his wheelchair for an hour in the morning and again in the afternoon.

It was a hard summer for Florence. In addition to her worry about her husband, she had to arrange for doctors' visits and nurses to care for TWL, with transportation to the island by ferry service and motorboat sharply curtailed by fuel rationing. Nancy Lamont, Austin's competent and lovely wife, helped her mother-in-law care for the patient before the nurses arrived. For ten days Florence censored Tom's daily mail from the bank to remove any items that might upset him before the office staff took on the task itself. The doctors would not let their patient consider business matters or even write letters for several weeks.

In a letter to TSL in London, Florence discussed the necessary restrictions on TWL's future activity. "I think he is going to be difficult to manage. For instance, all this presiding and speech making is awfully bad for him, and he adores it."

At the end of August, Lamont wrote his oldest son as he sat outside on the lawn in the afternoon sunshine watching the Austin Lamonts sail by toward Pulpit Harbor after a picnic at Barred Island. His mood was decidedly upbeat.

> As I cabled you, it was stupid of me to come down with this crack of anemia and I feel especially badly that at the start it scared your poor Mother half to death. Then of course there was the great excitement of doctors and nurses dashing in from all over. The Island full of gossip. "Well, well, I hear they got another new doc over to Mista Lamont's, from New York way or somewhere. Must be pretty bad, I guess. Allus was a pleasant gentleman." Then reams of nice letters all full of good advice: Take it easy old man, watch your step, make haste slowly, don't try to turn mutton into lamb, etc. . . . I was hoping to go to 23 day after Labor Day but they put it off a bit. Enough of all that. . . . First real illness in 50 years!

TWL continued to recuperate at the 70th Street house during September. He stayed on the sidelines as his name was bandied about in a political exchange between Wendell Willkie, who was considering another run for the Republican presidential nomination, and a group of conservative Missouri Republicans who were determined to stop him. Edward Monsanto Queeny, the head of Monsanto Chemical in St. Louis, had publicly chided Willkie for his association with Lamont through their common membership in Freedom House, an organization promoting international cooperation in the postwar era. To the Republican right wing, any link with J. P. Morgan & Co. had sinister implications, a political fact of life that Willkie recognized. In a public statement he played down the Lamont-Willkie connection, terming Queeny's charge as "strong condemnation by frail association."

In October, Lamont returned to the office on a reduced schedule, accepted evening engagements sparingly, and devoted more time to reading and his correspondence. In a *Saturday Review of Literature* article in December, "What a Capitalist Reads," TWL gave high marks to Willkie's best-selling *One World*, John P. Marquand's *So Little Time*, and Walter Lippmann's *U.S. Foreign Policy*. Lamont was a voracious reader—largely of nonfiction, along with a sprinkling of novels and mysteries; Hercule Poirot supplanted Sherlock Holmes as TWL's favorite detective. Low-brow forms of popular culture like most Hollywood movies and radio comedy hours bored him.

At the end of December, TWL suffered a heart attack, and this time there was no doubt. Under doctors' orders he did not leave his room for a month, and no visitors were permitted. Lamont did not want the outside world to learn of his heart attack, and while his family knew the truth, the party line to others was that he had been struck down by a severe case of influenza.

The Lamonts rested at Yeamans Hall during March, accompanied by a trained nurse, Miss Dahl. Golf was out for TWL, and he did a lot of reading and writing. In a letter to Corliss he said, "As for myself, despite wars and cruelties and confusion incredible, I am glad to be living at this hour. If I had to choose, I should choose no other day nor generation. *This* is the time to be alive!" By mid-April Lamont was putting in a shortened day at the office three or four times a week.

Florence wrote TSL that "everything is different and will never be the same." For years Florence had been the one who was in and out of doctors' offices. Now their roles were reversed. TWL's heart condition was like the sword of Damocles, but she would get used to it.

Letters to the Editor

In 1938 Lamont had sold his interest in the *Saturday Review of Literature* which, practically speaking, had imposed the duty to fund its depression years' deficits totaling about half a million dollars. However, under a new editor, Norman Cousins, the magazine prospered, and TWL was happy to accept Cousins's requests for book reviews from time to time.

In May 1944, Lamont reviewed a new biography of his old friend Jan Christiaan Smuts and wrote a statement for an Office of War Information broadcast to South Africa commemorating his seventy-fourth birthday. Lamont never flagged in his admiration for General Smuts. In 1939 Smuts had been the pivotal figure in persuading the dominion parliament to join Great Britain in declaring war on Germany, in the face of strong resistance from anti-British pro-German elements of the Afrikaner population. Smuts had once again become his country's prime minister and was still its leader almost five years later, after placing the country on a wartime footing and organizing the South African forces for their part in fighting the German and Italian armies. A confidant of Winston Churchill, he had strongly urged the opening of the French North African front by the American and British armies. Lamont and Smuts continued to correspond on the progress of the war and the prospects for eliminating mankind's age-old scourge after the victory.

Smuts also wrote to Florence about his philosophic and religious thoughts, and TWL exchanged letters with "Isie" Smuts. A chatty correspondent, with a neat and clear hand, she reported on the latest changes in the life of the Smuts family brought on by the war and their daily regimen of long hours of hard work. "But we shall never have another chance of service. So never mind," added the general.

Smuts had longed to lead the Lamonts on another African excursion, perhaps to Nyasaland, Kenya, or Albert National Park, with its Gorilla Reserve. But war broke out first. "And so the caravan passes once more into the night. May God be with us and take the hands of His erring children," wrote the general in 1939. And in 1942: "I value your and Florence's letters very much and look rather wistfully to the times when we may meet again and perhaps see more of this great continent."

After the outbreak of war Smuts had written Lamont:

> Of course for me the issue is at bottom a large human and spiritual one. I believe in the Spirit which has led humanity on and blossomed on all the great ideas which underlie our Western culture. The things Hitlerism stands for are the negation of all this, and if Nazi-ism is a crusade, no less is that great crusade of the Spirit on which we have set out. Victory is not guaranteed us, the Right oftener than not is defeated. But still the spirit beckons and leads us on, and we cannot but follow as the moth follows its candle light. It is the Divine in us which shapes our course through the world.

And later:

> So much is at stake for the whole world and the future of our civilization. . . . Freedom for the individual to hold up his head against the omnipotent state, the responsibility of the individual to his own conscience in all the deepest concerns of life and thought, self-government as we have evolved it in our Western Democracy, all these are at stake. I consider the Nazi or Fascist system as it has been working these last years as the quintessence of evil—Gestapo, spying, oppression by the state, and the reduction of the human to the insect level.

But the general was not confident about the prospects for a lasting peace after the victory was won. The postwar organization to maintain peace would be worked out. "It is the spirit animating the machine that will matter," he wrote TWL in 1942. "May it come—that dawn of the spirit?"

Ultimate victory seemed assured by the time the Lamonts saw Smuts again. In mid-April 1945, the general spent a few days with his friends at their New York home, stopping off on his way to San Francisco to attend the historic conference to complete the charter of the United Nations, the proposed new organization for international cooperation and world peace. It was a happy reunion.

On May 25, 1944, at the invitation of Eugene D. Kisselev, the Russian consul general in New York, Tom and Florence dined with Andrei A. Gromyko, the new ambassador from the U.S.S.R., and his wife. Only the three couples were present. In his memorandum TWL noted that "water was at a high premium." Four kinds of spirits, including "fiery vodka" and "first class champagne," were served along with mounds of black caviar.

The dour-faced young ambassador was very upset at the Catholic Church which, he charged, was attempting to undermine the new ties between Russia and the U.S. Catholic criticism of the U.S.S.R. had died down since Russia had become an American ally in fighting the Nazis, said TWL, but Americans were worried about Russia's political intentions toward Poland when it was reoccupied by the Russian army.

Since its 1943 summer offensive, the Red Army had been driving the shattered and demoralized German forces back toward eastern Europe and seemed certain to recapture Poland in a matter of months. Poland's postwar boundaries and national independence were the critical questions Americans hoped to see promptly and fairly settled.

Gromyko responded, in so many words, that questions about Poland should be decided by Russia alone, as they were vital to her national security. The Polish leaders were hard to deal with, including the so-called government-in-exile in London.

The ambassador was mainly interested in TWL's view of the postwar prospects of good commercial relations between the U.S. and Russia. Lamont replied that until the war was over, it was impossible to estimate Russia's potential to export goods to Western markets. While it was unlikely that American investors would supply loans to Russia, large manufacturing companies might extend credit for the purchase of their products in the hope of opening up a profitable new market. Ambassador Gromyko invited Lamont to visit Russia to discuss future business relations, which TWL said he would consider when the war was won.

In June, Lamont sent the consul general a memorandum, which he might show the ambassador, elaborating on the points he had made at dinner. A tolerant and humane settlement of political differences between Russia and her Polish, Baltic, and Balkan neighbors would have a direct bearing on the goodwill and confidence of Americans in developing commerce with the U.S.S.R. The settlement should not be imposed ruthlessly by Russia, and it would be wise for the Soviet government to secure the endorsement of the U.S. administration, which would carry great weight with all Americans, including millions of Polish descent.

Lamont traced the history of U.S.–U.S.S.R. relations since the 1917 revolution, noting his own part in recommending vainly that President Wilson send a mission to Petrograd to encourage the new Soviet leaders to fight on against the German invaders. TWL had also supported the American recognition of the Soviet government in 1933. He concluded with a personal note: "I may add for my own satisfaction that the high-spirited Russian poet, Lermontov, was of Scottish descent, his Lamont forefathers coming from the same district in Scotland that all of us Lamonts hailed from originally." However, TWL's attempt to soften the iron-fisted strategy of a brutal regime was doomed to the same oblivion as his previous efforts with Mussolini and the Japanese warlords.

The Harvard commencement on June 29 had a definite military cast as 5,200 young army officer candidates and midshipmen received certificates of achievement. Wartime Harvard was a large military training center, and the commencement audience in the huge quadrangle was a sea of tan and navy blue uniforms. The temperature was ninety-five degrees, and Florence persuaded TWL to sit under the shade of a tree and not on the stage in the broiling sun with Harvard's elder statesmen in high hats and heavy frock coats.

TWL, who had received an honorary degree from his alma mater in 1931, mounted the stage briefly to be presented with the Harvard Alumni Medal for Distinguished Service. Two good friends, Walter Lippmann and Federal Judge Augustus Hand, received honorary degrees at the 1944 commencement, and Lippmann gave the main address. Florence applauded heartily as the columnist called for an alliance of the United Nations, "the only conceivable foundation on which we can begin to build international order."

Tom and Florence left for North Haven right after the exercises. TWL looked forward to a good rest to restore his health fully. He also had a new literary project he was working on—reminiscences of his boyhood in the parsonages along the Hudson.

*   *   *

TWL corresponded regularly with his eldest son in London, who had been promoted to Lt. Colonel. As a procurement officer his job was to obtain British-source supplies and equipment for the U.S. Eighth Air Force, assigned to bombing missions over Germany. TWL had made contributions of his own to the Eighth Air Force before he became ill. In 1942 Secretary of War Henry Stimson had appointed Lamont to head a civilian committee to collect maps, photographs, and other data on manufacturing plants in Europe. The group gathered a considerable amount of information, mainly from American companies with prewar operations in Europe, that was helpful to the Air Force in selecting its targets.

During TSL's years in London, 1942–1944, the city was frequently the target of German planes that dropped high-explosive bombs and incendiaries. After D-Day, the Germans bombarded London with thousands of V-1's, jet-propelled flying "buzz bombs," and later V-2 missiles, which caused devastating damage and over 30,000 casualties. TSL, along with most Londoners, had some close calls.

Despite the threat of air raids, the social life for a well-connected Air Force officer like TSL was lively. The atmosphere of wartime London, the center for launching the epic campaign to liberate Europe, was one of excitement as well as anxiety over the daily dangers and those that lay ahead. Many of TSL's American friends passed through London on military assignments, and it was good to see them and compare notes over a few drinks. There were gregarious English hostesses ready to entertain the visiting comrades-in-arms, and if the party were interrupted by the mournful wail of sirens warning of approaching German bombers, no matter: the guests would scurry to the nearest shelter to wait out the air raid. Searchlight beams crisscrossed the night sky searching for the intruders, and anti-aircraft guns and rocket barrages thundered. The spirit of the embattled city was indomitable and inspiring, as broadcaster Edward R. Murrow stirringly reported to millions of Americans, including Tom and Florence.

In early July, TSL crossed over the channel to Normandy in his new supply assignment with the Ninth Air Force, which provided tactical support to the American armies in France. He wrote that life was much less tense than in London, where the residents were constantly exposed to the deadly buzz-bomb attacks. TSL retired from the Air Force in October 1944 and returned to New York and his banking career.

Young Tommy's naval career had taken an abrupt turn. In September 1943, he "washed out" of flight training school in Holbrook, Arizona; his instructors had decided that he lacked flying aptitude. Rejecting the chance to train as a officer candidate in the college-based Naval V-12 program, Tommy went through boot camp at San Diego Naval Training Station. He then attended Quartermaster School, followed by Submarine School, and on June 20, 1944, said good-bye to his San Diego girl and sailed for Pearl Harbor. In early July he was assigned to a submarine tender bound for Midway Island. Tommy had wanted sea duty as soon as possible and was happy to join the crew of the U.S.S. *Snook*. The *Snook*, a 307-foot submarine with ten twenty-one-inch torpedo tubes, had sunk or damaged thirty Japanese ships on previous patrols. TWL II's morale was high.

The sudden death from a heart attack of George Metcalfe, the major-domo of the Lamont household for thirty years, was "a terrible blow" TWL wrote his children, who felt the same way. Metcalfe had been a loyal, efficient, and selfless aide, almost part of the family. Florence added, "Father and I feel we have lost our best friend and most devoted."

At Lamont's time of life the obituary columns often carried sad news. On July 3, 1944, Norman H. Davis died. TWL's close friendship with Davis went back to the days of the Paris Peace Conference. His death closed a long career of distinguished public service culminating in his leadership of the wartime Red Cross.

Following his defeat in the Wisconsin Republican presidential primary in the spring of 1944, Wendell Willkie had dropped out of the race, and the G.O.P. convention chose New York Governor Thomas E. Dewey as its standard-bearer. Willkie, who continued to pursue a strenuous schedule of speaking engagements across the country, suffered a series of heart attacks and died on October 6 at the youthful age of fifty-two. Lamont issued a public eulogy for the man whose global vision he had so greatly admired.

TWL donated $10,000 to the major Republican campaign committees—national, state, and county—but did not seek to counsel the party's candidate. Dewey was cordial and respectful to the elderly banker, but Lamont probably sensed that his advice would fall on deaf ears. As a campaigner Dewey was stiff and uninspiring. The Dewey campaign seemed plodding, and furthermore, the governor was running against the "champ," and a wartime leader to boot. The American people saw no reason to "change horses in midstream," and FDR won a fourth term, handily capturing 53.4 percent of the popular vote.

Lamont's closest friend at the office was Russell Leffingwell, who was most solicitous about TWL's fragile health. When Lamont first became ill, Leffingwell had advised that he should delegate less important tasks to others and "conserve his strength for the important things of leadership in public and private life." Furthermore, he should "stop galloping around like a colt."

Lamont was no longer galloping; in fact at his doctor's orders he had given up his favorite recreation—playing golf—perhaps the cruelest blow of all. At his reduced gait TWL found his greatest pleasure in writing— his boyhood memoirs, letters to the *New York Times*, book reviews, and the like. TWL now went to the office mainly to attend to his prolific correspondence and other literary efforts. The Morgan staff writer in residence who ably assisted Lamont was R. Gordon Wasson, who had replaced Martin Egan after his death in 1938.

Lamont and Leffingwell, the two "wise men" at 23 Wall Street, exchanged papers on economic history, public policy issues, and so forth, sometimes sending copies to their powerful columnist friend Walter Lippmann. With a few notable exceptions, TWL's and RCL's viewpoints had long been in concert. TWL had tremendous respect for Leffingwell's intellect and wisdom. One morning at the senior officers' meeting, Leffingwell had expounded at length his views on a complex issue concluding with "Does anybody disagree with what I have said?"

Lamont quickly replied: "Would anybody dare?," and the room exploded with laughter.

Lamont had cleared his letter of November 19 to the *New York Times* with Under Secretary of State Edward R. Stettinius, Jr., the son of his deceased partner. In it Lamont noted that the question of how the victors should treat the vanquished was uppermost in people's minds. In considering the issue Americans should remember that it was the militaristic nature of Germans, not a vengeful Versailles Treaty, that had spawned the Nazi movement and belligerence. In fact, the Allies had been moderate and indeed naive in dealing with Germany after World War I.

The Nazis' brutal aggression was a violent restatement of Germany's international conduct going back in modern history to the conquests of Bismarck in the 1860s. The German people were easily persuaded by their leaders then and later in 1914 and 1939 that wars of subjugation were a noble course to pursue. The German cry for "Lebensraum" had always been specious. Germany's repeated attacks on inoffensive neighbors were not due to lack of "living space."

TWL saw no advantage in splitting up Germany into several parts or reducing it to an agricultural state, as proposed by Treasury Secretary

Morgenthau. The important thing was to keep Germany disarmed and prevented from ever again "running amuck."

Once more Lamont pleaded for close cooperation with the other great powers, especially Great Britain and Russia. The U.S.S.R. would meet America halfway "if we would quit complaining about the system of government which happens to suit her." Because of America's strength, the U.S. more than any other country had the responsibility for maintaining world peace.

The letter's closing bore the unmistakable Lamont stamp.

> The dignity and freedom of the individual man is a simple, everlasting truth, something to be lived for, to be fought for, and, if necessary, to die for.
>
> That is the faith that during these last five terrible years has outfaced the shadow of death; that will, despite evil and aggression by warlike states, always save the world, redeem it and make it whole. For well do we know that in the last analysis liberty lies not in international machinery to prevent aggression but in the heart of man.

Of all the momentous decisions taken by FDR, Churchill, and Stalin at the Yalta meeting in February 1945, those concerning the political future of Poland aroused the most public concern. While Poland would gain German territory to the north and west, about a third of prewar Poland would be turned over to Russia. Free elections were pledged for Poland and other liberated Eastern European states, but by mid-March it was evident that the Russians were seizing control of these countries in violation of their agreement at Yalta.

In his letter of March 18, 1945, to the *New York Times* TWL appealed to Americans to understand Russia's special strategic needs. Lamont observed that the Russian people "having twice within thirty years suffered from Germany the most sweeping devastation and loss of life . . . do not intend to be caught in the same way again." It was regrettable that the Russians had not shown "a less intransigent attitude towards their weaker neighbor." But it was understandable that Russia considered it critical to protect itself against "a third attempt at world domination by a fresh Germany."

After all, America had its own Monroe Doctrine to protect Latin America, including the vital Panama Canal, from outside aggressors. So Americans should not complain if Russia wanted to be bordered by friendly neighbors. Having been far removed from "bloody invasion and the imminent threat of hideous force," Americans should be tolerant of the desperate attempts of their Allies to meet "most pressing difficulties that chance not to be so immediate to America."

FDR thanked TWL for his support of the administration's position on Poland, and his personal physician, Dr. Miller, wrote, "Your pump may miss a beat once in a while, but the old bean is working on all four cylinders."

"They Are Not Dead, Our Sons Who Fell in Glory"
(from "In Memoriam" by Joseph Auslander)

The world was stunned by the news of President Roosevelt's death on April 12, 1945, from a cerebral hemorrhage while vacationing at Warm Springs, Georgia. Vice President Harry S. Truman assumed the presidency and the role of a world leader in winning the war and planning the global organization for peace, the objective of the United Nations meeting in San Francisco to be held later in April.

In a real sense FDR was a war casualty as much as any fallen soldier or sailor. Lamont wrote his widow: "To all of us who had known Franklin . . . who had seen his gallantry and courage and felt the inspiration of his great war leadership, his death at the hour of his triumph seemed hard to bear." Eleanor Roosevelt replied, "It was very sad that he could not have lived to see the day of victory."

The U.S.S. *Snook*'s seventh war patrol, and Tommy's first, was highly successful, and Tommy reported with a sense of exhilaration that he had heard his "first shot fired in anger." Northeast of the Philippines the *Snook* joined a pack of three other American submarines to cut off a Japanese convoy heading north. Attacking on the surface in the darkness of the early morning hours of October 24, 1944, the *Snook* torpedoed and sank three freighters and severely damaged another one. A few days later off Formosa the *Snook* sank another Japanese vessel and then picked up a downed American fighter pilot floating in his rubber raft off Luzon.

Tommy had noted the endless drabness and boredom of navy life in his earlier letters home. But now he wrote his father, "I came out of action with a deep sense of satisfaction, something I hadn't felt before."

On November 18 the *Snook*, with its battle flag flying proudly, received a triumphant welcome as it docked at Pearl Harbor. All hands were awarded the U.S. Navy Combat Pin and Citation.

The Navy, taking good care of its elite submariners on leave, billeted Tommy at Honolulu's deluxe Royal Hawaiian Hotel for two weeks. TWL II drank beer, slept a lot, and swam off the hotel's famous beach.

Before long Tommy was ready to return to sea. As a Seaman I/C striking for a quartermaster rating, TWL II served his watches topside. He wrote his father, who had returned to civilian life: "At sea I'm pretty happy. I like the sea, the roll of the ship, the bright southern stars at night." On Christmas night the *Snook* sailed from Pearl Harbor bound for Midway before heading north.

The next patrol off the Kurile Islands was a "stinker," wrote Tommy. The *Snook* encountered heavy gales and seas, poor visibility, extreme cold, and drifting ice floes. The freezing temperatures and icy spray made the topside watches a torment for Tommy and his mates. One night the submarine collided with a small iceberg, which damaged its superstructure. Worst of all, no enemy shipping was sighted. The *Snook* returned empty-handed to Midway on February 17, 1945.

A month later the *Snook* began its ninth war patrol, heading for Guam, where Tommy mailed a letter to an old friend stationed at Midway.

> Well, think of me shifting from one tired leg to another all night (for four hours to be exact) while you guzzle beer. Dulce et decorum est pro patria mori. Horum omnium fortissimi sunt submarinae. J'espere que ça retarde le censeur.*

The *Snook* left Guam on March 28, receiving orders three days later to join a "wolf pack" of American submarines headed by the U.S.S. *Tigrone*. On April 8 the *Snook* radioed her position, just east of Hainan, to the *Tigrone*. When the *Snook* did not acknowledge radio messages the next day, it was assumed that she was moving toward the Luzon Straits. Other attempts to raise the *Snook* in the coming days and weeks were futile. She was never seen or heard from again.

On May 14, 1945, Tommy's parents received the customary dreaded

---

*Roughly translated: "To die for one's country is sweet and seemly. Of all young men, those of the submarines are the finest. I hope that these words will baffle the censor."

telegram: "The Navy Department deeply regrets to inform you that your son Thomas William Lamont II Seaman First Class USNR is missing following action while in the service of his country."

Tommy's loss was a terrible shock to TWL. Tommy almost seemed more like a son than a grandson to him, and he may well have suspected that he might turn out to be the brightest star among his Lamont successors. In a letter to General Smuts, Lamont said: "It was a hard blow for Florence and for all of us, the first break in our circle, and he was an unusually promising boy of only twenty. They say that some of our servicemen do not know what they are fighting for. Certainly young Tommy did."

His spiritual beliefs had become a new source of strength for Tommy in the Navy, as he told his mother. "The Church is like one of our new battlewagons. It is impregnable. No matter what happens to me, when I can go to Church, the world is like North Haven on a Northwest day— for a while at least." He also wrote, "North Haven is my Tivoli, my Mandalay, my favorite place on earth."

A memorial service was held for TWL II in the island church on August 11, 1945. To his family the final lines of the Navy hymn, "O Hear Us When We Cry to Thee For Those in Peril on the Sea" were never sung with more feeling.

The Germans surrendered on May 7, 1945. On August 14, after the two atom bombs had devastated Hiroshima and Nagasaki, Japan surrendered, and the long night that followed the day of infamy ended.

Lamont spent a quiet summer at Sky Farm working on the book about his childhood, *My Boyhood in a Parsonage*, and recording his memories of early days in business, financing the Allies during World War I, the Paris Peace Conference, and the political battle over the League of Nations. A secretary from his office, Katherine McGuirk, was on hand each morning to take dictation or type up his manuscript and letters, and the mail pouch went back and forth each day between Sky Farm and 23 Wall Street. Miss McGuirk did her typing in a small cottage located about fifty yards down a steep path leading from the house to the beach. When TWL, sitting on the porch of the main house, needed her assistance, he rang a large dinner bell, and the secretary would come scrambling up the path. "It's funny but he acts as though he's been ringing the dinner bell all of his life and having a secretary come puffing along," Miss McGuirk wrote a colleague at the office, diplomatically expressing her frank opinion of the arrangement.

During the fall TWL and Florence spent many days at Palisades. They enjoyed walks along the forest trails to cliff lookouts over the broad river flowing below with its banks aglow in autumn colors. On September 30 Lamont passed another milestone, his seventy-fifth birthday.

Lamont, the largest stockholder of J. P. Morgan & Co., did not plan to preserve a major family interest in the bank, preferring more diversification in his holdings and those of his heirs. As the war wound down, the market became more receptive, and on July 12, 1945, TWL sold 5,000 shares in a public offering led by Morgan Stanley and Smith Barney, for about $1.5 million. On November 13, 1945, Lamont donated 5,020 shares of Morgan stock to Harvard College with a market value of $1.5 million. The two transactions lowered Lamont's ownership in the bank to under 20 percent. TWL was especially enthusiastic about the project he was undertaking at Harvard.

For some months Lamont had discussed with President Conant and Keyes D. Metcalf, the college librarian, Harvard's need for a new library. For years the college students had used the huge Widener Library along with graduate students and faculty. It was not a satisfactory arrangement. The undergraduates should have a smaller library of their own, which would alleviate the capacity shortage facing the whole university library system. The estimated construction cost was $1.5 million for the new building, the first separate undergraduate library in a university.

No philanthropy ever brought TWL more pleasure. Scores of Harvard men, who had seen the story announcing the gift in the newspapers, wrote to congratulate him. He followed the site and architectural planning with great interest, but wisely stayed out of the inevitable debates that arose over the site and design. President Conant planned to announce the official designation of the Lamont Undergraduate Library at the 1946 commencement exercises in June, and TWL wrote him that he would certainly be there if the doctors would let him go.

TWL's heart condition, which he called "a circulatory disturbance," was not improving. Both he and Florence, who suffered from high blood pressure, were ready for a warmer climate during the winter months than that of Yeamans Hall. In 1946 they chose the Gasparilla Inn at Boca Grande on Florida's west coast, where J. P. Morgan had wintered in the past and where he died in 1943. Gasparilla was a small, quiet resort featuring a rambling white hotel, a bit run-down, a golf course, and a fine beach.

Tom and Florence went walking on the beach together and cruising in the calm waters of the Gulf and Pine Island Sound in the motorboat TWL had chartered for their stay. The mail pouch arrived regularly from New

York, and Lamont worked on editing the proofs of *My Boyhood in a Parsonage* for Harper and Brothers and a spin-off article for the *Atlantic Monthly*. Florence suspected he was getting a bit bored with their quiet existence, but they stayed on for two months before returning to New York.

Lamont's good friend Lord Halifax was resigning as ambassador to return to England. Lord and Lady Halifax stayed with the Lamonts on the occasion of the Pilgrims dinner in honor of the ambassador, following the custom that the Pilgrims, having given the first dinner in New York for an incoming British ambassador, gave the last one as well. The splendid affair, calling for white tie and decorations, was held in the Grand Ballroom of the Waldorf-Astoria. TWL sat next to Halifax on the dais, and at the close of the evening Lamont rose to pay a brief tribute to his friend: Americans were grateful that during the last five arduous years they had had a British ambassador with the character and understanding of Lord Halifax. Edward and Dorothy Halifax had lunch with Tom and Florence at the 70th Street house before sailing home on the *Queen Mary* and invited the Lamonts to visit them soon.

Phillips Exeter Academy was preparing to honor the two men whose collaboration had contributed so much to its development into one of the nation's foremost secondary schools. With the war over and the school returning to normal operations, it was time for Dr. Lewis Perry, the principal, and Thomas W. Lamont, the president of the board of trustees, to step aside for younger men. Dr. Perry had been principal since 1914; Lamont had been a trustee since 1917 and head of the board for the last eleven years.

On June 1, 1946, the Annual Alumni Day was renamed Perry-Lamont Day as a thousand alumni returned to their old school for the first postwar reunion. Perry and Lamont addressed the large crowd of alumni, over seven hundred students, faculty, and townspeople. TWL praised Perry, waxed nostalgic over his student days at P.E.A., and eased into his sermon, quoting his old friend General Smuts's eloquent words: "There is in man an inward glory of the spirit, something eternal that in the due course of events, even after every setback, will come to heal the world."

But the world would not become tranquil by itself alone, and Lamont declared that Exeter men would do their part to solve its pressing problems. At the trustees' meeting, William G. Saltonstall, an Exeter history teacher, was chosen to be the new principal, and Thomas S. Lamont was elected to succeed his father as president of the board of trustees.

TSL had long been proud to follow in his father's giant footsteps, on

Exeter's and Harvard's governing boards and down other paths. He lacked his father's dynamism and readiness to take on bold initiatives. He was prudent, hardworking, amiable, and well-liked, and his selection to head the Exeter board was a popular choice.

Because of TWL's heart condition, the doctors would not let him join Florence in May on a trip to England to visit old friends they had not seen since before the war. Tom and Florence spent the summer in North Haven, and TWL felt poorly much of July. When he felt up to it, he doggedly continued his research and writing about his experiences in international politics and business, perhaps fearing that time was not on his side.

Miss McGuirk was on hand again in August, when Lamont felt better, to provide secretarial assistance. She noted in a letter to Edward Saunders, Lamont's personal assistant at the office, that "Mr. L." tired quickly. He didn't seem at all well to her, and she wondered if he should even be on the island. However, Lamont was in good hands: his son Austin, a physician doing medical research at Johns Hopkins, spent the whole summer at North Haven to be near his father.

Fitting the Final Pieces

Developments on the Mexican front were reported periodically to Lamont, still the chairman of the Committee of International Bankers on Mexico. Arthur Anderson at the bank and the lawyers had made some slow progress: a new agreement to settle the outstanding railway debt was concluded on March 20, 1946. The bondholders, as in the government debt agreement, would fare poorly: the complex pact with the National Railways of Mexico would bring them no more than about twenty cents on a dollar of principal.

Since 1932 the distribution of over $6 million received from Mexico had been blocked by lawsuits filed by both the Mexican government and later by bondholders questioning the expenses the committee had incurred. On August 30, 1946, New York Supreme Court Judge Ferdinand Pecora, the tenacious interrogator of the Morgan partners in the 1933

Senate hearings, ruled that the account of the committee was in order as of April 1942, thus permitting a distribution to the bondholders. The disbursement brought the total funds received by the bondholders after expenses to about $40 million since the first debt agreement of 1922, when the total outstanding government and railway debt amounted to $500 million in principal and $200 million in unpaid interest. It was a minuscule return to the investors. And still the larger question remained unanswered: how could a poor country like Mexico repay its foreign debt if the cost was reducing the already impoverished living standard of its people, causing suffering, anger, and even violent protest? And if it didn't, what foreign investors would be willing to supply it with the fresh capital it needed for development?

A major obstacle to economic growth in backward countries was the lack of competent leaders dedicated to improving the welfare of their burgeoning populations mired in peasant-class poverty. The ruling classes paid little heed to the concept of creating a society of economic opportunity for all citizens. The governments were often tantamount to army-backed dictatorships, with rampant corruption at all levels, and the small elite upper class that dominated agriculture and business was devoted to amassing and enjoying family wealth. Lamont was the forerunner of a parade of twentieth-century bankers who would tackle the frustrating problem of lending to Third World countries.

Bennett Cerf, head of Random House, had wanted to publish *Boyhood*, but Lamont chose the venerable Harper and Brothers, led by his friend Cass Canfield. Parts of the book appeared in the *Atlantic Monthly* and *Saturday Review* during the summer.

In September 1946, *My Boyhood in a Parsonage* was published and received warmly. Said the *New York Times Book Review*:

> These memoirs are uneven in quality and occasionally verge on the sentimental. But they have much of the charm that made Clarence Day's "Life With Father" memorable. . . . These quiet pages from an earlier, more dignified America should evoke nostalgia.

The *Herald Tribune*, noting that the book was slight at two hundred pages, and even puffed a little, concluded:

> These pages are full of quiet charm, but they also contain much of the best of America, and for that reason this book, too, is high romance.

TWL was pleased with the many letters he received praising *Boyhood*, including those from his literary friends in England, where the book was later published by William Heinemann Ltd. "Charming" was the adjective used most often to describe the little book, which by year-end had sold 20,000 copies and just squeaked onto the *Herald Tribune* best-seller list.

Following his regular practice, Lamont urged the new British ambassador, Lord Inverchapel, to stay at the 70th Street house in New York and invited him to his annual dinner for the trustees of the Carnegie Foundation for the Advancement of Teaching on the eve of their yearly meeting in November. Lamont also wrote to the ambassador about a gift he was considering. TWL had seen a pamphlet describing the urgent financial needs of Canterbury Cathedral, which had been damaged by German bombs in 1942 and its library destroyed. In addition, substantial restoration work, neglected since the beginning of the war, was badly needed. Postwar Britain was financially prostrate, and it was hoped that American friends would come to the rescue.

Lamont saw an opportunity to demonstrate his lifelong admiration and affection for England and its people. Ambassador Inverchapel put TWL in touch with the Archbishop, the Most Reverend Dr. Geoffrey Francis Fisher, and on February 3, 1947, a gift of $500,000 by Lamont for the restoration of the cathedral was announced in the press.

Said Lamont in his letter to the archbishop:

> We Americans of all others can never forget that in the darkest days of 1940 and 1941 it was only British courage and the blind faith of free men, undismayed by disaster, that saved the world from the evil of the Teutonic onslaught.
>
> Canterbury is the heritage of the whole Christian world. It was centuries ago that your workmen painstakingly erected this monument of beauty and worship, and always since that time it has been cherished by the English-speaking race. It is you with whom we share our fundamental religious convictions, brought to the New World with our forebears at Jamestown and Massachusetts Bay. We have followed the way as they followed it. We have looked forward, as they looked, to a city not built with hands.

The archbishop replied, "There is nothing so important in the troubled world as the maintenance of the Christian tradition on the one hand and the fellowship of our two nations on the other. Your gift . . . cannot but do untold good."

Lamont avoided contact with the Dean of the Cathedral, Dr. Hewlitt Johnson. The "Red Dean," so dubbed by the tabloids for his pronounced leftist views, had implied in a statement that his acquaintanceship with Corliss, with whom he shared a sympathetic opinion toward the goals of the U.S.S.R., may have inspired the gift. It simply was not true.

TWL was deluged with English "fan mail," as he called it, with many letters from "common folk" that moved him. He thanked Helen Reid of the *Herald Tribune* publishing family for the paper's graceful editorial tribute.

> Mr. Lamont's gift recognizes and honors this common inheritance. It is the man who was a boy in Methodist parsonages of Hudson River Valley villages who can' best agree today with the Archbishop of Canterbury that it is the "spiritual realities" which constitute the true life of nations—and their fellowship in the restoration of a cathedral and a world.

The London *Times* noted ·that the son of a Methodist parson had demonstrated again the unity of Christendom.

In January 1947 a private car, hitched onto the rear of the regular train to Tampa, transported the Lamont party to Boca Grande, which Tom and Florence had chosen as their future winter home. They had just bought a house with a balcony overlooking the beach and blue waters of the Gulf.

Lamont, who had brought his own doctor with him, now slept under an oxygen tent to ease his breathing at night, and he had his good days and his poor days. He worked on his memoirs, when he felt up to it, and answered the heavy fan mail he continued to receive about his gift to Canterbury Cathedral. The office mail pouches arrived regularly, and "Mr. L." had ample dictation and typing to keep Miss McGuirk busy, including a message of greeting to the annual Morgan staff party dining and dancing at the Starlight Room of the Waldorf-Astoria. It turned out to be an especially high-spirited occasion, perhaps because the word was out that the practice of partially manning the bank on Saturday mornings would be ended.

TWL probably did not read the item of family news reported in the *Boston Herald* while he was at Boca Grande. His second grandson, Ted, at Harvard, had entered a singing contest at Loew's State movie theater, held to promote its current attraction, *The Jolson Story*. He had signed up under a fictitious name, but an alert reporter uncovered his identity. "Lamont Scion Shows Rich 'Mammy' Voice" was the headline of the story, which reported, "Harvard student, Edward M. Lamont, added mammy singing, Jolson style, to the famous banking clan's accomplishments last night." Nor would Lamont have read the sports page stories about another Harvard student at the time—hockey star Lewis T. Preston, who as Morgan's chief executive four decades later spearheaded the bank's campaign to reenter the securities business and later became president of the World Bank.

TWL gradually regained vitality at Boca Grande. The Lamont house-keeper reported to TWL's executive secretary, Edward Saunders, "One feels that he lives very near to God and has been given the strength to carry on."

For many years the Lamonts had attended the Easter service at the First Presbyterian Church in Englewood, and they timed their return from Florida to spend the weekend at Palisades and go to their old church on Easter Sunday. Tom was feeling better than he had in months and started going downtown to his office once or twice a week for meetings or lunches with his colleagues.

The bank's postwar look was gradually changing. There were many more women on the staff, mainly in secretarial positions, although a few male secretaries like Saunders lingered on. While female staff members were advised to wear hats and gloves when they went outside the bank, some informality was developing in men's wear. The mandated prewar stiff collar was gone, and T. S. Lamont was the first to startle his colleagues by appearing in a seersucker suit one summer morning.

While the firm was small in size relative to its rivals, the Morgan name still carried a special cachet. The Morgan "bird dogs," well-trained Ivy Leaguers in Brooks Brothers suits who traveled the country to talk to clients and solicit new accounts, made regular calls on the executive officers of corporations, even though their calling cards bore no officer's title. It was well known that Morgan was stingy in handing out titles, contrary to general practice in the industry.

But Lamont was now rarely seen at his rolltop desk on the banking floor. In his private office upstairs he planned his philanthropy and reminisced in letters to old friends. He also updated his will. His school and college would receive generous bequests. So would the Metropolitan Museum of Art, where Lamont served on the board of trustees. The Flemish tapestries and the portrait of "The Sackville Children" by John Hoppner at the 70th Street house would go to the museum when Florence died. TWL left bequests to a number of other New York institutions—museums, hospitals, and charities, including the New York Conference of the Methodist Episcopal Church—and to the Town of North Haven, Maine, reflecting Lamont's gratitude to his island neighbors for many happy summer holidays.

In June 1947 ground was broken for the Lamont Library at Harvard, and at the end of the month Tom and Florence went up to North Haven, where they were later joined by their children and spouses and fifteen grandchildren. To the family's great relief, Tom's health held up well.

Tom's latest craft, a new forty-foot motor cruiser, the *Little Reynard*, led a flotilla of vessels transporting the clan to the Lamont island, Big White in Hurricane Sound, for the annual picnic on the pink-white granite slabs ringing the island. Swimming by the venturesome, trail clearing, and poetry reading were regular features of this occasion; Masefield's "Sea Fever" was the family favorite, capturing the ocean surroundings perfectly;

> *And all I ask is a windy day with the white clouds flying,*
> *And the flung spray and the blown spume and the sea gulls crying.*

Tom and Florence also enjoyed quiet times—walking about their farm and lovely garden with its white picket fence and masses of flowers covering the slopes of the ravine running down toward the shore. They often sat on their lawn with its sweeping view of the bay dotted with spruce-covered islands and sailboats tracking across the white-capped waters. In the evening they watched the golden western sky giving way to darkening shades of blue and finally starry night as the sun went down behind the Camden Hills on the far shore. All was still, except for the chug of a fisherman's boat returning from mackereling and the wash of its wake on the rocky beach below.

Tom worked steadily on the memoirs of his career in international finance, aided by the cheery Miss McGuirk. He was proud of the Morgan bank's performance and his own role in organizing foreign loans and credits and laid out the record in his manuscript. After all, the ultimate measure of a bank was its lending record—the ability of its officers to select sound projects and borrowers who repaid their debts. The bulk of the Morgan-led foreign loans and credits since World War I had already been retired, and only the Axis powers had stopped payment on their obligations, defaults that were cured after the war.

Lamont also reflected on the dramatic change in the global financial scene. After the Great War, American bankers, led by J. P. Morgan & Co., had mobilized the capital needed to rehabilitate Europe and stabilize national currencies. In the aftermath of World War II, the U.S. government would direct the first huge outflow of capital overseas. Only the United States had the undamaged productive capacity and capital reserves needed to restore the war-ravaged nations of Europe and Asia, help develop the backward economies of the world, and provide foreign credits to bolster currencies under pressure. The International Bank for Reconstruction and Development (the World Bank), which would market its bonds to private investors to finance its loans, and the International Monetary Fund had just been established for these very purposes. In June Secretary of State George C. Marshall had articulated his historic plan advocating a multibillion-dollar U.S. program of economic aid for Europe. American economic power was dominant in the world. No one could possibly foresee that some forty years later the U.S. would become the world's leading debtor nation in head-to-head economic competition with its wartime enemies.

However, to rebuild and develop the world's economies vast sums were needed in the form of grants or long-term loans, whose repayment was far from assured, in the early postwar years. It was a job for governments, not private bankers.

TWL continued his writing as he passed a quiet autumn in New York and at Palisades. His doctors had tightened their restrictions on his activities, ruling out all large social functions. Lamont did not disagree, but put aside thoughts of death. He was determined to finish the story of his career, and even when tired he would force himself to write or dictate a few hours.

Lamont had visibly aged in the last few years. He was frail and wore a waistcoat or sweater under his jacket even on warm days. His wisps of hair were white; his face was wan, its expression benign but lacking animation. Gone was the alertness, the ready smile, and cheerful vitality. TWL now sat quietly listening to others' conversation, straining to overcome the barrier of growing deafness. The flaming zest for life had become a flickering candle.

On December 17 Lamont attended the regular J. P. Morgan & Co. board meeting at the bank. Postwar lending was growing, but slowly; U.S. government securities still comprised about half of the bank's total assets of $666 million. Morgan's 1947 earnings had fallen off 10 percent from 1946 to just under $3 million, and there would be no year-end bonuses for the bank's 657 staff members and 49 officers.

On December 22, 1947, Lamont wrote George Whitney, Morgan's president.

Dear George,

I have always felt a deep sense of gratitude to the members of the staff of the office for all they have done for me and been to me over the last thirty-seven years. Even if some faces have changed, the spirit of all is the same.

Because this has been, with increased living costs, an exceptionally difficult year, I am turning over to you a sum sufficient to enable you to divide it among the staff so that each member will receive a Christmas gift from me equivalent to five percent of the 1947 salary.

TWL gave special attention to planning his 1947 Christmas gift list. Presents of books, wine, cigars, flowers, chocolates, and sometimes checks went out to a host of friends, business acquaintances, secretaries, nurses, and others who had cared for him. He sent food packages to friends in England, still gripped by shortages and austerity. The patriarch gathered his family and a few old friends at Palisades to celebrate Christmas, and following tradition, poems, songs, and toasts were rendered by young and old. Midway through dinner TWL suddenly felt weak and retired to the oxygen tent in his bedroom, where family members dropped in quietly to wish him a Merry Christmas and thank him for his presents.

"Time, Like an Ever-Rolling Stream"

Lamont's sojourn in Florida a year earlier had renewed his strength, and TWL looked forward to spending the early months of 1948 in the sunny climate of his winter home at Boca Grande. Florence's 1939 Ford sedan had been sent down by train, and the *Little Reynard* was also on hand for cruising and fishing in the Gulf and inland waterways.

However, the train trip south proved very tiring for TWL, and the weather was cold and damp when the party arrived at the resort on January 10. TWL came down with the flu, and his doctor administered penicillin. Miss McGuirk was also in attendance to take down his letters. Lamont dictated his comments on George Whitney's annual letter to the Morgan stockholders and thanked the Morgan staff for their many letters to him expressing gratitude for his year-end gift.

During the last week in January, Lamont's heart condition steadily worsened. He lay in bed, often under the oxygen tent, too weak to talk, and Florence sat beside him holding his hand and praying.

Miss McGuirk reported to Saunders, "Mr. L. is far from well." She went out for a run in the *Little Reynard*. "Had a nice time, but there is no heart in anything with Mr. Lamont ill."

TSL and Austin came to visit their father and were spelled in a few days by Corliss and Eleanor Cunningham. They were with their mother at Lamont's bedside when the end came. Lamont died peacefully in his sleep just before midnight on February 2, 1948. He was seventy-seven years old.

A thousand people filled the English oak pews of the Brick Presbyterian Church at Park Avenue and 91st Street for the funeral service of Thomas W. Lamont on Saturday, February 7. After the congregation sang the final hymn, "For All the Saints, From Whom Their Labors Rest," the coffin, blanketed with red roses, was carried slowly down the center aisle of the church behind the clergy and honorary pallbearers. Lamont was buried in the family plot at the Brookside Cemetery in Englewood.

There were many news stories and editorials about Lamont's life and his bequests of some $10 million, including $5 million to Harvard and $2 million to Exeter. His generosity was considerable, as was his estate, about $25 million, which netted out to $4.4 million after bequests and taxes. The articles noted that Lamont had been one of the nation's most respected private citizens and a leader in international finance at a time when America became the foremost financial power in the world. Some writers saw Lamont's rise from Methodist parsonage to Morgan partnership in patriotic terms—an outstanding example of the American way of life not possible in most countries. Others noted Lamont's special gift for friendship.

The *New York Herald Tribune* said:

> The simplicity, the clear thought, the warm heart that the friends of Thomas W. Lamont knew so well were the core of his being. They governed his manner of life, they ordered his actions, they shaped his long and distinguished career.
>
> His competency in finance was complete, the product of years of experience and association with the ablest experts. But it was not for any special wisdom that his advice was sought by the great corporations and the strongest nations. It was his practical judgement on the one hand and his skill in meeting and handling individuals on the other which made him a leader. Economics is not the exact science we wish it could be; at the heart of every financial crisis there stands an intensely practical problem which must be solved by shrewdness, by imagination, by an expert guess. It was the great talent of Mr. Lamont that when all the experts had spoken he could approach the final choice with a clear eye and the confidence born of a nature at ease.
>
> His skill in negotiation was far more than the ingenuity of a craftsman. It was part of his zest for human beings. He liked all kinds of people, from poets to prime ministers; when he found a companion he made a friend. His home was rich with varied and distinguished visitors whom he chose by the simplest of tests—that he liked them. His old friends were the best, but he never ceased to meet new minds and form new interests.

Two institutions held an especial place in his heart, and the first of them was Exeter. It was typical of his way of life that he gave as generously of his time and effort to his school as he did of his money. His years as president of the Exeter board of trustees covered the period of that academy's rise to its present distinguished leadership. Mr. Lamont played an active role in that period of progress. At Harvard his monument is the new undergraduate library, a fitting symbol of Mr. Lamont's genius for the practical, the useful.

The record of his early years was set down by him in his lifetime. "My Boyhood in a Parsonage" is a rare and precious document of American history. The spirit of Mr. Lamont lives in his narrative, modest, friendly, loyal—an American success story without a false note, the hero an American of whom the whole country can be proud.

Said Carlton A. Shively of the *New York Sun*:

Wall Street has had more colorful, more spectacular figures than Thomas W. Lamont. . . . It has had none of greater ability, of deeper human understanding, of more inbred kindliness and of truer friendship. They don't come any better than "TWL."

The editorialists were right; friends were important to Lamont, and he gathered them around him in his full and pleasant life. His homes and yachts were filled with guests; his correspondence was prodigious, extending over decades with some friends, and going beyond exchanges of personal news, developed into a valuable intelligence network. Lamont also wrote his children regularly throughout his life; the Lamonts, like their forebears, were a close family.

TWL thought in terms of public policy and took a long, broad view of his business; bank loans were building blocks of a structure reflecting a strategic vision. He was a cultivated man whose speeches and writings on large issues were sprinkled with history and literary and biblical quotations. The Morgan bank was already noted for sound practices and moral leadership, and, not withstanding the occasional lapse in business judgment, Lamont, along with colleagues like Morrow and Leffingwell, added a unique intellectual stature to the firm.

In the early 1920s with Davison gone, the Morgan bank needed a dynamic executive to lead the way—seek out new business and plan new strategies. With audacity, imagination, and a strong awareness of public image, Lamont became the firm's guiding light and power behind the throne, and under his leadership the Morgan bank amassed enormous authority, especially in dealing with governments at home and abroad.

While taking ample time to enjoy the good life, Lamont worked hard at his business, calling on the very capable Morgan staff experts to furnish the necessary research and analysis. Resolving the problems of domestic and international finance became a stimulating high-stakes game, and from his early days in business, when the going was hard, TWL was not averse to risk-taking when his calculation of the odds was favorable. Lamont was confident in his judgments and pursued his objectives relentlessly. No nagging doubts or anxious nights for TWL; he slept well.

Analysis of loan proposals is one thing, foreseeing stock market and economic trends another—an attempt to chart a course across a murky and dangerous sea whose surface can be storm-tossed or calmed by changing political and economic winds and stirred by mysterious currents flowing from the decisions of millions of consumers and investors. The rise and fall of the stock market would always confound investors, and some forty years after Lamont's death it was battered by the greatest single-day sell-off in history during another disastrous October session.

Economic forecasting was clearly not TWL's forte. The 1929 crash and ensuing depression stunned and baffled everyone and ushered in the new era of massive government intervention to treat the nation's ills. The power of Wall Street flowed to Washington. Lamont was slow to confront the surge of unsound and unfair trading practices in the stock market, even lagging behind the conservative Hoover in the president's concern over needed reforms. A staunch Republican in domestic affairs, TWL feared the effect of government initiatives to intervene and regulate the economy and financial markets, and when the Morgan bank, his formidable base of operations, was threatened by legislative proposals to curb its powers, Lamont rose to lead the resistance to change.

Lamont's advocacy for fewer and stronger well-managed banks and nationwide branch banking went unheeded—to the nation's misfortune. Many banks continued to court disaster in their lending policies and rush like lemmings to join the latest lending fad, be it loans for Third World countries or office building construction. In 1982 Mexico triggered a wave of bank loan defaults by Third World borrowers, and later hundreds of banks lacking geographic diversification in their lending were hard hit by a concentration of bad loans in their regional markets when they suffered an economic downturn. A little over four decades after Lamont's death, the greatest wave of loan defaults and failures of banks and savings institutions since the Great Depression swept across the country. Despite its losses from Latin American loans during this banking meltdown, the Morgan bank's overall performance enhanced its reputation as the leader among its peers.

In 1989 the Federal Reserve finally granted the bank the authority to underwrite corporate securities, the flourishing business of Lamont and his partners more than half a century earlier before the Glass-Steagall Act. Over the next several years the bank forged ahead in underwriting new issues of corporate debt and stock, and in 1992 J. P. Morgan Securities Inc. became the first bank securities affiliate to lead a public offering of corporate stock in the United States since 1933.

The human suffering and enigma of the Great Depression stretched on through the thirties, short-lived gains sinking to new lows. Lamont had warned that U.S. tariff escalation would bring down swift retaliation on American business, with disastrous consequences flowing from world-wide protectionism. He was dead right about this grievous wound to the economy. Tariff walls went up and trade went down. The depression deepened and spread at home and abroad, and billions of dollars of loans to Latin America and Europe went unpaid. Morgan-led foreign loans, TWL's special area of interest, held up well in contrast to the wave of defaults experienced by other lenders.

Lamont did not hesitate to express his views on foreign economic issues, such as tariffs and the handling of international debts, even if they clashed with administration programs. Bankers had expert knowledge in these areas, and they should speak up. However, he believed that the U.S. government and not bankers should direct foreign policy in matters of national security. If dictators needed punishing, Lamont would take his lead from the administration. Morgan's foreign loans were cleared with the State Department, and from the late 1930s on, as the war became global, TWL submitted his speeches and articles on foreign policy to the department for prior screening. Sometimes he floated ideas that the government backed but did not yet choose to propose. A Lamont speech or letter to the *New York Times* was a good way to test the political waters.

In foreign affairs Lamont was naive in judging the intentions of the dictators, too ready to join the business-as-usual mentality of the British prime ministers and establishment with whom he hobnobbed during the thirties. The slaughter of the Great War was a vivid memory, and appeasement was not yet disgraced as the shameful ally of ruthless aggression, symbolized by Chamberlain's return from Munich with his rolled-up umbrella and a pact with Hitler for "peace in our time." Lamont had witnessed the horror and carnage of Flanders battlefields and understood the British feelings of revulsion at the thought of another war. His innate optimism blinded him as he held fast to his faith that the power of reason, abetted by the arts of persuasion, would deter would-be aggressors.

TWL was a rational businessman, and war was irrational and therefore unthinkable. "All my business life," he wrote, "I have been engaged . . . in convincing the other fellow that for one reason or another he should adopt my views. . . . That sort of thing is what life is made up of."

International disputes, like business deals, should be negotiated by political leaders sitting down together and striking a bargain. He couldn't believe that intelligent leaders of great nations were ready to plunge the world into the horrors of a second great war. Even Hitler could be appeased and Mussolini enticed away from his evil influence. Lamont's views on Japanese aggression in China developed in a parallel fashion: he long misjudged the power and determination of the Japanese militarists for territorial expansion.

Looking back in 1945, TWL tried to explain his blindness to the menace of the dictators. In an essay he wrote:

> We have all refused to believe until the last moment that there were Dillinger nations prowling about with completely laid out plans of evil intent. . . . For in the makeup of the Anglo-Saxon there is that extreme of humanness that abhors cruelty and will have none of it.

Lamont had misread the signals, along with the leaders of Britain and France, as Winston Churchill's cries of warning went unheeded. But when the Nazi threat became clear to all in early 1939, Lamont was quick to call for repeal of the Neutrality Act to enable Britain and France to buy U.S. military supplies to build their defenses. And when war broke out he championed all-out aid to Britain in her desperate struggle, American's fight, too, he maintained.

Championship of aid to Britain and China was the climax of TWL's long battle against the fervent isolationist policy pursued by most of his fellow Republicans. On the aid issue, tariff protection, and other matters of foreign policy, Lamont left his party behind at the water's edge. His internationalist outlook, developing from his earliest days in business to his role as a world banker shuttling between New York and Europe, led to his conviction that international cooperation and world trade expansion were the foundation stones of peace and prosperity. Those were themes that Democrats, not Republicans, traditionally endorsed. So TWL joined Woodrow Wilson's call for American leadership in world affairs and membership in the League of Nations, although it took a new world war a generation later and another Democratic president to make it happen. In similar fashion Lamont welcomed President Roosevelt's program to reduce trade barriers.

TWL was armed with a sturdy set of principles drawn from experience and individuals who in different ways had uniquely influenced him. Surely the list would include his father, the lettered and steadfast parson; J. P. Morgan the elder, whose accomplishments and strength of personality and character he so admired; Harry Davison, his forceful friend and banking mentor; Woodrow Wilson, whose vision of international cooperation TWL shared; and Jan Christiaan Smuts, an inspirational leader and friend. And he would have joined his Morgan partners in declaring Russell Leffingwell the wisest of them all.

Lamont had long been the bank's chief spokesman, aiming to erase the legacy of suspicion and demonstrate that the Morgan firm stood for constructive operations in the public interest. He was also the partner who dealt with presidents and their cabinets and, traveling abroad regularly, worked with high foreign officials to resolve financial crises and disputes and undertake important new loans.

On these missions and during domestic calamities like the stock market crash, Lamont was the one chosen to explain the complex and disturbing events to the public. His invariable style was never to alarm and make things worse, but always to seek to calm people's fears and restore their confidence, the bedrock of financial stability.

During the depression years the bankers came under severe attack, and the New Deal programs feared by many businessmen began to flower. Politicians and writers denounced the Morgan firm for its role in World War I. More than ever the bank and Wall Street needed a persuasive defender.

Lamont's personal forays into behind-the-scenes peacemaking in Japan and Europe were well-meaning attempts that, like children's sand castles, were soon swept aside by the tide of history. On the other hand, his advice on international finance carried considerable weight with the White House. In his public utterances during the period leading up to Pearl Harbor and the war years, TWL was a forceful advocate of administration foreign policy, which the president appreciated.

Always eager to shape large policies and events, Lamont cultivated important journalists, welcomed opportunities to expound his views to an audience on the issues of the day, and was not shy in offering his advice to presidents, prime ministers, and their lieutenants. The most influential banker of his era was the Ambassador from Wall Street.

Sources

The main original sources for this book are the Thomas W. Lamont Papers in Baker Library at the Harvard Graduate School of Business Administration and a collection of family letters, largely from TWL and Florence to their parents and children, held by the Lamont family. The Lamont Papers, contained in 276 separate boxes, are lodged in the Manuscript and Archives Division of the library. A valuable guide and index compiled by John V. Miller, Jr., is available. Mrs. Florence Lathrop, the curator, and her staff were most helpful to the author.

The material covers TWL's career—the early days in business and banking before joining the Morgan firm, personal correspondence, Morgan bank affairs, foreign trips, TWL's outside interests, his articles and speeches, and miscellaneous items, including diaries of special episodes, photographs, and newspaper clippings. The family letters are also voluminous, starting when TWL went off to Exeter and continuing throughout his life.

The Papers of J. P. Morgan, Jr., at the Pierpont Morgan Library were extremely useful, and I am grateful to David Wright, curator, for his guidance. I would also like to thank Melanie Smith of the Morgan Bank library and Peter Eisenstadt of the New York Stock Exchange for their valued assistance.

The interviews, privately printed books, and documents listed in the bibliography were essential primary sources, and the published books listed provided necessary biographical and historical background. I am indebted to the late Professor Vincent P. Carosso of New York University for sending me an excellent list of books relating to my subject and to Joan Nordell of the Harvard University Library for procuring books for my study.

Three books by Lamont—*My Boyhood in a Parsonage*, *Henry P. Davison*, and *Across World Frontiers* were key secondary sources. For the sake of brevity, I will refer to them as *Parsonage*, *Davison*, and *Frontiers*. The most important reference books and materials I used are listed at the head of each section. Family letters were relied on throughout the book and are noted in the text. Lamont Papers box and file numbers or other sources are provided for key unidentified quotations in each chapter.

Book I: The Rising Path, pages 3–64

Parsonage, Frontiers, Davison; diary of Thomas Lamont, TWL's father; C. Lamont, *Thomas Lamonts in America*; 1888 Pean (Exeter yearbook); Williams, *Story of Phillips Exeter Academy*; Crosbie, *Phillips Exeter Academy, A History*; 1892 50th reunion Report containing excerpts from Harvard Crimson 1888–92; Bentinck-Smith, *The Harvard Book*; Wagner, *Four Centuries of Freedoms*; Flandrau, *Harvard Episodes*; Pier, *Story of Harvard*; Blanchard, *H Book of Harvard Athletes*; Chandler, *Benjamin Strong*; Logan, *George F. Baker and His Bank*; *Bankers Trust Company, 75 years*; Forbes, *Morgan*; Allen, *The Great Pierpont Morgan*; Allen, *The Lords of Creation*; Chernow, *The House of Morgan*; Morgan Guaranty Trust, *23 Wall Street*; Wheeler, *Pierpont Morgan and Friends*; Satterlee, *J. Pierpont Morgan*; U.S. House Committee on Banking and Currency Testimony Before Money Trust Investigation, 1913; TWL account books; Harvard Class of 1892 25th Reunion Report; Nicholson, *Dwight Morrow*; J. P. Morgan & Co., *America and Munitions*; Lamont Papers.

Along the Hudson
Lamont-Davison conversation: page 35, *Frontiers*; quotation about childhood memories: page 4, *Parsonage*.

Huc Verite Pueri, Ut Viri Sitis
Translation of inscription: "Come Hither, Boys, That Ye May Become Men."

Fair Harvard and Its Sons
Professor Royce quotation: page 189, *Parsonage*.

Member of the Press
Lamont Papers, Box 121.

Perils of Business
Lamont Papers, Boxes 150, 232, 235, 236, 239, 240, 256, 274.

Down a New Road
Quotation describing Morgan's handling of money panic: pages 37–39, *Frontiers*; Lamont Papers, Boxes 81, 83, 133, 142, 232.

Mr. Morgan's Choice
Conversations with Morgan: pages 40–43, 46, 47, *Frontiers*; Lamont Papers, Boxes 109, 142.

The Money Trust Hearings
TWL comments on Morgan's death from letter of March 17, 1938 to Henry Steele Commager: Partners file, J. P. Morgan, Jr. Papers; Lamont Papers, Boxes 20, 106, 125, 210; J.P.M. & Co. letter to U.S. House Committee: Box 210–26.

Changes at 23 Wall
Lamont Papers, Boxes 110, 126, 231; Morgan press release on directorships: Box 110–111; TWL letter to FDR: Box 231–13.

Book II: The Trials of Peacemaking, pages 67–150

Frontiers; *Davison*; Forbes, *Morgan*; Nicholson, *Dwight Morrow*; Chernow, *House of Morgan*; Morgan firm, *America and Munitions*; Forbes, *Stettinius, Sr.*; Babington-Smith, *John Masefield*; C. Lamont and L. Lamont, *Letters of John Masefield to Florence Lamont*; Baruch, *The Public years*; House and Seymour, *What Really Happened at Paris*; Hoover, *The Ordeal of Woodrow Wilson*; Walworth, *Wilson and His Peacemakers*; Lloyd George, *Memories of the Peace Conference*; Hogan, *Informal Entente*; Pruessen, *John Foster Dulles*; Bailey, *Woodrow Wilson and the Lost Peace*; Baruch, *Making of the Reparations and Economic Sections of the Treaty*; Seymour, *Papers of Colonel House*; Grant, *Bernard Baruch*; Lamont Papers; Peace Conference diaries of TWL and Vance McCormick: Box 164-18, 19; TWL diary contains conversations with various figures in Book II.

Europe in Flames

TWL quotation on outbreak of war: page 53, *Frontiers*; TWL quotation on neutrality: letter to *New York Times* October 14, 1935; Lamont Papers, Boxes 91, 121, 136, 248, 249.

Arming the Allies

Anonymous death threat to TWL: page 192, Chernow, *House of Morgan*; James J. Hill statement: page 66, *Frontiers*; Lamont Papers, Boxes 81, 136; TWL memorandum of Chicago trip, including exchanges with Dawes et al.: Box 81-15; Morgan statement on loans: Box 81-20.

Family Affairs

Lamont Papers, Boxes 18, 236, 249, 253, 266, 267.

America Goes to War

Lamont Papers, Boxes 91, 260, 264; TWL speeches, Boxes 141, 143, 148, 149, 151, 155, 162.

Touring the Front

Dawes quotation, battlefield description: page 81–82, *Frontiers*; Lamont Papers, Boxes 91, 122, 127, 134, 142, 143, 151, 155; Woodrow Wilson letter to TWL on Russia: Box 134-9.

The Whipping Post

Lamont Papers, Boxes, 117, 118; conversation with Woodrow Wilson: Box 118-1.

Paris Peace Conference

Lloyd George reference to "pips squeak" quotation: page 244, Bailey, *Woodrow Wilson and the Lost Peace*; Lamont Papers, Boxes 164, 165.

Reparations

Lief quotation: page 75, Walworth, *Wilson and His Peacemakers*; Baruch quotation on Cunliffe: page 103, Baruch, *The Public Years*; quotation from armistice agreement and American position paper on reparations: page 19, Baruch, *Making of the Reparations and Economic Sections of the Treaty* and other standard sources; Hughes quotation: page 89; Bailey, *Woodrow Wilson and the Lost Peace*; Wilson quotation on war costs: page 174, Walworth, *Wilson and His Peacemakers*; Lamont Papers, Boxes 164, 165, 166, 167, 168, 171; Wilson quotation on "Logic": page 281, Walworth, *Wilson and His Peacemakers*, Box 164–18.

The Specter of Famine

Lamont Papers, Boxes 164, 165; Lloyd George quotation about Klotz and description of meeting with Germans: Box 164–18.

Hard Bargaining

Lamont Papers, Boxes 164, 165, 166.

A German View, A View of Germany

Lamont Papers, Boxes 164, 170, 171; M. Warburg memorandum: Box 171–27.

The Allies Dispute and Entertain Each Other

Wilson conversation about Fiume: page 114, *Frontiers*; Lamont Papers, Boxes 85, 164, 165, 166, 168, 169, 170, 171; quotations and description of debate over Belgium: Boxes 164-18, 168-1,2,3; Keynes plan and TWL memorandum to Wilson: Box 165-12,13; dinner conversations with Orlando and Paderewski: Box 164-18.

Political Flak and Danger Signals

Admiral Grayson quotation: page 309, Walworth, *Wilson and His Peacemakers*; Lamont Papers, Boxes 164, 165, 171; letters from Woodrow Wilson to TWL: Boxes 171-28, 29, 165-30.

The Treaty of Versailles

Conversation with Clemenceau: page 178, *Frontiers*; Lamont Papers, Box 164.

Lobbying for the League

Quotation from Morgan letter to mother: page 108, Forbes, *Morgan*; Lamont Papers, Boxes 118, 119, 138, 149, 172; quotation from Case letter: Box 118-9; Borah statement on TWL and League: *New York Morning Sun*, July 1, 1919; TWL statement on League: Box 173-28; letters from Wilson to TWL: Box 138-3; Wilson quotation on China: page 214, *Frontiers*.

Book III: Finance and Diplomacy Intertwined, pages 153–244

Frontiers; Cohen, *The Chinese Connection* (the authoritative secondary source on this subject); Florence Lamont, *Far Eastern Diary*; *Davison*; Bailey, *A Diplomatic History of the American People*; Davis Polk, *International Committee of Bankers on Mexico*; Forbes, *Morgan*; Leffler, *Elusive Quest*; Cecil, *All the Way*; Baruch, *Public Years*; Nicholson, *Dwight Morrow*; Matz, *Otto Kahn*; Cowles, *Mike Looks Back*; Allen, *Lords of Creation*; Josephson, *Money Lords*; Brooks, *Once in Golconda*; Chernow, *House of Morgan*; "Harvard 50th Reunion Report"; Lamont Papers.

The Chinese Consortium
Secretary Bryan quotation: page 542, T. W. Lamont article, *Atlantic Monthly*, October 1923; Shao-yi quotation: page 240, *Frontiers*; Sun Yat-sen conversation: page 242 *Frontiers*; Hsu Shih-Ch'ang conversation: page 248, *Frontiers*; Lamont Papers, Boxes 143, 144, 161, 162, 164, 183, 184, 185, 186.

Case Closed
Lamont Papers, Boxes 139, 141, 143, 149, 160, 183, 184, 185, 186; TWL speech to American Manufacturers Export Association: Box 141-24; TWL speech to Academy of Political Science: Box 139-6.

The Republicans Take Over
Lamont Papers, Boxes 97, 98, 118, 119, 158; letters to Harding: Box 97-9; letter to *Post*: page 218, *Frontiers*; conversation with Harding at White House: page 219, *Frontiers*.

The Mexican Debt Dilemma
Lamont Papers, Boxes 118, 119, 192, 193, 194, 195, 196, 197, 198, 199, 201, 202, 203, 204, 205, 241, 250; letters to Hughes and Mexican government proposing mission: Box 192-5; cable to TWL from Morgan: Box 192-7; de la Huerta debt proposal: Boxes 201-26, 203-16; TWL press release: Box 203-16; conversation with Munsey: page 101, *Frontiers*; Dutch Treat Club speech: Box 146-24; quotations from TWL letters to de la Huerta and Hughes after settlement: Box 204-12.

Financing European Recovery
Lamont Papers, Boxes 82, 86, 108, 120, 141, 142, 190, 249; TWL A.B.A. speech: Box 141-16; Baruch quotation on Lord Cecil: page 123, Baruch, *The Public Years*; TWL call on Mussolini: Box 190-13; interview with Curtis in *Editor and Publisher*: Box 120-5.

A New Client
Lamont Papers, Boxes 185, 186; TWL letters to Inouye: Box 186–14.

A Settlement Unravels

Lamont Papers, Boxes 192, 193, 194, 195, 197, 198, 202, 204, 205, 208; Pani-Lamont correspondence: Box 204-15; Pani-Cochran correspondence: Box 204-25.

The Dawes Loan

Lamont Papers, Boxes 115, 139, 146, 176, 177, 178; TWL-Macdonald letters: Box 176-13, 19, 21; Morrow-Hughes letters: Box 177-13, pages 276, 277; Nicholson, *Dwight Morrow*; Clementel quotation on French allocation: Box 177-11; Morgan quotation on attitude toward Jews: page 117, Forbes, *Morgan*; Morgan cable exchange about Speyer: Box 177-22, 23; Lord Cecil quotation: pages 185–186, Cecil, *All the Way*.

New Loans and Bad Debts

Lamont Papers, Boxes 84, 96, 111, 115, 131, 147, 149, 190, 203, 204, 243; memorandum on January 1925 Pani meetings: Box 204-27; TWL April 1925 speech to Italian American Association of Italy: Box 149-31; TWL 1922 letter to Hughes: Box 94-18; TWL quotation from October 1925 meeting with Pani: interview with Leighton H. Coleman; TWL November 1925 speech to Italy-America Society: Box 149-3; Otto Kahn quotation: page 250, Matz, *Otto Kahn*; TWL speech to Foreign Policy Association: Box 147–29; letter to H. Croly: Box 115-17, TWL July 1926 speech to Italy-America Society: Box 149-38.

The Good Life

Cowles quotation: page 17, Cowles, *Mike Looks Back*; Lamont Papers, Boxes 94, 95, 107, 126, 149, 150, 186, 244.

Japan's Wall Street Friend

Lamont Papers, Boxes 183, 186, 188, 189, 190; Lamont Japan Society speech, December 1926: Box 150-6; TWL letter to Olds, November 11, 1927: Box 189-30; TWL cable to Inouye, December 1, 1927: Box 189-32; TWL Institute for Pacific Relations speech: Box 149-21.

Banking on the Corner

Lamont Papers, Boxes 149, 190; TWL International Chamber of Commerce speech: Box 149-22.

Egyptian Kings, Past and Present

Conversation with King Fuad: Harvard 50th Reunion Report; Lamont Papers, Boxes 189, 244, 245; TWL letter to Inouye, January 9, 1928: Box 189-33.

Book IV: Boom and Bust, pages 247–332

Pusey, *Charles Evans Hughes*; Steel, *Walter Lippmann and the American Century*; Allen, *Lords of Creation*; Amory, *The Last Resorts*; Forbes, *Morgan*;

Brooks, *Once in Golconda*; Josephson, *Money Lords*; U.S. Senate Committee on Banking and Currency Hearings, 1933; Bailey, *A Diplomatic History of the American People*; Case, *Owen D. Young and American Enterprise*; Chernow, *House of Morgan*; Dawes, *Journal as Ambassador to Great Britain*; Leffler, *Elusive Quest*; Sloate, *1929*; Hoover, *Memoirs of Herbert Hoover*; Allen, *Only Yesterday*; Thomas, Morgan-Witts, *The Day the Bubble Burst*; Galbraith, *The Great Crash*; Grant, *Bernard Baruch*; Wigmore, *The Crash and Its Aftermath*; C. Lamont, *The Thomas Lamonts in America*; Tyack, *Cliveden and the Astor Household*; Masters, *Nancy Astor, A Life*; Nicholson, *Dwight Morrow*; Davis Polk, *International Committee of Bankers on Mexico*; Cohen, *The Chinese Connection*; Elson, *Prelude to War*; Carosso, *Investment Banking in America*; Davis, *FDR The New Deal Years*; Lamont Papers.

Domestic Affairs

Hughes quotation: page 628, Pusey, *Charles Evans Hughes*; quotation about Yeamans Hall: page 164, Amory, *The Last Resorts*; Lamont Papers, Boxes 239, 245.

Running With the Bulls

TWL letter to Albert H. Wiggen: page 189, Brooks, *Once in Golconda*; G. Whitney quotation: Columbia University Oral History; Lamont Papers, Boxes 84, 126.

The Young Plan

Quotation from S. Parker Gilbert report on Germany: *Time*, January 14, 1929; Lamont Papers, Boxes 91, 96, 104, 138, 178, 179, 180; memorandum of meeting with Root, April 9, 1929: Box 179–27; Young statement about Lamont: *New York Times*, June 15, 1929; Lamont statement on Bank of International Settlements: *New York Herald Tribune*, July 5, 1929.

Advice for the White House

Quotations of I. Fisher and C. E. Mitchell: *Time*, November 2, 1987; Lamont Papers, Boxes 52, 98, 179, 274; TWL letter to Hoover, September 20, 1929: Box 98-14; TWL letter to Hoover, October 19, 1929: Box 98-16.

The 1929 Crash

Lamont Papers, Box 131; newspaper reports of TWL public statements: Box 131-26, 27, 28; John D. Rockefeller statement: *Time*, November 11, 1929; Mitchell toast and Baruch cable to Churchill, November 15, 1929: page 241, Grant, *Bernard Baruch*; TWL statement to Stock Exchange governors: *Time*, February 26, 1940.

The International Inn and Other Diversions

Lamont Papers, Boxes 82, 129, 131, 181, 191, 239, 245; memorandum of meeting with Mussolini: Box 245-25.

Clash Between Friends

Lamont Papers, Boxes 192, 194, 195, 196, 197, 198, 200, 201, 202, 203, 204, 205, 208; meeting with Pani, January 21, 1925: Box 204-27; Morrow letter to Monroe, February 2, 1929: Box 192-14; TWL cable to partners, March 2, 1929: Box 192-15; TWL letter to Monroe, May 31, 1929: Box 192-16; TWL letter to Morrow, July 24, 1930, Morrow letter to TWL, August 20, 1930: Box 192-18.

The Deepening Depression

Lamont Papers, Boxes 98, 104, 137, 140, 154, 155, 246, 250; TWL Academy of Political Science speech, November 14, 1930: Box 140-13; Senator Smoot statement: Box 140-2; TWL remarks at Academy dinner in honor of Lippmann, March 25, 1931: Box 140-5.

Financial Disarray in Europe

Lamont Papers, Boxes 96, 98, 144, 158, 159, 181; telephone talks with Hoover, June 1931: Box 98-18; TWL letter to Hoover, October 20, 1931: Box 98-19.

The Senate Has Questions

Lamont Papers, Boxes 98, 147, 211, 274; TWL letter to Hoover, August 26, 1931: Box 98-19; TWL speech to EURC, October 2, 1931: Box 147-10; copy of TWL Senate testimony: Box 211-5; Morgan press release: *Wall Street Journal*, December 19, 1931.

Japan's First Target: Manchuria

Lamont Papers, Boxes 79, 187, 188; TWL memorandum to Lippmann, October 1, 1931: Box 187-10; TWL letter to Sonoda, March 10, 1932: Box 187-14; Lamont letter to Lowell, March 10, 1932, TWL letter to Takahashi, March 30, 1932: Box 188-22; TWL letter to Stimson, October 11, 1932: Box 209-25.

Keeping New York Solvent and Florence Happy

Lamont Papers, Boxes 98, 274.

A Debate Over the Market

Lamont Papers, Boxes 98, 116; TWL letter and memorandum on short selling to Hoover, April 1, 1932: Box 98-21; Hoover letter to TWL, April 2, 1932, TWL reply to Hoover, April 8, 1932: Box 116-7.

The Reparations—War Debt Minuet

Lamont Papers, Boxes 95, 98, 103, 107, 181; MacDonald letter to TWL, May 26, 1932: Box 107-8; Stimson letter to TWL, May 27, 1932: Box 181-25; Egan memorandum to TWL, July 14, 1932: Box 98-22; Lippmann column quotation: page 293, Steel, *Walter Lippmann and the American Century*; MacDonald letter to TWL, February 17, 1933: Box 107-8.

The Domestic Banking Crisis

Lamont Papers, Boxes 103, 127, 140, 274; TWL speech on banking, November 18, 1933: Box 140-7; TWL letter and memorandum to FDR, February 27, 1933, Morgan statement on gold standard: Box 127-22.

Book V: The Defensive Years, pages 335–432

Forbes, *Morgan*; Wigmore, *The Crash and Its Aftermath*; Brooks, *Once in Golconda*; Carosso, *Investment Banking in America*; Papers of George L. Harrison; U.S. Senate Committee on Banking and Currency Hearings, 1933 (report of testimony, exhibits, memoranda presented at hearings); T. Morgan, *FDR*; Leffler, *The Elusive Quest*; Nicholson, *Diary and Letters 1930–39*; Schlesinger, *Coming of the New Deal*; Chernow, *House of Morgan*; Josephson, *The Money Lords*; J. P. Morgan, Jr. Papers; Bailey, *A Diplomatic History of the American People*; Seymour, *American Neutrality 1914–1917*; Davis Polk, *International Committee of Bankers on Mexico*; U.S. Senate Special Committee Investigating the Munitions Industry Hearings Record, 1934–1936; Tyack, *Cliveden and the Astor Household*; Masters, *Nancy Astor*; Hancock, *Smuts—The Fields of Force*; Steel, *Walter Lippmann and the American Century*; Elson, *Prelude to War: World War II*; Lundberg, *America's Sixty Families*; Cohen, *The Chinese Connection*; Case, *Owen D. Young and American Enterprise*; E. Roosevelt, *FDR, His Personal Papers*; Davis, *FDR The New Deal Years*; Schwartz, *Liberal—Adolfe A. Berle*; The United States of America before the Securities and Exchange Commission, 1938 (report of testimony at hearings); Meyer, Hinton, and Rodd: *Some Comments About the Morgan Bank*; Morgan Stanley, *Morgan Stanley, 50th Anniversary Review*; Lamont Papers.

Confrontation in Washington

"Gabriel Over Wall Street": *New York American*, March 13, 1933; Lamont Papers, Boxes 80, 211, 212, 274; conversation with FDR, March 23, 1933: Box 211-13; Morgan partners testimony at Senate hearings: report of U.S. Senate Committee on Banking and Currency Hearings, 1933; Morgan letter to Lawrence, June 30, 1933: page 179, Forbes, *Morgan*.

Handling the Press

L. Gould column: *New York Journal*, February 4, 1948; quotation of Franz Schneider: personal interview; Lippmann articles: *New York Herald Tribune*, May 26, 31, 1933; Lamont Papers, Boxes 85, 105, 120, 212, 274; TWL memorandum on Lippmann articles: Box 105-6; TWL memorandum on meeting with Lippmann: Box 212-26.

Holiday in England; Troubles in New York

Lamont Papers, Boxes 104, 105, 107, 110, 115, 246, 274; MacDonald letter to TWL, August 11, 1933: Box 107-8; Lippmann letter to TWL, January 27, 1934: Box 105-7.

Germany Threatens Default

Lamont Papers, Boxes 129, 182, 246; TWL-Schacht letters, April 1934: Box 182-2; Morgan aide-mémoire to State Department: Box 182-3; TWL memorandum of Chamberlain meeting: Box 182-4; TWL memorandum to U.S. embassy: Box 182-5.

The Lord of San Simeon and Other Acquaintances

TWL conversation with Hopkins: page 498, Schlesinger, *Comng of the New Deal*; Nicholson quotations about Lamont and Morrow biography: pages 181, 182, 204, Nicholson, *Diary and Letters 1930–39*; Lamont Papers, Boxes 98, 182, 247; TWL memorandum of talk with Hearst: Box 98-4; TWL memorandum of July 16 talk with Schacht: Box 182-10.

Launching a New Enterprise

Key sources on formation of Morgan Stanley: *Morgan Stanley, 50th Anniversary Review*, interview with Perry E. Hall; Meyer, Hinton, and Rodd, *Some Comments About the Morgan Bank*, page 29.

Senator Nye Attacks

Lamont Papers, Boxes 214, 215, 216, 274; Nye speech, May 27, 1935: Box 214-14; Duffus letter: October 22, 1935, *New York Times*; Villard articles: *The Nation*, October 16, November 13, 1935; Morgan letter to partners, October 28: Box 214-14; Baker letter to *New York Times*, November 1935: Box 215-11.

The Mexican Muddle

Lamont Papers, Boxes 192, 195, 196, 198, 199, 202, 203, 204, 205; TWL correspondence with Mexican finance ministers Pani and Gomez, 1932–34; President Rodriguez report, September 3, 1934: Box 205-14; TWL phone conversation with Suarez, December 17, 1935: Box 205-15.

A Question of History

Morgan and Lamont testimony: U.S. Senate Special Committee Investigating the Munitions Industry Hearings Record, 1934-1936; Lamont Papers, Boxes 210, 213, 214, 215, 216, 217; J. P. Morgan summary of Senate Munitions Committee hearings: Box 216-32.

A Royal Affair

This chapter is largely drawn from family letters; Lamont Papers, Boxes 82, 191, 247; TWL letter to Nancy Astor: Box 82-5; TWL letter to Fummi: Box 191-8.

South African Safari

Hancock, *Smuts—The Fields of Force*, Volume 2; Lamont Papers, Boxes 247, 274; TWL journal of trip: Box 247-17.

The Senate Summons Again

Lamont Papers, Boxes 217, 247, 274; TWL interview on possibility of war in Europe: *New York Times*, *New York Sun*, August 22, 1936; statement's effect on market: *New York Journal*, August 22, 1936; testimony at Senate Committee on Interstate Commerce hearings: *New York Times*, *Wall Street Journal*, March 6, 1937; Robert R. Young quotation: page 202, Josephson, *The Money Lords*.

Mussolini's Olive Branch

Lamont Papers, Boxes 191, 247; TWL memoranda and letter to TSL about meeting with Mussolini: Box 191-13.

After-Dinner Message

Lamont Papers, Boxes 144, 151, 247, 248, 274; Lindbergh Dinner speech: Box 151-14; Morgan quotation: page 189, Forbes, *Morgan*; Lundberg quotation: page 33, Lundberg, *America's Sixty Families*; TWL press interview: *New York Herald Tribune*, September 7, 1937; TWL speech to Commercial Club of Chicago: Box 144-10.

War in China

Lamont Papers, Boxes 184, 197, 188; TWL October 1934 memorandum to Sawada: Box 187-29; TWL letter to Fukai: Box 197-32; Johnson letter to TWL: Box 184-11; TWL letter to Wakasugi: Box 188-4; Saito letter to TWL: Box 188-5; TWL letter to Johnson, February 26, 1938: Box 184-14.

Partisan Passion

Lamont Papers, Boxes 89, 128, 157, 185, 274; TWL speech to National Institute of Social Sciences, May 5, 1934 with quotation about "robots": Box 155-2; TWL University of Pennsylvania speech, January 17, 1938: Box 157-14; TWL February 25 letter to FDR: Box 128-3.

Richard Whitney's Shocker

J. P. Morgan letter on Kennedy to Montagu Norman, March 18, 1938: page 189, Forbes *Morgan*; TWL testimony at S.E.C. hearings: The United States of America Before the Securities and Exchange Commission, 1938; Lamont Papers, Boxes 82, 217, 248, 279, 282; Nancy Astor letter to TWL: Box 82-5; Willkie letter to TWL: Box 217-8.

Book VI: Again: the Devil's Madness, pages 435–524

Forbes, *Morgan*; Elson, *Prelude to War: World War II*; Heiferman, *World War II*; Morgan, *FDR*; A. M. Lindbergh, *War Within and Without*; C. Lindbergh, *The Wartime Journals of Charles A. Lindbergh*; Josephson, *The Money Lords*; Morgan, Rodd, Hinton, *Some Comments About the Morgan Bank*; Morgan Stanley, *Morgan Stanley 50th Anniversary Review*; Chernow, *House of Morgan*; Cohen, *The Chinese Connection*; Hinton, *Cordell Hull*; Johnson, *William Allen White's America*; Johnson, *Selected Letters of William Allen White*; Reston,

Deadline, A Memoir; Harvard Class of 1892 Fiftieth Anniversary Report; C. Lamont, *Things to be Remembered*, and *The Thomas Lamonts in America*; Bailey, *A Diplomatic History of the American People*; Barnes, *Willkie*; Masefield, *Salt Water Poems and Ballads*; Lamont Papers.

Calm Before the Storm

Lamont Papers, Boxes 49, 127, 147, 160, 182, 209, 248, 250; TWL June 30, 1938 letter to FDR on U.S. Steel: Box 127-22; TWL letter to Hull: Box 209-29; Nancy Astor letter to TWL: Box 82-5; TWL University Club speech: Box 160-44; Brinkmann letter to TWL: Box 182-22; TWL letter to Brinkmann: Box 182-24; Kennedy quotation on Chamberlain and Churchill: unpublished family letter; TWL-Puhl letters of August 1939: Box 182-26.

Conflict Over Neutrality

Lamont Papers, Boxes 127, 140, 141, 209; Lindbergh radio speech: *New York Times*, September 15, 1939; Lindbergh quotation: page 269, *Wartime Journals of Charles A. Lindbergh*; FDR letters to TWL: Box 127-23; TWL Academy of Political Science speech: Box 140-19.

New Look at the Corner

Whitney quotation on partnership: *New York Times*, September 21, 1939; Lamont Papers, Boxes 110, 274; quotation from Morgan letter of March 30, 1940: page 198, Forbes, *Morgan*.

The War and American Politics

Anne Lindbergh quotation: page xxviii, *War Within and Without*; Lindbergh radio speech: *New York Times*, May 20, 1940; Lamont Papers, Boxes 21, 86, 89, 104, 123, 124, 137; Betty Morrow letter to TWL, May 25, 1940; TWL letter to Lindbergh, May 29, 1940; Lindbergh letter to TWL, June 7, 1940: Box 104-24; TWL correspondence with Cowles, Root, April 1940: Box 123-25; TWL letter to Willkie: Box 124-13; TWL letter to FDR: Box 127-25.

Menace on Both Oceans

Lamont Papers, Boxes 21, 49, 50, 84, 90, 94, 98, 100, 127, 141, 146, 147, 151, 152, 184, 188, 191; FDR letter to TWL: Box 191-10; TWL letter to Fummi, May 31, 1940: Box 191-11; TWL speech "The Far Eastern Threat": Box 141-3; Grew letter to TWL, December 26, 1940, Matsuoka letter to TWL: Box 141-5; TWL letters to Halifax: Box 97-6; Churchill quotation on Halifax: page 569, *Second World War (Their Finest Hour)*; Committee to Defend America by Aiding the Allies goals statement: Box 21-12; White letter to TWL of December 10, 1940: *William Allen White's America*; La Guardia letter to White and Lamont statement about Committee: December 29, 1940 *New York Herald Tribune*; TWL Merchants' Association speech: Box 151-27; TWL Economic Club of Detroit speech: Box 146-25; phone calls and letters to FDR: Box 127-25.

From Pulpit Harbor to Pearl Harbor

Lamont Papers, Boxes 84, 105, 127, 274; TWL notes on FDR meeting, August 15, 1941: Box 127-26; TWL letter to Halifax, October 15, 1941: Box 84-23; TWL memorandum to Lippmann: Box 105-3; TWL letter of December 15, 1941 to FDR and FDR reply: Box 127-27; TWL memo of FDR meeting, January 26, 1942: Box 127-27.

On the Home Front

Lamont Papers, Boxes 4, 5, 19, 143, 145, 239; TWL talk Council on Foreign Relations: Box 145-6.

TWL II

Senior Class Oration: page 216; C. Lamont *Things to Be Remembered*; Lamont Papers, Box 238.

A New Father-Son Team

Lamont Papers, Boxes 144, 151, 155; TWL speech to Congress of American Soviet Friendship: Box 144-16.

Good Neighbor Policy

Lamont Papers, Boxes 192, 193, 194, 207, 208; TWL letter to Hull; TWL conversation with Wells, March 5, 1942; TWL letter to Lord Bicester, December 2, 1941: Box 208-17.

Pen in Hand

Lewis quotation: *New York Times*, April 18, 1943; Lamont Papers, Boxes 89, 104, 127, 142, 144, 155, 208, 274; FDR letter to TWL, November 10, 1941 about Lewis: Box 127-26; Committee for Economic Development speech, April 13, 1943: Box 144-14; NBC radio speech: *New York Times*, June 27, 1943.

Reduce Speed

Quotation from Willkie letter to Queenie, October 1943: page 342, Barnes, *Willkie*; Lamont Papers, Boxes 159, 250, 274.

Letters to the Editor

Lamont Papers, Boxes 90, 104, 105, 124, 127, 128, 131, 137, 139, 156, 157, 159, 162, 250, 274; Smuts letters to TWL of June 9, 1939, December 22, 1939, August 11, 1940, and April 8, 1942: Box 131-3, 4; memoranda on Gromyko meeting: Box 128-16.

"They Are Not Dead, Our Sons Who Fell in Glory"

Lamont Papers, Boxes 85, 90, 127, 131, 239, 251, 266, 274; Eleanor Roosevelt letter to TWL of May 3, 1945: Box 127-20.

Fitting the Final Pieces

Quotation from "Sea Fever": Masefield, *Salt Water Poems and Ballads*; TWL letter to George Whitney: Meyer, Rodd, Hinton, *Some Comments*

About the Morgan Bank; Lamont Papers, Boxes 14, 15, 85, 152, 153, 154, 205, 251, 274; TWL letter to Archbishop and Archbishop's letter of February 7, 1947: Box 14-15.

"Time, Like an Ever-Rolling Stream"

Lamont Papers, Boxes 251, 274.

Bibliography

Allen, Frederick Lewis. *The Great Pierpont Morgan*. Harper & Brothers, New York, 1949.

———. *The Lords of Creation*. Harper & Brothers, New York and London, 1935.

———. *Only Yesterday*. Harper & Brothers, New York and London, 1931.

———. *Since Yesterday*. Harper & Brothers, New York and London, 1939.

Amory, Cleveland. *The Last Resorts*. Harper & Brothers, New York, 1952.

Babington-Smith, Constance. *John Masefield; A Life*. Macmillan, New York, 1978.

Bailey, Thomas A. *A Diplomatic History of the American People*. Prentice-Hall, Englewood Cliffs, N.J., 1974.

———. *Woodrow Wilson and the Lost Peace*. Macmillan, New York, 1944.

Bankers Trust Company. *Bankers Trust Company, 75 Years*. BTC, New York, 1978.

Barnes, Joseph. *Willkie*. Simon and Schuster, New York, 1978.

Baruch, Bernard M. *The Making of the Reparations and Economic Sections of the Treaty*. Harper & Brothers, New York and London, 1920.

———. *Baruch: My Own Story*. Henry Holt, New York, 1957.

———. *The Public Years*. Holt, Rinehart and Winston, New York, 1960.

Bentinck-Smith, William. *The Harvard Book*. Harvard University Press, Cambridge, 1953.

Bertagna, Joe. *Crimson in Triumph, A Pictorial History of Harvard Athletics, 1852–1985*. Stephen Greene Press, Lexington, Mass., 1986.

Birmingham, Stephen. *Our Crowd: The Great Jewish Families of New York*. Harper & Row, New York, Evanston, and London, 1967.

Blanchard, John A. *The H Book of Harvard Athletes*. Harvard University Club, Cambridge, 1923.

Blum, John Morton. *From the Morgenthau Diaries*. Houghton Mifflin, Boston, 1957–67.

Brooks, John. *Once in Golconda, A True Drama of Wall Street 1920–1938*. Harper & Row, New York, Evanston, and London, 1969.

Burner, David. *Herbert Hoover, A Public Life*. Alfred Knopf, New York, 1979.

Burns, James MacGregor. *Roosevelt: The Lion and the Fox*. Harcourt Brace, New York, 1956.

Carosso, Vincent P. *Investment Banking in America: A History*. Harvard University Press, Cambridge, 1970.

————. *The Morgans, Private International Bankers 1854–1913*. Harvard University Press, Cambridge, 1987.

Case, Everett N. and Josephine Y. *Owen D. Young and American Enterprise*. David R. Godine, Boston, 1982.

Cecil, Viscount Cecil of Chelwood. *All the Way*. Hodder and Stoughton Ltd., London, 1949.

Chandler, Lester V. *Benjamin Strong, Central Banker*. Brookings Institution, Washington, D.C., 1958.

Chernow, Ron. *The House of Morgan: An American Banking Dynasty and the Rise of Modern Finance*. Atlantic Monthly Press, New York, 1990.

Churchill, Winston S. *The Second World War*. Houghton Mifflin, Boston, 1948.

Clay, Sir Henry. *Lord Norman*. Macmillan, London, 1957.

Cohen, Warren I. *The Chinese Connection*. Columbia University Press, New York, 1978.

Coit, Margaret L. *Mr. Baruch*. Houghton Mifflin, Boston, 1978.

Cory, Lewis. *The House of Morgan: A Social Biography of the Masters of Money*. G. Howard Watt, New York, 1930.

Cowles, Gardner. *Mike Looks Back*. Gardner Cowles, New York, 1985.

Crosbie, Lawrence M. *The Phillips Exeter Academy, A History*. Plimpton Press, Norwood, 1924.

Cruikshank, Jeffrey L. *A Delicate Experiment: The Harvard Business School 1908–1945*. Harvard Business School Press, Boston, 1987.

Current, Richard N. *Secretary Stimson*. Rutgers University Press, New Brunswick, 1954.

Davis, Kenneth S. *F.D.R. The New York Years 1928–33*. Random House, New York, 1985.

————. *F.D.R. The New Deal Years 1933–37*. Random House, New York, 1986.

Dawes, Charles G. *Journal as Ambassador to Great Britain*. Macmillan, New York, 1939.

Elson, Robert T. *Prelude to War: World War II*. Time-Life Books, New York, 1977.

Flandrau, Charles M. *Harvard Episodes*. Copeland and Day, Boston, 1897.

Forbes, John Douglas. *J. P. Morgan, Jr. 1867–1943*. University Press of Virginia, Charlottesville, 1981.

———. *Stettinius, Sr.: Portrait of a Morgan Partner*. University Press of Virginia, Charlottesville, 1984.

Frieden, Jeffrey A. *Banking on the World*. Harper & Row, New York, 1982.

Galbraith, John Kenneth. *The Great Crash*. Houghton Mifflin, Boston, 1972.

Garraty, John A. *Right Hand Man: The Life of George W. Perkins*. Harper & Brothers, New York, 1957.

George, David Lloyd. *Memoirs of the Peace Conference*. Little Brown, Boston, 1937.

Goodwin, Doris Kearns. *The Fitzgeralds and the Kennedys*. Simon and Schuster, New York, 1987.

Grant, James. *Bernard Baruch, The Adventures of a Wall Street Legend*. Simon and Schuster, New York, 1983.

Hancock, W. K. *Smuts—The Fields of Force*. Cambridge University Press, Cambridge, U.K., 1968.

Heiferman, Ronald. *World War II*. Derbibooks, Secaucus, N.J., 1973.

Hinshaw, David. *Herbert Hoover, American Quaker*. Farrar Strauss, New York, 1950.

Hinton, Harold B. *Cordell Hull, A Biography*. Doubleday, Doran & Co., Garden City, 1942.

Hogan, Michael J. *Informal Entente: The Private Structure of Cooperation in Anglo-American Economic Diplomacy, 1918–1928*. University of Missouri Press, Columbia, 1977.

Hoopes, Townshend. *The Devil and John Foster Dulles*. Little Brown, Boston, 1973.

Hoover, Herbert. *The Memoirs of Herbert Hoover*. Macmillan, New York, 1952.

———. *The Ordeal of Woodrow Wilson*. McGraw-Hill, New York, 1958.

House, Edward M. and Charles Seymour. *What Really Happened at Paris, Story of the Peace Conference 1918–1919*. C. Scribner's Sons, New York, 1921.

Hoyt, Edwin P., Jr. *The House of Morgan*. Dodd, Mead and Company, New York, 1966.

Hull, Cordell. *The Memoirs of Cordell Hull*. Macmillan, New York, 1948.

Ingo, Walter. *Deregulating Wall Street: Commercial Bank Penetration of the Corporate Securities Market.* Wiley, New York, 1985.

Isaacson, Walter, and Evan Thomas. *The Wise Men: Six Friends and the World They Made.* Simon and Schuster, Touchstone Books, New York, 1986.

Jackson, Stanley. *J. P. Morgan.* Stein and Day, New York, 1983.

Jensen, Amy La Follette. *The White House and Its Thirty-two Families.* McGraw-Hill, New York, Toronto, London, 1958.

Johnson, Arthur Menzies. *Winthrop W. Aldrich: Lawyer, Banker, Diplomat.* Graduate School of Business Administration, Harvard University, 1968.

Johnson, Walter. *Selected Letters of William Allen White.* Henry Holt, New York, 1947.

———. *William Allen White's America.* Henry Holt, New York, 1947.

Josephson, Matthew. *The Money Lords: The Great Finance Capitalists 1925–1950.* Weybright & Talley, New York, 1972.

Kneisel, William J. *Morgan Stanley & Co., Inc. A Brief History.* Morgan Stanley, New York, 1977.

Lamont, Corliss. *The Thomas Lamonts in America.* A. S. Barnes, South Brunswick and New York, 1962.

Lamont, Corliss, ed. *Things to Be Remembered.* Privately printed, 1946.

Lamont, Corliss and Lansing Lamont, eds. *Letters of John Masefield to Florence Lamont.* Columbia University Press, New York, 1979.

Lamont, Edward M. *Thomas Stillwell Lamont.* Privately printed, Horizon Press, New York, 1969.

Lamont, Florence. *Far Eastern Diary.* Privately printed, Horizon Press, New York, 1951.

Lamont, Thomas W. *Across World Frontiers.* Harcourt Brace & Co., New York, 1951.

———. *Henry P. Davison: The Record of a Useful Life.* Harper & Brothers, New York and London, 1933.

———. *My Boyhood in a Parsonage.* Harper & Brothers, New York and London, 1946.

Leffler, Melvin P. *The Elusive Quest—America's Pursuit of European Stability and French Security 1919–1933.* University of North Carolina Press, Chapel Hill, 1979.

Lindbergh, Anne Morrow. *Hour of Gold, Hour of Lead, Diaries and Letters 1929–1932.* Harcourt Brace Jovanovich, New York and London, 1973.

———. *War Within and Without, Diaries and Letters 1939–1944.* Harcourt Brace Jovanovich, New York and London, 1980.

Lindbergh, Charles A. *The Wartime Journals of Charles A. Lindbergh.* Harcourt Brace Jovanovich, New York and London, 1970.

Logan, Sheridan F. *George F. Baker and His Bank 1840–1955.* Privately printed, 1981.

Lundberg, Ferdinand. *America's Sixty Families.* Citadel Press, New York, 1946.

Manchester, William. *The Last Lion, Winston Spencer Churchill. Visions of Glory 1874–1932.* Little Brown, Boston, Toronto, London, 1983.

———. *The Last Lion, Winston Spencer Churchill. Alone 1932–1940.* Little Brown, Boston, Toronto, London, 1988.

Masefield, John. *Salt Water Poems and Ballads.* Macmillan, New York, 1926.

Masters, Anthony. *Nancy Astor, A Life.* Book Club Associates, London, 1982.

Matz, Mary Jane. *The Many Lives of Otto Kahn.* Pendragon Press, New York, 1963.

Mayer, Martin. *The Bankers.* Weybright & Talley, New York, 1974.

Mitchell, Broadus. *Depression Decade.* Rinehart, New York, 1947.

Moley, Raymond. *After Seven Years.* Harper & Brothers, New York, London, 1939.

Morgan Grenfell and Company. *George Peabody & Co.; J. S. Morgan & Co.; Morgan Grenfell & Co.; Morgan Grenfell Co. Ltd; 1838–1958.* Privately printed, Oxford University Press, 1958.

Morgan Guaranty Trust Company. *23 Wall Street.* Morgan Guaranty Trust Company, 1983.

Morgan, Stanley. *Morgan Stanley 50th Anniversary Review.* Morgan Stanley, New York, 1985.

Morgan, Ted. *F.D.R., A Biography.* Simon and Schuster, New York, 1985.

Morison, Samuel Eliot and Henry Steele Commager. *The Growth of the American Republic.* Oxford University Press, New York, 1937.

Morrow, Elizabeth Cutter. *The Mexican Years.* Privately printed, Spiral Press, New York, 1953.

Nicholson, Harold. *Dwight Morrow.* Harcourt Brace, New York, 1935.

Nicholson, Nigel, ed. *Harold Nicholson—Diary and Letters 1930–1939.* Atheneum, New York, 1966.

———. *Harold Nicholson—The War Years 1939–1945.* Atheneum, New York, 1967.

Pecora, Ferdinand. *Wall Street Under Oath: The Story of Our Modern Money Changers.* Simon and Schuster, New York, 1939.

Pier, Arthur S. *The Story of Harvard.* Little Brown, Boston, 1913.

Pruessen, Ronald W. *John Foster Dulles: The Road to Power.* Free Press, New York, 1982.

Pulling, Edward, ed. *Selected Letters of R. C. Leffingwell.* Exposition Press, Hicksville, N.Y., 1980.

Pusey, Merlo. *Charles Evans Hughes*. Macmillan, New York, 1951.

Reston, James. *Deadline, A Memoir*. Random House, New York, 1991.

Roosevelt, Elliot, ed. *F.D.R., His Personal Papers*. Duell Sloane and Pierce, New York, 1947.

Saltonstall, William G. *Lewis Perry of Exeter*. Atheneum, New York, 1980.

Satterlee, Herbert L. *J. Pierpont Morgan*. Macmillan, New York, 1939.

Schlesinger, Arthur M., Jr. *The Age of Roosevelt*. Houghton Mifflin, Boston, 1960.

———. *The Coming of the New Deal*. Houghton Mifflin, Boston, 1959.

———. ed. *The Almanac of American History*. G. P. Putnam's Sons, New York, 1983.

Schwartz, Jordon A. *Liberal—Adolfe A. Berle and the Vision of an American Era*. Free Press, New York, 1987.

Seldes, George. *Witness to a Century: Encounters with the Noted, the Notorious and the Three SOBs*. Ballantine Books, New York, 1987.

Seymour, Charles. *Summary of the Intimate Papers of Colonel House*. Houghton Mifflin, Boston, 1926.

———. *American Neutrality 1914–1917: Essays on the Cause of American Intervention in the World War*. Yale University Press, New Haven; Oxford University Press, London, 1935.

Shermer, David. *World War I*. Derbibooks, Secaucus, N.J., 1975.

Silverman, Dan P. *Reconstructing Europe After the Great War*. Harvard University Press, Cambridge, 1982.

Sloat, Warren. *1929 America Before the Crash*. Macmillan, New York, 1979.

Steel, Ronald. *Walter Lippmann and the American Century*. Atlantic Monthly Press–Little Brown, Boston, 1980.

Stimson, Henry L., and McGeorge Bundy. *On Active Service in Peace and War*. Harper, New York, 1948.

Sullivan, Mark. *Our Times, The Twenties*. C. Scribner's Sons, 1926–1935.

Sulzberger, C. L. *The American Heritage Picture History of World War II*. American Heritage, New York, 1966.

Tarbell, Ida M. *Owen D. Young*. Macmillan, New York, 1932.

Thomas, Gordon and Max Morgan-Witts. *The Day the Bubble Burst*. Doubleday, Garden City, 1979.

Tyack, Geoffrey. *Cliveden and the Astor Household: Between the Wars*. Willmot Printers, Ltd., High Wycombe, U.K., 1982.

Wagner, Charles A. *Harvard—Four Centuries of Freedoms*. Dutton, New York, 1950.

Walworth, Arthur. *Wilson and His Peacemakers: American Diplomacy at the Paris Peace Conference, 1919.* W. W. Norton, New York and London, 1986.

Warburg, James P. *The Money Muddle.* Alfred A. Knopf, New York, 1934.

Wheeler, George. *Pierpont Morgan and Friends: The Anatomy of a Myth.* Prentice-Hall, Englewood Cliffs, N.J., 1973.

White, William Allen. *The Autobiography of William Allen White.* Macmillan, New York, 1946.

Wigmore, Barrie A. *The Crash and Its Aftermath: A History of the Securities Markets in the U. S. 1929–1933.* Greenwood Press, Westport and London, 1985.

Williams, Myron C. *The Story of Phillips Exeter Academy.* P.E.A., Exeter, 1957.

Winkler, John K. *Morgan the Magnificent: The Life of J. Pierpont Morgan.* Vanguard Press, New York, 1930.

Unpublished Papers and U.S. Government Reports

The Papers of Thomas W. Lamont. Baker Library, Harvard University

Family letters held by the Lamont family

Diary of Thomas Lamont (T.W.L.'s father)

Harvard College Class of 1892 Reunion Reports

The Papers of George L. Harrison. Butler Library, Columbia University

U.S. House Committee on Banking and Currency Testimony Before Money Trust Investigation, 1913

U.S. Senate Committee on Banking and Currency Hearings on Stock Exchange Practices, 1933

U.S. Senate Special Committee Investigating the Munitions Industry Hearings Record, 1934–1936

The United States of America before the Securities and Exchange Commission, Volume 1, November 1, 1938

The Papers of J. P. Morgan, Jr. The Pierpont Morgan Library

Morgan Papers. J. P. Morgan & Co. Library

America and Munitions. The Work of Messrs. J. P. Morgan & Co. in the World War. Privately printed by J. P. Morgan & Co.

News releases on the deaths of J. P. Morgan, Jr., S. Parker Gilbert, and Russell C. Leffingwell, from the files of J. P. Morgan & Co., Inc.

Morgan & Cie., N. D. Jay, Morgan Guaranty Trust Company

The Seniors, Partners, and Aides. A conference paper by Vincent P. Carosso. Sleepy Hollow Press, 1981. Reprinted by Morgan Guaranty Trust Company.

Some Comments about the Morgan Bank by John M. Meyer, Jr., Longstreet Hinton, and Thomas Rodd. Privately printed by J. P. Morgan & Co., Inc.

U. S. Submarine Losses World War II, U. S. Navy Department

International Committee of Bankers on Mexico. Collection of agreements between Committee and Government of Mexico, compiled by Davis, Polk, and Wardell.

Interview with George Whitney, Columbia University Oral History Research Office.

List of People Interviewed for This Book

Vincent P. Carosso (deceased), Professor of History, New York University and author of books and articles in investment banking.

Leighton H. Coleman, former senior partner of Davis, Polk law firm. (deceased)

Stuart Cragin, former Executive Vice President and director of J. P. Morgan & Co., Inc.

Daniel P. Davison, former chairman and CEO of United States Trust Company.

Gerhard H. Gesell, Judge U. S. District Court for District of Columbia. (deceased)

Bert C. Gordon, former Vice President Morgan Guaranty Trust Company.

Perry E. Hall, former managing partner of Morgan Stanley & Co.

Longstreet Hinton (deceased), former Chairman of Trust Committee and director of J. P. Morgan & Co., Inc.

Corliss Lamont, son of T.W.L.

Lansing Lamont, grandson of T.W.L.

Margaret Lamont, granddaughter of T.W.L.

Nancy S. Lamont, daughter-in-law of T.W.L. (deceased)

John M. Meyer, Jr., former Chairman and CEO of J. P. Morgan & Co., Inc.

Charles F. Morgan, former partner of Morgan Stanley & Co.

John P. Morgan II, former Vice President of Morgan Guaranty Trust Co.

Walter H. Page, former Chairman and CEO of J. P. Morgan & Co., Inc.

Ellmore C. Patterson, former Chairman and CEO of J. P. Morgan & Co., Inc.

DeWitt Peterkin, Jr., former Vice Chairman of J. P. Morgan & Co., Inc.

Edward Pulling, son-in-law of Russell C. Leffingwell. (deceased)

Franz Schneider, Jr., former financial editor of *New York Evening Post* and other newspapers, executive of Newmont Mining Co., and corporation director. (deceased)

Peter Vermilye, Senior adviser, Baring America Asset Management Co., Inc., and former Vice President of Morgan Guaranty Trust Co.

A. Vernon Woodworth, North Haven summer resident

Photo Credits

Book jacket portrait by Charles Hopkinson, Courtesy of Harvard Club of New York City.

1, 2, 3, 4, 5, 6, 7: Lamont family collection.

8: Reprinted with the permission of Macmillan Publishing Company from *J. Pierpont Morgan* by Herbert L. Satterlee. Copyright 1939 by Junius S. Morgan, renewed 1967 by Mabel Satterlee Morgan.

9: Photograph from Henry P. Davison: *The Record of a Useful Life* by Thomas W. Lamont. Copyright, 1933, by Thomas W. Lamont. Copyright renewed 1961 by Thomas S. Lamont. Reprinted by permission of Harper Collins Publishers Inc.

10, 11: Baker Library, Harvard Business School.

12: Lamont family collection.

13: Lamont family collection (*New York Herald Tribune* photo).

14: New York Stock Exchange Archives.

15: Courtesy of Estate of Harold Nicholson.

16: *Cape Times*

17: Phillips Exeter Academy.

18: Lamont family collection.

19: The Bettman Archives, *United Press International* photo.

20: Lamont family collection.

21: Harvard Magazine.

22: Brown Brothers.

23: Lamont family collection (*N.Y. Daily Mirror* photo)

24: Courtesy of Leffingwell family.

Index

Across World Frontiers (Lamont), xiii
Act of 1925, 302
Addis, Sir Charles, 169–70
Albany City Evening Journal, Lamont as reporter on, 18
Albert (king of Belgium), 148
Aldrich, Amey, 406
Aldrich, Chester, 406
Aldrich, Nelson, 49
Aldrich, Winthrop, 336, 364
Alexander, Henry C., 439
Alfonso (king of Spain), 226
Alleghany Corporation, 253–54, 343–44, 380, 405–6. *See also* Van Sweringen Brothers
Allied debt, and the United States, 186–87
Alston, Beilby, 157
America First Committee, 464, 467
American Foreign Securities Co., 83
American Group, and China, 194
American Neutrality 1914–1917 (Seymour), 384
American Viscose Co., 468
America's Sixty Families (Lundberg), 411–12
Anderson, Arthur M., 207, 240, 283–84, 510
Argyllshire, Lamont clan in, 229

Armour, J. Ogden, 76–77
Armstrong, Helen, 404–5
Arno, Peter, 418
Article 27, 175–77, 184–85, 197
Article X, 135–37
Astor, Lady Nancy, 279–80, 323, 396–97, 426–27
Astor, Lord, 279–80, 396–97
Austria: bank failure in, 294; bond issue completed for, 192; economic status of, 189; foreign loan to, 191, 439–41, 443;

Bacon, Robert, 106
Baker, George, Jr., 3, 37, 85, 230, 265; farewell letter from Lamont to, 42; money trust hearings and, 53–54
Baker, Newton D., 384–85
Banco Agricola, 386
Banco Nacional de Mexico, 197
Bankers Trust Company, 3–4, 35, 40, 51
Bank failures, statistics of, 329–31
Bank for International Settlements, establishment of, 258–60, 278–79, 367
Banking and Currency Committee, 318

Bank of England, 73
Barney, Charles T., 36
Bartow, Francis D., 240
Baruch, Bernard M., 101, 106, 108, 110, 130
"Bear raids," 318
Beech Corporation, 411
Belgium, foreign loan to, 218–19
Bell, Johannes, 139
Benes, Edward, 129
Benet, William Rose, 224
Berenson, Bernard, 216
Berle, Adolf A., 419
Beverage, John, 92
Bicester, Lord, 489
Big Four, 107
"Bird dogs," 514
Blagden, Dorothy, 399
Blagden, Linzee, 399
Bliss, General Tasker H., 105, 116
Bombing, the Morgan bank as a target of, 169
"Book of Friendship" awards, 486
Borah, William E., 135, 142
Boston Advertiser, Lamont as correspondent for, 18
Boston Herald, Lamont as reporter for, 18–20
Bound Brook, N.J., Lamont family reunion at, 7
Bound Brook LaMontes. *See* Lamont, George; Lamont, Rebecca
Bowers, Arthur F., 23–25
Brainard, Morgan, 351
"Brain trust," 361
Brandeis, Louis, 57
"Breaking the Money Trust," (Brandeis), 57
Brest-Litovsk talks, 98
Brinkmann, Dr. Rudolf, 440
British government, foreign loan to 74–82, 92–93
Brooks, Phillips, 17
Brown Bros. Co., 83
Bryan, William Jennings, 70, 153–54

Butler, Dr. Nicholas Murray, 265, 323, 355

Cadogan, Sir Alexander, 472
Canby, Henry Seidel, 224, 396
Canfield, Cass, 511
Canham, Erwin D., 455
Carnegie Trust Company, 45–46
Carranza, Venustiano, 176–77
Case, George, 3, 141
Cecil, Lady, 212–13
Cecil, Lord Robert, 190–91, 212–13, 293
Century Club, 464
Cerf, Bennett, 511
Chamberlain, Neville, 369–70, 397; criticism of, 438; at Munich conference in 1938, 436; and policy of conciliation, 427; praise for, 437
Chicago business community, and the Anglo-French loan, 76–82
Child, Richard W., 192
China: American interest in, 194; foreign investment in, 153–54; Japanese aggression in, 414–17
Chinese consortium, 153–66
Chinese Famine Committee, 167
Churchill, Winston S., 265, 397, 398, 462–63; shipboard meeting with FDR and, 470–73, 476–77
Cilley, Bradbury, 16
Clark, Senator Bennett Champ, 391, 393–94
Clavernack, 5
Clemenceau, Georges, 96–97, 107, 113, 118, 121–22, 126–27, 139
Clémentel, Étienne, 204, 209
Cochran, Thomas, 88, 200, 240, 302, 425
Colefax, Lady Sibyl, 397
Coleman, Leighton H., 220
Collier's Weekly, 346, 355
Committee of Experts, 255
Committee on Banking and Currency of House of Representatives, 48

Committee to Defend America by Aiding the Allies, 450, 464, 466–67
Commonwealth and Southern, 422
Conant, James B., 390, 445
Congressional Joint Committee on Tax Evasion and Avoidance, 411
Congress of American-Soviet Friendship, 486
Consortium for the Assistance of China, 169
Converse, Edmund C., 39, 85
Coolidge, Calvin, 192, 196, 212, 247
Corey, Lewis, 347
Corliss, Charles (brother-in-law), 4, 27, 30, 31, 39–40
Corliss, Coon & Co., 21–22
Corliss, Florence. *See* Lamont, Florence
Corliss, Lamont (son), 33
Corliss, Mrs. Wilbur Fisk (mother-in-law), 21–22
Corliss, Wilbur Fisk (father-in-law), 21–22, 24, 242
"Corner, the", 239
Corn Exchange Bank Trust Company, 424
Costigan, Edward P., 347
Council of Four, 121
Council on Foreign Relations, 354
Cousins, Norman, 497
Covington, Burling, 388
Coward, Noel, 398
Cowles, Gardner, 227, 355
Cowles, John, 453
Cox, Governor James M., 171, 361
Credit-Anstalt, 294
Creel, George, 98
Crimson, Lamont as editor on the, 18–19
Crocker, William H., 235
Croly, Herbert, 222
Crosby, Oscar T., 93
Cubit, Lady Olive, 467
Cunliffe, Lord Walter, 95, 108–9

Cunningham, Charles C. (son-in-law), 323, 490
Cunningham, Eleanor A. (daughter), 40, 249, 323, 490
Curtis, Cyrus H., 193–94
Cushman, Townshend, 27, 30
Cushman, William, 27, 31
Cushman Bros., 26, 28, 33. *See also* Cushman, William; Cushman, Townshend

Dahl, Miss, 497
Daladier, Edouard, 436
Damrosch, Walter, 365
Dan, Dr. Takuna, 232, 311
Dassau, John, 425–26
Davies, Joseph E., 486
Davies, Marion, 375
Davis, John W., 212, 265, 337, 391
Davis, Norman H., 106, 108–9, 111; as ambassador-at-large, 344; as chairman of Red Cross, 462; death of, 502; and *New York Evening Post,* 181
Davison, Henry (Harry) P., 3–4, 33, 43, 61, 115; and Bankers Trust, 35–39; as chairman of War Council of Red Cross, 89; and copy of draft treaty, 134–35; illness and death, 174, 182
Davison, Henry P., Jr., 188, 251
Dawes, Charles G., 77–79, 81, 95, 201, 261. *See also* Dawes Plan
Dawes Plan, 201–13, 254–55, 377, 378, 439–40. *See also* Dawes, Charles G.
Dawson, Geoffrey, 427
De la Huerta, Adolfo, 178, 182–85, 197–200. *See also* Mexico, foreign loan to
de Oca, Louis Montes, 281–87, 385
Depression era, 288
De Rivera, Primo, 226
Dewey, Thomas E., 452, 502

Díaz, Porfirio, 175
Dill, Sir John, 472
Dillon, Clarence, 207, 227
Dillon, Read, 191, 227, 468
Dingley Tariff, 29
Draper, Ruth, 399
Drexel, Morgan & Co., 43
Duane, William, 435
Duffield, Pitts, 27
Duffus, R. L., 382–83
Dulles, John Foster, 107, 110, 111, 113, 129
DuPont, Pierre S., 480
Dwight Morrow (Nicholson), 382–83

Eccles, Marriner, 422
Eden, Anthony, 427, 438
Edge, Walter E., 146
Edward VIII (king of England), 397–98, 404
"Effect of the War on America's Financial Position, The," 89
Egan, Martin, 155, 231–32, 324–25, 503
Eglee, Dr. E. P., 231
Eichelberger, Clark M., 465
Eliot, Charles W., 22–23
Elizabeth (queen of Belgium), 148
Elliott, William Y., 222
Emergency Banking Act, 331
Emergency Unemployment Relief Committee of New York, 306
Equitable Life Assurance Company, 52
Erie Railroad, 71
Ewing, William, 379

Famine in China, 167
FDR. *See* Roosevelt, Franklin D.
Federal Reserve Act of 1914, 62
Federal Reserve Board, 83, 84
Ferber, Edna, 291
Ferdinand, Archduke Franz, assassination of, 67
Field, Marshall, 181

"Financial Illusions of the War," 90
Financial panic of 1907, 36–37
"Fireside chat," 332. *See also* Roosevelt, Franklin D.
First National Bank, 3, 40, 51
Fisher, Irving, 265–66
Fisher, Most Reverend Dr. Geoffrey Francis, 512
Fiume situation, 125
Fletcher, Duncan, 339
Fletcher, Henry P., 176
Foch, Marshal, 114
Forbes, Bertie C., 354
Forbes, John Douglas, on Lamont, xiv
Forbes, W. Cameron, 91–92, 480
Ford, Henry, 351
Foreign Affairs, 354
Foreign bond, to British and French governments, 74–85
Foreign lending, U.S. government proposals for, 217–18
"Foreign Loans, an Essential Instrument of Commerce," 90
Forgan, James B., 77–79
Foster, John Watson, 70
Fourteen Points, 105, 107, 115, 120, 123. *See also* Wilson, Woodrow
France, declares war on Germany, 442
Franckenstein, Baron, 189
French government: request for loan from, 74–82; sale of treasury bills by, 83
Freres, Lazard, 211
Frontier Corporation, 263
Frost, Robert, 477–78
Fuad (king of Egypt), 242
Fukai, Governor Eigo, 414
Fummi, Giovanni, 223, 397, 407–8, 412, 457–58
Fummi, Lady Anne, 457

"Gabriel over Wall Street," 375
Galsworthy, John, 183
Gannett, Lewis S., 384
Gary, Elbert, 38

Gavit, Jack, 287
Gavit, Lucy (Lucy Lamont), 287–88
Gay, Edwin Francis, 141–42, 170, 181
George, Lloyd, 69, 71, 97, 107, 109–11, 113–14, 121
George VI (king of England), 410
Germany: and default on loans, 367–70; economic blockades and, 119–20; new plan for payments and, 378; reduction in reparations and, 324; reparations and the Committee of Experts and, 255; surrender of, 507
Gesell, Gerhard, 428
Gilbert, S. Parker, 206, 211, 370, 377–78, 425
Glass, Senator Carter, 105–6, 342, 351. *See also* Glass-Steagall Act
Glass-Steagall Act, 352, 365, 375
Gomez, Martes, 386–88
Good Neighbor policy, 488
Gore, Senator Thomas, 307
Goring, Hermann, 444
Gould, Leslie, 353
"Government Bond for Everybody, A," 90
Gow, Betty, 317
Grayson, Admiral Cary T., 138, 146
Great Britain: and war with Germany, 442; foreign loan to, 301; *See also* British government
Grenfell, Edward C., 67, 82, 97, 109, 293, 492
Grew, Joseph C., 414, 460
Grissell, Captain Michael, 467–68
Gromyko, Andrei A., 499
Guaranty Trust Company, 51

Halifax, Dorothy, 509
Halifax, Lord Edward, 462–63, 473, 474, 491, 509
Hall, Perry E., 379
Hammond, Ogden, 226

Hand, Learned, 250–51, 265, 448, 500
Hapgood, Norman, 57
Hara, Takashi, 156–57
Harding, Senator Warren G., 170, 173, 192, 217
Harjes, Herman, 207, 209, 216
Harkness, Edward B., 390
Harrison, George E., 265
Harvard Business School, Baker Library, xiv
Harvard College, class of 1892 50th reunion, 480–81
Harvard Monthly, 20
Hauptmann, Bruno Richard, 372
Hearst, William Randolph, 336, 374–76
Helvering, Guy T., 411
Hendershot, Ralph, 353, 421
Herriot, Édouard, 203, 204
Hess, Jerome, 388
Hibbard, Susan, 435
Hill, James J., 41, 75
Hirohito, Emperor, 233–34
Hitler, Adolf, 370, 378, 426–27, 436–38, 461–62
Hoffman, Miss, 226, 227
Hoffman, Paul, 479
Hoover, Herbert C., 92, 107, 115, 118, 148, 297–99, 318–20; and the Allied debt, 187–88
Hopkins, Harry L., 72–73, 371, 470–71
Houghton, Alanson B., 206
House, Colonel Edward M., 93, 105, 108–9, 114, 118, 132–33
Howe, Louis, 363
How to Win Friends and Influence People (Carnegie), 437
Huddleston, Dr. John, 72–73
Huerta, General Victoriano, 175, 177
Hughes, William, 110
Hughes, Charles Evans, 173, 185, 188, 194, 196, 203, 217

Hukuang Railway, 153, 163, 167
Hull, Cordell, 361–63, 368, 407, 416, 439, 462, 477, 488
"Hunt for a Money Trust, The," 56
Huxley, Julian, 477
Hymans, Paul, 126, 127

Ickes, Harold, 444, 494
Inouye, Inosuke, 157–59, 166, 195–96, 232, 234, 236–37, 310–11
Inter-Allied Reparations Commission, 121
Interborough Rapid Transit Company, 315
International Committee of Bankers, 385–87
International Consortium for the Assistance of China, 153
Inverchapel, Lord, 512
Irish, Margaret (Mrs. Corliss Lamont), 248, 291
Italy, foreign loan to, 191–92, 221
Iwasaki, Baron, 156–57
Iwasaki, Baroness, 156–57

James, Henry, 292
James, William, 17
Japan: foreign loan to, 195–96; militarism in China by, 243–44, 414–17, 458; South Manchuria Railway loan to, 236, 237; Pearl Harbor and, 475
Jay, Nelson Dean, 207
Jayne, Caroline Deuel. See Lamont, Caroline
Johnson, Dr. Hewlitt, 512
Johnson, Henry "Red," 317
Johnson, Hugh, 466
Johnson, Nelson T., 236, 414–5
Johnson Act, 464
Joint High Loan Commission, 74

Kai-shek, General Chiang, 244
Kellogg, Frank B., 203, 206, 218, 231, 236

Kellogg-Briand Pact, 265, 311
Kennedy, Joseph P., 427, 441
Kerr, Philip, 118, 442
Keyes, Leonard, 355
Keynes, John Maynard, 115, 128
King, Edward, 38–39
"Kingfish, the," 345
Kisselev, Eugene D., 499
Kittredge, George Lyman, 16
Klotz, Louis-Lucien, 113, 117, 119–20, 121
Knickerbocker Trust Company, 36–37
Knowles, R. E., 354
Knox, Frank, 459, 477, 484
Knutson, Harold, 455
Kohler, Peter Cailler, 33, 40
Konoye, Prince Fumimaro, 414, 460
Kristallnacht, 438
Krock, Arthur, 384
Kuhn, Loeb & Co., 195–96, 210

LaGuardia, Fiorello H., 465
Lamont, Archibald, 8
Lamont, Austin (son), 36, 228, 495, 510
Lamont, Caroline (Caroline Deuel Jayne) (mother): birth of, 6; death of, 87; marriage to Lamont, 6; personality of, 9–10
Lamont, Corliss (son), 248, 291, 478
Lamont, Corliss & Company, 3, 33, 39–40
Lamont, Edward (Ted) M. (grandson), 513
Lamont, Eleanor A. (daughter), 40, 249, 323, 490
Lamont, Elinor (Ellie) B. (daughter-in-law), 181–82, 191, 249
Lamont, Elizabeth (grandmother), 7
Lamont, Florence (Florence Corliss) (wife): birth of first grandchild, 212; births of children, 32, 33, 36, 40; enjoys good life, 275–77; evening pastimes and, 315–17; flies with Lindbergh, 372; hospitalized,

215, 224; impressions of FDR, 180; in Egypt, 241; in Greece, 292–93; in Spain, 226; marriage to Lamont, 27; meets Lamont, 21–23; member of committee to help children, 172; outing with R. MacDonald, 279; received degree, 32; shopping in Peking, 164; surgery, 329–30; at Treaty of Versailles, 138–39

Lamont, George (uncle), 7–8

Lamont, Hammond (brother), 7, 11, 13, 58

Lamont, Lucy (sister), 287–88, 492

Lamont, Margaret (daughter-in-law), 248, 291

Lamont, Nancy (daughter-in-law), 495

Lamont, Thomas, Pastor (father): as church fundraiser, 6–7; in Charlotteville, 5; death of, 87; education of, 5; family geneology of, 8; memorial statement about, 88; moving to new parsonages, 11, 12; retired, 87

Lamont, Rebecca (aunt), 7–8

Lamont, Thomas Stilwell (son), 32, 86, 251, 483; engagement of, 181; first born child to, 212; graduation from Harvard, 174; joins J. P. Morgan & Co., 188; president of Board of Trustees at Exeter, 509–10; wedding of, 191

Lamont, Thomas W.: his admiration for Wilson, 190; against Japanese aggression, 459; on American Commission to Negotiate Peace, 105–6; as an Anglophile, 28, 491; as an avid reader, 11; at Bankers Trust Co., 35; becomes a Morgan partner, 41–42; birthplace of, 5; brief summary of life and work, 519–23; childhood years of, 5, 7–8, 9, 10, 11–13; in China, 159–64; Chairman of Chinese Famine Committee, 167; Chairman of Class

Committee, 22; Chairman of International Committee of Bankers, 183; Chairman of Red Cross National Advisory Committee, 476; Chairman of Red Cross War Fund, 479; Chairman of Reparations Commission for Austria, 129; Chairman of Special American Committee, 321; his Christmas list, 516–17; as city editor at *New York Tribune*, 23–25, 27; and *Crimson*, 18–19; cruising the Caribbean, 228–29; and Cushman Bros., 26–34; dating, 24–25; death of, 517–18; on the death of J. P. Morgan, 56; his earnings of 1913, 58–59; at Exeter, 13–16; and *Exonian*, 15; at family reunion, 7–8; and FDR at Pulpit Harbor, 470–73; and the financial panic of 1907, 36; first trip abroad, 28; friendship with Lady Astor, 280; gift to Harvard, 390; gift to restoration of Canterbury Cathedral, 512; and golf, 190; and good life, 275–77; and good works, 225; graduation from Harvard College, 22; and *Harvard Monthly*, 20; illness of, 495, 496–97, 508, 510, 513; in Italy, 192, 215–16; in Japan, 155–59; joins Bankers Trust, 3–4; joins First National Bank, 40; as a journalist, 18–19; leaves Bankers Trust, 40; and *Literary Monthly*, 15; meets Emperor Hirohito, 233; meets King Fuad, 242; meets Mussolini, 407; member of Methodist Church, 10; in Mexico, 177–79, 182; money trust hearings, 49–55; and pastimes, 36–37; and *Pean*, 15; becomes president of Cushman Bros., 32; purchased *New York Evening Post*, 100–102; received Harvard Alumni Medal for Distinguished Service, 500; received

honorary degrees, 296, 323, 368; as reparations consultant, 108–14; and R. Whitney incident, 427–31, 423–25; in South Africa, 398–403; and student pranks, 14–15; student years at Harvard College, 17–23; in support of Russia, 484–87; testifies at Senate Banking and Currency Committee, 345–50; underwrites Lamont Undergraduate Library, 508; viewpoint on World War I, 67–68; on War Council, 118–19; his will, 514; his work habits, 240–41; writes Davison biography, 248; and Young Plan, 254–62
Lamont, Thomas William, II (grandson): becomes Naval Aviation Cadet, 484; gives class oration, 482–83; graduation from Exeter, 481–82; joins crew of U.S.S. Snook, 502; missing in action, 505–7
Landon, Alfred M., 404, 453, 454
Landon, Hugh, 480
Lansing, Robert M., 70, 84, 105, 156
Lausanne agreement, 324–25
Laval, Pierre, 303–4
Lawrence, Bishop William, 351
League of Nations, 116, 134
League of Red Cross Societies, 134
Leffingwell, Russell C., 93, 98, 106, 188, 227, 239–40, 265, 378, 502–3
Lehman, Governor Herbert, 331, 363
Leith, C. K., 109
Lend-Lease bill, 466, 468, 469
Lewis, John L., 419, 420, 492–93
Liberty loan bond issues, 89–91
Liberty Loan Committee, 89
Lilienthal, David, 422
Lindbergh, Anne Morrow, 300
Lindbergh, Charles A., 300, 317, 372, 443–44, 445–46, 450–52, 464, 466
Lindbergh, Charles A., Sr., 48

Lippmann, Faye, 250–51, 292, 404–5
Lippmann, Walter, 250, 258–59, 292, 293, 308–9, 325–26, 356–58, 404–5, 500
Little Reynard, 514, 517
Litvinov, Maxim, 478, 486
Lockett, Arthur, 26, 30, 31, 40, 43, 59
Lodge, Henry Cabot, 142
Logan, James A., 203, 206
London Economic Conference, 360–62
Long, Breckinridge, 155, 156, 158
Long, Huey P., 345–46
Lothian, Lord, 442–43, 460–61, 462
Loucheur, Louis, 108–9, 121, 126
Low, David, 427
Lowden, Governor Frank, 170
Lowell, A. Lawrence, 92, 296, 312
Luce, Henry, 459
Lundberg, Ferdinand, 411–12
Lusitania, 71
Lytton Report, 313

McAdoo, William G., 73, 84, 93, 98, 344, 391, 393
McCormick, Colonel Robert R., 467
McCormick, Vance, 106, 108, 110, 111
MacDonald, Ramsay, 203, 205, 261, 264–65, 279, 302, 327, 362, 368
McFadden, Louis T., 290
McGuirk, Katherine, 507, 510, 513, 515, 517
McKee, Earle, 435
McKinley, William, 29
MacMurray, J.V.A., 155
MacVeagh, Charles, 235, 236
MacVeagh, Charlton, 235
Madero, Francisco, 175
Manchukuo, 313
Manchuria, and the Japanese, 154–58, 195, 309–13
Marshall, George C., 472, 515–16
Masefield, John: meets the Lamonts,

97; comments on Lamont, xiv–xv;
received honorary degree, 100
Masunosuke, Adagiri, 154–55
Matsuoka, Yosuke, 460
M-Day (Stein), 396
Mellon, Andrew W., 203, 218, 411
Merchant's Review, 32, 33–34
Metcalfe, George, 202, 226, 228,
276–77, 361–62, 399, 401, 425,
502
Mexico, foreign loan to, 175–79,
183–85, 197–200, 220, 280–87,
385–90, 487–89, 510
Meyer, John M., Jr., 468
Michelson, Charles, 455
Millay, Edna St. Vincent, 477–78
Miller, Dr. James A., 495
Millis, Walter, 380
Mills, Edgar, 28–29, 31–32, 34
Miner, Edward G., 181–82
Miner, Elinor (Ellie) B. (daughter-in-
law), 181–82, 191, 249
Ministry of Munitions, 82
Missouri Pacific, 253, 380, 405
Mitchell, Charles E., 236, 266, 335,
341
Moley, Raymond, 361
"Money trust," 48–54
Mongolia, and the Japanese, 154–58
Monnet, Jean, 120–21, 447
Monroe, Vernon, 282
Moore and Schley, 37–38
Morgan, Henry Sturgis, 188, 251, 379
Morgan, J. P., & Co., 36; and Bel-
gium's loan, 218–19; and Carnegie
Trust Company, 45–46; description
of daily activities, 239; and France's
loan, 74–82, 203; and Germany's
loan, 211, 212, 280; and Great
Britain's loan, 300–301; and heavy
losses, 364; incorporation of,
448–50; and Italy's loan, 221, 238;
and Japan's loan, 196; and Jewish
people, 210; as member of Federal
Reserve, 479; and Mexico's debt,

286–87; nepotism and, 188–
89; opening files for examination,
337; and postwar look, 514; and
practice of offering stock to select
list, 252–53; as purchasing agent
during World War I, 69; releases
first financial statement, 365; sale of
American securities, 443; sale of
Standard Brands stock, 264; and
Senate Munitions Committee, 391–
95; and three sons as partners,
251; and the Vaness Corporation,
225–26
Morgan, J. Pierpont: asks Lamont to
be a partner, 41–42; astuteness in
business, 47–48; banking background of, 43–44; compassion for
people and, 46; death of, 55–56;
and financial panic of 1907, 36–39;
and money trust hearings, 48–53;
his presence, 46–47; success and,
44
Morgan, J. P., Jr.: attempted murder
of, 72; death of, 492; description
of, 60; at Harvard College, 17;
heart attack of, 410; as head of
Morgan house, 56; in a money
pinch, 373, 448; personality of,
340–41; view on the Germans, 262
Morgan, Junius, 43
Morgan, Junius S., Jr., 169, 188, 392
Morgan bank building, description of,
63
Morgan Grenfell & Co., 67–68, 366,
368, 402
Morgan Harjes & Co., 68, 95
Morgan, Henry (Harry) S., 379
"Morgan Inquiry, The," 357
Morgan Stanley & Co. Incorporated,
379–80, 447–48, 468
Mori, Kengo, 231
Morley, Christopher, 224
Morris, Roland S., 156–57, 167
Morrow, Anne. *See* Lindbergh, Anne
Morrow

Morrow, Dwight D., 62–63, 80, 205, 206, 248, 250; as ambassador, 229; death of, 303; fundraiser for Japan, 196; and Mexico's debt, 281–87

Morrow, Elizabeth (Betty), 250, 371–72, 450–51

Muller, Hermann, 139

Mullers, Adrian H., and Sons, 380

Munsey, Frank A., 101, 181, 193–94

Murray, Philip, 419, 420

Murray, Gilbert, 292–93

Murrow, Edward R., 501

Mussolini, Benito, 192, 215, 221–23, 278, 382, 407–10, 436, 457–58

My Boyhood in a Parsonage (Lamont), xiii, 13, 507, 509, 511

National City Bank, 51, 70

Nemaha, 86–87

Neutrality Act of 1935, 382

Neutrality Act of 1937, 443

Neutrality Act of 1939, 446

New Deal, 371, 418–19

New Haven Railroad, 71

New York, New Haven, and Hartford Railroad, 60–61

New York Central Railroad, 71

New York City, financial woes of, 314–15, 363–64

New York Evening Post, 100, 141, 181, 192–93, 194

New York Tribune, Lamont as city editor of, 23

Niagara Hudson Power Corp., 263

Nicholson, Harold, 372, 382, 397, 427

Nickel Plate, 225

1929 crash, of Wall Street, 269–75

Nogara, Bernadino, 458

Norman, Montagu, 97, 202–5, 207–8, 377, 439

Northcliffe, Lord, 94–96

Northern Pacific, board of directors for, 41

North Wind, 92, 100

Norton, Charles Eliot, 17

Norton, Jane (Jessie) (Mrs. J. P. Morgan), 219

Nye, Senator Gerald P., 381, 384, 391–92, 394–96

Nye Committee hearings, 385

Obregón, Álvaro, 176–78, 197–200, 281

Ochs, Adolph, 355

Ogden, Rollo, 101, 105

Olds, Robert E., 236

O'Leary, Jeremiah, 81

One World (Willkie), 496

"Open Door" policy, for China, 153

Oppenheimer, Lady, 402

Oppenheimer, Sir Ernest, 402

Orlando, Premier (of Italy), 107, 122, 125, 127, 132–33

Other People's Money and How the Bankers Use It (Brandeis), 57

Paderewski, Jan, 132–34

Padilla, Dr. Ezequiel, 489

Page, Walter Hines, 94

Paley, William S., 411

Palmer, A. Mitchell, 148

Palmer, George Herbert, 17

Pani, Alberto J., 197–200, 213–14, 220, 385–86

Paris Peace Conference, 105–7

"Peacock Point, The," 156

Pearl Harbor, 475

Pecora, Ferdinand, 335, 337–38, 510–11

Pennypacker, John G., 479

"Pennywise by War," 90

Perkins, George W., 35, 37, 42–43

Perkins, Thomas Nelson, 255

Perry, Dr. Lewis, 86, 390, 509. *See also* Perry-Lamont Day

Perry-Lamont Day, 509. *See also* Perry, Dr. Lewis

Pershing, General John J., 95

Peters Chocolate Co., 40

Phillips, William, 409
Phillips Exeter Academy, Lamont's student years at, 13–16
Pirelli, loan to, 238
Pittman, Senator Key, 361
Plumer, General, 118
Polk, Frank, 156, 158
Polk, Fred L., 98
Porcellian Club, 17, 228
Porter, William H., 45
Presbyterians, in contrast to Methodists, 6–7, 10
Prince of Wales, 172, 361
Pritchett, Henry S., 100, 265
Prittwitz, F. W., 304
Puhl, Dr. Emil, 441, 443
Pujo, Rep. Arsene P., 48

Queeny, Edward Monsanto, 496

Raskob, John J., 344
Raushenbush, Stephen, 95, 96, 391–92, 394
Reading, Lord, 74, 76–77, 78, 81, 94, 100, 293
Reciprocal Trade Agreements Act, 411
Reconstruction Finance Corporation, 330
Red Cross National Advisory Committee, 476
"Red Dean," 512
"Red scare," 148
Reid, Helen, 292, 513
Reid, Ogden, 292
Remington Arms Company, 82
Reston, James, 467
Reynard, 230, 248, 317, 325
Reynard II, 276
Reynolds, George M., 57, 77–79
Road to War, The (Millis), 380
Rockefeller, John D., Jr., 265
Rome, city of, foreign loan to, 238
Rome-Berlin Axis, 413
Roosevelt, Eleanor, 480, 505

Roosevelt, Franklin D., 404, 458, 469–70, 470–73; castigates bankers, 337; Churchill and, 476–77; death of, 505; the Lend-Lease bill and, 466; the Neutrality Act of 1937 and, 443; *New York Evening Post* and, 181; wins election, 326; wins third term, 456; wins fourth term, 502
Roosevelt, Theodore, 35, 44–45
Root, Elihu, 135, 257, 265
Root, Oren, Jr., 453
Royce, Josiah, 23
Rubinstein, Arthur, 398
Rubio, Ortiz, 284, 286, 287
Rublee, George, 388–90, 487
Ruhr, occupation of, 201, 202
Runyon, Damon, 355
Ruth, Babe, 326

"Sage of Emporia, The," 461
Saito, Hiroshi, 415–16
Salter, Sir Arthur, 189
Saltonstall, William G., 509
San Simeon, 374–75
Sardi, Baron, 221
Sarnoff, David, 257
Satterlee, Herbert, 51
Satterlee, Louise, 51, 55
Saunders, Edward, 231, 514
Savage, Philip, 249
Schacht, Dr. Hjalmar, 211, 256–57, 262, 367, 376–78
Schiff, Mortimer L., 210
Schneider, Franz, Jr., 193, 353–54
Scott, Walter A., 15–16
Second District Public Service Commission, 71
Second Federal Reserve District, 89
Securities Act of 1933, 366
Sedgwick, Ellery, 100, 181
Seymour, Professor Charles, 384, 396
"Shall America's Prosperity Continue?", 90

Shao-yi, T'ang, 160
Sherman Anti-Trust Act, 44–45, 50, 61
Shih-ch'ang, Hsü, 162
Short selling, practice of, 318
Simmons, E. H. H., 269
Simpson, Thatcher & Bartlett, 63
Simpson, Mrs. Wallis Warfield, 397–98
Sloan, Alfred P., 411
Smith, Governor Alfred E., 247, 445
Smith, Howard C., 30–32, 33, 34, 43
Smith, Captain Jeremiah, Jr., 95–96, 106, 155, 165, 169, 231, 390
Smith Barney & Co., 479
Smoot, Senator Reed, 289–90
Smoot-Hawley Tariff, 289, 411
Smuts, General Jan Christiaan, 111, 398, 400–402, 497–98
Smuts, Mrs. Jan Christiaan, 400–402
Snowden, Philip, 261, 262
Sokolsky, George, 159
So Little Time (Marquand), 496
Sonada, Saburu, 311
South Manchuria Railway, 155, 158, 195, 234, 236, 243–44, 309–10
"Speculative orgy" theory, 266–67
Speyer & Co., 210–11
Stamp, Sir Josiah, 293
Standard Brands, 264
Stanley, Harold, 240, 378–79
"Star Spangled Banner, The," 291
Stassen, Harold E., 454
Steel, Ronald, 293
Steele, Charles, 61, 88, 373, 379, 448
Stein, Rose M., 396
Stettinius, Edward R., 69, 84, 89, 128–29, 219
Stettinius, Edward R., Jr., 503
Stillman, James, 37
Stimson, Henry L., 257, 259, 283, 311, 477
Stock exchange practices of, investigation of, 318–20

Strauss, Albert, 117
Strong, Benjamin, 37, 39, 216
Suarez, Eduardo, 385, 388, 389, 487–89
Sub-Committee No. 2, 108
Sulzberger, Arthur Hays, 467
Summary of Conditions of Peace, 129
Sumner, Lord John, 108
Swope, Herbert Bayard, 115

Taft, Senator Robert A., 452
Taft, William Howard, 45
Takahashi, Korekiyo, 312
Tarbell, Ida, 56–57
Tardieu, André, 322
Taussig, Charles, 419
Taylor, Myron C., 265, 488
Temporary National Economic Committee, 447
Tennessee Coal and Iron Co. stock, 37, 38
Tennessee Valley Authority, 422, 452
Thompson, William Boyce, 97, 136, 390
Tildsley, Bertha, 241
Tildsley, John, 241
"Today and Tomorrow," 356
Tojo, General Hideki, 475
Toward Castle, 229
"Tragic Drama, The," 97
Treaty of 1839, 125
Treaty of Versailles, the signing of, 138–39
Tripartite Pact, 459
Trowbridge and Livingston, 63
Truman, Harry S., 505
TSL. See Lamont, Thomas Stilwell
Tugwell, Rexford G., 419
Tumulty, Joseph P., 146
TWL. See Lamont, Thomas W.

"Uncle Shylock," 324
"United Nations," 477
U.S. Foreign Policy (Lippmann), 496

U.S. Senate Banking and Currency Committee, 332, 335, 340–50
U.S. Senate Committee on Interstate Commerce, Subcommittee on Railroads, 405–6
U.S. Senate Finance Committee hearings, 306–7
U.S. Senate Foreign Relations Committee, 134
U.S. Senate Investigating the Munitions Industry, Special Committee of, 381
U.S. Senate Munitions Committee, 391–96
United States: war on Germany, 88; war on Japan, 476
United States Steel Corporation, 45
U.S.S. *Snook*, 502, 505–7
Untermyer, Samuel, 50–54

Vail, Theodore N., 100
Vaness Corporation, 225
Van Schaik, Frances, on Lamont, xv
Van Sweringen, Martin J., 225–26, 253–54, 345, 380, 405
Van Sweringen, Orvis P., 225–26, 253–54, 345, 380, 405
Van Sweringen Brothers. *See* Van Sweringen, Orvis P.; Van Sweringen, Martin J. *See also* Alleghany Corporation
Victor Emmanuel III (king of Italy), 192, 215
Villard, Oswald Garrison, 100–101, 383, 384

Wakasugi, K., 415
Walker, Mayor James, 314–15
Walker, Sybil, 277, 321
Walker and Gillete, 179
Wallace, Henry A., 477, 486
Wallenberg, Marc, 115
Wall Street, crash of, 268–75
Warburg, Max M., 122, 123

Wasson, R. Gordon, 503
Watson, Colonel Edwin "Pa," 445, 450, 470
Welles, Sumner, 444, 472, 488
Wells, H. G., 180, 183, 308, 323
Wemyss, Admiral Sir Rosslyn, 119
Wentworth, George A., 14, 15, 16
Wheeler, Senator Burton K., 405–6
White, Henry, 105
White, William Allen, 445, 450, 461–62, 463–64, 465
Whitney, George C., 423–25, 427–31, 438–39. *See also* Whitney, Richard
Whitney, Richard, 269, 270, 318–19, 423–26, 427–31. *See also* Whitney, George C.
Whitney, Richard, and Company, 423
Wiggin, Albert, 364
Williams, Jesse L., 155
Williams, Mrs. Jesse L., 155
Willkie, Wendell L., 422, 452–56, 502
Wilson, Woodrow, 67–88, 93–94, 98, 113–14, 128; declares war on Germany, 88; the German reparation problem and, 109, 110–11; and the *New York Evening Post*, 102–5; redraws national boundaries, 124–25; signs the Treaty of Versailles, 139; on speaking tour, 143; suffers a stroke, 146
Winchester Repeating Arms Company, 82
Winlock, Herbert, 243
Wood, General Leonard, 170
Woodin, William H., 337–38, 344
Woodworth, A. Vernon, 240
World War I: famine and, 116–19; impact of, on U.S. finance, 67–73, 74–82, 82–85; outbreak of, 67; German reparations and, 108–14

XYZ Corporation, 378–79

Yamamoto, Isoroku, 414, 475
Yat-sen, Dr. Sun, 160–61
Young, Owen D., 181, 204, 211–12,
    255, 257–59. *See also* Young Plan
Young, Robert R., 406

Young, Sir Hubert, 401
Young Plan, 254–59, 260, 262, 367–
    68, 370, 376–78. *See also* Young,
    Owen D.
Yung, Guido, 191–92